# FOREIGN POLICY
# IN
# WORLD POLITICS

**CONTRIBUTING AUTHORS**

*Robert J. Art*
*Vernon V. Aspaturian*
*Leon D. Epstein*
*Josef Joffe*
*Roy C. Macridis*
*Richard L. Park*
*Robert A. Scalapino*
*Kenneth W. Thompson*
*Allen S. Whiting*

# FOREIGN POLICY
# IN
# WORLD POLITICS

**5th edition**

*ROY C. MACRIDIS, editor*

PRENTICE-HALL, INC., ENGLEWOOD CLIFFS, NEW JERSEY

*Library of Congress Cataloging in Publication Data*

Macridis, Roy C.   ed.
   Foreign policy in world politics.

   Includes bibliographies and index.
   1. International relations.   I.   Art, Robert J.
II. Title.
JX1391.M32   1976        327        75-44190
ISBN 0-13-326488-2

© 1976, 1972, 1967, 1962, 1958 by Prentice-Hall, Inc.
Englewood Cliffs, New Jersey

PRINTED IN THE UNITED STATES OF AMERICA

10   9   8   7   6   5   4   3   2   1


Prentice-Hall International, Inc., *London*
Prentice-Hall of Australia Pty. Limited, *Sydney*
Prentice-Hall of Canada, Ltd., *Toronto*
Prentice-Hall of India Private Limited, *New Delhi*
Prentice-Hall of Japan, Inc., *Tokyo*
Prentice-Hall of Southeast Asia Pte. Ltd., *Singapore*

# CONTENTS

# PREFACE

The first edition of this volume appeared in 1958 when the subject of comparative foreign policy was something of an academic novelty. This fifth revised edition is presented with the knowledge that it has now become a recognized field of study. We have maintained the original format of the book that seems to have served so well students and teachers alike. We have updated our material and present two new essays on German and American foreign policy written by Dr. Josef Joffe of the Center of European Studies at Harvard and Professor Robert Art of Brandeis University, respectively. The British, French, Soviet and Chinese sections include new material and have been extensively overhauled. We have revised our introductory chapter and have tried in our bibliographical references to keep up with the voluminous literature, without, I am sure, doing justice to it.

Again, as in the past, my warmest thanks go to the contributors whose staying power has been a source of particular satisfaction to me and, I hope, to those who will again use this volume.

*Roy C. Macridis*

Waltham, Mass.
Oct. 1,1975

# FOREIGN POLICY
# IN
# WORLD POLITICS

# THE COMPARATIVE STUDY OF FOREIGN POLICY

1

*Kenneth W. Thompson*
*Roy C. Macridis*

## INTRODUCTION

No aspect of policy making is more intriguing and complex than foreign policy. As the world has become increasingly a maze of interdependent relationships, with economic, cultural, military, social, and even ethnic considerations making their weight felt upon every decision, from its inception down to its execution and implementation, so have the agencies of decision making become increasingly numerous and complex, if not always interdependent. It is hard to trace a policy decision to one single actor; it is difficult to apply a rational model of means and ends to a decision taken; it is virtually impossible to evaluate a decision, i.e., to say when it has succeeded and when it has failed; it is

hazardous to try to impute clear motives to the policy makers and trace the origins of decisions to such motives.

The relatively simple world of the past, consisting of independent and sovereign states pursuing their relations with each other through their ambassadors and through diplomatic channels, has given place to transnational economic and military organizations and arrangements that transcend the individual nation states. There is more reality and weight to the OPEC countries than to the individual sovereign states that comprise it, and it has a direct or indirect bearing on United States or European foreign as well as on the policies of all individual countries in the world today. The same is the case with NATO, with the European Economic Community, and with the Warsaw Pact countries.

The student of foreign policy today must take into consideration this new factor—what may be called an interpenetration of individual states by interests and forces that necessarily restrain or limit the freedom of action of their political leaders and decision makers. No state—not even the so-called superpowers—is immune. United States foreign policy to Israel, or Turkey, or Greece, is intimately associated with internal politics; our energy policy with international, financial, and monetary considerations. Our military and defense posture is associated with national and international industrial interests. The student must understand from the very start that foreign policies are often a result of multiple forces rather than the jinn produced by the magic wand of a Secretary of State or a President. Restraints upon action are more frequent than the freedom to act. Deliberate and authoritative decision making gives place to "muddling through." No clear blueprints can be drawn and no action can follow them. "Contingency planning" means the preparation of a series of possible plans to face possible situations—yet reality, in its complexity, fails to follow the course for which the plans were made.

The puzzle for the student becomes even more complex since not infrequently policies are pursued in the name of a given principle when in fact they render the principle totally meaningless. How, for instance, do those who claim that American policy is "imperialist" interpret our attachment to Israel? The answer is that they cannot. The explanation offered by others is that Israel is a democratic country and that we have a moral obligation to protect that small country to live in peace and security in the land its people were forced to abandon a long time ago. But if it is not economic interests but rather attachment to democracy that shapes our foreign policy, why did we support for seven years a ruthless military dictatorship in Greece? Because our strategic interest demanded it, is the standard answer. So that foreign policy is "explained" by some in terms of economics, by others in terms of ideological factors and by many in terms of strategic grounds to cover different situations. Similarly the Soviet Union supports the development of what amounts to a dictatorship in India in the name of freedom, while China opposes it on the same grounds. This doesn't stop China from supporting Prince Sihanouk, an old time ruler in Cambodia, but a close friend, and trying to impose him upon the revolutionary government of this country! Is there a common thread that can put some order in this confusion and provide an explanatory frame if not for each and every individual foreign-policy decision at least for the major foreign-policy strategies nations pursue? To seek an answer is the purpose of this essay and the central theme of this volume.

## TWO BASIC APPROACHES TO FOREIGN POLICY

Two approaches to foreign policy have vied with one another in Western thought at least since the days of the French Revolution. One is the *ideological* approach, according to which the policies of states vis-à-vis the rest of the world are merely expressions of prevailing political, social, and religious beliefs. In this approach, foreign policies are classified as democratic or totalitarian, libertarian or socialist, and peaceloving or aggressive. The second approach to foreign policy is *analytical.* At the heart of this viewpoint is the proposition that policy rests on multiple determinants, including the state's historic tradition, geographical location, national interest, and purposes and security needs. To understand foreign policy, the observer must take into account and analyze a host of factors.

## The Ideological Approach

In the twentieth century, it has been commonplace for critics to proclaim that the United States, or Britain, or France has no foreign policy or has been unfaithful to liberal or socialist or conservative principles, as the case may be. This is one way to think about foreign policy; to the present day it is perhaps the prevailing approach. Periodically, the domestic political arena rings with angry charges that a set of political leaders, a political party, or an administration is opportunistic in foreign affairs and faithless to its political creed or ideology. Governments are condemned for not supporting democracy, or free enterprise, or a particular social class everywhere around the world. This dominant approach views foreign relations primarily in psychological terms; it looks to the motives or ideologies of leaders or governments as the essential, if not the sole, determinant of policy. It maintains that a democratic regime pursues one type of foreign policy, an autocratic government another, a communist government a third, and

a democratic-socialist administration still another. There is a fairylandlike simplicity about this that makes it widely acceptable and easily understood. Foreign policy is considered a function of a political system in action or of the preferences or convictions of political leaders who carry out its programs.

## The Analytical Approach

There is a second approach to foreign policy, however, which has at least as respectable a heritage. It was a ruling point of view throughout much of the eighteenth and nineteenth centuries, whether in doctrines of raison d'état or in broader historical interpretations, and it is being revived in our day by a handful of analysts and scholars.

Its renaissance is partly an outcome of the apparent shortcomings of the psychological or ideological approach, especially in accounting for present-day international developments. That approach has been shaken and discredited by inner contradictions, and it has faltered and failed in describing the continuities of objective and purpose in the policies of states. Regardless of the party in power or the leaders and their private or public philosophies, British, American, French, and Russian foreign policies display unities that transcend individual beliefs or ideologies. In the early postwar period, the Labour government in England, despite long-standing protests against Tory imperialism and power politics, turned inevitably to the protection—in Western Europe, in the countries of the British Commonwealth, in the Iberian Peninsula, and in the Near and Middle East—of substantially the self-same interests that Tories and Whigs had considered vital for several centuries. In the United States, the Kennedy, Johnson, and Nixon foreign policies have looked to the central goals with which the administrations of Roosevelt and Truman were concerned. The means, methods, or techniques may have changed, but the interests and objectives have been relatively constant.

Therefore, in a period of a little more than two decades there has been a reaction against the ideological approach to the study of international relations. It should perhaps have been obvious that a conception in which foreign policy is nothing more than a by-product of domestic politics could hardly do justice to the elements of continuity in national policy. At some point, it became necessary to recognize that objective requirements of the national interest place certain irremovable limits upon any statesman seeking to formulate foreign policy. Regardless of the intentions, social philosophy, or religious outlook of individuals, there are broad strategic interests intimately bound up with a nation's geographic position and international role that must be safeguarded if its independence is to be preserved. Not only are these interests permanent for Bolsheviks as well as Tsars, but continuity also appears in the approach  a nation's statesmen, who stand guard over their country's security and whose conception of that security has been formed and molded by the same institutions and traditions. However intangible, the "national mind," which interprets the national interest, is itself a factor in the permanence of foreign policy. Out of the interplay of a durable international position with permanent traditions

and institutions, the larger nation-states have fashioned foreign policies that, in broadest outline, have been consistently maintained over long periods, even in the face of drastic changes on the domestic political scene.

According to this second approach, foreign policy demands, of policy makers, choices and discriminations of a basic order. Not only are the interests of a nation permanent in character, but they range themselves in a hierarchy of greater and lesser interests. In a classic statement intended as a guide in the formulation of Belgium's foreign policy but with relevance for all foreign policy, M. Paul-Henri Spaak observed:

There must be a hierarchy in international obligations. The nations of a continent cannot reasonably be asked to consider with the same realism and sincerity of judgment affairs which directly concern them and events which are taking place thousands of kilometers away in regions where they have neither interests nor influence.

Certain interests must be defended at all costs; others should be safeguarded under particular circumstances; and certain others, although desirable, can almost never be defended. It is the task of foreign policy, in the first instance, to determine its own hierarchy of interests and, next, to examine the scale of interests revealed in the principles or practice of other nations' foreign policies. Even when national leaders forswear the formulation of hierarchies of interests, the hard tests of practice often evoke underlying conceptions of vital interests. The United States' decision, in World War II, to bring the fighting to a successful conclusion in Europe and the North Atlantic before turning to destroy the enemy in the Pacific, or Britain's waiting, at the turn of the nineteenth century, until Poland was attacked and other nations were invaded before forming coalitions against Napoleon—these are examples of action in terms of a basic perception of interests.

The interests of states, and their power to pursue their claims, are of course immutable for any given historical period only in the sense that they set broad limits within which choices in foreign policy are made. They set the framework within which the domestic political contest over external policies must be waged. In the same way that no Soviet government is likely to relinquish its hold over Eastern Europe, no American government can take steps that would compromise the security of the Western Hemisphere. It is obvious that both power and interests can be made responsive to the forces of change. For example, a so-called peace-loving nation, faced by threats to its security, can translate its resources into military power, its influence into foreign bases and real estate, and its industrial and military potential into forces in being. This has, in effect, been the trend of postwar American foreign policy. Or a state may suffer a loss of power, as Britain did in World War II, with the consequent need for revising its estimates of national interest. Technology can require continuing reappraisals of national security and of the means of preserving it, and may lead to changes in the ranking of the great powers. Britain may have fallen in the hierarchy of powers as other nations belatedly experienced the industrial revolution, but it may recapture at least some of its vaunted supremacy in an era of atomic energy and hydrogen bombs. The existence of continuities in the foreign policies of states is admittedly more subject to debate in an era when one of the few certainties is the continual unrelenting pace of technological change.

## THE ELEMENTS OF FOREIGN POLICY

The study of foreign policy, despite the two major approaches described above, provides no ready-made categories that can be applied to every nation. Perhaps even in the physical sciences, the effort to uncover total systems, at least in these terms, is less fruitful than is sometimes imagined. In any event, there is marked diversity in the categories of analysis by which foreign policy has been studied in the present volume. To a considerable extent, this results from differences in national context. For example, social stratification has implications for the making of foreign policy in Britain that it seems not to have in the Soviet Union, and the policy-making process in Britain has greater continuity and tradition even than the American system. A fortiori, the newer states cannot point to the same political experience and diplomatic tradition in which the older nations can take pardonable pride. Despite these individual variations in the species, the nation-states whose policies are described have much in common. Their foreign policies are susceptible of analysis in terms of a checklist of elements that exist, that can be identified, and that merge and compromise the bases of foreign policy.

The elements of foreign policy may be thought of in terms of concentric circles. At the center are certain elements that are more or less material in character. Some of these are relatively permanent, such as geography and natural resources. Others, like the economic, industrial, and military establishments, are more responsive to change and human manipulation. Then there are human factors, largely quantitative in the case of population, and qualitative as regards national character, social structure, national morale, political institutions and experience, and an effective tradition of diplomacy. From these elements and the instrumentalities of the policy-making process, the substance of foreign policy derives, and major historic policies and the vital interests of countries emerge.

It may be worth at least passing mention that students of international politics have for the most part concentrated their attention on the elements of foreign policy. By contrast, writers on comparative politics have dealt more particularly with the policy-making process, including the influence of political parties, interest groups, effective political ideologies, and the peculiar executive-legislative relations in a country. The attempt has been made in the present volume to marry these two approaches, and to combine the study of objective factors in foreign policy with the study of processes by which decisions are reached and policies implemented.

Significant Factors in the Study of Foreign Policy

*The Elements of Foreign Policy*
A. The relatively permanent material elements
  1. Geography
  2. Natural Resources
    *a.* Minerals
    *b.* Food production

    *c.* Energy and power
B. Less permanent material elements
  1. Industrial establishment
  2. Military establishment
  3. Changes in industrial and military capacity
C. The human elements: quantitative and qualitative
  1. Quantitative—population
  2. Qualitative
    *a.* Policy makers and leaders
    *b.* The role of ideology
    *c.* The role of information

*The Foreign Policy-making Process*
A. The governmental agencies
  1. Executive (e.g., prime minister, relevant ministries, and interministerial or interdepartmental organizations)
  2. Legislature (including relevant committees)
B. The nongovernmental agencies
  1. Political parties
  2. Interest groups
  3. Media of communication
  4. Characteristics of public opinion

*Trends and Issues*
A. National purposes
  1. Peace as national purpose
  2. Security as national purpose
  3. Power as national purpose
  4. Prosperity and economic development as national purpose

*Foreign Policy in the Context of the Cold War . . . and After*

*Evaluation of Foreign Policy*

*Patterns of Foreign Policy*

The Relatively Permanent Material Elements

*Geography.* The more or less permanent elements of foreign policy obviously include geography, perhaps the most stable factor undergirding a nation's policies. It is not without significance that "except for Japan . . . Britain has been the only major power of modern times to be based on an island rather than a large continental area."[1] Its separation from the European continent by a narrow but strategic body of water, the English Channel, proved as decisive in frustrating the designs of Hitler and Napoleon as it had those of Julius Caesar or Philip II. No less an authority than Sir Eyre Crowe observed: "The general character of England's foreign policy is determined by the immutable conditions of her geographical situation on the ocean flank of Europe as an island State with vast oversea colonies and dependencies, whose existence and survival as an independent community are inseparably bound up with the possession of preponderant sea power."[2] This passage gives a clue to an important source of one of the most successful foreign policies in history. Going back to the fifteenth and sixteenth centuries, England, with but two exceptions, has neither been invaded nor defeated; and the exceptions—the American Revolution and the Afghan Wars—are hardly impressive evidence to challenge the importance of its geographic position. Until quite recently, England remained an island with what Winston Churchill described as threefold commitments to Europe, the British Commonwealth, and the "New World." Historically and down to the present, it has striven to retain for itself sufficient freedom of action to harmonize its commitments in each of these orbits, and only at points

where they overlapped have new undertakings been possible. It is true that technology, through inventions like the airplane and submarine, has transformed the character of Britain's location, and that its interests today are drawing it ever closer to Europe. In part, political factors have prompted this trend, including the British failure to pursue a successful independent foreign policy when its interests were in conflict with those of the superpowers, as in the Suez crisis in the autumn of 1956. But in Arnold Toynbee's apt words, "in this postwar age, the English Channel is no broader—in the subjective human terms of measurement which have to be applied in this context—than a Dutch dyke in the age of Alva and William the Silent; and the Atlantic itself is no broader than the Channel at the time when Napoleon's army of invasion was encamped at Boulogne."[3] Nonetheless, there are reasons for treating with some reserve claims about the annihilation of distance, for this statement dates back to 1934 —only a few short years before the backbone of Nazi strategy was broken by an island state whose geography continued to make a difference.

No one would doubt that communications and modern warfare have shifted the emphasis that can properly be laid on geographic location, but its influence continues in various ways, not least in the case of the great powers. The territorial expanse of the Soviet Union, whose land mass extends over one-seventh of the land area of the earth, or the vast reaches of the Chinese empire —both make military conquest and

---

[1]See chap. 2.

[2]Eyre Crowe, "Memorandum on the Present State of British Relations with France and Germany, January 1, 1907," in *British Documents on the Origins of the War: 1898–1914*, ed, G. P. Gooch and H. Temperley (London: Her Majesty's Stationery Office, 1938), 3:402–3.

[3]Arnold J. Toynbee, *A Study of History* (London: Oxford University Press, 1934), 3:353.

control problematical even with absolute weapons. The policies that the United Nations was able to pursue in Korea were circumscribed by the magnitude of the military effort of fighting a successful war on the seemingly endless terrain of the mainland of China. At the same time, the difficulties of maintaining communication networks within these vast areas can be a source of weakness in defense. For Russia, the lack of natural frontiers in the west or of natural obstacles to invasion across the plains of Poland and eastern Germany has been a source of conflict and weakness from the fourteenth century up to the present day. This condition must be considered at least partly responsible for Soviet policies toward the satellites and for the insistence of the late Premier Stalin that "Poland is a matter of life and death."

*Natural Resources.* The crisis in the Middle East provides a reminder that natural resources continue to be a vital element in foreign policy. The decisive importance of the countries in the Arabian peninsula rests primarily in the control they exert over oil. In practice, modern technology has made Middle Eastern oil production an increasingly vital necessity, especially for regions like Western Europe. Instruments of production, transportation, and war require oil as a source of energy—Clemenceau once observed that "one drop of oil is worth one drop of blood of our soldiers"—and its importance has led to a shift in the relative power of major regions of the world (as in the rise to importance of the Middle East) and of some of the major nations. Self-sufficiency in this natural resource has enhanced the power of Russia and the United States while Britain and other European nations have been made weaker by their want of oil. The Middle East still furnishes a large proportion of Western Europe's oil supplies and, barring major conflicts, this fact will continue to influence policy. Other estimates suggest that with the expansion of industrial production and national income and the flagging output of Europe's coal industry, Western European oil consumption may be trebled in twenty years. Hence control of oil becomes a crucial stake in world politics, and "oil diplomacy" has emerged as a term of art among policy makers.

Other natural resources influence foreign policy; the most basic has tended to be food production. Germany's military and political strategy in two world wars influenced by the need to gain a comparatively early victory before its limited food reserves were exhausted. For much the same reason, Britain, which before World War II produced only 30 percent of its food, ran the risk of destruction when its external lines of communication were threatened by submarines and air power. Britain, by economic enterprise, had extended its influence until, by the 1930s, there was no part of the world not economically linked in some way with London; but its security became more precarious in proportion to its dependence on tenuous and extended lines of communication. Liberals, prompted by their zeal for international trade, frequently decry a nation's quest for autonomy and self-sufficiency, yet in wartime self-sufficiency becomes a decisive source of strength. Food and energy are the lifeblood of a nation; its leaders must find ways, whether domestically or internationally, to satisfy these needs.

### Less Permanent Material Elements

*Industrial Establishment.* The twin forces of the Industrial Revolution and the contemporary political revolution, symbolized by the fact that approximately seventy new nations have gained recognition since World War II, underscore the vital importance of another element of foreign policy. In the nineteenth and twentieth centuries, the industrial establishment of a country has been the most basic index of world power. So long as Britain had no equal as an industrial power, its weight in the balance of power was bound to be decisive. With the increase in industrial strength of Germany and the Soviet Union or of Italy and Japan, to say nothing of the United States, Britain's capacity to influence the course of world politics was substantially reduced. Britain, having lost its industrial supremacy, also lost its capacity to serve as a balancer. France's industrial decline in relation to Germany meant that it was no longer able to resist German expansionism. Industrial capacity in both world wars, even more than peacetime military preparedness, proved to be the *ultima ratio.* It was the latent power of the United States, reflected in its industrial resources, that tipped the scales and gave the victory to the allied powers in World War II:

In any comparison of the potential resources of the Great Powers the United States, even before Hitler's war, far outstripped every other nation in the world in material strength, in scale of industrialization, in weight of resources, in standards of living, by every index of output and consumption. And the war, which all but doubled the American national income while it either ruined or severely weakened every other Great Power, has enormously increased the scale upon which the United States now towers above its fellows.[4]

The realities of industrial capacity, can therefore be ascertained and measured, at least in approximate terms. India, for example, seems to have been lacking in the industrial resources essential to a great power. Although it has substantial deposits of coal and iron and ranks high in manganese production, it has in the past lagged far behind the first-rate powers in the level of its industrial establishment. Only a tiny percentage of its total population has been engaged in industry, and its industrial plants have been severely limited. India is but one of a number of new nations whose rising political expectations are echoed in their demands for expanded industrial capacity. Its five-year plans are in part the expression of the drive for economic development and industrialization. Most of the nations that have only recently attained independence seek economic growth as the indispensable prerequisite of status in the international society. For some, the quest for rapid industrialization cannot be other than abortive. The observer can suggest that they might play a more significant role if they held to a more modest view of their destiny and cast their lot with neighboring states in a regional development program. In so doing, however, they would accept a permanently inferior position in which their freedom of action would be hedged about, and this they are unwilling to do.

*Military Establishment.* The military establishments of nations comprise

[4] *The Economist* (London), May 24, 1947, p. 785.

another, and possibly the most explicit, element of foreign policy. Diplomacy and military strength go hand in hand. In an earlier day, the great powers sent gunboats up the rivers of states they were seeking to influence; today a show of strength involves air forces, fleets, and satellites. The postwar distribution of power was an outcome of the position of the Red Army at strategic points in the heart of Europe. Germany's demoniacally successful diplomacy in the period between the two world wars was clearly the direct outgrowth of superior military preparedness. The explosion and testing of atomic weapons by the Soviet Union has been joined with strategic moves in the Cold War. The frontiers separating the spheres of influence of warring states often demarcate the limits of their effective military forces, as, for example, in both Korea and Indochina. As long as force remains the final arbiter of rivalries among nations, the comparative strengths of military establishments will set boundaries to actions in foreign affairs.

Military strength quite obviously lacks the permanence of the elements of geography or natural resources. Throughout history it has been subject to the compulsions of technological changes that have brought far-reaching shifts in power. The phalanx was the key to Sparta's victory over Athens in the Peloponnesian War of 431–404 B.C. Its effectiveness lay in the use of heavy infantry in close-order formation and in reliance upon shock techniques. The Athenians recovered from their defeat and, thirty-three years later, employed swarms of light infantry to conquer the Spartans. Somewhat later, the Thebans improved the phalanx by distribut-

ing its power in depth, thus introducing an element of surprise that had been missing. The Macedonians revamped the Spartan phalanx, made use of Greek mercenaries, and put their stress on a war of movement. But Macedonia was succeeded by the military genius and mobile legions of Rome. Hardened in civil and border wars, the Roman army proved versatile enough to fight as skirmishers or heavily armed infantrymen in open country and in villages and towns. However, the battle of Adrianople against heavily armed cavalrymen from the east brought the challenge Roman military leaders had foreseen but for which they were unprepared. In modern times, technology has given dramatic opportunities to those military leaders who proved capable of adaptation and innovation. By contrast, failure to respond to change has usually meant failure even for those whose traditional military resources appeared to be adequate. The Germans were defeated in World War I because they used the strategy of 1870 against their opponents' order of battle of trench warfare and economic blockade. The French, expecting another costly and brutal war of attribution, built the Maginot Line in the 1930s to fight the kind of struggle that military technology had already rendered obsolete. Short of warfare itself, the failure of military establishments to keep pace with fast-moving technological changes can also reduce nations' influence in the chancelleries of the world. This was the tragedy of France before World War II.

The difficulties inherent in maintaining military establishments that will not suffer defeat are more complex than mere responses to technological change. A nation may recognize the need for military organs capable of supporting the foreign policies it pursues but be limited in the margin of its economic resources that can be turned to military use. Some countries exhaust their resources in attaining a viable economy; others, like the United States, have a surplus with which to meet foreign military and political commitments. Belgium cannot afford to devote the same part of its gross national product to military ends as can the Soviet Union or the United States. Thus, both in absolute and relative terms, the military establishment of smaller powers must lag behind.

However, it should be remembered that technology is not the only important element in military strength. A technically weaker nation can, if it is sufficiently determined, tie down if not defeat outright a stronger nation in a guerilla combat. Most recently, the effectiveness of this method has been shown in Algeria and in Indochina.

Three errors are commonly made in appraising the military component of foreign policy. First, military power is often confused with national power, and a nation's capacity to impose its will is equated with its military establishment. Military power is like the fist whose force depends on the health and vitality of the body politic and the whole society. Troops are an important determinant of a successful foreign policy, but without other foundations they will not suffice. Second, the military element is often viewed in more static terms than is appropriate. The democracies, although the last to arm in two world wars, rallied their forces to gain the victory in the end. Third, it is difficult to analyze and foresee, in advance of a particular war, the most effective distribution of the components of military force. For example, what comprises a strong military force today? Is it large ground forces, hydrogen bombs, or intensive research? Is a small, highly specialized army more desirable than a large number of ground forces? Or are both essential for a nation that seeks to be strong? The answers to these questions will probably be decisive in determining a state's future influence in the world, yet it is sobering that estimates must be made on the basis of contingencies that cannot now be foreseen. We know in a general way that an effective foreign policy must be supported by a military program that can safeguard national security. But this leaves those who make decisions with the painful task of distributing resources among alternative means of defense without any certainty of the kind of war they may have to fight.

### The Human Elements: Quantitative and Qualitative

*Quantitative—Population.* Students of foreign policy have stressed another set of elements that make up a third concentric circle of factors of policy. They constitute the human forces—both quantitative and qualitative. Population is a quantitative factor that obviously must be considered in every calculation of the capacity of states. The importance of China and India rests partly in the size of their populations, which exceed 500 million people; both the Soviet Union and the United States, numbering less than half the populations of these countries, have shown respect for their potential. Conversely, nations with falling birth rates have lost influence among the society of nations, as France did after World War I. In the past, the wide diversity in technological skills, for instance, between an Englishman and a Chinese, meant that population was not a factor. In recent years, this situation has been changing. The 50 million people now living in the United Kingdom enjoy a high degree of scientific skill, but there is no longer any certainty that the peoples of underdeveloped areas may not eventually approach them, or even that the combined skills of so large a population may not compensate for a persistent technological lag.

The use of population statistics and forecasts suggests that the science of estimating and predicting the relative populations of states is simple and precise. Yet demography is subject to many of the vicissitudes to which other research in the social sciences is exposed. For example, World War I virtually wiped out a whole generation of Frenchmen. France's casualties from 1914 to 1918 numbered 1,400,000 young men. By 1938, the French birth rate no longer compensated for the death rate, and in World War II, France lost 625,000 men—almost three times America's losses in a country one-fourth America's size. Yet, since World War II, the French birth rate has reversed direction, and, since 1946, the surplus of births over deaths has been about 225,000 a year—a surplus greater than that of Italy or West Germany. France, which had been static and immobile between the world wars, has witnessed a renewal of its rate of growth. In more general terms, then, population is an element of foreign policy that is not absolutely predictable and that depends on other related elements. It may en-

able or prevent a state from achieving its national purposes, but, in either role, it is also subject to change and fluctuation.

*Qualitative—Policy Makers and Leaders.* Another crucial element of policy is the role of policy makers within a political system. The study of the methods, style, and quality of the process by which policies are implemented is the concern of students of both international and comparative politics. Moreover, the capacity for rational and responsible foreign policy varies greatly from state to state.

From a formal point of view, a policy maker is the official empowered with making the relevant decisions in foreign policy. In some political systems, the officials are the effective decision makers, as is the case in stable democratic systems and well-established authoritarian systems. In other cases, the officials are not the effective decision makers. The matter is one for empirical observation, knowledge of existing domestic systems, and study of historical patterns of foreign policy action. In most cases, observation will disclose the effective wielders of power and the real centers of decision making, but there will always be some doubt, especially when competing groups and elites have different views or when there is conflict on goals or on the means of achieving them. In societies where the officials are not the true wielders of power, the search for the centers of power may lead us to the political party, the military, the trade unions, the tribal chiefs, or the intellectuals. No prediction about foreign policy trends can be made, for many countries, without a careful assessment of the relative strength of the students, the trade unions, the military, the church, and the business groups.

Political leadership, in most societies, acts in order to maintain the security of the national state. An indispensable ingredient of security is power. The "realists" in international relations claim that power is a primary consideration in the behavior of the ruling groups of any nation-state, and that ideology and all other considerations are subordinate. This is undoubtedly true, and the quest for power often comes into conflict with national welfare or even internal status; thus, groups in power, in order to increase the power of the nation-state, may sometimes undermine their own position. The extent to which considerations of power will come into conflict with considerations of internal status, wealth, and leadership is a matter for empirical and historical study. In order to study comparative foreign policy, we ought to know how well entrenched are the effective wielders of power, and how likely is it that their decisions will be obeyed. International conflict will strengthen or weaken leadership, depending on the existing constellation of the various groups in a society. It is important to discover the circumstances under which an external threat leads to the consolidation of the power of an existing leadership group and when it leads to an undermining of that leadership.

It is also important to define the relations between the various decision makers or wielders of power. The question applies with equal relevance to the "Soviet world" and the "free world."

*The Role of Ideology.* What is the role of ideology within the international system? The term *ideology* applies not only to the manner in which objectives are shaped, but also to how the given objectives will be pursued.

There is a range of means, extending from outright violence to attachment to the established procedures. As long as international rules for the adjustment and accommodation of conflict have a very low degree of legitimacy, conflict will always involve a threat of violence. At what point is conflict likely to lead to war? It is difficult to make an accurate prediction, but certain obvious alternatives can be envisaged.

The available instruments of violence are an important consideration in assessing the likelihood of war. The more destructive the weapons available, the less likely their use; hence, the effort will be to accommodate conflict. "Total" destructive power in the hands of only two powers may lead to a number of alternatives: progressive disarmament of all other political systems; progressive polarization, in the form of alliances under the leadership of the two states, or an effort to redress the balance by the manufacturing of weapons by a third power or bloc, as was true with de Gaulle's France. Polarization may be stable if it brings about either complete disarmament of the rest of the world, with the express or tacit agreement of the two states involved, or the physical division of the world into two clearly demarcated and integrated spheres. All other situations are bound to be highly unstable.

This appears to be the case more than thirty years after the end of World War II. The two superpowers, unable to reach an agreement, have permitted a slow drift towards multicentrism. France and China have developed their atomic weapons while the Atlantic alliance and the Russian-controlled bloc are going through a process of disintegration. Thus, we have again entered a period of instability mitigated only by the continuing predominance of the United States and the Soviet Union. The Sino-Soviet conflict; the United States involvement in Southeast Asia; far-reaching social and political changes in South America, as in Chile; the *Ostpolitik* initiated by Willy Brandt in West Germany; and growing resentment of U.S. and Soviet influence—all are indications of the fluidity of the present situation in which the only discernible pattern is the reassertion of national aspirations by independent sovereign states.

*The Role of Information.* What importance does information have in shaping policy? The problem of available information, which forms the basis of the policy maker's decision, is very complex. Game theory postulates its free flow, much as the liberal economics assumed perfect mobility and price competition. The "liberal model" is useful because, on its basis, we can make inferences about events and developments even when empirical reality does not fit the model. Game theory does not have this advantage, because it assumes a game without telling us what the game is about—i.e., whether it is war, peace, accommodation, maintenance of the status quo, surprise attack, or annihilation. Despite the theory's emphasis upon the "rules," we cannot understand what they are unless we assume that the participants have similar objectives, norms, and leadership characteristics, a situation that obviously never obtains. If the participants all play different games with different rules, we have no game amenable to rational observation. Therefore, where and how reality differs from the model cannot be shown in any

terms. Game theory, useful in military analysis when we consider the use of weapons and force, is less relevant to the study of foreign policy.

To undertake a discussion of the relationship between information and policy making or formulation of objectives, we would have to consider: (*a*) information available to decision-making and governing elites; (*b*) information as a source of conflict among elites; (*c*) possession of information as a source of power and influence among certain of the political elites or decision makers; (*d*) the manner in which information is perceived; and (*e*) the serious problem of the disparity between the information available to the public and that available to various public policy-making and leadership groups. A subsidiary problem is that of the manufacturing of "information" in different degrees in all political systems.

### Diplomacy: National Purposes

Another element of foreign policy is the quality of a nation's diplomacy. At one level, this involves a clear conception of national purposes; at another, it involves prudence and skill in the use of the tools of statecraft. For purposes of analysis, both can be examined in the context of American foreign policy.

It is well to remind ourselves that issues confronting the makers of American foreign policy compete for attention, crowding out and succeeding one another in headlines of the daily press. Turkey, Greece, Egypt, Syria, Cambodia, Israel, Laos, and Cuba and continuing attention to the Middle East and Vietnam, flash kaleidoscopically across each of our horizons as we seek to understand international affairs. Sensing this process, it is tempting to second-guess the future. When one is asked what will be the most compelling and troublesome problems of the next six months or a year, he can prophesy the continued threat of war in the Middle East or agreement on arms controls. But behind these issues and affecting their resolution are deep-seated, underlying questions relating to this country's basic goals and national purposes. What do Americans seek in the world? Is it peace? Power? Prosperity? Each of these goals is often set forth as a national fundamental aim. Sometimes peace, especially in this atomic age, is made an absolute purpose; prosperity sometimes seems to emerge as the one end Americans seek above all others in the conduct of their affairs in the world. We shall look in turn at each of these goals, seeking to ascertain its relevance to the real issues in America's foreign affairs.

*Peace as National Purpose.* It is sometimes considered a mark of bad judgment to recite a succession of "great generalities" at the outset of any discussion. However, the present crisis imposes upon us responsibilities of perceiving more clearly the ebb and flow of certitude and truth with respect to the root principles of world affairs. Recent events have shaped and molded the dimensions of the international problem in a manner that few anticipated. Take, as an example, the issue of peace. For the first time in centuries, rational men have been claiming—apparently with some accord—that war has become obsolete as an instrument of national policy. President Eisenhower reiterated his

view, and he maintained again at the First Geneva Conference that victor and vanquished alike would be casualties in any thermonuclear war. His successor, President Kennedy negotiated a Limited Nuclear Test Ban Treaty, which was signed and ratified by the Senate in 1963. President Nixon undertook protracted negotiations, which were continued by President Ford at Vladivostok. But does this mean that peace is inevitable and atomic warfare impossible? Apparently not, if we consider recent policy statements, the informed opinions of experienced leaders, or events in the Middle East and above all, in Southeast Asia—without mentioning, of course, the Sino-Soviet conflict.

*Power as National Purpose.* The most celebrated and controversial policy statements in the mid-fifties were those attributed by *Life* writer James Shepley to Secretary of State John Foster Dulles. In discussing the policy of "massive retaliation," Mr. Dulles observed: "The ability to get to the verge without getting into the war is the necessary art. If you cannot master it, you inevitably get into war. If you try to run away from it, if you are scared to go to the brink, you are lost." Earlier he had said that a potential aggressor must know that his acts would be met by such retaliation and that he would lose more than he could gain. Specific targets for retaliation had to be selected and agreed upon in advance: "The way to deter aggression is for the free community to be willing and able to respond vigorously at places and with means of its own choosing." Its response should be massive and overwhelming.

If we separate the chaff from the grain, the political from the inescapable truth in this contested statement, it seems clear that the possibility of resort to military measures has not been cast out from the armory of American foreign policy. Since the Eisenhower administration stressed, wherever possible, the replacement of manpower with decisive weapons, the risk of warfare with ultimate weapons can hardly be said to have passed. Nor is this possibility made any less ominous by the boasts of Soviet leaders that they too have developed a strategy of retaliation. The Soviet resistance to a neutral administrator of a disarmament agreement and their refusal to accept other suggested procedures are further evidence. In this situation an accident, a miscalculation, or an act of desperation could easily set off the conflict that Geneva was said to have made impossible. The "Nixon Doctrine," which preserved American commitments to come to the aid of allies who suffer aggression while reducing conventional American military resources for supporting these commitments, has not decreased the risk of using ultimate weapons in conflicts. Secretary Kissinger's statement on the use of force in the event of economic strangulation in the Middle East is but the most recent expression of this approach.

*Prosperity and Economic Development as National Purpose.* Turning to the issue of prosperity, we enter the presence of the most appealing of the current trends of informed thinking on our foreign policy. This trend of thought maintains, with varying reservations, that most of the tensions between the West and the uncommitted countries of the world are the result of mutual suspicions, and that these can be composed through economic cooperation and aid. Put in the proper perspective, a policy of contributing modestly and consistently to prosperity and the raising of standards of living in the world is a viable, if not an utterly essential, goal of American foreign policy. Its emphasis is all the more crucial because of the neglect of this facet of American thinking in the past. However, prosperity, like peace, is at best a proximate guide to action. It offers no panacea to the ills that engulf the world. Tensions may be eased when the fruits of economic development and growth are more widely shared at home and abroad, yet American experiences of intense strife and national division during the 1950s and 1960s should caution us against excessive optimism.

On a world scale, the limits of a form of inverted Marxism that looks to economic development as a miraculous device for purging tensions and strife are even more graphic. Japan and the United States have not been deterred from misunderstandings by Japan's phenomenal economic growth. Similarly, while India has literally raised herself by her own bootstraps, and has increased real income 28 percent in the period from 1949 to 1965, and attained, in 1953/54, the highest rate of economic growth in the world, this has, if anything, prompted her to press claims more vigorously, even when they conflicted with those of the West.

Furthermore, those who would lay the disparities in standards of living throughout the world on the conscience of the West sometimes seek to exact a heavier tribute than any nation or civilization can fulfill. These developments in other countries are intimately bound up with cultural traditions, with political order and stability, with resources, attitudes, population pressures, and a thousand local conditions that Western powers can only slightly shape or affect. If Western efforts can assist others to inch their way to a happier and more promising state of economic well-being and political justice, this will be enough, and it may even stem the advance of hostile forces. However, it can lead at best to public disillusionment and perhaps a deep and festering embitterment with the West's role in the world if public justification of these programs claims more than is warranted.

That the West should be left to find its way gropingly, painfully, and with uncertainty can come as a shock only to those who forever seek simple absolutes and an easy pathway. Peace, more than ever before in America's history, is a paramount goal of American foreign policy. However, it is a goal that knows its limits. Power throws a spotlight on those dark corners of American action that were but dimly lighted throughout the era of intellectual pacifism and political neutralism. Prosperity—especially in Asia, Africa, and the Middle East—must be as much America's aim as military security. Yet prosperity is a means and not an end. The interests of progressive, no less than oppressed, states clash and must be accommodated. Diplomats and not the experts in technical assistance must be called to this task.

We will be on surer ground if we recognize that peace, power, and prosperity are rough guidelines to action. They show us the perimeters within which to work, but in no way remove the demands placed on leaders for political judgment and practical wisdom.

## FOREIGN POLICY IN THE CONTEXT OF THE COLD WAR ... AND AFTER

Theories of social science run the risk of departing too sharply from social reality. By contrast, advances in the medical sciences are often accounted for by the phrase "the scientist is never too far from the patient in the sickbed." The scientist is close to nature so long as he poses relevant and researchable questions. The focus of his interest must be "operationally relevant." Economics, particularly since Walras and more notably since Keynes, has become at once more scientific and more useful. Practitioners of foreign policy are often critical of the unfortunate irrelevance of much theorizing in such approaches as the theory of decision making and behaviorism. They charge that theories remain on the drawing board without being tested or applied against reality.

At the same time, policy makers are the first to signal the need for principles of wider application or for a manageable body of doctrine on foreign policy. Public leaders need help, not merely from efficiency experts, but also from political and constitutional theorists, on problems involved in the organization of the government for the conduct of foreign policy. How should foreign policy be carried on in a democracy? Who takes responsibility and who should be the coordinator of policies and programs? What aspects of foreign policy are the appropriate concern of appointed or elected officials? What part is the responsibility of the whole of the body politic? What are the objectives of foreign policy, how should they be ranged, and in what hierarchical order? For example, how should statesmen order and relate the goals of most

Western countries, which include national security, avoidance of thermonuclear war, the preservation of Western values, and support for the rising expectations of newly independent peoples?

These issues are clearly amenable to study, to the ordering of facts and data, to trial and error in testing alternative hypotheses, and to building a body of more generalized theory with relevance for practice. Propositions put forward by one observer will invariably be challenged by others. This is the story of evolving knowledge. If scholars and writers with commitments to rigorous and systematic analysis leave this rich field to others, understanding will suffer. Yet it is disheartening to note how many serious scholars prefer the simpler if tidier tasks of abstracting from reality those problems on which great masses of data are at hand, regardless of their significance.

*Policy and Public Opinion.* The first obstacle is inherent in the problem of marshalling domestic support for American policies while at the same time putting America's best foot forward in the eyes of the rest of the world. To mobilize support for policies, Americans say things to themselves that, from the standpoint of other peoples, might better be left unsaid. (In this the United States is, of course, not unique.) America is a vast sprawling continent of great diversity of political and religious beliefs; in its constitutional system, power and responsibility are broadly diffused, although less so in foreign affairs than in the conduct of domestic affairs. Thus Americans speak in many voices, some raucous and strident, as they seek to persuade one another of the right course to follow. The language of domestic politics is not the language of political theory. It aims to unite as many as will join to support policies or programs. It looks to a common denominator that can more often be found in broad principles and moral generalities than in specific directives of strategy that, like military policies, must be cast in practical alternatives to meet circumstances. It prefers militant slogans to qualified truths, a crusade to public conversations about a problem.

Above all, it is a permanent part of the landscape of international relations that American foreign policy must draw its support from a union of the experts, the public, and friends and allies abroad. History demonstrates that no American statesman can ignore any point on the triangle without courting disaster. Before World War II, the public ostensibly lagged behind the thinking on foreign affairs of experts and allies. Following World War II and up to 1950, American policy—especially with respect to Europe—was acceptable alike to the authoritative views of the experts, to the public, and to the members of the postwar Grand Alliance. This day has passed, and the demands of the three groups have tended increasingly to go their separate ways, especially on Vietnam.

*Colonialism.* Another obstacle to effective policy making stems from the colonial dilemma, which reached beyond America's national life and touched conflicting interests at work throughout the rest of the world. We know that the colonial problem stood at the top of every agenda for discussion of American foreign policy. Responsible officials were encouraged to issue proclamations and to throw America's weight behind independence movements. In this setting, it was tempting to take general and sweeping positions and to express an American doctrine on the rights of peoples everywhere to independence and self-government. However, the record of America's efforts to align itself squarely with either colonial or anticolonial powers is sprinkled with as many failures as successes.

Nevertheless, Americans face new situations today that demand new and more vigorous policies. Nationalism is on the march in Asia, the Middle East, and Africa, and Americans implore one another to identify their country with these movements rather than appearing to stand in their pathway. Unhappily, the colonial problem has been less tractable than those exhortations suggest. For at the same time as the fight has been waged to end old imperialisms, a new expansionism has threatened. To meet it, some feel that America must cleave to its trusted friends and allies with whom it has interests and military bases in common, striving to preserve a more stable world balance of power. Yet, in itself, this is not likely to be enough. The present equilibrium of power will be upset unless America can join with new forces in the so-called underdeveloped areas. We may say, therefore, that the United States faces the triple challenge of stemming the tide of Russian imperialism and Chinese communism, uniting the other Western states, and drawing closer to non-Western peoples only recently emerging as independent states. In a manner of speaking, policy makers must keep three balls in the air. This is the unenviable task of American statesmanship.

The pathos of America's position may be illustrated briefly from events in the last two decades. First there was the U.S. statement on Goa, recognizing Portugal's authority in the tiny enclave in India, prompted doubtless by the zeal of European officers in the State Department to display a sense of community with Portugal. This provoked deep resentment in India and, perhaps, throughout much of Asia. Next came the expression of "sympathy" for Greek feelings in the Cyprus dispute, which loosed a torrent of British protest. Then the Dutch voiced dismay at Dulles' warm and friendly comments during a visit to the Indonesian Republic. The United States aroused its European friends when it appeared to take sides with Egypt and Middle Eastern friends by reassuring Turkey against Syria and Russia, and more and more in the past few years by supporting Israel in its conflict with the Arabs. More recently the changing objectives of Soviet foreign policy, the emergence of a new and independent but powerful Communist China in Asia, and the specter of communism in the Castro variety in Latin America have underscored the predicament of American foreign policy. The Soviet image has changed for ourselves and our Western allies, and the need for accommodation with the Soviet Union is a view that is now largely shared by American experts. Yet we remain somehow still committed to earlier positions and policies that paralyze our reflexes and make negotiations on common interest between the two countries more difficult. Similarly, there was a tendency to view conflict in Vietnam in global and absolute terms—as the extension of communist aspirations for domination and expansion instead of considering it as a manifestation of a limited and negotiable area of conflict. Events in Latin America have provoked an increasing nervousness with popular revolutions—which we often championed in the past—and a tendency to equate them with anti-American subversive moves directed and inspired by "worldwide communism." Such attitudes have accounted for the progressive decline of our influence and position in Western Europe.

Perceiving these problems, can we say anything about this perplexing picture that will offer some guidance to the juggler or policy maker of whom we have spoken? Perhaps there are guidelines or principles we can enunciate to spotlight a few of the darker corners of this colonial problem. First, we must start with the presumption that the colonial problem is fraught with dilemmas with which America must learn to live. Dogmas for or against colonialism will not waft them away: solutions must be worked out case by case. Second, timing is of the essence. The statement supporting Indonesia stirred up a hornets' nest because Dutch-Indonesian tensions at that time were great. Third, if any general solution can be found, it rests in the coordinating of mutual interests, not in the wholesale sacrifice of one set of interests to another. In North Africa, the French, American, and African interests appeared to coincide, in that all wanted "liberal solutions." Likewise, in other regions, the goal should be the harmonizing of interests. This calls for a judicious balancing of claims. Fourth, it is one of the ironies of history that force may be necessary to preserve colonial arrangements, not in order to perpetuate them, but so that their orderly liquidation may be achieved.

Finally, conflicts of interest—as past conflicts between Britain and India or between the Dutch and the Indonesians—may be swept along by powerful historical movements until one side emerges supreme. It may be necessary for American policy makers to choose sides, and so inevitably give offense. These facts need not preclude prudence and restraint, but the end of the colonial era has changed the form, if not the substance, of choices Western leaders must make.

As the Cold War has moved into a period of some relaxation of tensions and détente, the same dilemmas have reasserted themselves. American policy makers striving for peace in the Middle East have proceeded with Soviet-American relations clearly in view. Détente in Sino-American relations has been balanced against prospects for improved Soviet-American relations. When the United States tilted toward Pakistan in 1972 at the expense of relations with India, it did so because Pakistan was a channel through which Secretary Kissinger was seeking to open up relations with China. The opening up of relations with China, which the Nixon Administration judged required a high degree of secrecy, was carried out at the expense of the close relations which had been built up with Japan. The announcement of President Nixon's trip to China was described in Japan as "shock diplomacy."

Thus in the era of détente, the same conflicts between competing relationships has continued. Policy makers have felt called upon to *choose* at particular stages, and almost always deterioration has set in, in relationships with some nation-states. It would seem that for détente, as for the end of colonialism, the possibility of simple and unequivocal choices among alternatives does not exist. There must be a balancing process, and this is the essence of foreign policy for a great power.

## The Concept of "Patterns"

A few words need be said about the meaning of "foreign-policy patterns." It is a term that refers to the behavior of nation-states and more specifically to the foreign policy-making institutions and officials of a nation-state. It denotes the manner in which they define their positions and that of their State vis-à-vis the outside world—the world of other nations—over a given period of time. A "pattern" implies the existence of goals to be realized and the mechanisms and practices through which such goals are realized. Above all the term connotes the existence of intellectual equipment—something like a filter mechanism or lenses—through which policy makers look at the outside world, sift information that comes in, and take steps that relate to the goals of the nation-state. A military coup in Ethiopia; uncertainty about the future regime in Portugal; invasion of northern Cyprus by the Turks—these are events that mean different things to different nations and their policy makers. They are events that are viewed in terms of the goals of their respective nation-states. As a result reactions to them will differ from one state to another.

Objectively speaking no nation-state can expect to realize fully all its goals all the time. There are irreducible goals that are associated with clear-cut patterns of action and reaction. They generally involve the minimum requirements of security

and defense as defined by the policy makers and the nation's political elite. Not much compromise is possible. The Soviets reaction to an effort on the part of Poland to join NATO is obvious. They will use force rather than allow it. The reaction of the USA to the installation of Soviet missiles on Cuban territory is equally certain. The harder and clearer the definition of minimum and irreducible goals and the means of action to bring them about, the higher the level of predictability in international relations and, as a result, the stability of the international system. In contrast, the situation in the Mideast is highly volatile because of the *lack* of clear-cut goals and of anticipated forms of action on the part of the various protagonists. Another illustration was the war in Korea in 1951 that may have originated in the inadvertent remarks made earlier by the Secretary of State Dean Acheson according to which South Korea was not within the perimeter of U.S. defense.

There are, however, goals that call for adjustment and compromise. They are what a nation-state considers desirable but not indispensable. They do not directly involve matters of security and survival but rather the expansion or consolidation of power. Such goals may be graded on a scale of priorities beginning with what is of particular importance and ending with those that can be dispensed with under pressure. For instance, the former Secretary of Defense in France, an ardent Gaullist, defined the goals of France to be the security of Europe, the avoidance of "certain dominations" in the Mediterranean, in Africa and in certain parts of the world where our flag flies." Obviously this implied a ranking of interests and goals in which

Europe, North Africa, French-speaking Africa and "certain parts" of the world would be ranked in that order.

How are patterns shaped? There is one and only one answer: by history. And by this we mean the existence over a long period of time of analogous, if not identical, reactions to analogous, if not identical, stimuli. It is only then that a "pattern" becomes firmly crystallized. It involves a goal shared widely by the elites, and it is associated with an equally accepted set of actions to bring it about. In the discussion of the individual foreign policies of the countries we cover, we identify basic patterns and indicate the force they have acquired over a given period of time.

One fundamental risk in every society and system is that a pattern once crystallized may become rigid and axiomatic, thus hindering debate on foreign policy and binding the system to a course of action that is out of tune with the international environment or its capabilities. But patterns can change due to both internal and external factors. The political elites may gradually reshape the goals of foreign policy in the light of circumstances—political, economic, or ideological. Some reasons may be compelling—i.e., drastic decline in the "power" of the nation involved, as has been the case with Great Britain. In other cases change may be the result of deliberate choice on the part of the political elites—as may well be the case with the U.S.—Soviet or Sino-American relations. Or it may be the outcome of drastic change of the regime of a country, where it is not impossible to witness (even if temporarily) a complete reversal of alliances and a redefinition of goals and tactics. External factors, on the other hand, are

associated with significant changes in the international environment. When Canning, in the early nineteenth century, "appealed to the new world in order to redress the balance of the old"—he was already taking into consideration the emergence of extra-European powers in the international equation of forces —an emergence that became the dominant phenomenon of the twentieth century. Technology and rapid technological changes call for a restructuring of foreign policy patterns, too. In the same way in which the British channel no longer provides an insurmountable barrier, nuclear weapons and ICBMs have radically changed the strategy of alliances and the deployment of forces.

As technological, economic, strategic, and political changes occur, and the international environment becomes transformed, two major dangers are ever present. We have already mentioned one, that is, the political elite may remain blind to these changes and follow patterns that were valid under different conditions in the past. The common saying that armies are always prepared to fight the *last* war—even if an exaggeration—illustrates the point. The elites become ensnared in the stereotypes of the past and assume that the *same* goals are to be implemented by the *same* actions. The second danger is equally ever-present. Elites—and not only in democracies —may divide sharply on goals and means. A division may lead either to inaction or to sudden changes that create an element of unpredictability and instability.

There is a need for careful analysis of the existing patterns, their scope, their intensity, the conditions under which they change, and the penalties

—both for the nation-state and the international community—that result from prolonged rigidities and from divisions among the elites.

## EVALUATION OF FOREIGN POLICY

When it comes to studying foreign policy in its various manifestations, and most particularly international conflict—including war—the social scientist is in a difficult position. He is asked to explain and predict attitudes whose complexity makes a mockery of the few "scientific" tools we have. The layman presses us to predict American or Chinese foreign policy; to unwrap the famous riddle of the Soviet foreign policy; or to explain the nature and conditions of conflict in our contemporary world.

The more stubborn and complex the material, the greater the temptation to move into the realm of abstraction. The canons of science call for simplicity and economy in the formulation of hypotheses that are to be tested. It is only when simple hypotheses are tested that the scientist moves into the more complex, slowly relating and checking his findings with the outside world. We, in contrast, find that we cannot test. As a result, many of us today find it easier *not* to relate our speculations to the outside world at all, and to create propositions, conceptual schemes, and models that have logical coherence, but fail to pass the test of empirical relevance. There is much futility in this.

The way out, in our opinion, is to assume from the start that the range of indeterminacy in our social and political world is great. This is even more applicable to the behavior of states that goes under the name of "foreign policy." To attempt to construct generalizations and models that will give us a rigorous scientific understanding and prediction of foreign policy is a hopeless task.

As we move more into the realm of abstraction in the name of "science," we become more likely to evade—and perhaps evasion is the basic reason for the "scientific" trend toward a high degree of abstraction and conceptualization— our responsibilities in advancing an understanding of politics, notably in international relations and conflict. Therefore, we would, for instance, suggest a better understanding and study of the existing laboratory, i.e., history. We cannot understand why simulated war games are more important to devise and study than actual or historical conflict from which all degree of simulation is eliminated by the stark and brutal necessity of real choice and decisions. Second, we believe that case studies of the individual foreign policy-making process, including conflict of various states in terms of the descriptive categories suggested, would give us considerable food for thought and might lead us to more fruitful hypotheses.

One of our aims should be to find regularities in the behavior of nations and to develop general propositions by setting forth carefully the conditioning factors that account for types of behavior. Thus we may hope to reduce the range and degree of indeterminancy. But ours is also a world where exercise of will and choice calls for more than a scientific knowledge of man and nations.

The analytical approach to foreign policy, as distinct from the ideological approach, is no miracle-working device for understanding the complex problems of international affairs. It gives no clue to the specific decisions that must be reached daily. It is not a cookbook with recipes for action to fit every contingency. It does, however, provide a way of thinking about the foreign policy of any country and ordering the factors that contribute to the conduct of foreign relations. If prediction is still beyond the reach of scholars, analysis in the face of varying contingencies may be attainable. In some form or another, this method is useful in studying the acts of great and small powers. Amid all the variations of individual scholars writing about unique national policies, this book serves to demonstrate the role and the limits of the systematic analysis of foreign policy.

### Evaluation of Foreign Policy Decisions

As the reader goes through the analysis of the foreign policy making of individual countries, he unavoidably is concerned with evaluating them. Have the policy makers made a "good" or a "bad" decision? Has the foreign policy pursued by a given country been "successful" or "unsuccessful"? In terms of what criteria and what canons shall we judge and render a verdict? The intense debate that went on over U.S. policy in Vietnam, just as in France over Indochina and Algeria, clearly demonstrates that clearcut and objective tools for analysis and judgment are not always available.

To begin with, there is the perennial problem of "good" and "bad" —i.e., of *normative* criteria and goals. Such goals generally indicate the overall commitment of a society to a way of life and naturally influence policy making and foreign policy as well. The aversion of the average cit- izen in the United States to the Nazis or to the invasion of China by Japan in the 1930s was real and reflected a normative posture on the part of the American people and its policy makers. There is no doubt that some of the same values and normative criteria play an exceedingly important role in the minds of those who have been critics of involvement in Vietnam and its military manifestations. For a long time American isolationism was based squarely on normative considerations—primarily the belief that the American way of life was distinct and superior to those of the European countries, and that any involvement in their affairs and any involvement on their part in the affairs of the American continent would "contaminate" and perhaps corrupt the American democracy. By the same token, many French political leaders and intellectuals believed that the French colonies were a major challenge for the dissemination of the French culture and the French language through which the "natives" would be assimilated to a higher and better way of life.

The student generally is inclined to be very sympathetic to foreign policy analysis in terms of basic ethical criteria. This is not, however, an easy job—nor is it analytically satisfactory. The first difficulty is that of agreeing on ethics. For those who consider an ethical principle more important than human life, outright destruction in its name is preferable to peace; for those who consider communism a danger far outweighing the well-being of any given generation, war and sacrifice is above that of welfare and well-being; for those who consider democracy and an open society more valuable than one man's life, again, war and destruction may be inevitable to preserve what is so highly valued. In other words, it is not always easy to find people agreeing on the highest normative goal. Even if we found agreement on the goal, a second difficulty would emerge: how to implement it. As we noted, isolationism was for a long period of time a policy related to the preservation of American democracy. The Cold War and our intervention in Vietnam are related exactly to the preservation of the same ideals. So is NATO. The same normative goal, in other words, may be pursued by foreign and military policies that appear to be on their face antithetical. There is a second difficulty—that of the choice of the means to the pursuance of an accepted goal. Means can be proximate; they can be intermediate. To illustrate what we have in mind: Is it possible in the name of a given ethically accepted goal to pursue means that appear to be incompatible with it? The argument is a very old one—and in foreign policy the illustrations are abundant. Richelieu had no scruples in allying himself with Protestant powers against Catholic Spain. And Churchill in the war against Nazi Germany solemnly proclaimed that he would ally himself not only with Stalin but with the Devil himself, if he could find him! In the pursuit of freedom and democracy, American foreign policy makers seemed to have gone just as far in forming alliances or giving support to some of the most repressive regimes in the world. At what point—and again, in terms of what criteria—can we convincingly argue that certain means distort the end? That certain policy or policies are incompatible with the posited ethical values? If human life is the highest end, is slavery to be preferred to loss of life? If freedom

is the highest end, is it higher than life itself?

The truth is that as in domestic politics there are many values, many ethical norms, and many ways of life that claim primacy in our international community. We live in a pluralistic universe, and nothing can destroy our world more easily than the unqualified assertion of one ethic or one way of life over all others. It is clear that there is a relativist ethic. In the words of Pascal, "what is 'good' [acceptable] on one side of the Pyrenees Mountains may well be 'bad' [unacceptable] on the other." This may be so without there being a compelling necessity for either country to extirpate by force what each considers bad and therefore to fight with each other to the ultimate destruction of one or perhaps both. Many nation-states today seem to hold values that are antithetical to each other. Many can live side by side without attempting to impose their will upon the other. That which many hold to be the epitome of morality and their demands that policy must be harnessed to it may well lead directly to conflict and war.

In a pluralistic universe, then, judgment and evaluation in terms of ethical considerations is hazardous and highly unpredictable. We prefer and we suggest here a more instrumental approach to the evaluation of foreign policy. It is based on the assumption that, at least for the time being, nation-states are here to stay and that their foreign policy must be evaluated in terms of the success and failure to implement the goals they pursue. In the international community each and every state is allotted some power, which alone or in combination with others allows it to keep its autonomy and way of life or, conversely, prevents its destruction by others. The international community has been in this sense a world of power relations differing in degree rather than in kind from domestic politics.

Power relations, it must be noted, express themselves in a number of ways, of which war is the extreme form. Alliances, international law, cooperative schemes, and even integrative schemes express and regularize power relations just as a constitution, a judiciary, and a police system do at the domestic level. A world based upon power relations is not a jungle. Systems providing for balance or limitations or deterrence often are more stable and less likely to lead to the use of force than situations where power relations are unrecognized and ignored. For power, while occasionally erupting in the outright use of force, more often seeks to find, in the world of nations, affinities, compatibilities, and safeguards that will prevent it from becoming destructive. The problem is not to negate power or to ignore it, but to build restraints and to prevent its potentially destructive manifestation by the use of force. The recognition and legitimation of one nation-state's power means, in the last analysis, its preservation in order to exclude the use of force.

Finally, an analysis based upon power must also take into consideration that it is not an end in itself. It is an instrument for preserving a national community and its way of life. Its use, therefore, must always be subjected to this test: Does it preserve the national community? Does it enhance its security and well-being? Is its use consistent with the basic interests of the national community? Was dropping the atomic bomb on Hiroshima, for instance, necessary for the United States' *preservation,* in the broadest sense of the term? By presumably shortening the war in the Far East, did its use safeguard basic American interests? Was its use indispensable for the preservation of such interests? Undoubtedly, the student will now raise objections to the trend of this argument. He will point out that we have reintroduced normative considerations just after arguing in favor of their exclusion. *Who* can decide, and *how,* whether the use of the bomb was necessary or indispensable? Some will say that it was if one American life was saved at the cost of hundreds of thousands of Japanese civilians. Others will argue precisely the opposite. However, the normative argument need not enter into the picture (despite our abhorrence of the sacrifice of human life that the use of the bomb entailed); indeed, it cannot be answered even if it is allowed to enter into the picture. The question can be answered by a careful analysis of means and ends. Our purpose was to bring the Japanese to terms—to force them to unconditionally surrender. If the use of the bomb had been the only way to do it, then and only then can we differ about its ethical connotations. The analysis we suggest, however, involves a number of steps *before* we confront the thorny ethical question. Were there other means available to make the Japanese come to terms? Were they used? If not, why not? If so, with what results? Did the policymakers balance carefully the damage to the image of the United States by the use of a new weapon that destroyed and maimed many, many thousands against the benefit that was to be derived from its use? Did other considerations enter into the picture—our desire, for instance, to finish the war there before the Russians were able to join our forces in full force and create serious dissension and problems—as the case proved to be in Europe? Whatever the answers, the questions raised suggest the approach we follow in evaluating a foreign policy: we link the policy to a goal and discuss it in terms of the implementation of the posited goal.

We propose simply to suggest a set of instrumental criteria in terms of which "success" or "failure," or at least a discriminating bill of particulars, can be determined. Foreign-policy decisions are generally made in order to alleviate a country's predicaments or to create favorable conditions for it—specifically, in terms of the United States, to increase our security, power, or influence in the world. In this sense, a decision may be simply defensive in nature (i.e., to remove a perceived predicament, as in the 1973 all-out U.S. military alert to prevent Soviet troops from moving into the Middle East) or promotive (i.e., to create conditions conducive to the exercise of American influence and power). Very often a defensive policy cannot be easily distinguished from a promotive one.

To assess the success or failure of a decision—or a set of decisions that constitutes a policy—the outside observer must have a series of unambiguous facts and figures before him. This is not always an easy situation to come by. First, we must have a fairly explicit statement of the goals desired by the decision maker. Second, we must try to establish a connection between a series of acts and decisions that are made to implement the major goals posited. Third, in assessing the nature and effectiveness of such a series of intermediate decisions, we must be constantly aware that the goal posited remains the same, or that, if it has changed in response to changes in the international environment, there is a clear awareness of such a change. Fourth, we must undertake a cost-factor analysis—that is to say, we must try to assess the nature of the means used and their effectiveness in terms of the costs they entail. Given a scarcity of resources, a high-cost policy, even if successful, may be a failure if it is shown that it has deprived a given system of the means required to meet other and perhaps more pressing predicaments. By the same token, a low-cost policy that has succeeded may be considered to be a failure if it has created conditions that render its future use ineffective or has created unanticipated difficulties that entail high costs. Last but not least, whether a given policy has succeeded or failed, it is incumbent upon the analyst to show that success could not be obtained by any other means, or, alternatively, that failure could have been averted by the choice of different means. Otherwise, no conclusive and coherent explanation can be given regarding the relationship between means and ends.

The difficulties in evaluating foreign policy, it should now be clear, may well be insurmountable. They are only compounded by the following requirements, which alone can provide the proper context in which we may dare evaluate:

1. We must first provide a clear description of the predicament; for instance, what was exactly the predicament for the United States in the rebellion in the Congo? But this is not always relevant. It is more important to identify how the predicament was perceived

—in other words, to determine why a certain situation was or is considered by policy makers to be a predicament.

2. The next step, related to the first, is to make an effort to assess the flow of information and intelligence that goes into the formation of the perception of the policy makers: Is there only one source? Which one? Are there many sources? Do they provide the same facts and figures, or do they differ? If they differ, how are differences resolved in accepting one set of information flows and rejecting another?

3. This leads us to our third required piece of information: Which governmental units are most responsible for coping with the predicament? And if it falls (at least technically) within the jurisdiction of more than one, what types of intergovernmental and interunit arrangements exist to allow for a concerted action?

4. At this stage, assuming that the information sources, the nature of the predicament, the perception of the predicament, and the particular governmental units and procedures used in order to make a decision are known, we need to have a clear statement and description of the action resulting from the decision actually made—e.g., an ambassador was recalled; economic aid was offered; an official was bribed; the Marines were dispatched.

5. A knowledge of the action taken (or contemplated) must be coupled, at least when analyzing democratic foreign policy making, with the possession of an unambiguous declaration of the anticipated consequences of the action or decision. The simpler and the smaller the number or numbers of consequences anticipated, the easier the evaluation. The greater the number and the more complex the goal, the more difficult the assessment—unless one is able to peel off the rhetoric that often accompanies a decision from its substance, or unless we can establish a set of priorities of

goals ranging from the imperative ones through the desirable ones down to the least-expected but simply hoped-for. Such priority assessments are not always easy to make, for the time dimension within which policies are implemented constantly forces reconsideration and reshuffling of priorities.

Only after the above steps have been carefully followed can the analyst survey the actual consequences that flowed from the policies made and arrive at a very quiet, and always highly qualified, verdict. Our frame of analysis, in other words, is *instrumental*, relating means to ends and linking the two by study of decision-making procedures and intermediate steps. It is based on a power theory of international politics in which the ultimate analysis of "success" and "failure" can be measured in terms of the plusses and minusses in the increments of power and influence for a given nation.

To summarize: Foreign-policy evaluation involves: assessment of the goals of a given country; analysis of the various predicaments that seem to endanger these goals; an examination of the instrumentalities (policies) pursued to alleviate the predicaments; a careful examination of the manner in which such policies were formulated, with regard to both the predicament involved and the manner in which the policy was to be implemented; an account of the major governmental organs responsible for the implementation of a policy; a careful examination of the availability of alternate means and instrumentalities (were they considered? were they rejected after being considered, and if so why?); and finally, an assessment—i.e., did the policy as formulated and implemented bring about the desired goals? If so, then our verdict is positive—as may be the case with the Marshall Plan for aiding the European nations. If not, we must then ask: Why not?

Even a negative verdict to a given foreign policy, however, calls for a reevaluation, which should take at least two major forms. First, we must determine whether failure was due, not to implementation or to the means used, but rather to the goals posited. Generally, we must assume that, if the goals were completely or considerably beyond the available means at the disposal of a country, the policy was doomed to failure, no matter how well it was implemented. By the same token, even if the policy is successful at a very high cost, it must be considered a failure because it makes the country involved vulnerable to other potential predicaments. But even if the goals posited are compatible with the power resources of a given nation, failure may be due to a number of factors and reasons already mentioned: the given predicament may have been alleviated, but the policy responsible may have caused a series of unanticipated predicaments; or the policy pursued may have alleviated the predicament temporarily, only to allow it to appear in a more virulent form later on; or, finally, the policy used may be so far at odds with the posited goals as to insidiously distort the goals themselves. As an illustration, we might cite the case of U.S. foreign policy respecting Greece formulated in 1947 by President Truman, who promised aid to Greece (and Turkey) in order to safeguard their security from communist aggression and infiltration and in order to promote free, democratic institutions. Twenty-five years later, Greece was a military dictatorship and Turkey appeared to be in the process of becoming one. American presence and help has, all along, so emphasized the military importance of these countries at the expense of all the other goals explicitly stated by President Truman in 1947 that one of the overt goals of American foreign policy makers—the preservation of free institutions in the "free world"—was perverted and distorted.

## SELECTED BIBLIOGRAPHY

ALLISON, GRAHAM T. *Essence of Decision: Explaining the Cuban Missile Crisis.* Boston: Little, Brown, 1971.

ALMOND, GABRIEL A. *The American People and Foreign Policy.* New York: Praeger, 1960.

ARON, RAYMOND. *A Century of Total War.* Garden City, N.Y.: Doubleday, 1954.

————. *Peace and War: A Theory of International Relations.* Garden City, N.Y.: Doubleday, 1966.

BELOFF, MAX. *Foreign Policy and the Democratic Process.* Baltimore: Johns Hopkins, 1955.

BOULDING, KENNETH. *Conflict and Defense.* New York: Harper & Row, 1961.

BROWN, SEYOM. *New Forces in World Politics.* Washington, D.C.: The Brookings Institution, 1974.

BUCHANAN, WILLIAM. *How Nations See Each Other: A Study of Public Opinion.* Urbana: University of Illinois Press, 1953.

CLAUDE, INIS. *Power and International Relations.* New York: Random House, 1962.

DESTLER, I.M. *Presidents, Bureaucrats, and Foreign Policy.* Princeton: Princeton University Press, 1972.

DE JOUVENEL, BERTRAND. *The Art of Conjecture.* New York: Basic Books, 1967.

DEUTSCH, KARL W. *The Analysis of International Relations.* Englewood Cliffs, N.J.: Prentice-Hall, 1968.

DE VISSCHER, CHARLES. *Theory and Reality in Public International Law.* Princeton: Princeton University Press, 1956.

DUROSELLE, JEAN-BAPTISTE. *La Politique etrangere et ses fondements.* Paris: Librairie Armond Colin, 1954.

FALK, RICHARD A., and MENDLOVITZ, SAUL H., eds. *Toward a Theory of War Prevention.* New York: World Law Fund, 1966.

FARRELL, R. BARRY, ed. *Approaches to Comparative and International Politics.* Evanston, Ill.: Northwestern University Press, 1966.

FEHRENBACH, T. R. *This Kind of Peace.* New York: McKay, 1966.

GROSS, FELIKS. *Foreign Policy Analysis.* New York: Philosophical Library, 1954.

HAAS, ERNST. "The Balance of Power: Prescription, Concept, or Propaganda?" *World Politics* 5 (1950): 459–479.

HAAS, ERNST B., and WHITING, ALLEN S. *Dynamics of International Relations.* New York: McGraw-Hill, 1956.

HALLE, LOUIS J. *Civilization and Foreign Policy.* New York: Harper & Row, 1955.

HALPERIN, MORTON H. *Bureaucratic Politics and Foreign Policy.* Washington, D.C.: The Brookings Institution, 1974.

HINSLEY, F. H. *Power and the Pursuit of Peace.* New York: Cambridge University Press, 1963.

HOFFMAN, STANLEY, ed. *Contemporary Theory in International Relations.* Englewood Cliffs, N.J.: Prentice-Hall, 1960.

HUNTINGTON, SAMUEL P. *The Common Defense: Strategic Programs in National Politics.* New York: Columbia University Press, 1961.

KAHN, HERMAN, and WEINER, ANTHONY J. *The Year 2000—A Framework for Speculation.* New York: Macmillan Co., 1967.

KAPLAN, MORTON A., ed. *New Approaches to International Relations.* New York: St. Martin's, 1968.

KENNAN, GEORGE F. *American Diplomacy: 1900–1950.* Chicago: University of Chicago Press, 1951.

———. *Realities of American Foreign Policy.* Princeton: Princeton University Press, 1954.

KISSINGER, HENRY. "The Policymaker and the Intellectual." *Reporter,* March 5, 1959, pp. 30–35.

KISSINGER, HENRY, ed. *Problems of National Strategy.* New York: Praeger, 1965.

LALL, ARTHUR. *Modern International Negotiation.* New York: Columbia University Press, 1966.

LEVINE, ROBERT. *The Arms Debate.* Cambridge: Harvard University Press, 1963.

LISKA, GEORGE. "Continuity and Change in International Systems." *World Politics* 16 (1963): 118–36. [Review of Richard Rosecrance, *Action and Reaction in World Politics.*]

MARSHALL, C. B. *The Limits of Foreign Policy.* New York: Holt, Rinehart & Winston, 1955.

MEEHAN, EUGENE. *Explanation in Social Science: A System Paradigm.* Homewood, Ill.: Dorsey, 1968.

———. *The Theory and Method of Political Analysis.* Homewood, Ill.: Dorsey, 1965.

MORGENTHAU, HANS J. *Politics Among Nations.* New York: Knopf, 1954.

———. *The Purpose of America.* New York: Knopf, 1960.

———, and THOMPSON, KENNETH W. *Principles and Problems of International Politics.* New York: Knopf, 1951.

NEUSTADT, RICHARD E. *Presidential Power: The Politics of Leadership.* New York: John Wiley, 1960.

NICOLSON, HAROLD. *Diplomacy.* New York: Harcourt, Brace & World, 1933.

———. *The Evolution of Diplomatic Methods.* New York: Harper & Row, 1955.

ORGANSKI, A. F. K. *World Politics.* 2d ed. New York: Knopf, 1968.

ROSECRANCE, RICHARD. *Action and Reaction in World Politics.* Boston: Little, Brown, 1963.

ROSENAU, JAMES N., ed. *International Politics and Foreign Policy.* Glencoe, Ill.: Free Press, 1964.

ROSENBAUM, NAOMI. *Readings in the Western Political Systems.* Englewood Cliffs, N.J.: Prentice-Hall, 1970.

RUSSETT, BRUCE M., ALKER, HAYWARD R., JR., DEUTSCH, KARL W.; and LASSWELL, HAROLD D. *World Handbook of Political and Social Indicators.* New Haven: Yale University Press, 1964.

SCHELLING, THOMAS C. *Arms and Influence.* New Haven: Yale University Press, 1966.

———. *The Strategy of Conflict.* New York: Oxford University Press, Galaxy Edition, 1963.

SPANIER, JOHN. *Games Nations Play: Analyzing International Politics.* New York: Praeger, 1972.

THAYER, CHARLES W. *Diplomat.* New York: Harper & Row, 1959.

THOMPSON, KENNETH W. *American Diplomacy and Emergent Patterns.* New York: New York University Press, 1962.

———. *Christian Ethics and the Dilemmas of Foreign Policy.* Durham, N.C.: Duke University Press, 1959.

———. *The Moral Issue in Statecraft.* Baton Rouge: Louisiana State University Press, 1966.

———. *Political Realism and the Crisis of World Politics.* Princeton: Princeton University Press, 1960.

———. *Understanding World Politics.* Notre Dame: University of Notre Dame Press, 1975.

ULLMAN, RICHARD H., and TANTER, RAYMOND. *Theory and Policy in International Relations.* Princeton: Princeton University Press, 1972.

# BRITISH
# FOREIGN POLICY

2

*Leon D. Epstein*

Americans especially have often admired British foreign policy making for its method if not its substance, believing that diplomatic wisdom and shrewdness prevailed over political emotions and parochial concerns. Prestige of this kind was understandable during the centuries when so small an island kingdom stood as a major world power and even, at times, as the leading world power. The evidently successful acquisition of imperial territory, international trade, and general influence enhanced the reputation of the process by which British foreign policy was made, supported, and executed. There had to be, it seemed, special political attributes to explain how the limited British population could exert power over vast overseas populations, notably in the late nineteenth and early twentieth centuries, while maintaining a leading influence among European nations.

Sustaining this reputation was less likely during Britain's decline in status among the great powers of the mid-twentieth century. Apparent failures in foreign policy, such as the collapse of the attempt to appease Hitler in the 1930s or the frustrated effort to reoccupy the Suez Canal zone in 1956, were charged against the political process and not simply regarded as the product of diminished relative power. So too was the expensive perpetuation into the 1950s and 1960s of the increasingly unsubstantial, even if symbolically useful, policies of independent nuclear deterrence, Commonwealth leadership, and responsibility flowing from a "special relationship" with the United States. A sympathetic observer, it is true, could have discerned even during the decades of decline that Britain adjusted successfully to second place in a military alliance and accomplished its massive imperial withdrawal with relative graciousness. No other nation ever surrendered so much in so short a time as did Britain in the fifteen or twenty years after 1945, but this accommodation was hardly awesome, as had been the old accumulation and maintenance of power. In particular, it was not awesome to Americans who, during the very years of British decline and withdrawal, were concerned with the enormous expansion of the American nation's role in the world. A policy-making process associated with decline attracted little admiration. And no postimperial successes were evident even in the early 1970s. Instead Britain's decline relative to other nations became more striking, especially in economic terms, and its prolonged uncertainty about membership in the European Economic Community suggested a failure to find a place in the contemporary world. Consequently Americans, however disenchanted lately with their own nation's role as a world power and so with its policy-making process, may not readily perceive Britain even as a model for adjustment to diminishing power and responsibility. Nevertheless Britain's policy-making process, in foreign as in domestic affairs, deserves attention within the Western democratic context, as a long-established alternative to American institutional arrangements. Moreover, Britain's decline in status is both so recent and so significant that it needs to be comprehended in any survey of world politics.

## THE NATIONAL BACKGROUND

### Economic Geography

Except for Japan, whose days of imperial glory were few, Britain has been the only major power of modern times to be based on an island rather than a large continental area. It is easy to forget how small the British island home is. The whole of the United Kingdom, including the six counties of Northern Ireland plus England, Wales, and Scotland, comes to just over 94,000 square miles—an area smaller than Oregon and only slightly larger than Minnesota. Almost 56 million people now live in the United Kingdom, and over 49 million of this total are in England and Wales, which together have one of the highest population densities of any white community of comparable size. About 10 million persons live in London and its immediate environs, and almost every Englishman is within a day's rail journey of London.[1] This densely populated island is separated from the northwest coast of Europe by only 21 miles of open water, but even this distance has been sufficient for British life to develop its own distinctive pattern. Although isolation from European power struggles (in the nineteenth-century American manner) has never been feasible, the British long avoided identification as a purely European power.

Britain's island location and the absence of a nearby frontier, either in Britain or on the Continent, made it natural for Englishmen to seek their fortunes in faraway places. This meant sea trade as well as colo-

[1]Demographic and economic data are published by the Central Statistical Office, *Annual Abstract of Statistics* (London: Her Majesty's Stationery Office).

nial settlement, and both ventures were highly developed before the Industrial Revolution. Almost from the start, British factories supplied an established overseas trade in addition to a domestic market. By the mid-nineteenth century, the large-scale exchange of domestic manufactures for overseas raw materials and foodstuffs had become the cardinal feature of the British economy. Abundant coal, originally inexpensive to mine, provided an important base for the early British industrial supremacy. Not until 1870 did this supremacy begin to fade in relation to the more rapid industrial growth of Germany and the United States.[2]

Nineteenth-century industrialization made the British almost entirely an urban people, and reduced agriculture to a decidedly secondary status. Workers engaged in agriculture have long constituted a lower proportion of the gainfully employed than in almost any other country in the world.[3] Despite recent successful efforts to increase agricultural production, the British must remain predominantly a manufacturing people and also a people largely dependent on outside sources of food and raw materials. It is true that Britain's complete dependence on imported oil is expected to diminish and perhaps disappear in the 1980s when its own North Sea wells are successfully exploited. But with the continued need to import much of the nation's food, along with many other commodities available only from abroad, Britain must still plan to export a very high percentage of its manufactured products, even if it will also export some oil, in order to earn its way in the world.

## Social Structure

Class differentiation, on various bases, is treated more openly as a fact of life in Britain than in the United States, and this may lead to an exaggeration of the relative importance of class in British politics. It is true, however, that working-class consciousness has remained definite and substantial. Despite the occupational rise of many Englishmen in each generation,[4] a rise resembling American patterns of mobility, the working class long retained a distinctive status resting on the assumption that most children of workers would themselves become workers. Status may now be more fully identified with occupation than with income, and also with intangibles such as style of life or manner of speech. These cultural marks have only begun to lose their significance.

The British educational system has played an important part in preserving class distinctions. Best known in this respect are the "public schools," which are really private secondary schools operating on a boarding or day basis for children whose parents can afford the fees. These schools include the limited number of famous and prestigious institutions such as Eton, Harrow, Winchester, and Rugby, but altogether the fee-paying private sector has enrolled no more than about 5 percent of all secondary-school-age students. Government-sup-

[2]W. Stanford Reid, *Economic History of Great Britain* (New York: Ronald Press, 1954), pp. 337, 377.

[3]P. Sargent Florence, *The Logic of British and American Industry* (London: Routledge & Kegan Paul, 1953), p. 5

[4]D. V. Glass, ed., *Social Mobility in Britain* (London: Routledge & Kegan Paul, 1954), p. 20.

ported grammar schools, also designed to provide academically superior secondary education, enrolled a much larger minority—over three times as large in the mid-1960s. This minority, selected by competitive examination of children at about age eleven, was characterized by its intellectual promise rather than by the fee-paying capacity of parents. But this minority was drawn much more heavily from middle-class backgrounds than were the *majority* of secondary students. The majority of secondary students were assigned, also as a result of examination, to less academically distinguished government schools. Thus the system, until very recently, separated students, at an early age, in paths that seemed related to demonstrated abilities partly associated with family backgrounds.

Whatever the social and educational disadvantages, especially for the majority consigned to schools of lesser status and quality, there is no doubt that the government grammar schools provided at least some lower-income students with a first-class education, enabling them to compete with the products of the fee-paying schools for the limited number of places in British universities and for the financial support to attend these universities. The pattern seemed designed to produce an able and trained intellectual elite, selected largely on the basis of merit.[5] But it is challenged by the growing movement for comprehensive secondary schools in which, as in American high schools, courses are conducted under one roof for students of different abilities. Developed in many communities particu-

larly after World War II, these comprehensive schools remained the less conventional and less frequent path before the late 1960s, when the Labour government sought to establish them as the norm for planning secondary education. Although the Conservative government of 1970–74 was not similarly dedicated, a trend toward comprehensive schools in most areas continued and received new impetus when Labour returned to power in 1974.

British universities remain a bulwark of education available for the talented minority. Following a decade of what was, by past British standards, an enormous expansion, these universities enrolled fewer than 250,000 students in the early 1970s. Even if all other postsecondary students, particularly those in teacher training, are added so as to provide figures comparable to 'enrollment figures for American colleges and universities, there were no more than 450,000 British postsecondary students compared with about 9 million American—or about one-twentieth as many students from a total population over one-fourth that of the United States. Numerical comparisons between Britain and most other developed nations are only *somewhat* less unfavorable.[6]

Apart from social class and the related differentiation of an educational elite, the British people appear relatively homogeneous. The population, despite substantial immigration in the 1950s and early 1960s from the West Indies, India, and Pakistan, remains almost 98 per-

[5]Michael Young, *The Rise of the Meritocracy* (London: Thames and Hudson, 1958).

[6]Charles L. Taylor and Michael C. Hudson, *World Handbook of Political and Social Indicators* (New Haven: Yale University Press, 1972), pp. 229–31.

cent white, and the near-elimination, by recent restrictive legislation, of further immigration of Asian and African peoples will not allow this proportion to change greatly from the present level. So much of the nation's overwhelmingly white population is ethnically "British" that this century's immigrants from Ireland and from continental Europe, while fairly numerous, are exceptional as minority groups insofar as they are not fully assimilated. Unlike Americans, the great majority of Britain's inhabitants have no national background save their present one. However, "national background" means something different in Scotland, Wales, and Northern Ireland than it does in England. The difference is sufficient to nourish a strong nationalist movement especially in Scotland and also in Wales, and to make Northern Ireland a place in which only about two-thirds of the population associate themselves with Britain. Consequently the United Kingdom appears to have some of the qualities of a multinational state. But the fact remains that England alone, apart from Scotland, Wales, and Northern Ireland, has about 83 percent of the U.K. population, and that it will tend to characterize Britain even if it concedes regional autonomy at its geographical fringes.

Britain's considerable religious homogeneity should be observed. The nation is largely Protestant, with historically important distinctions between the Church of England and various other Protestant denominations (lumped together as "nonconformist"). There are fewer than a half-million Jews. The approximately five million Roman Catholics are a more substantial minority, but they are not often politically conspicuous now that, in Brit-

ain itself, the old Protestant concern to protect the nation against papal power has virtually disappeared. Of course, the half-million Catholics of Northern Ireland, inevitability identified with their Irish co-religionists of the Republic of Ireland, are by no means at peace with the one million Protestants who have, at least until recently, dominated Northern Ireland. This circumstance, while one in which Britain generally became heavily involved in the late 1960s and into the 1970s, is genuinely exceptional in that there is no similarly consequential division between Protestants and Catholics in the rest of the United Kingdom.

## Political Experience

Not only are the British old as a people, but they are also old as a nation. The unity of England and Wales goes back to the Middle Ages, and the union with Scotland dates from the beginning of the eighteenth century. The island was small enough to be dominated early by a single political authority, mainly representing the numerically superior English population. National political institutions are of such long standing that loyalty to them has, at least in England itself, been taken for granted in a way that would be difficult in a more recently created nation.

The supremacy of Parliament, in relation to the monarch, has been constitutionally established since 1688. Traditionally, the parliamentary regime was liberal and aristocratic—liberal in the sense of standing for the liberty of individuals and of property, and aristocratic in that relatively few were eligible to choose parliamentary representatives. Like

British society in general, the political system remained nonegalitarian until the late nineteenth century, when the vote was extended to the mass of the population. That the political institutions, managed over centuries by a special ruling class, should thus have been democratized without revolution distinguishes British history from much of the European continent's.

Persistent External Concerns

Historically, Britain has had two major international concerns. The first has been to maintain oceanic access to the rest of the world, and the second to prevent any potentially hostile power from dominating the continent of Europe.

In the days when the British Empire was at its zenith and when most of the currently equal partners in the Commonwealth were imperial colonies, the simplest way for Britain to maintain overseas access was to command the seas. This is just what Britain did on its own until about the time of World War I. As long as "Britannia ruled the waves," the nation's trade routes were secure, as were its military communications with the empire. The growth of American naval power ended exclusive British control of the seas, but the advantages of that control remained because the United States became an ally and not an enemy. The most direct threat first came from the German navy, and especially from German submarines in both world wars. For the first time in modern history, an enemy was equipped with a force that could just possibly cut the British lifeline to the outside world. And this was not yet all. The airplane and the rocket

bomb threatened the island even more dramatically during World War II.

The classic British concern with the European balance of power has sometimes been explained as a corollary of the nation's general position in the world. In his famous Foreign Office memorandum of 1907, Eyre Crowe assumed that Britain's capacity to command the seas, which he regarded as essential, would inspire fear and jealousy among other countries.[7] To avert an anti-British combination based on such fear and jealousy, Crowe thought, Britain needed to make special efforts to develop a policy that harmonized with the interests of other nations. First among these interests, he wrote, was independence, and therefore Britain had rightly championed (and should continue to champion) the independence of nations against any single powerful and ambitious state. In practice, this meant a grouping of forces against first one strong European power and then another, "but ever on the side opposed to the political dictatorship of the strongest single State or group at a given time."[8]

Neither of Britain's major concerns has diminished in the nuclear age. Access overseas, even without large imperial possessions, remains vital for economic reasons, and the avoidance of hostile domination of continental Europe is politically as well as economically important. It is the means for dealing with these

[7]Memorandum by Eyre Crowe, in *British Documents on the Origins of the War, 1898–1914,* ed. G. P. Gooch and Harold Temperley (London: Her Majesty's Stationery Office, 1928), vol. 3.

[8]*Ibid.,* p. 403. On the balance of power, see also Harold Nicolson, *Diplomacy* (London: Oxford Unversity Press, 1950), p. 135.

concerns that have changed. With limited resources in a new world of superpowers, Britain's old command of the seas is impossible. Even when allied to the much greater American naval strength, Britain is now unable to achieve its earlier kind of security. Similarly, the problem of preventing hostile domination of the European continent has greatly changed. Britain itself cannot supply the crucial element in a coalition against the single strongest continental power. This is even clearer when that power is the Soviet Union, as after World War II, than when it was Germany. In both instances, the United States became the decisive force.

## THE POLICY-MAKING PROCESS

Traditionally, in considering the conduct of British foreign affairs, American observers tended to admire what appeared to be the capacity of a well-informed executive to act without frustrating pressures from legislative authority or other domestic political forces. This capacity might in part have been attributed to British aristocratic customs, more characteristic of the nineteenth than of the twentieth century, as well as to the greater experience of an old European power. But it has also been associated, in American minds, with the parliamentary-cabinet form of government as opposed to the separation of executive and legislative powers, and with the special British development of a nonpopulist yet responsible democratic government. Perhaps British politics were thus idealized by the once-prevailing Anglophiles in the American intellectual community. There might always

have been significant political pressures at least indirectly influencing British foreign policy, and these pressures could well have come from a fairly large section of the public whose support, in recent times, would have been essential in fulfilling any major national commitment. But the picture of strong, effective, and coherent British policy making remained dominant until the 1950s and 1960s, when the decline of Britain's national fortunes caused even the effectiveness of its political process to be challenged. It was then that an American political scientist could argue that British government had performed less well in foreign policy making, during the twenty years following World War II, than had the American system, and that the inferior performance resulted in large part from weakness rather than strength in executive leadership.[9]

### Governmental Agencies

*The Executive Authority.* Legally the political executive, representing the crown, is supreme in foreign policy making. Foreign policy is ordinarily presented to Parliament at some stage, but there are no constitutional provisions resembling the American requirements for congressional—particularly Senate—approval of certain significant international commitments. The present-day political leadership of prime minister and cabinet is heir to the traditional prerogative of the crown in making Britain's foreign policy.

The search for restraints must, therefore, enter the political instead of the legal sphere. It is common to assert that prime minister and cabi-

[9]Kenneth N. Waltz, *Foreign Policy and Democratic Politics* (Boston: Little, Brown, 1967).

net conventionally hold office only while supported by a parliamentary majority, and are limited by the threat of ouster from office as the result of unpopular or unsuccessful policies, foreign as well as domestic. The assertion is of doubtful relevance for twentieth-century British politics, at least until 1974. Apart from brief transitional periods, there has been a sufficiently stable two-party pattern producing a majority party in the House of Commons, as well as a sufficiently cohesive majority party to preclude the kind and the number of parliamentary defections necessary to vote its own political leadership out of office. Only the electorate, every five years—or sooner at the prime minister's option—decides whether to have a new executive by returning a majority of M.P.s from what had been the opposition party. Between general elections, it must be stressed, a parliamentary majority party has effectively protected its leadership from ouster by formal votes of censure or no confidence in the House of Commons. But this is still to speak of the most readily observable formalities, although no longer merely of the legalities, of the governmental process. The political sphere also involves the possibility of more subtle restraints. Four prime ministers since 1940 have left office without losing general elections and without losing majority support in parliamentary voting. Although age and illness account, at least in part, for three of the four resignations, even these instances suggest a flexibility of tenure that the American presidency lacks. More pointedly, in the fourth instance, Neville Chamberlain's departure in 1940 was the known political consequence of a revolt in which members of the prime minister's own party refused their support in such numbers as effectively to threaten, without actually destroying, Chamberlain's majority. Smaller and less dramatic revolts, only surfacing partly in parliamentary voting, are reasonably assumed to have been factors in the resignations of Eden in 1957 and Macmillan in 1963, if not in the departure of the aging Churchill in 1955. Even without the evidence of open revolts through parliamentary speeches or voting abstentions, many of which may only pressure without threatening a government, there are other intraparty limits on the policy-making power of a leadership that hopes to retain its position. Continued parliamentary-party support must often be sought by persuasion, compromise, and concession.

A prime minister seeks and obtains that support within the context of the collegial leadership represented by the cabinet. The word is the same as the American term for the president's chief administrative appointees, but the political significance of the British cabinet is almost entirely different. The difference has been obscured in recent years by the growth of the prime minister's authority, especially as party leader and dominating public figure; and for a time in the 1960s, observers began to describe Britain as having "prime ministerial" rather than cabinet government.[10] Granting that the prime minister is now a great deal more than merely "the first among equals," as supposed in the original conception of cabinet government, nevertheless it is almost

[10]The question of prime ministerial government is debated in Anthony King, ed., *The British Prime Minister* (London: Macmillan, 1969).

certainly an exaggeration to consider the prime minister so dominantly responsible for executive policy making as is the American president. Politically the prime minister cannot be nearly so independent of a cabinet as an American president. The prime minister shares executive authority with cabinet colleagues even though, like the president, the prime minister appoints these colleagues. What is crucial is that British cabinet members, by custom amounting to political necessity, are chosen so as to include almost all of a parliamentary party's important leaders. It is their support, or that of most of them, that is essential. With it the prime minister maintains a parliamentary majority; without it the prime minister can be isolated and driven to resign or to change policy to accord with that of cabinet colleagues. Nothing about this description denies the likely predominance of a prime minister in cabinet policy making. As the party leader elected by parliamentary-party colleagues in the first place, the prime minister has both the political status and the personal respect to be able ordinarily to persuade colleagues to accept policies; but the prime minister has so to persuade or, as may happen, to accept policies emerging from cabinet discussions. The cabinet, and especially its most important members, is thus itself a kind of restraint in relation to the policy-making authority of a chief executive. Britain, then, has collective rather than strictly individual responsibility for the executive decision making that is so characteristic of foreign affairs. Or, to be more careful, since the prime minister's special importance should not be disregarded, Britain has greater collective responsibility in these matters than has the United States.

A closer look at the cabinet should help explain its complexities. There are about twenty members, varying by two or three in either direction as recent prime ministers have found politically convenient. Always included are the heads of the most important ministries (*departments* in American terminology), some of which, such as the Foreign Office, Defense, Home Affairs, and the Treasury, are consistently so defined while others might be important enough only in certain periods. There are, in other words, some ministers, as well as junior ministers (undersecretaries, for example), outside the cabinet but in the larger "government" of about seventy executive appointees from parliamentary ranks. Because the most important political figures in the majority party are naturally chosen to head the most important ministries, they thus are cabinet members. So often are a few other similarly important politicians assigned traditional cabinet-status titles without specific departmental responsibility, but perhaps with special assignments (such as for the Rhodesian problem or for Common Market pre-entry negotiations). In this way, the prime minister can include in the cabinet the party members who are the ablest, most experienced politicians, and simultaneously the chief officers of the major departments of state. The basic political character of the appointments is not substantially qualified by the inclusion of a few members of the House of Lords, named either because of their political consequence in that body or because of special skills justifying a new peerage to accompany ministerial appointment. The latter suggests freedom to name a cabinet member who lacks prior parliamentary experience, but this is a freedom sparingly exercised. Certainly parliamentary experience, ordinarily meaning lengthy membership in the House of Commons, is a virtual prerequisite for cabinet appointment. On the other hand, such experience, however long, does not itself guarantee either cabinet or junior ministerial appointment.

Most directly concerned with foreign affairs in the cabinet are the prime minister and the foreign secretary (whose full title is now secretary of state for foreign and commonwealth affairs, following the merger in 1968 of the Foreign Office with the previously separate Commonwealth ministry, which had earlier absorbed the old Colonial Office). The relationships between prime minister and foreign secretary vary considerably from government to government. One can even hold both positions, but the last time that the prime minister was also foreign secretary was in 1924. But a prime minister, if a strong-minded leader experienced in foreign affairs, can act as foreign secretary while the title is held by a close and loyal confidante. At the other extreme, a prime minister more fully absorbed in domestic affairs can appoint a foreign secretary possessing considerable independent authority in Parliament. That authority need not flow from specialized expertise; for example, it was primarily political in the case of Ernest Bevin, the powerful trade unionist who was the Labour government's foreign secretary under Prime Minister Clement Attlee, and also in the case of James Callaghan, whose popularity in the Labour party helped to make him foreign secretary in 1974. A considerable standing within the parliamentary majority party (and probably a measure of respect from the Opposition) is useful for any foreign secretary—at least as much as it is for any other cabinet member. The standing may well combine specialized experience with personal popularity in the parliamentary party. So it did for Sir Alec Douglas-Home when he returned to the foreign secretaryship in Heath's Conservative government of 1970. Still, the prime minister must share in the parliamentary defense of foreign policy as well as in the making of it. The prime minister is always the leading member of the collegial group responsible for policy and cannot avoid that responsibility.

Other cabinet members are regularly involved in foreign policy. Since 1964 the defense secretary heads a unified military establishment (without the formerly coexisting Admiralty, War Office, and Air Ministry). Under the defense secretary, besides a minister of state, are three undersecretaries, one for each service. But only the defense secretary has cabinet status—much like the foreign secretary whose several subordinate ministers of state and undersecretaries are also outside the cabinet. Another member of the cabinet, the chancellor of the exchequer, is necessarily involved in all policies that require government funds and thus has to be mentioned as concerned with foreign affairs. International commitments have been known to be expensive, even prohibitively so, for a nation whose economy is as strained as Britain's. Responsible for the political direction of the Treasury, which in Britain combines budget making and many other tasks of administrative supervision along with the more limited functions of the U.S. Treasury Department, the chancellor of the exchequer is often in a position to be the crucial decision maker. The chancellor is always a leading figure in the majority party or certainly becomes so by virtue of being made chancellor.

It is reasonable to assume that the chancellor of the exchequer would be included—along with prime minister, foreign secretary, defense secretary, and perhaps a few others—in any "partial cabinet" organized to consider major foreign policy decisions. There is a good description of such a "partial cabinet" by a former participant, Patrick Gordon Walker, who also provides a careful analytical position of its relation to other cabinet groupings.[11] It differs, he explains, from what has been called an "inner cabinet" of the prime minister's friends who meet only informally. The partial cabinet is an organized committee, of a kind often used to expedite business by having only the relevant ministers meet on a given interdepartmental problem before bringing a policy proposal to the full cabinet. In significant foreign affairs, the committee seems more impressive because of its likely membership, and so the aptness of the term *partial cabinet* in such instances, although probably also in the case of a somewhat differently constituted committee contemplating a major domestic decision. Regardless of the term, some such collegial group, smaller than the whole cabinet, is an important part of the British decision-making process: it represents cabinet authority without usurping it. As Gordon Walker, himself a former foreign secretary, rightly observes, this constitutes the "very opposite of Prime Ministerial government; it presupposes that the Prime Minister carries influential Cabinet colleagues with him, and

that these will, with the Prime Minister, convince the Cabinet if policy is questioned when the Cabinet is informed."[12] The same British collegial principle is illustrated most persuasively by the testimony that Labour's prime minister and foreign secretary, in the 1960s, were once overruled by the cabinet on a matter of great importance.[13]

*The Foreign Service.* So far only the political leadership of the government has been discussed. Under its executive authority is a sharply differentiated career service that does not change with political turnovers. As in other nations, foreign-service officers are international subject-matter specialists in a way that politicians need not be (although they occasionally are). The career members of the British Foreign Office appear to have a greater prestige and influence than their American counterparts. The prestige is partly traditional and, until the 1960s, closely associated with heavy recruitment, by competitive examination, from the upper layers of the educational elite produced by the fee-paying public schools and by Oxford and Cambridge universities.[14] The foreign service has been separated from the domestic civil service both in its recruitment and in its managerial direction.[15] Its relative influence, however, depends on more than traditional educational elitism and the presumably associated professional competence. There is also the structural fact that the most experienced

[11]Patrick Gordon Walker, *The Cabinet* (New York: Basic Books, 1970), pp. 39–40, 88–90.

[12]*Ibid.,* p. 91.
[13]*Ibid.,* p. 92.
[14]Anthony Sampson, *The New Anatomy of Britain* (New York: Stein and Day, 1972), p. 288.
[15]On recruitment, see Lord Strang, *The Foreign Office* (New York: Oxford University Press, 1955), chaps. 4 and 5.

and successful foreign-service officers occupy crucial positions in relation to the foreign secretary and to other ministerial policy makers. Compared to the United States—where an administration appoints a substantial layer of its own politically chosen specialists, in the relevant departments as well as in the White House—a new British government brings with it little more than the limited number of ministerial and junior ministerial appointees already noted. And most of these are chosen for their parliamentary political talents rather than for their specialized knowledge of a given field. They are more directly dependent on career service advisers than are American presidents and cabinet members.[16] Understandably, this works to increase the influence of the foreign service (much as the similar situation works in the same direction for Britain's domestic civil service). Yet it is well to remember that the role remains that of influence; however weighty the advice from career officials, policy making is the responsibility of the political executive—prime minister, foreign secretary, and others functioning within the cabinet.

*Parliament.* British legislative authority, embodied now overwhelmingly in the popularly elected House of Commons, provides the most significant arena for debate and controversy concerning foreign as well as domestic policy. It does so even though, as previously observed, it does not itself make the policy or customarily exercise power to reject either a government policy or the government that makes a policy. Except in the most extraordinary circumstances, the influence of the

Commons is exerted within the context of parliamentary voting in which a majority party formally supports the government.[17] The context is not as limiting as it might appear from parliamentary voting itself. Government policy is formulated in the cabinet with some concern for the explicit and implicit preferences of the more than three hundred M.P.s who compose the majority parliamentary party. Intraparty discussion and pressures are common, and regular opportunities exist for communication between backbenchers and their leaders. All of a party's M.P.s meet from time to time, while some meet regularly in their own party committees, including one devoted to foreign affairs. The M.P.s of the majority party will later vote in sufficient numbers ordinarily to support the government policy, even though they may have argued against it in intraparty councils. A few will abstain or, more rarely, vote against their government without causing it to lose its parliamentary majority; these are danger signals for the leadership, which is thereby being told of the extent of disaffection with its policy. Admittedly, such parliamentary behavior is far different from the independent exercise of power by American members of

---

[16]Waltz, *Foreign Policy,* p. 137.

[17]An extraordinary circumstance in which a government policy was not supported sufficiently by the majority parliamentary party did occur in October 1971 when Heath's Conservative government proposal to join EEC was approved only with the help of enough opposition M.P.s to compensate (actually more than compensate) for the loss of a minority of Conservative rebels. Uwe Kitzinger, *Diplomacy and Persuasion* (London: Thames and Hudson, 1973), pp. 400–413. The import of this incident, along with the Labour government's parliamentary division in 1975, is discussed later, in this chapter's treatment of the EEC.

Congress either on the floor or in their decision-making committees.[18] British M.P.s of the majority party are so likely to observe the political exigencies requiring public support for their executive leadership that their influence must be exerted more subtly, usually behind the scenes when policy is formulated, or by a critical speech, or by an abstention designed to affect the next policy formulation.

Members of Parliament of the opposition party, both individually and collectively through their leadership, have a different and perhaps immediately even less consequential role to play. In parliamentary voting, of course, they regularly lose and are meant to lose to a cohesive majority party backing its government's policies. Individual M.P.s of the opposition party are only rarely potential participants—as are many American congressional representatives of the nonpresidential party—in a bipartisan majority supporting foreign policy. For support of its policy, in foreign or in domestic affairs, the government almost always depends on its partisan majority. On an important occasion, the government's policy will usually be presented and defended by the foreign secretary, one or two political aides, and the prime minister; the Opposition will then be represented by appropriate members of its "shadow cabinet"— that is, particularly by its prospective foreign secretary and its prospective prime minister (the opposition leader). Thus a Commons debate is mainly between those responsible for policy and those who would like to be, and might well become, re-

sponsible. It is a discussion between a government and its alternative.[19]

In addition to full-fledged debates on foreign affairs, the government is subject to attack during the regularly scheduled Commons question period—the first hour of each of the first four meeting days of the week. During this period, questions are addressed to ministers concerning their various policies. Foreign affairs receives its share of questions, both from opposition members and from members of the majority party. Sometimes the questions are directed to the prime minister instead of to the foreign secretary. More often than is possible for other subjects, foreign affairs questions can be turned away on the ground that to answer would violate national security. However, there are many questions, sometimes difficult and embarrassing, that government leaders attempt to handle, for it is politically unwise for ministers to dodge too many questions. The question period, as well as the general debate, serves to exemplify the usefulness of Parliament's role with respect to policy making: to question and criticize, but not to defeat the government.

The same can be said for the parliamentary performances reflecting individual and intraparty dissent

---

[18]Max Beloff, *Foreign Policy and the Democratic Process* (Baltimore: Johns Hopkins Press, 1955), pp. 25–26.

[19]The most dramatic example was the prolonged debate between the Labour opposition and the Conservative government over Britain's Suez intervention, reported in 558–560 *House of Commons Debates, passim* (October 30–November 8, 1956). See also Leon D. Epstein, *British Politics in the Suez Crisis* (Urbana: University of Illinois Press, 1964), chap. 5. For a strong argument concerning the efficacy of the parliamentary role in general, see Alexander J. Groth, "Britain and America: Some Requisites of Executive Leadership Compared," *Political Science Quarterly* 85 (June, 1970): 217–39.

concerning world affairs: M.P.s, simply because they are M.P.s, command a certain amount of public attention for their views, whether presented in or out of the House of Commons. There is a fairly good chance that what is said in the House will be reported outside. The most famous twentieth-century example is Winston Churchill's use of the Commons, as well as of other public arenas, to expound his critical view of the governing Conservative party's policy toward Hitler's Germany in the 1930s. Churchill was then a dissident nonministerial member of that governing party. More recently, there have also been dissenting M.P.s within each major party. Left-wing and pacifist-minded Labour M.P.s disputed their party's military commitments—particularly those involving the American alliance—throughout the decades of the Cold War, and they did so both with Labour in office and—perhaps more vigorously and on a larger scale—when their party was in opposition. On the other side, imperialist Conservative M.P.s attacked their party's policies during Britain's nearly steady postwar retreat from its former power and glory, and this often meant criticism of their own government when it, instead of Labour, happened to be managing the retreat (from Suez, for example). Always, as with the Labour left M.P.s, the imperialist Conservative M.P.s used the Commons as the place to let their leaders and the country know that there were nonconsensual views that had to be taken into account, if not followed, in making foreign policy.

### Nongovernmental Agencies

*Political Parties.* As their parliamentary behavior indicates, British parties, despite internal disagreements, function as collective adversaries with respect to foreign as well as domestic policy. The considerable interparty consensus about the general lines of policy does not, except during wartime coalitions, keep the opposition party from criticizing, conventionally and legitimately, either the substance or the execution of the government's policy. Related to this function, as well as to a majority party's defense of government policy, are the large membership organizations that each major party (and also the Liberal party during its periods of revival) maintains outside of Parliament in loosely defined connection with the strictly parliamentary groups. The extraparliamentary organizations are not simply cadres of officeholders and prospective officeholders;[20] nor are they skeletonized structures to be filled out only during election campaigns. Rather, they contain large numbers of regular dues-paying members—although fewer in the 1970s than in the 1950s.

On this score, the Conservative structure is simpler than Labour's. Conservative membership is entirely individual and direct. The member joins a Conservative constituency association, which is affiliated to the National Union of Conservative and Unionist Associations. Total membership in recent years has been about 1.5 million. Labour's more complicated structure allows both direct and indirect memberships. In addition to about one-half million who belong to Labour constituency associations, over 5 million are counted as members because they

[20] The fullest account of the relationship of mass membership to parliamentary parties is R. T. McKenzie, *British Political Parties* (London: William Heinemann, 1963).

belong to trade unions that are affiliated to the Labour party and that pay dues to the party.

From the viewpoint of each party's parliamentary leadership, the principal purpose of the mass membership is undoubtedly to help win elections. Advice, let alone direction, on policy questions is hardly desired, but this does not prevent the organized membership from offering and even urging such advice. Regular dues-paying members have often become active in the first place in order to have a role affecting policy. There are two levels at which rank-and-file members can try to influence decisions. The first is through the Conservative or Labour constituency organization, which selects its parliamentary candidate, and would therefore appear to have the means of influencing decisively the position of an M.P. How much and how often this channel of influence is used cannot readily be discovered. There have been some instances in which sitting M.P.s have been locally rejected for subsequent candidacy because of policy disagreements, notably after the Suez crisis of 1956 or after the EEC debate of 1971.[21] Ordinarily, at least before 1975, such rejections tended to reflect a super-loyalty to national party positions more or less as championed by parliamentary leaders.

The second level for rank-and-file influence is the national conference held annually by each major party. Delegates to each conference, chosen by the various units of the national party, have the opportunity to present, discuss, and vote on policy resolutions. On foreign affairs as on other matters, the mass membership of each party has had distinctive views which it has sought, via conference resolutions, to persuade or pressure party leaders to adopt. The Conservative conference has passed resolutions without claiming the power to fix the parliamentary leadership's policy. The Labour conference, however, has often acted as though it and the executive committee elected by the conference did have such power. The Labour party constitution does give the external mass organization the power to decide general policy, but this is at odds with the usual British conception that policy is made by parliamentary representatives who are individually and collectively responsible to the electorate. It is also at odds with much of Labour's own practice, notably in the significant periods of 1945–51 and 1964–70, when the party formed the government. Labour government leaders usually succeeded in getting the party conference to support foreign policy positions already adopted by the government. And the parliamentary leaders were able, during most of Labour's opposition years of 1951–64, to keep the initiative and to persuade the conference delegates to accept official policy, occasionally in compromised form. In 1960 the Labour conference did adopt foreign policy resolutions advocating unilateral nuclear disarmament, which were flatly opposed by the parliamentary leadership. The leader, Hugh Gaitskell, and most of the parliamentary party refused to be bound by these resolutions. Whether Gaitskell would eventually have been forced either to adopt the conference's policy or to resign was never answered, because he suc-

---

[21]Epstein, *Suez Crisis,* chap. 6. The Labour M.P. rejected by his local party after his 1971 parliamentary deviation in favor of EEC membership tells his story in Dick Taverne, *The Future of the Left* (London: Cape, 1974), Part I.

ceeded in getting the next annual conference, in 1961, to reverse the 1960 position. His persistence, along with the bulk of Labour M.P.s, in a year's defiance of conference resolutions is usually considered evidence for the primacy of the parliamentary party in Labour policy making.

Yet this primacy is certainly challenged when Labour is in opposition. In 1970–73 the party conference and its national executive committee opposed British membership in the European Economic Community (EEC) despite the parliamentary party leadership's own previous effort, when governing in the late 1960s, to obtain entry. No direct conflict occurred, however, since most of the parliamentary party, under Harold Wilson, decided to oppose British entry at least under the terms the Conservative government had negotiated in 1971. When he returned to power in 1974–75, Wilson and most of his cabinet, while observing the party's electoral commitment to renegotiate EEC-membership terms and to present these terms to a national referendum, were willing to make the case for continued membership despite predictable conference disapproval and very substantial dissent within parliamentary ranks. In this respect, the Wilson leadership was seeking to make government policy as it had on most occasions in 1964–70 when its primacy in foreign affairs had been more easily maintained in relation to conference resolutions. Moreover, Wilson's policy making succeeded when his government's renegotiated EEC terms were approved by a two-to-one margin in the unprecedented referendum of June 1975.

Regardless of their disputed role in determining policy, organized parties do serve as media for the expression of public opinion and as agencies of popular pressure if not control much more regularly than in the United States. This is plainer and more significant in the Labour party. The left-wing critics within the Labour party have been numerous and persistent—whether defeated, as on a variety of resolutions in the 1950s, or temporarily successful, as on unilateral nuclear disarmament in 1960 or EEC in the early 1970s. They represent a strong tendency among many Labour party activists and trade union leaders, and their persistent left-wing advocacy in foreign affairs is rooted in both socialism and pacifism. Opposition to "power politics" and "imperialism" has been traditional Labour party ideology; so has a commitment to a distinctively "socialist foreign policy." Thus the left wing opposed German rearmament following World War II, suspected the Anglo-American alliance (most of the time and especially during the Vietnam war), and rejected nuclear weapons.[22] Such left-wing views did not often become official Labour policy, and they seemed to exert less influence than ever during Prime Minister Wilson's governments of the late 1960s. Yet they remained to be faced by Labour leaders at most party conferences and to arise more formidably in the 1970s when Labour was again in opposition and then marginally in office.

A comparable, although ideologically opposite, campaign formerly sought to move the Conservative party leadership from its usually

[22]Labour conference debates are reported verbatim in *Annual Reports* published by the party.

moderate position of accepting Britain's diminishing status in world affairs. More accurately called "imperialist" than "right-wing," it represented a substantial force at party conferences as well as among Conservative M.P.s until the late 1950s.[23] "Empire" long remained the emotive word for Conservatives, as "socialist" has been for Labour, but efforts to save the empire or to halt its "scuttling," ceased to be relevant in the 1960s, when virtually all of the large British dependencies of the past had become self-governing nations. The new multiracial Commonwealth, to which these nations belonged along with Britian and the old white dominions, did not have the same imperialist appeal. More significant for many rank-and-file Conservatives were the remaining ties to British settlers in Africa—notably in Southern Rhodesia, where the effort of the white minority to maintain its dominance was met with less hostility among Conservative activists than it was among Labour activists. Somewhat similar sentiments could be associated with Conservative party support for the sale of arms to the Union of South Africa. Another kind of residual imperialist sentiment was displayed in Conservative willingness to support or even encourage the use of British military force when the nation's overseas interests appeared to be challenged; thus there was strong rank-and-file party sympathy for the abortive campaign of Eden's government in 1956 to reverse the Egyptian seizure of the Suez Canal. Much less dramatically, this kind of sympathy could be counted on by Conservative leaders

who, in the early 1970s, sought to postpone Britain's military departure from positions east of Suez already scheduled for abandonment by the previous Labour government.

Party membership has played an even less certain part in the development of policy concerning British entry into the EEC. During the periods in which this was a live issue in British politics (often in the 1960s and again in the 1970s), the decision to seek British entry was first taken by the government, Conservative or Labour, and then subject to debate within each party. At certain times, as in the early 1960s, when the Conservative government was negotiating entry (eventually vetoed by de Gaulle), there was an apparent interparty divergence. Conservatives supported their leadership's efforts (with some reluctance), and Labour conferences backed their leadership's evident opposition—at least to the supposed terms of entry. In the late 1960s, when Wilson's Labour government sought to join the EEC, the party was carried along with the government position, while Conservatives did not oppose what they had so recently tried themselves. Yet even when both parties formally approved of entry, there can be no doubt that at almost all times, including 1969–70, there was considerable dissent within each major party. It was expressed at both party conferences. In order to obtain at least majority support on this issue, each party's leadership had to present its policy so as to stress negotiations without firm commitment in the absence of favorable terms. Each party contained both nationalist and practical economic critics, often reflecting widespread opposition outside party channels. There were also ideological dissenters—

[23]Conservative conference debates are reported verbatim in *Annual Reports* published by the party.

socialists who disliked the big-business orientation of the Common Market and residual imperialists who disliked the European (as opposed to an overseas) involvement. Neither of these latter forces was strong enough on its own, after the early 1960s, to cause a major party to adopt a doctrinal line against joining the EEC, regardless of the terms of entry that might be negotiated. While socialist and nationalist principles contributed in 1971 to Labour opposition to the Conservative government's negotiated entry, the Labour party conference as well as the parliamentary Labour party then officially opposed only the specific terms of entry. In practice, of course, this meant opposing the only terms evidently obtainable for Britain to enter the EEC during the early 1970s. Yet, by confining official opposition to the specific economic terms, Labour avoided a flat commitment to withdraw Britain from the EEC. By pledging to submit renegotiated terms to a popular vote, the party probably satisfied some of its more ideological anti-EEC activists whose rank-and-file pressure seemed indirectly influential.

Rank-and-file pressures in constituencies and in party conferences are often closely related to differences of opinion between the party's M.P.s. It is really the M.P.s who are the direct objects of whatever influence the external organizations can bring to bear. Despite the advantages of the party's leaders in maintaining parliamentary cohesion—especially when they hold government office—the fact remains that the few hundred M.P.s who compose a majority party have a final authority: their backing for a policy has to be secured by a government. And when a party is out of power, its M.P.s even have room for some initiative. Labour formally gives control of its opposition policy to its M.P.s. The Conservative party maintains an equivalent, though less clearcut, means for backbenchers to express their opinions (which may also be the opinions of their constituency followers).

In discussing the role of parties it should be pointed out that, despite extremists within each party, the moderate Conservative and moderate Labour leaders have occupied a good deal of common ground with respect to Britain's postwar foreign policy. The important matters of maintaining a substantial if now limited defense establishment, preserving the American alliance, and surrendering imperial possessions have not been basically at issue between the two major parties (or between them and the Liberal party). Insofar as the parties have disagreed on these matters, it has ordinarily been at the margins of policy. For example, while the Labour party officially disputed, from 1960 to 1964, the Conservative government's policy favoring an independent nuclear arsenal for Britain, Labour's alternative was to place Britain's nuclear force in a joint Atlantic force with the United States and to rely openly on American military capacity. Much more unusual was the sharp and nearly total Labour opposition to the Conservative government's Suez campaign of 1956. Even in 1971, when Labour opposed the terms of EEC entry, its party solidarity was much less substantial, as it was also when advocating renegotiation in the election campaigns of 1974.

There is a danger of overstating the importance of British parties in foreign policy. Despite their greater organization and cohesion around policy positions in comparison with American parties,[24] the fact remains that British parties do not regularly present competing foreign policies to the electorate. Even when they seem to present different policies, as on the independent nuclear force in the 1964 general election, the issue may not be especially relevant to the voters. Party appeals have usually focused on domestic issues, and there is convincing evidence from opinion surveys in 1964 that the British electorate regarded these issues as much more important than any defense or foreign policy question.[25] The 1964 electorate is probably not exceptional in this respect. Without a notable crisis in world affairs, it now seems that most British voters are unlikely to make their electoral decisions primarily on international questions. The 1974 general elections, when Labour proposed at least a possible reversal of the Conservative commitment to EEC membership, are special cases, but it is by no means clear that the EEC was a dominant issue even in those campaigns. Certainly foreign affairs more generally, including defense, appears to have played hardly any part in the February 1974 election campaigning.[26] Perhaps international questions were more salient several decades ago, while Britain was more consequential in world

affairs, but whatever the situation in the past it seems unrealistic now to expect British voters to rest their electoral choices very heavily on foreign policy issues.

*Interest Groups.* Major British interest groups tend to have direct connections with a political party. The outstanding example is that of the trade unions, most of which are affiliated with the Labour party and thus share directly, often dominantly, in that party's policy making. The unions also have a general organization, the Trades Union Congress, which is not part of the Labour party and which confers with the governments, regardless of which party is in power, in behalf of union interests. Somewhat similarly, the cooperative movement works both within and outside the Labour party. The Conservatives have no precise organizational counterparts, but industrial leaders maintain close connections with the party. This they do personally, as important Conservatives themselves, and through the usual business organizations established in particular trades and in general categories such as manufacturing. Trade associations, like individual trade unions, may maintain communication with party leaders on policy matters of direct concern. A distinctive feature of this political communication, from the American point of view, is that individual M.P.s often openly serve as agents for interest groups—business, union, farm, and others; M.P.s are even subsidized for this purpose by the groups they represent. There is ready access and, therefore, influence—but not overwhelming influence. For example, the British farm organization, working closely with the Conservative party, might have contributed to the delay in the Macmillan govern-

[24]This view of British parties is advanced most vigorously by Samuel H. Beer, *British Politics in the Collectivist Age* (New York: Knopf, 1965).

[25]National Opinion Polls, Ltd., *Political Bulletin* (London), October, 1964, Appendix A. See also David E. Butler and Donald Stokes, *Political Change in Britain* (New York: St. Martin's Press, 1969), pp. 343–44.

[26]David Butler and Dennis Kavanagh, *The British General Election of February 1974* (London: Macmillan, 1974), pp. 61–65.

ment's decision to negotiate for entry to the Common Market, but it did not prevent the decision or set all the terms for entry.

Generally, the most substantial interest groups concerned with foreign policy decisions are not organized primarily to influence such decisions. This holds for the important domestic economic groups noted above, and also for other types of organizations. Churches are plainly in this category; through their official representatives, they express opinions bearing on British foreign policy, although the expression of such opinions is only incidental to their main role. Veterans' groups are another case in point, although their efforts to influence general policy are less prominent in Britain than the efforts of comparable groups in the United States. The same can be said, for a different reason, of the activities of ethnic groups. Such groups are simply less significant in Britain because of the absence of large ethnic minorities of the sort that compose so much of the American population. Although there are, and almost always have been, continental refugees in Britain, their numbers have not been sufficient to constitute serious pressure on British foreign policy making. Even the Jewish population of a half-million cannot be said to be an electoral factor in determining British policy toward Israel, despite a vigorous Zionist movement—represented particularly in the Labour party. Neither is the Irish minority, largely centered in a few seaports and manufacturing centers, a major influence, although it does, like the Zionists, have parliamentary members.

In addition to the groups whose varying influence on foreign affairs is incidental to their main purpose, there are also many British groups organized entirely around foreign policy issues. These may be less substantial, but they are often most active propagandistically. Some organizations are devoted to particular causes, such as justice or freedom for certain people in a certain place, and they wax and wane with the excitement of the issue. Others are broader in scope and more durable. One example is the United Nations Association; another, operating at a scholarly and almost official level in order to influence opinion makers, is the Royal Institute of International Affairs; a third, also of limited membership, is the newer Institute of Strategic Studies, which combines key government personnel with other selected persons who are professionally concerned with the analysis of foreign and defense policies. At an altogether different level of activity was the mass-membership organization, the Campaign for Nuclear Disarmament. Developed in the late 1950s to oppose Britain's retention of nuclear weapons, the CND undoubtedly mobilized the residual pacifism and neutralism of socialists, students, intellectuals, and miscellaneous middle-class citizens. Their most spectacular tactic was a well-publicized protest march each spring from a nuclear weapons center to a Trafalgar Square rally. The Nuclear Disarmers became active not only in this way and through a flood of speeches and literature, but also in the Labour party, where their position was accepted by important trade union leaders as well as by many constituency party workers. More recently both pro-EEC and anti-EEC organizations were major ad hoc participants in the 1975 referendum campaign.

*Media of Mass Communication.* The most basic point to note about British mass media is their national character. Strictly local and regional newspapers are of minor importance in relation to the media centered in London. The British magazine, radio, and television audience is essentially national. Opinion concerning foreign policy, like that concerning most domestic policy, is formed nationally and not regionally.

British communication has also taken on a special character by virtue of the continued monopoly (broken only at the local level in the 1970s) of radio broadcasting by the government-owned British Broadcasting Corporation (BBC), and by a similar monopoly of telecasting, which lasted until 1955, when supervised commercial television began to compete with the BBC. The government-owned service has avoided the editorialized commentary on the news typical of American radio and television. The news is reported straight and without dramatization, and a similar standard is expected of commercial television. Radio and television facilities are used by government spokesmen, particularly the prime minister and the foreign secretary, for official expositions of foreign policy, the importance of this means of communication with the nation having been firmly established by the successful wartime speeches of Winston Churchill. Some radio and television time is divided, according to an agreed-upon formula, between political parties for a presentation of their views on international as well as other issues. Occasionally, too, there are programs devoted to discussion of foreign policy. Television, as in the United States, is the most important means of reaching a mass audience; but in no case is there any purchase of time for the presentation of opinions.

The neutrality of British radio and television stands in contrast to the sharply partisan attachments of the press. A majority of newspapers lean toward the Conservatives, but the largest London paper, the *Daily Mirror,* is often pro-Labour. Although none of the mass-circulation dailies (such as the *Daily Mirror* and its several pro-Conservative counterparts) give much serious attention to international affairs, it is through their headlines, often slanted by partisan considerations, that a large share of the British population forms its perspective on international policies. Nevertheless, the quality press, even with its small circulation, deserves more attention as a molder of opinion. Except in Scotland, where there are equivalent newspapers, almost every person seriously concerned with national or international affairs reads the *Times* of London, the liberal *Guardian,* or the Conservative *Daily Telegraph.* Moreover, at least one of three London Sunday papers —the *Observer,* the *Sunday Times,* and the *Sunday Telegraph*—is read by virtually the whole of the serious English public. In addition, the special importance of the weekly *Economist* should be noted; more so than other intellectually oriented weeklies (such as the *Spectator* and the left-wing *New Statesman*), the *Economist* reaches the influential. Although these various papers and periodicals often present divergent views, there is an intimacy about the English circle of discussion that is absent in larger and less centralized political communities.

Other media of communication also play an important role in Britain. Pamphlets, for instance, are still widely used by party and party-affiliated groups to reach the public. Furthermore, Britain is a book-reading nation, and it is worth mentioning that both scholarly and popular volumes on foreign policy reach the attentive public. Speeches at public meetings, even though they are declining into popularity as a result of television, are still a means of influencing political audiences. A speech by a major public figure remains an important occasion, at least for the membership of a political party.

### The Role of Public Opinion

Many of the "nongovernmental agencies" discussed in the preceding section are often conceived as representing public opinion, in contrast to the official agencies of governmental policy making. For analytical purposes it has been useful to adhere to this distinction, although there is a considerable overlapping of persons and functions. This overlapping seems to be an especially significant feature of Britain's small, homogeneous community of important ministers, top civil servants, editors of quality newspapers, and certain academic and other public persons capable of informal consultation. Possessing common social and educational backgrounds, members of this limited community are often thought both to make and expound policy, especially in the somewhat detached international field. Specifically, during the 1960s and early 1970s, they seemed, to dissenters, to be a dominating elite favoring Britain's membership in the EEC when national surveys of public opinion showed substantial and sometimes majority opposition. In a very real sense, the Labour party's commitment to a referendum on continued EEC membership represented an effort to reject policy making by a foreign-affairs leadership—or at least to subject such policy making to a more direct popular check than that of the parliamentary process.

Populism of this kind is a novelty in Britain. Generally there has been a frank recognition of the leadership groups that, in Gabriel Almond's phrase, "carry on the specific work of policy formulation and policy advocacy."[27] As Almond has also pointed out (although in reference to the United States), an elite of this sort does not operate independently of "certain policy criteria in the form of widely held values and expectations."[28] The British public, like the public elsewhere, sets such criteria, and the policy makers are limited thereby—as, for instance, by the public's manifest desire for peace. The subtlety of these relations has been well described by Kenneth Younger, a former minister of state for foreign affairs. Control of foreign policy, he says, is more oligarchic than control of domestic policy, and on first reflection he could think of no occasion when he or his superiors "had been greatly affected by public opinion in reaching important decisions."[29] But this first impression, he realized, was misleading, because public opinion did affect ministers in a general way. "The Government," he writes, "tends to identify itself almost un-

[27]Gabriel Almond, *The American People and Foreign Policy* (New York: Harcourt, Brace, 1950), p. 5.
[28]*Ibid.*, p. 6.
[29]Kenneth Younger, "Public Opinion and Foreign Policy," *British Journal of Sociology* 6 (June, 1955): 169.

consciously with a vaguely sensed general will, and no clear formulation of the pressure of public opinion upon Government policy ever occurs."[30] Younger believes that a government identifies itself especially with its own supporters.

## THE SUBSTANCE OF FOREIGN POLICY

Ordinarily, it is assumed that major tendencies in British foreign policy are not subject to drastic change as a result of general elections or other internal political events. No such change can be observed in any of the shifts in party government during the twenty-five years after World War II—from Conservative to Labour in 1945, to Conservative in 1951, back to Labour in 1964, and again back to Conservative in 1970. Each of these successive governments faced a world situation in which Britain had limited choices, often confined to methods, timing of a military withdrawal, or marginal issues such as whether to sell arms to the Union of South Africa or how hard a line to take against Southern Rhodesia's white government. Not regarded as reversible by the dominant forces in either major party were policies related to close association with the United States, continued membership in the North Atlantic Treaty Organization, and the gradual withdrawal from imperial responsibilities. Nor, once negotiations were begun to enter the European Economic Community, was it thought likely that a subsequent

government would abandon negotiations altogether or seek to reverse a negotiated entry when actually accomplished. Admittedly, Labour's 1974 commitment on renegotiations and a referendum risked, although it did not actually produce, a major policy reversal.

### Commonwealth Relations

Especially in the past, Britain's relations with the other member nations of the Commonwealth and with its strictly imperial dependencies, might not have seemed properly to belong within the sphere of foreign affairs. Now, however, that the British government itself blurs the distinction by having only one merged ministry to deal with foreign and Commonwealth relations as well as with what remains of colonial affairs, it is clearly reasonable to consider policy toward the Commonwealth as an aspect of British foreign policy. The term *Commonwealth of Nations* is of recent coinage, succeeding *British Commonwealth of Nations* as well as the still older *British Empire.* For a time during the years between the two world wars and just afterward, Englishmen often spoke of *Commonwealth and Empire,* meaning by the first part of the phrase the already self-governing member nations (or "dominions," as they were also called), and by the second part the still vast areas and populations that were British dependencies governed in some degree from London. Gradually, however, *Commonwealth* has come to be used almost exclusively as most of the formerly imperial dependencies have become self-governing member nations; the word *British* was simultaneously dropped as the prefatory adjective

---

[30] *Ibid.* p. 171. See Bernard C. Cohen's distinction between the absence of governmental responsiveness in the short run with an apparent responsiveness in the long run. *The Public's Impact on Foreign Policy* (Boston: Little, Brown, 1973), p. 206.

for a group of nations now so largely Asian and African.

*Commonwealth,* it can be seen, is the single general name for an entity consisting of and developed from two very different elements of modern British overseas expansion. The first element is largely British in the literal sense of those nations—Canada, Australia, and New Zealand—which were settled and dominated numerically and politically by peoples from the British Isles, and augmented by other European immigrants. The Union of South Africa, which along with Canada, Australia, and New Zealand joined Britain in the original Commonwealth and remained a member until the early 1960s, was always a special case, since its British-derived population was not dominant over time in relation to the white settlers of Dutch descent—and certainly not in relation to the black African population. But even taking into account the Union of South Africa and the large French minority in Canada, the Commonwealth before 1945 was principally British in many significant ways. The spacious, remote, and growing nations of Canada and Australia, however British in origin, were bound to develop and pursue interests of their own, for which reason they had become self-governing even in the nineteenth century; but they also shared many interests with Britain and consequently displayed considerable support for British policy, as in their almost immediate move to participation in both world wars. Whether this kind of cohesion would have continued after World War II, even in an old Commonwealth, is doubtful; it was surely too much to expect in the newly enlarged and extremely diverse Commonwealth. The new mem-

ber nations were overwhelmingly Asian and African by population, not just by geographical location. Neither India (by far the largest) nor any of the other new Commonwealth states had ever been so heavily populated by British settlers as to make for a British nation. Mainly, these nations had simply been governed by Britain following military conquest and economic involvement by way of trade and industry. Only in certain parts of eastern and southern Africa were there substantial settlements of Britishers, and even in these exceptional instances the colonial settlers were no more than a large privileged minority whose capacity to dominate, in Southern Rhodesia or the Union of South Africa, depended on sternly enforced racial discrimination. Much more characteristic in Africa were Ghana and Nigeria, which, like India and Pakistan and almost all of the other former African and Asian dependencies of any size, had no large minority of British or other white settlers. The thin line of British civil servants, military officers, and business people did not realistically constitute a colonial settlement. Therefore, self-government could only mean non-British government without any claims to the contrary. The most the former British governors could hope for was that the new, indigenous government would be in the British style, which they had usually sought to implant through the establishment of elected parliaments and native civil services before the achievement of complete self-government. This hope was (perhaps surprisingly) fulfilled during the first decades of Indian government in particular, but its achievement, now apparently unsure, could not substitute for common interest flowing from a common national origin. In short, the Commonwealth ceased to be British in much more than name when it became multiracial in the decades after World War II.

Some exposition is required in order to understand the maintenance of this Commonwealth and its apparent significance in recent British experience. It is a residual symbol of two old British ambitions. One ambition was to lead a "Greater Britain" that combined, in a kind of union—economic as well as political—Britain itself and the British-populated overseas dominions (and perhaps the United States). The other ambition, really meaningful only for a few decades of the late nineteenth and early twentieth centuries, was to possess an imperial power through domination of huge Asian and African portions of the globe. There did not appear to be any other way for Britain to achieve great-power status once it became clear, as it did even before 1900, that it had to compete with the larger continental states of Germany and Russia, and with the United States. But neither ambition, it also became clear, could be fulfilled after World War II. The possibility of a reintegration of English-speaking dominions was obviously remote, given the increasingly national identities of Canada and Australia, not to mention the Union of South Africa; in any event, Britain could hardly expect to lead these nations when it was economically weak and militarily dependent on the United States. And, of course, Britain had neither the will nor the capacity to hold, for a prolonged period, the large imperial territories against their now-rebellious Asian and African populations. It did not follow, however,

that Britain was obligated to encourage Commonwealth membership for these territories when they became self-governing. It would have been possible, while extending self-government in Asia and Africa, perhaps still more rapidly than was actually done, to have eliminated even the residual special ties to Britain, and so to have kept the Commonwealth exclusively, or almost exclusively, a grouping of "British" nations. This would have meant an effort to achieve a somewhat closer community even if well short of a union of "Greater Britain." The British rejection of this option reveals how postwar Britain still sought greatness in the world through a liberalized mid-twentieth century version of "empire." A Commonwealth large enough to include India and most of the other formerly Asian and African dependencies was necessary in order to magnify Britain's role commensurate with the old ambitions. Moreover, the very multiracial character of the new Commonwealth seemed itself an accomplishment in a world otherwise divided so sharply along racial lines. With pride, then, a British ambassador to the United States could say, in 1956: "Britain lies at the heart of the Commonwealth, and the Commonwealth contains over six hundred million people, more than a third of the population of the free world."[31]

Unquestionably there does remain, even now, a genuine if limited association of nations called the "Commonwealth." Thirty-two nations, including Britain, are members (as of 1973), and about thirty other territories, mainly very small,

[31]Roger Makins, "The Commonwealth in World Affairs," *Labour and Industry in Britain* 14 (September, 1956):116.

remain "dependencies" with varying degrees of self-government. The total Commonwealth population has risen to 800 million, and is now even more overwhelmingly Asian and African than it was twenty years ago. Each member nation acknowledges the queen of England as the symbolic head of the Commonwealth, but the new Asian and African nations do not accept the queen as their own crowned head of state. There is no central authority, in any practical political sense, above that of the respective governments themselves, although there are essentially administrative arrangements, including a Commonwealth Secretariat, for a multitude of cooperative ventures.[32] There are also regular meetings of prime ministers and other political leaders at Commonwealth conferences, at which efforts are made to adopt common policies at least on matters of intra-Commonwealth concern. It has not been possible, however, for the Commonwealth to present a united front on many of the most important international issues of concern to Britain. Not only have the African and Asian member nations been at odds with any seeming reassertion by Britain of an imperialist role, as at Suez in 1956, but the established Afro-Asian position in the Cold War has been neutralist, under Indian leadership, and thus distinct from Britain's alignment with the United States. Broadly speaking, the new Commonwealth nations have defined their global interests differently from Britain's—no doubt because those interests are in fact different in many basic respects.

Yet Britain has exerted considerable effort, often at considerable expense, to maintain the multiracial Commonwealth. It loosened what was already a loose intergovernmental structure in order to accommodate first India and then other Asian and African nations when they insisted on republican regimes without the British queen as their crowned chief of state. Britain also accepted the Commonwealth's numerically predominant antagonism to the Union of South Africa, and joined in policies leading to the Union's exit from the Commonwealth. It is true, of course, that by the 1960s many British people shared the African and Asian hostility toward the Union's racist domestic policies, but there remained (and still remain) many closer British ties with the Union and the people in it than with the newer Commonwealth nations. These ties are economic as well as ethnic and personal—at least with respect to the large English-speaking white minority. Yet such ties have been overridden with respect to Southern Rhodesia, whose white minority is almost completely British in origin. Britain rejected the claim of a regime based on that minority to become self-governing and, as such, presumably a member nation of the Commonwealth. In fact, after rejecting the asserted independence of that regime in 1965, Britain attempted to give effect to the rejection by economic sanctions along with withdrawal of legal recognition. Again, it must be said that the British policy reflected widespread antiracist sentiments in Britain itself. But it is by no means clear that Britain would have taken quite so hard a line without the desire to maintain its Commonwealth ties with Asian and

[32]J. D. B. Miller, *Survey of Commonwealth Affairs* (London: Oxford University Press, 1974), chap. 17.

African nations. There were limits, of course, to the policies Britain would adopt because of Afro-Asian pressure; thus Britain refused to use its military force to attempt to overthrow the white minority government of Southern Rhodesia and, as a result, received more adverse criticism than credit from the Afro-Asian members of the Commonwealth.[33] However, apart from the expense of launching a military expedition in Africa, there was another reason Britain could not seriously contemplate such an action to please most of the Commonwealth: sending British soldiers to fight British settlers in behalf of a black majority was hardly attractive politically in Britain itself.

An even clearer indication of the inherent limits on an Afro-Asian orientation for Britain's Commonwealth policy is to be found in the postwar history of Britain's immigration legislation. Adhering at first to an idealistic conception of Commonwealth citizenship, Britain was open throughout the 1950s to immigrants from the African, Asian, and West Indian member nations and dependencies, just as it was to immigrants from the old British dominions. And this was at a time when Britain was by no means open on the same basis to immigrants from southern and eastern Europe. Commonwealth citizens were treated as British citizens rather than as foreigners. Consequently, during the years of full employment in Britain and of unemployment or underemployment in other parts of the Commonwealth—in the overpopulated Asian and West Indian nations particularly—there was a fairly large-scale movement of nonwhite people to British cities, bringing their total numbers near the 2-percent figure, as noted earlier, and producing, in certain cities, considerable popular agitation against the immigration. Responding to this pressure in the 1960s, successive British governments, Conservative and then Labour, acted first to curtail the immigration and then to try to eliminate it almost altogether. Governmental leaders, it is likely, acted reluctantly insofar as they were committed to Commonwealth ideals, but politically they appreciated that they had little choice, even though they might well have been able to cite strictly economic benefits for Britain in securing additional workers.

In other instances, Britain has pursued a Commonwealth policy that could be questioned on purely economic grounds and that, on such grounds, has recently been limited. Overseas economic aid to the less-developed nations of the Commonwealth is an obvious case in point, although it might be argued that Britain continued to be relatively generous in this respect. Military commitments have seemed more burdensome partly because they may have derived from an older imperial role rather than from a strictly contemporary Commonwealth purpose, even though serving it as well. Britain sought to defend territories not only while they were still dependencies—as in providing a military force in Malaya during the earlier postwar years—but also afterward, as when, in the middle 1960s, Britain helped the self-governing Commonwealth nation of Malaysia fight Indonesian attacks. More generally, Britain maintained expensive overseas bases—the so-called East-of-Suez policy—for such purposes, and only in 1967 scheduled their abandonment or near-abandonment for

[33] *Ibid.*, chap. 10.

the 1970s. Perhaps Britain would have wanted in any case to retain these tangible signs of influence in the postwar world, but the Commonwealth tie surely encouraged and legitimized the expenditure for at least two extra decades. The virtual withdrawal that has now occurred may thus be understood as reflecting a diminishing Commonwealth emphasis as well as Britain's generally diminishing influence in world affairs.

From an American and perhaps also from a broader Western viewpoint, Britain's postwar involvement in the new Commonwealth appeared useful if only because it meant that Britain assumed some of the military burden, east of Suez and elsewhere, that might otherwise have become the sole responsibility of the United States. Much of this could also have been justified from a strictly British viewpoint on the widely held assumption that Britain, as a Western power, has a considerable stake in the American-led effort to contain hostile forces and to preserve Western communication with less-developed nations. But it is not clear that quite as much of the actual British overseas undertaking could thus have been justified during the quarter-century after World War II. It was one thing for an economically weakened but still substantial power like Britain to contribute, as it did on a large scale, to the military defense of Europe, where British interests were most directly involved. Large-scale military expenditures elsewhere seemed less obviously necessary, and they were not forthcoming on a similar scale for so long a time from other Western European nations of similar size. It is hard to escape the conclusion that Britain retained a disproportionate overseas commitment, and that it did so partly because of its residual imperial attachment to Commonwealth responsibilities. That attachment may now have diminished, at least in its capacity to influence material commitments. After all, the generation of Englishmen growing up since World War II has not really lived in the era of imperial glory or even of great-power status. On the other hand, preceding generations, including those in policy-making positions until now, must have found the symbolism of Commonwealth a useful mid-twentieth-century substitute for imperialism. Especially during the decades of Britain's withdrawal from territories it had once governed, the existence of the Commonwealth could assuage what was aptly called a "sense of personal loss —almost of amputation,"[34] which Englishmen felt when a colony became independent. Substitution of the Commonwealth association for the empire could thus help account for the relatively slight resistance to the withdrawal process and so to the absence of persistent attempts to hold territory that had become unmanageable for Britain.

### English-speaking Ties

Britain's links with other English-speaking nations are based on a political heritage along with a common language and an ethnic background associated with the language. These links are not everywhere identical with those of the Commonwealth. Most of the present multiracial Commonwealth is no more English-speaking than it is British; on the other hand, the largest and most

[34]John Strachey, *The End of Empire* (New York: Praeger, 1964), p. 204.

powerful English-speaking nation, the United States, is not a Commonwealth nation. Ireland also is not a Commonwealth nation. Yet its association with Britain, despite centuries of religious and political animosity, is a fact dictated by proximity and economic dependence as well as by the common use of the English language. Ireland, no less than Canada, Australia, and New Zealand, has parliamentary institutions clearly derived from British tradition. Chiefly, however, it is Britain's overseas linguistic ties that are unusually significant in comparison with those of other European nations. They are not the ties of a political union or even of an economic union. Yet there can be little doubt that many British people are able more readily to identify their own nation with the other English-speaking nations than with the multiracial Commonwealth. Americans are less likely to be considered foreigners than are Indians and Pakistanis, or even Europeans whose language if not race seems more foreign than that of the more geographically distant English-speaking American. Sir Winston Churchill was not alone among his countrymen in cherishing Britain's status among the "English-speaking peoples." [35] The very phrase, perhaps partly because it is a twentieth-century euphemism for "Anglo-Saxon world," conveys, especially in Britain, much of the feeling associated with a racial or ethnic bond. As such, the ties may readily be exaggerated. Neither in Canada nor in the United States, and no longer in Australia, is the national background of the population so

completely British. In addition to Canada's French (and French-speaking) population, there are large numbers of people of various continental European backgrounds in all of the English-speaking overseas nations except New Zealand. The United States in particular is surely not British except in its origins.

Dealing with the United States represents a very special problem in Britain's relations with the English-speaking world if only because the United States has over twice as many people and twice the power of all the rest of that English-speaking world. Thus British identification as part of this world means that Britain, even if joined by Canada, Australia, and New Zealand, is distinctly a junior partner in an American-led or American-dominated combination. Earlier in the twentieth century this was by no means so evident; during World War I and even during World War II, Britain primarily regarded American power in terms of helping further British policy—or at least the policy of the English-speaking nations. After World War II and especially since the first few postwar years, Britain had to face the fact that the United States was now so greatly predominant in the Western alliance that Britain was being asked to assist in pursuing policies that often seemed primarily American in conception even if designed to serve general Western purposes. Understandably, Britain was uneasy in this new and unaccustomed relationship. Generally, Americans seemed, to the British, brash and inexperienced in international affairs—especially so in the Middle East, where the United States was perceived as a usurper of Britain's old leading role and as unwilling to back what Britain believed to be its own interests (as in

[35] As, for instance, in Winston Churchill's famous Fulton, Missouri, speech. See the *New York Times*, March 6, 1946, p. 4.

Iran or the Suez Canal). Moreover, the American involvement in Asia, whether with regard to nationalist China, Korea, or Vietnam, was not one that many Englishmen wanted to share. Always the preference was for the maintenance of American power and interest in Europe in order to hold the line where it had been drawn, in 1945, between Eastern and Western Europe. Here Britain feared, at different times, either that the United States would be too belligerently anti-Soviet, or that the United States would weary of the Cold War task of containment and simply withdraw into isolationism or into deeper Asian involvements. But neither uneasiness nor irritation with American ways kept Britain from maintaining its place in the alliance. This did not mean that critics ceased to question the terms of the alliance or the particular policies of American leadership. There is no doubt, for example, that broad sections of British opinion were troubled about the involvement of the United States in Vietnam, and that the official governmental unwillingness over several years openly to criticize American policy concealed misgivings beyond those vigorously asserted by the left wing of the Labour party.

Perhaps what is suggested by Britain's tendency in such a circumstance to go along with, or to acquiesce officially in, American policy is that the dependence on American power militarily and economically had become so great as to leave virtually no other national choice. If so, what has this to do with "English-speaking ties" as such? Surely it is not the simple fact that Americans and Englishmen speak the same language that then accounts for maintenance of the alliance. Nor is it likely

to be the association of ideology, culture, and institutions with the language. Such common grounds were not always sufficient in the nineteenth century for Anglo-American agreement on international matters. On the other hand, given the contemporary facts of British and American power, it can be argued that the ties of language and associated factors facilitate the alliance just as they probably made it seem natural in the first place. It has been possible for Englishmen, especially those in government leadership positions, to believe that their country had a "special relationship" with the United States, different from that of the continental European nations that appeared similarly joined in the North Atlantic Treaty Organization.[36] Within this special relationship, which from time to time seemed to be recognized by American officials, the British government sought throughout the postwar era to exert its influence on American policy—often privately and informally—and to maintain a distinctive place for Britain in the highest councils of the Western world. Good personal communication between a prime minister and the American president has been an important part of the special relationship. To maintain such communication and its effectiveness as a means of exerting influence appeared to require that British officials avoid public dispute with American policy.

As with the British attachment to the Commonwealth, so the English-speaking ties and notably the special

[36]Britain's Washington embassy has had a staff of 700, more than twice the size of any other Western European nation's embassy in the U.S. Sampson, *Anatomy*, p. 293.

American relationship often seemed to be juxtaposed against Britain's integration in Western Europe. American policy did not suggest that Britain should choose between the United States and Western Europe; on the contrary, postwar American policy had been to urge Britain to join Western European integration, specifically that of the Common Market, while at the same time maintaining ties with the United States. It often seemed as though the American government wanted to deal with Britain as one of several Western European allies rather than as a special kind of partner. Britain, rather than the United States, had emphasized the special relationship, and in such a way as to stress an extra-European role for itself.

This role, as a member of an Atlantic community of primarily English-speaking nations, is in many cultural and ideological respects a more congenial one for many English people that is a more fully integrated European role. Apart from an intellectual minority who occupy cultural as well as linguistic common ground with continental Europeans, there are fewer barriers of "foreignness" for the English in working with English-speaking nationals, even with Americans. Perhaps this will change as more British people visit continental countries and if the image of unstable political institutions in France, Germany, and Italy recedes with prolonged continental democratic experience. Or, put the other way, perhaps the English-speaking ties will diminish in relative significance if American democratic institutions, never entirely equated with their own by the British, should be perceived as increasingly unstable. By the 1970s the capacity of American government was already being questioned in a way that it had not been since World War II. Such questioning coincided with the increasingly European identification sought by Prime Minister Heath, but not by Prime Minister Wilson, through EEC membership. For the first time, though perhaps briefly, Western European status seemed to be pursued as a partial alternative to the special relationship with the United States.

### Foreign Economic Policy and the EEC

Britain's dependence on overseas trade means that economic matters are always in the forefront among foreign policy issues. Since World War II, the most consistent national concern has been the maintenance of a sufficient volume of manufactured exports, along with so-called invisible earnings from various services, to pay for needed imports of food and raw materials, as well as to compensate for Britain's overseas expenditures for military and economic-aid purposes. This represents the well-known balance-of-payments problem with which Britain has struggled from crisis to crisis during the last thirty years. At first, in the decade of general European recovery after World War II, Britain received loans and assistance under the American Marshall Plan primarily to help bridge a dollar gap—meaning that Britain needed more dollars than could then be earned in order to purchase goods principally from the United States and Canada, while rebuilding and modernizing manufacturing industry from its war-damaged state.

But Britain's balance-of-payments problem has persisted long after the postwar recovery period and despite a considerable degree of success, in that period, in the effort to increase manufacturing output and its sale abroad. The success in this respect has often been offset by increased domestic demand both for Britain's own products and for imported goods, and so the government has restrained this demand by various fiscal measures. In the early postwar years there was a stringent austerity program which, through the use of high purchase taxes and other means, prevented the British from buying their own exportable products (cars, for example) and which virtually prohibited the importation of many foreign products. Even after this program was relaxed, there remained restrictions on foreign-travel expenditures, made more or less stringent from time to time, and various other controls designed to limit domestic consumption, especially when exports lagged behind imports. Moreover, recurrent crises, signified by the declining value of the British pound sterling in international exchange, pushed the British government to devalue its official currency rate and at various times to arrange international loans, economies in government expenditures (particularly overseas), and even a slowdown in domestic economic growth in order to curb the inflation that raised the price of British products sold abroad. Although measures of this kind achieved temporary successes, in the late 1960s and the very early 1970s, Britain's international economic difficulties appeared to be nearly chronic. In fact, they seemed to have worsened in the mid-1970s as the rate of inflation rose more rapidly than in many other Western nations, economic growth lagged behind continental Europe's, and continued deficits in

its balance of payments made Britain increasingly a debtor nation.

These difficulties were associated, to some extent, with Britain's virtual abandonment in 1972 of its long effort to serve as a banker for what was called the "sterling bloc" of nations—the Commonwealth (except Canada) and a few small non-Commonwealth nations closely tied to British trade.[37] Within the bloc, free exchange was encouraged, and gold and dollars were pooled for dealing with other countries. The bloc's success obviously depended on the international usefulness of sterling—the British currency—and that usefulness declined along with Britain's economic power. A good case can be made that Britain clung too long to its leading role in the sterling bloc just as it had to its associated Commonwealth position. It is not even certain that Britain had to be the sterling-bloc banker in order for London to continue to serve as an international financial center.[38] Any sacrifices that Britain made in order to maintain the sterling bloc in the 1950s and 1960s might, therefore, have been needless. Even if the sacrifices involved no readily measurable financial loss, they did add to the delay in British adjustment to modest economic status as one of several Western European powers. The new reality allowed no place for British leadership of any overseas grouping and no hope for reestablishing the old nineteenth-century economic supremacy on a residual imperial base.

An important portion of Britain's economic policy in the first half of

[37]Miller, *Survey*, p. 296.
[38]Susan Strange, *Sterling and British Policy* (London: Oxford University Press, 1971), pp. 71, 203.

the twentieth century had rested on that hope. Empire and then Commonwealth trade was supposed to act as a substitute for the vanished capacity of Britain to compete successfully in free-world markets as it had against the less-developed competing nations of the mid-nineteenth century. What Britain faced, even before 1900 but certainly after that, was the competition of newer and more efficient industrial powers, at a time when Britain already had to export manufactured goods in order to obtain necessary food and raw materials. After World War II, the problem was simply more acute. Britain had been seeking a solution for several decades. Its situation dictated the continued encouragement of food imports because, even with the considerable revival of domestic agriculture in the twentieth century, foreign food in large quantities was going to remain essential for the large and still growing urban population. Thus the old policy of no tariff—or at least a very low tariff—on food imports remained desirable. But it could be so applied as to discriminate in favor of Commonwealth nations; that is, their foodstuffs could be allowed to enter Britain at a tariff level much lower, if a tariff were in existence at all, than that used for the foodstuffs coming from non-Commonwealth nations. In return, the Commonwealth nations could discriminate in favor of British manufactured exports. Some such system was part of a grandiose scheme at the turn of the century, when Joseph Chamberlain urged an imperial economic customs union. But it was not until the decades between the world wars that Britain developed the tariffs and accompanied them with what was called "imperial preference" ("Commonwealth preference"

after World War II) to implement the objectives of intra-Commonwealth trade.

It is true that these arrangements, chiefly made in the 1930s, constitute the British variant of the economic nationalism of the interwar era; other nations, led by the United States, were raising their tariffs to protect home markets against foreign competition. Britain was trying to enlarge its home market, in effect, so as to coincide with the imperial boundaries. However well imperial preference seemed to work in the 1930s, associated as it was with British economic recovery from the interwar depression, its further development after World War II could not be realized either materially or in the broader political sense desired by its staunchest champions. Other Commonwealth nations—particularly Canada and Australia, with whom the preferences of the 1930s had been important—did not find it in their postwar interest to extend the preferences on a broad scale, and Britain's own need for more American trade and aid was not compatible with any increased discrimination in favor of Commonwealth producers. The alternative presented by the new American encouragement of general free trade was more attractive and more feasible. Consequently, imperial preference, although not abandoned, declined greatly in relative importance after 1945. Not only were no new preferences negotiated, but the existing ones ceased to be as significant, in terms of competitive advantage, as they had been in the 1930s.[39]

In view of their limited significance, it is not surprising that the

[39]Political and Economic Planning, *Commonwealth Preference in the United Kingdom* (London: Allen & Unwin, 1960), p. 5.

remaining special Commonwealth trade relationships, while perhaps contributing to Britain's delay in negotiating for EEC entry and to the terms of negotiation, did not preclude British commitments to Europe in the 1960s and early 1970s. Commonwealth trade could not now determine British economic policy. There was simply not enough of it. Trade with Western Europe not only was much greater by the 1960s, but it was growing much more rapidly than Britain's trade with the Commonwealth.[40] No reversal of this trend was probable. The less developed Afro-Asian nations of the Commonwealth were unlikely soon to have the capacity of Western Europe to purchase British goods. And the English-speaking Commonwealth nations, while highly prosperous, would constitute only limited markets for British products because of their relatively small populations, their proximity to other developed nations (Canada to the United States and Australia to Japan), and their desire and ability to expand their own manufacturing industries. Economically Britain could not rest its future primarily on Commonwealth trade, and certainly it could not afford to continue to discriminate in favor of Commonwealth trade at the expense of the greater opportunities in Western Europe and in the rest of the world.

Understandably, then, the best that Britain did for its Commonwealth connections when negotiating and renegotiating with the EEC was to arrange for transitional adjustments of certain surviving preferences. Especially important for Britain itself were provisions for duty-free food. Entirely apart from pro-Commonwealth sentiment, it was in Britain's own interest to ask the EEC to exempt Commonwealth food imports from a common levy on non-European products. In this respect, British policy reflected a general national concern to retain the advantages of inexpensive food supplied by overseas producers, in the United States as well as in the Commonwealth, rather than to become dependent on the highly protected and therefore possibly more expensive continental agricultural production. Britain also had genuine concern for the Commonwealth producers. These producers had depended on a preferential entry to the British market. Not only would they lose their advantage, but they would also suffer a disadvantage from continental competition when Britain accepted charges against all but intra-EEC products. For the Commonwealth's tropical foodstuffs, most of which did not compete directly with EEC products, Britain was able to make relatively successful arrangements. Adjustments for temperate-zone overseas imports proved to be much more difficult, and especially for New Zealand's food products. New Zealand had long depended on Britain's preferential trade to market its butter, cheese, and other agricultural products. Any sudden curtailment of this market would have been a hard blow not only for New Zealand, but also for Britain because of the consequent inability of New Zealand to purchase British manufactured goods.

[40]Miller, *Survey*, p. 290. The trend toward greater European than Commonwealth trade was plain before British entry into EEC, but it became even more marked after entry. Thus in 1974 Britain's exports to its eight EEC partners were worth twice as much as its exports to the Commonwealth. *The Economist* 254 (March 15, 1975):16.

Britain did secure substantial short-run concessions for New Zealand's food products in 1971, when negotiating EEC entry, and a further concession in 1975, when renegotiating continued membership. Otherwise, most of the old conflict between Commonwealth and EEC interests had disappeared in the 1970s. In fact, by 1975 many Commonwealth nations seemed to prefer that Britain remain an EEC member. There were now potential advantages in trading relations with all of Western Europe, instead of with an isolated and diminishingly important Britain, and these advantages might better be secured for Commonwealth nations if Britain, as a Commonwealth nation, were inside the EEC.[41]

Especially in retrospect, the Commonwealth preference system does not seem to have been crucial in the long British debate over EEC membership. Certainly after 1961, when a British government first made it plain that the old preferences would at least gradually be surrendered as the price of EEC entry, the more potent arguments about membership were largely domestic—some economic and some broadly political. These arguments differed in emphasis from the case that had been made for Britain to stand apart from the earliest continental European integration, the Schuman Plan of 1950, which placed the coal and steel industries of France, Italy, West Germany, and the Benelux countries

under a supranational European authority. Conceiving itself as a great world power, Britain saw little reason at that time to merge its national identity, or a portion of its sovereignty, with the still economically depressed and politically unstable continental powers. And in the immediate postwar years, Britain remained more prosperous than most of continental Europe. Even in the mid-1950s, when the six continental nations first proposed extending their integration to a common market for all agricultural and industrial products (not just coal and steel), Britain found no compelling argument for joining the integration plans.

But by the late 1950s, the economic situation dictated a much greater British concern with European trade. Continental growth was now plainly more rapid and impressive—especially in Germany, and becoming so in France—and the integrated coal and steel community was already a functional success. Commonwealth trade had not developed on any massively enlarged scale. Moreover, Britain's confidence in its future as a Commonwealth leader and overseas power was shakier than in 1950, notably after the display of weakness during the Suez crisis of 1956. Consequently, Britain was ready for some intra-European preferential trade arrangement, but not yet for the supranationalism or the common external tariff being developed by the six continental nations after 1955.

As the EEC, or Common Market, began to succeed, the first British response was to try in 1957–58 to persuade the six nations to join Britain and several other European nations

---

[41]Commonwealth leaders were quoted to this effect by *The Economist* 254 (March 15, 1975):16. More generally the Commonwealth's growing realization of its stake in British membership in EEC is explained by F. S. Northedge, *Descent from Power* (London: Allen & Unwin, 1974), pp. 236–37.

in a looser free-trade organization that would afford only mutual tariff preferences for those countries unwilling to accept the other features of the EEC. The advantage for Britain was plain: It would be able to sell its products within any EEC country, as it had done before, without being discriminated against, but it would not have to abandon any of its other trading advantages by virtue of adopting the EEC's common external tariff. After this suggestion was rejected by the six continental nations, Britain led in the separate development of the European Free Trade Association, which in the early 1960s reduced tariffs among its seven members (Sweden, Denmark, Norway, Portugal, Austria, Switzerland, and of course Britain). Although this association worked effectively to increase trade among the nations involved, it was hardly much of a rival to the EEC. The total population was much smaller than that of the six continental nations, and so the economic growth potential was much more limited. The political potential was meant to be limited, and the noncontiguous character of the association's membership worked in the same direction.

From its inception (or at least separate development), the EFTA was plainly not an economic alternative to the EEC. It was not so for Britain or for the other EFTA member nations, several of which, like Britain, sought membership or association with the EEC as that organization shortly proved itself as the dynamic market of Europe. Britain's own effort to reverse its initial decision against joining the EEC came in 1961 when Prime Minister Harold Macmillan led his Conservative government to begin negotiations for entry.[42] These negotiations lasted until early 1963, when President de Gaulle made it painfully clear that France was vetoing British admission. This veto, abrupt and contemptuous of Britain's continued conflicting desire to be a non-European Anglo-Saxon power, came only after persistent British efforts to obtain economic concessions.[43] These concessions involved a transitional period for reducing the Commonwealth preferences (previously noted), as well as arrangements for adjusting domestic British agriculture to the EEC's price-support structure. This latter point was not a trivial matter either in British politics or in the negotiations. Britain's method of subsidizing agriculture had been to keep prices for domestic farm products at low levels, like the imported tariff-free products, and to pay British farmers, from the government treasury, the difference between their costs plus profits, on the one hand, and the lower prices of the marketplace. British consumers were thus accustomed to apparently inexpensive food. The EEC method is radically different. There is a common external tariff (and other restrictive measures) against food imports, while consumers pay more nearly the actual cost of relatively expensive farm products from continental European countries (especially France). As taxpayers they contribute in other ways as well, through their governments, to the subsidy of farming. The net cost of one method is not clearly greater than that of the other, but there is no doubt that the

[42]Miriam Camps, *Britain and the European Community, 1955–1963* (Princeton: Princeton University Press, 1964), chaps. 9–10.
[43]Waltz, *Foreign Policy*, chap. 9.

EEC method seemed more expensive to British consumers. Altogether there was no politically painless way for a British government to accept the EEC's agricultural arrangments; a period of transition would only ease the pain.

So it was that Prime Minister Macmillan, from 1961 to 1963, and then Prime Minister Harold Wilson in 1967, sought to gain British admission to the EEC. Perhaps Wilson was able to negotiate with less concern for adversely affected domestic economic interests. Once he committed his own government and party, he had a measure of bipartisan support that Macmillan lacked in the early 1960s when the opposition Labour party seemed hostile to entry.[44] But special transitional arrangements of some kind, for both Commonwealth and domestic agriculture, were still necessary in 1970 when Prime Minister Heath's government began Britain's third effort to join. What was changed in 1970 was that de Gaulle, who vetoed Wilson's and Macmillan's earlier attempts, no longer commanded French policy. Conceivably his successors, not sharing all of de Gaulle's feeling that Britain was too non-European for the EEC, were much more willing to grant the transitional economic arrangements that Britain still desired. Much depended on Britain's own posture. Was the nation in fact ready to assume a more definitely European role? Economically it seemed so. Although British economic interests would suffer, especially in the short run, there was a widespread realization in industry and government that Britain needed to belong to a larger in-

ternal market in order to share in the growth of modern technology and that, in this respect, there was no alternative to the EEC. Politically also, the time appeared right, since the Commonwealth mirage had receded and, temporarily at least, the American connection had lost some of its counterattraction as the United States had become increasingly troubled by its internal difficulties. Britain may have finally become more fully European because it had nowhere else to turn.

At any rate, the Heath government in 1971 did negotiate EEC-entry terms that it regarded as satisfactory. The entry was not supported by widespread popular enthusiasm. Most opinion polls during 1971 showed a majority against entry, although there was a surge of support when the government presented its accepted terms.[45] Moreover, the Labour party, both through its external organization and its parliamentary members, decided to oppose Heath's negotiated terms of entry, and thus oppose entry itself. Harold Wilson, the Labour Leader, and only recently the prime minister who had sought British entry, asserted that Heath's terms were not ones that he would have accepted. Others in his party, especially in leadership positions, took the same opposition line, thus avoiding any recantation of an earlier general willingness to secure British membership. But the pressure for Labour's opposition was undoubtedly greatest from those who disliked EEC entry on any terms. Such root-and-branch opponents were to be found among major trade-union leaders and generally, but not solely,

[44]Robert J. Lieber, *British Politics and European Unity* (Berkeley: University of California Press, 1970), chap. 9.

[45]Kitzinger, *Diplomacy and Perssuasion*, pp. 362–63.

among left-wing Labour party members, in and out of the House of Commons. The Labour left always regarded the EEC as an essentially capitalist institution. It did not want Britain to surrender any of its own governmental power to socialize its economy. Trade unionists, while sometimes sharing this socialist perspective, were also fearful of continental manufacturing competition and of more expensive European food for British workers. More broadly, both in the Labour party and in the Conservative party (especially in its right-wing), any prospective transfer of national sovereignty to Brussels was disliked.

Despite the sharp division of British opinion, institutionalized by Labour's partisan opposition, the Heath government proceeded in 1971 and 1972 to lead Britain into the EEC, officially assuming membership at the start of 1973, without submitting its terms of entry to the British electorate either in a general election or in a referendum. Heath could claim substantial parliamentary support, ordinarily all that the British constitution required. In fact, his parliamentary support in this instance was greater than his own party's usual majority because, on the decisive parliamentary vote in October 1971, there were more Labour M.P.s who broke from their party to support Heath's policy than there were Conservative M.P.s opposing EEC entry. And most of the handful of Liberal M.P.s, representing a reviving third party committed to EEC, also voted with Heath. Yet Britain's membership could not be regarded as permanent as long as the major opposition party rejected the negotiated terms. The importance of this continued rejection became clear when Labour was re-turned to power in 1974, first in February as a minority government and then in October with a bare majority. The new Labour government acted on its electoral campaign commitments to renegotiate the terms of entry before their submission to the British electorate for approval or disapproval.

Renegotiations were conducted, chiefly by Foreign Secretary Callaghan,[46] until early 1975, when both Callaghan and Prime Minister Wilson decided that they had obtained enough concessions to present a favorable recommendation to their colleagues and to the British people. Chiefly these concessions reduced Britain's expected contribution to the EEC budget, so as to be more nearly commensurate with Britain's newly diminished economic status, and softened some of the EEC's agricultural policies (including those affecting New Zealand imports) that Britain found objectionable. Furthermore, the EEC seemed to have pulled back from earlier projects for additional financial and economic union that had troubled defenders of British national sovereignty.[47] Although some of these changes were mainly symbolic and others would have been likely without dramatic renegotiation, the Labour government leadership could and did claim that it had bargained for better terms than those that it

[46]Foreign Secretary Callaghan, as chief renegoitator, was important both because his long and popular standing in the Labour Party would help to attract support for membership terms that he could secure, and because his governmental position meant that now foreign and economic policies were merged in a way that they had not always been at an earlier period. William Wallace, "The Management of Foreign Economic Policy in Britain," *International Affairs*, 50 (April 1974): 251–67.

[47] *The Economist* 254 (March 15, 1975):12.

had opposed in 1971–73. About two-thirds of Wilson's cabinet agreed, and the Labour government, fulfilling the rest of its electoral pledge, presented the issue to a national referendum in the hope that the public would approve the new bargain. Although some Labour cabinet members, about half of the Labour M.P.s, and most of the external Labour party organization still opposed EEC membership, the government leaders, with the help of Conservative and Liberal leaders plus much of the business community, were able to secure an overwhelming majority (17, 378, 581 to 8, 470, 073) in the June 1975 referendum. British membership in EEC was finally settled.

### Security Policy

The reasons for Britain's assumption that it cannot protect itself against aggression without help are obvious. The island's location, vulnerability, and limited resources require that protection come from collective arrangements with other nations. Strictly speaking, modern Britain has never relied solely on its own military capacities. Its tradition of trying to maintain a European balance of power has necessarily involved joining alliances with some nations against others. Before World War I, this policy, combined with command of the seas, allowed Britain considerable freedom of action and certainly a sense of having the national destiny in its own hands. The change in Britain's relative position may not have been fully appreciated until World War II, but in 1940 even the magnificent stand against Hitler could not conceal Britain's inability to protect its far-flung interests without the aid of a stronger power.

After World War II, and partly as its consequence, Britain appeared distinctly less imposing than either of the superpowers, the Soviet Union and the United States. Security against Soviet domination of the continent required American help. Accordingly, the cornerstone of Britain's postwar European policy was to obtain an American commitment, of a sort denied before World War II, to defend Western Europe and by this means to deter aggression. Thus the act of securing American involvement in the North Atlantic Treaty Organization (NATO) was considered a prime diplomatic success. As a leading British diplomatic historian wrote of the treaty, "It is indeed in one sense the culmination of British policy during the last half century."[48] Britain had at last, through an outside ally, succeeded in righting the European balance of power. From this viewpoint, British participation in the military arrangements of the Western European Union, though a sharp departure from British policy, became decidedly subordinate to membership with America in NATO.

The North Atlantic Treaty Organization has continued to be Britain's principal instrument of military security. There has been no tendency to follow France's more nationalistic policy, developed by de Gaulle, of withdrawing from NATO commitments and specifically rejecting American predominance within the alliance. Even outside Europe, and apart from NATO itself, British security policy has ordinarily been pursued in conjunction with American power rather than indepen-

[48]Charles Webster, in *United Kingdom Policy*, ed. Charles Webster (London: Royal Institute of International Affairs, 1950), p. 26.

dently. The abortive Suez expedition of 1956 was a striking exception, since Britain was actually at odds with the announced policy of the United States. Otherwise, even distinctively British actions were consonant with American policy, as in Malaysia and, for the most part, the campaigns to preserve order in remaining British dependencies.

Yet there have been general strains in Britain's security relations with the United States. Some derive from the relative novelty of Britain's junior-partner status in an alliance. The inherent difficulty of such status has been exacerbated by a persisting economic dependence on the United States. Needing American aid for general as well as for military purposes has at times caused Britain to seem, or perhaps just to feel, more a satellite than a partner of any kind. Certainly Britain has sought to avoid such an appearance; the best-known instance of this was Britain's long-standing policy of recognizing Communist China despite the United States' refusal to do so. Less plain but probably more significant has been the fairly steady British effort to stand apart, privately if not officially, from any large-scale involvement in apparently aggressive American military policies in Asia. Britain's objective has always been to concentrate military efforts in Europe and closely related areas. Britain has not wanted either itself or the United States to be distracted from the task of European defense, which remained primary even after the late 1950s, when the Soviet military threat became less ominous.

Heavy dependence on American power did not make for an inexpensive British security policy. Partly this was a matter of Britain wanting some independent force of its own to avoid complete dependence; partly it was a matter of doing enough within the alliance to encourage the continued American commitment and trying, on these terms, to influence American policy. In other words, maintaining the "special relationship" with the United States as well as remaining a distinctively British power meant substantial military expenditures. As late as the mid-1960s, Britain was calculated to be spending more proportionately on defense than any other nation of comparable size.[49] Expenditures included overseas military bases east of Suez as well as in the Mediterranean, large contributions of armed forces to NATO in Western Europe, and nuclear weapon development on a partially independent basis. There is no question that these expenditures strained British resources. In fact, the strain was so great that the bases east of Suez were scheduled for early abandonment, or token maintenance, and almost all non-European naval, air, and army expenditures were sharply reduced by plans announced in 1975. Also, the nuclear development was pooled, in effect, with American deterrent capacity after it became apparent that Britain could not afford its own delivery system even though it had its own nuclear bombs. American missiles had to be obtained if Britain was to have a deliverable nuclear weapon capacity.[50]

In other ways as well, British military efforts, while still large in relation to limited national resources, continue to be gradually reduced. The navy has ceased to be a really

[49]Waltz, *Foreign Policy*, p. 179.
[50]Andrew J. Pierre, *Nuclear Politics* (London: Oxford University Press, 1972).

large force in any comparative sense; and it was finally decided in the late 1960s that the air force would not be modernized through the purchase of the latest American aircraft. Conventional ground troops have been cut back to the point where there is no substantial home reserve ready for military action. Conscription, which ended in 1960, has not been necessary in light of the decisions to limit total military force levels in accord with financial necessities. As of 1975, Britain's only continuing major commitment was its contribution to NATO, especially in the form of troops stationed in West Germany—and there is increasing British concern about the expensiveness of this contribution. Reducing it, or persuading Germany to pay for more of it, must be considered at least a possibility in the near future. But it is significant that it remained substantial after Britain decided drastically to reduce, almost to eliminate, its capacity for major overseas military action. Thus the current emphasis of security policy is plainly on home or close-to-home defense, so far as conventional British forces are concerned, and on American capacity, nuclear or otherwise, in the larger world arena. This latter reliance involved Britain as a base for American bombers, as a launching site for intermediate-range ballistic missiles, and as a supplier of harbors for missile-carrying submarines. Admittedly, these involvements lessened in importance with the development of intercontinental missiles, but some remain as visible signs of the significance of the alliance.

A point that remains to be discussed is British membership in the United Nations. As one of the founding Big Five, Britain is a permanent member of the Security Council and a prominent participant in U.N. affairs generally. Like other Western democracies, including the United States, Britain has had to accustom itself to a U.N. Assembly dominated increasingly by an Asian-African majority. But it has never been official British policy to rely primarily on the United Nations as the agency for securing Britain against aggression. Although many, particularly liberals and Labour party members, display a considerable emotional attachment to U.N. ideals, British policy makers have understandably found alliances such as NATO sturdier shields than the U.N. Charter. Britain has been anxious primarily to maintain the United Nations as a gathering place for all nations, so that opportunities for discussion, negotiation, and compromise are readily available.

## CONCLUDING REMARKS

During much of the period since World War II, British foreign policy attempted to meet immense residual responsibilities with limited resources. Only slowly were these responsibilities reduced in accord with a realization that a necessarily nonimperial Britain lacked the economic and military capacity for exercising world power and leadership. Now, however, the nation undoubtedly accepts a much more modest role in international affairs than it played throughout modern history. This means that Britain, while retaining its important trade relations with the overseas world, ceases to patrol the oceans or otherwise protect militarily its non-European interests. And it means that, within the Commonwealth, Britain becomes only one of several contenders for influence instead of the accepted leader, while the Commonwealth itself more nearly resembles the United Nations than it does a British bloc or any other bloc of like-minded peoples.

Furthermore, without overseas power, Britain's claims for a special relationship with the United States, in NATO and in other respects, must also diminish. No longer does Britain seem even the plainly second-place partner of the United States. Now it is but one of several Western European allies, and perhaps not even the most powerful. Like the other allies, Britain is bypassed when the United States pursues its own détente with Russia and with China, as it began to do in the early 1970s.[51] Britain does not belong with the superpowers as it did in 1945 and as it seemed to claim during the first decade or two after 1945. This will hardly trouble a new generation of British leaders, coming of age after 1945, in the way that it has older policy makers, accustomed to the nation's traditional status and who are now beginning to move out of the policy-making positions.

The question for new British leaders, as for their community generally, is "How shall Britain function as a nation with limited power?" Even in answering this question, there may be little choice as to general direction. Geographical location and economic facts dictate a priority for special Western European arrangements of some kind, and

given overseas trading interests and continued military dependence by Britain and the rest of Western Europe on the United States, the arrangements cannot be exclusionary. What is probably still open to choice is the way in which Britain functions as a middle-size European power. Until 1975, this choice was expressed as one between membership in the European Economic Community and close but outside collaboration with that Community. Now, at last settled in the EEC, Britain might either foster or retard efforts to achieve a more substantially integrated Western Europe for political as well as economic purposes. Although Britain has preferred limited integration, virtually as a condition for continuing membership, it is by no means clear that this will always be its preference if Britain should find that it could exert leadership within the EEC.

A more drastic policy choice ought to be noted despite its present improbabilities. Retaining only EEC trade ties but otherwise going it alone, without NATO, the Commonwealth, or a special American connection, could conceivably appeal to a new British public. Removed long enough from world power status, Britain might also want to withdraw from responsibility for the military defense even of Western Europe, perhaps adopting the neutrality of Sweden or Switzerland if not the cold war neutralism of many Asian and African nations. Such a "little England" policy would indeed be a departure from the way in which British interests have been perceived and pursued not just in the past but especially in the most recent decades of closer involvement in Western Europe and in-

[51]Northedge, *Descent from Power*, pp. 270–71.

creased dependence on the United States.

Currently, however, nothing about Britain is taken for granted in the old way. Not only is the substance of its foreign policy less certainly continuous than we once believed, but the process of making that policy may also be changing. The fact that EEC-membership was submitted to a popular referendum is only one—and probably a nearly unique—break with traditional practice. Divisions in party ranks over the EEC were significant because they occurred along with other indications that neither the Conservative nor the Labour party was able to function in the cohesive manner so characteristic of most of the postwar parliamentary experience described earlier in this chapter. Still more disruptive of the established pattern of alternative governing parties was the inability, particularly in 1974, of either of the two major parties to mobilize sufficient electoral support to produce a decisive parliamentary party majority. Although these difficulties may be transient, it is also possible that Britain's largely two-party system, at least in its Conservative-versus-Labour form, is to be succeeded by political competition that makes for something other than the stable party government we have associated with twentieth-century Britain. Explaining how Britain's long established system has worked is not a sure guide for the next few decades. But it is the best we have in a world where established Western democratic policies and processes have generally become insecure and uncertain.

## SELECTED BIBLIOGRAPHY

BELOFF, MAX. *The Future of British Foreign Policy.* London: Secker and Warburg, 1969.

CAMPS, MIRIAM. *Britain and the European Community, 1955–1963.* Princeton: Princeton University Press, 1964.

DARBY, PHILIP. *British Defense Policy East of Suez 1947–1968.* London: Oxford University Press, 1973.

FRANKEL, JOSEPH. *British Foreign Policy, 1945–1973.* London: Oxford University Press, 1975.

GOWING, MARGARET. *Independence and Deterrence: Britain and Atomic Energy, 1945–1952.* London: Macmillan, 1974.

KITZINGER, UWE. *Diplomacy and Persuasion.* London: Thames and Hudson, 1973.

LIEBER, ROBERT J. *British Politics and European Unity.* Berkeley: University of California Press, 1970.

MILLER, J. D. B. *Survey of Commonwealth Affairs.* London: Oxford University Press, 1974.

NEUSTADT, RICHARD. *Alliance Politics.* New York: Columbia University Press, 1970.

NORTHEDGE, F. S. *Descent from Power.* London: George Allen and Unwin, 1974.

PIERRE, ANDREW. *Nuclear Politics.* London: Oxford University Press, 1972.

SAMPSON, ANTHONY. *The New Anatomy of Britain.* New York: Stein and Day, 1972.

STRANGE, SUSAN. *Sterling and British Policy.* London: Oxford University Press, 1971.

VITAL, DAVID. *The Making of British Foreign Policy.* New York: Praeger, 1968.

WALTZ, KENNETH. *Foreign Policy and Democratic Politics.* Boston: Little, Brown, 1967.

# FRENCH
# FOREIGN POLICY

*Roy C. Macridis*

3

The dilemma facing France at the end of World War II may be stated in rather simple terms: France, one of the great powers in the world, found her position drastically weakened. But the aspirations of greatness and rank have persisted. These aspirations were expressed succinctly by the architect of France's post-World War II policy, General Charles de Gaulle. "I intended," he wrote in his *Memoirs,* referring to the period immediately after the defeat of Germany,

to assure France primacy in Western Europe by preventing the rise of a new Reich that might again threaten her safety; to cooperate with the East and West and, if need be, contract the necessary alliances on one side or another without ever accepting any kind of de-

pendency; to transform the French Union into a free association in order to avoid the as yet unspecified dangers of upheaval; to persuade the states along the Rhine, the Alps and the Pyrenees to form a political, economic and strategic bloc; to establish this organization as one of the three world powers and, should it become necessary, as the arbiter between the Soviet and the Anglo-Saxon camps.[1]

This was an ambitious scheme, and, as he admitted, the means available to his country "were poor indeed." But it was a goal widely shared by the majority of the French elites. In fact right after the Liberation of France in 1944, while the war was still going on the French people

[1] *War Memoirs,* vol. 3, *Salvation* (New York: Simon & Schuster, 1960), p. 204.

75

were asked in a survey whether they thought their country was still a "great power." Eighty percent said "yes."

In 1944, after the liberation of Paris, with the return of General de Gaulle and the establishment of his provisional government on the French territory, France and her overseas possessions were in a state of dependency. Drained of manpower, with her economy seriously undermined after four years of occupation, facing urgent problems of social and economic reconstruction at home and powerful centrifugal forces in the empire, the power and even the political will to fashion the instruments that would lead to an independent course of action were lacking. France was dependent upon Britain and, primarily of course, upon the United States. In terms of Walter Lippmann's axiom that commitments in foreign policy must be commensurate with strength, it was very clear that there were few commitments that France could undertake and carry out successfully without Anglo-American support. France's liberty of action, therefore, was limited. Her aspiration to remain a top-rank power seemed to be at variance with her capabilities.

Thus the dilemma confronting France's post-World War II governments and her political elites was either to accept the situation as it developed after World War II or to continue to seek "greatness" and "rank" without the physical, military, and economic resources to implement it. It called for difficult political decisions and choices; it demanded the rapid reconsideration of some of the traditional French foreign policy patterns; and, above all, it required a meaningful debate among political leaders and elites about alternatives and choices. Neither the political system under the Fourth Republic nor the political parties and the press managed to provide for such a debate. There was no "great debate" to redefine the French position and status in the world. Strangely enough, it was only after the return of General de Gaulle to power in 1958 and the establishment of the Fifth Republic that foreign policy themes began to be stated with enough clarity to invite debate, to elicit support or to provoke criticism. The Fifth Republic under de Gaulle was a decade during which options were examined, choices made, and instruments for their realization fashioned. It was the decade during which many of the goals felt and shared by many of the French elites were given shape, form, and direction. Curiously enough, the leadership of the Fifth Republic (from 1958 to the present) does not differ fundamentally in its foreign policy aspirations from that of the Fourth Republic (1946–58). The difference lies primarily in its clearcut and authoritative—if not authoritarian—formulation of goals and in the stability of its political leadership to implement them.

In this chapter we shall examine the background factors that have shaped France's foreign policy—her geographic position, her economic and social development, her ideology and culture, the persistent national interests pursued in the past, and the foreign policy objectives, as they were reformulated in the years of the Fourth Republic and, more particularly, as they have been restated in the years of the Fifth Republic under de Gaulle and under his successors—Georges Pompidou (1969–74) and Giscard d'Estaing, since June 1974.

## BACKGROUND FACTORS

A number of interacting factors constitute the setting in which foreign policy operates. Some of these factors are objective ones; they can be easily measured and compared. Others are subjective, and constitute a community's image of itself in the world. Among the objective factors, the most important are the nation's economic strength, its geographic position, its military potential, its technological skill, its culture, and the diffusion of its culture in other parts of the world. The subjective factors are primarily ideological; they can be studied with reference to the various elites of the system and to the particular conception the elites have of their country's role in the world. Important among those elites is, of course, the political leadership.

Subjective and objective factors constantly interact to give to foreign policy a dynamic and ever-changing pattern; however, such interaction may be impeded for various reasons, so that reality—i.e., the objective factor—may be at variance with ideology—i.e., the subjective factor. As we have pointed out, this might be a tenable hypothesis for the study of French foreign policy in the twentieth century.

### The Economic Foundations

The most significant feature of the French economy was, until the last two decades, its relative decline. While industrialization went forward rapidly throughout the nineteenth century in England, Germany, Japan, and the United States, and also in the Soviet Union in the twentieth century, France's economy advanced at a snail's pace.

Yet France began with a marked head start over *all* other countries. During the Napoleonic era and until the middle of the nineteenth century, France was one of the best economically developed nations of the world. From then on, despite a wealth of resources and skilled labor, her economy declined in comparison with almost all the other countries of Western Europe. Her total national income, between 1870 to 1940, rose by about 80 percent; that of Germany increased five times; that of Great Britain, three-and-a-half times. In the years between the two world wars (1918–1940), investment declined to a point below zero—that is, France was living on her capital, using her factories and equipment without replacing them in full. She was going through a period of disinvestment. The destruction wrought by World War II, estimated at approximately $50 billion, was an additional setback. With her industrial equipment destroyed or dilapidated and her transportation network paralyzed, France's economy was in a state of collapse.

There were many long-range factors associated with this stagnation —notably, the very slow growth of population, a backward agriculture, the protectionist policies of the state and, finally, the attitudes of the business groups.

*Population.* In 1800 France had the largest population of any country in Europe and the Americas, excepting only that of Russia. The Napoleonic armies were recruited from, and supported by, 26 million French men and women, when England had only 11 million inhabitants, the United States 5.5 million, and the German states, including Austria, about 23 million. France maintained this advantage until about 1860, when she had about 38 million. From then on, her population remained virtually static. In 1940, for instance, it was almost exactly 40 million, while that of the United States was close to 150 million, that of Great Britain was 50 million, and that of Germany (West and East, but without Austria) was 65 million. In the years between 1930 and 1940, the French population actually declined—that is, there was an excess of deaths over births. Two wars had taken a heavy toll, also, of the young and active part of the population. The percentage of the aged (over sixty-five) became disproportionately heavy, thereby contributing to economic stagnation.

*Agriculture.* Difficulties became apparent in the period between 1870 and 1940. The proportion of farmers—about 30 to 35 percent of the active population—was the largest in Western Europe excepting Italy and Spain, but their productivity was one of the lowest in Europe. There were a great number of small, marginal farms, divided and subdivided into parcels to which new techniques and mechanization could not be applied. Until 1940 France used less fertilizer than any other Western European country, and the use of tractors remained insignificant.

*Protectionism.* That much of the population remained on relatively unproductive farms was due partly to the tariff policies of the state. Agricultural interests formed powerful lobbies which demanded and got a high protectionist tariff, sheltering French business and agriculture from foreign competition. They also received special subsidies and guaranteed price supports. Those profiting from these measures were not

only wheat producers and growers of beets (from which large quantities of alcohol are distilled), but wine growers, fruit growers, and dairy interests as well. High tariffs also sheltered manufacturing concerns. The state was perpetuating and supporting a situation that consecrated the weakness of the economic system.

*Business Attitudes.* Industrialists and business groups did not show, in France, the initiative and willingness to take risks that we generally associate with capitalism. Many business enterprises were family affairs. Production remained geared to a limited demand instead of seeking new markets. Profits were often saved instead of being reinvested.

A particularly vulnerable part of the economy was in the distribution sector. Large chain stores were the exception, and small merchants and shopkeepers eked out a living through a limited volume of trade. As a result, efficient techniques to reduce costs and bring prices down were not developed. Retail prices kept far ahead of wholesale prices, with the many middlemen who handled the product making small profits. This unduly inflated the price the consumer paid. The middlemen in France, like the agricultural population, formed an oversized and relatively unproductive sector of the economy. They, too, organized in strong pressure groups and demanded subsidies and protection.

The end of World War II brought to light the weaknesses of the country and accentuated a number of them. The greater part of the foreign assets and investments of France had been wiped out, millions had lost their lives or health as a result of the war and the enemy occupation, and the industrial equipment of the country had reached obsolescence. The tasks ahead were to stop inflation and put the currency back on a healthy basis; to rebuild the communication systems as well as the schools, factories, and homes; to improve the productive resources in order to bring production up to the prewar level and surpass it; to rationalize and reorganize the agriculture; and, above all, to catch up with the "world outside" and to build strength without which survival as a nation might well be impossible.

## Geographic Position

France's geographic position had created contradictory interests and commitments. On the one hand, she has been a continental power with frontiers that include, to the east, Belgium, Germany, Switzerland, and Italy, and, to the southwest, Spain; on the other hand, she has had a colonial empire with possessions throughout Asia and Africa and in the Pacific, Indian, and Atlantic oceans.

The French Empire had been developed and consolidated by the end of the nineteenth century. On the Continent, the Spanish frontier and Switzerland presented no problems. The threat came from Germany—a Germany that after 1870 had been unified and that after 1930, despite its defeat in 1918, confronted France once more with a population of some 65 million and an economic and industrial system more productive than her own. At the same time, the empire called for everlasting vigilance against potential marauders, particularly England, and against nationalist independence movements so that France needed a strong army at home as

well as a strong navy. This involved heavy economic sacrifices.

From whichever point of view one looks at the situation as it developed in the latter part of the nineteenth century, one cannot help but realize that the French predicament was a serious one. France, more than any other country of the world, had to assume the heavy burdens both of a continental power and of an empire. The end of World War II and the subsequent developments indicate, as we shall see, that France stubbornly attempted to preserve both positions.

## Persistent Patterns

A number of patterns underlie the French conception of foreign policy. In the nineteenth century they reflected France's strength, but they slowly crystallized into dogmas and myths that were ultimately separated from twentieth-century reality. It is, nonetheless, in terms of such myths that France's foreign policy was shaped—immediately after World War II—rather than in terms of the new factors that developed partly as a result of the war and partly as the result of a number of social, economic, and ideological forces that stirred the world.

The basic objectives of foreign policy remained (a) the continuation of France's imperial position, and (b) continental strength. The first meant, as we have seen, the maintenance of the far-flung empire with all the financial difficulties and obligations it entailed. Not for a moment was the notion of federalism and self-government for its members seriously entertained. Maintenance of the empire was conceived as a part of France's mission and as a continuous challenge to French culture and influence. The resurrection of France as a continental power was also an automatic reflex; no political leader doubted it. The end of World War II by the defeat of Germany was, in a sense, their revenge for the German occupation of France. Victory, it was thought, simply reestablished the prewar balance. To implement France's continental position, the same alliances with the West and with the East were contemplated— all of them directed against a Germany that lay prostrate and divided. The fact that the Soviet Union had gained a foothold in the heart of Europe did not alter the traditional French reflexes; Germany was the enemy of France. A weak Germany and a Franco-Russian alliance remained the conditions for French security. When General de Gaulle visited Moscow and signed the Franco-Russian treaty in December, 1944, he was preserving French security according to the best traditions of the nineteenth century.

## THE SUBSTANCE OF FOREIGN POLICY: TRENDS AND PROBLEMS

France has followed two basic foreign policy objectives ever since the eighteenth century. The first is the policy of *natural frontiers* and the second is the policy of what might be called *European status quo,* or *balance of power* in Europe.

The natural frontiers of France have been considered to be on the Rhine and on the Alps. They include Belgium, Holland, Luxembourg, and the German territory that lies west of the Rhine. This was interpreted to mean that France's strategic and military interests extended to those areas, and that no other

power could set foot there without jeopardizing her interests. The continuity of this policy is remarkable. Danton stated in 1793, "The frontiers [of the Republic] are marked *by nature.* . . . They are the Rhine, the Alps and the Pyrenean mountains." Clemenceau affirmed in 1919, "The move towards the Rhine was the tradition of our ancestors. . . . It was the tradition to create a frontier, a *true* frontier marking the French territory." General de Gaulle, in 1944, stated, in the name of a weak and defeated country, "The Rhine *is* French security and I think the security of the whole world. But France is the principal interested party. . . . She wishes to be solidly established from one end to the other of her *natural frontier.*" [2]

The policy of status quo, on the other hand, was based upon three assumptions that became in turn three basic objectives of policy:

1. France was not interested in any European conquest.
2. No single power should gain preponderant strength in Europe. The status quo—consisting of a number of competing political units, small if possible —should be maintained so as to give France the role of an arbitrator.
3. France became the protector of small states throughout Europe, since it was owing to the existence of many of them that she could effectively play the role of arbitrator and maintain her position of supremacy in Europe. As Vergennes wrote, in 1777, "France, placed in the center of Europe, has the right to influence all the great developments. Her King, like a

[2]See the excellent article by J. Raoul Girardet, "L'influence de la tradition sur la politique étrangère de la France," in *La Politique étrangère et ses Fondements,* ed. Jean-Baptiste Duroselle (Paris: Librairie Armand Colin, 1954), pp. 143–63.

supreme judge, can consider his throne as a tribunal established by Providence to guarantee the respect for the rights and properties of the sovereigns." [3]

This providential role of France has been restated many times.

In 1919 the two policies converged. The theory of natural frontiers led to the demilitarization of the territory west of the Rhine to the control of the Saar, and to the military oversight of France over the Low Countries. The policy of the status quo, as redefined, led to an effort to divide Germany, to the breakup of the Austro-Hungarian Empire, and to the establishment of a number of new nations all over eastern and south-eastern Europe, with which France established close political, economic, and military ties. Of course, a number of other factors entered into the picture. The Wilsonian idea of self-determination encouraged the establishment of small states which France was only too pleased to take under her protection, while the creation of a number of small states east of Germany formed a *cordon sanitaire* against the Soviet Union and, at the same time, prevented Germany from moving east.

By 1919, then, the two traditional French foreign policies had found a happy reconciliation. Despite a number of difficulties (the dismemberment of Germany did not take place, for instance), the general settlement gave France both a position of preponderance in Europe and a great degree of security and safety. If only the world had stood still, France might have maintained that position.

[3]Quoted in J. Raoul Girardet, Ibid.

The policy of a European balance of power, plus security, also became France's worldwide policy. The empire had been consolidated by end of the nineteenth century and World War I. The imperial vocation, and with it the world vocation of France, continued side by side with its continental vocation in the years after World War II–years that we intend to discuss now. We shall divide our discussion into two parts: France and Europe; France and the empire.

France and Europe:
The Insoluble Dilemma

The immediate reaction of France after liberation in December, 1944, was to attempt to reestablish her traditional position of security in Europe and of independence as a world power. From 1944 until mid-1947, a policy was followed that for all practical purposes was identical to that of 1919. France proposed the following:

1. The dismemberment of Germany and prolonged occupation of the country
2. Heavy reparations and tight control of German industrial output
3. The reestablishment of French control in the area west of the Rhine by the detachment of these territories from Germany
4. A prolonged occupation, if not annexation, of the Saar
5. The independence of the small nations of Europe
6. An alliance with the Soviet Union directed against a threat to French security from Germany
7. An alliance with Great Britain

Under the first government of General de Gaulle (1944–46) this policy was pursued with great tenacity. After the liberation, a

Treaty of Mutual Assistance was signed with the Soviet Union. The two countries agreed to take "all the necessary measures in order to eliminate any new menace coming from Germany and to take the initiative to make any new effort of aggression on her part impossible" (Article 3). Immediately after the signing of the pact, General de Gaulle declared, "Because two of the principal powers of the world—free from any conflict of interest in any part of the world—decide to unite under specific conditions, it does not mean that either the one or the other envisages to organize the world and even its security without the help of other nations." [4]

But one might ask whether the haste with which General de Gaulle went to Moscow to sign the treaty was not motivated by considerations other than the security of France from an attack by Germany, which lay literally prostrate before the Anglo-American and Soviet armies. By the treaty with Moscow, France was indeed serving notice to her former British and American allies that she intended to pursue an independent policy.

In fact, until the beginning of 1947, every effort was made by France to gain the support of *either* the Soviet Union *or* the United States (along with Great Britain) in the implementation of her German policy. Neither of her two allies, however, responded favorably, since they both hoped to see, ultimately, an economically and politically unified Germany *on their side,* something that would have meant the end of French aspirations for European security and leadership. When Soviet Foreign Minister Molotov declared

himself, in July, 1946, in favor of a politically unified Germany, *Année Politique* commented, "There was reason for France, which could count on the support of her ally in the East *against* the Anglo-Americans, to be disappointed." [5]

*The Cold War and the Development of Western Alliances.* The Cold War, whose origin can be traced to Yalta and Potsdam, erupted in the beginning of 1947. Conferences in Moscow and London had failed to produce any kind of agreement on the problem of Germany. The lines were being drawn, and the division of Germany into two zones—Soviet and British-American—became a certainty. The conflict implied the strengthening of both zones, and hence the development of a strong West German Republic supported by the United States and England.

France managed to maintain control over the Saar, but failed in all her other claims. After June, 1947, the whole of Western Europe and Great Britain received massive American aid to develop their economy. In 1948 the Brussels Pact brought together the Benelux countries, France, and Great Britain. It provided for a permanent consultative council and negotiations to promote economic development of the countries concerned, and included a military clause calling for immediate consultations to take common action against a German attack or aggression and to cope with a situation that constituted a menace to peace, no matter where it occurred or from where it came. In 1949 the creation of a large military umbrella was logically called for. Not only the Brussels signatories, but also all the

---

[4] Quoted in *Année politique, 1944–45,* p. 89.

[5] *Année politique, 1946,* p. 400.

Western countries, including ultimately Greece and Turkey, participated. The United States became a permanent part of this alliance that still continues as the North Atlantic Treaty Organization (NATO). Article 5 stipulates that an attack against any one of the signatories, either in Europe or in North America, would be considered an attack against all. It further provides (in Article 9) for a permanent deliberative organization and the establishment of a common military command. West Germany was orginally excluded from NATO.

These developments determined France's position. She became a member of NATO and of the various Western alliances, under the overall leadership and military direction of the United States. Such an alliance underwrote her security and, in general terms, the integrity of her empire. The exclusion of Germany continued to give her a strategic position in Western Europe, as well as the semblance, if not the reality, of national power and independence. But the question of Germany's future had been only postponed. A military Western alliance without Germany hardly represented a solution of the problems of military defense. Furthermore, as the struggle between the East and the West not only continued but was intensified with the Berlin blockade, the takeover of Czechoslovakia by the Soviets, and the Korean War, the prize of Germany became more important for the two major opponents. For the United States, the rearmament of Germany seemed the logical step in the construction of a strong defensive line against a potential Soviet attack.

*The European Defense Community and Its Al-*ternatives. It was, strangely enough, the French who came forth with the answer: the creation of a West European army, the European Defense Community (EDC), involving a genuine integration of national forces and a unified—and, if possible, a supranational—command. The United States endorsed this policy as an alternative to the rearming of West Germany within NATO.

No sooner had the European Defense Community (EDC) been announced and formulated, however, than it provoked a storm of protest in France. The political parties came out actively either for or against it. Extreme right-wing and extreme left-wing parties joined hands against the treaty, which was defended by a sharply divided center. To French public opinion, the most controversial part of the treaty was the envisaged German rearmament. A majority of the members of the National Assembly considered German rearmament, even within the EDC, a direct challenge to French sovereignty, clearly spelling the end of France's aspirations to remain a leading European nation. The memory of Nazi Germany was too fresh in the minds of many; the possibility that West Germany, once rearmed, might attempt to provoke a war with the Soviet Union in order to achieve its unification, and thus drag the whole of Europe into a war, was pointed out; the assumption by Germany of a predominant role in Europe, at a time when France was heavily engaged in protecting her empire, was also mentioned. Each party and each parliamentary group saw specific reasons for refusing to accept the treaty, while its proponents defended it also for different reasons. Since there was no genuine majority for or against the treaty,[6] it was on a procedural motion that, in August, 1954, the EDC was rejected by the French National Assembly. In the meantime, all the other prospective members had honored the signature of their governments. Only the French assembly used its constitutional prerogatives and refused to ratify the treaty. The rejection climaxed four years of equivocation. It was only in December, 1954, that the National Assembly, six months after defeating the EDC for fear of German rearmament, allowed Germany to become a member of NATO and to rearm herself within the framework of the NATO alliance.

### France and the Empire

The French Empire extended over every continent of the world. Its administration was a vestige of the Napoleonic conceptions of a highly centralized bureaucratic system—an administration in which Paris, through the colonial officials, made the ultimate decisions and legislated for the whole empire. Its cementing ideology was that of "assimilation"—the notion that ultimately every inhabitant would become a French citizen and be represented in the French Parliament—a notion at marked variance with the Anglo-Saxon conception, according to which political and cultural evolution of the colonial peoples would

ultimately bring about political autonomy and self-government.

In 1944 the basic charter of colonial policy had been drafted at the Brazzaville Conference. There it was decided that "the purpose of the civilizing work accomplished by France in the colonies excludes any idea of autonomy, any possibility of an evolution outside of the French Empire. The establishment, even in the remote future, of 'self-government' in the colonies must not be considered." [7] In 1945, when a trusteeship committee was appointed within the United Nations, the French made it quite clear that they would not accept its jurisdiction. The empire was French, and hence a matter of domestic policy.

In almost every case, the French insisted upon assimilation and maintenance of French sovereignty. In 1945 France refused to withdraw her army from Syria and Lebanon. Within a year she had to give in. In 1947 she refused to enter into negotiations with Ho Chi-minh, and engaged in a war that lasted until 1954. The war in Indochina cost France more than a billion dollars a year, retarded her internal investment policy, and paralyzed her alternate plans for an economic and social reconstruction of the North African territories. It was in part responsible for France's inability to keep pace with German economic reconstruction in Western Europe.

But the Indochinese war brought other problems to a head. In Algeria, Tunis, and Morocco, the independence movements were gaining strength. These movements, however, envisaged continued cooperation with France. In every case, the

---

[6]The division of the political system in the French Parliament and in the various coalition cabinets reflected very closely the division of public opinion: in July, 1954, 36 percent of those asked were "for" or "rather for" the EDC, 31 percent were "against" or "rather against," and 33 percent did not answer.

[7] *Année politique, 1944–45.*

French political leaders and representatives and the various military leaders in command of the French troops reiterated the philosophy of the French vocation. Time after time, the legitimate interests of France were evoked. Time after time, the representatives of the French government and army intervened. By 1956, both Morocco and Tunisia became independent. The refusal to grant self-government left only one alternative: secession.

This situation was most evident in Algeria, where there was a very strong movement in favor of self-government after the liberation of France in 1944. It gained strength after the independence of Morocco and Tunisia. Yet there were many opportunities to cope with the Algerian situation, and progress was made in 1947, when special legislation granting considerable political autonomy to Algeria was passed, although never implemented. Claims of French sovereignty in Algeria and assertions that France "intends to stay there," made in the last years of the Fourth Republic, sounded very similar to the assertions made about Syria, Lebanon, Indochina, Tunis, and Morocco.

## THE LEGACY OF THE FOURTH REPUBLIC (1946–1958)

### ELEMENTS OF STABILITY

Speaking on October 28, 1966, in his fourteenth press conference, General de Gaulle, now back in office as President of the Fifth Republic, stated with remarkable succinctness the objectives of French foreign policy in terms that applied to the Fourth Republic (1946–1958) as well:

In the world as it is people sometimes feign surprise over the so-called changes and detours of France's action. And there are even those who have spoken of contradictions or Machiavellism. Well, I believe that while the circumstances are changing around us, in truth there is nothing more constant than France's policy. For this policy, throughout the extremely varied vicissitudes of our times and our world—this policy's essential goal is that France be and remain an independent nation.[8]

Despite the divisions of the political system under the Fourth Republic and the fact that they often spilled over into the area of foreign policy, there was continuity in the pursuit of basic objectives of foreign policy. The political elite, the political parties (with the exception of the Communists), and the public remained steadfast in their attachment to the traditional interests of France, in spite of rapidly changing world conditions. Discontinuities were occasionally introduced, but only in the form of decisive choices. This was the case in 1954–55, with the termination of the Indochinese war, the granting of autonomy and later independence to Morocco and Tunisia, and the Paris agreements that consecrated West German sovereignty and allowed for German participation in NATO. The political system remained, by and large, committed to the following objectives: (a) the maintenance of an Atlantic and world position that implied a weak Germany and a militarily independent France; (b) a European rapprochement in terms of which France could gain strength at the

[8]Charles de Gaulle, *Discours et Messages*, vol. 5 (Paris: Plon, 1970), 97.

head of Western Europe; and (*c*) the maintenance of a top-rank world position.

What has been called *la politique du grandeur* ("the policy of greatness"), according to which France's vocation is that of a world power and therefore a partner in the development of world strategy or—under propitious conditions—an independent force, was ever present. General de Gaulle's policy, after he returned to power on June 1, 1958, was a faithful expression of the broad objectives pursued by the political leadership of the Fourth Republic.

*The Empire: The Foundation of a New Policy.* It was only in the last two years of the Fourth Republic, between 1956 and 1958, that France's leadership decided to move ahead of the irresistible trend of colonial emancipation rather than attempt to oppose it. In 1956, the French Parliament began consideration of new legislation to put an end to the theory and practice of assimilation. A *loi-cadre* ("framework law") empowered the government to enact executive orders in order to give considerable autonomy to the African republics and Madagascar. They became semi-independent republics, with their own parliaments and responsible executives. France retained jurisdiction over important areas of policy making such as defense, foreign policy, trade, and education. But the first path toward gradual political emancipation had been made, and it proved to be irreversible.

*Economic and Military Policy.* The Fourth Republic also laid the groundwork of France's economic and military recovery. The Atomic Energy Commissariat, founded in 1945, continued in operation throughout the many years of cabinet instability,

and it was endowed with adequate credits. The possession of an atom bomb in a world in which only three powers had developed nuclear weapons became associated, in the eyes of the French political leaders and public alike, with France's national independence and security. Throughout the latter years of the republic, all French governments favored the suspension of the fabrication of the bomb *and* the gradual destruction of nuclear weapons. Only if the latter condition were accepted would France have been willing to abandon her manufacture and testing of the bomb.

Although favoring the Atlantic alliance, the political leaders of the Fourth Republic never agreed to play a secondary role and acquiesce to American or British and American supremacy. They did not accept any genuine integration of military command within NATO and, alleging their colonial obligations, insisted on maintaining autonomy over their military forces. They remained reluctant to permit the United States to establish stockpiles of nuclear weapons or to construct launching sites on French soil. The same fear of integration of the military forces applied to a purely European army, as we have seen.

Thus, while accepting participation in an Atlantic and European military alliance, the French governments made sure that these alliances never took a form that undermined France's independence and freedom to use her own military forces at her own discretion. By the same token, they were unwilling to participate in any defense system with the British and the Americans unless France were given full and equal power on all global decisions and strategy.

## Public Opinion[9]

Studies of opinion throughout the Fourth Republic indicate that there was a striking coincidence of the action of the political leaders and public opinion. French attitudes toward the Cold War, the Soviet Union or the United States, the problem of French military independence and West Germany, and European cooperation show stability and continuity.

*The Cold War.* Generally, the attitude of the French with regard to the Cold War can be summed up as one of neutrality and considerable hostility toward both protagonists. One out of every ten Frenchmen polled believed that the United States was to be blamed, two out of ten put the blame on the Soviet Union, and four out of every ten on both. At the same time, the French public thought that neither the United States nor the Soviet Union was doing all it could to avert the Cold War. Fifty-two and 57 percent of those interrogated in 1957 believed that the United States and the Soviet Union, respectively, were not doing as much as possible. From 1952 until 1957, the public expressed itself as follows:

*Europe.* While the French continued to fear West Germany and to be reluctant to see her rearm, there was a general resignation to Germany's participation in European cooperation schemes. From 1947 until December, 1957, French public opinion favored a European union. Fifty-five to 70 percent were in favor, and those opposed never exceeded 21 percent. In only two polls, taken

**To which camp should France belong?**

|  | The West | The East | Neither |
|---|---|---|---|
| Sept., 1952 | 42% | 4% | 43% |
| Nov., 1954 | 36 | 2 | 39 |
| June, 1955 | 18 | 3 | 57 |
| Aug., 1955 | 23 | 4 | 51 |
| Dec., 1955 | 35 | 5 | 45 |
| May, 1957 | 28 | 4 | 39 |
| Dec., 1957 | 21 | 3 | 51 |

**If there were a war between the United States and the Soviet Union, to which camp should France belong?**

|  | U.S. | USSR | Not take part |
|---|---|---|---|
| Sept., 1952 | 36% | 4% | 45% |
| Nov., 1954 | 22 | 2 | 45 |
| June, 1955 | 19 | 3 | 58 |
| Aug., 1955 | 25 | 5 | 51 |
| Sept., 1957 | 15 | 3 | 62 |

in 1955, did less than 50 percent favor a European union. Support for the European Common Market, for the Schuman Plan, and for the European atomic cooperation program was equally strong. The rearmament of West Germany, however, was considered, until 1954, to be a danger, and the consensus of opinion favored a demilitarized Germany. In 1955, 53 percent were against the participation of West Germany in the defense of Western Europe.

*Atomic Weapons, NATO, and the United States.* Although they still chose neutrality and condemned the manufacture and potential use of atomic weapons, the French, in December, 1957, favored "giving more attention to atomic weapons" for the defense of their country. Forty percent were in favor and 20 percent were opposed; 40 percent declined to answer.

In December, 1957, the French were also asked, "Under the present circumstances, how can France best

[9]For a good summary of public opinion trends, see: "La politique étrangère de la France et l'opinion publique, 1954–1957," *Sondages: Revue Française de l'opinion publique,* nos. 1 and 2 (1958).

assure her security?" Sixteen percent favored the maintenance of the existing alliances in Western Europe, within NATO and with the United States; 5 percent favored a military alliance limited to Western Europe only; 21 percent favored a general security system including the United States, Western Europe, and the Soviet Union; and 34 percent favored withdrawal *from all alliances* and the assumption of an independent and neutral posture.

In the same context, the general reaction of the French public with regard to NATO was one of relative indifference. Not more than 50 or 60 percent were prepared to answer on the basis of any knowledge of the organization. Of those answering, only a small percentage favored the organization and considered it important for the security of France. Such a reaction stemmed primarily from the realization that the United States was exerting too much influence on French foreign policy. Forty to 42 percent of the French interrogated between 1952 and December, 1956, thought that the United States had too much influence. In the same manner, more than 60 percent believed, in 1956 and 1957, that France was not treated by the United States as an equal in matters concerning the two countries. Some 27 to 40 percent believed that Americans and French had common interests, while some 25 percent believed that the interests of the two countries were different. More than 33 percent of those asked in December, 1956, believed that a European union would diminish American influence, and 35 percent of them believed that such a diminution of American influence would be "a good thing."

Thus, throughout the period of the Fourth Republic, the public, even if badly informed, reacted with a remarkable degree of unity in favor of neutrality and European cooperation, feared Germany, suspected NATO, and in general agreed that independence and security could be based only on national strength and freedom of action. Despite an underlying realization of France's reduced world status, the public continued to cling to the image of a strong and independent France. They deplored the reduction of French strength and accepted European unity as an instrument for the realization of national security vis-à-vis both the United States and the Soviet Union.

*A New Economic Policy.* There was a clear perception among most of the political leaders of the Fourth Republic that France could not recover its prewar position without drastic economic effort. A rapid modernization of the French economy and a gradual movement toward increasing European cooperation were required. A strong France in a well-integrated western European economy could be far stronger than if she acted alone. Therefore, the Fourth Republic, after many equivocations, moved after 1956 in the direction of the European Economic Community (EEC) providing for liberalization of trade, lowering and ultimately eliminating all tariffs, and free movement of capital and labor among West Germany, Italy, France, and the Benelux countries. The treaty formalizing the EEC ("Common Market") was signed in Rome in 1957 and put into effect on January 1, 1959.

*The Beginning of Economic Modernization.* The task facing the country immediately after World War II was two-fold: reconstruction and productive investment, to renew the industrial equipment of the nation and to expand its weak sectors. This was the objective of the first Monnet Plan (1947–1950).

Production and modernization programs for six basic industries—coal mining, electric power, steel, cement, farm machinery, and internal transportation—were adopted for 1947, 1948, 1949, and 1950. A second and a third plan were developed. These began to build upon healthier foundations. Whatever the weaknesses of the Fourth Republic, whatever the vacillations of the various governments, massive public investment was followed scrupulously and expansion and growth became the commonly accepted policy. By 1956–57 the impact of the economic plans was clearly discernible. France was modernizing fast, at a tempo that began to compare favorably with that of Germany in 1952–56. By 1958 the gross national product had almost doubled. The population also began to grow, registering a rise for the first time since 1870. It has grown by about 15 percent since the end of the war, and now exceeds the 52 million mark.

## ELEMENTS OF INSTABILITY

The governmental institutions of the Fourth Republic adversely affected the implementation of the long-range objectives, but only to a degree. Despite the instability of the cabinet—there were twenty cabinets under the Fourth Republic—foreign policy was directed by only a very small number of foreign ministers. Under the Fourth Republic there were, in all, five ministers of foreign affairs: Robert Schuman and

Georges Bidault, Edgar Faure and Pierre Mendès-France (from the Radical Socialists), and Christian Pineau (of the Socialist party). Divisions, however, in domestic and colonial issues and growing parliamentary interference provided serious internal difficulties and a marked immobility in policy making. This was the cause, for instance, of the equivocation on the European Defense Community. The instability of the cabinet undermined consistency in execution of policies.

The formulation of foreign policy, like the formulation of any other policy at the governmental level, involved the cooperation of the prime minister and his cabinet with the Parliament. As a result, its formulation suffered because of certain inherent weaknesses of the governmental process in France. These weaknesses were (a) the coalition character of the cabinet, and (b) the instability of the cabinet.

*Coalition Cabinet.* Throughout the Fourth Republic the cabinet was composed of the leaders of a number of political parties. In fact, ever since the establishment of the Third Republic, hardly a party or a combination of two parties managed to provide a majority in the legislature. The cabinet was a coalition of the leaders of many parties and groups. As a result, the desired homogeneity of views on policy in general and on foreign policy in particular was lacking. Very often, the members of one and the same cabinet held opposing views on matters of foreign policy. That happened, for instance, between 1952 and 1954, when members of the same cabinet were in favor of and against the European Defense Community.

*Instability of the Cabinet.* Under the Third and Fourth Republics, the average life of a coalition cabinet was short. In the last two decades of the Third Republic, the average life of a cabinet hardly exceeded eight months. From the establishment of the Fourth Republic to the middle of 1958, there were twenty cabinets. The succession of cabinets at this rate was responsible for the following consequences:

1. Lack of continuity in the implementation of foreign policy
2. Lack of planning

Both these evils were to some degree alleviated, as we have noted, by the relative independence of the minister of foreign affairs and by his continuity in office. However, this continuity in office of the minister of foreign affairs could not compensate for the instability of the cabinet, since issues of foreign policy could not be dissociated from other issues of policy.

Such a situation could not but invite growing parliamentary interference, which aggravated the situation. Disagreements on foreign policy inevitably reached the Parliament and became, in turn, matters over which political parties and parliamentary groups took sides, thus intensifying party warfare in the National Assembly, causing frequent dislocations of the existing majorities, and accentuating the instability of the cabinet.

### Overview: Policy of the Fourth Republic

Tenacity and continuity in the perception of common goals; inability to implement these goals because of great disparity between aspiration and means, a disparity brought about by the influence of stronger powers, notably the United States; and a deadlock created by the sharp internal divisions that produced discontinuities and vacillations in the overall carrying out of foreign policy —this is perhaps the best way to summarize the foreign policy of France in the twelve-odd years of the Fourth Republic.

It was only at the very end that, after numerous setbacks, a new note of realism was injected into the relations between France and her Western neighbors. The domestic economic efforts were beginning to pay off, and the French business elite became increasingly reconciled to the notions of decolonization and of European unity. By 1957 most political parties were willing to go along with the establishment of the Common Market. For many, however, close economic and political European cooperation implied something else—the creation of a strong European bloc, possibly under the leadership of France, that would give her an opportunity to play a genuinely independent role in world affairs.

Colonial disengagement, economic modernization, the abandonment of a protectionist economic policy, the rapid development of resources—including the discovery of rich deposits of oil and gas on the soil of France and in Sahara—were beginning to provide a sense of strength and recovery where in the past there had been only a feeling of weakness and frustration. The dismal way in which the Fourth Republic came to an end, and the difficulty of finding a solution to the Algerian problem, did not hide from the vast majority of French men and women the promise that lay ahead.

## THE FIFTH REPUBLIC AND GENERAL DE GAULLE (1958-1969)

The failure of the Fourth Republic rapidly and effectively to translate into action the commonly shared foreign policy objectives was one of the major reasons for its ultimate downfall. France's diminished status in the world, the successive defeats or withdrawals in the many and elusive colonial wars, the failure of France and Great Britain in Suez, the growing strength of West Germany in NATO and in Western Europe under a stable political leadership were all factors in the growth of a spirit of nationalism in the country, contrasting sharply with governmental instability. Parliament and coalition cabinets continued to mirror the perennial and multiple divisions of the body politic at the very time when the public demanded unity and the realization of national objectives.

Whatever the factors and the immediate causes associated with the military uprising of May 13, 1958, in Algeria, it was to General de Gaulle that most of the political groups and leaders turned. Army officers, veterans, the political parties from the Socialists to the Independents, and a great number of intellectuals—some with considerable misgivings—turned to de Gaulle as the symbol and the person around whom this new spirit of French nationalism could find expression.

### The Basic Assumptions

De Gaulle's basic assumptions—what we may call his overall philosophy—begin and end with the notion that there is one social force—the "reality of the nation" (*le fait national*)

—that overshadows all others. No other force or forces—ideological, social, or economic—have succeeded in undermining the nation-state as the focal point of the ultimate loyalty of man.

From the postulate of national reality a number of inferences flow. They do not always have the logical consistency that an academician would desire; but consistency is not a necessary ingredient of statecraft. Situations change so fast in our world that the only consistency lies in the ability to adjust.[10] Consistency means, in the last analysis, realism. Yet the inferences that follow from the postulate on national reality constitute guides to action and must be spelled out.

*The Reality of the Nation and the Means of Achieving Independence.* The reality of the nation requires power in order fully to manifest itself. Surveying the world situation before the Allied victory in Europe, de Gaulle could not restrain his bitterness: "How dull is the sword of France at the time when the Allies are about to launch the assault of Europe." [11] Although not the only one, the basic ingredient of power is the military. In the ruins of France after the liberation, de Gaulle set himself to recreate the French army. He was haunted with the certainty that the Allies were blocking his efforts because they were unwilling to allow France to develop the military strength that would enable her to become an

[10]Almost always, for instance, de Gaulle, speaking on international issues, inserted the phrase "given the present conditions in the world," or "in the actual state of developments," or "things being as they are."

[11]*War Memoirs*, vol. 2, *Unity* (New York: Simon & Schuster, 1959), p. 245.

equal. When the matter of Germany's occupation seemed in doubt, he ordered his divisions onto German soil, suspecting, perhaps rightly, that the Allies might prevent France from participating in settling the future of Germany and remembering, also, that in war possession is nine-tenths of the law. His vision remained the same throughout the months following the liberation—to recreate the French armed forces. When there was not enough gas to heat French stoves, he established a Commission for Atomic Energy.

But there are other important factors in the equation of power. De Gaulle recognized many and used them all: alliances; diplomacy and skill in negotiations; cultural relations; spiritual influence; economic resources and population.

A strong ingredient of power—indeed, the only valid expression of a nation—is the state and its political organization. Gaullist revisionism, both before and throughout the Fourth Republic, was predicated upon de Gaulle's ideas about world relations and the role of the French nation. To play the proper role, France needed a strong state. In this state, one man, the president of the republic, should make foreign policy on behalf of the nation—the "real France"—incarnating the national interests over and above the welter of particular interests and ideological factions.

A third ingredient of power that de Gaulle evoked very frequently led him to follow policies to which he had seemed firmly opposed. This is what he called the imperative of the *grands ensembles* ("great wholes"). Nations must establish cooperative "wholes" that provide the structural bases and the resources for the economic development and defense of each one and all. This is not contrary to his emphasis upon national uniqueness, nor did it lead him to the espousal of projects of military integration. The building of large wholes creates something that is more than an alliance and less than a federation. It is a close association and cooperation between nation-states which, by pooling some of their resources, find the strength to sustain a common purpose.

*The Idea of Balance.* De Gaulle's emphasis upon the reality of the national phenomenon and its concomitant accessories—power, both military and political—led him to a theory of international relations that is often referred to as "realist." International relations comprise an arena of conflict in which every participant nation-state attempts to increase its strength at the expense of the other. Every political leadership, no matter what ideology inspires it, acts in terms of national consideration. *If so, it is only power that can check power—and the only possible international world is one in which an equilibrium of powers is reached.* This led de Gaulle to follow conclusions that directly shaped his actions and are likely to influence his successor.

The present balance is unnatural, precarious, and unwise—unnatural, because it involves a polarization of the world and the creation of political satellites, which are inconsistent with the secular realities and interests of nations; precarious, because both the big and small nations are continuously on the brink of war; unwise, because it gives to the two of the less qualified nation-states (the United States and the Soviet Union) full liberty to act, the independence to decide their fate and with it the fate of the world.

Both the American and the Soviet

efforts are expressions of national power, in one form or another. If they are allowed free sway, they might enter upon armed conflict. If they find a temporary accommodation, it will be in order to establish a joint hegemony over the world. *Either eventuality will be to the detriment of the other nation-states* including, of course, of France and Europe as a whole. This can be avoided only by creating a balance of power consistent with the growing realities of the world, in which the economic and political development of Europe is bound to play a growing role.

General de Gaulle's conception of a balance was a permanent trait of his thinking and action. It took a number of forms. In the third volume of his *Memoirs*, de Gaulle pointed out that the only way to keep the Soviet Union out of the heart of Europe was to dismember Germany. Thus the threat of a new Germany would be eliminated, and the fears of the Soviet Union and the Eastern European nations alleviated. Moreover, a treaty with the Soviet Union, directed against the revival of German power, would free France to pursue her other world obligations. It was the failure of Yalta to revive the pre-World War II arrangement in Europe that also accounted for the bitter denunciations against the settlement. Although France received a number of compensations, perhaps far beyond what the French leadership had a right to expect in terms of her real power at the time, Yalta became slowly identified with a betrayal of Europe and France by the Anglo-Saxons.

As late as August of 1968 the response of de Gaulle to the Soviet invasion of Czechoslovakia was a condemnation of Yalta! He then stated that:

the armed intervention by the Soviet Union in Czechoslovakia shows that the Moscow Government has not freed itself from the policy of blocs that was imposed on Europe by the effect of the Yalta Agreements, which is incompatible with the right of peoples to self-determination and which could and can only lead to international tension. . . . France, who did not take part in these Agreements and who does not adopt that policy, notes and deplores the fact that the events in Prague—besides constituting an attack on the rights and the destiny of a friendly nation—are of the kind to impede European détente, such as France herself practices and in which she urges others to engage, and that, alone, can ensure peace.[12]

De Gaulle made an open offer to Churchill in November, 1944, to combine forces so that the two countries with their far-flung empires would be able to act independently of the Soviet and the Americans. It is worth quoting his remarks to Churchill:

You can see, France is beginning to recover. But whatever my faith in her is, I know that she will not recover soon her former strength. You, English, will finish this war on the other hand with glory. But nonetheless your relative position may well be weakened in view of your losses and sacrifices, the centrifugal forces that undermine the Commonwealth and above all the ascendancy of America and Russia, and later on of China. Well then, our two ancient countries are both weakened at the time when they are to confront a new world. . . . But if England and France agree and act together in the future negotiations, they will have enough weight to prevent any decision that will not be acceptable to them. . . . It is this common will that

[12]Ambassade de France, Service de Presse et d'Information, no. 1121, August 21, 1968.

must be the basis of the alliance that you are proposing to us. . . . The equilibrium of Europe, . . . the guarantee of peace on the Rhine, the independence of the states on the Vistula, the Danube and the Balkans, the keeping on our side of the peoples to whom we opened up civilization in all parts of the world, the organization of the nations in a manner that will provide something else than a battlefield for the quarrels of the Russians and the Americans, finally the primacy in our policy of a certain conception of man, despite the progressive mechanization of the societies, . . . is it not true that these are the great interests of the Universe? These interests, let us put them together and safeguard them together.[13]

A third scheme involved an alliance with the Soviet Union, directed against German recovery and guaranteeing the status quo of Europe. Speculating before his trip to the Soviet Union in December, 1944, only a few weeks after he had made his offer to Churchill, de Gaulle wrote wistfully, "Perhaps it might be possible to renew in some manner the Franco-Russian solidarity, which even if misunderstood and betrayed in the past, was nonetheless compatible with the nature of things *both with regard to the German danger and the Anglo-Saxon efforts to assert their hegemony.*"[14]

A fourth and perhaps more persistent effort to recreate a balance is the revival of Europe as a "third force." What "Europe" meant to de Gaulle, exactly, is a difficult matter. In his *Memoirs* he spoke of an organization of the peoples of Europe from "Iceland to Istanbul and from Gibraltar to the Urals." Sometimes Russia is part and sometimes it is

not, although emphasis is often put on the European destiny of Russia. Sometimes it is Western Europe and sometimes the whole of Europe. Sometimes "Europe" implies a dismembered Germany, sometimes a divided Germany, and sometimes a Franco-German rapprochement without qualifications. Two things are certain: "Europe," whatever it is, is distinct from the "Anglo-Saxon powers." It is also separate from Soviet Russia, without, however, always denying the European position of Russia and hence its participation.

With the economic recovery of West Germany and the continuing division of this country into two blocs, de Gaulle's conception of Europe became clearer. A strong France in Western Europe could assume the leadership of the Western bloc and speak for it. But to be strong in Western Europe, France must maintain good relations with a West Germany that is, all the same, never to be allowed to match France's leadership. So, underlying the new conception of balance in which Western Europe is perhaps to become for the first time a genuine third force, there is always an emphasis on France's interest, which means France's strength. A leader of Western Europe, France, can put all her weight, in the name of the new force, into world strategy and world leadership.

In the name of balance, de Gaulle envisaged in the course of less than twenty years the following alliances: (*a*) with the British, in order to create an independent bloc vis-à-vis the Soviets and the Americans; (*b*) with the Soviet Union, in order to maintain French supremacy in Europe vis-à-vis Germany; (*c*) with all against the revival of a unified,

---

[13]Quoted in *War Memoirs*, vol. 3, *Salvation* (New York: Simon & Schuster, 1960), p. 52.
[14]*Ibid.* p. 54, italics supplied.

militarized, and strong Germany; and (d) with West Germany and the other Western European states, in order to create an independent bloc —a third force in Europe that might lead to drastic changes in the balance of power.

*The Constitution of the Fifth Republic.* As we noted, one of the serious difficulties throughout the Fourth Republic was the lack of strong executive leadership to formulate and implement policy and to translate overall foreign policy goals and aspirations into effective decisions. The Constitution of the Fifth Republic provides that the cabinet "shall determine and direct the policy of the nation" and that "it will be responsible to Parliament."; in addition, "the Prime Minister is responsible for national defense" (Articles 20 and 21). The president of the republic, on the other hand, "shall be the guarantor of the national independence, of the integrity of the territory, and of the respect . . . of treaties" (Article 5). He "shall negotiate and ratify treaties" and "he shall be informed of all negotiations leading to the conclusion of an international agreement" (Article 52). All major treaties, however, must be "ratified by law" (Article 53).

The contrasts with the constitutional arrangement of the Fourth Republic lie primarily in the conception of the role of the president. He was given both implicitly and explicitly broader powers. The president is the guarantor of the national integrity; the commander-in-chief, presiding over the meetings of the various defense councils; and the possessor of large emergency powers. He is the "moderator" (*arbitre*), making presumably final decisions whenever there appears to be division and conflict in the country or his cabinet. He has the power to dissolve the legislature and to ask the public, in a referendum, to endorse or reject his policy.

Under de Gaulle, the presidency became the coordinating office for the major decisions: military policy, foreign policy, and colonial policy. His successors endorsed this position. Cabinet meetings are simply for the execution and implementation of the decisions made by the president and his immediate advisers. The president is not simply informed of foreign policy negotiations. He negotiates directly with foreign representatives, prime ministers, and heads of state; he outlines the goals of the government—at times taking even the cabinet and the prime minister by surprise. Matters pertaining to NATO, to the ties among the members of the Common Market, to negotiations concerning suspension of atomic tests, to the advisability of a summit meeting—all are decided by the president.

The role of Parliament is greatly diminished. Negotiations and formulations of policy are kept secret in the best tradition of the old diplomacy. Only general developments and overall policy have been discussed. Since the establishment of the Fifth Republic, there have been a number of major foreign policy debates, lasting two or three days each. Debate, however, is limited to the exposition of the prime minister's or the minister's views and to foreign policy pronouncements by various party leaders.

The parliamentary Committee on Foreign Affairs of the National Assembly has heard the minister of foreign affairs frequently, and many questions on foreign policy have been addressed to the prime minister and the minister. They have been perfunctory, however. Since the possibility of engaging the responsibility of the president of the republic and the cabinet is lacking, in the first place, and highly restricted in the second, debate is little more than academic.

Occasions for the expression of dissatisfaction have not been lacking, however. For instance, when the debate on the government's program on atomic weapons and the development of a retaliatory atomic force for France took place (in connection with the voting of military credits), the Senate twice defeated the measure that had been passed in the National Assembly. The opposition in the National Assembly had the opportunity to introduce motions of censure which were defeated. Again, in the spring of 1966, de Gaulle's decision to withdraw from NATO led to a full-dress debate triggered by a censure motion against the government. Not more than 140 deputies out of 482 voted for the motion.

## THE GAULLIST YEARS: THE SUBSTANCE OF FOREIGN POLICY

The Gaullist years will no doubt be considered by future historians to have set the guidelines for French foreign policy. Both de Gaulle's philosophy (which we discussed briefly earlier) and his actions set a pattern that can be described in one simple phrase—the reassertion of independence. In a highly fluid and everchanging world it was the vocation of a nation-state to establish its freedom to act—to seek its allies and pursue its interests. The objective of independence and of independent action became almost an obsession often obscured by the changing tactics in order to preserve and maximize all possible options and never to create a situation or to allow an arrangement to develop that took ultimate choices and decisions away from the hands of France. The obsession often led the country, under de Gaulle, perilously close to isolationism, to a Maurassian *France seule* posture, in a world where the solitary state—even for the superpowers—is an anachronism. At times in an effort to keep all choices open, France, unable to both please its allies and placate possible enemies, found herself ignored by both. In Europe unwilling to commit herself to a genuine political union but always anxious to speak on behalf of Europe and the European interest, de Gaulle antagonized his partners without being able to provide them with leadership and strength. If one were to single out one connecting thread in de Gaulle's actions, it would be his desire and his efforts to see both American and Soviet forces withdraw, in one form or another, from Eastern and Western Europe.

In his last press conference, on September 9, 1968, de Gaulle summed it up thus:

Since 1958, we French never ceased to work in order to put an end to the regime of the two blocs. Thus, while building close relations with the countries of Western Europe, even to the extent of transforming our former estrangement with Germany into cordial cooperation, we have slowly detached ourselves from the military organization of NATO which subordinates the Europeans to the Americans. Thus, while participating in the Common Market we have never consented to the establishment of a supranational system which will drown France in a . . . whole which will have no other policy but the one of the protector from across the seas. . . . By the same token, . . . we have restored our relations with the countries of Eastern Europe and above all with Russia. ... We have given to the great Russian people to understand ... that the whole of Europe expects from them something much better than to shut and chain their satellites within the barriers of a crushing totalitarianism.[15]

We shall discuss the Gaullist decade with regard to (a) colonial and economic policy, (b) NATO, (c) Europe and the Common Market, (d) the atom bomb, and (e) relations with the Soviet Union.

### End of Empire; Economic Growth

In 1958, General de Gaulle pledged to all overseas territories a new political arrangement—the French Community—and, if they wished it, their independence. All of the territories, with the exception of Guinea, entered the French Community. They became republics federated with France. They were governed by the president of the French republic, who was also president of the community, with the assistance of an Executive Council which consisted of the president of the republic, a number of French ministers charged with community affairs, and the prime ministers, or their delegates, of the African republics and Madagascar. A Community Senate, with primarily consultative powers, was also established, as well as a community arbitration court, to hear and pass on controversies among the member states. In the course of 1959–60, the community was abandoned. Speaking in Dakar, Senegal, in December, 1959, de Gaulle promised to grant "international sovereignty" —that is, complete independence—

[15]Quoted in *Année politique, 1968*, p. 392.

to all of France's African territories. All the African republics have become independent, and all of them have become members of the United Nations as independent, individual states with the freedom to vote as they please in the United Nations General Assembly and to participate in its organs and specialized commissions.

Thus France, under de Gaulle, put an end to colonialism. In doing so, she improved her position in Africa, where she is assured of a reservoir of good will. Large subsidies to the African republics and Madagascar guarantee a good rate of modernization and industralization there, which is bound to favor French trade and investments in Africa and improve the living standards of the Africans themselves. Thus, politically and economically, the road was paved for better relations.

*Algeria.* It was not until July 3, 1962, after a series of zigzags and equivocations into which we need not enter here, that Algeria was finally granted her full independence. The leaders of the rebellion were released from jail, and the French settlers began their return to France. Between 1962 and 1965, almost 1 million European French citizens and a sizeable number of Algerians who had fought in the French army or in territorial units were resettled in the metropolis with substantial financial aid from the state. Thus the war in Algeria (1954–1962) that, like the war in Vietnam, had sapped the energy of the country, that had provoked sharp and, at times, irreconcilable conflicts, that had seriously qualified France's freedom of action, that had gravely undermined her prestige among her former colonies, particularly in Africa, came to an end. In 1962, for the first time since World

War II, French soldiers were no longer fighting anybody, anywhere. Relations with Algeria itself rapidly improved, and France continued to extend considerable economic and cultural aid to the newly created state.

## NATO: Participation; Reform; Withdrawal

Immediately after his return to power, de Gaulle asserted that it was not the purpose of France to limit her foreign policy "within the confines of NATO." On September 23, 1958, he addressed a memorandum, still technically secret, to Belgian Prime Minister Paul-Henri Spaak, Prime Minister Macmillan, and President Eisenhower. It is, however, common knowledge that the memorandum contained a diagnosis of the problems facing NATO and a statement of French policy. De Gaulle indicated the common responsibilities imposed upon the alliance in case of war, but pointed to the inequality in armaments and, what is more, to the disparity in the freedom of the member states to make decisions. Events in Egypt and Algeria contrasted sharply with those in the Near East, Formosa and, later, Vietnam. He proposed, therefore, the establishment within NATO of a "directorate" of three— England, France, and the United States—with responsibility for elaborating a common military and political strategy for the whole of the planet, for the creation of allied commands for all theaters of operation, for joint deliberations about strategy, and for joint decision on the use of atomic weapons. "The European states of the continent," he stated on April 11, 1961, ". . . must know exactly with which weapons and under what conditions their overseas allies would join them in battle."[16] He reminded President Kennedy, who was to visit him within a matter of weeks, that "the threats of war are no longer limited to Europe" and that NATO should accordingly revise its organization to meet joint non-European problems. There was also a threat in the memorandum: France would reconsider its NATO policy in the light of the response of England and the United States.

Although ostensibly addressing problems related to NATO, de Gaulle was actually attempting to place France on a level to which no other continental European power in NATO could aspire. NATO was to remain a broad organization, according to his proposal, but with three of its members—France, England and the United States—jointly in charge of global strategy. The three great powers were, in the best tradition of the old diplomacy, to be in charge, at the NATO level, of the Atlantic problems, and jointly in charge of planetary strategy. De Gaulle remained adamant. When his suggestions were rejected, France withdrew its Mediterranean fleet from NATO command; she refused to integrate her air defense with NATO; she prevented the building of launching sites and the stockpiling of atomic warheads over which she could have no control. But this stand against military integration was to bring France in conflict with West Germany. This became painfully evident during Chancellor Adenauer's visit in December, 1959, and

[16]News conference, April 11, 1961, in *Speeches and Press Conferences*, no. 162, pp. 7–8.

throughout 1960, when de Gaulle and his advisers talked freely about an "independent" Western European strategy and apparently foresaw even the possibility of the withdrawal of American forces.

With the end of the Algerian war, there was no doubt at all as to where de Gaulle stood and what he wanted. First, European problems had better be left to the European nations. This involved even the problem of German reunification. Second, European nations, notably France, had worldwide commitments that transcended the regional limits of NATO, just as did the United States. Hence the future of the national armed forces and their deployment and posture was a national matter belonging to France. Third, without ever stating it, de Gaulle seemed to infer that the presence of American troops in Europe was becoming, at least politically, a liability. Fourth, NATO and its integrative aspects were to be thrust aside and replaced, at most and on the basis of expedience and contingency, by a classic alliance among individual and separate states—an alliance that was to be negotiated and renegotiated as the circumstances demanded. De Gaulle never rejected the desirability of such a classic alliance, but while insisting on its form—a pact between individual sovereign states —he never specified its content. It has seemed clear, however, that such an alliance was to be construed narrowly. The partners would be free to differ on everything that did not involve their defense against a specified foreign attack under the stipulated conditions. France would be free to move in her own way in China, in Southeast Asia, and in Latin America, as well as reconsider her relations with the Eastern European countries or the Soviet Union. De Gaulle's revisionist policy with regard to NATO was, in other words, an explicit reformulation of France's full-fledged independence to act as a world power. If and when the interests of the United States and France converged, so much the better; if they diverged, each would be free to act independently of the other. In three separate memorandums—on March 11, March 29, and April 22, 1966—the French government communicated its decision to withdraw its forces from NATO on July 1, 1966, and demanded the withdrawal, by April 1, 1967, of all United States armed forces and military personnel and of all NATO instrumentalities from the French soil. The only remaining possibility was that American forces could be stationed in France, and French forces in Germany, on the basis of bilateral arrangements. The alternative left to the United States was to persist in the continuation of NATO without France, but with the support of England and West Germany.

## The Common Market

Under de Gaulle, the economic development of the country continued to improve. The improvement was partly due to measures, originally suggested by a "special" committee of experts, designed to eliminate inflationary tendencies and restore monetary stability. This plan aimed "to restore to France its international status" in the economic field and "to establish the nation on a foundation of truth and severity, which alone can enable it to build its prosperity."

In order to achieve a sounder monetary position and a better competitive position for French goods in foreign markets, the franc was devalued by 17.5 percent in December, 1958. France restored the convertibility of the franc, thus giving foreign companies the guarantees necessary to enable them freely to invest and remit profits. Foreign capital began to flow into the country, contributing appreciably to the improvement in the balance of payments. The new price of the franc made it again possible to liberalize trade, and enabled France to fulfill its commitments toward its Common Market partners. On January 1, 1959, France implemented, in full, the European Common Market treaty provisions for the reduction of customs duties and the liberalization of trade. Moreover, because devaluation had lowered the prices of French goods, the country's foreign trade improved rapidly. In May, 1959, for the first time in a very long period, France's foreign trade balance showed a surplus. Exports rose at a rapid rate. Industrial production, after a slight decline in 1963–64, resumed its upward trend and was followed by a steady rate of increase that averaged 4.5 percent until 1968, when, as a result of the May–June uprisings and strikes, production fell off sharply and the balance of payments was seriously affected. In August, 1969 (after de Gaulle had retired), France had to adopt restrictive policies and devalue the franc by some 13 percent; exports then began to rise again, causing a rapid improvement in the balance of payments.

De Gaulle's acceptance of the Common Market was motivated in part by economic reasons and in part by considerations favoring the development of a European "whole." The crucial reason, however, was political. This became abundantly clear after 1960. The Common Market suggested the possibility that a larger European whole could be placed under the leadership of France, armed with atomic weapons that were denied to Germany by virtue of the 1955 Paris accords. Britain's participation was highly desirable, provided Britain was willing to abandon the intimate Atlantic connections that underwrote the dominance of the United States, and also provided that Britain brought into a European pool—under some form of Franco-British control—her atomic and hydrogen weapons and knowhow. Britain's nuclear power was to be its dowry in the contemplated marriage with the Common Market. When it became clear that England was unwilling to cut her intimate ties with the United States, de Gaulle decided to refuse entry to England. In his now famous press conference of January 14, 1963, de Gaulle, alleging economic and cultural reasons, rejected England's entry. The heart of the matter, however, was political and strategic. England, de Gaulle feared, would remain under the domination of the United States, and her entry into the Common Market would thus reinforce America's influence.

With England at least temporarily out of the picture, de Gaulle turned to Germany. A Franco-German alliance providing for frequent consultations and possibly for the elaboration of common policy on military, foreign, cultural, and economic questions, would provide the hard core for consolidating Western Europe and, given France's military superiority, safeguard French leadership at the same time. In January, 1963, a Franco-German treaty, embodying the principle of consultations on matters of defense, foreign policy, and cultural affairs, was signed. However, the very logic of the treaty raised serious questions. It was again based on the assumption that West Germany would accept French, rather than American, leadership and protection. But in the light of its military and economic ties with the United States, and especially in the light of the overwhelming superiority of the United States in these areas, it was unlikely that any German political leader would acquiesce to this. Gradually, the treaty was bypassed and the policies of the two countries on military and foreign policy questions began to diverge, with Germany supporting the United States. Thus, what accounted for de Gaulle's rebuff of Britain seemed to be also called into play by Germany. It was only de Gaulle, and only France, that seemed to believe that Western Europe could do without the United States, and it was only France that pressed for a European solution of the European problems at the very time when the heart of the European defense establishment continued to lie across the Atlantic.

But the Common Market remained a successful economic arrangement. It had, by 1965, reached the stage when increasing commitments to supranationality were to be made, and when some decision could be made by a qualified majority of the participants. In other words, the Common Market had moved to the critical stage when it was about to assume, even to a limited degree, genuine supranationality. However, such a supranationality is, as we have seen, contrary to de Gaulle's basic assumptions about the nature of international relations. Alleging the unwillingness of the other five members to accept common agricultural policies (policies, incidentally, quite advantageous to French agriculture), de Gaulle instructed his ministers, in the middle of 1965, to withdraw from the Council of Ministers of the Common Market. He also attacked the supranational character of the Rome treaty establishing the EEC and claimed that the assumption of power by a body of "stateless" functionaries was prejudicial to the independence of the sovereign member states. The Rome treaty, he concluded, had to be revised in order to do away with all supranational clauses. In effect, he urged that the Common Market remain a purely economic arrangement, held together by the will of sovereign and independent states, and subject to the veto power of each and all.

## Nuclear Strategy

Since the Allies seemed unwilling to subordinate overall strategy and the use of atomic weapons to a "directorate," France proceeded with the explosion of her own atom bomb. A number of additional reasons were given: the uncertainty about the use of the bomb by the United States, except in self-defense; the need of a French deterrent to war; the injection of a new pride and a higher morale in an army that had experienced one frustration after another; and, finally, the world-wide commitments of France. As long as other powers have nuclear weapons, the only policy consistent with French interests, according to de Gaulle, was to develop nuclear weapons. At the Geneva disarmament conference, the French continued to favor the liquidation of stockpiles of weapons and delivery missiles before the suspension of manufacturing and testing of nuclear weapons.

On February 13, 1960, in accord with the timetable set before de Gaulle returned to office, France exploded her first atomic device in the Sahara. Since then, there have been seven additional atomic tests in the atmosphere and a number of underground ones. Nuclear devices were tested in the Polynesian possessions of France in the Pacific, with the latest tests in 1974.

By 1967, France had a minimum of a hundred atomic bombs, averaging in strength at least three times that of the first bomb which fell on Hiroshima. With nuclear capabilities to be added soon, it was estimated that France's force would attain a genuine deterrent. The army has been trimmed down, and increasing emphasis has been placed on atomic weapons and the production of delivery vehicles, some of which are now operational.

The reality of French nuclear capability, even if limited, was bound to cause a reconsideration of strategic thinking. General de Gaulle himself was particularly anxious not to allow France to meet a crisis with antiquated ideas and weapons. Atomic weapons are considered today to be the best deterrent against war, by giving to the nation possessing them the possibility of retaliating against the vital centers of the enemy's power. However, given the nuclear capabilities of the United

States and the Soviet Union, the confrontation of American and Soviet forces in the heart of Europe and, finally, the particular interests of France in Europe, the French hope to perform a number of interrelated and often contradictory strategic tasks. France wishes to maintain a special and privileged position in Western Europe, including West Germany, without, however, allowing herself to be overshadowed by Germany; to keep the substance of the Atlantic alliance, without conceding to the United States a free hand in Western Europe; and to promote a détente with Eastern Europe.

The French atomic weapons are of course not calculated to provide a solution to the above problems. The atomic weapon itself is only a means to *one* goal—independent French action—rather than part of a comprehensive strategy. The acquisition of military independence, or at least of a semblance of independence, can and will provide freedom for France to move in one or another direction as the world situation changes. This is the heart of Gaullist doctrine, and it is, of course, at odds with American efforts to reduce to a minimum anything and everything that might upset the United States' control and initiative.

### The Soviets: The "Opening to the East"

As we have seen, de Gaulle never accepted the arrangements made at Yalta. Yet it was quite obvious that, as long as the Soviet threat continued and Soviet power was countered by American power, the division of Europe along the lines laid down at Yalta was inevitable. With the emergence of the Sino-Soviet split, with the relative weakening of the Soviet Union's expansionist trends, with the growing preoccupation of the Soviets with many internal problems, and last, with the emerging aspirations of many Eastern European nations for independence, the time appeared propitious to reopen the Yalta settlement. This necessitated, first, a reconsideration of the problem of German reunification and, second, the assumption by Western Europe of a relative degree of independence vis-à-vis the United States. For as long as NATO remained what it was, and as long as there was direct Soviet-American confrontation in the heart of Europe, there would be no relaxation of Soviet controls in Eastern Europe.

De Gaulle's emphasis upon a "European Europe," his often-repeated statements about a Europe stretching from the Urals to the shores of the Atlantic, were designed to suggest such a relaxation. Its implementation proved to be a much harder problem. One way was to achieve a genuine Franco-German entente within the context of the Common Market, and then to begin a dialogue with the Soviet Union on matters of German reunification. This proved difficult because of the unwillingness of the Germans to substitute French protection for American, and because of the legitimate doubts of American policy makers about the advisability of such a course of action. De Gaulle then made repeated overtures in the direction of the Eastern European satellites. Cultural and economic ties were stressed; visits were exchanged, a number of leaders of Eastern European countries visiting Paris; and France refused to consider any arrangement that would give the Germans a say about nuclear arms. Thus, under de Gaulle, France was returning increasingly to the pre-World War II arrangements—in which an understanding with the Soviet Union is indispensable to the maintenance of peace in Europe, and in which Germany must reenter the concert of European powers, but without the ultimate weapons. This might well have been the objective of General de Gaulle's visit to the Soviet Union in the summer of 1966 and of Premier Kosygin's return visit to France six months later.

*  *  *

When he returned to power in 1958, de Gaulle did not innovate. He favored independence and a great power rank for France. Not a shred of national independence was to be sacrificed to integrative schemes—military, economic, or political. The Common European Market was accepted as a convenient scheme for economic cooperation. The Atlantic alliance was considered necessary but not its integrative military arrangements. The army was reorganized in a manner that emphasized the primacy of the nuclear weapon—with improved delivery capabilities and the development of some four nuclear submarines with missiles. France stood alone with the possibility of deploying the weapon against anybody "from wherever he came," as General Ailleret announced in 1967. The "opening to the East" to establish better relations with the soviet Union and make American military presence less imperative, but also to convince the Soviet Union to relinquish its hold over Eastern Europe, became a cardinal move in de Gaulle's diplomacy in the last years of his presidency.

## AFTER DE GAULLE:[17] THE POMPIDOU YEARS (1969–74)

When Pompidou came into office the Gaullist aspirations had not materialized. On the contrary, it seemed that the basic Gaullist design, to create an independent Europe under French leadership and protection, to undermine the Soviet and American positions in Eastern and Western Europe, respectively, and to prevent a Soviet-American cooperation that he equated with a "condominium," had failed. Even the remarkable industrial growth in France and her strong economic position in the world declined dramatically in 1968 in the wake of two months of revolutionary uprisings that left the economy crippled.

We shall examine the foreign policy under Pompidou with regard to the Common Market and Europe, the Atlantic Alliance, the Franco-Soviet relations, and the evolution of French strategy. First, we shall discuss briefly presidential dominance as it applies to foreign policy.

### Presidentialism and Foreign Policy

Continuity with the Gaullist practices was the rule. President Pompidou alone made foreign policy with the Prime Minister playing only a secondary role. The President of the Republic met personally with the leaders of other countries. He held biannual meetings with the German chancellor; had frequent meetings with the British Prime Minister; had three special meetings with President Nixon, including a visit to the

[17]For a fuller development see Roy C. Macridis, *French Politics in Transition: The Years After de Gaulle* (Cambridge, Mass.: Winthrop, 1975).

United States. He toured virtually every part of French-speaking Africa. Despite his ill health he visited China. Personal and direct diplomacy became the common practice. Presidential dominance was just as real as under de Gaulle. Yet a number of changes can be detected. Pompidou appeared more modest in his aspirations. The Gaullist challenges to the world were replaced by more practical considerations in which economic motives played an important role. The dominant issues were how to get oil; how to improve the position of the French farmers in the Common Market; how to establish economic cooperation with the Soviet Union; how to maintain Franco-American relations without flaunting American power or American policies in faraway areas—Vietnam or Latin America or Canada. No major new policies were outlined or suggested—except for the enlargement of the Common Market to which we shall return. Incrementalism was the rule. Pompidou continued by and large to act within Gaullist principles but qualified them as time went on in the light of changing international events and in terms of a more realistic appraisal of France's power and influence in the world.

### France and the Common Market

The ultimate goal of the founders of the Common Market was political union. They expected that ultimately decisions would be made by a qualified majority vote and that a European executive—the Commission—and a European Parliament would begin gradually and in specified areas to make decisions binding upon the member states. The ultimate dream of the founders was to establish a federation of European states with common political institutions endowed with supranational powers. As a candidate for the presidency, Pompidou ran as a European, and it was widely rumored that he favored not only stronger European ties but also the inclusion of Great Britain in the Common Market. Only *in* Western Europe and *with* Western Europe, i.e., the Common Market, could France again become a center of power. But what kind of Europe was it to be? And what would be the relations between such a Europe and the United States, the Soviet Union, and the rest of the world?

Pompidou's policies and objectives are clearly evidenced in the proceedings of three major European summit conferences—in Hague in 1969; in Paris in 1972, and in Copenhagen in 1973.

*The Hague Conference.* In the Hague conference Pompidou presented the famous "triptych" for the future of the Common Market: *Achèvement, approfondissement,* and *elargissement. Achèvement* meant the completion of the financial-agricultural arrangements to create a common agricultural market with an external tariff and a complex procedure of price controls and subsidies to farmers. It benefited the French farmers and was constantly declared by the French officials as absolutely necessary for the consideration of all other economic and social matters. *Approfondissement* meant the "development in depth" of the Common Market to cover banking and monetary policy, harmonize taxation, equalize social security legislation, and establish some political ma-

chinery through which Europe would speak "with one voice" in international affairs. *Elargissement* meant the expansion of the Common Market by the inclusion of other states—notably England—to full membership. It was a challenging presentation but the question of priorities was left unsettled. Would development in depth come before expansion? Pompidou opted for the broadening of the Community, and the inclusion of England, Ireland, Denmark, and Norway. But when the Common Market partners urged the strengthening of the political integrative institution by giving more powers to the Executive Commission and to the European Assembly, Pompidou demurred. He was willing to allow for the rapid exploration of means to "develop in depth" the Common Market in the direction of a monetary union, the establishment of a common patents office, and harmonizing taxation, but he opposed any form of political integration. Throughout his presidency this remained the dominant theme of the French.

*The Referendum of April 23, 1972.* In January 1972 the four candidate members of England, Denmark, Ireland, and Norway were admitted into the Common Market in a treaty that had to be ratified in one form or another by the Common Market countries and also by the new member states. "Having assumed personally the responsibility for this," stated Pompidou in his Press Conference, "first in Hague, then in my meeting with Prime Minister Heath (summer of 1971) and having authorized the signature of the Treaty, I consider it both my duty and in accordance with democratic principles to ask the

French people, who have elected me . . . to express themselves directly on this European policy." [18] The referendum was to be held on April 23, 1972, and was to be followed by a new European Summit meeting of all the members of the Community —including the new ones.

The question before the French voters was two-fold: a) the approval or disapproval of the Treaty enlarging the Community, b) the overall support or disavowel of Pompidou's European policy. In a clarifying document to all French voters it was stated that they had to decide whether or not Europe would move progressively in the direction of a confederation that would preserve the personality of the states that comprise it. To some, confederation was contrary to the Gaullist heritage; to others, Pompidou was not going far enough in the direction of a genuine political Europe. The matter was further confused by the strong national overtones that accompanied the call for the approval of Pompidou's foreign policy: it would serve French interests, promote France's strength, consolidate her independence. Opinion was divided. The Communist party had urged a "No" vote; the socialists had counseled abstention; the centrists voted "Yes," because they wanted European Union and favored the entry of England even though they opposed Pompidou's lack of willingness to go beyond vague phrases about a confederation. The results were disappointing for the President. For every hundred registered voters only 37 voted "Yes"; 17 voted "No," and the rest abstained. It was a political defeat, especially in comparison to recent polls in which more than 70 percent of the French favored England's entry.

*The Paris Conference.* The summit meeting of the nine European countries (Norway decided not to join the Common Market), represented by their top political leaders, took place October 19–20, 1972 to consecrate the entry of England, Denmark and Ireland into the European Economic Community, but also to face up to some new and urgent monetary problems and to consider the reform of its institutional structures.

The Nine (England, France, West Germany, Italy, Belgium, Holland, Luxemburg, Denmark, and Ireland) constitute a formidable economic, trading, industrial, and financial bloc, and potentially even military bloc. This community of two hundred and fifty million people enjoys a standard of living that ranks among the highest. It accounts for about 40 percent of the world's trade, produces more steel and more automobiles than the United States and operates about 50 percent of the world's merchant marine. Two of the countries (England and France) have mastered nuclear technology and have nuclear arms. Six of them had gone through almost fifteen years of close cooperation that brought important tangible and even more important intangible benefits: a common agricultural market and a common external tariff, the elimination of internal tariffs and trade barriers, massive and intensive cultural exchanges. The way had been opened for the preparation of some genuine integrative plans: a European common monetary system with perhaps even a common currency and a European bank; social and welfare harmonization; regional planning and regional

[18] *Annèe Politique*, 1972, p. 216.

development within a European framework; reciprocity to all educational degrees; free mobility of capital and labor.

However, little progress had been made in the establishment of an institutional arrangement that stops short of a genuine federation but is something more than a loose confederation. The Summit conference, then, failed to reach an agreement on the political future of Europe.

Ambiguity and studious delay were the rule when it came to institutional reforms and political cooperation. There was nothing except the expression of pious hopes for cooperation in the development of a common foreign policy. Nothing specific was decided on how to establish a common dialogue between the Nine as such and the United States. Lipservice, was paid to the need of consultations, but even the idea of a European political secretariat was discarded. What is more, nothing was decided about common defense and strategy and the relations of the Nine within or without NATO. As for the reform of institutions, it was simply agreed to proceed with studies for the strengthening of the "powers of control" of the European Parliament, but the question of its election by universal suffrage was sidestepped. The conference also agreed to study the prospects "of transforming before the end of the present decade and *with the fullest respect of the Treaties already signed* the whole complex of relations of member states into a European Union." By 1975 a report was to be prepared and submitted to a new summit conference.

A number of economic problems were discussed. The French insisted on a European monetary union or at least a commitment to go ahead with

it. It will not be "completed" until December 31, 1980. However, the word "completed" (achevè) is never defined to mean what it should, i.e., that by that time, if not sooner, *all* European currencies would be treated as a unit in their fluctuations vis-à-vis all outside currencies.

*The Summit at Copenhagen.* The European Summit meeting in Copenhagen in December 1973 was called because of a series of circumstances that required urgent common decisions: the situation in the Middle East, relations between Europe and the United States, and the energy crisis. Each and all of these items were related not only to economic and political but also to strategic developments that had placed France and Europe in severe difficulties. None of the hopes associated with the establishment of European institutions had materialized. Crucial monetary difficulties—the devaluation of the dollar, the reevaluation of the deutsch mark, the uncontrolled fluctuations of European currencies, the constant pressure on the part of the United States for commercial and trade arrangements to take into account the U.S. military expenses in Europe (evaluated at three billion dollars a year), strong divergencies among the European states with regard to Israel—all of these had undermined the spirit of European cooperation. Europe remained politically an entity consisting of nine relatively small, sovereign states.

It was at this juncture that Pompidou and his Foreign Affairs Minister, Michel Jobert, rose belatedly to the support of European solidarity; to the search for a European identity; to an effort to define it and give it its own defense; and finally to a search to solve the energy crisis by following a course independent of the United States. "The Nine affirm their common will to see Europe 'speak with one voice' when it comes to world-wide matters." The Conference adopted a declaration stressing the following:

a. The understanding that all bilateral arrangements made by the nine should take into greater consideration the common positions agreed by them;
b. The chiefs of state should meet more frequently;
c. The specific character of the European entity should be respected;
d. The institutions of the community must function fully, and rapid decisions must be made;
e. The relations among the Commission, the Council of Ministers, and the European parliament should be improved in order to expedite decisions and to reinforce the budgetary control powers of the latter.

Despite the overt professions of Europeanism, there was no tangible evidence in Pompidou's period that France had relinquished its stand against any political integrative arrangements in Europe. The ruling body remained the Council of Ministers and the individual veto of each of the countries comprising the Common Market reemphasized on a number of occasions. A political Europe endowed with some representative institutions that can speak on behalf of the Nine is still to be made. In this sense Pompidou remained as Gaullist as de Gaulle!

The Atlantic Alliance and Defense

Two basic propositions have shaped French foreign policy and defense with regard to the Atlantic Alliance: First, that the division of the world into two "blocs," under the respective control of the United States and the Soviet Union, is unacceptable; second that in our nuclear world possession of nuclear weapons is the only corollary to national independence. Hence, no integrative alliances should be made that qualify a country's freedom to act.

These two propositions have diametrically contradictory implications when they apply to the United States—the leader of the Atlantic world—and to other states, particularly in Europe that do not have the nuclear weapon. In the first case France's position is a call for independence against the United States; in the second it is a call for the dependence of the European states upon France for their protection and makes France (or at least so it is hoped) the leader of the Western European nations. It is this contradiction that has made European unity difficult to achieve and has also marred relations between France and the United States.

The French "revolt" against the United States[19] —a revolt that dates from the first exchanges between de Gaulle and Roosevelt—has taken every conceivable form: political, economic, cultural, diplomatic, and strategic. Powerfully supported by the Gaullists and the Communists (for different reasons) it has been popular among the French. It has led to the withdrawal of France from NATO and her unwillingness to consider permanent and binding consultative relations between the Common Market and the U.S. The

[19]Stanley Hoffmann, *Decline or Renewal: France Since the 1930s* (New York: Viking Press, 1974), pp. 332–62.

French never agreed to participate in a disarmament conference claiming that it was designed to keep the monopoly of nuclear weapons among those who already had them; they refused to participate in the negotiations for a balanced and mutual reduction of forces in Europe—anticipating a deal between the Russians and the Americans that would weaken the defense of Europe; they, of course, have had nothing to do with SALT. They have protested against the agreement for the prevention of nuclear war signed by the United States and the Soviet Union in the summer of 1973—because they were not consulted and also because they feared a lowering of the American commitment to defend Western Europe.

In 1973 it was primarily the effort made by the United States to develop a new Atlantic charter and reassert the solidarity of the Atlantic world that provoked strong reactions on the part of France. They saw in the United States efforts a design to again "control" and dominate Europe. When the United States Secretary of State, Henry Kissinger remarked that the European identity cannot be defined and expressed outside of the Atlantic whole he was repeating what in effect most European leaders, except the French, had argued. Nor was Kissinger implying that a "compatibility" between Europe, the United States, and the other members of the Atlantic Alliance called for United States domination. Rather, he was seeking a structured pattern of consultations. At this point Pompidou reverted to the Gaullist hard line by calling for the independence of Europe, the acknowledgement of a European identity, the need (conceded until then by all other members of the Community but France) to develop the proper political mechanisms so that Europe could speak with "one voice," and, finally, a common European defense.

## French Defense Strategy

But it was France's concept of defense and her strategy within the Atlantic Alliance that created more serious problems. French strategists have attempted to develop a theory that reconciles France's place in the alliance with her independent nuclear force. Their arguments run as follows: Supposing there is an aggression from the East—then the Alliance becomes operative and the NATO and French forces together engage the aggressor on the basis of the existing bilateral arrangements —presumably somewhere in Europe. If, however, during these forward operations it becomes clear to the French leaders that the aggressor is *aiming* at France's territory, that his *intent* is indeed to occupy France, or destroy her, or seriously imperil her vital interest then France will be free to act alone, by using her nuclear forces. This point, the so-called *critical threshold of aggressiveness*, is to be determined by the French leaders. The French can and will communicate to the aggressor through appropriate but unequivocal signals their readiness to use their nuclear weapons if the aggressor fails to respond appropriately. In other words, all cooperative arrangements that may exist between France and the "Alliance" are set aside in favor of French unilateral action the very moment the French leaders decide that the critical threshold of aggressiveness *for*

*France* has been reached. A nuclear retaliatory strike will presumably follow against the aggressor irrespective of what the allies do and even if they are still engaged in battle.

The French position is contrary to the inherent logic of the alliance. Why should allies agree to engage their forces in common against an aggressor while leaving one of them free to jeopardize and indeed to destroy the whole in the name of its vital interests? Why should France's allies act as France's first line of defense unless there is a common strategy that, while protecting France, protects also their forces and their interests? Why should they go along in a common effort that threatens the existence of their own forces by putting them at the mercy of one of them? Since France's position is not likely to find acceptance she may discover that what she considers her first line of defense—the Alliance— is unavailable. She may then be left with nothing but her nuclear weapons to fend off a direct threat to her territory.

This is perhaps the greatest weakness of the French position today and the most unfortunate legacy of the Gaullist years. Without integrative military alliances and without a political Europe that can elaborate a common strategy and defense, France is faced with the prospect of increasing her conventional forces rapidly and at high cost or of emphasizing her independent national nuclear capability and thus of moving even closer to a purely defensive posture that will underwrite her isolation. This is the dilemma: France cannot rely upon her nuclear force without strong cohesive and integrative alliances, but yet she cannot make integrative alliances without abandoning the grandiose and rigid emphasis upon military and nuclear independence.

### Relations with the Soviet Union

Pompidou continued to follow the guidelines laid down by de Gaulle in relations with the USSR. Frequent consultations between the leaders of the two states were held; however, economic arrangements were negotiated representing only a modest increase in the trade between the two countries. With the occupation of Czechoslovakia by the Russian troops in the summer of 1968 the last efforts on the part of France to provide an "opening to the East," based upon a withdrawal of Soviet political and military control there, had failed. There was little that the French could give and even less that the Russians wanted.

In the growing world of détente the French under Pompidou had even less to give. With the withdrawal of the French forces from NATO but the continuation of the Alliance there was little that could change the status quo. In the last year of the Pompidou presidency the remarks made by the French President and his Minister of Foreign Affairs about a Soviet-American "condominium," and more particularly an independent European defense, were sharply criticized by the Soviet leaders. Since there is no prospect for France to trade off her Atlantic alliance for a different one, there is very little that France can do to arouse genuine Soviet interest and support. The Gaullist strategy of using the one side against the other cannot be successful when the two superpowers manage to reach direct agreements to maintain the status quo.

## Overview: French Policy Under Pompidou

Continuity of the Gaullist policy under Pompidou seems to have been the rule. Even when he admitted England and the other three countries into the Common Market, the French President was not altering the course of French foreign policy. In the last year of the Gaullist presidency there were intimations that de Gaulle was prepared to do the same. He was both fearful of the success of political integrative mechanisms and disenchanted with the Franco-German treaty of 1962 which was to lead to a strong Europe under the joint leadership of the two (with France having the nuclear weapons). De Gaulle had begun to lose interest in the Common Market of the Six and to favor a looser arrangement with other European states including England.

The policy vis-à-vis the Arab world and against Israel remained the same; every effort was made to maintain relations with French-speaking Africa and to improve relations with Northern African states—Tunisia, Morocco, and Algeria; nuclear tests continued, and the nuclear weapon was improved, but its credibility remained as precarious as before. Despite some efforts to establish an understanding with NATO on technical strategic matters, the independence of France's nuclear posture and unilateral strategy was maintained. Within the European countries France refused to participate in the Eurogroup—the effort to provide for standardization of weapon and military procurement in the context of the Atlantic Alliance and in cooperation with it. While some joint projects with European states succeeded—such as the Concorde—no agreement was reached on a common nuclear energy policy. France under Pompidou became progressively isolated. The desperate search for a role in world affairs had brought no tangible results.

## IN SEARCH OF A ROLE—GISCARD D'ESTAING

The year 1973 was for President Pompidou similar to what 1968 had been for General de Gaulle. The oil crisis, the war in the Mideast, the negotiations between the two superpowers to put an end to the war there without any consultations with "Europe," the strong line taken by Henry Kissinger and President Nixon urging the Common Market countries not to make decisions without prior consultations with the United States, as well as the internal conflicts within the Common Market, and the decisions of individual countries, including France herself, to abandon common monetary policies and invoke special measures to protect their economies, showed not only the weakness of France but also her inability to play a role in Europe and the Mediterranean. It was perhaps this realization that led the dying President and his foreign Minister to return to the Gaullist hard line of national independence against the United States and to a belated search for a "European identity" and a "European defense."

But France's partners in the Common Market were unwilling to follow French leadership. The British election of a Labor Government committed to the renegotiation of the terms of England's entry into the

Market and the added economic difficulties caused by mounting inflation seemed to presage the dislocation of the Common Market, not only as a political entity—which it was never allowed to become—but also as an economic one.

Like Pompidou, Giscard d'Estaing ran in the Presidential election of May 1974 as a "European." But unlike Pompidou, he seems inclined to follow a different approach to the realization of the reconstruction of Europe. First and foremost he seems to be returning to de Gaulle's realization that it is only through a firm consolidation of the relationship between France and West Germany that a European vocation can be kept alive and prosperous. The first political leader to visit him in June 1974 was his former fellow Minister of Finance of West Germany, now Chancellor,Helmut Schmidt, and he returned the visit within a few weeks. The new Minister of Foreign Affairs, the former French Ambassador to West Germany, was appointed because of the great importance the new President attributed to Franco-German relations. There is every indication that European unity will not be pursued through Summit meetings, as with Pompidou, but in terms of careful and painstaking deliberations both in the Council of Ministers and in the Commission of the Common Market countries. The Council of Ministers *and* the Commission may begin to work together on both political and economic matters.

In the declaration of the NATO countries in Ottawa and subsequently in Brussels in the summer of 1974 the "identity" of Europe was recognized and so was her freedom to act and negotiate with others without any binding obligation to prior consultations with her Atlantic partners—notably the United States. But such consultations were deemed to be "necessary" and "highly desirable." Thus the declaration on "European independence" sought by the Gaullists in the past and especially by Pompidou's foreign Minister gave way to an assertion of an "identity" of Europe, in the context of the realities of the Atlantic Alliance.

Similarly in matters of defense the disagreements between France and virtually every other member of the Atlantic Alliance are being reconciled. There was no question of a European independent defense, as the French insisted, but of the "distinct" defense. There was a recognition of the contribution of the European (i.e., French and British) nuclear deterrence to the Common Atlantic defense. The General Chief of Staff, General François Maurin, continued to argue in favor of a French national nuclear striking force, but he conceded that it was the duty of France to foresee all possibilities, and if she were to engage in battle ". . . in the framework of the Alliance," to determine and define in advance the procedures in terms of which France will engage her forces. "Consultations for this purpose are going on with the appropriate NATO organs," he added.[20] This appears to be another step in the direction of closer cooperation with NATO.

There are indications that France is returning to the realities of the international situation in the realization that its new role is above all in Europe but within the framework of the Atlantic Alliance. The presence of American forces in Europe and

[20]In *Revue de Défense Nationale,* July 1974.

the support of such forces not only "presently" but for the future was explicitly accepted. The argument in favor of a separate and independent European defense for France, seems to have given place to the realistic demands of the other European countries in favor of both European cooperation *and* consultations with the United States in the framework of NATO. The use of terms such as the "specificity" and the "identity" and the "individual" European nuclear contribution to the Alliance satisfies the French.

### The "Summit" of Paris

The most important landmark in the progress of closer cooperation among the Nine was the Summit meeting of the heads of the nine governments held in Paris, December 9–10, 1974.[21] It was decided to regularize the convening of such meetings with the participation of the Foreign Ministers at least three times a year and to establish an "administrative secretariat" (the term political secretariat was not mentioned) to provide minimal liaison services. More important, it was agreed to bring into these deliberations the Executive Council of the Common Market and to coordinate diplomatic action in "all areas of international affairs which affect the interests of the Community" so that the Nine could speak through their periodically designated President with one voice. The French President stated that he would live up to

[21]For the full text of the agreements reached see "Summit Meeting of the Heads of Government of the Nine Countries of the European Community" Paris, Dec. 9 and 10, 1974 (New York City, N.Y.: Ambassade de France, Service de Presse et d'Information, 1975).

the timetable set at the Summit of Paris to establish such a European Union by 1980. The British are reluctant, and the economic problems facing individual countries and the Market as a whole are likely to have precedence over any ambitious political decisions. But as was the case with economic arrangements in the past, there is growing realization of the need for a joint foreign policy for the Nine. Ad hoc arrangements and consultations among the Nine with the participation of the European Commission, are more likely to lead to political union than a solemn drafting of a federal or confederational charter. But even here the new President has made two important policy commitments. First, he came out for the direct election of the European Parliament by the peoples of the nine countries and second, he renounced, together with the other heads of state, the practice of "unanimous consent," thereby allowing for some decisions to be made by qualified majority. These are important steps in the direction of better cooperation and more effective decision making on the part of the Council of Ministers of the Common Market countries and, barring major political and economic crises, may pave the way to continuing binding institutional arrangements. Europe cannot speak with "one voice" yet, but continuing consultations may provide for common foreign-policy positions. As it was with the economic Europe, a political Europe is likely to evolve gradually, step by step, and only when the need for unity is clearly perceived by the political leaders of the nations that comprise the Nine. France, under Giscard d'Estaing, seems closer than under any previous French leader to making the effort in a truly cooperative spirit no longer based on the expectation that she will assume a dominant role.

In summary, the new foreign policy of President d'Estaing may well put an end to the isolation of France —in Europe, in the Atlantic Alliance, and also in the Mediterranean. Above all, France may seek a new role as a member of the European Community and *in* the European Community in close cooperation with West Germany. The ambitious and grandiose projects to become a "balancer" between East and West, to undermine the position of the United States or the Soviet Union, to create an independent Europe under French leadership, and to provide for a credible national deterrent outside of the Atlantic Alliance, propounded by de Gaulle and occasionally nourished by Pompidou, especially in his last year in office, are no longer seriously entertained. The nostalgia for the glories of the past has given place to the realization of the opportunities of the present— France and Western Europe have a role to play in Africa, in the Mediterranean, and in the European continent within the context of an Atlantic cooperation that can ultimately lead to strength and independence. Yet the Gaullist aspirations not only die hard but are strongly urged upon Giscard d'Estaing (a non-Gaullist) by the Gaullist party in the National Assembly. Special relations with the Arab nations continue to be cultivated, and economic relations, including massive sales of military equipment, are being developed. The French Minister of Foreign Affairs met with the leader of the Palestinian Liberation Organization. France favors the Minister's participation in any conference that may be called to debate the issues dividing Israel and the Arabs. The new President reiterated the need for an "autonomous French defense" while his Foreign Minister has alluded to the "desire" on the part of the United States and the Soviet Union to establish a "condominium." Orthodox Gaullists are ready to portray the slightest concession on the part of France as a betrayal of the Gaullist goals and of French independence. They are joined by the Communists and many of the Socialists in the National Assembly. While Giscard d'Estaing seems to be motivated by a genuine desire to establish a European entity in the context of cooperation with the United States, powerful political forces and voices continue to invoke the "independence" and the "sovereignty" of France vis-à-vis both the United States and Europe.

## SELECTED BIBLIOGRAPHY

### Basic Sources

*Année Politique:* Annual survey of political and economic events and developments. Presses Universitaires de France, Paris.

DE GAULLE, CHARLES. *Discours et Messages.* This is a detailed compilation of the utterances of the General between 1940 and April 28, 1969—the day he resigned. (In five volumes; with comments and notes by François Goguel.) Paris: Plon, 1970–72.

————. *Memoirs of Hope: Renewal and Endeavor.* New York: Simon & Schuster, 1971. They cover the first four years of de Gaulle in office after he returned to power on June 1, 1958. Their completion was interrupted by the General's death on Nov. 9, 1970.

_____. *War Memoirs.* Vol. 1, *The Call to Honour.* New York: Viking Press, 1955. Vol. 2, *Unity.* New York: Simon & Schuster, 1959. Vol. 3, *Salvation.* New York: Simon & Schuster, 1960.

*Politique Etrangère de la France: Textes et Documents,* published by Documentation Française, 29 Quai Voltaire, Paris 75007. It contains all major addresses and foreign policy documents since 1966. There is an English translation for 1966, '67, '68, '69, and '70. The volumes for 1971, '72, '73, '74, and '75 are available only in French. Most of the speeches of President Pompidou and President Giscard d'Estaing are available in English through the French Press and Information Service, 972 Fifth Ave., New York, N.Y.

*Sondages:* The publication of the Institut Français de l'Opinion Publique (30 Rue d'Aumale, Paris 9e) provides invaluable survey material on French public opinion trends including occasional in-depth surveys on foreign policy.


Books

AILLERET, CHARLES. *L'Aventure atomique française.* Paris: Grasset, 1968.

ARON, RAYMOND. *The Great Debate: Theories of Nuclear Strategy,* trans. by Ernst Pawel. New York: Doubleday, 1965.

BEAUFRE, ANDRE. *NATO and Europe.* New York: Knopf, 1967.

_____. *Dissuasion et Stratégie.* Paris: Armand Colin, 1964.

_____. *Stratégie à l'action.* Paris: Armand Colin, 1966.

BUCHAN, ALASTAIR. *A World of Nuclear Powers.* Englewood Cliffs, N.J.: Prentice-Hall, 1966.

_____. *Europe's Futures, Europe's Choices: Models of Western Europe in the 1970's.* New York: Columbia University Press, 1969.

CHARLOT, JEAN. *Les Français et de Gaulle.* Paris: Plon, 1971.

COUVE DE MURVILLE, MAURICE. *Une Politique Etrangère.* Paris: Plon, 1971.

DE CARMOY, GUY. *Les politiques étrangères de la France, 1944–46.* La Table Ronde. Paris, 1967.

DE LA GORSE, ANDRE-MARI. *de Gaulle entre deux mondes.* Paris: Fayard, 1964.

DEUTSCH, KARL W., EDINGER, LEWIS, MACRIDIS, ROY, and MERRITT, RICHARD. *Elite Attitudes and Western Europe.* New York: Charles Scribner's Sons, 1966.

DUROSELLE, J. B. *La politique étrangère et ses fondements.* Paris: Librairie Armand Colin, 1954.

FURNISS, EDGAR, JR. *France: Troubled Ally.* New York: Harper & Row, 1960.

GROSSER, ALFRED. *La politique extérieure de la 4ième République.* Paris: Librairie Armand Colin, 1963.

_____. *French Foreign Policy under de Gaulle.* Boston: Little, Brown, 1965.

HOFFMANN, STANLEY, et al. *In Search of France.* Cambridge, Mass.: Harvard University Press, 1964.

_____. *Decline or Renewal: French Politics since the 1930s.* New York: Viking Press, 1974. Particularly chaps. 10, 11, and 12.

HUNT, K. *NATO without France: the Military Implications.* Adelphi Papers no. 32, London: Institute of Strategic Studies, 1966.

JOUVE, EDMOND. *Le Général de Gaulle et la construction de l'Europe, 1940–66.* 2 vols. Paris: Librairie générale de droit et de jurisprudence, 1967.

KERTESZ, STEPHEN D., and FITZSIMMONS, M. A. *Diplomacy in a Changing World.* South Bend, Ind.: University of Notre Dame, 1959. See the section by Prof. J. B. Duroselle, "French Diplomacy in Post-World War."

KISSINGER, HENRY. *The Troubled Alliance.* New York: McGraw-Hill, 1965.

KOHL, WILFRED. *French Nuclear Diplomacy.* Princeton: Princeton University Press, 1971.

KOLODZIEJ, EDWARD A. *French International Policy under de Gaulle and Pompidou.* Ithaca, N.Y.: Cornell University Press, 1974.

KULSKI, W. W. *de Gaulle and the World System.* Syracuse, N.Y.: Syracuse University Press, 1967.

MACRIDIS, ROY C. *de Gaulle—Implacable Ally.* New York: Harper & Row, 1966.

_____. *French Politics in Transition: The Years after de Gaulle.* Cambridge, Mass.: Winthrop, 1975.

MACRIDIS, ROY C. and BROWN, BERNARD E. *The de Gaulle Republic: Quest for Unity.* Homewood, Ill.: Dorsey Press, 1960.

MORSE, EDWARD L. *Foreign Policy and Interdependence in Gaullist France.* Princeton, N.J.: Princeton University Press, 1973.

NEWHOUSE, JOHN. *de Gaulle and the Anglo-Saxons.* New York: Viking Press, 1970.

NORTHEDGE, F. S., ed. *The Foreign Policies of the Powers.* New York: Praeger, 1968. See especially pp. 187–220.

STEEL, RONALD. *The End of Alliance: America and the Future of Europe.* New York: Viking Press, 1964.

VIORST, MILTON. *Hostile Allies: FDR and de Gaulle.* New York: Macmillan, 1965.

WHITE, DOROTHY S. *Seeds of Discord.* Syracuse, N.Y.: Syracuse University Press, 1964.

WILLIAMS, PHILIP. *French Politicians and Elections, 1951–1969.* Cambridge, England: Cambridge University Press, 1970.

_____. *Politics in Post-War France.* 2nd Ed., London: Longmans, 1958.

WILLIAMS, H. PHILIP, and HARRISON, MARTIN. *Politics and Society in de Gaulle's Republic.* New York: Doubleday-Anchor, 1973.

WILLIS, ROY. *France, Germany and the New Europe, 1945–1967.* New York: Oxford University Press, 1968.

# THE FOREIGN POLICY OF THE GERMAN FEDERAL REPUBLIC

*Josef Joffe*

4

## INTRODUCTION: THE LEGACY OF HISTORY AND GEOGRAPHY

There are few nations whose history contains as many broken threads as Germany's. In this century alone, Germany has undergone four radical changes of political personality—from Wilhelm II's Empire to the Weimar Republic, from Hitler's *Reich* of the Thousand Years to its two postwar successors, the Federal Republic of Germany (FRG) and the German Democratic Republic (GDR). Other nations, like France and Russia, have also experienced revolutionary transformations. Yet throughout modern history, they have preserved a fairly stable geographical and physical identity. Germany, by contrast, has not. Since the Middle Ages, "Germany" has stood for a kaleidoscopic pattern of political entities in the heart of Europe whose boundaries were forever changing.

From the tenth to the thirteenth century, the "Holy Roman Empire of the German Nation" saw itself as the heir of Rome. Yet its identity was more often than not based on a claim and a spiritual idea rather than on the realities of political control. For centuries afterwards, until its reunification under Bismarck in 1871, Germany has lacked an effective central political authority. This absence was both unique and crucial, setting Germany apart from the dominant historical trend in Europe. In the wake of the Middle Ages, the nation-state became the dominant form of political organization. Its model was provided by the evolution of England and France since the thirteenth century. From a central "core area,"[1] political authority was

[1]For the concept of the "core area" and its role in nation-building, see Karl W. Deutsch, *Nationalism and Social Communication* (Cambridge: MIT Press, 1966).

successively pushed outward through military conquest and dynastic marriage. Religious homogenization and the rise of national sentiment reinforced monarchical rule.

As England, France, Spain, and Sweden gradually acquired their geographical identities, the German Empire disintegrated into a crazy-quilt pattern of competing principalities and cities. In the wake of the sixteenth century's Reformation, political divisions accentuated by religious schisms added up to a power vacuum in Central Europe. By the time of the Thirty Years' War (1618–1648), Germany was no longer an "actor" on the European scene, but an object of manipulation and conquest. Ostensively a religious war, the Thirty Years' War was in fact a great power conflict fought in and over Germany. Even without modern weapons of mass destruction, the war had a more devastating impact on Germany than World War II. One third of the population perished, and some historians maintain that it set German economic development back by 100 years.

German "nation-building" did not resume until the eighteenth century, and then under unique historical auspices. The core area was the Kingdom of Prussia, which embarked on the road to expansion under Frederick the Great's leadership around the middle of the century. Compared to the Habsburg Empire or the established nation-states like England and France, Prussia's economic resources were as sparse as its population. Yet Prussia had thoroughly absorbed the lessons of Germany's endemic vulnerability. If insecurity was the basic condition of political life, then survival was the supreme imperative. The State would have to be strong, and the interests of the individual citizens would have to be subordinated to the demands of military prowess. A maximum state of readiness and the deftness of maneuver would have to compensate for geographic and economic disadvantage. Because of this, Prussia developed one great advantage over its neighbors: an efficient administration apparatus and a modern draft system that endowed Prussia's kings with a disproportionately large standing army.

Prussia's expansion was essentially completed in 1871 when Bismarck imposed unity on the remnants of the Holy Roman Empire outside the Habsburg dominions. German unity, however, remained as elusive as it had come late. It lasted seventy-four years—from 1871 to 1945, when the victorious armies of the United States and the Soviet Union met on the Elbe river at the close of World War II.[2]

[2]Chronological note: In 1871, Germany was unified under Bismarck (*Reich* Chancellor) and Emperor Wilhelm II. Since the new *Reich* (Empire) regarded itself as successor to the medieval "Holy Roman Empire of the German Nation," it came to be known as the Second German Empire. After the brief revolution at the end of World War I, the *Reich* was succeeded by the Weimar Republic. The first German Republic derived its name from the small town of Weimar where its constitution was drafted. It lasted from 1919 until 1933 when Adolf Hitler was elected Chancellor. The year 1933 marked the beginning of the dictatorial Third Reich (or Reich of the Thousand Years), which was destroyed by the Allied victory in 1945. After a four-year interregnum, the Federal Republic of Germany (FRG) and the German Democratic Republic (GDR) became the de facto successor states of the Third Reich. Both gained sovereignty in 1955. For a concise introduction to political change in Germany since Bismarck, see Guido Goldman, *The German Political System* (New York: Random House, 1974), esp. chaps. 1–3.

From its very beginning, the Second German Empire (1871–1918) was saddled with a triple handicap. It was a latecomer to the great-power scene, it was a latecomer to nationhood, and given the peculiar way in which unification was achieved, it remained an unfinished nation. Like Prussia, the German Reich had suddenly emerged among the established powers that for centuries had regarded the European center as proper object of domination. Its rise was inseparably tied to conquest, yet it was at a stage in the evolution of the European system where such dramatic increase in power could only appear as usurpation of the established order. Indeed, Germany's unification by "blood and iron" grew directly out of the Franco-Prussian war of 1870–1871, which ended in the annexation of Alsace and Lorraine against the wills of their populations. For centuries, the swapping of territories and populations had been a legitimate instrument of diplomacy. In an age of nationalism, however, annexation ran the risk of mobilizing entire nations for the cause of *revanche*. The absorption of two French provinces saddled Germany with a legacy of permanent conflict with France. It lasted three generations and took two world wars to resolve.

After 1871, Germany may have been the strongest nation on the continent, but it was only a "semihegemonial" power.[3] It was strong enough to defeat any single comer, but not strong enough to keep them all at bay at the same time. Given its vulnerable frontiers, its strength had to be predicated on speed, the offensive, and the concentration of power. Offensive capabilities always exceeded defensive ones, and in spite of vast disparities in population and size, the Reich had inherited Prussia's vulnerability. During the Seven Years' War (1756–1763) an all-Continental coalition had almost destroyed Frederick's Prussia. The "nightmare of coalitions," as Bismarck called it, became the abiding obsession of German leaders. The nightmare sprang to life twice in two world wars.

Germany remained an unfinished nation. Unification had not been achieved under the Liberal-Democratic auspices of the crushed 1848 Revolution. Instead, it was Prussia that had unified Germany by conquering it.[4] Prussia's political system, reared in the tradition of bureaucratic absolutism and dominated by the landed *Junker* oligarchy, was superimposed on Germany as a whole. The result was a unique discrepancy between extremely rapid industrialization and political backwardness.

The price of accelerated economic growth was a pattern of boom and bust. A swelling proletariat added class strife to the ancient cleavages between North and South, between Catholics and Protestants. Yet unlike England, the ruling nobility did not embark on a path of political reform which would have integrated successive layers of the population into the political process. The middle class was co-opted by protective State intervention; the working class

---

[3]This term has been borrowed from Ludwig Dehio, *Deutschland und die Weltpolitik im 20. Jahrhundert* (Munich: Oldenbourg, 1955), p. 15.

[4]Thus the apt heading of chapter six, "The Conquest of Germany by Prussia," in A. J. P. Taylor's *The Course of German History* (London: Hamish Hamilton, 1945).

was mollified by rudimentary welfare state measures. Yet conflict was not resolved. Contending factions were played off against each other. Social pressures were diverted by foreign policy crises and grandiose national projects. An almost mystical idea of national unity was substituted for the idea of freedom. There were those who begrudged Germany its new "place in the sun." The appeal to national solidarity in the face of threat and encirclement from abroad became a powerful surrogate for political equality.

Bismarck fully understood Germany's precarious position in the European system. He constantly assured his neighbors that the Reich was "satisfied." He avoided challenging England's supremacy at sea. He fought off domestic pressures for imperial conquest in Africa and Asia. And he remained on friendly terms with Russia, France's most likely ally. At the same time, Bismarck deftly diverted Europe's attention away from the European center, encouraging France to expand into North Africa and keeping Anglo-Russo-Austrian conflicts alive in the faraway Balkans and Near East.

After Bismarck's retirement in 1890, however, the Reich drifted into a collision course with the rest of Europe, aided by ineptness of Bismarck's successors, especially of that "maniac on the throne,"[5] Kaiser Wilhelm II. For not even a second Bismarck could have managed to freeze Europe's tenuous order, let alone prop up the obsolete and conflict-ridden domestic system of Imperial Germany. Certainly World War I was a war nobody wanted, but

[5]Alexander Gerschenkron, *Bread and Democracy in Germany* (New York: Howard Fertig, 1966), p. 88.

pent-up conflicts had been brewing for a long time. As the nineteenth century drew to a close, domestic strife—especially in the "premodern" societies of Germany, Austria and Russia—intensified diplomatic conflicts.

In Germany, for instance, aggressive nationalism was increasingly used to deal with unresolved domestic issues. Bismarck's earlier assurances gave way to colonial expansion in Africa, Asia, and the Middle East. It alarmed the European powers already established there and was bound to unify them against Germany. Colonies required a navy, so the implicit alliance with England was sacrificed for an intensive naval race. In addition to focusing popular attention on a grandiose national project, the naval program had the virtue of providing long-term stable demand for a young steel industry hard-hit by recurring depressions. Similarly, the agrarian aristocracy in the East clamored for protective measures against cheap Russian grain imports. Hence, successive turns of the tariff screw acted to alienate Russia and to push it into the French camp.

Germany's geographic situation has always provided an obsession as well as a temptation. The obsession was Bismarck's "nightmare of coalitions," and it seemed to have come true in 1907 when England, France, and Russia joined forces in the Triple Entente. The temptation (posed by encirclement) was to make the lightning strike against the most threatening opponent at any one time or, worse, an all-out war for hegemony which would break the stranglehold permanently. Thus the so-called "Schlieffen Plan" prior to World War I foresaw a quick victory in the West as prelude to a second strike in the East before the cumbersome Russian mobilization machinery was ready for war. A similar strategy was employed by Hitler during World War II. In both cases, it activated the coalition nightmare that it was designed to thwart once and for all.

In 1945, the seventy-four year experiment in German unity ended in cataclysmic defeat and six-fold dismemberment.[6] The Nazi Revolution had destroyed much of Germany's old social and political order. Having acted as a "modernizer," the Nazi dictatorship was in turn swept away by the Allied victory. In contrast to 1918, when defeat and short-lived revolution had barely affected the social foundations of German political life, surrender and occupation in 1945 wiped the slate almost completely clean. On the other hand, the war also left a legacy which was to shape and determine West German foreign policy for a generation and more to come.

## I. THE POLITICS OF IMPOTENCE: WEST GERMANY AS A SPECIAL CASE

The study of comparative foreign policy is based on the application of yardsticks by which we compare and contrast in order to distinguish the unique from the general. By virtue of, say, its size, population, and resource base, the Federal Republic of Germany (FRG) falls into the elusive category of "middle powers" like England, France or Italy. Yet if we look more closely at the peculiar origins and handicaps of the Federal Republic, we see that there are some conspicuous distinctions which suggest a special case.

To begin with, the very existence of the FRG represents something of a historical fluke. In 1945, when the four victor powers assumed "supreme authority"[7] over its affairs, Germany had virtually ceased to exist as a political entity. In the aftermath of the hatreds unleashed by the Third Reich, an indefinite period of punishment and subjection appeared as Germany's most likely fate. Yet in the wake of victory, the wartime alliance between East and West disintegrated. A new conflict, the Cold War, superseded the old one. The Cold War represented an inconceivable windfall gain for Germany. A "Super-Versailles" did not materialize. Instead, in 1949 Germany suddenly found itself doubly reincarnated on either side of the Elbe river.

Thus, the very establishment of the FRG was not so much an act of choice as it was the result of Allied fiat. The Federal Republic was an offspring of bipolarity, conceived and nurtured by the strategic imperatives of the West. Yet while the Federal Republic was bound to profit from the transformation of the dominant international conflict, it was also its prostrate captive and, by virtue of partition, its starkest symbol.

For a good part of its existence, the Federal Republic has been subjected to a unique degree of dependence and external constraints. In many ways it was more of an artifact than a nation state. Founded in

---

[6]The Federal Republic of Germany, the German Democratic Republic, East Berlin, West Berlin and the territories incorporated by Poland and the Soviet Union.

[7]Beate Ruhm von Oppen, ed., *Documents on Germany Under Occupation, 1945–1955* (London: Oxford University Press, 1955), p. 30. (This is a useful collection of documents on the first postwar decade.)

1949, it continued to lack sovereignty, the most essential attribute of a state, until 1955. Even after 1949, sovereignty was only delegated and subsumed under the Occupation Statute by which the United States, England and France retained supreme authority. After sovereignty was devolved in 1955, the three Western powers reserved important prerogatives, notably those pertaining to Berlin and Germany as a whole, which they retain to the present day. But even on the German side, there was a deliberate refusal of complete statehood. Apart from the amputation of its eastern territories, the nation was split into two political units. Accordingly, the officially proclaimed raison d'être of the FRG was that of a *Provisorium,* a transitional polity which would liquidate itself on the day reunification came.[8]

Dependence imposed itself in many guises. Most crucial, the FRG suffered from a unique disjunction between diplomacy and its moral and material wherewithals. Deprived of sovereignty, armed forces, economic strength and moral credibility, West German diplomacy was reduced to empty-handed bargaining. The main objective of policy was not the pursuit of concrete goals, but the accumulation of resources-in-being, which could be expended for political influence. Indeed, the overriding problem was to acquire the very *right* to conduct a foreign policy in the first place.[9] This predicament was adeptly expressed in Konrad Adenauer's (Federal Chancellor from 1949 to 1963) first declaration before the *Bundestag:* "For the German people there is no other way of attaining freedom and equality of rights than ... in concert with the Allies. There is only one path to freedom. It is the attempt to extend our liberties and prerogatives step by step and in harmony with the Allied High commission."[10]

Secondly, instead of domestic structures affecting the FRG's foreign policy, the foreign policies of others came to shape the evolution of domestic institutions and societal orientation. On the level of society, the widespread reaction against both National Socialism and Communism served as a fertile breeding ground for the seeds planted primarily by the American occupation in form of reeducation, denazification, federalism and free-enterprise economic development. While the Constitution—the Basic Law—was not imposed on the Germans (as it was on the Japanese), it did follow the guidelines laid down by the Military Government. Yet even if direct interference was limited, it was surely no coincidence that societies and institutions in both Germanies closely resembled those of their patron powers. In the end, Stalin's famous dictum was manifestly vindicated: "This war is not as in the past. Whoever occupies a territory also imposes on it his own social system. Everyone imposes his own system as far as his army can reach. It cannot be otherwise."[11]

---

[8]There is no Constitution but only a "Basic Law" which was enacted for a "transitional period" only. Its preamble explicitly charges the German people with the task of achieving reunification.

[9]Cf. Alfred Grosser, *Germany in Our Time* (New York: Praeger, 1971), p. 291.

[10]*Verhandlungen des Deutschen Bundestages* (the official record of West German parliamentary proceedings), September 20, 1949, p. 29.

[11]As quoted by Milovan Djilas, *Conversations with Stalin* (New York: Harcourt Brace Jovanovich, 1962), p. 114.

Thirdly, instead of its own foreign policy affecting the Federal Republic's international milieu, the bipolar structures of postwar Europe determined West German policy and interests. There was the escape from subjection; the shattered economy that had to be rebuilt; and as Stalin imposed ideological uniformity on Eastern Europe and made his unsuccessful bid for Berlin in the Blockade of 1948–49, security against subversion and invasion became an intense preoccupation. As the most exposed member of the Western coalition, the Federal Republic has tended to subordinate other concerns to the demands of Alliance cohesion and readiness. On the other hand, and in spite of the reversal of alliances in the Cold War, the FRG had to guard against the nightmare of coalitions which might still resurrect in the reassertion of Four-Power solidarity. Finally, the amputation of the Eastern territories and partition mortgaged the FRG with a powerful legacy of revisionism. Although reunification was deliberately postponed to another and better day, it remained the official raison d'être of the Federal Republic. As we shall see, the contradiction between an actual policy of integration into the West and the aspiration for reunification with the East posed the dominant dilemma of West German foreign policy for a generation to come.

## II. THE POLITICAL STYLE: SOVEREIGNTY THROUGH INTEGRATION

After its establishment in 1949, the FRG had to live without power and the capacity to reward or to punish. Yet it did retain one important bar-gaining counter: the capacity to *deny* cooperation to its would-be allies— a value that grew as a direct function of the West's determination to turn West Germany into a bulwark against the East. The repetitive gamble of West German diplomacy consisted of discovering and exacting the highest political price for voluntary collaboration.

Initially that price was not very high. Two world wars had saddled the young Federal Republic with a costly legacy of suspicion and fear. France, which had borne the brunt of three German attacks within three generations, was determined to keep the FRG weak and closely controlled. West German diplomacy confronted an all but impossible task. It had to build a tradition of trust; it had to gain recognition as a legitimate actor in the community of nations.

In his pursuit of international respectability, Adenauer consistently followed three basic principles. First, France needed reassurance that there would be no resurgence of the "German peril." Second, there was only one method of spanning the gap between Allied insistence on constraints and German aspirations for sovereignty. The West had to be persuaded to reverse Lenin's classic precept that "Trust is good, control is better." Accordingly, Adenauer's entire diplomacy was devoted to transmuting the constraints imposed unilaterally by the victors into mutual controls shared voluntarily by all. Finally, the best way to achieve both objectives was political and economic integration which would supersede the ancient logic of power politics by the new logic of community and mutual gain.

As a result, Adenauer became a compulsive joiner on the simple theory that voluntary compliance would make Allied imposition less likely, while membership in any international organization would bestow not only the trappings of equality, but also the real chance to influence the course of events. It is impossible to understand the success story of European integration without taking into account these basic facts of West Germany's postwar condition. For the FRG, integration was a low-cost, high payoff policy. Since the Occupying Powers retained supreme authority, West Germany's integrationist virtues carried their own tangible rewards. For the Federal Republic, integration merely involved sacrificing nonexisting, potential rights in exchange for actual, partial sovereignty. Since integration was predicated on the equal subjection to common rule, self-abnegation became the condition for self-assertion. As such, Adenauer's tactics were exactly the reverse of the early Europeanists such as Jean Monnet, one of the founding fathers of European integration. They saw partial integration as irresistibly spreading solvent of national sovereignty because each concrete integrative measure in any one area would force leaders to integrate more and more sectors. Adenauer, however, reversed the logic by using each concession to the FRG as a lever for lifting the restraints upon German statehood and freedom (i.e., upon German national sovereignty).

If the West insisted on reparations and control of the iron and coal industries of the Ruhr district, Adenauer complied, but also proposed that the FRG join the International Ruhr Authority. If the French were afraid of the FRG's superior economic potential, Adenauer suggested that American re-construction capital be channeled through France. When France moved to detach the iron-rich Saarland from West Germany, Adenauer countered with a call for complete Franco-German union.[12] In other words, the unique quality of Adenauer's style rested in his persistent attempt to transcend the normal diplomatic process which begins by haggling over each issue at hand and ends up by splitting the difference. Instead, his most elementary diplomatic technique was forever dedicated to "upgrading the common interest" and hence, to dwarfing a particular clash of interest by enlarging the framework for its solution.

This was certainly Adenauer's basic objective in the aftermath of World War II. It is doubtful, however, whether he would have succeeded in transforming the stakes as quickly as he did without another enormous windfall gain: North Korea's attack on South Korea in the summer of 1950. To trade cooperation for emancipation was one thing; to reduce West Germany's crushing impotence was a far more formidable task. "I began to understand," Adenauer was to reminisce many years later, "that in our days influence required power. Without power, one cannot conduct policy.

[12]This bold gamble did not work, or only to the extent that the French responded with the so-called "Schuman Plan" for the integration of West Europe's coal and steel industries which blossomed into the European Coal and Steel Community (ECSC), the forerunner of the Common Market. With French control instincts satisfied, Adenauer succeeded in persuading the French to postpone the formalization of the Saar's autonomy. A few years later France agreed to a Saar referendum. When the population rejected autonomy, the Saar became a *Land* of the Federal Republic in 1957.

Without power, our words will not be heeded."[13]

Acting on Machiavelli's dictum that strong armies make for reliable allies, Adenauer had taken a calculated risk as early as late 1949 when he floated his famous trial balloon on German rearmament. Against the background of the Prague Coup and the Berlin Blockade, he told an American correspondent in December of 1949 that "Germany should contribute to the defense of Europe in a European army under the command of a European headquarter."[14] Unperturbed by protests at home and abroad, he kept fishing for an Allied invitation to contribute integrated German contingents. In order to foreclose an easy way out for the West, which would have robbed him of the most crucial bargaining chip toward sovereignty, he was quick to brand the "idea of raising volunteers in Germany" as exploitation which would reduce Germany to a supplier of mercenaries.[15]

The North Korean attack succeeded where Adenauer had failed with his deflated trial balloon on German rearmament. It dramatized (if only by false analogy) the strategic and political logic inherent in the founding of NATO and the Federal Republic. By the late summer of 1950, the American decision to rearm West Germany finally delivered the vehicle on which Adenauer could coast towards sovereignty. Furthermore, it enlarged a primarily Franco-German contest over the extent of West German emancipation to a three-party game in which the United States switched from reluctant referee to tacit ally.

At first France responded with an ambitious project to supranationalize the very hard-core of sovereignty (i.e., defense) in a European Defense Community (EDC). The EDC and West German sovereignty were firmly linked in the settlement between the FRG and the West, concluded in 1952. Yet France could never make up its mind what was more important: the containment of the Soviet Union or the control of Germany. Thus, on August 30, 1954, the French National Assembly repudiated the entire settlement. The grandest design of European unity was sacrificed to the sturdier ideal of national sovereignty.

Yet the United States and Britain were now firmly committed to German rearmament. France was finally swayed by a host of new contractual and configurational constraints against the resurgence of a German threat. Among them, the most crucial guarantee was an Anglo-American commitment to maintain a substantial military presence ·in West Germany and Europe. In 1955 the occupation regime was terminated. With its sovereignty restored, the Federal Republic was admitted directly into NATO.

Only Talleyrand has done better than Adenauer in modern times. After Napoleon's final defeat, Talley-

[13]As quoted by Dieter Schröder in *Süddeutsche Zeitung*, January 7, 1960, p. 3.

[14]Interview with John Leacacos, *Cleveland Plain Dealer*, December 4, 1949. There is a rich literature on the story of German rearmament. On the German side, the best is Arnulf Baring's *Aussenpolitik in Adenauers Kanzlerdemokratie* (Munich: Oldenbourg, 1967). For treatments in English, see Laurence W. Martin's classic study "The American Decision to rearm Germany" in Harold Stein, ed., *American Civil-Military Decisions* (Birmingham: The University of Alabama Press, 1963) and the more recent analysis by Robert McGeehan, *The German Rearmament Question: American Diplomacy and European Defense After World War II* (Urbana: University of Illinois Press, 1971).

[15]Konrad Adenauer, *Erinnerungen*, 1 (Stuttgart: Deutsche Verlags-Anstalt, 1965), p. 343.

rand went to the Congress of Vienna (1815) as the representative of a pariah nation. He managed to have France rehabilitated by abjuring its revolutionary designs and subscribing to the principle of monarchical legitimacy. Ten years after World War II and total defeat, Adenauer succeeded in purchasing respectability and security for half of the nation at the price of an unprecedented policy of self-denial and dependence for the FRG and partition for the whole.

## III. REUNIFICATION VS. REALPOLITIK

In 1966, three years after his retirement from the chancellorship and one year before his death, Adenauer was asked: "Let us assume, though, that a reunified and neutral Germany had been possible, would you have wanted it?" Adenauer's answer was an emphatic "No, never."[16] As curt as this reply was, it probably contains the most concise explanation for the course of West German foreign policy in his thirteen-year tenure.

Why did Adenauer place a higher value on the Federal Republic's amalgamation into the West than on reunification? An answer must resist two facile theories which suffer from the imputation of either excessive idealism or excessive cynicism to his motives. According to the one, Adenauer reduced reunification to a second-order concern because Europe was more important to him than Germany. According to the other, he treacherously wrote off East Germany as a presumptive stronghold of the Social Democratic Party (SPD) and Protestantism and thus as a threat to his own tenure.

There probably were elements of both of these theories in his calculus. Adenauer's "Rhenocentrism" has been a source of persistent speculation. As mayor of Cologne in the 1920s, he had an ambiguous record of separatism in favor of a Rhenish Republic economically linked with Belgium and France and politically tied to a German federation.[17] If the Cologne Cathedral somehow symbolized the spiritual fount and the political center of an ancient European civilization, then the "Asian steppes"[18] began in Magdeburg, Berlin being a "heathen city."[19] Similarly, Prussia represented the very nemesis of Germany while the Social Democrats (whose electoral strength was concentrated in Protestant East Germany) were the latter-day political descendants of the power-hungry Prussian *Junker* class.[20]

Yet no foreign policy—not even the allegedly simple- and single-minded diplomacy of Adenauer—can ever be reduced to the ideology or psychology of its perpetrator. Since the problem was more complex than reunification, the explanation is also more complicated. Apart from the volitions of any German leader, reunification was an unrealistic goal. After the war, Germany was

---

[16]In an interview with Golo Mann on April 18, 1966. Golo Mann, *Zwölf Versuche über die Geschichtsschreibung* (Frankfurt: S. Fischer, 1973), p. 136.

[17]For the record, ambiguous as it is, see the painstaking account by Karl D. Erdmann, *Adenauer in der Rheinlandpolitik nach dem ersten Weltkrieg* (Stuttgart: Klett, 1966).

[18]Interview with Hans-Peter Schwarz as quoted in his *Vom Reich zur Bundesrepublik* (Berlin: Luchterhand, 1966), p. 433.

[19]As quoted by *Gazette de Lausanne*, July 15, 1947. See also *Hannoversche Presse*, July 16, 1957.

[20]As quoted by Schwarz, *op. cit.*, p. 432.

the "prize, the pivot, and the problem of European politics."[21] Accordingly, there was no way either side would voluntarily let go of *its* German half. Politically, bipolarity in Europe was strictly a zero-sum game; whichever superpower succeeded in incorporating all of Germany on its side would have scored an enormous, unacceptable gain against the other. Militarily, on the other hand, nuclear weapons had turned Cold War politics into a non-zero-sum game with an incalculable negative payoff for both. The use of force was out of the question, for no conceivable stake was worth the cost of potential nuclear devastation.

There was one logical alternative: a reunified and neutral Germany. Yet Germany was not Austria (which was neutralized in 1955). For good reasons, the West was not interested. A neutralized Germany would have bottled up Western defenses behind the Rhine while giving the Soviet Union all the strategic and psychological advantages of proximity. More generally, neutrality raised all the uncertainties of the ancient "German problem." Germany has always been either too strong or too weak. Before unification in 1871, the problem was posed by Germany's weakness and inability to stave off domination by others. After 1871 Germany was too strong to be contained by its neighbors, yet not strong enough to impose its lasting rule on the continent.

Given Germany's critical size, neutralization would have rolled both of these problems into one. If Germany were neutral and *disarmed*,

it would raise the dual problem of keeping it disarmed and others from dominating it. If Germany were neutral and *armed*, it would pose the reverse problem of keeping it neutral or from dominating Europe either alone or with another power.[22] By contrast, bipolarity and partition had paradoxically defused all of these risks in an order which was as novel as it was stable.

The Cold War alliance systems protected Germany not only against others, but also against itself. Contrary to the Bismarck Empire, Germany did not have to labor under the double-burden of projecting the main threat to Europe's order *and* of managing its stability from a solitary position at the center. Unlike the Weimar Republic, it did not have to (and could not) play East against West as the condition of survival. With *two* Germanies countervailing each other and their respective patron powers, German strength was at once neutralized and harnessed. At the same time, they were not left alone, but remained anchored in two antagonistic communities which gave them shelter as well as a role.

Yet what about German interests? Why did Adenauer refuse to grasp the opportunity for reunification-cum-neutralization as fleetingly offered by Stalin's notorious notes to the West in March of 1952?[23] In the first place, Adenauer did not have a choice except to cast the

---

[21]Pierre Hassner, "Europe West of the Elbe" in Robert S. Jordan, ed., *Europe and the Superpowers* (Boston: Allyn and Bacon, 1974), p. 103.

[22]For an interesting "internalization" of this reasoning on the part of German policy makers, see Heinrich von Brentano's address before the Bundestag. (He was Foreign Minister from 1955 to 1961) *Verhandlungen des Deutschen Bundestages*, February 27, 1955, p. 3883.

[23]For the exchange of notes, see the Council on Foreign Relations, *Documents on American Foreign Relations, 1952* (New York: Harper and Row, 1953), p. 248 ff.

FRG's lot with the West. West Germany's peculiar condition prejudged not only the style, but also the substance and direction of its diplomacy. By definition, sovereignty could only mean its devolution from the West, while security could only mean security against the East. Any *Schaukelpolitik* (a policy of maneuver and balance) between the two blocs carried the high risk of either postponing sovereignty forever or, worse, reactivating a collusive Four-Power policy. As Adenauer put it at the time: "One false step, and we would lose the trust of the Western powers. One false step, and we would be the victim of a bargain between East and West."[24] For if there was anything worse than partition, it was precisely the kind of neutralization extended by the Soviets just prior to the conclusion of the Western settlement with the FRG in May of 1952.[25]

The real problem of West German policy transcended the antinomy between integration and reunification. If we are to believe Adenauer, the real crux was the protection against yet another "nightmare of coalitions," the abiding obsession of modern German foreign policy. This priority was articulated by Adenauer in an interview given in 1953. It bears citing at length because it captures the articles of faith (or fear) on which his entire foreign policy was based. If Bismarck's obsession had been the "nightmare

of coalitions," Adenauer's horror was Potsdam:

It is no coincidence that the Soviets keep referring to this agreement over and over again. To them it represents an eternal Morgenthau Plan imposed by the Four Powers. . . . Every Soviet reference to this agreement constitutes a Soviet invitation to the West to conclude such a bargain on our backs. . . . Potsdam signifies nothing but: Let us strike a bargain at Germany's expense. . . . Bismarck spoke about his nightmare of coalitions against Germany. I have my own nightmare: its name is Potsdam. The danger of a collusive great power policy at Germany's peril has existed since 1945, and it has continued to exist even after the Federal Republic was established. The foreign policy of the Federal Government has always been aimed at escaping from this danger zone. For Germany must not fall between the grindstones. If it does, it will be lost.[26]

Or as Adenauer told John McCloy, the American High Commissioner in Germany: "Once . . . the question of a [West German] defense contribution is satisfactorily solved, the demilitarization and neutralization of Germany will no longer be possible."[27] Binding the Federal Republic's fate to the West would fetter *both* sides. Above and beyond delivering sovereignty and security, integration would undercut the Potsdam nightmare by drastically limiting the West's options toward the Soviet Union. The prime thrust of the settlement was defined quite bluntly by Franz Josef Strauss (Minister of Defense from 1956–1962) in response to Opposition

[24]Adenauer, *Erinnerungen* 2 p. 88.
[25]"I considered neutrality between the two power blocs as an unrealistic position for our nation. Sooner or later, one side or the other would attempt to incorporate Germany's potential on its side. . . . We had to join either one or the other side, if we wanted to prevent being crushed by both." Adenauer, *Erinnerungen* 1, p. 96.

[26]In a broadcast interview with Ernst Friedländer on June 11, 1953. Presse- und Informationsamt der Bundesregierung, *Mitteilungen an die Presse*, no. 561/53, pp. 3–4.
[27]As recounted in his *Erinnerungen* 1 p. 457.

complaints that reunification required an agreement among and with *all* the four victor powers: "Much more important than a Four-Power conference is the creation of a situation which makes a Four-Power bargain at our expense impossible."[28]

The settlement with the West as concluded in 1952 and amended in 1954[29] (after France had vetoed the original compact) ratified and unprecedented policy of dependence and self-denial on the part of the Federal Republic.[30] In exchange, the

West limited its own options by a number of pledges which explicitly or implicitly precluded the wrong kind of German settlement with the Soviet Union:

1. As the only government "freely and legitimately constituted," the Federal Government was "entitled to speak for Germany as representative of the German people in international affairs." By thus underwriting the FRG's *Alleinvertretungsanspruch* (its claim to be the sole representative of Germany as a whole), this declaration bestowed the title of succession to the German *Reich* to the Federal Republic and, by implication, precluded Western recognition of the GDR.

2. By agreeing that the "final determination of the boundaries of Germany" must await a *freely* negotiated peace settlement, the West not only refused the legitimacy of the postwar demarcation lines (i.e., the borders between the two Germanies and the Oder-Neisse line), but also reassured the FRG against a peace treaty imposed by fiat of the Four Powers.

3. By extending their security guarantee to Berlin, the former German capital now located within the territory of the GDR, the Western powers again demonstrated their refusal to recognize the finality of partition as well as their determination to preserve Four-Power responsibility in Berlin and Germany as a whole as anchor point for a reunification settlement.

4. "Pending the peace settlement, the Signatory Powers will cooperate to achieve by peaceful means their common aim of a reunified Germany enjoying a liberal democratic constitution like that of the Federal Republic and integrated within the European Community." This was theoretically the "efficient" part of the bargain. If the first three commitments were to hold open an unacceptable and presumably temporary status quo, the fourth pledge bound

---

[28] *Verhandlungen des Deutschen Bundestages,* July 16, 1952 p. 9853.

[29] For the documents, see Council on Foreign Relations, *Documents on American Foreign Relations, 1952* and the volume for 1954 (New York: Harper and Row, 1953 and 1955). For a succinct analysis of the 1954 settlement, see Charles E. Planck, *The Changing Status of German Reunification in Western Diplomacy, 1955–1966* (Baltimore: Johns Hopkins Press, 1967), pp. 6–10.

[30] In the first place, West German sovereignty was sharply circumscribed by the retention of Allied reserve powers relating to "Berlin and Germany as a whole." Second, the FRG bound itself to raise 500,000 troops and to intergrate them *wholly* into NATO. Third, the FRG renounced the right to manufacture nuclear as well as biological and chemical weapons. Fourth, the FRG undertook by a three-fold declaration of self-limitation to refrain from any action "inconsistent with the strictly defensive character of NATO," to "resolve by peaceful means" its disputes with other nations, and, most importantly, "never to have recourse to force to achieve the reunification of Germany." Lest there remain any doubt, these good-conduct pledges were reinforced by an Allied declaration which was certainly directed against the Federal Republic. Accordingly, "they will regard as threat to their own peace and safety any recourse to force which . . . threatens the integrity and unity of the Atlantic alliance . . . [and] . . . will consider the offending government as having forfeited its right to any guarantee and any military assistance. They will act . . . with a view to taking other measures which may be appropriate." *Documents on American Foreign Relations, 1954,* pp. 115–17.

the West to a joint policy dedicated to its transformation.[31]

Given these terms, especially reunification under "liberal," "democratic," and "integrated" auspices, the contractual pledges of the West could not (and did not) lead to national unity. By elevating the contradiction between integration and reunification to the level of solemn codification, the compact with the West was clearly a second-best solution. At best, the West's refusal to concede the finality of the status quo would keep the *prospect* of reunification alive while undercutting the danger of a collusive settlement with the Soviet Union. Similarly, if the West continued to demonstrate its commitment to German unity in word and deed, reunification would continue to serve as a vital myth at home.

On the domestic front, Adenauer was hounded by a Social Democratic opposition which was forever hammering home the contradiction between integration and reunification. Once Adenauer had secured his bargain with the West, he had to mobilize domestic support, or at least deflate the Opposition's best arguments against him. The neutralization of domestic opposition to his *Westpolitik* was outlined in a circle-squaring feat which represented the Western settlement as not only compatible with reunification, but also as its necessary precondition.[32] Rhetorically, the gap between aspiration and reality was spanned by the dominant myth of the 1950s— the "policy of strength." In its strongest version it echoed Dulles' "roll-back" policy:

Only the sufficient strength of the West will create a real basis for peaceful negotiations. Their objective is to liberate peacefully not only the Soviet Zone but also all of enslaved Europe east of the Iron Curtain.[33]

As a political promise, the "policy of strength" required tangible proofs and tests in the years to come, but no deadlines were suggested or spelled out. When *would* the West be strong enough to warrant a dialogue with the Soviet Union? By failing to define the time horizon for an active reunification policy, the departure point was left undetermined. The "policy of strength" precluded any method of comparing rhetorics with reality. Yet it did fulfill the vital function of stabilizing the domestic base of Adenauer's foreign policy. By suggesting that reunification would require time, it was a call for patience and did help to postpone domestic frustrations and the moment of truth.

Moreover, under the terms of the Western settlement, the Allies had assumed primary responsibility for reunification. Self-denial on the part of the Government could be transformed into a double-asset. Diplomatically, it evaded the risks of autonomy by dispatching the emotional reunification issue into the safe haven of Allied responsibility. Domestically it legitimized Adenauer's prudent passivity toward the Soviet Union. Since it was the Soviet Union that refused self-determination and free elections to the population of the GDR, Moscow could be

[31] See *Documents on American Foreign Relations*, *1954*, pp. 116, 117, 139.

[32] As Adenauer put it in 1952: "I assure you: we are convinced that this treaty is the first step toward reunification." Quoted in *Frankfurter Allgemeine Zeitung*, May 27, 1952.

[33] In a broadcast interview with Ernst Friedländer, *Bulletin*, no. 27, March 16, 1952, p. 262.

blamed for a stalemate which was not of German or Western making. But even if reunification was not achieved, the potentially most dangerous issue of postwar German politics was at least quarantined. The partition of Germany never acquired the demagogic potential which the territorial losses imposed by Versailles had presented in the Weimar Republic. Even if far more onerous for the Germans, it did not become a source of explosive nationalism.

## IV. DOMESTIC SOURCES AND FOREIGN POLICY

In many ways, the Federal Republic found itself in the same situation as the Weimar Republic. Both were tenuous democratic experiments, and both had to live with externally imposed restrictions. Similarly, the built-in revisionism of both was totally at odds with international realities. The Weimar precedent was hardly encouraging. As the rise of Hitler had shown, national grievances could become the breeding ground for ultra-nationalist revolt and dictatorship.

Yet Bonn did not repeat the Weimar experience, and it is perhaps Adenauer's greatest achievement that he managed to turn the conditions of potential disaster into the sources of social stability and democratic evolution. The most crucial difference between Weimar and Bonn was economics. Unlike the Weimar Republic, the FRG could *enjoy* the economic consequences of peace. In the 1920s, security for France spelled reparations and indefinite economic controls on Germany. In the 1950s, however, security for the United States spelled speedy recovery and sustained prosperity for West Germany and Western Europe. Instead of a staggering reparations burden, there were massive infusions of American capital. Instead of "beggar-thy-neighbor" policies, there was free movement of goods and capital, enforced and encouraged by the United States.

Having been robbed of its East German markets, West Germany, traditionally the Reich's industrial center of gravity, found itself in the same position as export-dependent England, minus its far-flung trading network. Although Adenauer pursued European integration primarily for its political pay-offs, integration and free trade were· also an enormous economic boon. They provided both markets and competitive pressures. Moreover, partition produced a blessing in disguise—a massive influx of skilled labor.

About ten million people came from the territories incorporated by Poland, Czechoslovakia, and the Soviet Union. Until 1961 when the wall sealed off the Berlin refugee conduit, about three million came from the GDR, among them a disproportionate number of the young and highly trained. Apart from feeding a sustained expansion process, the millions of refugees exerted a downward pressure on the level of wages. The sheer numbers of the population transfer surely explained the astounding "discipline" of West German labor unions, the high rate of investment, the long-term competitiveness of West German exports, and hence, the stuff from which the "economic miracle" was made.

With the economy set on a path of sustained growth, the political institutions of the Federal Republic could draw their legitimacy from an ever-expanding base of economic performance. In contrast to Weimar, democracy was not associated with national humiliation, inflation, and large-scale unemployment. The economic miracle compensated for the lack of historically grown legitimacy normally rooted in the continuity of institutions and national identification.

Unlike the leaders of Weimar, Adenauer succeeded in divorcing territorial revisionism from economic grievances. Although long forgotten (or precisely because it is), the deliberate and speedy integration of the refugees from the East was an impressive testimony to Adenauer's political farsightedness. Its antirevisionist thrust emerges most dramatically by contrast to the Palestinian refugees of 1948 who were just as deliberately interned in camps around Israel's periphery as pawns for territorial change.

With their economic problems rapidly divorced from their political complaints, the refugees never formed that reservoir of *déracinés* (the uprooted) which was turned against the Weimar Republic. Economic co-optation soon paid off politically. The refugee party managed to poll only 5.5 percent of the total vote in 1953, the only election in which it gained entry into the Bundestag. Eventually, the BHE membership was absorbed by the three major parties.

Nationalism, the less clamorous brother of revisionism, was similarly defused. After World War I, Germany was spared the trauma of total defeat and occupation. Defeat could therefore be transfigured through a "stab-in-the-back" legend. By contrast, the apocalyptic failure of the

Third Reich's ultranationalist experiment had certainly pulled the sting of aggressive German nationalism. Whatever potential was still left in the wake of demoralization and apathy could be safely enveloped in the *transnational* nationalism surrogates of Europeanism and anti-Communism.

Transcending national boundaries, the twin ideology of Europeanism and anti-Communism produced multiple domestic payoffs. In the first place, they dovetailed perfectly with the dominant conflict and the direction of West German diplomacy. In addition to legitimizing the truncation of West German foreign policy, they also served to underwrite the asset of diplomatic reliability which Adenauer had brought into his partnership with the West. Secondly, the "European fatherland" served as a safe and constructive outlet for the affective instincts of the population. Aggressive impulses, on the other hand, could be channeled into the *communal* ideology of anti-Communism. For the first time, Germany did not stand alone. And given the lack of autonomy, Adenauer could reap the benefits of a unifying ideology and an external threat without having to pay the price of actual conflict (as did German leaders before and after World War I). External tensions—the prime source of solidarity at home—were not of German making.

Thirdly, anti-Communism was an invaluable asset in the nation-building process and the domestic struggle for tenure. Insulated from the societal model implemented across the Elbe, nation-building could proceed under liberal-capitalist auspices toward what some commentators have called the "Adenauer

Restoration."[34] In terms of domestic politics, anti-Communism delivered a potent electoral weapon against the Social Democratic opposition. It did not matter that the SPD was staunchly anti-Communist. Yet its residual or reformist Marxism allowed the Government to discredit the SPD as the party of crypto-Communism and ultimately national treason.

## V. THE POLITICS OF DEPENDENCE

With the bargain struck in the 1954 agreements, the Federal Republic had acquired a certain veto power over the future course of East-West relations in Europe. At a maximum, the terms of the settlement enjoined the West to demonstrate its commitment to reunification by policy and proclamation. At a minimum, it precluded Western recognition of the German Democratic Republic and the demarcation lines drawn after World War. Both objectives came to be embodied in the *Politik des Junktim* (policy of linkage) which constituted the linchpin of German diplomacy throughout the 1950s and most of the 1960s. By linking *any* East-West negotiations to a resolution of the German question, it operationalized the West's reunification pledge.

In theory, any kind of East-West settlement would have to be preceded or at least paralleled by progress on reunification in peace and freedom. In practical terms, this

[34]"Restoration" is a suggestive but delusive description for postwar West German society. Power was certainly not "restored" to the Nazi clique or the quasi-aristocratic ruling class of Weimar. Instead, there was a great deal of upward mobility. "Restoration" should thus actually read "fractured continuity" plus "capitalist economic development" plus "expanding welfare state."

meant free elections in the GDR and freedom of alignment for a reunified Germany. Both conditions, if realized, would have delivered the German prize to the West. Hence the various quadripartite conferences of the 1950s (Berlin in 1954, Geneva in 1955 and 1959) ended in predictable stalemate. Yet in terms of West German interests, stalemate was better than the "wrong" kind of agreement. Since Soviet security proposals were always targeted on West German "revanchism" and the consecration of the status quo, *any* Four-Power conference tended to evoke the specter of Germany's discrimination and victimization. Even if it failed as an instrument for the transformation of the status quo, the *Junktim* served reasonably well in blocking its deterioration as long as the FRG managed to persuade its Western allies that *their* conflict with the Soviet Union was identical with the more special German-Soviet quarrel.

The FRG's veto power was therefore derivative. It was strength on lease, predicated on the long-run willingness of the West to subordinate its search for a modus vivendi with the Soviet Union to West Germany's quest for national unity. The ratification of the alliance system in 1955 marked the zenith of West German influence in the Western coalition. For both East and West, Bonn's integration into NATO terminated a six-year period of courting and concessions. If the FRG was now a bulwark for the West, it could always become a stumbling block towards accommodation with the East.

By the same token, the Federal Republic had lost its attraction for the Soviet Union. In the previous decade, Soviet policy had always oscillated between courting Germany's allegiance and controlling it in collusion with its wartime allies. Yet whether courtship or control, this ambivalence was at least centered on Germany as a whole, and therefore predicated on some kind of reunification. After 1955 this option vanished.

This switch in Soviet policy was hardly surprising. The West had settled for the second-best solution of half a Germany in its camp. The Soviet Union followed suit and began to consolidate its own German state. In 1955, the GDR was also granted sovereignty, joining the Warsaw Pact one year later. Having shelved its all-German option, the Soviet Union was now unequivocally wedded to a "two-state" theory on Germany and an unremitting campaign to gain international recognition for its junior partner and the postwar *faits accomplis.*

As reunification receded into a hazy future, the FRG was confronted with the hazardous dialectics of a changing nuclear balance. In 1953, the Soviet Union had acquired the hydrogen bomb, and it was only a matter of time until America's nuclear superiority, the cornerstone of the Atlantic Alliance, would give way to "peril parity." In the fall of 1957, the Soviets launched their first *Sputnik,* and the notorious "missile gap" was born. Years later, the "gap" was exposed as a sham, but in the meantime, the Soviets played their presumed technological advantage for all it was worth by gradually stepping up pressures against the West. In response, the United States sought to reassert the waning credibility of its deterrent threat by introducing medium-range ballistic missiles and tactical nuclear weapons

in Europe. With NATO about to go nuclear, the FRG was faced with yet another fateful choice like that between integration and national unity, which had already been made.

After a brief effort to resist the nuclear tide,[35] the FRG decided to acquire an atomic armory of sorts (i.e., dual-purpose delivery vehicles and a stockpile of tactical warheads under American control). To the West Germans, tactical nuclear weapons appeared as panacea for all the ills which had befallen the Alliance since 1955. Adenauer had never quite trusted American pledges to abstain from its past isolationist habits. As public opinion in the West began to speculate about the merits of disengagement in Central Europe (in the wake of the Hungarian revolt), Adenauer's fears were fueled by the specter of Soviet-American collusion whose seeds seemed to have been planted in the combined superpower pressure against the Franco-British Suez expedition in 1956. Tactical nuclear weapons for the *Bundeswehr* (Federal Forces) would forge an additional bond between the FRG and its senior American partner, forever prone to withdrawal symptoms. Second, they would strengthen the hostage function of American troops in Germany and prop up the tilting European balance. Third, given French and English determination to develop their own independent deterrents, nuclear weapons appeared as a crucial symbol of political status. Having no say over the Alliance's nuclear strat-

---

[35]Adenauer was afraid that the "New Look," that is, the Pentagon's attempt to save money by substituting nuclear firepower for conventional forces, would serve as a smokescreen for U.S. withdrawals from Europe.

egy was seen as a retrograde fallback to an earlier role of voiceless dependence.

The Soviet Union had minced no words in warning the FRG against a nuclear decision. Thereafter, events unfolded with inexorable necessity. In its very attempt to escape from inferiority, the FRG soon found itself entangled in even greater dependence on the West as a result of Khrushchev's Berlin Ultimatum[36] in the winter of 1958. The crisis over Berlin lasted four years until it was superseded by the new superpower crisis in Cuba. The atom in German hands may have been of puny military significance (especially since the Americans clutched both the trigger and the ammunition), but it became a formidable tool in the hands of the Soviets. German revanchism, an earlier tradition of international violence, *and* German nuclear weapons presented the Soviets with a tailor-made legitimization for a *Westpolitik* that sought to rally Europe around "peaceful coexistence" and their own vision of European security. If the former required the lasting acceptance of the status quo, the latter implied security not so much for, as against, Germany.

Although ostensibly targeted on the Allied presence in the former German capital, the Berlin crisis ultimately turned into the most dramatic crisis of confidence between the FRG and the West. Berlin was clearly well-chosen. The Soviets had all the advantages of geography on their side, and they could saddle the West with the psychological burden of having to fire the first and perhaps fateful shot. The Soviets were evidently trying to make the best of the Sputnik shock, knowing that the margin of Western concessions on Berlin—the prime locus and symbol of Western resistance in the Cold War—was so minute that, short of retreat or violence, they would have to offer compensation elsewhere. Hence, if the West were going to submit to the Soviet bluff, it would most likely yield on the "secondary theater" of, say, a tacit recogniton of the GDR, the nuclear armament of the *Bundeswehr,* or on a European security system which, as Adenauer claimed, would reduce the FRG to a "second class" state. In short, the Berlin Gambit was a brilliant opening bid towards a "moveable status quo,"[37] and for the time being, Khrushchev could simply sit back and wait for the payoffs which would soon come his way.

The ups and downs of the Berlin Crisis have been described at great lengths elsewhere.[38] Suffice it to say that it did not take much arm-twisting before the West began to cringe and offer concessions on European

[36]Khrushchev's message on November 27, 1958, called on the West to recognize the abnormality of its presence in West Berlin. If after 6 months, West Berlin was not turned into a demilitarized Free City, the Soviets would turn the control of access over to the GDR (subsequently flanked by the threat of a separate peace treaty). Thereafter the West would have to negotiate with the GDR but face the military might of the entire Warsaw Pact if it resorted to force. Furthermore, the best way to solve the entire German problem was the withdrawal of both German states from their alliance systems while their armed forces would be limited by the needs of maintaining domestic law and order.

[37]Herbert Dinerstein, *Fifty Years of Soviet Foreign Policy* (Baltimore: Johns Hopkins Press, 1968), p. 34.

[38]See for instance Philip Windsor, *City on Leave* (London: Chatto and Windus, 1963); Jean Smith, *The Defense of Berlin* (Baltimore: Johns Hopkins Press, 1963); Hans Speier, *Divided Berlin* (New York: Praeger, 1961); and Jack M. Schick, *The Berlin Crisis, 1958–1962* (Philadelphia: University of Pennsylvania Press, 1971).

security and the de facto recognition of the GDR in order to preserve its position in Berlin. As a result, the Federal Republic was confronted with a dual problem. In the short run, it was faced with the paradoxical prospect of having to pay the political price of Allied resistance in Berlin. The long-run problem was even more insidious. Like any client state, the FRG drew its derivative strength from an intimate association with its patron powers—in particular, the United States. The weak become strong if they can persuade their protectors that their interests are alike. Then a threat to the weak constitutes an obligation for the protector. And since the commitments of the strong powers are not only worldwide but also interdependent, they cannot easily retract any particular engagement for fear of damaging their credibility elsewhere. Until the Berlin Crisis exposed the heterogeneity of interests between the West and the FRG, the latter could extract leverage from impotence by identifying its own special conflict with the East with the global bipolar conflict as a whole.

The Berlin Crisis was a watershed because it began to unravel this "indivisibility of conflict."[39] Berlin was clearly a bipolar issue, and so were the security and Western ties of the Federal Republic. Yet reunification was not. As it turned out, the Geneva Conference of 1959 was the last time East and West met to discuss the reunification of Germany.

Allied policy began to draw an increasingly rigid distinction between its own and West Germany's conflict with the Soviet Union. England's temptation to compensate its

decline from Empire and power with a policy of splendid mediation between the blocs became a source of persistent concern for the FRG. While Bonn gained some solace in de Gaulle's refusal to negotiate under pressure, what mattered was the United States. In the 1960 Presidential campaign, Kennedy had forcefully attacked the Republican administration for its military weakness and lack of will, yet in terms of West German interests, the advent of the Kennedy administration in 1961 turned into a disaster in disguise.

While demonstrating his resolution to resist Soviet pressure through well-publicized increases in defense-spending and the reinforcement of the American garrison in Berlin, Kennedy was also obsessed by both powers' capability to inflict devastating nuclear damage on each other. "This had changed all the answers and all the questions."[40] Above all, the new situation required the scrupulous avoidance of confrontations and misperceptions. As a result, Kennedy placed a maximum value on superpower negotiations. Regardless of outstanding political issues, the military milieu had to be stabilized through arms control measures, such as a test-ban and a nonproliferation pledge. While Alliance cohesion was important, the realization of German national aspirations could no longer be allowed to define the touchstone of the East-West relationship.

Maintaining Western rights in Berlin was one thing, but "the reunification of Germany seemed to him an unrealistic negotiating objec-

[39]Richard Lòwenthal, *Vom kalten Krieg zur Ostpolitik* (Stuttgart: Seewald, 1974), p. 57.

[40]As quoted by Theodore C. Sorensen, *Kennedy* (New York: Bantam Books, 1966), p. 577.

tive."[41] Kennedy drew a clear distinction between preserving the FRG's loyalties to the West and the active pursuit of reunification:

Germany has been divided for sixteen years and will continue to stay divided. The Soviet Union is running an unnecessary risk in trying to change this from an accepted fact into a legal state. Let the Soviet Union keep Germany divided on its present basis and not try to persuade us to associate ourselves legally with that division and thus weaken our ties to West Germany and their ties to Western Europe.[42]

The Berlin Crisis marked a definite break in the evolution of West German foreign policy. In the first place, the climax of the Crisis—the erection of the Berlin Wall in August of 1961—shattered the vital myth of reunification. The wall not only sealed the status quo in the most drastic sense of the term, but also spelled the end of East Germany's accelerating depopulation, the most visible proof of the regime's failure and illegitimacy. (Prior to 1961, about 3 million East Germans had crossed over into the FRG.) By taking a high risk in Berlin, the Soviet Union had clearly demonstrated the extent of its commitment to the viability of the East German regime. Moreover, the closure of the refugee conduit foreshadowed an uninterrupted period of East German nation-building and ultimately, the slow convergence between totalitarian rule and popular consent. August 13, 1961 thus constituted the long-postponed moment of truth.

Henceforth, unity could only mean reassociation and coexistence, but no longer a unification effort which would turn Germany into a larger version of the Federal Republic. As Willy Brandt, then mayor of West Berlin, put it a few months after the wall was erected: "After 12 years, we must recognize our aspirations as illusions. . . . Today, there is no visible price of reunification except for the renunciation of freedom."[43]

The Crisis eroded the fundamental premises of German foreign policy. Again, in the words of Brandt: If in the 1950s the policy makers presumably really did believe that "integration and rearmament would also achieve the unification of our divided people . . . , everybody knows today that such automatism does not exist and that it has never existed."[44] If the West was ready to pursue détente regardless of a solution of the German question, then the FRG either had to go along or "go it alone." If the latter raised the traditional specter of isolation, the former required a fundamental transformation of policy. It required accepting the consequences of World War II which the Soviets exacted as price for accommodation.

The Crisis paved the way for domestic change. Surprisingly, the population displayed an impressive degree of political maturity in the face of manifest disappointment. Instead of an anti-Western reaction, there was a sharp rise in pro-West-

[41]Arthur Schlesinger, *A Thousand Days* (Greenwich, Conn.: Fawcett Crest, 1967), p. 371.

[42]Kennedy in a conversation with Finland's President Kekkonen in October 1961. As quoted by Schlesinger, *ibid.*

[43]Address to the Bundestag, December 6, 1961, as reprinted in Willy Brandt, *Der Wille zum Frieden* (Hamburg: Hoffmann & Campe, 1971), p. 68.

[44]"Denk ich an Deutschland . . . ," address at the Evangelische Akademie, Tutzing, July 15, 1963. *Pressedienst des Landes Berlin*, no. 135, July 15, 1963.

ern sentiment.[45] Frustration was not directed against the Alliance but against Adenauer, who lost 5 percent of his votes and hence the CDU/CSU's absolute majority in the September 1961 elections. Two years later, Adenauer was forced to resign.

Indirectly, the Crisis accelerated the conversion of the Social Democratic party from a vilified minority party to a broadly based left-of-center political force. As an extremely successful party leader of the Berlin SPD, Willy Brandt soon acquired stature in the party as a whole. In the face of the Soviet threat, his pragmatic and strongly pro-Western views gained ascendancy over the SPD's cherished ideological and diplomatic dogmas. As mayor of embattled Berlin, Brandt was assured continuous national and international exposure which he skillfully parlayed into his nomination for the Chancellor candidacy in 1961 (remaining his party's candidate in 1965 and 1969). In short, three lost elections and the Soviet pressure on Berlin coincided to persuade the SPD to shed the burden of residual Marxism and ambivalence to the West. Reform was soon honored by electoral approval. In 1961 the SPD received 4.5 additional percentage points. In 1966 the SPD entered the government under the aegis of the CDU/CSU-SPD "Grand Coalition." In 1969, Brandt's accession to the Chancellorship opened the way for the transformation of West German policy which came to be known as the New Ostpolitik—the new policy toward the East.

## VI. OSTPOLITIK: OLD AND NEW

### 1. Continuity: The "Policy of Movement," 1963–1966

The resolution of the Cuba Crisis in the fall of 1962 marked the most decisive watershed between the confrontation politics of the 1950s and the fitful search for détente of the 1960s and 1970s. In its wake, the FRG was confronted with some agonizing dilemmas. In part, these dilemmas grew out of the very ambiguity of détente itself. Was détente going to take place on the level of bipolarity or societies, blocs or states? Was détente supposed to trigger qualitatively different political relationship by *resolving* conflict, or was it merely going to stabilize the existing spheres of influence at a lower intensity of confrontation? Did détente imply more cooperative behavior between the states, or was the evolution of domestic regimes in fact the precondition for diplomatic progress?

The 1960s were to suggest that these processes were as contradictory as the policies pursued by the various protagonists. The superpowers were primarily interested in stabilizing their strategic relationship at a lower level of risk and in recentralizing their respective alliance systems. In essence, superpower détente consisted not "in resolving disputes but in ignoring them,"[46] or at best, in ratifying a narrow communality of interests as represented in the Non-Proliferation Treaty of 1968.

France, on the other hand, pursued an antibloc détente policy, addressed to the *States* of Europe and

---

[45]Confidence in NATO rose from 52 percent in December of 1958 to 73 percent in November of 1961. *Divo Pressedienst,* April 1962, p. 4.

[46]Philip Windsor, *Germany and the Management of Détente* (London: Chatto and Windus, 1971), p. 23.

dedicated to eroding the "twin hegemony" of the two superpowers. If a military threat was no longer imminent and nuclear weapons had made alliances impossible, the time had come for a "European Europe" from the "Atlantic to the Urals" according to Charles de Gaulle's vision.

The Federal Republic could travel neither road. Following the American lead would require acquiescence in the status quo and hence the acceptance of partition. Bonn initially balked at acceding to the Test Ban Treaty of 1963 because the signature of *both* German states might have implied the de facto recognition of the GDR. Neither could the FRG join the French effort which, in proclaiming the paramountcy of States, raised the risk of fragmenting the Western alliance while legitimizing the existence of the East German regime.

Finally, whereas everybody else could easily start with agreements on peripheral issues, the FRG immediately ran up against the central problem of the territorial questions and its relationship to the GDR. The very attempt at exploring some form of coexistence forever involved setting foot on the slippery slope of the de facto recognition. Neither could the FRG simply withdraw to the orthodoxy laid down in the heyday of the Cold War. While perpetually reminding its allies of their contractual commitments to German claims, the Federal Government was careful not to alienate them by setting forth demands which were too adamant or too restrictive. There was the pressing need to hold the West to its part of the 1954 bargain and the equally crucial imperative of avoiding diplomatic isolation.

The outcome of these dilemmas was an ambiguous blend of resignation and resistance. Thus the Federal Government gave its grudging acquiescence to détente for the sake of Alliance cohesion while hedging it with preconditions in line with the principles laid down in the previous decade. These principles proclaimed that "the German question is one of the principal causes of tension in the world, and one cannot hope to eradicate these tensions if the German question remains unsolved."[47] The traditional "linkage," according to which great power accords were always to subsume progress toward German unity, was slightly loosened to permit détente if—and only if—the resolution of "peripheral" issues did not prejudice the resolution of "central" problems like the German issue.[48]

At the same time, the FRG embarked on a cautious Ostpolitik which sought to circumvent rather than to solve the central dilemmas of German diplomacy. Gerhard Schröder's (CDU Foreign Minister from 1961–1966) "policy of movement" was concentrated on economic engagement in Eastern Europe which was presumably eager to partake of Western economic plenty and to lighten the burden of Soviet dominance. Since the "policy of movement" sought to bypass the

[47]Chancellor Ludwig Erhard, who had replaced Adenauer in 1963, in his inaugural address before the Bundestag. As quoted in a collection of documents issued by the Auswärtiges Amt (Foreign Office), *Die Bemühungen der deutschen Regierung und ihrer Verbündeten um die Einheit Deutschlands, 1955–1966* (Bonn: Bundesdruckerei, 1966) p. 461.

[48]See Foreign Minister Schröder's address before the Parliamentary Assembly of the Western European Union, December 4, 1963. Presse- und Informationsamt der Bundesregierung, *Bulletin*, no. 214, December 5, 1963. (Hereafter cited as *Bulletin*.)

hard-core problems of the intra-German and German-Soviet conflict, it was bound to assume an anti-Soviet and anti-GDR thrust.[49]

The premise underlying that policy was based on an overperception of East European stirrings of independence. It assumed that East European polycentrism was necessarily anti-Soviet and liberalizing, that the threshold of Soviet sensitivity was high enough to ignore West German probes; and that the isolation of the GDR would soften the target to such an extent that the FRG could define the terms of the relationship with the GDR and the measure of liberalization within.

Events were to bear out none of these assumptions. The establishment of trade relations with Eastern Europe did not "spill over" into political change. Trade missions were opened in Poland, Rumania, and Hungary in 1963 and in Bulgaria in 1964. Yet the failure of an economic agreement with Czechoslovakia already demonstrated the limits of economic diplomacy. Prague refused to discuss trade without any of the political downpayments (towards a resolution of the Munich legacy)[50] which Schröder had studi-

ously sought to avoid. Moreover, as the case of Rumania showed, "national communism" could go hand in glove with tight domestic discipline, making the GDR appear no more reactionary than some of its Warsaw Pact partners. Finally, the FRG's unwillingness to discuss any of the real political issues such as the territorial order of postwar Europe, while at the same time seeking access to nuclear sharing, did little to widen its narrow base of trust in Eastern Europe.

The ambiguity of West German posture, which sought to combine the retention of past claims with an opening to the East, made a Soviet intervention initially unnecessary. Bonn's refusal to concede the finality of the Oder-Neisse line and to dispense with the "Hallstein Doctrine"[51] allowed the Soviet Union and the GDR to cast the FRG into the role of the last cold warrior. The vilifications tended to be substantiated by the increasing attacks which the right wing of his own Christian Democratic party leveled

---

[49]For an excellent review of Schröder's policy, see Windsor, *op. cit.*, esp. chap. 3.

[50]The Munich Agreement by which Czechoslovakia was essentially forced to cede the Sudeten territory to Hitler-Germany in 1938 has been a persistent source of contention between the FRG and the CSSR. After the war, the Sudetenland reverted to Czechoslovakia, which proceeded to expel about three million Sudenten Germans. While the Erhard government fell short of conceding the invalidity of the Agreement, it did renounce all claims to the Sudetenland. Thereafter, the issue became whether the Agreement was invalid initially or only rendered void by the German occupation of Czechoslovakia in March 1939. The issue es-

sentially boils down to which government is legally accountable for the property claims of the expelled Germans. For a brief review of the legal complexities, see Lawrence L. Whetten, *Germany's Ostpolitik* (London: Oxford University Press, 1971), pp. 168–71.

[51]After the establishment of diplomatic relations between the Soviet Union and the FRG in 1955, the so-called "Hallstein Doctrine" was formulated which branded any diplomatic recognition of the GDR as "unfriendly act . . . tending to deepen the division of Germany" (Adenauer's declaration before the Bundestag, *Verhandlungen des Deutschen Bundestages*, September 22, 1955, p. 5647). If the intent of the Doctrine was to block the international recognition of the GDR through the threat of severing diplomatic ties, it also foreclosed diplomatic relations with Eastern Europe which, having already recognized the GDR, was by definition out of bounds.

against Schröder's policy of flexible orthodoxy.

Schröder had totally misunderstood the GDR's role in the Soviet scheme of things. True, the East German regime was more dependent on the support of the Soviet Union than any other East European leadership. Yet it did not follow that West Germany's encouragement of East European autonomy would somehow weaken the position of the GDR. In fact the opposite was true. As Philip Windsor has pointed out, "in reality, East Germany was the bastion of polycentrism." Precisely because the presence of a huge Soviet army in the GDR "enabled the Soviet Union . . . to encircle and contain the more independent regimes, East Germany buttressed the framework of polycentrism. . . ."[52] Rather than isolating East Berlin, the Policy of Movement accomplished the opposite: it made the GDR all the more important to the Soviet Union. The much advertised Soviet-East German Treaty of Friendship and Mutual Assistance of June 1964 clearly demonstrated the futility of Schröder's hopes.

Parallel developments in the West were to underline the irony of a situation where the isolator himself became isolated. The early 1960s had witnessed a tug-of-war between France and the United States for West Germany's allegiance. During the Berlin Crisis, Adenauer had demonstratively leaned toward de Gaulle, who had refused to grant any concessions to the Soviet Union. In his twilight days, he concluded a Treaty of Collaboration with France (January 22, 1963, one week after de Gaulle vetoed Britain's entry into the Common Market). The Treaty

was subsequently emasculated by a strongly worded pro-American preamble, added by an almost unanimous Bundestag.

Moreover, when faced with the specter of a Franco-German axis, the Kennedy Administration quickly shifted from coolness to courtship. In the summer of 1963, Kennedy embarked on a triumphant trip to Germany, bearing with him the promise of an equal Atlantic partnership between the United States and Europe. In addition, the Administration revived the dormant proposal for a Multilateral Force (MLF) —a fleet of nuclear missile-carrying freighters manned by NATO contingents—as a bid for Bonn's allegiance.[53] After a spectacular beginning, the new Franco-German friendship soon proved too strenuous for the FRG. Unwilling to support de Gaulle's increasingly strident anti-American course and gratified by American attention, the FRG returned to the American fold under Chancellor Erhard's leadership. (Erhard had replaced Adenauer in the fall of 1963.) If dependence was a fact of German life, it was at any rate more honorable to subordinate the FRG to a remote superpower like the United States than to a potential political peer and economic inferior like France.

The supreme irony was that Bonn did not succeed in stabilizing its special relationship with Washington. Having at first vacillated between France and the United States and then sought refuge with the latter,

[52]Windsor, *op. cit.*, pp. 62–63.

[53]"If de Gaulle meant to make West Germany choose between France and the United States, the MLF, in Washington's view, was the way to make it clear that Bonn would find greater security in the Atlantic relationship." Arthur Schlesinger, *A Thousand Days*, pp. 744–745.

the FRG was ultimately forced to realize that it had gained neither. When faced with the reassertion of German-American solidarity, France embarked on an outflanking maneuver by approaching its traditional partner, the Soviet Union. By early 1965, as a German editorial put it, there was "nothing left of the Gaullist concept that no concessions should be made to the Soviet Union as long as there is no sign of Soviet accommodation on the German problem."[54]

American policy under Lyndon Johnson did not honor the loyalty of its transatlantic junior partner. As de Gaulle turned toward the Soviet Union, the United States turned from Atlantic partnership toward escalation in Vietnam. Concomitantly, the superpower dialogue evolved to a higher level, a progression which was best symbolized by President Johnson's "bridge-building" speech of October 7, 1966.[55] In effect the President then proposed reconciliation with the Communist half of Europe while tacitly offering not to press German claims for the time being.

As a result, American policy manifestly shifted its priorities. In 1963, Schröder had tried to orchestrate his Ostpolitik with an attempt to mobilize the West for a reunification initiative. By 1965, after months of foot-dragging, Bonn's reunification venture collided for the first time with American unwillingness to engage in fruitless diplomatic exercises while other East-West issues were more urgent and more amenable to resolution. The MLF did not materialize. Instead, the speed with which the Johnson Administration set out

to conclude the Non-Proliferation Treaty with the Soviet Union was perhaps the most dramatic turn toward collaborative bipolarity—the fear of German foreign policy. Preoccupied with Vietnam, Washington not only withdrew 15,000 troops from Germany, but also insisted on full offset payments for the remaining contingents. Beset by his own fiscal troubles at home, Erhard traveled to Washington in an attempt to soften the American terms. His failure contributed decisively to his fall from power upon his return.

At the same time that the FRG was threatened with isolation in the West, the Soviet Union moved into the breach by launching an intensive campaign for a European security conference which would finally ratify the territorial status quo. By the fall of 1966, West German foreign policy was confronted with impasse on all fronts. Long-postponed change was now unavoidable. Fittingly enough, its beginning was symbolized by the emergence of the "Grand Coalition" between the CDU and the SPD. Its raison d'être and point of departure were aptly characterized by its architect and Minister for All-German Affairs, Herbert Wehner of the SPD: "Until now we have lived beyond our means—as if we had been a victor power by adoption."[56]

2. *Continuity and Change: The Ostpolitik of the "Grand Coalition"*

Because the CDU/CSU-SPD coalition formed in the fall of 1966 commanded over 90 percent of the Bundestag seats, it was more of an "uncertain" than a "grand" coalition. Combining two potential ma-

[54] *Die Welt*, April 29, 1965.
[55] Reprinted in the *New York Times*, October 8, 1966.

[56] Foreign Minister Willy Brandt before the Consultative Assembly of the Council of Europe, January 24, 1967. *Bulletin*, no. 8, January 26, 1967.

jority parties, it was programmed for dissolution almost from its conception. From the very beginning, the requirements of diplomatic flexibility were tightly circumscribed by the need to preserve a precarious consensus. At best, the coalition was able to reconsider the nature of détente. Having traditionally defined reunification as the touchstone of détente, the Government now reversed priorities with its avowal "not to burden the policy of détente in Europe with any preconditions" because "the problems of Europe like those of Germany cannot be settled in a Cold War atmosphere."[57] Aware of the counter-productiveness of its traditional braking efforts, the FRG gingerly set out to rejoin the mainstream of Allied policy.

In all other areas, however, the need to preserve coalition cohesion effectively prevented a clean break with past orthodoxy. While the Government made a demonstrative effort to leave the trenches of the Cold War, it clung to the legal claims staked out in the 1950s. If the Kiesinger-Brandt government assured Eastern Europe that it had no "territorial claims,"[58] it also insisted that the definitive status of Germany's borders had to await a comprehensive peace settlement. While assuring Poland that "we now understand far better than before [Poland's] desire to live at last in a territory with secure borders,"[59] the FRG did not concede the finality and legitimacy of the Oder-Neisse line. Admitting that Hitler's invasion of Czechoslo-

vakia had rendered the Munich Agreement null and void, Bonn did not concede its invalidity from the very start.

As a second substantial departure, the Government quietly dismantled the so-called "Hallstein Doctrine," although it was careful not to discard all the pieces. The principle which had precluded diplomatic ties with any state apart from the Soviet Union, which recognized the GDR, was modified. It now permitted formal relations with the Warsaw Pact countries on the "birthmark theory," according to which they never had a genuine choice in this matter. The Doctrine would still be invoked against non-Communist countries although its application would not necessarily lead to the massive retaliation of an automatic rupture of relations. Subsequently, Bonn moved from words to deeds, and as the first major success of the new Ostpolitik, exchanged ambassadors with Rumania in early 1967. Simultaneously, Bonn proceeded to sound out Czechoslovakia, Hungary, and Bulgaria.

While softened, the previously drawn distinction between the GDR and other Warsaw Pact members remained operative. "Détente in Europe ... must include détente in Germany," and hence, as Willy Brandt put it, "we aspire to an 'organized coexistence' in Germany."[60] Coexistence, however, did not include formal recognition. In short, in its quest to unshoulder the odium of Cold War obstructionism, the Grand Coalition sought conciliation while withholding codification of the status quo. This thrust was exemplified in its attempt to envelop the hard-core territorial issues in a com-

[57] *Ibid.*
[58] Willy Brandt on June 10, 1968. *Bulletin,* no. 73, June 12, 1968.
[59] Chancellor Kurt-Georg Kiesinger (CDU) in his inaugural address before the Bundestag, December 13, 1966. *Bulletin,* no. 157, December 14, 1966.

[60] *Bulletin,* no. 8, January 26, 1967.

prehensive offer of renunciation-of-force agreements.

Ambiguity exacted its price. The new Ostpolitik tended to raise more fears than it assuaged. If the FRG had no territorial claims, why did it refuse to acknowledge the postwar borders? If "organized" coexistence was the goal, why did Bonn withold recognition from the GDR?

Given the inroads West Germany had made in Eastern Europe, the GDR was now indeed faced with the specter of isolation. Proclaiming a Hallstein doctrine in reverse, the leaders of the GDR called on its allies to make diplomatic ties with the FRG contingent on the latter's recognition of the GDR. By March 1967, Ulbricht had succeeded in erecting a formidable barrier against further West German advances by concluding twenty-year treaties of friendship with Czechoslovakia and Poland. The Ulbricht-forged "Iron Triangle" manifestly raised the price for Bonn's access to Eastern Europe, notably the recognition of the GDR, the ratification of the Oder-Neisse border, the unequivocal renunciation of the Munich Agreement, and abstinence from any form of nuclear weapons sharing. Like Adenauer in the 1950s, Ulbricht had now acquired a veto over his bloc's policy to the other side.

3. *Change: Willy Brandt's "Policy of Peace"*

Détente in the 1960s exhibited a peculiar dialectical pattern. The destabilization of societies and blocs in the early 1960s led to the forcible reimposition of uniformity in Czechoslavakia. Yet it was precisely the consolidation of Soviet rule which opened the way for real, controlled movement. Moscow could allow movement because leaders in the East and West would now carefully attune their own policies to the drastically demonstrated limits of Soviet tolerance.

Several other factors also contributed to the new mobility after 1968. The Soviet Union was eager to repair its tarnished image. And, while the new Nixon Administration was eager to achieve some basic breakthroughs with Moscow (notably on SALT), it had also served notice that tensions in other areas like Berlin would affect détente as a whole. Also, the "Chinese connection" has been a source of much speculation. The relationship between a mellowing Soviet *Westpolitik* and mounting hostility with China was probably more complex than the Sino-Soviet clashes of early 1969 suggested. For in the years before, a hardline policy toward Europe had gone hand in hand with deteriorating relations with China. Conversely, signals of Soviet flexibility in the West had clearly preceded the outbreak of fighting in 1969. A more plausible interpretation would therefore go beyond the purely European framework and take into account the evolving triangular constellation between Moscow, Washington, and Peking. As China was emerging from the self-imposed isolation of the "Cultural Revolution," American policy under Nixon and Kissinger skillfully maneuvered into position between the two Communist giants. The specter of an implicit Chinese-American alliance (motivated by Chinese fears of the Soviets and the United States' quest for a settlement in Vietnam) therefore increased the Soviet Union's stakes in strengthening its relationship with the United States and the West.

The evolution of West German politics served as a crucial triggering factor. In the elections of September 28, 1969, the Social Democratic Party had captured the government for the first time since the early Weimar days. (Lacking an absolute majority, the SPD was forced to share power with the liberal Free Democratic Party, the FDP.) Since the elections had been dominated by Ostpolitik issues, the outcome suggested a new consensus as well as a mandate.

The new Brandt Government quickly began to signal its resolution to do what all previous Bonn governments had sought to resist: to accept the post-war status quo for what it was. The quest for reunification was reduced to a minimal policy of prophylaxis. It was no longer *the* stumbling block towards reconciliation but instead the refusal to legitimize policies that would definitively *preclude* reunification once and for all. Accordingly, Willy Brandt did not even mention "reunification" in his inaugural address, emphasizing instead the universal right to self-determination. Dispensing with the FRG's claim to "sole representation," he spoke of "two German states in one nation." While a joint heritage and nationality precluded the final step of formal diplomatic recognition, Brandt offered "contractually regulated cooperation" to the GDR. Significantly, in renewing his predecessors' offers of renunciation-of-force agreements, he emphatically included the GDR as well as the crucial stipulation that these compacts would be based on the "territorial integrity" of each signatory state.[61] Having served notice that it was ready to "unlink" and

"quarantine" the German issue, the Brandt Government signed the Non-Proliferation Treaty (NPT) in November of 1969. Bonn's signature was a signal as well as a turning point, since West German access to nuclear weapons had been a prime focus of the German-Soviet quarrel since 1957.

Against the background of the larger changes in the international system, the stage was set for an incredibly complex diplomatic exercise which amounted to a virtual settlement of World War II. Rather than in a formal peace conference, resolution unfolded in a crisscrossing pattern of multilateral and bilateral negotiations. The vehicles of reconciliation were renunciation-of-force treaties (based on the affirmation of the territorial status quo) with Moscow and Warsaw, a Basic Treaty with the GDR (regulating state-to-state coexistence without de jure diplomatic recognition), and a quadripartite Berlin agreement (ensuring access and the ties between the FRG and West Berlin).

Not surprisingly, the prime obstacle proved to be the GDR. Like the FRG in an earlier stage of détente, the GDR again mounted an all-out effort to retain its role as "guardian at the gate" between the two blocs. Both had gained their identity and derivative power through their struggle against each other. Monopolizing the national heritage, they had drawn their own legitimacy from denying to the other. Both had been able to harness their alliances to a hard-line approach to the other side by cultivating intimate links with their bloc leaders. However, as with the United States in the early 1960s, the Soviet Union was now no longer willing to subordinate its own interests to the claims of its junior partner. Indeed, Ulbricht's quiet ouster

---

[61]Bundesministerium für innerdeutsche Beziehungen, *Texte zur Deutschlandpolitik*, Vol. IV (Bonn: Vorwärts-Druck, 1970), pp. 11–13, 38–39.

in May of 1971 (no doubt with Soviet encouragement) evoked comparison with the fate of Adenauer, whose political decline began in earnest in the wake of the Berlin Wall and the United States' passivity after 1961.

Moscow's prime aim in the entire enterprise was a West German treaty and an all-European conference which would finally consecrate the territorial redistribution resulting from World War II. In its quest to escape from inferiority, the GDR's objectives were more demanding. It sought not only the long-withheld diplomatic recognition from the West and the FRG but also an explicit change in the status of West Berlin, a Western enclave whose political ties to the FRG posed a persistent challenge to its territorial sovereignty. Yet through a skillful diplomacy, which extracted leverage from Western support as well as domestic weakness, Bonn managed to outflank its hostile brother. At home, Brandt found himself confronted with a CDU Opposition which sought to recapture the governmental power it had held for twenty years by attacking his Ostpolitik as a "give-away" and treason to Germany's national cause. Domestic instability (Brandt's narrow parliamentary majority was soon whittled down to a margin of two) forced the Government to tie the ratification of the Eastern treaties to a satisfactory Berlin settlement.

Although Moscow had initially balked at including Berlin in its bilateral talks with Bonn, Berlin became the touchstone and focal point of the entire mosaic. For the three Western powers began to define Berlin as the prime test of Soviet intentions and therefore predicated the convocation of a European security conference and the recognition of the GDR on a Berlin agreement.

After years of resistance to Western détente efforts, Bonn's policy was now at last re-integrated into the larger framework of Western diplomacy. This was one of Brandt's greatest achievements. On the one hand, it helped to relieve earlier American anxieties about the haphazard pace of German Ostpolitik, which was now subject to some supervision by the West. On the other hand, the Berlin link strengthened Bonn's hand vis-à-vis the East. Failure in Berlin would threaten the entire edifice of détente, and hence the Soviet Union was forced to rein in its obstreperous East German ally.

The Berlin Agreement was signed on September 3, 1971. For the first time since the war, the Soviet Union pledged to ensure "unimpeded access" to Berlin. While reaffirming that West Berlin was not a "constituent part" of the FRG, the Agreement did concede the crucial point that the ties between both could be "maintained and developed."[62] The Eastern Treaties were ratified on May 17, 1972. On June 3, the Berlin Agreement entered into force. Having narrowly escaped from a parliamentary vote of no-confidence in April, Brandt called for a special election in November of 1972. It was again heavily dominated by Ostpolitik. Its outcome, a comfortable majority for the Brandt coalition, suggested that the quasi-ratification of the status quo abroad had been accompanied by a stable transformation of the ideological consensus at home. Thereafter, the de facto recognition of the GDR was formalized in the Basic Treaty between both German states concluded on December 21, 1972. Although the GDR

[62]For the German and English texts of the Berlin Agreement, see *Europa-Archiv*, 19/1971, pp. D 443–453.

now maintains diplomatic ties with the Western world, it did not succeed in gaining de jure recognition from the FRG. The fine distinction between de facto and de jure was drawn by the fact that both states now maintain "permanent missions" rather than embassies in each other's capitals.

## VII. CONCLUSION: RETURN TO NORMALCY

Having surmounted the tortuous obstacle course of negotiation and ratification, Brandt's Ostpolitik spelled the end of an era in post-war German politics. Yet in spite of evident differences in tactics between Adenauer and Brandt, both phases of West German foreign policy were linked by some profound continuities. First and foremost, Adenauer had sought to escape from subjection and isolation. Given the setting after 1945, partition was the price for security and emancipation. Adenauer's disingenuity may have been an act of true statesmanship: in suggesting that integration into the West would lead to reunification, he anchored the young Federal Republic in a community that softened the blow of partition and underwrote the stability of democratic evolution. When the moment of truth dawned many years later, West German society reacted with remarkable political maturity.

Brandt closely followed in the footsteps of the FRG's founding father. Domestically, his Ostpolitik forged a new consensus by carefully dismantling the vital myth of reunification. Both had sought to defuse the dangerous potential of revisionism, and both were haunted by the perils of Germany's position in the European center. In the course of

the ratification debates, Brandt again evoked the ancient nightmare of German diplomacy in defense of his Ostpolitik: "An anti-German coalition has been Bismarck's as well as Adenauer's nightmare. We, too, are faced with this problem, and we should make sure that our own policy does not turn this problem into a burden."[63] The détente of the 1960s had rent the previous consensus between the FRG and the West, confronting Bonn with the prospect of isolation or adaptation. As Adenauer had integrated the young German state into the Western community, Brandt's Ostpolitik re-integrated his country's policy into the mainstream of Western diplomacy.

In affirming the "inviolability" of Europe's postwar borders and in recognizing the existence of a second German state, the FRG merely ratified the unavoidable. Yet in resolving its special conflict with the East, the FRG did not embark on a new balancing act between East and West. Indeed, the Eastern treaties with the Soviet Union and Poland explicitly affirm the continued validity of previous "bilateral and multilateral" agreements concluded by the signatories. In other words, these treaties underlined rather than loosened the FRG's earlier commitments to the West as formalized in the 1954 settlement, its accession to NATO, and the various treaties of the European Community.[64]

The Federal Republic has remained anchored in the Western community, yet by setting aside its conflict with the East, it has also lightened the burden of its dependence on the West. Even among al-

[63] *Verhandlungen des Deutschen Bundestages,* May 17, 1972, p. 10897.
[64] Presse- und Informationsamt der Bundesregierung, *The Treaty of August 12, 1970 between the FRG and the USSR* (Bonn, 1970).

lies, solidarity exacts its price, and for the past three decades the FRG has paid frequent political and economic tribute for Western loyalty. As the most exposed member of the Alliance, the FRG has born the brunt of offset payments for American troops in Europe. German concessions on the Common Market's agricultural policy have been heavily conditioned by the need to preserve French support on East-West issues. To forestall the international recognition of the GDR, the Federal Republic has courted the developing world with foreign aid.

In the 1970s, the FRG could begin to afford a more "normal" foreign policy. For instance, in 1965 Chancellor Ludwig Erhard subordinated profits to politics by vetoing the shipment of German steel pipes to the Soviet Union in response to American complaints that these were "strategic" materials. In 1975, on the other hand, Bonn ignored American pressures and went ahead with the sale of a multibillion-dollar complete-fuel cycle nuclear industry to Brazil which might enable the latter to produce its own nuclear weapons in the next decade. In the early 1960s, Bonn undertook to ship American weapons to Israel, a brokerage task which eventually culminated in the severence of diplomatic relations between the Arab world and West Germany. During the Yom Kippur War of 1973, by contrast, Bonn publicly chastized its American ally for violating the FRG's sovereignty in the process of resupplying Israel with American materiel stationed in West Germany. Similarly, in 1974 Chancellor Helmut Schmidt served notice on France that West Germany would no longer automatically foot the bill for the European Community's Common Agricultural Policy whose subsidies tended to benefit primarily French farmers.

In other areas, the legacy of the past, however, still continues to bedevil West German foreign policy. Its peculiar problems have been muted, but not totally exorcized. The two Germanies will remain locked in an uneasy coexistence between "two states in one nation," as Brandt put it, and "two nation states" to which the GDR aspires. "Normalcy," if historical experience is a guide, is shrouded in a hazy future. It took centuries of intermittent strife before Austria and "Germany" could finally treat each other as two separate entities, regardless of their common heritage, language, and culture. That Willy Brandt should resign from the Chancellorship in May of 1974 because one of his assistants, Günther Guillaume, was exposed as an East German spy only underlines the peculiar conflict relationship between the two German states.

The mere existence of another German state constitutes a latent threat to one's own system. Treaties are insufficient to relieve fears of mutual subversion, especially since the tools of subversion are so easily mobilized and employed. Nowhere else but in Germany (and perhaps Korea) could an agent like Günther Guillaume cross borders, burrow into the other side's society and emerge many years later close to the center of political power. Similarly, even with a quadripartite agreement, Berlin will remain a lasting source of conflict. Its Four-Power status symbolizes one of the most important unresolved legacies of World War II. It is a permanent chink in the territorial sovereignty of the GDR, and at the same time the most vulnerable spot of West German diplomacy. After the conclusion of the Eastern treaties, diplomatic contention between the FRG and the East has predictably focused on the nature and extent of the ties between the Federal Republic and West Berlin.

While the old legacy is bound to resurface periodically, an entirely new set of problems will dominate West German foreign policy in the years to come. These problems are common to all the nations of the developed world. Indeed, the very nature of foreign policy seems to be changing. As the old dominant conflict between East and West is declining, a new conflict between the old rich (the industrial world), the new rich (the OPEC countries), and the old poor (the developing nations of Africa and Asia) has moved to the center of the stage.

The stakes of the conflict are no longer security in the narrow military sense, but the stability of resource supplies and prices. Domestic welfare and the "struggle for the world product"[65] has usurped the traditional primacy of the "high politics." The means of the new warfare are not military might but the manipulation of the raw material prices and currency surpluses. Similarly, the framework of policy is changing. For decades, the Atlantic Alliance constituted the prime forum of interaction for the Federal Republic and its Western partners. Today NATO has been whittled down to a residual defense organization against a residual military threat.

Theoretically, the new dominance of economic and monetary issues should pave the way for an enlarged West German role in world affairs. By all tokens, the Federal Republic is an economic superpower today. Its per capita gross national product is only slightly smaller than that of the United States (about $6600); it has the highest currency reserves in the world, the best record on unemployment and inflation, and it continues to accumulate balance-of-trade surpluses while everybody else is struggling with deficits.

Yet even with its new-found autonomy and its staggering economic strength, the Federal Republic has thus far chosen to play a relatively modest role. Bonn continues to rely on Washington for military protection. It has bailed out Italy with a large currency loan, but it has not employed its financial might to energize the languishing European integration venture. Caught between its moral obligation to Israel and its economic interests in the Arab world, the Federal Republic has charted a finely balanced course between the two. It has brushed aside calls for an economic "bigemony" with the United States, which might threaten its old partnership with France and its new relations with the Soviet Union.[66]

In short, the Federal Republic has acquired a few more balls to juggle but resisted a new role. Years ago it was fashionable to dub the FRG as "economic giant and political dwarf." For some twenty odd years

[65]Cf. Helmut Schmidt's "The Struggle for the World Product," *Foreign Affairs*, April 1974. (Helmut Schmidt replaced Willy Brandt as Chancellor in May 1974.)

[66]For an advocacy of such "axis," see C. Fred Bergsten's testimony in *American Interest in the European Community*, Joint Hearings before the Subcommittee on Europe and the Subcommittee on Foreign Economic Policy of the Committee on Foreign Affairs, House of Representatives, 93rd Congress, November 8, 1973, pp. 89ff.

the Federal Republic was constrained and content to conduct a nonautonomous foreign policy. Like Voltaire's *Candide*, it could cultivate its own garden. Today, given the changing nature of power, economic giants have accumulated political muscle almost by default. To be sure, in a period of transition, discretion is a counsel of prudence as well as economy. And like all the industrialized nations, the Federal Republic is turning inward. Yet it will become increasingly difficult to cultivate one's own garden in an unsettled world.

## SELECT BIBLIOGRAPHY

### I. PRIMARY SOURCES AND DOCUMENTS

AUSWÄRTIGES AMT, ed. *Die Auswärtige Politik der Bundesrepublik Deutschland.* Cologne: Verlag Wissenschaft und Politik, 1972.

EMBREE, GEORGE D., ed. *The Soviet Union and the German Question, 1958–1961.* The Hague: Nijhoff, 1963.

MEISSNER, BORIS, ed. *Die deutsche Ostpolitik, 1961–1970.* Cologne: Verlag Wessenschaft und Politik, 1970.

OPPEN, BEATE RUHM VON, ed. *Documents on Germany Under Occupation, 1945–1955.* London: Oxford University Press, 1955.

Press- und Informationsamt der Bundesregierung. *Bulletin* (a regular compilation of important speeches, documents, press conferences, etc., in a German and an English edition).

### II. BOOKS AND ARTICLES

ADENAUER, KONRAD. *Erinnerungen.* 4 vols. Stuttgart: Deutsche Verlags-Anstalt, 1965–1968.

_____. *Memoirs, 1945–1953.* Chicago: Regenery, 1966.

AUGSTEIN, RUDOLF. *Konrad Adenauer.* London: Secker and Warburg, 1964.

BIRNBAUM, KARL E. *East and West Germany: A Modus Vivendi.* Lexington, Mass.: Heath Lexington Books, 1973.

BRANDT, WILLY. *Aussenpolitik, Deutschlandpolitik, Europapolitik.* Berlin: Berlin-Verlag, 1968.

_____. *A Peace Policy for Europe.* New York: Holt, Rinehart & Winston 1969.

CHILDS, DAVID. *From Schumacher to Brandt: The Story of German Socialism, 1945–1965.* Oxford: Pergamon Press, 1966.

CRAIG, GORDON. *From Bismarck to Adenauer: Aspects of German Statecraft.* New York: Harper & Row, 1965.

CRAMER, DETTMAR. *Deutschland nach dem Grundvertrag.* Stuttgart: Verlag Bonn Aktuell, 1973.

DAHRENDORF, RALF. *Society and Democracy in Germany.* New York: Doubleday, 1967.

DEHIO, LUDWIG. *Germany and World Politics in the Twentieth Century.* New York: Norton, 1967.

DEUTSCH, KARL W., and EDINGER, LEWIS J. *Germany Rejoins the Powers: A Study of Mass Opinion, Interest Groups and Elites in Contemporary German Foreign Policy.* Stanford: Stanford University Press, 1959.

_____. "Who Prevailed in the German Foreign Policy Process?" in Dogan, Matthei and Rose, Richard, eds. *European Politics: A Reader.* Boston: Little, Brown, 1971.

EDINGER, LEWIS J. *Kurt Schumacher: A Study in Personality and Political Behavior.* Stanford: Stanford University Press, 1965.

GIMBEL, JOHN. *The American Occupation of Germany, 1945–1949.* Stanford: Stanford University Press, 1968.

GOLAY, JOHN. *The Founding of the Federal Republic of Germany.* Chicago: Chicago University Press, 1958.

GOLDMAN, GUIDO. *The German Political System.* New York: Random House, 1974.

GROSSER, ALFRED. *Germany In Our Time.* New York: Praeger, 1971.

HAAS, ERNST. *The Uniting of Europe.* Stanford: Stanford University Press, 1958.

HANRIEDER, WOLFRAM. *West German Foreign Policy, 1949–1963: International Pressure And Domestic Response.* Stanford: Stanford University Press, 1967.

———. *The Stable Crisis: Two Decades of German Foreign Policy.* New York: Harper and Row, 1970.

HARTMANN, FREDERICK H. *Germany Between East and West: The Reunification Problem.* Englewood Cliffs, N.J.: Prentice-Hall, 1965.

HEIDENHEIMER, ARNOLD J. *Adenauer and the CDU.* The Hague: Nijhoff, 1960.

HOFFMANN, STANLEY. *Gulliver's Troubles, Or the Setting of American Foreign Policy.* New York: McGraw Hill, 1968.

JOFFE, JOSEF. "Germany and the Atlantic Alliance: The Politics of Dependence, 1961–1968," in Cromwell, William et al. *Political Problems of Atlantic Partnership.* Bruges: College of Europe, 1969.

KAISER, KARL. *German Foreign Policy in Transition.* London: Oxford University Press, 1968.

———, and MORGAN, ROGER, eds. *Britain and West Germany: Changing Societies and the Future of Foreign Policy.* London: Oxford University Press, 1971.

Keesing's Research Report No. 8. *Germany and Eastern Europe Since 1945: From the Potsdam Agreement to Chancellor Brandt's Ostpolitik.* New York: Scribner, 1973.

KRISCH, HENRY. *German Politics Under Soviet Occupation.* New York: Columbia University Press, 1974.

LÖWENTHAL, RICHARD. *Vom kalten Krieg zur Ostpolitik.* Stuttgart: Seewald, 1974.

———, and SCHWARZ, HANS-PETER, eds. *Die zweite Republik.* Stuttgart: Seewald, 1974.

LUDZ, PETER C. *Deutschlands doppelte Zunkunft.* Munich: Hanser, 1974.

MERKL, PETER H. *The Origin of the West German Republic.* New York: Oxford University Press, 1965.

———. *German Foreign Policies, West & East.* Santa Barbara, Calif.: Clio Press, 1974.

MORGAN, ROGER. *The United States and West Germany, 1945–1973: A Study in Alliance Politics.* London: Oxford University Press, 1974.

NÖLLE, ELISABETH and NEUMANN, ERICH P. *The Germans: Public Opinion Polls, 1947–1966.* Allenbach: Verlag für Demoskopie, 1967.

PINSON, KOPPEL S. *Modern Germany: Its History and Civilization.* New York: Macmillan, 1966.

PLANCK, CHARLES E. *The Changing Status of German Reunification in Western Diplomacy, 1955–1966.* Baltimore: Johns Hopkins Press, 1967.

RICHARDSON, JAMES L. *Germany and the Atlantic Alliance: The Interaction of Strategy and Politics.* Cambridge: Harvard University Press, 1966.

SCHICK, JACK M. *The Berlin Crisis, 1958–1962.* Philadelphia: University of Pennsylvania Press, 1972.

SPEIER, HANS, and DAVISON, W. PHILLIPS, eds. *West German Leadership and Foreign Policy.* Evanston, Ill.: Row, Peterson, 1957.

STRAUSS, FRANZ JOSEF. *Challenge and Response: A Program for Europe.* New York: Atheneum, 1970.

VALI, FERENC. *The Quest for a United Germany.* Baltimore: Johns Hopkins Press, 1967.

WHETTEN, LAWRENCE L. *Germany's Ostpolitik.* New York: Oxford University Press, 1971.

WILLIS, FRANK R. *France, Germany and the New Europe, 1945–1967.* London: Oxford University Press, 1968.

WINDSOR, PHILIP. *German Reunification.* London: Elek Books, 1969.

———. *Germany and the Management of Détente.* New York: Praeger, 1971.

ZIEBURA, GILBERT. *Die deutsch-französischen Beziehungen seit 1945: Mythen und Realitäten.* Pfullingen: Neske, 1970.

ZINK, HAROLD. *The United States and Germany, 1944–1955.* Princeton: Van Nostrand, 1957.

# SOVIET FOREIGN POLICY

5

*Vernon V. Aspaturian*

## THE SOVIET UNION AS AN ACTOR IN THE INTERNATIONAL SYSTEM

At one time it was fashionable to emphasize the enigmatic aspects of Soviet foreign policy behavior, to accentuate its remarkable capacity for evoking the most variegated and contradictory responses to its diplomacy. Edward Crankshaw could write that while "in its distant objectives, the foreign policy of the Soviet Union is less obscure and more coherent than that of any other country," its immediate intentions and the motivations behind its day-to-day diplomacy often appeared incoherent, capricious, and almost always enigmatic.[1] As the Soviet state approaches its sixtieth anniversary,

[1] *New York Times Book Review,* July 3, 1949, p. 4.

we might observe that its distant objectives have become less clearcut, more ambivalent, and infinitely more complex, while its immediate purposes and goals in foreign policy have become less obscure, even though they are no less capricious and contradictory than its previous behavior.

Analysis of Soviet foreign policy behavior is no less difficult than before. As knowledge and information concerning Soviet foreign policy has expanded, the complexity and variety of Soviet behavioral patterns have grown at an even faster rate. Confusion about Soviet motives, misperceptions of her intent, and puzzlement in comprehending Soviet behavior still characterizes any attempt to analyze Soviet foreign policy. After six decades of existence, the Soviet state emerges distinctly as a complex, multidimensional, international actor, sharing certain characteristics with other actors in the international system, while displaying unique characteristics that set it apart from other states.

To understand Soviet foreign policy it is necessary to properly define the Soviet Union as an actor in the international system. This is by no means a simple task. The Soviet Union increasingly betrays many characteristics similar to those of other actors, particularly the United States, which has increasingly, although not always consciously or advertently, served as a model for the Soviet Union. This stems from the fact that during the past two decades the United States has stood at the apex of the international system, and the Soviet Union has been its principal rival and challenger for that status.

The many characteristics which the Soviet Union shares with the United States as a global power or with China as a sociopolitical system, however, should not obscure the significant characteristics of the Soviet Union that make it unique. Indeed, the two sets of characteristics the Soviet Union shares with the United States and China—global power and revolutionary center, respectively—emerge as only one source of confusion about Soviet foreign policy behavior. The duality of the Soviet Union as the center of a revolutionary movement, defined as its Party role, and as a State among states in the international system, has long been recognized. Yet the perception of the Soviet Union as a dual entity is an oversimplification of a more complicated existence. The Soviet Union is more than a dualistic entity. It is a multiple one, whose components have both contradictory and competing constituencies with intersecting, conflicting, and harmonious interests, inspired by a variety of motives. The Soviet Union as a Russian national state, its current manifestation as legal-constitutional multinational federal/confederal state representing the interests of its component nations individually in the international community, and its position as a commonwealth of nations representing their interests collectively, provide the content and substance for three additional Soviet roles.

The USSR is endowed with multiple identities in international affairs, influenced by a wide spectrum of elements that intersect to fundamentally impinge on the contours of Soviet behavior. Currently the Soviet Union is the only authentic multiple actor in international affairs. It reveals itself as an aggregate of five distinct but interrelated institutionalized personalities. These are 1) state, 2) party, 3) Russian nation, 4) non-Russian nation (variable), and 5) multinational commonwealth.

Multiple identities performing multiple functions in multiple environments in response to the multiple pressures and demands of multiple constituencies constitute a recipe for confusion and complexity for Soviet leaders and observers of Soviet behavior. The possible mutations of inputs and outputs are staggering in their variety and proliferation. The problem of analysis is complicated by the difficulty in securing reliable data concerning past Soviet foreign policy, to say nothing about acquiring information concerning current policy. Nevertheless, information on Soviet political behavior has been more plentiful in recent years. This, beside continuing changes within the Soviet Union, changing external perceptions and analytical models of the Soviet system, and fundamental alterations in alignments within the international environments in which the Soviet Union acts, have contributed to the complexity of Soviet foreign policy analysis.

All the identities developed in the periods of evolution in the Soviet system are not equally significant in assessing the behavior of the Soviet Union. Their relative importance varies not only with the changing goals of the leadership, but also with the changing alignment of internal forces, the corresponding demands and pressures of its various constituencies, and the opportunities and risks that manifest themselves in the international environment.

As a *state*, the Soviet Union functions in its broadest dimension, operating in four of the five environments to which it must respond. As a state, the Soviet Union plays no formal nor overt role in the world Communist movement. In its capacity as a state, the Soviet Union must articulate the interests of social constituencies within the sociopolitical system in accordance with a shifting structure of power and priorities. These, in turn, must be coordinated with the demands of the nationalities within the Soviet multinational order, and harmonized with the interests of other Communist states in the interstate subsystem, before it acts within the general interstate system.

In the general interstate system, the Soviet Union functions as one of the two global powers. In this capacity, it must accept minimum obligations in return for corresponding rights and privileges. The increasing importance of the Soviet Union as an actor in the international system has impressed itself on the consciousness of the Soviet leaders, imparting to Soviet behavior a measure of maturity, responsibility, and prudence that has, at the same time, served to erode its responsibilities as the center of a revolutionary movement.

In its capacity as a state, the Soviet Union is charged with defending and advancing the interests of the Soviet Union and its domestic constituencies against those of other states in the international community. The foreign policy outputs of the Soviet state are formulated internally in accordance with changing spectrum of priorities arrived at in response to the constituencies that can influence the process. These constituencies can be nationalities, institutions, bureaucratic structures, sociofunctional elites and social classes, and subgroups within them. The foreign policy of the Soviet state may assume the patterns of self-perpetuation (security and maintenance), self-extension (aggrandizement), or self-fulfillment (development, prestige, and status), either for the state as a whole or constituencies, individually and collectively.

The credentials of the Soviet state as a global power rest upon its powerful economic-technological foundations and the possession of advanced technological weapons systems, including thermonuclear warheads and ICBM delivery systems. The Soviet Union is thereby able to assert unilaterally an interest anywhere and take corresponding action, including intervention. As a global power, the Soviet Union has intervened successfully in the Caribbean and the Middle East, leading to the creation of allied states in both regions. It made an unsuccessful attempt to establish a presence in the Congo, but in recent years has been more successful in establishing itself peripherally on the African horn. It has successfully maintained a presence in South Asia and Southeast Asia, where its rivalry is increasingly with China, rather than the United States. The Soviet Union has supplemented its military prowess with diplomatic initiatives, economic assistance programs, and political support of selected states in an endeavor to shift its international influence from a military foundation to a more durable foundation of prestige.

The Soviet role as a global power is further enhanced by being the leader of an ideological-military coalition (institutionalized as the Warsaw Treaty Organization) that reigns supreme in its own region, Eastern Europe, in which it tolerates no external intrusion. Beginning in 1971, the United States and West Germany through a series of treaties have informally recognized Eastern Europe as a Soviet sphere of influence. The simultaneous immunity of the Soviet regional sphere from external intervention and the formalization of an exclusive Soviet right to intervene in Eastern Europe was consecrated in the enunciation of the so-called "Brezhnev" or "Socialist Commonwealth Doctrine" in 1968 after the military intervention and occupation of Czechoslovakia by the military forces of the Soviet Union, Poland, East Germany, Hungary, and Bulgaria.

Before the advent of the Soviet state there existed the Communist (Bolshevik) Party. It inspired and created the Soviet state in response to the values of its ideology, Marxism-Leninism. One of its important goals was to facilitate and encourage the communization of the world, allegedly in consonance with the imperatives of inexorable historical laws of development. Originally, the Soviet state was conceived as an instrument of the Party in its mission of communizing the world. The Soviet socialist order, the world Communist movement, and the Communist interstate subsystem were creations of the Soviet Union in its capacity as a revolutionary party in furtherance of this aim. Thus, the Party fashioned the very environments within which it functions, but the feedback effects of these creations have in turn influenced the changing roles and functions of the Party.

In its capacity as a revolutionary Party, the Soviet Union performs the following roles and functions as: (1) the ideological guardian of the existing Soviet sociopolitical order (socialist society) and the initiator and architect of its future development (Communist society); (2) the ideological and organizational leader of the ruling Communist Parties and (3) the ideological leader and source of inspirational and material support of the world Communist movement, made up of both ruling and nonruling Communist Parties. As a Party, the Soviet Union functions in the three environments of the Soviet sociopolitical order, the Communist interstate subsystem, and the world Communist movement.

In recent decades, the prominence of the Party has waned as that of the Soviet Union as a state has waxed. Since Stalin's death in 1953, the Soviet grip on the interstate subsystem and the world Communist movement has loosened. China has emerged as a rival of the Soviet Union in Communist environments as well as the general interstate system, while the East European states have achieved degrees of autonomy in domestic affairs (within parameters decreed by the Soviet Union). Under Khrushchev, Moscow unilaterally renounced its position as the leader of the world Communist movement, fragmented and divided since 1960, although the Soviet Union simply retrograded itself to be the leader of a truncated movement, of which China and Albania and a number of other parties are not formal members. While China is not the leader of a rival world Communist movement, it remains a rival of the Soviet Union within the world of communist states and parties.

The history of the relationship between the Party and state is a prerequisite to understanding Soviet behavior in world affairs. There has always existed a rivalry between the two, not only because their functions overlapped and were contradictory, but also because each identity had a tendency to inspire, attract, and respond to different internal and external constituencies and clients. Over the years the state identity has gained at the expense of the Party, largely because it is capable of appealing more effectively to the interests and demands of a larger constellation of constituencies than can the Party. Tension between the two identities in international affairs has been a chronic problem during the existence of the Soviet system. The Party was assigned the mission of subverting and transforming the international environment in which the state functioned in preparation for the disestablishment of the state as a distinct entity (the "withering away" of the state). But the Soviet state has adapted to the interstate system. It has developed a separate vested stake in its own perpetuation distinct from that of the Party; it has given rise to bureaucracies and structures whose interests and power are linked with the destiny of the state. Since 1956, the Soviet state has integrated itself into the international system as one of the two major global powers. This has served to intensify its stake in supporting the system. The mission of world Communism, vested in the Party, tends to undermine not only the interstate system, but to seriously complicate the role and effectiveness of the Soviet Union as a global power. With the emergence of Communist China, the Soviet stake in world Communism has been undermined while its role as a global power continues to grow in importance.

As a result of these changing relationships, the goals of the state and Party, as well as the intentions of Soviet leaders, have become increasingly differentiated as the two identities inspire the formation of factional differences and alignments. Furthermore, since the raison d'etre of the Party is to bring about World Communism, presumably in response to the dictates of history, its legitimacy lies in the fulfillment of this goal, rather than serving the needs of domestic constituencies. For this reason the Party responds to the needs of external constituencies (foreign Communist parties). The Party is a selective and restrictive organization whose membership includes only 10 percent of the adult population. Its principal domestic constituency is thus the Party membership, or perhaps more precisely, the coterie of permanent Party officials and functionaries called the

Party Apparatus, composed of some 250–300-thousand officials. The State, on the other hand, is a universal entity; the entire population is affiliated and identified with it in their capacity as *citizens*, 90 percent of whom are not Party members. They are inclined to perceive the State as the repository of their interests and the conduit for their demands and grievances.

In addition to these two major identities of the Soviet Union in international affairs, a brief word is in order with respect to the remaining three identities. The one conspicuous identity which has contributed to the confusion about Soviet foreign policy is its identity as a Russian national state. As the historical and juridical successor to the Russian imperial state, the Soviet Union functions as the heir and custodian of the interests of the Russian nation, the largest nation in the USSR (52 percent of the population), and a nation which has been an imperial and traditionally ruling nation. In this capacity, the Soviet Union fulfills the role of preserving and extending the values, goals, and interests of historic Russia. The Soviet Union includes within its domain the entire Great Russian nation and is territorially and demographically indistinguishable from the Russian Empire that preceded it as a Russian national state. Its constituency is thus the entire Great Russian Nation. In this role, the Soviet State manipulates patriotic symbols, commemorates national glories, venerates historic heroes (mostly Tsars and generals), worships at national shrines, extols Russian culture and language, and celebrates the lofty goals and achievements of Holy Mother Russia while rationalizing and downplaying the more negative features of the Russian tradition.

The Soviet State has registered high marks in its role as a Russian state under Soviet rule. Traditional Russian values and aspirations have not only been fulfilled in large part, but even more importantly, have been assimilated into Marxist ideology, "internationalized" and advanced in the name of Communism. In this way, Russian cultural norms have been "universalized" as Soviet norms and have been adopted, assimilated by, and imposed upon the non-Russian nationalities, who make up 48 percent of the population, not in the name of "russification," but under the banner of "progress."

The institutionalization of the Russian identity of the Soviet State is manifested most emphatically by the Russian language, which is not only the *lingua franca* of Soviet society, but the official language of state, diplomacy, and military command. Although the Soviet Union remains a multinational state, the Russian character of the state is unmistakable. Thus, the Russian share of membership in the Communist party has ranged as high as 75 percent (1926) to about 62 percent during the past decade, while the leadership of the Party and State institutions have remained overwhelmingly Russian in composition. The upper echelons of the armed forces are a monopoly of Russians and Russianized Ukrainians and Byelorussians, while the Foreign Ministry and diplomatic service are also virtually monopolized by Russians. Furthermore, ethnic Russians serve as high party, government, economic, and secret police officials in all of the non-Russian republics.

For all of these reasons, some observers have always maintained that the essential key to understanding the behavior of the Soviet Union lies in perceiving its basic identity as Russia, pursuing the traditional "national interests" of Russia, rather than its identity as an agent of world revolution or as the embodiment of a multinational state.

The powerful role of the Soviet Union as a Russian national state, however, should not be interpreted as meaning that the USSR does not play a meaningful role in its representation of the interests of the non-Russian nationalities. The Soviet Union is an authentic multinational state. It is the state embodiment of more than a dozen major nations and scores of smaller ones who have no role in the international community other than their representation through the Soviet State. Two major Soviet Union Republics, the Ukraine and Byelorussia, have partial separate representation in the interstate system as members of the United Nations and affiliated agencies, but the remaining Soviet nations are bereft of such recognition.

Under international law the Soviet Union is recognized as a single composite (plural, multiple) state entity in its capacity as a Union State. At the same time, however, two of its constituent republics, the Ukraine and Byelorussia, enjoy partial recognition under international law as members of the United Nations and other international and multilateral bodies and associations. The thirteen remaining Union Republics are equally endowed constitutionally with potential separate recognition, entitling them to act in the international community while remaining a part of the Union and retaining their representation as well.

As a composite juridically plural state, the Soviet Union consists of fifteen Union Republics and twenty Autonomous Republics, all of which are considered by Soviet jurists to be endowed with some form of state existence or sovereignty, although only the Union Republics are endowed with the legal capacity to secede from the Union, raise armies, contract treaties, and engage in diplomatic relations with the outside world (i.e., they are juridically invested with all the trappings of an actor in the interstate system). In addition to the Union and Autonomous Republics, eight Autonomous Oblasts and ten National Okrugs are endowed with lesser juridical powers. Although most of these powers remain "fictional," they retain powerful symbolic force and the various Soviet nations jealously guard whatever symbols of statehood they are allowed to enjoy.

The last identity of the Soviet Union is its manifestation as a unified aggregate of nations—its multinational commonwealth identity. In this capacity it represents the distilled and consensual interests of all its member nations and their permanent commitment to each other as parts of a juridical polyethnic entity. The multinational commonwealth identity is a residue of the original Soviet pretense that the USSR was the embryo or nucleus of a future universal federation of Communist nations.

## ANALYZING SOVIET FOREIGN POLICY BEHAVIOR

Irrespective of its identities, Soviet foreign policy is simultaneously reactive and initiatory, defensive and aggressive (i.e., responsive to both threats and opportunities), attentive to and shaped by both domestic and external constituencies, animated by both self-interest and ideology, and shaped by capabilities, risk perceptions, and cost/benefit calculations. The spectrum of variables and factors that constitute inputs into Soviet political behavior are enormous. Their complex relationships to one another are further complicated by the identities of the Soviet Union and its multiple environments. Identities and environments must thus be correlated not only with constituencies, but also with the variables and constants that contribute to Soviet political behavior and whose significance has varied so enormously.

Bearing this in mind, the conditioning factors can be summarized and categorized into five groups of variables:

1. *Motivations/Purposes:* These are subjective preferences defined in terms of ideology, goals, values, norms, interests, and belief-systems, organized into a dynamically related scheme of priorities, and formulated in terms of demands upon the outside world.
2. *Capabilities/Power:* These variables are subject to precise measurement if access to the data and information is possible, and include the means, instruments, institutions, structures, and resources whereby demands upon the outside world are asserted, activated, or realized.
3. *Risks:* The risk variables are defined in terms of three interrelated, perceived calculations of chance involved in the initiation of a voluntary action (demand, threat, lack of response), whose outcome is uncertain, but whose consequences can be harmful: (a) chance of success, (b) chance of harm, and (c) chance in the magnitude or level of harm.

4. *Costs/Benefits:* These represent perceptions of calculated or anticipated costs measured against perceptions of anticipated or certain benefits under three sets of circumstances: (a) if voluntary action is initiated to press or realize demands, (b) if responses are made to events or conditions taking place in the external environment, and (c) no action or response is taken.
5. *Opportunities:* These variables are perceived situations where optimal intersection of demands, capabilities, risk and cost variables occur.

These groups of variables are in constant dynamic interaction with each other and can be broken down into more discrete categories and individual factors, most of them qualitative and judgmental.[2]

The individual variables within the five groups or categories of variables are of two types: (1) voluntaristic (i.e., normative, volitional, subjective), and (2) deterministic (i.e., nonvolitional, objective). Voluntaristic variables are those whose weight and effect can be directly varied by human will. Deterministic variables are those whose effects and weight are independent of direct human will, but whose relative impact may vary because of conscious changes in the dimensions and value of the voluntaristic variables. For example, geographical location is not subject to significant change through human action, but the relative value of geography in contributing to Soviet behavior in foreign policy has been fundamentally altered by the advent of nuclear missile capabilities developed by human

[2]For a more detailed exposition of this framework, cf. Vernon V. Aspaturian, *Process and Power in Soviet Foreign Policy* (Boston: Little, Brown, 1971), pp. 56–83.

technology. Similarly, a state's natural resources may be fixed and finite, but its weight as a factor varies with the human ingenuity, effort, and will invested in their development.

Some variables betray both voluntaristic and deterministic characteristics. Political culture, including national character, for example, is the cumulative product of human volition and changes slowly. Nevertheless, it is essentially deterministic since desision makers cannot readily alter national character, nor easily shed its conditioning effects. In many instances, the deterministic or voluntaristic quality is a dominant rather than exclusive characteristic, but the transformational direction of change is generally for voluntaristic variables to assume deterministic characteristics. Religion and ideology, initially voluntaristic, tend to take on deterministic attributes as they are progressively assimilated into the political culture.

As pointed out earlier, Soviet mc tives have often been misrepresented; one must resist the temptation to readily equate intentions with foreign policy. The predisposition of scholars to construct a framework that can predict Soviet foreign policy stems largely from the fact that basic Soviet intentions are constantly expressed in speeches, documents, pronouncements, resolutions, books, laws, and articles. While all of this may constitute foreign policy inputs, it is not Soviet foreign policy.

The assumption that Soviet speeches and other published output are significant sources for clues to current or future intent is true in a limited sense. But Soviet speeches and writings are not exclusively concerned with intent, since they serve many purposes, only one of which is to reveal (deliberately or inadvertently) intent in foreign policy. There is the important time dimension to be considered as well: the relationship between *words* and *policy* varies from time to time, depending on the nature of the factional balance or conflict within the leadership itself. Since Stalin's death, the Soviet elite has been in a state of chronic factional conflict with the eruption of acute crises at periodic intervals, resulting in shifts, realignments, dismissals, promotions, and rotations of personalities. Hence, the relationship between words and policy has become considerably more complicated as compared to the Stalinist years, since statements contain not only possible intent, but conflicting possible policies. In other words, Soviet published output now communicates not only intent, but also controversy, debate, and dissent about future policy.

All published works by Soviet civilian and military leaders can be viewed as possible sources of information concerning current and future intentions. But whose intentions? Under Stalin, policy formulation and decision making were tightly centralized. Under his successors, the continuing struggle for power has resulted in the fragmentation of the decision-making structure, distributing power among individuals and factions, each influential in parallel institutional power structures. Ideological orthodoxy has been divorced from personalities and policy formulation. Policy formulation in turn has been frequently out of phase with the administration and execution of policy as rival factions assumed control over policy-making bodies. Personalities, factions, and eventually sociofunctional and socioinstitutional groupings assumed a more variable role in the shaping of Soviet behavior, and a new fluid relationship was established in the decision-making process.

It is no simple matter to elicit future intentions from Soviet words, uttered or printed. Three general observations should be stated at the outset: (1) long range intentions have always been more clearly discernible than short range, although even in this realm, as the Sino-Soviet conflict illustrates, long range Soviet intentions are by no means clearly charted and are constantly subjected to corrosive influences; (2) the more distant and remote in time a statement of policy intent, the more unified the outlook of the Soviet leadership is likely to be; and (3) debate and controversy over long range strategy are most likely to be explicitly echoed by contrasting statements and pronouncements issued by foreign Communist parties, most notably those of Communist China.

Thus, while Soviet words are not always statements of intention, they are vehicles of communication, often serving contradictory purposes. Soviet words may represent (1) propaganda, (2) deception, (3) concealment of actual intent, (4) rationalization or legitimization of actions and policies, (5) and internal controversy. Analyzing Soviet intentions on the basis of documents, speeches, and ideological statements give undue weight to "rational" factors, since the irrational, accidental, and fortuitous factors can hardly be divined from verbal sources. On the other hand, calculating Soviet motives on the basis of capabilities or past responses and patterns of behavior can also result in faulty and erroneous extrapolations and projections, since signifi-cant and crucial acts can depart from past behavioral patterns.

Estimates of the "human equation" in Soviet behavior, whether derived from personal observation, or biographical or psychoanalytical studies of the Soviet leadership, are essentially subjective; they originate with observers who are free from neither ignorance, prejudice (cultural or individual), nor gullibility. Any attempt to distill the essence of Soviet intentions solely from personality considerations is also likely to be seriously deficient. A sound analysis of Soviet intentions must take into consideration words, conduct, and personalities, not as independent articles, but as basic variables whose relative significance is in constant flux. Past experience has shown that predicting Soviet foreign policy on the basis of capabilities can be as unreliable as predicting it purely on the basis of stated intentions. As their capabilities have expanded, Soviet leaders have reevaluated original goals in the light of risks and possible returns. Furthermore, growing capabilities in a context of factional differences have created new options, giving rise to new perceptions of risks, interest, and priorities with the consequent erosion of commitment to earlier goals.

In recent years, the growth in Soviet capabilities, instead of intensifying commitment to ideological goals like "world Communism," has contributed to the erosion of such commitments and to redirection towards other purposes, more limited and traditional. Soviet commitment to ideological goals thus has been attenuated, not only because of factional conflict, but also because the commitment is now more widely diffused among the purposes generated by its five identities. It becomes increasingly difficult for the Soviet leaders to sacrifice the interests of one identity for another. Since intense commitment to ideological interests (party identity) seriously undercuts the interests of the other identities and their constituencies, they become increasingly reluctant to pursue it.

In analyzing Soviet foreign policy, the relevant variables from these five sets must be viewed in dynamic interaction with each other. Serious changes in one gross variable can alter the relevance of the others, which may then recombine to feed back, again altering the initial variable. Originally it was envisaged by the Soviet leadership that since the normative goals of its ideology were constant and absolute truths, their realization would be maximized by the development of Soviet resources. Theoretically, as Soviet capabilities grew, ideological goals would be progressively transformed into policy goals. But as capabilities developed, other variables were seriously affected. The risks of converting ideological purposes into policy goals appeared to grow even faster than Soviet resources. For as Soviet power grew, other powers revised their estimates of Soviet intent, assigned greater seriousness to ideological purposes, and reacted in a defensive or hostile manner. The rise of Hitler was largely attributable to the growing capabilities of the Soviet Union, which served to impart greater credibility to Soviet ideological intentions and to the "Bolshevik danger."

With the advent of nuclear weapons the risks of a forward ideological policy were sharply increased and assumed a different character. The development of thermonuclear weapons and the advent of missile delivery systems qualitatively transformed the risk and cost variables. The more powerful the Soviet Union became in terms of advanced weaponry, the riskier and more costly became its serious commitment to a policy of advancing world Communism. As a consequence, the commitment to ideological goals was seriously eroded and the Soviet leaders searched for new capabilities without running grave risks or involving potentially suicidal costs. This meant shifting away from serving the interests of external constituencies (ruling and nonruling Communist parties, particularly China), as the Soviet leadership under Khrushchev directed greater attention to serving domestic Soviet constituencies.

Technological advances in weapons systems or other factors that might seriously alter the existing strategic balance between the United States and the Soviet Union can also feed back to alter the equilibrium among the variables determining Soviet foreign policy. Just as the relative weight of ideology as a motivating factor diminished as risks multiplied and increased, a substantial reduction in the risk variable and/or potential costs could trigger a rise in the relative weight of the ideological factor. If this happens, the stage could be set for a rearrangement of the variables mix in the calculation of Soviet foreign policy.

## CONTINUITY AND CHANGE IN RUSSIAN FOREIGN POLICY

In order to draw a proper appraisal of Soviet diplomacy, the voluntaristic aspects of Soviet foreign policy must always be measured against its power to overcome the deterministic impediments of international reality. Thus, although the Soviet Union can plan the calculated growth of the economic and military foundations of its power, it cannot "plan" foreign policy. This fact was eloquently stated by Maxim Litvinov to the Central Executive Committee in 1929:

Unlike other Commissariats, the Commissariat for Foreign Affairs cannot, unfortunately, put forward a five-year plan of work, a plan for the development of foreign policy. . . . In . . . drawing up the plan of economic development, we start from our own aspirations and wishes, from a calculation of our own potentialities, and from the firm principles of our entire policy, but in examining the development of foreign policy we have to deal with a number of factors that are scarcely subject to calculation, with a number of elements outside our control and the scope of our action. International affairs are composed not only of our own aspirations and actions, but of those of a large number of countries . . . pursuing other aims than ours, and using other means to achieve those aims than we allow.[3]

The balance between the voluntaristic and deterministic components of Soviet foreign policy is neither fixed nor stable, but is in a state of continual and deliberate flux. In the initial stages of the Bolshevik Republic, its foreign policy was virtually at the mercy of external forces over which it could exercise little control, and Soviet diplomacy assumed the characteristic contours of a weak power struggling for survival under onerous conditions. As its economic and military position improved, it gradually assumed the characteristics of a great power and, given its geographical and cultural context, it took on the distinctive features of its tsarist predecessors and the impulse to subjugate its immediate neighbors.

## The Geographic and Historical Inheritance

"Marxism," wrote a more recent Soviet specialist on diplomacy, "teaches that economic factors determine the foreign policy and diplomacy of a state only in the long run, and that politics and diplomacy are, in a certain sense, conditioned by the concrete historical period and by many other elements (not excluding even, for instance, the geographical situation of a given country)."[4] Although Soviet writers may still tend to agree with the observation of the hapless Karl Radek that "it is silly to say that geography plays the part of fate, that it determines the foreign policy of a state,"[5] geography is nonetheless the most permanent conditioning factor in a country's foreign policy; for location, topography, and natural resources are significant—and often decisive—determinants of a country's economic and military power. Geography's effects, however, are relative, rarely absolute, always dependent upon the more variable factors in a country's character, such as its cultural traditions, political institutions, the size and diversity of its

[3] *Protokoly Zasedani Tsentralnovo Ispolnitelnovo Komiteta Sovetov,* Bulletin 14 (Moscow, 1930), p. 1.

[4] F. I. Kozhevnikov, "Engels on Nineteenth Century Russian Diplomacy," *Sovetskoye Gosudarstvo i Pravo,* December, 1950, no. 12, pp. 18–34.

[5] "The Bases of Soviet Foreign Policy," in *The Foreign Affairs Reader,* ed. M. F. Armstrong (New York: Harper & Row, 1947), p. 173.

population, the exploitation of its natural resources, and the skill of its statesmen. A country's geography, with rare exceptions, cannot be remade; it can only be utilized more effectively. Although Radek's contention that "the questions raised by geography are dealt with by each social formation in its own way . . . determined by its peculiar economic and political aims" remains incontestable, it was the blessing of providence that this vast empire secreted all the basic ingredients for the erection of a powerful industrial and military state, given the necessary will and determination of its leadership. Had Russia been a wasteland with limited raw materials, she would have been doomed to be permanently a preindustrial society. The character of her foreign policy—her very existence—would have been vastly different, and her vaunted ideology would have long been relegated to the ash cans of history.

The Soviet Union, like tsarist Russia before it, is the largest single continuous intercontinental empire in the world. Embracing fully half of two continents, the Soviet Union has the world's longest and most exposed frontier, which is at once both its greatest potential hazard and one of its prime assets in international politics. As a part of both Europe and Asia, and embracing more than 150 ethnic and linguistic groups ranging from the most sophisticated nations to the most primitive, the USSR achieves a unique microcosmic character denied any other country, including the United States with its ethnically variegated but linguistically assimilated population. Russia's serpentine frontier is both a consequence of the indefensibility of the central Russian plain and, at the same time, an important condition-

ing factor in the further evolution and execution of its foreign policy. For a weak Russia, such a frontier affords maximum exposure to attack, but for a powerful Russian state, this extended frontier, bordering on nearly a dozen states, offers an enviable and limitless choice for the exertion of diplomatic pressure. Since 1939, the Soviet Union has annexed four of its former neighbors, seized territory from seven more, and has made territorial demands upon two others; most of this territory was previously lost by a weakened Russia. Of all her bordering states, only Afghanistan has not been imposed on to cede territory to the Soviet Union.

In the past, Russia's geographical position has exposed her to continuous depredations and subjugation from all directions—an inevitable consequence of political disunity in a geographically indefensible community. But if geography simplified the conquest of a divided Russia, it also facilitated the expansion of a united and powerful Russian state, which pushed out in all directions until it was arrested by superior force.

In the absence of more obvious geographical obstacles to her enemies, Russia's physical security became irrevocably attached to land space, while her psychological security became inseparable from political centralization. This conviction was confirmed by Stalin, himself, on the occasion of Moscow's 800th anniversary in 1947:

Moscow's service consists first and foremost in the fact that it became the foundation for the unification of a disunited Russia into a single state with a single government, a single leadership. No country in the world that has not been able to free itself of feudal disunity and wrangling among princes can hope to preserve its independence or score substantial economic and cultural progress. Only a country united in a single centralized state can count on being able to make substantial cultural-economic progress and assert its independence.[6]

It is a persisting fact of Russian history that this dual quest for physical and psychological security has produced in Russian foreign policy a unique pattern. A divided Russia invites attack, but a united Russia stimulates expansion in all directions. The revolutions in 1917, and the terrible purges of the 1930s when Stalin undertook to enforce unity at home, exposed Russia's internal schisms to the world and stimulated foreign intervention. In each crisis, after surviving the initial assault from without, she embarked on a campaign designed to carry her beyond her self-declared national frontiers. The campaign failed in 1921, but she succeeded after World War II, bringing all of Eastern Europe under her hegemony.

The Bolsheviks fell heir not only to Russia's geography and natural resources, but also to the bulk of her population, her language, and the Russian historical and cultural legacy. Marxism gave Russia new goals and aspirations, but once the decision was taken to survive as a national state, even on a temporary and instrumental basis, the Soviet Union could not evade assuming the contours of a Russian state and falling heir to the assets and liabilities of its predecessors. Although Lenin thought that he had irrevocably severed the umbilical cord with Russia's

past, it was not entirely within his power to unburden the new Soviet Republic of the disadvantages of tsarist diplomacy. Foreign attitudes remained remarkably constant; fears and suspicions, sympathies and attachments were reinforced more than erased. Designs on Soviet territory still came from the same quarter, exposure to attack remained in the same places, and the economic and commercial lifelines of the tsars became no less indispensable to the new regime. In short, even if the Soviet Union refused to remain Russia, Japan remained Japan, Poland remained Poland, and the Straits remained the Straits. Moscow eagerly laid claim to all the advantages of historic Russia, and the outside world just as assiduously refused to permit her to evade the liabilities and vulnerabilities of the Russian past. Thus, partly by choice and partly by necessity, the foreign policy of the Soviet Union could not but assume some of the contours of its predecessors.

The impact of a voluntaristic doctrine like Marxism on the geographical facts of Russia and her messianic traditions not only reinforced the psychological obsession for security, but provided an ideological rationale for assuming the implacable hostility of the outside world and sanctified Russian expansion with the ethical mission of liberating the downtrodden masses of the world from their oppressors. The hostile West of the Slavophils became the hostility of capitalism and imperialism; instead of the parochial messianism of the pan-Slav enthusiasts, Marxism provided Russia with a mission of universal transcendence—transforming the outside world into her own image, in fulfillment of her historic destiny and as the only per-

---

[6] *Pravda*, September 11, 1947.

manent guarantee of absolute security. Up until the Twentieth Party Congress in 1956, the Leninist-Stalinist thesis that "the destruction of capitalist encirclement and the destruction of the danger of capitalist intervention are possible only as a result of the victory of the proletarian revolution, at least in several large countries,"[7] continued to be in force. Although "capitalist encirclement" was declared ended by Stalin's successors, the 1956 events in Poland and Hungary and the 1968 events in Czechoslovakia may have convinced some of the leaders in the Kremlin that this proclamation was premature.

To assume, however, that Soviet foreign policy is merely Russian imperialism in new garb would be a catastrophic mistake on both sides. Soviet foreign policy was bound to assume "Russian" characteristics during one phase of its metamorphosis, but now that the maximum, but still limited, aims of tsarist imperialism have been virtually consummated, the militant (no longer necessarily expansionist) aspects of its foreign policy will assume a purely Marxist character, while only the defensive aspects (i.e., the preservation of its present power position) of its diplomacy will retain distinctively "Russian" features. That these two aspects of current Soviet foreign policy are in flagrant contradiction is self-evident, even to the Kremlin and other communist leaders. Chinese accusations of "great-power chauvinism," the de-Stalinization campaign, the uprisings in Poland and Hungary, and the 1968 occupation of Czechoslovakia are all manifestations of this fundamental schism in Soviet foreign policy.

[7] *Kommunist,* January, 1953, no. 2, p. 15.

Whereas in the past, when the Soviet Union was weak, indiscriminate emphasis on the revolutionary aspects of its foreign policy tended to undermine its basic instinct to survive, now, its defensive reflexes tend to subvert not only its continuing leadership of world communism, but the eventual success of the movement itself.

### World Revolution and National Interest in Soviet Diplomacy: Prologue

Deciphering Soviet motives is an elusive and hazardous undertaking, yet it must be done systematically and with calculation, otherwise ad hoc and unconscious assumptions acquire priority by default. Miscalculation of motives can often be catastrophic, since foreign policy expectations are built upon assumptions concerning the motives and capabilities of other powers, and diplomatic success or failure often depends on the degree of accuracy with which these assumptions approach actuality. Much of the agony of postwar Western diplomacy can be traced directly to illusory expectations resulting from false calculations of Soviet motives by Western leaders. Diplomacy, however, is not an intellectual exercise, and motives are not always susceptible to rational and logical analysis. In any event, assessment of motives is rarely certain and in most cases calls not only for acute analytical intelligence, but also for espionage and, above all, for the intuitive wisdom of long experience in statecraft.

Information concerning Soviet motives is derived from three principal sources: word, conduct, and personal contact with the Soviet leadership. In general, whenever there exists a discrepancy between publicly stated intention and conduct, the latter is a more reliable indicator of motives on a short-run basis. Actually, there are three possible relations between speech and practice in Soviet diplomacy: (1) *identity;* (2) *approximation,* usually implying a temporary accommodation or modification of a preconceived intention, unless the latter itself receives explicit reformation; and (3) *divergence.* Cleavages between word and conduct may, in turn, result from faulty execution, misinformation, miscalculation, or deliberate confusion.

One question that inevitably arises is whether Soviet policy is actually motivated by ideological ends, such as world revolution, or by some other more mundane consideration, such as "power" or "national interest." Soviet ideology itself defines *national interest, power,* and *world revolution* in such a way as to make them virtually as indistinguishable and inseparable as the three sides of an equilateral triangle. The transcendental goal of Soviet foreign policy —world revolution—was defined by Lenin even before the existence of the Soviet state, when he declared in 1915 that "the victorious proletariat of [one] country . . . would stand up against . . . the capitalist world, . . . raising revolts in those countries against the capitalists, and in the event of necessity coming out even with armed force against the exploiting classes and their states."[8] "The fundamental question of revolution is the question of power," wrote Stalin, quoting Lenin, and he went on ·to say that, as the effectiveness of the Soviet Union as an instrument of world revolution is measured in terms of power, "the whole point is to retain power to consolidate it, to

make it invincible."[9] As a contrived and temporary nation-state, the Soviet Union assumed particular interests, but "the USSR has no interests at variance with the interests of the world revolution, and the international proletariat naturally has no interests that are at variance with the Soviet Union."[10] Stalin's final fusion was to identify the consolidation and extension of his own power with the interests of the world revolution.

The abstraction of a Soviet national interest outside the context of Soviet ideology, no matter how superficially attractive it may appear to be as a useful analytical tool, ruptures the image of Soviet reality and results in the calculation of Soviet foreign policy on the basis of false assumptions. Soviet foreign policy is based on the image of reality provided by the Marxist-Leninist ideological prism. Whether this image be faulty or not is totally irrelevant in the calculation of Soviet motives, although such a foreign policy will eventually reap its toll in diplomatic failure. The Soviet conception of "interest" cannot be separated from class categories, and its determination is essentially horizontal rather than vertical. Although the legal expression of class interests is temporarily articulated through the nation-state and assumes the character of a "national interest," nonetheless in the Soviet view there exist within each state not one but several parallel "national interests," corresponding to its socioeconomic development. The "national interest" reflected by the state in its diplomacy, however, can only represent

[8]V. I. Lenin, *Selected Works* (New York: International Publishers Co., n.d.), 5:141.

[9]J. V. Stalin, *Problems of Leninism* (Moscow: Universal Distributors, 1947), p. 39.

[10]W. K. Knorin, *Fascism, Social-Democracy and the Communists* (Moscow, 1933).

the interests of the "ruling class," and no other, regardless of its pretensions.

Marxism tenaciously holds to the view that the community of interests that binds identical classes of different nations is more fundamental and decisive than that which binds different classes within the same nation-state. Although division and disunity are inherently characteristic of the bourgeois classes of different states, whose conflicts of interest are periodically expressed in war, the interests of all proletarians (together with their peasant and colonial allies) are considered to be in total harmony, their basic identity being temporarily obscured by artificially stimulated national distinctions.

Given the premise of the total identity of interests on a class basis, the Soviet Union, as the only avowed proletarian state in existence and the self-proclaimed embryo of a universal proletarian state, pronounced its interests to be identical with those of the world proletariat:

The Communist Party of the Soviet Union has always proceeded from the fact that "national" and international problems of the proletariat of the USSR amalgamate into one general problem of liberating the proletarians of all countries from capitalism, and the interests . . . in our country wholly and fully amalgamate with the interests of the revolutionary movement of all countries into one general interest of the victory of socialist revolution in all countries.[11]

Although this view is vigorously contested, is far from universally recognized, and does not correspond to actual facts, it nevertheless remains as a residual basis for diplomatic action or analysis.

[11] *Kommunist*, January, 1953, no. 2, p. 15.

The presence of one of two factors, both capable of objective verification, is sufficient to impart to the national interests of a particular state an authentic international quality. These factors are (1) the creation of appropriate forms of political organization designed to articulate the national interests of one state as those of the world at large; and (2) mass recognition in other countries that the national interests of a foreign state are identical with a higher transcendental interest. Not one but both of these desiderata have characterized Soviet foreign policy. It was a cardinal aim to replace the nation-state system with a world communist state by shifting allegiance and loyalty from the nation-state to class. This not only invited the nationals of other countries to recognize a higher class loyalty to the Soviet Union, but meant active engagement in fostering the appropriate political institutions, such as the Comintern, foreign communist parties, front organizations, and the like, to implement this fusion.

The Soviet invitation to commit mass disloyalty has elicited wide response in the past. The formula identifying Soviet interests with the interests of the world proletariat had been accepted by millions of communists throughout the world as a basis for political action. This gave to Soviet national interests an undeniable transcendental quality denied to the national interests of any other state except China. No matter how persistently a state may claim to be motivated by the interests of all mankind, if such a claim is accompanied neither by a serious effort at implementation nor evokes a response in other countries, it remains an empty and pious pretension.

Transcendental ethical ends in foreign policy, irrespective of their substantive nature, have relevance only if they function as effective instruments or stimulants for the limitation, preservation, or further accumulation of power, or as instruments for its focalization. Otherwise they are meaningless slogans and utopias, devoid of anything but peripheral significance in the calculation of a country's foreign policy. Expansionism is thus inherent in the Leninist-Stalinist ideology, since the Soviet state was conceived as an ideological state without fixed geographical frontiers. Not only did this idea of the Soviet Union as the nucleus of a universal communist state receive expression in the basic documents of the Comintern,[12] but the Soviet constitution of 1924 proclaimed the new union to be open to all future Soviet republics and a "decisive step towards the union of workers of all countries into one World Socialist Soviet Republic."[13] And at Lenin's bier, Stalin vowed "to consolidate and extend the Union of Republics."[14]

Stalin's attempt to preserve the dominant and privileged status of the Soviet proletariat in the postwar communist fraternity of nations resulted in a specific form of Soviet imperialism that brought about Tito's defection and unleashed corrosive forces within the orbit as a whole. The subsequent failure of Khrushchev and Mao Tse-tung to reconcile their divergent national interests may have produced an irreparable schism in the movement as a whole. The failure of Stalin and his successors to calculate accurately the persistence and vitality of the community of interests based on national peculiarities is actually a reflection of the inadequacy of Marxist categories to deal with the conflicting interests of national communities, whether they be communist or bourgeois.

Paradoxically, as long as the Soviet Union was the only communist state, its universalistic pretensions were unchallenged by foreign communist parties. But with the eclipse of the Soviet monopoly of the interests of the world proletariat, occasioned by the emergence of a Communist China and national communism in Eastern Europe, the universalistic pretensions of the Leninist doctrine have been blunted, while, at the same time, stimulating a more limited "regional interest" aimed at synthesizing the various national interests of the communist orbit. The transmutation of several national interests into a single supranational interest remains an insuperable difficulty in the communist world, so long as the incompatibility of individual communist national interests, which the Marxist dogma fails to perceive accurately, prevails:

---

[12]See W. H. Chamberlin, ed., *Blueprint for World Conquest* (Chicago: Human Events, 1946).

[13]Full text in M. W. Graham, *New Governments of Eastern Europe* (New York: Holt, Rinehart & Winston, 1927), p. 608.

[14]*History of the Communist Party of the Soviet Union* (New York: International Publishers Co., 1939), p. 269.

Marxism-Leninism has always strongly advocated that proletarian internationalism be combined with patriotism. . . . The Communist Parties of all countries must . . . become the spokesmen of the legitimate national interests and sentiments of their people [and] . . . effectively educate the masses in the spirit of internationalism and harmonize the national sentiments and interests of these countries.[15]

Less than seven years after this statement, however, it had become quite clear that "the spirit of internationalism" could not prevail over the conflicting and incompatible national interests of the two great communist powers, each with its own national goals, aspirations, and image of the outside world. In 1963, Moscow denounced with eloquence the very vice which she had hitherto practiced with such consummate skill:

The statements of the Chinese leaders reveal a growing tendency to speak on behalf of the peoples of practically the whole world, including the Soviet people, the peoples of other socialist countries, and also the young national states of Asia, Africa, and Latin America. "Yet, who has given the Chinese leaders the right," the Soviet people inquire with indignation, "to decide for us, for the Soviet government, for the communist party, what is in keeping, and what is not in keeping with our interests? We have not given you the right and we do not intend to give it to you."[16]

With great reluctance, Soviet observers now concede that persisting national interests can prevail over a common ideological outlook in the behavior of states. One Soviet writer ruefully—almost pathetically—ruminates over the shattered theory that a common Marxist-Leninist ideology would eliminate conflicts of national interests between states:

Let us recall the state of theory before

the opening of the sixties. A formula of approximately this sort was set forth: All socialist states are of the same socioeconomic nature, they have the same type of political power, and the same ideology prevails in them; consequently, there should not and cannot be any disagreements or contradictions in the relations among the countries of socialism. The very fact of the establishment of socialist production relations in a number of countries was considered to be an adequate guarantee of good relations among them, a guarantee that national and international interests would somehow be harmonized.

But this became the reality:

Life has proved to be more complicated and contradictory than this formula. The actual practice of contact among the countries of socialism has shown that this homogeneity of socioeconomic, political, and ideological structures is a necessary but insufficient prerequisite for the real establishment of the principles of fraternity and cooperation, complete trust, and mutual understanding in the relations among socialist states.[17]

## SOVIET IDEOLOGY AND FOREIGN POLICY

The exact relationship between Soviet ideology and foreign policy has been subject to great controversy, ranging from the view that it is substantially irrelevant to the conviction that foreign policy is rigidly dictated by ideology. Actually, aside from providing the transcendental objectives of Soviet diplomacy, Soviet ideology performs five distinct, additional functions in foreign policy:

[15]Statement by the Chinese Communist Party, "Once More on the Historical Experience of the Dictatorship of the Proletariat." Full text in *Pravda*, December 31, 1956.

[16]Soviet government statement of August 21, 1963, *Pravda*, August 21, 1963.

[17]A. Bovin, "The International Principles of Socialism," *Izvestia*, September 21, 1966.

1. As a system of knowledge and as an analytical prism, it reflects an image of the existing social order and the distinctive analytical instruments (dialectical laws, and categories like the "class struggle," "historical stages," and so on) for its diagnosis and prognosis.
2. It provides an action strategy with which to accelerate the transformation of the existing social order into the communist millennium.
3. It serves as a system of communication, unifying and coordinating the activities of its adherents.
4. It functions as a system of higher rationalization to justify, obscure, or conceal the chasms that may develop between theory and practice.
5. It stands as a symbol of continuity and legitimacy.

This compartmentalization of Soviet ideology is frankly arbitrary, and actually ruptures its basic unity, which is not necessarily to be found in its logic or reason, but in the intuitive faith and active experience of its partisans—factors which often elude rational analysis. Elements of Soviet ideology that appear logically incompatible, in fact, are, but these rational contradictions can be unified only in the crucibles of revolutionary action, not in the intellectual processes of the mind. The true meaning of the Marxist-Leninist insistence on the "unity of theory and practice" is that contradictions cannot be resolved by logic, but by action, which is the final judge of "truth." Communist "truth" cannot be perceived without intuitive involvement—i.e., revolutionary action and experience.

## The Soviet Image of the World

The Soviet ideological prism reflects an image of the world that is virtually unrecognizable to a noncommunist, yet it is on this image that Soviet foreign policy is based. It reflects a world of incessant conflict and change, in which institutions, loyalties, and philosophies arise and decay in accordance with the convulsive rhythm of the dialectic, which implacably propels it on a predetermined arc to a foreordained future —world communism. This image is accepted as the real world by Soviet leaders. Their foreign policy rests upon the conviction that Marxism-Leninism is a scientific system that has uncovered and revealed the fundamental and implacable laws of social evolution, and, hence, that affords its adherents the unique advantage of prediction and partial control of events. This conviction has imparted to Soviet diplomacy an air of supreme confidence and dogmatic self-righteousness:

Soviet diplomacy . . . wields a weapon possessed by none of its rivals or opponents. Soviet diplomacy is fortified by a scientific theory of Marxism-Leninism. This doctrine lays down the unshakeable laws of social development. By revealing these norms, it gives the possibility not only of understanding the current tendencies of international life, but also of permitting the desirable collaboration with the march of events. Such are the special advantages held by Soviet diplomacy. They give it a special position in international life and explain its outstanding successes.[18]

The history of Soviet diplomacy, however, is by no means a uniform record of success, although "errors" in foreign policy are ascribed not to the doctrine, but to the improper apprehension and application of these infallible laws. Failure to apply these

[18]V. P. Potemkin, ed., *Istoriya Diplomatii* (Moscow, 1945), 3:763–64.

laws properly, according to the Soviet view, divorces foreign policy from international realities. Although it is true that "the record of Soviet diplomacy shows an inability to distinguish between the real and the imaginary, a series of false calculations about the capabilities and intentions of foreign countries, and a record of clumsy coordination between diplomacy and propaganda,"[19] still, Marxism-Leninism, on the whole, has furnished a system of analysis that gives a sufficiently accurate comprehension of power. The dogmatic reliance on techniques and methods that have proven successful under other conditions, the frequent refusal to jettison concepts that either have outlived their usefulness or consistently produce dismal results in terms of foreign policy aims, and the concentration of all decision-making authority in one man or in a tight oligarchy—these practices at times tend to convert Marxism-Leninism from a unique asset for Soviet diplomacy into a strait-jacket.

*The Dialectical Image of History.* Soviet ideology exposes the forces and tendencies operating in international politics, but it is up to the leadership to calculate these forces properly, seek out the most decisive trends, and coordinate Soviet diplomacy with the inexorable march of history. The success of Soviet diplomacy, according to the Soviet view, is maximized as it is attuned to the rhythm of the historical dialectic, and its failures are multiplied as it falls out of harmony. Conversely, the occasional successes of bourgeois diplomacy are due to fortuitous and haphazard coordination with historical development, or to the equally accidental deviation of Soviet foreign policy from the implacable dictates of history. These accidental deviations are attributed to faulty application of historical laws by individual leaders.

Without attempting any extended discussion of Soviet dialectics, it can be said that, in the communist view, history progressively exfoliates as a series of qualitative stages, each with its own peculiar economic organization of society, which gives rise to corresponding social, political, and religious institutions. This inexorable movement from lower to higher forms of economic and social organization is propelled by means of a dialectical duel between perpetually developing economic forces of society and the social and political institutions that attempt to preserve the economic order in the interests of a particular ruling class, whose servants they are. The class struggle, which is the principal motivating force of historical revolution, comes to an end only with the overthrow of the capitalist system by the proletariat, after which class distinctions, conflict, and war are finally eliminated. Once communism achieves victory on a world scale, the state itself and its coercive institutions are supposed to "wither away."[20]

The communists recognize five qualitative historical stages—primi-

[19]Max Beloff, *Foreign Policy and the Democratic Process* (Baltimore: Johns Hopkins Press, 1955), p. 98. See also Vernon V. Aspaturian, "Diplomacy in the Mirror of Soviet Scholarship," in *Contemporary History in the Soviet Mirror*, ed. J. Keep (New York: Praeger, 1964), pp. 243–74.

[20]For a more elaborate statement of the author's views on the nature of Soviet ideology, see Vernon V. Aspaturian, "The Contemporary Doctrine of the Soviet State and Its Philosophical Foundations," *American Political Science Review* 48 (December, 1954).

tive communism, slave-system, feudalism, capitalism, and socialism-communism—all of which, except for the first and last, are characterized by the institution of private property, two main contending classes (owners of the means of production and workers), and a state that represents the interests of the ruling class. Although the movement of history is from lower to higher stages, this movement is neither uniform nor without complications, and it does not pursue a uniform and rigid chronological evolution. This has been particularly true of the twentieth century. At the present time, communists acknowledge the coexistence of all historical stages; and this recognition has had a profound influence on Soviet foreign policy.

Soviet ideology is not self-executing; that is, it does not interpret itself automatically and does not reflect images of reality that can be unambiguously perceived, but rather it is based upon an authoritative interpretation of changing events by the Soviet leaders, who must choose from among a variety of possible interpretations, only one of which can be tested at a time for truth in the crucible of action. As long as Stalin was alive, interpretation of doctrine was a monopoly reserved for him alone: it was his interpretation.

*The Two-camp Image.* Stalin's image of the world after the Russian Revolution was one of forced "coexistence" between a single socialist state and a hostile capitalist world surrounding it—a coexistence imposed on both antagonists by objective historical conditions. Neither side being sufficiently powerful to end the existence of the other, they were fated to exist together temporarily on the basis of an unstable and constantly shifting balance of power:

> The fundamental and new, the decisive feature, which has affected all the events in the sphere of foreign relations during this period, is the fact that a certain temporary equilibrium of forces has been established between our country . . . and the countries of the capitalist world; an equilibrium which has determined the present period of "peaceful co-existence."[21]

The establishment, in a capitalistic world, of a socialist bridgehead which was inevitably destined to envelop the entire globe was, for Stalin, the supreme and ineluctable contradiction in the international scene. Although the capitalist world was infinitely stronger and could overwhelm the Soviet Republic if it could embark on a common enterprise, it was viewed as torn by internal divisions and conflicts that prevented the organization of an anti-Soviet crusade. Beside the overriding contradiction between the socialist camp and the capitalist camp, the bourgeois world was plagued with four additional inescapable contradictions: the contradiction between the proletariat and the bourgeoisie in each country; the contradiction between the status quo and the revisionist powers (Stalin referred to them as "victor" and "vanquished" capitalist states); the contradiction between the victorious powers over the spoils of war; the contradiction between the imperialist states and their colonial subjects.

The contradiction between the socialist and capitalist camps was considered by Stalin the most funda-

[21]J. V. Stalin, *Political Report of the Central Committee to the Fourteenth Congress of the Communist Party of the Soviet Union (B)* (Moscow, 1950), p. 8.

mental and decisive, but it was not to be aggravated so long as the Soviet Union was in a weakened condition. War between the two camps was viewed as inevitable; however, it could be temporarily avoided and delayed by astute maneuvering within the conflicts raging in the capitalist world.

Stalin's postwar policy appeared to be predicated on an inevitable conflict with the West, organized by the United States. The organization of the Cominform and the forced unity of the communist orbit, the expulsion of Tito from the communist fraternity, the extraction of public statements of loyalty from communist leaders in all countries, the urgency with which Stalin sought to eliminate all possible power vacuums between the two blocs along the periphery of the communist world, all were preparatory measures based on the false assumption that the American ruling class was betraying anxiety at the growth of Soviet power and was preparing to launch Armageddon. At the founding convention of the Cominform the late Andrei Zhdanov revealed the authoritative Soviet interpretation of the emerging bipolarization of power:

The fundamental changes caused by the war on the international scene and in the position of individual countries have entirely changed the political landscape of the world. A new alignment of political forces has arisen. The more the war recedes into the past, the more distinct become two major trends in postwar international policy, corresponding to the division of the political forces operating on the international arena into two major camps; the imperialist and antidemocratic camp, on the one hand, and the anti–imperialist and democratic camp, on the other. The principal driving force of the imperialist camp is the U.S.A. . . . The cardinal purpose of the imperialist

camp is to strengthen imperialism, to hatch a new imperialist war, to combat Socialism.[22]

During the Korean War and just prior to the Nineteenth Party Congress in 1952, a "great debate" had apparently taken place in the Politburo concerning the validity of the expectation of imminent war between the two camps. Two divergent views were discussed by Stalin in his *Economic Problems of Socialism:* (1) that wars between capitalist countries had ceased to be inevitable and hence war between the two camps was imminent, the view that was then current; and (2) that wars between capitalist states remained inevitable, but that war between the two camps was unlikely. Although the first view was the basis of Soviet postwar policy, Stalin ascribed it to "mistaken comrades," and elevated the second to doctrinal significance:

Some comrades hold that the U.S.A. has brought the other capitalist countries sufficiently under its sway to be able to prevent them going to war among themselves. It is said that the contradictions between capitalism and socialism are stronger than the contradictions among the capitalist countries. Theoretically, of course that is true. It is not only true now, today; it was true before the Second World War. . . . Yet the Second World War began not as a war with the USSR, but as a war between capitalist countries. Why? . . . because war with the USSR, as a socialist land, is more dangerous to capitalism than war between capitalist countries; for whereas war between capitalist countries puts in question only the supremacy of certain capitalist countries over others, war with the USSR must certainly put in question the existence of capitalism itself. . . . It is said that Lenin's thesis that imperialism

[22]Full text reprinted in *Strategy and Tactics of World Communism* (Washington, D.C.: Government Printing Office, 1948), pp. 216–17.

inevitably generates war must now be regarded as obsolete.... That is not true. ... To eliminate the inevitability of war, it is necessary to abolish imperialism.[23]

Stalin's only modification of his two-camp image was thus to concede that war between the two blocs was no longer imminent, but might be preceded by a series of wars among the capitalist powers themselves—between the United States and its satellite allies, France and Britain, on the one hand, and its temporary vassals, Germany and Japan, on the other. The resentment of the ruling classes of these vassal countries over American domination would provoke national revolutions and a renewed war over the ever-shrinking capitalist market, occasioned by the emergence of a parallel communist market, which would remain outside the arena of capitalist exploitation. The Soviet Union would remain outside the conflict, which would automatically seal the doom of world capitalism.

*The Post-Stalin Image.* At the Twentieth Party Congress (February, 1956) Stalin's image of the world was considerably modified in an attempt to bring it into closer focus with the realities of international politics. These modifications were made to eliminate the threatening schisms in the communist camp, to break up the unity of the non-Soviet world and dismantle anti-Soviet instruments like NATO, to head off the impending nuclear war that Stalin's doctrines and policies were unwittingly encouraging, and to enhance the flexibility of Soviet diplomacy in exploiting the contradictions of the capitalist world.

In place of Stalin's fatalistic image of a polarized world, the Twentieth

[23]J. V. Stalin, *Economic Problems of Socialism* (New York: International Publishers Co., 1952), pp. 27–30.

Party Congress drew a more optimistic, and, in many respects, a mellower picture:

1. "Capitalist encirclement" was officially declared terminated, as major speakers like Molotov echoed the Titoist doctrine that "the period when the Soviet Union was ... encircled by hostile capitalism now belongs to the past." The permanent insecurity of the Soviet Union, pending the worldwide victory of communism, as visualized by Stalin, was replaced with the image of a permanently secured Soviet Union, surrounded by friendly communist states in Europe and Asia, embracing nearly one-third of the world, with imperialism in an irrevocable state of advanced decay.

2. In place of Stalin's fixed vision of coexistence between two irreconcilable camps poised in temporary balance, which was declared obsolete and inapplicable to the postwar world, his successors recognized a third, "anti–imperialist" but nonsocialist, group of powers, carved out of decaying colonial empires, which had separated from the capitalist camp but had not yet joined the communist. Stalin's inflexible two-camp image needlessly alienated these new states and tended to force them into the capitalist orbit. This belt of neutralist states—a concept which Stalin refused to recognize—insulated the entire communist orbit from the capitalist world and, together with the socialist states, was viewed as constituting "an extensive 'zone of peace,'" including both socialist and nonsocialist peaceloving states of Europe and Asia inhabited by nearly 1,500,000,000 people, or the majority of the population of our planet."

3. Stalin's doctrine of the "fatal inevitability" of wars was pronounced antiquated, since its emphasis on coercive and violent instruments of diplomacy tended to render the Soviet peace campaign hypocritical, accelerated the formation of anti-Soviet coalitions, and, in an era of nuclear weapons, appeared to doom

both worlds to a war of mutual annihilation.

4. Stalin's five main contradictions were retained as valid and persistent, but the radical shift in the equilibrium of class forces in the world dictated a change of emphasis and the reordering of priorities. Stalin stressed the conflicts among the major capitalist countries as the main object of Soviet diplomacy, relegating other contradictions to minor roles, but his successors saw the main contradiction of the current historical stage to be that between the anticolonial and the imperialist forces. In short, the world has moved out of the stage of the "capitalist encirclement" of the Soviet Union and, during the current phase of coexistence, is moving into the stage of the "socialist encirclement" of the United States, as a prelude to the final victory of communism.[24]

The new image of the world drawn by Khrushchev at the Twentieth Party Congress was by no means the consequence of a unanimous decision. It was opposed by at least four, and possibly five, full members of the eleven-man Presidium. Aside from his vigorous opposition to Khrushchev's adventurist innovations in industry and agriculture, Foreign Minister Molotov and the so-called Stalinist faction bitterly resisted the demolition of the Stalin myth and the entire de-Stalinization program; and they systematically sabotaged the foreign policy decisions of the Twentieth Party Congress, which they publicly accepted.

Molotov objected to the decisions to seek a reconciliation with Marshal Tito and to meet President Eisenhower at Geneva. When Khrushchev and Bulganin returned from

[24]Full text broadcast by Moscow Radio, February 18, 1956. See also *New York Times*, February 19, 1956 (Mikoyan report).

Geneva, Molotov was waiting with sarcastic and biting comments on their personal diplomacy. As a result of his persistent criticism and obstructionism, he was disciplined by the Central Committee in July, 1955, and his "erroneous stand on the Yugoslav issue was unanimously condemned." This was followed shortly by his forced and pained confession of doctrinal error, which superficially appeared to have no connection with foreign policy but appeared designed to tarnish his ideological orthodoxy and was an unmistakable sign that he was on his way out. His unrelenting sabotage through the Foreign Ministry, in particular his determination to poison relations with Tito, finally led to his ouster as foreign minister in favor of Shepilov on the eve of Tito's visit to Moscow in June, 1956. Apparently, Shepilov also fell out of sympathy with the foreign policy he was supposed to execute. For when Khrushchev regained control at the February, 1957, plenum, Shepilov was summarily dismissed as foreign minister in favor of Andrei Gromyko, a professional diplomat who could be counted upon not to pursue a personal foreign policy.

In the bill of particulars against Molotov, the following charges were made:

1. For a long time, Comrade Molotov in his capacity as Foreign Minister, far from taking through the Ministry, of Foreign Affairs measures to improve relations between the USSR and Yugoslavia, repeatedly came out against the measures that the Presidium ... was carrying out to improve relations with Yugoslavia.

2. Comrade Molotov raised obstacles to the conclusion of the state Treaty with Austria and the improvement of relations with that country, which lies

in the center of Europe. The conclusion of the Austrian Treaty was largely instrumental in lessening international tension in general.

3. He was also against normalization of relations with Japan, while that normalization has played an important part in relaxing international tension in the Far East.

4. Comrade Molotov repeatedly opposed the Soviet Government's indispensable new steps in defence of peace and security of nations. In particular he denied the advisability of establishing personal contacts between the Soviet leaders and the statesmen of other countries, which is essential for the achievement of mutual understanding and better international relations.[25]

"Molotov," Khrushchev bluntly stated in a later speech, "found more convenient a policy of tightening all screws, which contradicts the wise Leninist policy of peaceful coexistence."[26] Thus, it can be assumed that Molotov advocated a continuation of the basic foreign policies of the Stalinist era, as modified during the Malenkov regime, based on a perpetuation of the two-camp image. It was Molotov's contention that Soviet policy could reap its greatest dividends by maintaining international tensions at a high pitch and running the risks of nuclear war on the assumption that an uncompromising, cold-blooded policy would force Western statesmen, through lack of nerve and under pressure of public opinion, to continually retreat in the face of Soviet provocation, for fear of triggering a

war of mutual extinction. It appears that he considered as un-Marxist the idea that the ex-colonial countries could be regarded as having deserted the capitalist camp and as constituting an "extensive zone of peace" together with the Soviet bloc. Rather, he believed that their behavior in international politics was motivated purely by considerations of opportunism and expediency. The main arena of rivalry for Molotov remained in Western Europe and the Atlantic area—the bastions of capitalism—and not in Asia or Africa. He continued to view the new countries of Asia and Africa with hostility and suspicion as appendages to the capitalist camp.

Molotov's policy of "tightening all screws" was opposed by the Soviet army, and also by Peking, which had its own reasons, although it was later revealed that the Chinese and Molotov seemed to agree on a wide range of issues. Speaking in Peking, Anastas Mikoyan, reputedly the principal Kremlin architect of the new diplomatic strategy, invoked Lenin in support of the current policy. Quoting Lenin's famous formula that "in the last analysis, the outcome of the struggle will be determined by the fact that Russia, India, China, etc. constitute the overwhelming majority of the world's population," he roundly condemned the Stalinist two-camp image to which Moltov still subscribed.

Soviet diplomatic strategy in the underdeveloped countries of Asia, Africa, and Latin America appears to contradict the basic revolutionary strategy of communism. Although Moscow's support of the so-called bourgeois-nationalist (roughly, "neutralist" under existing conditions) independence or revolutionary movements in the underdeveloped regions (colonies and

[25]The last point is probably a reference not only to the Geneva Conference but also to the various junkets of Bulganin and Khrushchev throughout Asia and Europe, none of which included Foreign Minister Molotov. Cf. *Pravda*, July 4, 1957.

[26]*New York Times*, July 7, 1957.

"semicolonies") against Western colonialism, economic dependence upon the West, and internal feudalism is fully compatible with Leninist-Stalinist doctrine on revolution in the underdeveloped world, the Soviet pattern of political and economic assistance to regimes like those in India, Egypt, Iraq, Ghana, and, to a lesser extent, Cuba, does not fully conform to communist doctrine. Red China has stepped into this breach and has challenged Moscow's refusal to encourage and support indigenous communist parties in their efforts to overthrow native "bourgeois-nationalist" governments and establish authentic communist-controlled regimes. Instead, according to Peking, Moscow supports governments which persecute and imprison local communists.

The Soviet position on this point is extraordinarily nondoctrinaire and pragmatic, for whereas China stresses the view that the Communist party is the only reliable instrument of revolution, Khrushchev and his successors appear to be toying with the idea that under favorable circumstances, particularly when the balance of power has shifted decisively in favor of the communist world, native bourgeois-nationalist leaders may be won over to communism and the revolution could be consummated from above rather than below. The transformation of the Castro regime in Cuba, from an anti-imperialist, nationalist regime into a communist regime, was apparently viewed by Khrushchev as a prototype of this process. As a practical diplomatic position, Moscow feels that any move to encourage communist insurrection in these areas would simply stampede them all into the capitalist and anticommunist camp.

## THE FORMULATION OF SOVIET FOREIGN POLICY

Any attempt to describe the formulation of Soviet foreign policy in the crucibles of its decision-making organs is bound to be a hazardous and frustrating enterprise. The absence of periodic or systematic publication of documents, the inaccessibility of archives and officials, the virtual nonexistence of memoirs or diaries of retiring statesmen, the puzzling duplication of state and party institutions, the perplexing fluctuations in their relationships, the ambiguity of Soviet ideology and the wide discrepancy between theory and practice, the bewildering profusion of constitutional and institutional changes, the arbitrary tendency to ignore or short-circuit elaborately detailed institutional channels, and, finally, the capricious and convulsive turnover of personalities are the more familiar impediments that must be contended with.

The Soviet political superstructure prior to 1953 was a complicated mosaic of shifting and interlocking institutions resting on an entrenched foundation of one-man dictatorship, in which all powers were delegated from above. The institutions of both party and state, as well as their relationship to one another, were essentially creatures of the late Joseph Stalin and were designed, not to limit his own power, but to limit that of his subordinates and rivals, and to facilitate the solidification of his own authority. As the instruments of his creation and manipulation, they could not, and did not, function as restraints on his latitude of decision. Both institutions and subordinates were liquidated with remarkable dispatch when the occasion demanded.

The system of duplicating and overlapping political organs between the party and state allegedly reflects a division of functions between the formulation and execution of policy, with policy formulation a monopoly reserved exclusively for the party, while the function of the government was to be restricted to formalizing and legalizing the decisions of the party into official acts of state. This dichotomy was never either rigid or absolute, but constantly varied in accordance with the degree of interlocking of personnel at the summits of the party and state hierarchies.

### The Party Congress

In theory the most exalted, but in practice the most degraded, of the central party institutions in the formulation of policy is the party congress. Traditionally, the most important fundamental pronouncements on foreign policy have been made before the party congress, which is empowered to set the basic line of the party and state, but which in actual fact merely hears and rubber-stamps the decisions made elsewhere. All higher organs of the party, including the Politburo and Secretariat, are responsible and accountable to the party congress, which theoretically can remove and replace their membership.

The actual role of the party congress in foreign policy has varied throughout its existence. Under Lenin, and, in fact, as late as the Sixteenth Party Congress (in 1930), serious debate on foreign policy and international revolutionary strategy frequently ensued, although never with the same intensity or wide range of diversity as on domestic policy. Because of its massive size (nearly 2,000 delegates), the party congress became increasingly unwieldy as an organ of debate and discussion, and it gradually was converted into a forum which heard various sides and finally into a subdued sounding board for Stalin's deadly rhetoric. Discussion and debate first slipped behind the doors of the Central Committee and eventually vanished into the Politburo. All decisions were made in the Politburo, then reported to the Central Committee and, with increasing infrequency, to the party congress. The principal function of the party congress was reduced to hearing the reports of prominent party figures.

The two most important reports to party congresses relating to foreign policy are the Main Political Report of the Central Committee, delivered in the past by Stalin (except at the Nineteenth Party Congress), and a report on the activities of the World Communist Movement. At the Nineteenth Party Congress, Malenkov delivered the Main Political Report. However, Stalin had ordered published his *Economic Problems of Socialism* on the eve of the party congress, and this set the tone and dominated the entire proceedings. At the Twentieth Party Congress, Khrushchev delivered the Main Political Report, incorporating radical doctrinal innovations affecting foreign policy, while Molotov confined himself to praising reluctantly the new policy and resentfully subjecting his own past conduct of foreign policy to self-criticism. The activities of foreign Communist parties were reported by their own representatives.

A close examination of the Main

Political Reports betrays an almost rigid uniformity in organization. The entire first section is devoted to international affairs; an authoritative interpretation of the world situation; an appraisal of the Soviet position; trends, developments, and opportunities to watch for; warnings, threats, boasts, and invitations to bourgeois powers; congratulations and words of praise for friendly countries; and, finally, a summary of the immediate and long-range objectives of Soviet foreign policy. This report, before the emergence of polycentric tendencies in the world communist movement and the onset of the Sino-Soviet dispute, set the line to guide Communists everywhere in their activities, and, thus, the party congress became not a forum for debate, but a unique medium of communication.

Debate and discussion vanished after 1930, and meetings of the party congress became so infrequent that they threatened to vanish altogether. In his secret speech to the Twentieth Party Congress, Khrushchev gave this vivid description of the deterioration of the party congress:

During Lenin's life, party congresses were convened regularly; always when a radical turn in the development of the party and country took place, Lenin considered it absolutely necessary that the party discuss at length all basic matters pertaining to ... foreign policy. ... Whereas during the first years after Lenin's death, party congresses ... took place more or less regularly, later ... these principles were brutally violated. ... Was it a normal situation when over 13 years [1939–1952] elapsed between the Eighteenth and Nineteenth Congresses? ... Of 1,966 delegates [to the Seventeenth Congress in 1934] with either voting or advisory rights, 1,108 persons were arrested on charges of revolutionary crimes.[27]

### The Central Committee

As the body that "guides the entire work of the Party in the interval between Congresses ... and ... directs the work of the Central and Soviet public organizations [i.e., the government],"[28] the Central Committee became the principal arena of debate and discussion of foreign policy during the period preceding 1934. According to the party rules at that time, the Politburo was obliged to report to this body at least three times a year, so that its decisions might be examined, criticized, and judged. The Central Committee elected the members of the Politburo, the Orgburo, and the Secretariat, and theoretically was empowered to appoint, remove, or replace its members. The Central Committee, itself elected by the party congress, was empowered to replace its own members by a two-thirds vote, but Stalin removed and appointed members of the Central Committee virtually at will.

On some occasions, the foreign commissar (who invariably is at least a full member of the Central Committee), as well as high Soviet functionaries of the Comintern, reported to the Central Committee on foreign policy and international communist activities. More often, the secretary general (Stalin) would deliver a report on the nature and scope of the

[27]This extract and all subsequent references to Khrushchev's secret report to the Twentieth Party Congress are taken from the full text, *New York Times*, June 5, 1956. The speech has been widely reprinted elsewhere.
[28]*The Land of Socialism Today and Tomorrow* (Moscow: International Publishers Co., 1939), p. 473.

Politburo's work and explain the precise application of the "line" under changing international conditions. A fairly large body, composed of full and alternate members (about equally divided), the Central Committee was empowered to alter the policies of the Politburo and support the views of the minority. Only full members exercised the right to vote, but candidates had the right to participate in debate. Some of these reports, but not all, were made public, particularly if important modifications of the policies announced at the previous party congress were made. The records of the Central Committee's proceedings during the Stalin era remain generally unpublished and inaccessible for examination.

The Central Committee too, in time, was reduced to little more than a sounding board; its meetings became increasingly infrequent, and there is reason to believe that, after 1934, its decisions were unanimous. In Khrushchev's secret speech, he said:

> Even after the end of the war . . . Central Committee plenums were hardly ever called. It should be sufficient to mention that during the years of the Patriotic War [i.e., World War II] not a single Central Committee plenum took place. . . . Stalin did not even want to meet and talk with Central Committee members. . . . Of the 139 members and candidates of the Party's Central Committee who were elected at the Seventeenth Party Congress [1934], 98 persons, i.e., 70 percent, were arrested and shot.

### The Party Politburo

There is no question but that the most important organ of decision making in the Soviet Union has been, and continues to be, the Politburo[29] of the Communist party. In accordance with the principle of "democratic centralism," the ultimate power of the party is entrusted to this organ. Its internal organization and recruiting procedures, the composition and convictions of its factions, and its voting practices remain essentially a mystery. No proceedings of its deliberations have been made public in decades, and, in the absence of any recent defections from this body, information concerning its procedures and activities can be derived only from the following sources: (1) fragmentary records of very early meetings; (2) public exposure of its deliberations by Leon Trotsky and other rivals of Stalin during the period before 1930; (3) accounts by high-ranking diplomats or government and party officials whose activities brought them to within close range of the Politburo, and who have defected from the Soviet Union; (4) personal accounts and memoirs of foreign statesmen who negotiated with members of the Politburo or with Stalin; (5) accounts of renegade officials of the Comintern and foreign Communist parties; (6) secrets spilled as a result of the Stalin-Tito feud; (7) Khrushchev's secret speech at the Twentieth Party Congress and its aftermath; (8) calculated leaks by the Polish Communist party and government since the rise of Gomulka; (9) examination of the decisions already taken; (10) rare public disputes between leading press organs of the party and government; (11) shifts in party and

---

[29]The party's highest organ was called the *Politburo* from 1917 to 1952, and the *Presidium* from 1952 to 1966. In 1966, the name *Politburo* was restored, and this term will be used throughout.

government officials; and (12) rare Central Committee resolutions, like that of June 29, 1957.

Under Stalin, all decisions of the Politburo on questions of foreign policy were, in one form or another, his own. All rival and dissident views were quashed and their adherents liquidated. The membership of the body was hand-picked by him. In his relations with the Politburo, Stalin could either announce his decisions and expect unanimous approval; submit them for examination and ask for discussion, with or without a vote; simply act without consulting his colleagues; or consult with various members on certain questions, to the exclusion of others. According to a former Soviet diplomat who was an eyewitness to some Politburo meetings in 1933,

a thin appearance of collective work is still kept up at Politburo meetings. Stalin does not "command." He merely "suggests" or "proposes." The fiction of voting is retained. But the vote never fails to uphold his "suggestions." The decision is signed by all ten members of the Politburo, with Stalin's signature among the rest. . . . The other members of the Politburo mumble their approval of Stalin's "proposal." . . . Stalin not only is generally called "the Boss" by the whole bureaucracy, but *is* the one and only boss.[30]

This general description of Stalin's style of work has been confirmed many times by diplomats and statesmen of many countries who observed that Stalin often made important decisions without consulting

[30]Alexander Barmine, *One Who Survived* (New York: G. P. Putnam's Sons, 1946), p. 213. Barmine adds that "thousands of relatively unimportant, as well as all-important, problems, must pass through Stalin's hand for final decision. . . . Weeks are spent in waiting; Commissars wait in Stalin's office."

anyone, while Molotov and others would request time to consult with their "government." The role of the other members of the Politburo could best be described as consultative, although within the area of their own administrative responsibility they exercised the power of decision. Testimony concerning Stalin's intolerance of dissent is uniformly consistent. "Whoever opposed . . . his viewpoint," complained Khrushchev, "was doomed to be removed."

The relationship between the Foreign Ministry and the Politburo has always been unique. Since relations with other states are viewed in terms of a struggle for power among various "ruling classes," and thus directly involve the security and the very existence of the Soviet state, the party center has always retained a tight supervision over the Foreign Ministry. This supervision assumes different forms, depending upon the party rank of the individuals who hold the posts of foreign minister and of premier. The premier has always been a party figure of the highest rank, while the foreign minister may or may not be a member of the party Politburo.

During the period when Maxim Litvinov was foreign commissar, his work was supervised by Molotov, the premier of the government and his formal superior. Matters of routine interest, not involving questions of policy or fundamental maneuver, were decided by Litvinov himself in consultation with his collegium. More substantial questions were taken to Molotov, who, depending upon the nature of the question, would make a decision or take it to Politburo.

The Politburo itself was broken down into various commissions dealing with different aspects of policy. Questions of foreign policy were first considered by the Politburo Commission on Foreign Affairs, which included the Politburo specialists on the Comintern, foreign trade, and defense. In matters involving exceptional or immediate importance, Molotov would deal directly with Stalin and get a decision.

The procedures of the Politburo were neither systematic nor rigid. Often Stalin would personally consult with the foreign commissar and his chief advisers; and Litvinov, on a few occasions, would be asked to make a report to the Politburo. The principal function of the Commission on Foreign Affairs was to act as a coordinating agency of all the departments concerned with foreign relations; assemble and evaluate intelligence information flowing from different channels; devise strategy and policy; examine analyses, projects, and reports drawn up by specialists in the Foreign Commissariat; study reports of diplomats abroad; and then make a comprehensive report either to Stalin or to the Politburo as a whole.

Once the decisions were made, they would be transmitted in writing or verbally by Molotov to Litvinov for execution. These bureaucratic channels were often ignored. Stalin would act directly with Molotov, his principal agent, and they would personally give instructions to Litvinov. Deviation or improvisation from instructions by the foreign commissar or his subordinates in the commissariat was neither permitted nor tolerated. According to Khrushchev, the system of Politburo commissions was not primarily for organizational efficiency, but was a sinister device whereby Stalin weakened the authority of the collective body:

The importance of the ... Political Bureau was reduced and its work disorganized by the creation within the Political Bureau of various commissions—the so-called "quintets," "sextets," "septets" and "novenaries."

When Molotov replaced Litvinov in May 1939, this cumbersome procedure was simplified. The Nazi-Soviet Pact was worked out principally by Stalin and Molotov, with Zhdanov and Mikoyan the only other members of the Politburo apparently apprised of the crucial decisions contemplated. The Politburo Commission on Foreign Affairs gradually increased in size until, by 1945, it was large enough to be converted by Stalin from a "sextet" into a "septet." As it grew in size, so its importance diminished. During the war, Stalin appeared to consult only Molotov on questions of foreign policy and frequently made decisions on the spot at the Big Three conferences.

Khrushchev's description of how decisions were made by Stalin and the Politburo is probably exaggerated and self-serving, but accurate in its outline:

After the war, Stalin became even more capricious, irritable, and brutal; in particular his suspicion grew. His persecution mania reached unbelievable dimensions. Everything was decided by him alone without any consideration for anyone or anything. ... Sessions of the Political Bureau occurred only occasionally, ... many decisions were taken by one person or in a roundabout way, without collective discussion. ... The importance of the Political Bureau was reduced and its work disorganized by the creation within the Political Bureau of various commissions. ... The result of this was that some members of the Political Bureau were in this way kept away from participation in the decisions of the most important state matters.

Decision Making in the Post-Stalin
Period: The Agonies of Collective
Leadership and Factional Conflict

The death of Stalin unleashed a struggle for power among his successors. Six months before his death, at the Nineteenth Party Congress, Stalin radically reorganized the party summit, abolishing the Orgburo and replacing the eleven-man Politburo with a Presidium of twenty-five members and eleven candidate members as the key decision-making organ of the Soviet system. Since many of the new members of the Presidium were burdened with permanent administrative responsibilities far from Moscow, and since it was much too large to function as a decision-making body, there was secretly organized, in violation of the new party charter, a smaller Bureau of the Presidium, whose membership has never been revealed. Whether expansion of the Presidium was designed by Stalin to widen the area of decision making and prevent a struggle for power after his death—thus preparing the conditions for orderly transition from personal to institutional dictatorship—or whether it was a sinister device for liquidating his old associates in favor of a generation ignorant of his crimes remains an intriguing enigma. According to Khrushchev,

Stalin evidently had plans to finish off the old members of the Political Bureau. . . . His proposal after the Nineteenth Congress, concerning the selection of 25 persons to the Central Committee's Presidium, was aimed at the removal of the old Political Bureau members and the bringing in of less experienced persons so that they would extol him. . . . We can assume that this was a design for the future annihilation of the old Political Bureau members, and in this way, a cover for all the shameful acts of Stalin.

Immediately after Stalin's death, the old members of Stalin's entourage reduced the Presidium to its former size. The removal of Beria and the dismantling of his secret police apparatus introduced an uneasy equilibrium among the various factions in the Presidium, none of which was powerful enough to overwhelm the others.

In the post-Stalin Presidium, decisions often were taken only after stormy controversies and agile maneuvering among the various factions. As a consequence, necessity was converted into ideology, and conflicting opinions, within carefully circumscribed limits, were given official sanction. The authoritative theoretical journal *Kommunist*, however, warned that "views that are objectively directed toward dethroning the leadership elected by the Party masses" would not be tolerated.[31] This danger is adumbrated in the party statutes, article 28 of which reads:

A broad discussion, in particular on an all-Union scale concerning the Party policy, should be so organized that it would not result in the attempts of an insignificant minority to impose its will on the majority of the Party or in attempts to organize fractional groupings which would break down Party unity, or in attempts to create a schism that would undermine the strength and the firmness of the socialist regime.[32]

The party statutes, however, were revised in 1961 at the Twenty-second Party Congress, in order to reflect more realistically the more

[31] *Kommunist*, August, 1956, no. 10, pp. 3–13.
[32] *Pravda*, October 14, 1952.

fluid situation which had developed since Stalin's death and, while factionalism was still proscribed, greater emphasis was placed on ensuring the expression of divergent views within the party. Thus, article 27 of the 1961 party statutes stipulates that

wide discussion, especially discussion on a countrywide scale, of questions of Party policy must be held so as to ensure for Party members the free expression of their views and preclude attempts to form fractional groupings destroying Party unity, attempts to split the Party.

*The Proliferation of Factional Politics.*
Diversity and clash of opinion were allowed, initially, to filter down only to the level of the Central Committee. Eventually, however, differences of opinion which reflected various factional views erupted—at first gingerly, and then more boldly, in party congresses, lower-level party bodies, the Supreme Soviet, various professional conferences, newspapers and periodicals, and in professional organizations. The disagreements within the Politburo which were unleashed after Stalin's death threatened to crack the party pyramid down to its very base. It was even possible to envisage the development of a multiparty system, and authoritative voices were openly advocating the nomination of more than one candidate for elective offices.

Decisions in the Politburo are reached by simple majority, with only full members entitled to vote, although alternate members participate in the debate and discussion. Meetings of the Politburo are held at least once a week and, according to what both Khrushchev and Mikoyan have said, most decisions are unanimous. Mikoyan has further elaborated by stating that if a consensus were unobtainable, the Politburo would adjourn, sleep on the matter, and return for further discussion until unanimity was achieved. Since five full members out of eleven were expelled on June 29, 1957, for persistent opposition to and obstruction of the party line, the unanimity of the Politburo's deliberations appears to have been exaggerated.

In view of Khrushchev's bitter attack on the organization of Politburo commissions under Stalin, the Politburo's internal compartmentalization may not be as rigidly demarcated as before; foreign policy decisions, instead of being merely the concern of the Commission on Foreign Affairs, are discussed and made by the body as a whole. "Never in the past," said Molotov at the Twentieth Party Congress, "has our Party Central Committee and its Presidium been engaged as actively with questions of foreign policy as during the present period."

The sharp and close factional divisions in the Politburo have revived the prominence and activity of the moribund Central Committee. Factional differences have been displayed before plenums of the Central Committee (held at least twice a year) where the actions of the Politburo have been appealed. In this relatively large body of 241 full members and 155 alternates, discussion of the views current in the Politburo is still more ritualized than free, with each faction in the Politburo supported by its own retainers in the Central Committee. Voting is conditioned not only by divisions in the Politburo, but also by considerations of political survival and opportunism, with members being extremely sensitive to the course that the struggle assumes in the higher body. "At Plenums of the Central Committee," according to the revealing statement of one low-ranking member, "Comrade Khrushchev and other members of the Presidium . . . corrected errors in a fatherly way . . . regardless of post occupied or of record."[33]

It was in the Central Committee that Malenkov reputedly indicted Beria and where, in turn, he and Molotov were disciplined and attacked by the Khrushchev faction. Shifts in the balance of factions in the Politburo are almost always immediately registered in the Central Committee, whose proceedings inevitably sway with those of the higher body. The Central Committee, whose decisions are invariably reported as unanimous, is empowered to alter its own membership and that of its higher bodies by a two-thirds vote; and in the June 1957, plenum it expelled three full members and one alternate from the Politburo and the Central Committee, demoted one to alternate status, and cut off still another at full membership in the Central Committee. Correspondingly, the Politburo was expanded to fifteen full members and nine alternates.

The Central Committee assumed increasing importance during the Khrushchev era, and it is likely that, after the "antiparty group" episode of June 1957, he considered this body as a counterweight to the opposition which might congeal against him in the Politburo. Khrushchev was almost fastidious in his zeal to enshrine the Central Committee as the ultimate institutional repository of legitimacy in the Soviet system. The body was enlarged and convened regularly by Khrushchev,

[33]Speech of Z. I. Muratov, first secretary of the Tatar Oblast Committee, Moscow Radio broadcast, February 21, 1956.

and all changes in personnel and major pronouncements of policy were either confirmed by or announced at Central Committee plenums.

Immediately after the expulsion of the "anti-party group," in mid-1957, and the removal of Marshal Zhukov, the Khrushchev faction appeared to be in full control of both the Politburo and the Central Committee and Khrushchev appeared to be in full command of the ruling faction. Proceedings of the Central Committee were also published more or less regularly under Khrushchev, although selective censorship and suppression persisted. Khrushchev's behavior at Central Committee proceedings was often crude, rude, and earthy; commanding, but not domineering. He would deliver a report on the main item on the agenda, which was then discussed in speeches delivered by the other members. These were freely interrupted by the first secretary, who might affirm, criticize, chastise, admonish, correct, and even warn the speakers, and they would respond with varying degrees of deference, familiarity, meekness, fear, or audacity. At the December 1958, plenum, for example, seventy-five speakers discussed Khrushchev's report, and Bulganin, Pervukhin, and Saburov used the occasion to denounce themselves for complicity in the "antiparty group" conspiracy to oust Khrushchev from power.

*Factional Conflict in the Politburo.* Differences in the Politburo arise as a result of both personal ambitions for power and fundamental conflict over doctrine and policy. Both factors are so intricately interwoven that attempts to draw fine distinctions between personal and policy conflicts are apt to be an idle exercise. Although Soviet ideology neither recognizes the legitimacy of factional groupings in the party nor tolerates the doctrinal schisms that are their ideological expression, the party, throughout its history, has been constantly threatened with the eruption of both. After Stalin's death, the rival cliques he permitted —and may even have encouraged— to form among his subordinates developed into factions, each with its own aspirations and opinions. Since no single faction was sufficiently powerful to annihilate the others, necessity was converted into virtue and the balance of terror in the Presidium was ideologically sanctified as "collective leadership."

Even before the revelations of the resolution that hurled Molotov and his associates from their places of eminence, it was unmistakable that serious factional quarrels kept the Politburo in a continual state of turmoil. At least three factions appear to have existed in the Politburo before June 1957, although the members of each faction were not permanently committed to issues; and personality and tactical shifts, although not frivolous, were also not unusual. The Politburo was divided on four major issues that had important foreign policy repercussions: the Stalinist issue; the relations between the Soviet Union and other communist states and parties; economic policy and reorganization; and relations with the ex-colonial states.

With the Politburo so sharply and evenly divided, "collective leadership" threatened to abandon Soviet foreign policy to the mercies of an inconclusive see-saw struggle plunging the Kremlin into a condition of perpetual indecision. While key Khrushchev supporters were out of town, Stalinist forces, by engineering a rump meeting of the Politburo —ostensibly to discuss minor matters—regrouped and resolved to unseat Khrushchev through a parliamentary ruse. When the meeting took place on June 17–18, 1957, the first secretary found himself momentarily outmaneuvered and apparently irrevocably outvoted. Refusing to resign, Khrushchev conducted a filibuster while his supporters quickly assembled a special meeting of the Central Committee and its auditing commission (a total of 319 members), which sat June 22–29, 1957.

After a bitter ventilation of all the contentious issues of doctrines and policy, during which sixty members reportedly took part in the debate and 115 filed statements, the anti-Khrushchev coalition was overwhelmed by a unanimous vote tarnished only by a single obstinate abstention by Molotov—the first such publicly admitted dissonance in a Central Committee vote in almost thirty years. The Stalinist wing of the coalition was charged in the resolution which expelled them with engaging in illegal factional activity and cabalistic intrigue:

Entering into collusion on an anti-party basis, they set out to change the policy of the Party, to drag the Party back to the erroneous methods of leadership condemned by the Twentieth Party Congress [i.e., Stalinism]. They resorted to methods of intrigue and formed a collusion against the Central Committee.

The victorious group itself soon betrayed signs of splitting on a wide range of domestic and foreign policies. The leadership tended to polarize into two main factions, a "moderate" group, led by Khrushchev, and a "conservative" group, whose leaders appeared to be M. A. Suslov and F. R. Kozlov, later apparently supported by traditional elements of the professional military and representatives of heavy industry. Generally speaking, the moderate faction sought a relaxation of international tensions and a détente with the United States, even at the expense of alienating China; the conservative faction saw little value in a détente with the United States, especially at the expense of alienating the Soviet Union's most important ally. Domestically, Khrushchev and the "moderates" were willing to tolerate greater relaxation of controls at home and advocated a change in the economic equilibrium in the direction of producing more consumer goods at the expense of heavy industry. The "conservatives" were opposed to further relaxation at home and may have even demanded some retrenchment, and they were virtually dogmatic in their insistence that priority continue to be given to heavy industry over light industry and agriculture. Under these conditions, formalized debate in the Central Committee gave way to a genuine, if largely esoteric, articulation of divergent factional viewpoints, which was also evident from the content of the speeches delivered at the Twenty-first and Twenty-second party congresses in January 1959, and October 1961, respectively.

As long as Khrushchev's policy of seeking a relaxation of international tension and a détente with the United States seemed to be bearing fruit, he was able to isolate and silence his critics in the leadership, particularly after his meeting with President Eisenhower at Camp David, in mid-1959. Relations with China simultaneously deteriorated catastrophically when Khrushchev unilaterally nullified a secret 1957 Sino-Soviet agreement on nuclear technology, just prior to his meeting with President Eisenhower. Since an improvement in relations with the United States inevitably meant a further deterioration of relations with China, this became an important and crucial issue which agitated the Soviet leadership. The factional opposition to Khrushchev was strengthened in January 1960, when the Soviet leader alienated the traditional military by calling for a reduction of the ground forces by one-third and shifting the main reliance for Soviet security to its nuclear deterrent capability. This new strategic policy was based upon the expectation of an imminent settlement of all outstanding issues between Washington and Moscow on the basis of the "spirit of Camp David."

After the U-2 incident, Khrushchev's grip on the Central Committee and its Politburo was weakened and came under increasing attack at home, while criticism in Peking mounted simultaneously. Khrushchev's foreign policy was based upon a fundamental restructuring of the image and character of the American "ruling class," which according to the "moderates" had split into a "sober" group, on the one hand, and an intractable group made up of "belligerent," "aggressive," "irrational," and even "mad" elements, on the other. The sober group—whose leader, according to Khrushchev, was President Eisenhower—was dominant, and it appeared ready to negotiate a settlement with the Soviet Union on a realistic basis, which to Khrushchev meant a détente based on supposed Soviet strategic superiority. Neither the "conservative" faction, nor the traditional military, nor the Chinese leaders subscribed to this image. The Soviet Union's leader was, in effect, relying upon the self-restraint of the sober forces in the American ruling class, and his opposition viewed his call for troop reductions and cutbacks in heavy industry with considerable alarm. From the Chinese viewpoint, Khrushchev's search for a détente with Eisenhower indicated an erosion in Moscow's commitment to revolutionary goals and a tacit alliance with Peking's principal national enemy.

Kennedy was unknown to the Russians, but Nixon was a well-known and heartily disliked personality, and so Moscow placed its reliance on a Kennedy victory and a reversal of post-U-2 policy. But the Soviet leader was to be disappointed once again, as the new president embarked on a course of strengthening U.S. military capabilities, supported an attempt to overthrow the Castro regime in Cuba, and refused to be bullied into negotiating a settlement on Soviet terms. The Soviet failure to win a Berlin victory and the steadily growing power of the United States increased the pressures upon Khrushchev both at home and from Peking, and at the Twenty-second Party Congress he adopted a harsher line toward the United States.

From the time of the Twenty-second Party Congress until Khrushchev's ouster in October 1964, the Soviet leadership was plagued by constant factional squabbles, and these often found expression in the Central Committee plenums. Khrushchev stayed in power only because the factional balance was extremely delicate, with some leaders supporting him on some issues and opposing him on others. Thus, Soviet factional politics was not only institutionally and functionally oriented, but issue oriented as well. It was the existence of issue-oriented factionalism which provided Khrushchev with the margins necessary to stay in power.

Khrushchev once again narrowly missed being ousted as a consequence of the Cuban missile crisis of October 1962, when his opposition at home and his critics in Peking seemed perilously close to holding a common point of view. His problems were also aggravated by President Kennedy's initial rejection of a Soviet proposal for a limited test-ban treaty based on three annual inspections. The Soviet premier gained a temporary extension of power, however, when the leader of the "conservative" faction, F. R. Kozlov, suffered an incapacitating stroke in April 1963. Although Khrushchev mused in public about his possible retirement, the incapacitation of Kozlov gave him a new lease on political power, and he quickly took advantage of President Kennedy's offer, made in a speech at American University, to reach an agreement on a limited test-ban treaty, which was signed the following month.

Khrushchev thus appeared to have vindicated himself, for the "sober" forces were indeed in control in Washington. While the détente was based not upon the assumption of Soviet strategic superiority, but upon the implied assumption of U.S. strategic superiority, it enabled Khrushchev to turn his attention to pressing economic problems at home and to the dispute with Peking. The Chinese called the limited test-ban treaty an act of Soviet betrayal. There was strong evidence that the treaty was not enthusiastically accepted by the "conservative" faction or the traditional military.

Khrushchev's inept handling of the dispute with China, his generally crude and unsophisticated behavior as a politician, and his constant boasting in public apparently finally alienated some of his supporters, who saw in him an impediment to a reconciliation with China and an obstacle to a rational approach to domestic problems. In October 1964, he was ousted in a coup engineered largely by his own trusted subordinates, Brezhnev, Kosygin, and Mikoyan. He was indirectly accused of concocting "harebrained schemes," "boasting," and general ineptness. Khrushchev's ouster allegedly took place at a Central Committee plenum, but the proceedings were not made public. The manner and abruptness of his dismissal caused considerable commotion and disturbance in other communist countries and parties, whose leaders received an explanation in a series of bilateral conferences.

The Chinese, the conservatives, the traditionalistic military, and the moderates all seemed to have a common interest in removing Khrushchev—if for widely differing and even contradictory reasons—and there seems to be little question that the factional situation at home and the criticisms from Peking combined to bring about the Soviet premier's political ouster.

The Central Committee thus began emerging as the most important political organ of power and authority in the Soviet system, although it has not yet eclipsed the Politburo, which, however, must be increasingly responsive to its deliberations. The growing power of the Central Committee reflects the increasingly pluralistic character of the Soviet social order. This body is composed of representatives from the most powerful and influential elite groups in Soviet society. It includes the entire membership of the Politburo and the Secretariat; the most important ministers of the government; the first secretaries of the several republics' party organizations and of important regional party organizations; the most important officials of the Soviet Union's republics; the marshals, generals, and admirals of the armed forces and the police; the important ambassadors; the trade union officials; cultural and scientific celebrities and leaders; the leading party ideologists; and the top Komsomol officials. Increasingly, these representatives perceive attitudes reflecting their institutional or functional roles and status in Soviet society, and this provides the social basis for the political factions which now characterize the Soviet system.

The transition from Stalinist, one-man rule to quasi-pluralistic political behavior is now all but complete. The Khrushchev decade emerges as a sort of transition period between these two types of political behavior. Under Stalin, conflicts were rendered into decisions after a blood purge in which potential opponents were physically destroyed; under Khrushchev, conflicts were resolved into decisions by the clearcut victory of one faction and the expulsion of the others from important positions of power. The blood purge was replaced with public condemnation and disgrace, demotion, or retirement; but since the execution of Beria in 1954, no fallen leader has been executed or even brought to trial. With the element of terror removed from the political process, however, the risks of opposition and dissent were considerably reduced. Victorious factions divided into new factions; the factional conflict resumed on a new level, around new issues. By late 1959, no single group could establish dominance, and control gradually came to be exercised by a kind of consensus, based on compromise, bargaining, and accommodation. This has introduced an element of instability and uncertainty with respect to any given government or administration, but it has simultaneously stabilized and regularized the Soviet political process and has removed much of the uncertainty which hitherto prevailed.

No formal charges of factionalism have been made against any group or individual in the Soviet Union's hierarchy since 1959. Such a charge can only be leveled if a particular faction is soundly defeated and expelled from the leadership, and this was characteristic of the rule by a single faction which flourished between 1957 and 1959. Factionalism is still prohibited by the party rules, but its existence was tacitly admitted by Kozlov at the Twenty-second Party Congress:

Under present circumstances, need the statutes contain any formal guarantee against factionalism and clique activity? Yes, . . . such guarantees as needed. To be sure there is no social base left in Soviet society that could feed opportunistic currents in the Party. But the sources of ideological waverings on the part of particular individuals or groups have not yet been entirely eliminated. Some persons may fall under the influence of bourgeois propaganda from the outside. Others having failed to comprehend the dialectics of society's development and having turned . . . into dying embers, will have nothing to do with anything new and go on clinging to old dogmas that have been toppled by life.[34]

*Interest Groups and Factional Politics.* It is at once obvious that factions could neither arise nor flourish unless they received constant sustenance from powerful social forces in Soviet society. Just as party factions do not organize into separate political organizations competing with the party for political power, so interest groups in Soviet society do not constitute separate organizations, but rather seek to make their influence felt as formless clusters of vested interests. Within the context of Marxist ideology, an interest group can only be a social class with economic interests that conflict with the interests of other classes. After the revolution, only the interests of the working class, as distorted by the Marxist prism, were given legitimate recognition—although the concrete political articulation of these interests was usurped by the Communist party—and all other interests and parties were condemned to oblivion. In 1936 Stalin declared the eradication of class conflict in Soviet society, but he continued to recognize the existence of separate social classes, whose interests had merged into a single identity. The Communist party was transformed from a party representing only the interests of the working class into one representing the transcendental interests of all Soviet social classes. Consequently, Soviet ideology neither recognizes the legitimacy of competing interest groups nor tolerates their autonomous existence. In Soviet jargon, an interest group that develops interests that deviate from the party line is a hostile class; the faction that represents it in the party is an attempt to form a party within a party, and its articulated views on policy

[34] *Pravda,* October 29, 1961.

and doctrine constitute an ideological deviation.

Separate interest groups, however, continue to flourish in Soviet society, but not in conformity with the doctrinaire and contrived premises of nineteenth-century Marxism, nor within the synthetic social divisions given official sanction. The collective-farm peasantry and the working class constitute the numerically preponderant classes in Soviet society, but the major interest groups with sufficient power and influence to apply political pressure do not follow the artificial constructions of Soviet ideology. In accordance with the unique dynamic of Soviet society, the privileged elites find their social differentiation within a single recognized group, the *intelligentsia,* which is not recognized as a social class, but is euphemistically called a *stratum.*

Although the Soviet intelligentsia (roughly identical with what Milovan Djilas labeled the "New Class") is a variegated congeries of differentiated elites, they all have a mutual desire to perpetuate the Soviet system from which they have sprung and from which they benefit as privileged groups. But each group is immediately concerned with its own vested stake in Soviet society, and seeks to force doctrine and policy to assume the contours of its own special interests. Since these groups do not enjoy official recognition, they all seek to exert their influence through the Communist party, not outside it, and political rivalry assumes the form of competing for control of the party's decision-making organs and its symbols of legitimacy. Because Soviet ideology rigidly and inaccurately insists on the existence of a single monolithic interest, representing that of society in its collective entity, conflicts between major groups were resolved not by political accommodation, but by mutual elimination and by the attempt of one interest group to establish its supremacy and to impose its views as those of society as a whole. Thus the Communist party, under the pressures of diverse groups seeking political articulation and accommodation, has become a conglomeration of interests whose basic incompatibilities are only partially obscured by a veneer of monolithic unity.

Not all interest groups in the Soviet Union are sufficiently powerful to exact representation for their views by factions in the party hierarchy. There are six principal groups within Soviet society that have accumulated sufficient leverage, either through the acquisition of indispensable skills and talents or through the control of instruments of persuasion, terror, or destruction, to exert pressure upon the party. These are (1) the party apparatus, consisting of those who have made a career in the party bureaucracy; (2) the government bureaucracy; (3) the economic managers and technicians; (4) the cultural, professional, and scientific intelligentsia; (5) the police; (6) the armed forces.

These major groups are by no means organized as cohesively united bodies, speaking with a single authoritative voice, but rather made up of rival personal and policy cliques, gripped by internal jealousies, and often in constant collision and friction with one another in combination or alliance with similarly oriented cliques in other social groups.

The party apparatus itself has been thus divided into rival cliques, the two main contending groups being those led by Khrushchev and Malenkov. After the denouncement

TABLE 5.1   Major Groups Represented in the Central Committee (Full and Candidate Members)

|  | 1952 | 1956 | 1961 (%) | April, 1966 (%) | 1971 (%) |
|---|---|---|---|---|---|
| Party apparatus | 103 | 117 | 158 (.43) | 155 (.43) | 172 (.43) |
| State and economic officials | 79 | 98 | 112 (.34) | 136 (.38) | 144 (.36) |
| Military officers | 26 | 18 | 31 (.10) | 33 (.10) | 33 (.08) |
| Cultural and scientific representatives | ... | ... | 18 | 15 (.04) | 25 (.06) |
| Police | 9 | 3 | 2 | 2 (.005) | 4 (.01) |
| Others | 19 | 19 | 9 (.19) | 19 (.053) | 25 (.06) |
| Totals | 236 | 255 | 330 | 360 | 396 |

of Malenkov, his supporters in the party apparatus were replaced with followers of Khrushchev. Although the function of the party bureaucracy is essentially administrative rather than policy making, it has a tendency to feel that it "owns" the party, and thus seeks first to subordinate the party to its control and then to force the other major groups to submit to the domination of the party. After Stalin's death, the serious and imminent threat posed to the party by Beria and his secret police caused Khrushchev and Malenkov to temporarily bury their rivalry in the apparatus of the party in order to crush the secret police, which had developed into an independent center of power and threatened to subjugate the party to its will. The secret police was dismembered with the aid of the army.

There appears to be no systematic attempt to select members of the Central Committee and its Politburo from among the major forces in Soviet society; the composition of these bodies appears to depend upon the balance of forces at any given time (see tables 5.1 and 5.2). Ample evidence exists, however, that their composition reflects deliberate recognition of these major interest groups. Traditionally, the party apparatus accounts for slightly less than half the total membership of the Central Committee, with the government bureaucracy (including the economic administrators) following close behind. The representation of the other groups is substantially less, although because virtually all members of the party's two highest bodies who are not career party bureaucrats are employed by the state, it is often difficult to distinguish the main line of work pursued by a particular member of the Central Committee. This is especially

TABLE 5.2   Major Institutions Represented on the Presidium or Politburo

|  | 1952 | 1953 | 1956 | 1957 | 1961 | 1963 | 1966 | 1970 | 1975 |
|---|---|---|---|---|---|---|---|---|---|
| Party apparatus | 13 (5) | 2 (2) | 4 (3) | 10 (6) | 7 (3) | 8 (4) | 6 (6) | 6 (7) | 9 (6) |
| State officials: |  |  |  |  |  |  |  |  |  |
| Economic sector | 5 (3) | 4 | 4 | 1 (2) | 2 | 2 | 1 | 0 | 1 |
| Other | 4 (2) | 3 (1) | 3 (1) | 3 | 2 (2) | 2 (2) | 4 (1) | 5 (1) | 4 (1) |
| Military | 0 | 0 | 0 (1) | 1 | 0 | 0 | 0 | 0 | 1 |
| Police | 2 | 1 (1) | 0 | 0 | 0 | 0 | 0 | 0 (1) | 1 |
| Other | 1 (1) | 0 | 0 (1) | 0 (1) | 0 | 0 | 0 (1) | 0 | 0 |
| Totals | 25 (11) | 10 (4) | 11 (6) | 15 (9) | 11 (5) | 12 (6) | 11 (8) | 11 (9) | 16 (7) |

true of individuals who move from one group to another. Consequently, all distinctions are provisional and, in some cases, arbitrary. The composition of the Politburo is more accurately differentiated, although even there, because of the interlocking of the top organs of state and party, some ambiguity prevails.

Since the membership of the Central Committee is normally determined by the party congress, which meets every five years, its composition is not normally affected by day-to-day changes in the factional equilibrium. The Politburo, whose membership can be altered by the Central Committee, is particularly sensitive to the fluctuations in the balance of power, and is a fairly accurate barometer of changing political fortunes.

Formerly, it could be said that the composition of the Central Committee was determined from the top, by the Politburo, but the relationship between the two bodies is becoming increasingly reciprocal. Changes in the composition of the Politburo now reflect, to some degree, changes in the factional balance in the Central Committee as groups and individuals maneuver for position and advantage—bargaining, negotiating, and accommodating. The Central Committee's authority becomes crucial, and perhaps even decisive, when the factional balance is delicate. Then, rival groups seek to gain wider support and alter their policies to meet the demands of wider constituencies. Thus, while the Politburo is the more accurate gauge of day-to-day politics, the composition of the Central Committee is apt to reflect more durable, long-range trends. Table 5.2 shows only institutional representation on the Politburo, and it should be noted

that interest groups tend, increasingly, to cut across institutional entities.

The party apparatus continues to be the dominant institutional actor in both the Central Committee and its Politburo, but its absolute and relative strength in both bodies, after reaching a post-Stalin high point in 1957, seems now to be diminishing as other groups demand greater representation. As factional cleavages develop within the apparatus, opportunities are created for other groups as they become targets of appeal for support by rival apparatus factions and in turn make demands upon the apparatus. The year 1957, after the expulsion of the "antiparty group," represented the zenith of single-faction rule, which was sustained substantially unimpaired until Khrushchev's assumption of the premiership in the following year. Factionalism, however, infected the victorious Khrushchev group itself, and the overall representation of the apparatus in the Presidium started to decline until, by the time of the Twenty-second Party Congress in October 1961, two main factions had once again materialized: a "moderate" faction led by Khrushchev and a "conservative" faction, supported by the traditional military, led by F. R. Kozlov, an erstwhile Khrushchev satrap. Khrushchev managed to hang on as both premier and first secretary, first in order to present a united front to both the United States and China, and second because he adjusted and accommodated his publicly stated views and policies to accord more with the demands of the "conservative" faction, without at the same time abandoning his leadership of the "moderate" faction. From the Twenty-second Party Congress until his ouster in October 1964, he presided over a regime which was characterized not by single-faction rule but by consensus and accommodation among a number of factions.

The fall of Khrushchev in 1964 did not produce any immediate major dislocations or dismissals in the Soviet Hierarchy, except for the demotion of a few individuals who were personally close or related to the Soviet leader. The most conspicuous was his son-in-law, Alexei Adzhubei, who was unceremoniously booted out of the Central Committee and relieved of his job as chief editor of *Izvestia*. Shelepin and Shelest, neither of whom were candidate members, were admitted as full members of the Presidium, and Demichev was appointed a candidate member. Shelepin and Demichev were also members of the Secretariat, and their appointment broadened the overlapping membership in the two bodies. There were other dismissals and appointments at lower levels, but they were accomplished with little fanfare.

In March 1965, after a Central Committee plenum, further changes were made. Mazurov was elevated from candidate membership to full membership in the Presidium, and D. F. Ustinov was added as a candidate member. Ustinov's star had appeared to rise after the Cuban missile crisis, when Khrushchev seemed to be in deep trouble, but it dimmed after Kozlov's stroke and Khrushchev had made a temporary political recovery.

Further changes were made in the party summit in December 1965, when Ustinov, Kapitonov, and Kulakov were appointed to the Secretariat to replace the three members who had been dropped after Khrushchev's political demise, raising its number once again to eleven. Six members of the Secretariat were also full or candidate members of the Presidium, which suggested a resurgence of the party apparatus's representation at the party summit. Podgorny, at this time, also replaced Mikoyan as chairman of the Presidium of the Supreme Soviet (the Soviet legislature), and subsequently relinquished his membership in the Secretariat.

The definitive post-Khrushchev composition of the party summit was achieved at the Twenty-third Party Congress in April 1966, when Mikoyan and Shvernik were retired from the Politburo and Pelshe, a Latvian party secretary, was appointed a full member over the heads of all the candidate members. Two new candidate members were appointed—Kunayev, a Kazakh party leader, and Masherov, a Byelorussian party secretary who had become a full member of the Central Committee only in November 1964. The composition of the Secretariat remained unchanged, except that Kirilenko, also a full member of the Politburo, replaced Podgorny in the Secretariat, since the latter's new post as chairman of the Presidium of the Supreme Soviet is traditionally disassociated from the Secretariat.

The restructuring of the party summit at the Twenty-third Party Congress strongly suggested that Brezhnev, the general secretary of the party, had strengthened his position and that he enjoyed a factional majority or consensus, but by no means had assumed the power of a Khrushchev or a Stalin, irrespective of the symbolic manipulation of nomenclature at the party congress. Of the eleven full members of the Politburo, four were members of the Secretariat, while of the eight candidate members, two were members of the Secretariat. This meant that six members of the eleven-man Secretariat also sat on the Politburo. The clear dominance of the party apparatus in the Politburo was further indicated by the presence of six party secretaries of republics (Ukrainian, Latvian, Georgian, Uzbek, Byelorussian, and Kazakh) as full or candidate members, thus broadening its ethnic base to include representation from six of the fourteen major non-Russian nationalities, including two central Asian Moslem nationalities, the Uzbek and Kazakh, and giving the apparatus a total of six full members and six candidate members of the Politburo, or twelve votes out of nineteen, a clear majority. In addition to this, career party bureaucrats like Podgorny and Mazurov moved into key state offices.

The rapid and utter defeat of Moscow's Arab client states by Israel in June 1967, was a traumatic diplomatic debacle for the Soviet leadership and triggered another round of acrimonious debate and controversy in the Politburo and Central Committee. While no major shake-ups resulted in the Politburo or Central Committee, significant reassignments of their personnel were further evidence of factional maneuvering for position. The major consequence of the shifts during this period, which were closely linked to foreign policy issues, was the conspicuous downgrading of the youngest and perhaps most threatening member of the Politburo, Alexander Shelepin, and his coterie of ambitious young *apparatchiki*, who were apparently pressuring the leadership for a more dramatic or militant response to the Egyptian defeat. Although the circumstances leading to

the occupation of Czechoslovakia in the following year further aggravated the factional alignments in the Kremlin, no perceptible major changes were registered at the apex of the system.

Changes in the party summit made at the Twenty-fourth Party Congress (1971) reflected even more the emerging dominance of Brezhnev within the Soviet leadership. Aside from the elevation of the general secretaryship to virtually an institutional role at the apex of the party and symbolically listed ahead of the Politburo, Brezhnev's increasing authority was also indicated by changes in the composition of the Politburo and the interlocking membership between it and the Secretariat. Four new full members were added to the Politburo, while members like Kosygin, Voronov, Polyansky, Shelest, and Shelepin suffered a decline in importance. The unexpected appointment of Kulakov, a close associate of Brezhnev and a relatively junior member of the Secretariat, to full membership on the Politburo over the heads of six sitting candidate members was the clearest indication of Brezhnev's growing authority. All of the candidate members advanced to full membership—Kunayev, Grishin, and Shcherbitsky—have had close relations with Brezhnev in the past.

All ten sitting members of the Secretariat were reelected, with six of the ten also sitting on the Politburo, four of them as full members and two as candidate members, thus giving the Secretariat four votes out of fifteen on the Politburo. Among the full members were four other full-time party functionaries: Pelshe, chairman of the Party Control Committee; Kunayev, first secretary of the Kazakh party; Shelest, first secretary of the Ukrainian party; and Grishin, first secretary of the Moscow city party organization. Thus, of the fifteen full members of the Politburo, no less than eight—a majority —were full-time party functionaries under the administrative authority of the general secretary. Of the six candidate members of the Politburo, two (Demichev and Ustinov) were central party secretaries, while three were first secretaries of union republic party organizations: Rashidov (Uzbek), Mzhavandadze (Georgia), and Masherov (Byelorussia). The remaining candidate member, Andropov, was also a veteran party functionary who was a member of the Secretariat until his appointment as head of the secret police in 1967. Thus, of the twenty-one members of the Politburo elected at the Twenty-fourth Party Congress, eight full members and five candidate members were full-time party officials.

In the 1971 reshuffling of Politburo membership, the representatives of state officialdom clearly suffered a setback, with only Podgorny, Kosygin, Mazurov, and Polyansky representing the central state officialdom among the full members, and Voronov (Russian SFSR) and Shcherbitsky (Ukraine) representing republican officials.

The elevation of Gromyko to full membership in the Politburo in 1973, without even a short period of apprenticeship as a candidate member, is unprecedented in Soviet history. Gromyko is a professional diplomat, who entered the diplomatic service during the Stalinist purges at age thirty-three and has served continuously in high diplomatic posts since 1943. He has served as foreign minister longer than any other incumbent—nineteen years—and has not been considered to be a heavyweight in the Soviet political arena. Gromyko is the first professional diplomat to be admitted to the Party's highest body. Thus the foreign ministry and the diplomatic service have achieved professional representation in this body for the first time.

At the same time that Gromyko was admitted to the Politburo, another precedent was established with the promotion of the Defense Minister, Marshal Andrei Grechko, to this body. Grechko is a professional soldier and is the first military professional to sit on this body as a full member in his capacity as a professional. To be sure, Marshal Georgi Zhukov was briefly a full member of this body in 1957, but by the time of his elevation, the Marshal was clearly more a political figure than a professional one, and he was removed abruptly and retired only three months after his appointment.

Thus, for the first time in Soviet history, the two government ministries most deeply involved in the administration of foreign policy are headed by professionals who have been admitted to the inner sanctum of Soviet power. This clearly suggests the increasing reliance of the regime upon professional expertise in the highest levels of politics and probably signifies at the same time the intricate balancing act being performed by Brezhnev. Gromyko and Grechko were admitted to the Politburo along with a third key figure, Yuri Andropov, the Secret Police Chief, who, however, was promoted from candidate membership. Andropov is a veteran party bureaucrat and not a professional policeman, but the simultaneous elevation of the highest representatives of three key institutional structures in the Soviet system reinforces the view that institutional structures are being increasingly recognized as aggregates of interest demanding direct and formal representation. These institutional representatives perform a dual function: they represent their institutional interests in the Politburo, and the Politburo's interests in their respective institutions.

As the Soviet Union moves uneasily into a world of increasing détente with the United States and increasing hostility with China, it becomes imperative that diplomatic and military policy are closely coordinated and in tune, and that the domestic situation be under close control. Gromyko's presence in the Politburo provides professional guidance to détente diplomacy; Grechko's presence guarantees that the voice of the professional military will be heard with equal audibility; while Andropov's presence signifies the anxiety of the regime that détente will foster domestic expectations for greater relaxation of internal ideological controls and the police will play a crucial role in policing these expectations and keeping them in check.

Secretary-General Brezhnev had formed unusually intimate ties with President Nixon and Secretary of State Kissinger in the implementation of his détente policies. President Nixon visited Moscow to sign the SALT and related agreements, while Brezhnev visited the President in the United States just as impeachment proceedings were getting under way in Congress. The forced resignation of President Nixon in 1974 and the passage of the "Jackson Amendment" by Congress requir-

ing that the Soviet Union revise its emigration policies before it could be accorded "most favored nation" status in commerce with the U.S., appeared to weaken Brezhnev's position in the Soviet leadership and exposed his policies to internal criticism. The Secretary-General met with Nixon's successor, President Gerald Ford, in Vladivostock, where another milestone in the Soviet-American détente was registered, thus strongly suggesting that Brezhnev intended to continue along the same course irrespective of the succession problem in the United States.

In April 1975, it was revealed that Alexander Shelepin, the youngest and probably the most ambitious member of the Politburo, had been dropped from the apex of the Soviet leadership, thus removing one of Brezhnev's most dangerous rivals and persistent critics. As noted earlier, Shelepin since 1965 has suffered a number of setbacks, but managed to remain within the leadership. Accompanying Shelepin's removal was a resolution of the Central Committee Plenum, hailing Brezhnev's leadership and reaffirming the détente policy.

It is normal practice to divorce membership in the Secretariat from membership in the Council of Ministers, since the Secretariat is supposed to exercise an independent audit of the government's work and check on the execution and implementation of party directives and resolutions. The only consistent deviation from this practice occurs when the same personality functions as general secretary (first secretary) of the party and as chairman of the Council of Ministers, as was the case during the later years of the Stalin

**TABLE 5.3  Interlocking of Government and Party Institutions and Personnel in the Soviet Political System, 1975**

| PARTY | | | | STATE | | | |
|---|---|---|---|---|---|---|---|
| Other | Republic Secretaries | Secretariat | Politburo | Council of Ministers | Presidium of Supreme Soviet | Premiers of Republics | Other |
| | | Brezhnev (General Secretary) | Brezhnev | | Brezhnev | | |
| | | | Kosygin | Kosygin (Chairman) | | | |
| | | Suslov | Suslov | | | | Suslov[5] |
| | | | Podgorny | | Podgorny (Chairman) | | |
| | | Kirilenko | Kirilenko | | | | |
| Pelshe[1] | Pelshe (Latvia) | | Pelshe | | | | |
| | | | Polyansky | Polyansky | | | |
| Shelepin[2] | | | Shelepin | | | | |
| | | | Mazurov | Mazurov | | | |
| | Kunayev (Kazakh) | | Kunayev | | Kunayev | | |
| | Shcherbitsky (Ukraine) | | Shcherbitsky | | | | |
| Grishin[3] | | | Grishin | | Grishin | | |
| | | Kulakov | Kulakov | | | | |
| | | | Andropov | Andropov | | | |
| | | | Gromyko | Gromyko | | | |
| | | | Grechko | Grechko | | | |
| | | | Solomentsev | | | Solomentsev (R.S.F.S.R.) | |
| | | Demichev | Demichev | | | | |
| | Masherov (Byelorussia) | Masherov | Masherov | | Masherov | | |
| | | Ponomarev | Ponomarev | | Rashidov | | Ponomarev[6] |
| | | | Rashidov | | | | |
| | | Ustinov | Ustinov | | | | |
| Romanov[4] | | Kapitonov | Romanov | | | | |
| | | Rudakov | | | | | |
| | | Katushev | | | | | |

1 Chairman, Party Control Commission  
2 Chairman, All-Union Council of Trade Unions (Dropped in 1975)  
3 Moscow Party Secretary  
4 Leningrad Party Secretary  
5 Chairman, Foreign Affairs Commission, Council of Union  
6 Chairman, Foreign Affairs Commission, Council of Nationalities

and Khrushchev eras. Similarly, the chairmanship of the Presidium of the Supreme Soviet is considered to be incompatible with membership in the Secretariat. Both Brezhnev and Podgorny relinquished their membership in the Secretariat upon their appointment as chairman of the Presidium of the Supreme Soviet. It is traditional, however, for the general secretary to be an ordinary member of the Presidium of the Supreme Soviet if he holds no other state post, and it is usual for the Presidium to include several other members of the party Secretariat, thus ensuring party audit and control over its activities. It is also customary for membership in the Presidium of the Supreme Soviet to be incompatible with membership in the Council of Ministers, since the latter is juridically responsible to the former. Since the death of Stalin, it has been normal practice to include high state and party officials of the R.S.F.S.R. and the Ukraine in the Politburo. (See Table 5.3.)

*The Party Secretariat and the General-Secretary in Soviet Foreign Policy.* Although the formal authority to make policy is vested in the Politburo, this power is clearly shared with the Secretariat, which at times tends to overshadow the Politburo. At the Twenty-third Party Congress in 1966, Stalin's old title of "general secretary" was revived to replace the more modest title of "first secretary," which Khrushchev employed. While the suggestion was rejected that the general secretary also be formally named "head" of the Politburo, Secretariat, and Central Committee, which would have transformed it into an institution rather than a mere title, the idea was apparently successfully resurrected and implemented in indirect form at the Twenty-fourth Party Congress five years later. The

proceedings and resolutions of the Twenty-fourth Party Congress and the behavior of Brezhnev there strongly suggest that the general secretaryship is now more than a title and more akin to an institution or organ, distinct from and superior to the Secretariat, Central Committee, and Politburo. Its precise position at the top of the Soviet institutional hierarchy has not yet been definitely demarcated, but seems nevertheless destined to be so. At the Twenty-third Party Congress, when Brezhnev first assumed the title of general secretary, it was used simply to identify him as the senior member of the Secretariat, and apparently carried no special significance in his capacity as a member of the Politburo: it was essentially a Secretariat title, not a party, Central Committee, or Politburo title. Since Stalin's death, the general and/or first secretary has increasingly assumed a more direct role in Soviet foreign policy and diplomatic negotiation. With the advent of Khrushchev to the counterpart post of first secretary, the role, functions and status of the first secretary started to change. Unlike Stalin, Khrushchev, as first secretary, was highly visible on the diplomatic scene and even before he, too, assumed the post of premier in 1958, Khrushchev participated in a number of diplomatic junkets and summit conferences, but always in the company of Bulganin, who was premier from 1955 to 1958. Khrushchev's presence on these occasions created problems of diplomatic protocol, for Khrushchev made it quite evident that he was invested with the substance of power of which Bulganin was a mere shadow.

In 1966, Brezhnev reinstituted the title of general secretary and this position was considerably strengthened in 1971 when he was reappointed to this position. At the outset of the Brezhnev/Kosygin regime, a scrupulous regard was maintained for diplomatic protocol. Kosygin, as head of the government, and Podgorny, as head of state, conspicuously and jealously preserved their diplomatic and official prerogatives. Gradually, however, Brezhnev intruded his person more and more into official diplomacy, initially restricting himself to Communist states, then extending his activities to Third World countries (Podgorny's jurisdiction) and then to Western Europe and the United States (Kosygin's jurisdiction in the diplomatic division of labor). Brezhnev, in his capacity as general secretary, is now normally accorded all the ceremonial trappings associated with a chief of state by foreign countries, although he holds no official executive or administrative office in the state, aside from ordinary membership in the Presidium. A special authorization was issued by the Presidium of the Supreme Soviet investing Brezhnev with plenipotentiary powers so that the documents signed by him were legal and met all the juridical tests of international law and the protocol norms of diplomacy.

### Internal Politics and Soviet Foreign Policy: Interest Groups and Factional Polarization on Foreign Policy Issues[35]

As the Soviet system matures and becomes inextricably identified with the interests of its various privileged elites, the decision makers must give

[35]This section is adapted from the author's "Internal Politics and Foreign Policy in the Soviet System," in *Approaches to Comparative and International Politics*, ed. B. Farrell (Evanston, Ill.: Northwestern University Press, 1966).

greater consideration, in the calculation of foreign policy, to factors affecting the internal stability of the regime; and they will show greater sensitivity to the effects of decisions on the vested interests of the various elites in Soviet society. The rise of powerful social and economic elites in the Soviet Union, and their insistent pressure for participation in the exercise of political power, could only introduce stresses, strains, conflicts, and hence new restraints into Soviet diplomacy.

Within the context of an ideology that imposes a single interest representing society as a whole, each interest group will tend to distort ideology and policy in an endeavor to give them the contours of its own interests; the next step is to elevate these to transcendental significance. Under these conditions, Soviet ideology may be constantly threatened with a series of fundamental convulsions if one interest group displaces another in the struggle for the control of the party machinery. Hence, a rational system of accommodating conflicting interests appears to be evolving. As the vested stake of each major group becomes rooted in the Soviet system, the contours of Soviet diplomacy and national interest will inexorably tend to be shaped more by the rapidly moving equilibrium or accommodation of interests that develop internally than by abstract ideological imperatives.

Although, ideologically, the basic purpose of external security and state survival is to develop into a power center for the purpose of implementing ideological goals in foreign policy (world communism), increasingly the purpose becomes to protect and preserve the existing social order in the interests of the social groups which dominate and benefit from it.

It must be realized that the relationship between internal interests and external ideological goals is a dynamic one. It fluctuates in accordance with opportunities and capabilities, but in the long run the tendency is that ideological goals which threaten internal interests erode and are deprived of their motivating character. The persistence of ideological goals in Soviet foreign policy reflects sociofunctional interests which have been traditionally associated with the party apparatus and professional ideologues. The fact that the concrete policies which have resulted from the pursuit of ideological goals in foreign policy have created special vested interests for other sociopolitical or socioinstitutional groups, like the secret police, the armed forces, and the heavy-industrial managers, should not obscure the fact that the definition, identification, and implementation of ideological goals, whether in foreign or domestic policy, has been the special function of the party apparatus and its attendant ideologues. An area of common interest among some members of the party apparatus and the armed forces and heavy-industrial managers in pursuing policies which are tension-producing has thus come into being. Tension-producing policies in an era of increasing technological complexity, however, not only tend to enhance the power of professionalized and technologically oriented groups in the Soviet Union, to the relative detriment of the status and power of the party apparatus, but also tend to alienate from the apparatus other more numerous social groups in society whose interests are more in consonance with tension-lessening policies. Such groups involved are the consumer goods producers and light-industrial managers; the intellectuals, artists, professionals, and agricultural managers; and finally, the great mass of Soviet citizenry, comprising the lower intelligentsia, workers, peasants, and others, whose priorities are always lower during periods of high international tensions. Since these latter social forces are more numerous than those whose interests are served by tension-producing policies, the party apparatus was in danger of alienating itself further from the great masses of the Soviet citizenry and becoming increasingly dependent upon the traditional military and heavy industry.

The Soviet Union, like the United States, is thus involved in a great debate over foreign policy and national security matters, centering around the issue of whether heightening or lessening international tensions better serves the "national interest."

The foreign policy and defense posture of the Soviet state establish a certain configuration of priorities in the allocation of money and scarce resources. Various individuals and groups develop a vested interest in a particular foreign policy or defense posture because of the role and status it confers upon them. Correspondingly, other individuals and groups in Soviet society perceive themselves as deprived in status and rewards because of existing allocation of expenditures and resources and, hence, they might initiate proposals which might alter existing foreign policy and defense postures or support proposals submitted by other groups or individuals.

A particular interest group or social formation may often have a role or function imposed upon it by events, circumstances, policies, and the mechanism of a given social system in response to certain situations that were not of its own making, or, in some instances, which provided the basis for its very creation and existence. While particular interest groups may not have sought such a role, nor have taken the initiative in acquiring it, nor even have existed before the function was demanded, once this role is thrust upon them they adjust to it and develop a vested interest in the function imposed upon them, since it constitutes the source of their existence and status. As individual members adjust to their role, develop it, and invest their energies and careers in it, they almost automatically resist the deprivation or diminution of this role in their self-interest.

The same is true of groups to which are assigned limited or arrested functions in society, except that these develop a vested interest in expanding their role, dignifying it with greater prestige, and demanding greater rewards. Consequently, it is extremely difficult to distill from Soviet factional positions those aspects of thought and behavior which express conflicting perceptions of self-interest on the part of various individuals, factions, and groups as opposed to authentic "objective" considerations of a broader interest, whether national or ideological, since they are so inextricably intertwined and interdependent.

All that we can assert at this point is that certain individuals and socioinstitutional functional groups seem to thrive and others to be relatively deprived in their development under conditions of exacerbated international tensions, while the situation is reversed when a relaxation of international tensions take place. Therefore, it might be assumed that groups that are favored by a particular policy or situation have a greater inclination to perceive objective re-

ality in terms of their self-interest. Groups that are objectively favored by heightened international tension might have a greater propensity to perceive external threats and a corresponding disinclination to recognize that the nature of a threat has been altered or eliminated, thus requiring new policies which might adversely affect them. On the other hand, groups that are objectively favored by relaxation of international tensions or a peace-time economy might be more prone to perceive a premature alteration of an external threat and a corresponding tendency to be skeptical about external threats which arise if they would result in a radical rise in defense expenditures and a reallocation of resources and social rewards.

The groups in Soviet society which appear to benefit from an aggressive foreign policy and the maintenance of international tensions are (1) the traditional sectors of the armed forces; (2) the heavy-industrial managers, and (3) professional conservative party *apparatchiki* and ideologues. By no means do all individuals or subelites and cliques within these groups see eye-to-eye on foreign policy issues. Some individuals and subelites, for opportunistic reasons or functional adaptability, are able to adjust to a relaxation of tensions by preserving or even improving their role and status. The significant point is that the impetus for an aggressive policy and the chief opposition to a relaxation of tensions find their social and functional foundations within these three sociofunctional or socioinstitutional groups, whose common perception of interests results in an informal "military-industrial-apparatus complex." Their attitudes stem almost entirely from the role they play in Soviet society and the rewards in terms of prestige and power which are derived from these functions in time of high international tensions as opposed to a détente.

The professional military, on the whole, has a natural interest in a large and modern military establishment and a high priority on budget and resources; the heavy-industrial managerial groups have a vested stake in preserving the primacy of their sector of the economy; and the party apparatus traditionally has had a vested interest in ideological conformity and the social controls which they have rationalized, ensuring the primacy of the apparatus over all other social forces in the Soviet system. All of these functional roles are served best under conditions of international tension. Consequently, this group, wittingly or unwittingly, has developed an interest in either maintaining international tensions or creating the illusion of insecurity and external danger.

To the degree that individuals or subelites within these groups are able to socially retool their functions and adapt them to peacetime or purely internal functions, then do they correspondingly lose interest in an aggressive or tension-preserving policy.

For purposes of analytical convenience, those social groups which would seem to benefit from a relaxation of international tensions can be classified into four general categories: (1) the state bureaucracy, in the central governmental institutions as well as in the republics and localities; (2) light-industrial interests, consumer goods and services interests, and agricultural interests; (3) the cultural, professional and scientific groups, whose role and influence seem to flourish under conditions of relaxation both at home and

abroad; and (4) the Soviet "consumer," who will ultimately benefit most from a policy which concentrates on raising the standard of living. The technical-scientific branches of the professional military, including the nuclear-missile specialists, also appear to benefit during periods of relaxed international tensions, when the main reliance for national security is on them and the traditional forces are subject to severe budget reductions.

While the contradiction between Soviet security interests and ideological goals in foreign policy has long been recognized by observers of the Soviet scene, a new variable in Soviet policy is the contradiction between enhancing economic prosperity at home and fulfilling international ideological obligations. In Soviet jargon, this emerges as a contradiction between the requirements of "building communism" and the costs and risks of remaining faithful to the principle of "proletarian internationalism."

This new factor has not gone unnoticed by the Chinese, who accused Khrushchev of abandoning Soviet ideological and material obligations to international communism and to the national-liberation movement in favor of avoiding the risks of nuclear war and building an affluent society to satisfy the appetites of the new Soviet "ruling stratum," in the guise of pursuing peaceful coexistence and "building communism." Thus, in a long editorial entitled "On Khrushchev's Phoney Communism and Its Historical Lessons For the World," the authoritative Chinese organ *Jen Min Jih Pao* charged on July 14, 1964:

The revisionist Khrushchev clique has usurped the leadership of the Soviet party and state and . . . a privileged bourgeois stratum has emerged in Soviet society. . . . The privileged stratum in contemporary Soviet society is composed of degenerate elements from among the leading cadres of party and government organizations, enterprises, and farms as well as bourgeois intellectuals. . . . Under the signboard of "peaceful coexistence," Khrushchev has been colluding with U.S. imperialism, wrecking the socialist camp and the international communist movement, opposing the revolutionary struggles of the oppressed peoples and nations, practicing great-power chauvinism and national egoism, and betraying proletarian internationalism. All this is being done for the protection of the vested interest of a handful of people, which he places above the fundamental interests of the peoples of the Soviet Union, the socialist camp and the whole world.

The same charge has also been leveled at Khrushchev's successors, who, Peking maintains, are simply practicing "Khrushchevism without Khrushchev."

## The Fragmentation of the Decision-Making Process

Under Stalin, policy formulation and decision making were tightly centralized in Stalin's person: thought and action were coordinated by a single personality. Under his successors, however, the inconclusive struggle for power has resulted in the fragmentation of the decision-making structure, distributing power among various individuals and factions, each in command of parallel institutional power structures. Ideology has been divorced from policy formulation which in turn has been frequently out of phase with the administration and execution of policy as rival factions have assumed control over policy-making bodies. The fragmentation of the decision-making structure was

initially concealed by the figleaf of "collective leadership," as factional politics replaced one-man decisions in the Soviet leadership. Personalities, factions, and eventually sociofunctional and socioinstitutional groupings assumed a more variable role in the shaping of Soviet behavior, and a new fluid relationship was established among Soviet capabilities, ideology, personalities, and institutions in the decision-making process. While this made it even more difficult to judge Soviet intentions and predict Soviet behavior, it was compensated for by the corresponding inability of the Soviet Union to pursue the single-minded and precisely calibrated type of foreign policy which was characteristic of the Stalin era, since Soviet leaders are apparently as uncertain as Western Kremlinologists in charting the course and outcome of internal factional conflict.

Factional conflict in the Soviet hierarchy has thus introduced a new element in Soviet behavior, since it is by no means predictable that a given Soviet personality or faction will continue, repudiate, or modify the policies of its predecessors. Even more significantly, Soviet policy may fluctuate not only in accordance with obvious institutional and personality changes, but also with the changing equilibrium of factions within the hierarchy on a more or less continuing basis. As Soviet capabilities expand, these factional conflicts register changing and conflicting perceptions of risks involved in relation to possible returns; they represent shifting configurations of interest, both domestic and external; and finally they represent conflicting and changing sets of priorities as new choices and options proliferate out of expanded capabilities. In the absence of a stable consensus in the policy-making Politburo, the tendency in the post-Stalinist Soviet Union has been for various factions to implement their own policies through institutions and organs under their direct administrative control, thus conveying the impression of inconsistent and ambivalent behavior in Soviet Policy.

The fragmentation of the decision-making process combined with the erosion of Soviet ideology has produced a new element of both instability and uncertainty in Soviet behavior—an institutionalized irrationality, particularly in crisis situations. Collective leadership, therefore, may not necessarily contribute to more rational or controlled action, but may, under certain conditions, be even more dangerous and difficult to contend with than one-man rule. Under some circumstances, collective leadership may turn out to be collective irresponsibility as decisions are made and unmade by shifting conditions or autonomous action is taken by powerful socioinstitutional bodies in the face of factional paralysis or bureaucratic inertia. The deliberations of a divided oligarchy are not only secret, but anonymous as well, and can yield many surprises. If, as in Czechoslovakia, the Soviet Union could unleash massive military forces *after* tensions had been presumably dissipated, the Soviet leadership is capable of virtually any kind of rash and irresponsible behavior. More than ever, Soviet decisions in foreign policy may reflect the anxieties, fears, insecurities, and ambitions of individual factions and personalities involved in secret and faceless intrigue and maneuver.[36]

[36]See Vernon V. Aspaturian, "The Aftermath of the Czech Invasion," *Current History* 55, no. 327 (November, 1968):263.

## THE ADMINISTRATION AND EXECUTION OF SOVIET FOREIGN POLICY

### Party Policy and State Administration: Conflict and Harmony

Responsibility for the actual *execution* of foreign policy, as distinct from its *formulation*, rests with the Council of Ministers and its Presidium, which is nominally accountable to the Supreme Soviet and its Presidium, but in fact is subordinate to the party Politburo, with which it normally shares key personnel. The relationship between the party's highest body and the Council of Ministers and its Presidium in the decision-making process, depends more upon the degree of interlocking membership between the two organs than upon constitutional forms. Under Stalin, particularly after he became premier in 1941, interlocking membership was virtually complete and was designed to ensure maximum harmony between party policy and state administration. Distinctions between formulation and execution of policy were ambiguous to the point of complete irrelevance under these conditions. Before Stalin held any formal executive position in the government, the institutions of the party were the chief decision-making bodies of the regime. But with his assumption of the premiership, Stalin, the secretary-general of the party, made policy, and in his capacity as premier he was also in charge of its execution and administration. As head of both party and government, he did not need to employ all the institutions of decision making, and those of the party virtually withered away. Since all diplomatic relations with the outside world are carried on through state institutions, the organs of the state had to retain sufficient vitality to legalize Stalin's decisions into formal acts of government.

## The Constitutional Basis of Soviet Foreign Relations

Under the Soviet constitution of 1936, as amended, foreign policy is administered and executed at four different institutional levels: (1) the Presidium of the Supreme Soviet, (2) the Supreme Soviet, (3) the Council of Ministers, and (4) the Union Republics, of which there are now fifteen. Although the Soviet constitutional setup is based on the principle of complete fusion of executive, legislative, and administrative power, each institutional level is invested with certain foreign policy functions, which may be permissive, exclusive, or concurrent. These legal relationships, however, do not function in any way as limitations on Soviet diplomacy.

*The Presidium of the Supreme Soviet.* The Presidium of the Supreme Soviet is vested under the constitution with a wide range of ceremonial, executive, and legislative functions. Juridically a creature of the Supreme Soviet, for which it acts as legal agent, it is its institutional superior and surrogate, since it is empowered with virtually the entire spectrum of authority granted to the Supreme Soviet during the long and frequent intervals between sessions of the Soviet legislature. Technically, all of its actions are subject to later confirmation by the Supreme Soviet, but in practice this is an empty ritual.

In the area of foreign affairs, the Presidium, in the person of its chairman, functions as the ceremonial chief of state, much like the British monarch:

In accordance with the universally recognized doctrine of international law, the supreme representation of the modern state is vested in the chief of state, whether he be an actual person (monarch, president of the republic) or a collective body (Presidium of the Supreme Soviet of the U.S.S.R., Federal Council of Switzerland).... As a general rule, the competence of the chief of state includes the declaration of war and conclusion of peace, nomination and reception of diplomatic agents, granting powers for the conclusion of international treaties and agreements of special significance, and the ratification and denunciation of these treaties and accords.[37]

In its ceremonial capacity, the Presidium confers all diplomatic ranks and titles of a plenipotentiary character, formally appoints and recalls diplomatic representatives of the USSR, and receives the letters of credence and recall from foreign envoys. Although foreign representatives almost always present their credentials to the chairman of the Presidium, they are, in fact, accredited to the Presidium as a collective entity.

The Presidium's substantive powers are considerable. Article 49 of the constitution authorizes it to interpret all Soviet laws, convene and dissolve the Supreme Soviet, annul decisions and orders of the Council of Ministers, appoint and remove the higher commands of the armed forces, and issue decrees in its own right, virtually without limits. Furthermore, the Presidium, during intervals between sessions of the Supreme Soviet, "proclaims a state of war in the event of armed attack ... or whenever necessary to fulfill international treaty obligations concerning mutual defense against aggression," can order general or

[37] Potemkin, *Istoriya Diplomatii*, 3:765.

partial mobilization, and can proclaim martial law in individual localities or throughout the country. The exercise of many of these powers is not subject to later confirmation by the Supreme Soviet, although the Presidium remains technically accountable for all its activities to the Soviet legislature, which theoretically can replace its personnel.

Certain important powers vested in the Presidium are provisional and delegated. Thus, the Presidium, during periods when the Supreme Soviet is not in session, can appoint and dismiss ministers upon the recommendation of the chairman of the Council of Ministers, but this is subject to later confirmation. Similarly, if the Presidium promulgates decrees of a fundamental nature outside its formal constitutional competence, they also are subject to confirmation, although this may be several years later.

Although the constitution appears to give the Presidium a monopoly on the ratification and denunciation of treaties, a law of the Supreme Soviet, "On the Procedure for Ratification and Denunciation of International Treaties," passed on August 19, 1939, defines as treaties requiring its ratification the following: (1) treaties of peace, (2) mutual-defense treaties, (3) treaties of nonaggression, and (4) treaties requiring mutual ratification for their implementation.[38] By implication, and in accordance with past practice, all treaties not specifically enumerated as requiring ratification by the Presidium are left to the discretion of the Council of Ministers. On the other hand, on rare occasions the Supreme Soviet has been asked to ratify or to grant preliminary approval to particularly

[38] *Second Session of the Supreme Soviet of the U.S.S.R.* (New York: International Publishers Co. 1938), p. 678.

important treaties, although there exists no constitutional imperative. *The Supreme Soviet.* As the "highest organ of state authority in the USSR," the Supreme Soviet has power under the constitution which is coterminous with that of the state.

Composed of two coordinate chambers of approximately equal size—the Council of the Union and the Council of Nationalities—the constitutional competence of the Soviet legislature in foreign affairs surpasses that of any other organ. In practice, it has abdicated most of its powers to the Presidium and has been left only with the empty shell of ceremony, which may sometimes border on consultation. Both chambers are equally potent or impotent, singly or together, and neither has specific functions or powers denied the other.

The formal authority of the Supreme Soviet in foreign policy falls into seven categories: (1) the enactment of basic legislation and constitutional amendments; (2) the confirmation of the decisions and decrees of the Presidium and the Council of Ministers; (3) ratification of selected treaties; (4) declaration of war and peace; (5) confirmation and authorization of territorial changes and of the creation, admission, promotion, demotion, and abolition of republics; (6) hearing and approving of foreign policy reports delivered by the premier or the foreign minister; and (7) the preliminary examination of treaties prior to ratification by the Presidium. Since Stalin's death, all these activities have been accorded greater publicity.

The sessions of the Supreme Soviet are short. Between 1946 and 1954, the Supreme Soviet sat for a total of only forty-five days, the longest session lasting seven days (June 1950), the shortest sixty-seven minutes (March 1953); its performance before and during World War II was even less auspicious. By far the most significant function of the Supreme Soviet is to hear reports on the foreign policy of the government. It is customary that the foreign minister review the government's foreign policy before this body, usually before joint sessions. It listens attentively and enacts the desired legislation. There is "discussion," but a close examination of the official records discloses not a single note of criticism, to say nothing of a negative vote, in all the deliberations of the Supreme Soviet.

In the words of *Kommunist*, "until recently [the Supreme Soviet's] sessions concerned for the most part consideration of budget questions and approval of the decrees of the Presidium"[39] ; but after the replacement of Malenkov with Bulganin in 1955, it was given a more conspicuous role in foreign affairs. At that time, the Supreme Soviet issued an appeal to the parliaments of other countries for a program of parliamentary exchanges in the form of visiting delegations addressing each other's legislatures; more than a dozen such exchanges have taken place. In July 1955, the Supreme Soviet adhered to the Inter-Parliamentary Union (ITU) and sent a delegation to its forty-fourth annual conference in Helsinki.

Although the two Foreign Affairs Commissions of the two chambers of the Supreme Soviet are supposed to make "a preliminary examination of all matters connected with foreign affairs to be considered by the Supreme Soviet (and its Presidium),"

this function had all but withered away, and the existence of these bodies was rendered virtually superfluous. They were suddenly brought back to life when the Soviet-Iranian agreement of 1954, the denunciation of the Anglo-Soviet and Anglo-French treaties of alliance, the Warsaw Pact, and the agreement to establish diplomatic relations with West Germany were all submitted to joint sessions of the two commissions (the Supreme Soviet was not in session) for consideration. After hearing reports by Molotov and his deputies, they recommended approval to the Presidium of the Supreme Soviet. At about the same time, the two chairmen of the chambers, together with reputedly prominent members of the two commissions, appeared at diplomatic receptions, received foreign dignitaries, and pompously pontificated on foreign policy in patent, but bogus, imitation of their counterparts in the U.S. Congress.

It was the Supreme Soviet which proclaimed an end to the state of war with Germany, on January 25, 1955. On August 4, 1955, it was called into special session to hear Bulganin's report on the summit conference at Geneva, a procedure that had not been used since Molotov addressed a special session on the Nazi-Soviet Pact of 1939. On this same occasion, the Supreme Soviet, after "debating" the policy of the government and "interpellating" the foreign minister, issued an appeal to the parliaments and governments of the world to "put an end to the arms race." The regular session of the Supreme Soviet coincided with the return of Bulganin and Khrushchev from their tour of Southeast Asia, and both addressed the Supreme Soviet on the results of their trip.

Although the activities of the Su-

[39] *Kommunist*, August, 1956, no. 10, pp. 3–15.

preme Soviet have been stepped up, there is little reason to believe that there has been a corresponding enhancement of its influence and power. It hears more reports on foreign policy, but it has also retained its absolute unanimity. The invocation of the formal prerogatives of the Supreme Soviet, however, is no idle exercise, since it creates certain advantages for Soviet diplomacy: (1) it serves to infuse the citizenry with the notion that their representatives participate in the formulation of foreign policy decisions; (2) as a propagandistic maneuver, it strives to create the illusion of evolving constitutionalism in the Soviet system; (3) as a purely diplomatic device, it permits the Kremlin to invoke constitutional procedures as a stumbling or delaying mechanism in negotiations, and affords a basis for demanding reciprocal action in the ratification of treaties and other diplomatic instruments.

The possibility, no matter how slight, that ceremony may some day be replaced with substance cannot be ignored, but this expectation must yield to the realization that the flurry of activity we have noted can be arrested as abruptly as it began. Yet it must be stated that periodic suggestions are made in the Soviet press that the Supreme Soviet be given more legislative authority.

*The Council of Ministers.* As the "highest executive and administrative organ" of the government, the Council of Ministers[40] "exercises general supervision" over the execution and administration of the country's foreign policy, and also directs the state's foreign trade monopoly. Constitutionally, since 1944 the central government no longer exercises a monopoly over foreign affairs, but merely represents the Soviet Union as a whole and establishes the "general procedure in mutual relations between the Union Republics and foreign states," and thus shares the conduct of diplomacy with its fifteen constituent republics. In practice, however, foreign policy in the Soviet Union is the most tightly centralized activity of the Soviet government.

The Council of Ministers has the power to (1) grant or withdraw recognition of new states or governments; (2) sever and restore diplomatic relations; (3) order acts of reprisal against other states; (4) appoint negotiators and supervise the negotiation of international treaties and agreements; (5) declare the adherence of the Soviet Union to international conventions not requiring formal ratification; (6) conclude agreements not requiring ratification with other heads of governments (similar to American executive and administrative agreements); (7) ratify all treaties and agreements not requiring ratification of the Presidium; (8) make preliminary examination of all treaties submitted to the Presidium for its ratification; (9) oversee "the current work of the diplomatic organs, effactually direct that work and take the necessary measures in that field"; and (10) appoint and accredit all diplomats below plenipotentiary rank and foreign trade representatives.[41]

Actually, there appears to be a great area of overlapping activity between the Presidium and the Council of Ministers in the conduct of diplomacy, and were it not for the fact that the one-party system makes all basic decisions, rivalries and jeal-

---

[40]Formerly the Council of People's Commissars, or *Sovnarkom.*

[41]See A. Y. Vyshinsky, *The Law of the Soviet State* (New York: Macmillan, 1948), p. 376; Potemkin, *Istoriya Diplomatii,* 3:767–68, 806–7.

ousies would almost certainly develop between these two organs, rendering coordination of diplomatic activity virtually impossible.

The most influential member of the Council of Ministers is its chairman, referred to in the West as the *premier*, who is always an important figure of the highest rank in the party hierarchy. This office, under the present and previous constitutions, has been filled by only eight men since the establishment of the Soviet state: Lenin (1917–1924); Rykov (1924–1930); Molotov (1930–1941); Stalin (1941–1953); Malenkov (1953–1955); Bulganin (1955–1958); Khrushchev (1958–1964); and Kosygin (1964–   ). Immediately after Lenin's death, when Stalin refused to hold formal office, this post was reduced to a mere shadow of the secretary-general of the party; but after Stalin assumed formal responsibility for the policies of the government in 1941, the post reassumed its former prestige and power. The rivalries that were unleashed after Stalin's death in 1953 temporarily revived the division of power between the premier and first secretary of the party, and the two positions were again separated, then reunited, and later reseparated. Khrushchev's assumption of the office after Bulganin's resignation reflected the internal and external symbolic significance which it acquired during Stalin's long tenure as well as the fact that it was too risky to permit it to be separately occupied.

The chairman (premier) has primary responsibility for the conduct of foreign policy and, presumably, the authority to appoint and remove the ministers concerned with its day-to-day execution. Immediately below the chairman are his first deputy chairmen and deputy chairmen, who normally are in charge of specific ministries, or may be without portfolio. The chairman, his first deputies, and his deputies constitute the Presidium (cabinet) of the Council of Ministers.

The Presidium has undergone serious transformations in size and composition in recent years, varying in size by more than a dozen members. Under Stalin the Presidium became so large that a Bureau (inner cabinet) of the Presidium was secretly organized, the composition and membership of which have never been made public. After Stalin's death, the Bureau of the Presidium was technically abolished, but, in fact, the Presidium was reduced to the smaller size of the Bureau.

The Council of Ministers and its Presidium are actually subordinate to the party Politburo and, in theory, to the Supreme Soviet and its Presidium. If the premier of the government loses a vote of confidence in the Politburo, the decision is reviewed by the Central Committee; if it is unheld there, he submits his resignation to the Presidium of the Supreme Soviet. The Central Committee, through its general secretary, nominates the next premier to the appropriate state organs and a new government is thus formed.

With Khrushchev's ouster in 1964, the stage was set for renewed rivalry between the Secretariat and the Council of Ministers. Kosygin took over Khrushchev's role as chairman of the Council of Ministers (Premier) and Brezhnev occupied Khrushchev's position as First Secretary, later to be changed to General Secretary. Beginning in 1968, the role of the Premier (Kosygin) in foreign policy has been substantially diminished, while that of Brezhnev, especially after his elevation to General Secretary in 1966, has been enhanced. Since the Twenty-fourth Party Congress in 1971, Kosygin has been all but eclipsed in foreign policy, particularly in the area of Soviet-American relations, by Brezhnev, who now performs many of the roles previously carried out not only by the Chairman of the Council of Ministers, but the Chairman of the Presidium of the Supreme Soviet (Podgorny) as well.

In nearly sixty years of Soviet diplomacy, there have been only seven foreign ministers: Leon Trotsky (November, 1917–April, 1918); Georgi Chicherin (1918–1929); Maxim Litvinov (1929–1939); Vyacheslav Molotov (1939–1949 and 1953–1956); Andrei Vyshinsky (1949–1953); Dimitri Shepilov (during 1956); and Andrei Gromyko (1957–    ). The typical tenure of a Soviet foreign minister is ten years. Nearly fifty-five years of Soviet diplomacy have been directed by only four individuals, thus giving Soviet diplomacy an enviable continuity—except for a few years after Stalin's death, when the changes reflected the bitter conflicts that have raged over foreign policy in the past few years.

### The Ministry of Foreign Affairs

*Evolution of the Foreign Ministry.* The Ministry of Foreign Affairs,[42] the government department directly charged with the daily administration of Soviet diplomacy, does not materially differ in its structure and organization from its counterparts in the other Great Powers, although its evolution is unique. Since its establishment, it has undergone a triple metamorphosis.

[42]Formerly the People's Commissariat for Foreign Affairs, or *Narkomindel.*

In the beginning, its primary purpose was to trigger a world revolution and thus create the conditions for its own extinction. It was thought that if the world revolution failed, a Soviet diplomacy would be impossible, and, if it succeeded, unnecessary. It was Leon Trotsky's boast: "I will issue a few revolutionary proclamations to the people of the world, and then close up shop."[43] On November 26, 1917, a decree from Trotsky's Foreign Affairs Commissariat virtually disestablished the diplomatic apparatus of the Russian state: all members of the Russian foreign service abroad were summarily dismissed unless they expressed loyalty to the Bolshevik regime. In their places, Bolshevik émigrés abroad were appointed as "unofficial" agents of the new government (Litvinov was such an appointee to Great Britain). Trotsky even neglected to establish a permanent home office; he appeared at his office only once—to dismiss all employees reluctant to pledge loyalty to the new regime and to set up a committee to publish the secret treaties in archives of the Russian Foreign Office.

The Treaty of Brest-Litovsk imposed upon the new regime diplomatic relations with Germany and its allies, so the Council of People's Commissars was forced to re-create a provisional diplomatic service. With obvious petulance, in a decree of June 4, 1917, it attempted to rewrite unilaterally the principle of diplomatic ranks adopted by the Congress of Vienna in 1815, by abolishing all Soviet diplomatic titles in favor of a single designation, "plenipotentiary representative"

[43]Quoted in E. H. Carr, *The Bolshevik Revolution, 1917–1923* (London: Macmillan, 1953), 3:16.

(*Polpred*). In a naïve attempt to impose Soviet egalitarian principles upon foreign envoys, the decree peremptorily announced that "all diplomatic agents of foreign states ... shall be considered equal plenipotentiary representatives regardless of their rank."[44]

Pending the eventual liquidation of the Foreign Affairs Commissariat, the functions of Soviet diplomacy during this initial period fell into three principal categories: (1) the publication of "secret treaties" in order to expose the duplicity and hypocrisy of the Allies and compromise them in the eye of their own people; (2) the conduct of necessary negotiations and diplomatic relations, on a temporary basis, with those capitalist states in a position to impose them; and (3) the utilization of Soviet embassies and legations abroad as centers of revolutionary propaganda, conspiracy, and activity (in clear violation of treaty obligations). In this connection, the Soviet government announced that

the Council of People's Commissars considers it necessary to offer assistance by all possible means ... to the left internationalist wing of the labor movement of all countries [and] ... for this purpose ... decides to allocate two million rubles for the needs of the revolutionary international movement and to put this sum at the disposal of the foreign representatives of the Commissariat for Foreign Affairs.[45]

Since the revolutionary and conspiratorial activities of Soviet diplomats complicated the establishment of desirable trade and political connections with the bourgeois world, the new commissar of foreign affairs, Georgi Chicherin (who succeeded Trotsky in April 1918), was instrumental in shifting the function of revolutionary agitation from the foreign office to the party. A new diplomatic service was organized from scratch by Chicherin, and shortly after he assumed office the Foreign Commissariat was organized into more than a dozen departments. The first "Statute on the Commissariat for Foreign Affairs" was issued by the Council of Ministers on July 6, 1921; it defined the sphere of competence of each of the departments. After the formation of the Union and the centralization of diplomacy in Moscow, the commissariat on November 12, 1923, received its definite statute which still constitutes the juridical basis for the organization and structure of the Foreign Ministry. However, it was not until 1924 that Soviet diplomacy was juridically relieved of its revolutionary mission and entered into its current phase. According to a decree issued November 21, 1924, and still effective:

It goes without saying that diplomatic missions abroad are appointed by each of the parties establishing diplomatic relations for purposes which exclude propaganda in the country to which they are accredited. The Soviet diplomatic missions follow and are to follow this principle with absolute strictness.[46]

Although, technically, the Soviet foreign office is supervised by the Council of Ministers, it has always enjoyed a unique, direct relationship

[44]Full text in T. A. Taracouzio, *The Soviet Union and International Law* (New York: Macmillan, 1936), p. 383.

[45]Jane Degras, ed., *Soviet Documents on Foreign Policy* (London: Royal Institute of International Affairs, 1951), 1:22.

[46]Full text in Taracouzio, *The Soviet Union and International Law*, pp. 389–90.

with the party Presidium. Unlike the other departments of government in the new Bolshevik regime, the Foreign Commissariat was unencumbered with holdovers from the old bureaucracy, Chicherin being the only prominent figure who had previous diplomatic experience. Consequently, from the very beginning, it was cherished by Lenin:

The diplomatic apparatus . . . is quite exceptional in the governmental apparatus. We excluded everyone from the old Tsarist apparatus who formerly had even the slightest influence. Here, the whole apparatus, insofar as it possesses the slightest influence, has been made up of Communists. For this reason this apparatus has acquired for itself . . . the reputation of a Communist apparatus which has been tested and cleansed of the old Tsarist bourgeois and petty bourgeois apparatus to a degree incomparably higher than that attained in the apparatus with which we have to be satisfied in the other people's commissariats.[47]

This quality, in the words of a Soviet diplomat, "helped make it a peculiarly well-fitted apparatus for the expression of new policies."[48]

The statute governing the Foreign Affairs Commissariat, decreed on November 12, 1923, which has been frequently amended but never superseded, defined its principal duties as follows:

(a) The defence of the political and economic interests of the USSR . . . (b) The conclusion of treaties and agreements with foreign countries in accordance with the decisions of the government. (c) Supervision over the proper execution of treaties and agreements concluded with foreign states, and enabling the corresponding organs of the USSR and the Union Republics to exercise rights conferred by these treaties. (d) Supervision over the execution by the competent organs of treaties, agreements, and accords concluded with foreign states.[49]

*The Foreign Minister and his Collegium.* The administration of the Foreign Commissariat was initially entrusted to a collegium in accordance with the Bolshevik principle of collective responsibility. The foreign commissar was forced to share authority and responsibility with a board of three or four other senior officials of the commissariat.

By 1934, defects of collective responsibility became so serious that Stalin condemned the collective principle as obsolete and subversive of efficient administration; the collegium was abolished and the foreign minister given complete charge of his department; in turn, he assumed full personal responsibility for its work.

Four years later, in March 1938, the collegium was restored in modified form, but was clearly divested of its former tyrannical power over the commissar. The Council of Ministers, which was too large and unwieldy as a decision-making or even advisory body, was retained as a convenient institution for the diffusion of policy and administrative decisions, and the collegium retained its

---

[47] *New York Times,* July 1, 1956. Extract is from suppressed Lenin documents distributed at the Twentieth Party Congress and later made public.

[48] Alexi F. Neymann, in *The Soviet Union and World Problems,* ed. S. N. Harper (Chicago: Chicago University Press, 1935), p. 279.

[49] The full text of this statute, with amendments through 1927, is reprinted in *Yezhegodnik Narodnovo Komissariata Po Inostrannym Delam Na 1928 God* (Moscow 1928), pp. 182–93. All subsequent references and extracts refer to this text. See also Potemkin, *Istoriya Diplomatii,* 3:770–71.

character as the executive committee of the commissariat. The commissar retained his plenary authority and responsibility, but the formal prerogatives of the collegium remained considerable.[50]

The institutional relationship established in 1938 between the foreign minister and his collegium has survived, substantially unaltered, till now. The size and composition of the collegium appear to vary, depending upon the discretion of the foreign minister (except in unusual circumstances), although appointments to the collegium continue to be made by the Council of Ministers. The collegium is presided over by the minister or one of his first deputies. It includes not only the first deputy and deputy ministers, but also about four to six senior officials in the department, one of whom frequently is the chief of the Press and Information Division. The number of first deputies has varied from one to three; their rank roughly corresponds to that of the undersecretary in the American State Department. Immediately below the first deputies are the deputies, whose rank corresponds to that of assistant secretaries in the American hierarchy; there may be up to six deputies (in 1966 there was one first deputy and six deputies). The other members of the collegium are normally department heads. Thus, the size of the collegium may vary by more than a dozen members.

The institutional prerogatives of the collegium fall just short of the power of actual decision, but without weakening in any way the full responsibility of the minister. It cannot overrule the minister's decisions, nor issue orders in its own name, but it is mandatory for the minister to report any disagreement with his collegium to the Council of Ministers for disposition. The collegium retains the right, individually or collectively, to appeal to the Council of Ministers or to the Central Committee of the party.[51]

*The Organization and Structure of the Foreign Ministry.* The basic organization and structure of the Soviet Foreign Ministry remain governed by the statute of 1923, which established a flexible system of administration, permitting a wide latitude for internal reorganization at the discretion of the minister. The ministry is organized into "divisions according to the main geographical divisions of the world and the main functions of the department and ... this apparatus both in its offices in Moscow and its missions in foreign countries does not present any striking differences in structure compared with similar departments in other countries."[52]

At the apex of the ministry stands the minister with his collegium, which is provided with a central secretariat—headed by a secretary general—performing routine secretarial and staff administrative work for the minister, his deputies, and other members of the collegium. The functional divisions, which have become increasingly differentiated with the expansion of Soviet diplomatic activity, have been conventional: Protocol, Political Archives, Courier and Liaison, Passport and Visa, Treaty and Legal, Economic, Consular Affairs, Administration, Personnel, Finance, Supplies, and Press and Information. Several related functional divisions are grouped together and supervised by

---

[50]See Vyshinsky, *The Law of the Soviet State,* pp. 387–89.

[51]Ibid.

[52]Neymann, in Harper, *The Soviet Union and World Problems,* pp. 226–27.

deputy ministers, and perhaps also by other collegium members. As Soviet power and influence in international affairs has increased, the functional divisions have undergone substantial reorganization in recent years. There are now seven functional divisions: Protocol, Press, Treaty and Legal, Consular Administration, Archives Administration, Personnel Administration, and Administration for Servicing the Diplomatic Corps. In addition, attached to the Foreign Ministry are two training institutions, the Institute of International Relations and the Higher Diplomatic School. The old Economic Division has since proliferated into a separate ministry called the State Committee for Foreign Economic Relations, which is in charge of the extensive Soviet foreign aid program. Two other ministries closely related to the Foreign Ministry are the old Ministry of Foreign Trade and the State Committee for Cultural Relations with Foreign Countries.

The political changes of the past twenty years, the massive expansion of Soviet diplomatic relations, and the creation of many new states in Asia and Africa have profoundly affected the internal organization of the foreign office. In the past few years, the number of geographical divisions has been increased, while the number of functional divisions has remained fairly constant. As compiled from press accounts, there are now eight "Western" divisions and eight "Eastern" divisions, plus two separate departments for international organizations and international economic organizations. The present geographical divisions, which closely resemble those of 1925, are as follows:

*Western divisions*

1. United States of America Division
2. Latin American Countries Division
3. First European Division (France, Benelux, Italy)
4. Second European Division (United Kingdom and white Commonwealth countries)
5. Third European Division (the two Germanies, Austria, Switzerland)
6. Fourth European Division (Poland and Czechoslovakia)
7. Fifth European Division (Balkan countries)
8. Sixth European Division (Scandinavian countries and Finland)

*Eastern divisions*

1. First African Division (North African states with the exception of Egypt and Sudan)
2. Second African Division (black African states)
3. Third African Division (black African states)
4. Near Eastern Countries Division
5. Middle Eastern Countries Division
6. South Asian Countries Division
7. Southeast Asian Countries Division
8. Far Eastern Countries Division (China, Mongolia, North Korea, and Japan)

Normally, a deputy minister exercises general administrative supervision over the work of several contiguous geographical divisions, and usually he is a former ambassador with diplomatic experience in the geographical area in question.

The appearance of kindred communist states in Eastern Europe and in the Far East has not modified the geographical divisions of the ministry. Relations with communist countries through the Foreign Ministry, however, have been reduced to the bare minimum required by international law and protocol, since substantive and policy questions are handled through corresponding party organizations. Soviet envoys to other important communist countries are considered primarily as functionaries and emissaries from the party, and secondarily as government agents. This has been confirmed and emphasized since Stalin's death, with the adoption of the practice of dispatching high party functionaries as ambassadors to other important communist states.

In view of the deterioration of relations with China, however, party relations between the two countries have virtually ceased, and contact has been limited almost exclusively to formal state relations. Already in 1959, Moscow had replaced a highly placed party official (Yudin) functioning as the Soviet ambassador with Chervonenko, a lower-level party functionary. And in April 1965, Chervonenko was replaced by a career diplomat, S. G. Lapin, who is not even a candidate member of the Central Committee. Lapin was withdrawn to become head of Tass, the Soviet news agency, in 1967, at the height of China's Great Proletarian Cultural Revolution, when the Soviet embassy was barricaded and its personnel abused and insulted by the rampaging Red Guards. Peking also withdrew its ambassador, and relations were not restored until late 1970, when V. S. Tolstikov, a veteran party functionary and member of the Central Committee since 1961, was appointed to Peking. Tolstikov's party ranking, nearer Chervonenko's level than Yudin's, is nevertheless sufficiently high to suggest that Moscow would prefer to employ him as a conduit to the Chinese party as well as state, in line with its general diplomatic pattern of relations with other communist countries. In sum, there is little question but that the party standing of Soviet ambassadors to other communist countries is indicative of the state of party relations existing between them.

*The Soviet Diplomatic Service.* The decree of 1918 reducing all diplomatic ranks to the single and equal rank of plenipotentiary representative remained technically in force until 1941, although it was neither possible nor desirable to honor it in practice. The principle of diplomatic equality was based on the discarded theory that "the representatives of ... the USSR do not personify a quasi-mythical Leviathan state, but only ... the plenipotentiary of the ruling class," and that diplomats from bourgeois countries were likewise emissaries of their ruling classes.[53] This view was condemned as doctrinaire and subversive of Soviet prestige and diplomacy since, in practice, it amounted to unilateral renunciation of all the privileges and prerogatives of seniority and rank under traditional norms of diplomatic intercourse.

Soviet diplomacy gradually accommodated itself to existing international practice through the extralegal exchange of supplementary protocols granting informal recognition of rank, so that Soviet diplomats might avoid forfeiting recognized privileges accorded those of rank and seniority. On May 9, 1941, the Presidium issued a decree establishing three diplomatic categories: (1) ambassador extraordinary and plenipotentiary, (2) minister extraordinary and plenipotentiary, and (3) chargé d'affaires. This decree gave legal sanction to de facto distinctions. Two years later, on May 28, 1943, the Presidium decreed the establishment of eleven grades in the diplomatic service and thus brought Soviet diplomatic ranking into complete focus with general diplomatic practice: (1) ambassador extraordinary and plenipotentiary;

[53]E. Korovin, *Mezhdunarodnoye Pravo Perekhodnovo Vremeni* (Moscow, 1924), p. 63.

(2) minister extraordinary and plenipotentiary of the first class; (3) minister extraordinary and plenipotentiary of the second class; (4) counselor, first class; (5) counselor, second class; (6) first secretary, first class; (7) first secretary, second class; (8) second secretary, first class; (9) second secretary, second class; (10) third secretary; and (11) attaché.[54]

*The Channels of Soviet Diplomacy.* It is general practice for Soviet envoys to report to the ministry through routine bureaucratic channels—that is, through the appropriate geographical divisions in the ministry—but ambassadors in important posts frequently report directly to the foreign minister. Reports of an exceptionally important character are also sent directly to the foreign minister or his first deputies, rather than through normal channels. The close supervision of the diplomatic service by the party center cannot be overemphasized; and diplomatic channels remain deliberately flexible.

Not all Soviet representatives abroad report to the Foreign Ministry. Envoys to other communist states, particularly those holding high party rank, probably report to the Central Committee or the Presidium, except for reports of essentially protocol or legalistic significance, which are funneled through normal channels. The jurisdiction of the Foreign Ministry over envoys to communist countries appears marginal at best.

Although the ambassador, as the chief legal representative of the Soviet Union in foreign countries, is charged with general supervision over the activities of Soviet representatives and missions abroad to ensure that they are in accord with the general policy of the government, this responsibility is often of little more than formal or legal significance. According to defectors like Igor Gouzenko and Vladimir Petrov, Soviet missions abroad are organized into five separate divisions, each with separate and independent channels of communication: (1) the ambassador and his staff, reporting directly to the Ministry of Foreign Affairs; (2) the commercial counselor, reporting to the Ministry of Foreign Trade; (3) the secret police representative, disguised as a minor diplomat, reporting directly to the foreign section of the Security Ministry (now Security Committee); (4) the attachés, reporting directly to the director of military intelligence in Moscow; (5) the party representative, also disguised as a minor diplomatic functionary, communicating directly with the foreign section of the Central Committee of the party.

All of these representatives, with the exception of the ambassador and the embassy staff proper, may be actively engaged in the overt or clandestine collection of intelligence information. In order to comply with the letter of their agreements with foreign countries, the ambassador is scrupulously insulated from all knowledge of illegal espionage activities organized by the other sections, and although the Foreign Ministry statute gives him the power to determine whether their activities are in accordance with government policy, in practice the ambassador rarely sees the reports dispatched by the other sections through their respective channels.

In addition to espionage and intelligence activities, the secret police and party sections maintain general surveillance over the other members of the mission and over each other.

[54]See Potemkin, *Istoriya Diplomatii,* 3:778–80. The date of the decree is mistakenly given as June 14, 1943, in this work.

If the accounts of high-ranking defectors from the diplomatic and police service are accurate, Soviet missions abroad are often centers of intrigue, personal vendettas, and institutional rivalries and jealousies.

Information coming through various channels is screened, coordinated, and evaluated by a special agency of the Central Committee, which then submits its reports to the Presidium to be used as a factor in the formulation of foreign policy and in the making of decisions.

As instruments, rather than makers of policy, Soviet professional diplomats play a minor role in the formulation of foreign policy. Their work is essentially technical and legalistic; their reports are concerned primarily, if not exclusively, with observations and suggestions for more effective implementation of existing policy. Their area of initiative is carefully circumscribed, and often they are ignorant of the exact intentions of their superiors in the Kremlin. Their reports constitute but a minute fraction of the information on which the Presidium acts, and final disposition of all information from routine diplomatic channels and intelligence sources is made by the Presidium as it sees fit.

## CONCLUSIONS

The balance sheet of Soviet foreign policy over the past fifty-five years shows an impressive range of accomplishments when measured against a comparable period for any other power of similar magnitude. An outlaw state in 1917, governed by a pariah regime, beset on all sides by powerful enemies, racked internally by social convulsions, civil war, fragmentation, and foreign occupation, the Soviet Union, whose chances for survival then were extremely poor, stands today as a modernized global power, second only to the United States in power, prestige, and influence. This evolution was no orderly unilinear development, preordained by history, but rather the outcome of periodic collisions between utopian hopes generated by ideology and the limitations imposed by the interests and ambitions of other states.

Throughout most of its history, Soviet foreign policy has operated within a self-defined framework of a two-camp or bipolar world with two basic players, Communism (the Soviet Union) and capitalism (everybody else), so that all losses in the capitalist world were automatic gains for the Soviet Union. While such an image of the world was a crude distortion of reality, it is true that the Soviet addiction to this grim view could only redefine the international situation and superimpose upon international politics the synthetic impression of a zero-sum game whereby a loss for one player was automatically a gain for the other. For nearly two decades the Cold War was pursued within this framework as the bipolarization of power around Moscow and Washington increasingly assumed the objective character of a zero-sum game. The disintegration of the European colonial empires, the advent of weapons of instantaneous and universal destruction, the progressive dissolution of the Soviet bloc, the erosion of the NATO alliance, and the eruption of the fraticidal Sino-Soviet conflict, however, have all but destroyed the bipolarized international community in which gains and losses could be registered with zero-sum gamelike simplicity.

The Soviet Union's current status and position in the world community represents a blend of objective success and subjective failure. That is, the Soviet Union has been a resounding success when its achievements are measured against the traditional yardstick of power politics, but a conspicuous failure when measured against its initial ideological inspiration and purpose. Instead of transforming the world, it is the Soviet Union that has been transformed. From a self-annointed center of world revolution dedicated to the destruction of the existing social and political status quo, it has been objectively transformed into a mature global power whose interest in stabilizing the status quo now virtually matches its dedication to revolution. From a self-perceived instrument of history ordained to save mankind from the injustices of capitalism and mandated to construct a new World Communist society of universal justice, liberated from class, national, and racial conflict, the Soviet Union is now content to offer itself as a model for rapid modernization and industrialization of underdeveloped societies, with its eschatological and apocalyptic rhetoric largely muted. Finally, its ideology has been transformed from a vehicle legitimizing world revolution into one legitimizing Communist rule in Russia; instead of raising the standard of revolution abroad, Moscow emphasized raising the standard of living at home in the name of ideology; instead of justifying further social changes in the Soviet system, it rationalizes the social status quo; instead of inspiring the masses to charge the barricades, Soviet ideology now erects barricades against the heresies of Peking.

If we employ the traditional criteria of success in foreign policy (power, influence, and prestige), it is indisputable that the Soviet Union has been more successful than any other state in the past fifty years, save the United States. The most significant factor in the simultaneous rise of Soviet power and decline of the power of other states was the Second World War. Germany was dismembered and occupied; Japan was squeezed back into her main island and disarmed; Italy was shorn of her colonial empire, while a weakened France, Great Britain, and Netherlands progressively relinquished theirs. During the same period, the Soviet Union annexed 250,000 square miles of territory in Europe and Asia, established vassal and subservient states in East Asia and Eastern Europe, displacing Japan and Germany respectively as the dominant powers in those two regions. It supported a successful Communist takeover in China; sponsored the growth and proliferation of Communist parties abroad, which it manipulated as instruments of its foreign policy; continued to maintain the largest military establishment in the world; and posed to move into new vacuums which might be created by the convulsions and agonies of colonial empires in dissolution and by the internal turmoil which swept Western Europe in the postwar period.

Although the Soviet Union has certainly failed in its original ideological mission of communizing the world, its half-century attempt has left a lasting imprint upon the physiognomy of the globe. It has fundamentally restructured the social, political, economic, and ideological configurations of one-third of the world and reoriented the direction in which the rest is moving. As a consequence of its endeavors, an international subsystem of fourteen Communist states has been established. These states not only share a common ideology, but a common socioeconomic system with a distinctive set of property relationships, giving rise to a shared social structure, governed and regulated by highly similar political institutions and processes.

Furthermore, Communist parties, are to be found in some seventy additional countries on every continent, ranging from miniscule and furtive illegal conspiratorial groups to large mass parties, such as those in France, Italy, and India. All these parties are inspired by variants of a common ideology, Marxism-Leninism, and are thus derivative emanations from the Bolshevik Revolution of 1917.

## SELECTED BIBLIOGRAPHY

ASPATURIAN, VERNON V. *Process and Power in Soviet Foreign Policy.* Boston: Little, Brown, 1971.

———. *The Union Republics in Soviet Diplomacy.* Paris: Libraire Droz, 1960.

———. *The Soviet Union in the International Communist System.* Stanford, Calif.: Hoover Institution Studies, 1966.

BARGHOORN, F. C. *The Soviet Cultural Offensive.* Princeton: Princeton University Press, 1960.

———. *The Soviet Image of the United States.* New York: Harcourt Brace Jovanovich, 1950.

———. *Soviet Russian Nationalism.* New York: Oxford University Press, 1956.

BELOFF, MAX. *The Foreign Policy of Soviet Russia, 1929–1941.* New York: Royal Institute of International Affairs, 1947.

———. *Soviet Policy in the Far East, 1944–1951.* London: Royal Institute of International Affairs, 1953.

BRZEZINSKI, ZBIGNIEW K. *The Soviet Bloc.* 2d ed. Cambridge: Harvard University Press, 1967.

CARR, E. H. *The Bolshevik Revolution, 1917–1923.* Vol. 3. London: Macmillan, 1953.

———. *German-Soviet Relations between the Two World Wars.* Baltimore: Johns Hopkins Press, 1951.

DALLIN, ALEXANDER, ed. *Soviet Conduct in World Affairs.* New York: Columbia University Press, 1960.

DALLIN, ALEXANDER, et al., eds. *Diversity in International Communism.* New York: Columbia University Press, 1963.

DEGRAS, JANE, ed. *Soviet Documents on Foreign Policy.* 3 vols. New York: Oxford University Press, 1951–1953.

DEUTSCHER, I. *Stalin.* New York: Oxford University Press, 1949.

DINERSTEIN, HERBERT. *War and the Soviet Union.* 2d ed. New York: Praeger, 1963.

FAINSOD, M. *How Russia Is Ruled.* 2d ed. Cambridge: Harvard University Press, 1963.

FISCHER, LOUIS. *Russia's Road From Peace to War.* New York: Harper & Row, 1969.

———. *The Soviets in World Affairs.* 2 vols. Princeton: Princeton University Press, 1951.

FLOYD, DAVID. *Mao Against Khrushchev.* New York: Praeger, 1963.

GITTINGS, JOHN. *Survey of the Sino-Soviet Dispute.* New York: Oxford University Press, 1968.

HILGER, G., and MEYER, A. G. *The Incompatible Allies.* New York: Macmillan, 1953.

HOFFMANN, E., and FLERON, F., eds, *The Conduct of Soviet Foreign Policy.* Chicago: Aldine, 1971.

HORELICK, ARNOLD, and RUSH, MYRON. *Strategic Power and Soviet Foreign Policy.* Chicago: Chicago University Press, 1966.

KEEP, JOHN, ed. *Contemporary History in the Soviet Mirror.* New York: Praeger, 1965.

KENNAN, GEORGE. *Soviet Foreign Policy Under Lenin and Stalin.* Boston: Little, Brown, 1961.

LOWENTHAL, RICHARD. *World Communism.* New York: Oxford University Press, 1964.

LEITES, NATHAN. *A Study of Bolshevism.* New York: Free Press, 1953.

MACKINTOSH, J. M. *Strategy and Tactics of Soviet Foreign Policy.* New York: Oxford University Press, 1962.

MARX, KARL, and ENGELS, FRIEDRICH. *The Russian Menace to Europe.* New York: Free Press, 1952.

MOORE, BARRINGTON. *Soviet Politics: The Dilemma of Power.* Cambridge: Harvard University Press, 1950.

MOSELY, PHILIP E. *The Kremlin and World Politics.* New York: Knopf, Vintage Books, 1960.

_____, ed. *The Soviet Union, 1922–1962: A Foreign Affairs Reader.* New York: Praeger, 1963.

*Nazi-Soviet Relations, 1937–1941.* Washington, D.C.: Government Printing Office, 1948. Selected documents from the German archives.

RESHETAR, J. S., JR. *Problems of Analyzing and Predicting Soviet Behavior.* Garden City, N.Y.: Doubleday, 1955.

ROSSER, RICHARD. *An Introduction to Soviet Foreign Policy.* Englewood Cliffs, N.J.: Prentice-Hall, 1970.

ROSSI, A. *The Russo-German Alliance, 1939–1941.* Boston: Beacon Press, 1951.

RUBINSTEIN, ALVIN Z. *The Foreign Policy of the Soviet Union.* New York: Random House, 1960.

SCHWARTZ, MORTON. *The Foreign Policy of the USSR: Domestic Factors.* Encino, Calif.: Dickenson, 1975.

SHULMAN, MARSHALL. *Stalin's Foreign Policy Reappraised.* Cambridge: Harvard University Press, 1963.

SOKOLOVSKII, V. M., ed. *Soviet Military Strategy.* Translated by H. S. dinerstein, L. Goure, and T. Wolfe. Englewood Cliffs, N.J.: Prentice-Hall, 1963.

SOVIET INFORMATION BUREAU. *Falsifiers of History.* Moscow, 1948. Official explanation of the diplomacy of the Nazi-Soviet Pact and its aftermath.

STALIN, J. V. *Economic Problems of Socialism.* New York: International Publishers Co., 1952.

_____. *The Great Patriotic War of the Soviet Union.* New York: International Publishers Co., 1945.

_____. *Problems of Leninism.* Moscow: Universal Distributors, 1947.

TARACOUZIO, T. A. *The Soviet Union and International Law.* New York: Macmillan, 1936.

_____. *War and Peace in Soviet Diplomacy.* New York: Macmillan, 1940.

TOMA, PETER, ed. *The Changing Face of Communism in Eastern Europe.* Tucson: Arizona University Press, 1970.

TRISKA, JAN F., and FINLEY, DAVID D. *Soviet Foreign Policy.* New York: Macmillan, 1969.

TRISKA, JAN, and SLUSSER, ROBERT. *The Theory, Law and Policy of Soviet Treaties.* Stanford, Calif.: Stanford University Press, 1962.

ULAM, ADAM B. *Expansion and Coexistence.* 2d Ed. New York: Praeger, 1974.

_____. *Titoism and the Cominform.* Cambridge: Harvard University Press, 1952.

WOLFE, B. D. *Khrushchev and Stalin's Ghost.* New York: Praeger, 1957. Khrushchev's secret report in full text, with commentary.

WOLFE, THOMAS W. *Soviet Power and Europe, 1945–1970.* Baltimore: Johns Hopkins Press, 1970.

_____. *Soviet Strategy at the Crossroads.* Cambridge: Harvard University Press, 1964.

ZIMMERMAN, WILLIAM. *Soviet Perspectives on International Relations.* Princeton: Princeton University Press, 1960.

# FOREIGN POLICY OF COMMUNIST CHINA

6

*Allen S. Whiting*

## CONCEPTUAL FRAMEWORK

Although China is the world's oldest continuous civilization, our analysis of Chinese foreign policy must be largely inferential. Very little primary research in Chinese archival materials has been completed to provide us with an evidential base for understanding the perceptual framework, the organizational interaction, and the political determinants which combine to make foreign policy. Too few detailed case studies exist of specific interactive situations involving the People's Republic of China (PRC) to lay a foundation for systematic generalization about behavior. Even the conventional historical record provides relatively little help. Although its political systems date back more

than 2,000 years, China is a relative newcomer to contemporary foreign relations. For centuries, its relations with the outside world remained tributary in nature. No concept of sovereignty or equality interfered with domination by the Middle Kingdom over dependencies such as Tibet and Mongolia, or vassal states such as Korea and Annam.

The collapse of the Manchu empire and the birth, in 1912, of the Republic of China failed to produce a united nation entering the world community on equal terms. Foreign governments continued to post their own troops and police in enclaves of extraterritoriality, enjoying foreign law and privilege on Chinese soil. Civil war rent China apart during the decade 1918–1928, as a northern government at Peking, dominated by shifting military factions, vied for power with a southern government at Canton, headed by Sun Yat-sen and his Kuomintang cohorts. Officially, Peking enjoyed recognition as the legal voice of China until its final defeat by the Nationalist (Kuomintang) army in 1928. Its actual power, however, extended through only a small section of the country. During the turbulent twenties, most of South China, Tibet, Sinkiang, Mongolia, and the northeast (Manchuria) lay beyond control of the capital. No sooner was the new government of Chiang Kai-shek established at Nanking in 1928, however, than Soviet troops fought to protect Soviet interests in Manchuria against the local warlord. In 1931 Japan overran this rich industrial area to create the puppet state of Manchukuo. Then, at the opposite end of China, Soviet authorities gave military and economic assistance to the local governor of Sinkiang, concluding formal agreements without reference to Nanking and informally extending influence over its policy and army. Warlord autonomy, Japanese invasion, and growing Chinese communist dissidence combined to deprive Chiang of control over more than a dozen provinces throughout most of the period 1931–1945. Meanwhile, each of these uncontrolled areas enjoyed varying degrees of independence in its relations with foreign powers.

In fact, not until 1949 and establishment of the People's Republic of China did the world's most populous nation achieve sufficient sovereignty and unity throughout its vast domain to enjoy a monopoly of full control over foreign relations in the central government. This provides a natural starting point for our analysis. Unlike its immediate predeces-

sor, however, the People's Republic was not formally admitted to "the family of nations" for many years, lacking diplomatic recognition from most countries outside the Soviet bloc, and denied participation in the United Nations until the 1970s. Thus, on the one hand, we have historical evidence of foreign policy conducted by a somewhat fictitious central government, ruling largely in name only from 1911 to 1928, followed by a highly fragmented regime from 1928 to 1949. This approximates forty years of seemingly "normal" international relations for a weak and divided China, formally allied with the victorious powers in two world wars and a member of the League of Nations. On the other hand, our principle object of interest, the PRC, spans more than two decades of semi-isolation from much of the international system, including the United Nations and such traditional Great Powers as the United States, Britain, and Japan.

These historical anomalies obviate the standard approach of focusing on the nation-state as actor. Despite appearances, foreign governments were not dealing with a highly stable and continuous regime prior to 1949. To be sure, the entity "China" was an obvious empirical referent for whatever group assumed authority at whatever point in the society. Treaties were negotiated, commerce carried out (albeit through foreign-controlled customs until the 1930s), and wars fought in the name of China. However, our inquiry will concern itself primarily with the perceptions and behavior of Chinese elites, particularly the communist, which have tried to manage China's foreign relations over the past half-century. It is their values and views, rather than the inheritance of tradition or the bureaucratic inertia of continuing organizational entities within government, which have shaped the ends, means, and style of Chinese foreign policy.

Our general conceptual framework begins with the physical environment, both real and perceived, into which these elites moved as international actors. In addition to actual size and geography, policy is shaped by perceptions of spatial relationships. Borders may be seen as secure or threatened, as inviolate or flexible, as indisputable or contentious and negotiable. Space may be conceived as providing isolation or inviting attack. Size may be held an asset of strength or a liability for defense. Perceptions, in turn, are in part a function of received experience, of history as it is transmitted within a culture or political system. Received experience provides "lessons" from the past whose "truth" may be reinforced through the "real experience" of the present. Just as there are objective inputs of wars and diplomacy, as in the physical attributes of geography, to shape perception and behavior, so too there is the subjective element of anticipation, which may create a "self-fulfilling prophecy" effect whereby expected hostility from an outside power is prepared for in such a way as to cause or increase hostility. Alternatively, "selective perception" focuses only on evidence of behavior which conforms with expectation and dismisses that which does not fit anticipation. These inputs of geography, history, and psychology combine to constitute what we shall call the *Chinese components* of foreign policy.

In addition, we must consider ideology or the *communist component*

of policy. Ideology is not unique to elites and cultures which articulate it in the highly formalized and conscious manner of communist systems, but its explicitness and omnipresence in their political communications makes it even more of a determinant than in less ideologically structured systems. From Marx to Mao, a corpus of literature provides definitions of goals and prescriptions of means that shape the view of the world from Peking.

These basic factors in the Chinese and communist components do not explain everything. They will be differentially affected by specific organizational roles and responsibilities such as defense, trade, diplomacy, and revolutionary activity abroad. Moreover, they will have an idiosyncratic impact upon policy as filtered through the different "operational codes" of such individuals as Mao Tse-tung, Liu Shao-ch'i, Lin Piao, and Chou En-Lai. The sum of these internal interactions constitutes the decision-making process, but this in turn must interact externally for the dynamic of international relations to be complete. Foreign policy does not operate in a vacuum, nor is it the exclusive initiative of one country, least of all China over the past half-century. Unfortunately, however, in the absence of any concrete data on the effect of organization and personality in Chinese foreign policy, we must remain content with a larger, looser inferential framework that deals primarily with the factors we have subsumed under the Chinese and communist components. Moreover, in the space at our disposal we cannot hope to do justice to interaction analysis except for selective illustrative purposes. Within these limits, nevertheless, we can appreciate the goals of recent

Chinese foreign policy and assess the means available and likely to be adopted by present and future elites in pursuit of these goals.

### Physical Factors—Real and Perceived

We cannot look at any map of the world, regardless of its projection, and not be awed by the proportion encompassed by China. So extensive is its reach from north to south and from east to west as to conjure up images of supracontinental domination "over-shadowing" Southeast Asia and India, while "menacing" the Soviet Far East and Japan. Coupled with emphasis on China's population of roughly 800 million, "expansionism" seems the inevitable threat confronting China's neighbors.

These images receive reinforcement from Chinese official statements. Although the days of the Chinese empire are long past, contemporary Chinese leaders continue to pay obeisance to the memory of vanished glory in their delineation of China's territorial goals. Chiang Kai-shek, borrowing Adolf Hitler's concept of *Lebensraum* ("living space"), laid claim to past holdings on the basis of population pressure as well as of historical possession:

In regard to the living space essential for the nation's existence, the territory of the Chinese state is determined by the requirements for national survival and by the limits of Chinese cultural bonds. Thus, in the territory of China a hundred years ago [i.e., c. 1840], comprising more than ten million square kilometers, there was not a single district that was not essential to the survival of the Chinese nation, and none that was not permeated by our culture. The breaking up of this territory meant the undermining of the nation's security as well as the decline of the nation's culture. Thus, the people as a whole must regard this as a national humiliation, and not until all lost territories have been recovered can we relax our efforts to wipe out this humiliation and save outselves from destruction.[1]

Although Chiang did not specify his "lost territories," a Chinese textbook published shortly after his statement contains a table listing them (see table 6.1).

Nor do communist leaders remain indifferent to China's past holdings, although they temper their immediate claims according to time and place. Thus, Mao Tse-tung staked out his future realm in an interview more than thirty years ago:

It is the immediate task of China to regain all our lost territories. . . . We do not, however, include Korea, formerly a Chinese colony, but when we have reestablished the independence of the lost territories of China, and if the Koreans wish to break away from the chains of Japanese imperialism, we will extend them our enthusiastic help in their struggle for independence. The same thing applies for Formosa. . . . The Outer Mongolian republic will automatically become a part of the Chinese federation, at their own will. The Mohammedan and Tibetan peoples, likewise, will form autonomous republics attached to the Chinese federation.[2]

True to his word, at least in part, Mao, despite Indian protests, sent the People's Liberation Army (PLA) into Tibet after the establishment of the People's Republic of China in 1949. His implicit definition of Korea as within China's sphere of interest received implementation

[1]Chiang Kai-shek, *China's Destiny* (New York: Roy Publishers, 1947), p. 34.
[2]Quoted in Edgar Snow, *Red Star over China* (New York: Random House, 1944), p. 96. Interviews with Mao Tse-tung in 1936.

when Chinese armies hurled back United Nations troops from the Yalu River to the 38th parallel during 1950–51. Sinkiang, which is presumably the region referred to above as "the Mohammedan people" (because of its predominantly Moslem population), became an autonomous region in 1955 after considerable pacification by the PLA garrison. Only Taiwan ("Formosa"), the Nationalist refuge, and Outer Mongolia, recognized as independent by the Treaty of Friendship and Alliance concluded between the Nationalist government and Moscow in 1945 and adhered to in this particular by Peking, have remained beyond Mao's control.

Similarly, both Nationalist and communist maps place China's borders far down in the South China Sea, off the shores of Borneo. Mao would subscribe to the statements of the official Nationalist handbook:

Both the southernmost and westernmost borders remain to be defined. The Pamirs in the west constitute a contested area among China, the U.S.S.R., and Afghanistan. The sovereignty of the Tuansha Islands [Coral Islands] in the south is sought by China, the Republic of the Philippines, and Indo-China.[3]

At least some of these are more than mere verbal aspirations. In the

[3] *China Handbook, 1955–56* (Taipei, Taiwan, 1955), p. 15. Although this was modified in later editions, continued Nationalist claims to the Paracel Islands 150 miles south of Hainan were forcefully paralleled by the PLA in January 1974 when its navy ousted South Vietnamese units from the area.

TABLE 6.1 China's "Lost Territories"

| DATE | AREA, IN SQUARE KILOMETERS | LOCATION | NEW OWNERSHIP |
|------|---------------------------|----------|---------------|
| 1689 | 240,000 | North side Khingan Mountains | Russia |
| 1727 | 100,000 | Lower Selenga Valley | Russia |
| 1842 | 83 | Hong Kong | United Kingdom |
| 1858 | 480,000 | North of Heilungkiang | Russia |
| 1858 | 8 | Kowloon | United Kingdom |
| 1860 | 344,000 | East of Ussuri River | Russia |
| 1864 | 900,000 | North of Lake Balkhash | Russia |
| 1879 | 2,386 | Liuchiu Islands | Japan |
| 1882–1883 | 21,000 | Lower Ili Valley | Russia |
| 1883 | 20,000 | Irtysh Valley east of Lake Zaysan | Russia |
| 1884 | 9,000 | Upper Koksol Valley | Russia |
| 1885–1889 | 738,000 | Annam and all Indochina | France |
| 1886 | 574,000 | Burma | United Kingdom |
| 1890 | 7,550 | Sikkim | United Kingdom |
| 1894 | 122,400 | West of the upper Salween | United Kingdom |
| 1894 | 91,300 | West of the upper Yangtze | United Kingdom |
| 1894 | 100,000 | Upper Burma, Savage Mountains | United Kingdom |
| 1895 | 220,334 | Korea | Japan |
| 1895 | 35,845 | Taiwan | Japan |
| 1895 | 127 | Pescadores | Japan |
| 1897 | 760 | The edge of Burma | United Kingdom |
| 1897 | 2,300 | The edge of Burma | United Kingdom |
| Total | 4,009,093 | | |

Source: Hou Ming-chiu, Chen Erh-shiu, and Lu Chen, *General Geography of China* (in Chinese), 1946, as reproduced in G. B. Crassey, *Land of the 500 Million* (New York: McGraw-Hill Book Co., 1955), p. 39.

past decade Chinese Communist troops have twice fought over disputed border areas. The movement of Peking's forces into Indian-claimed checkpoints along the Himalayas following the Tibetan revolt of 1959 triggered small clashes with Indian border guards that year. Subsequent Indian efforts in 1962 to recoup claimed land, long unoccupied until the advent of Chinese road building and patrols in 1958–61, ignited a smoldering confrontation which finally exploded that fall in a massive Chinese offensive at both ends of the 1,500-mile frontier. While larger strategic considerations than the border itself underlay the Chinese attack, the tenacity with which Peking bargained—and finally fought—with New Delhi over marginal land of little economic or political value illustrates the persistence of "lost territories" in shaping perceptions and goals of foreign policy.

An even more dramatic example of this phenomenon came in March, 1969, when Chinese border troops fought Soviet armored units over unoccupied islands in the Ussuri River along China's northeast frontier. These incidents, while far smaller in scope and briefer than the 1962 war with India, had far more threatening implications for China's security, since they involved the much more powerful Soviet military capabilities, potentially including nuclear weapons. Again, as with India, more was perceived to be at stake than the islands themselves. Nonetheless, the role the border played throughout 1969, both here and in Sinkiang, reminded the world that Chinese sensibilities and sensitivities can hearken back to times past to a degree unique among the major powers on the world scene today.

Does this necessarily mean that irredentism—the drive to recover "lost territories"—literally impels Chinese leaders to restore control over thousands of square miles ruled by Russia and the Soviet Union for a century or more? In the tense summer of 1969, the official English-language journal *Peking Review* suddenly introduced a heretofore neglected quotation from Mao, "We the Chinese nation have the spirit to fight the enemy to the last drop of our blood, the determination to recover our lost territory by our own efforts, and the ability to stand on our own feet in the family of nations." Although various sources, especially Soviet, imputed a grandiose irredentist design to Peking, supporting this charge with alleged statements made privately by Mao, their analysis was contradicted by the consistent caution with which Peking deployed force beyond its borders since its initial intervention in the Korean War in October, 1950. Certainly, the strategic imbalance between China and the USSR is so great, now and in the foreseeable future, as to make incredible a major move against Moscow's central Asian, Siberian, or Far Eastern holdings that were once ruled from Peking. And indeed, when Sino-Soviet border negotiations began in the fall fo 1969, the People's Republic issued the following declaration:

On May 24, 1969, the Chinese Government issued a statement [which] . . . pointed out that although the treaties relating to the present Sino-Soviet boundary were unequal treaties imposed on China by tsarist Russian imperialism in the latter half of the 19th century and the beginning of the 20th century, . . . the Chinese Government was still prepared to take these treaties as the basis for an overall settlement of the Sino-Soviet boundary question and proposed that, pending a settlement, the status quo of the border should be maintained and armed conflicts averted.... The Chinese Government has never demanded the return of the territory tsarist Russia had annexed by means of the unequal treaties.[4]

As in the Indian case, the border problem is both less and more than the question of "lost territory" per se. It is less so in terms of the amount of land actually at issue as compared with that carried on maps and tables as the maximal extent of past Chinese rule. The problem involves more than the land, however, insofar as it involves the principles of politics, both domestic and foreign, which impinge on the posture adopted by Chinese leaders vis-á-vis questions of "unequal treaties" and "lost territory." One such principle is the traditional Chinese definition of a government possessing the "Mandate of Heaven" as capable of defending the frontiers against barbarian incursions while maintaining the peace against domestic insurrection. Thus, so remote and undesirable an area as Outer Mongolia became the subject of political controversy in 1912, when young Nationalists agitated against Peking's concessions to Mongolian demands for autonomy under Russian protection, using the issue as a political weapon against the regime of Yuan Shih-k'ai. In 1950 Chinese Nationalist propagandists sought to embarrass the new communist regime in Peking in a similar manner. They charged it with "selling out" Chinese soil to the Soviet Union by accepting Outer Mongolian independence despite alleged Soviet violations of the 1945 agreements.

[4]Statement of October 7, 1969, in *Peking Review*, October 10, 1969.

In these agreements, Chiang Kaishek had promised to abide by a "plebiscite" in Outer Mongolia, knowing it would confirm the area's self-proclaimed independence under Soviet domination but hoping thereby to woo Stalin away from supporting the Chinese Communists. Seen in this perspective, Outer Mongolia is primarily a political issue to be exploited in domestic or foreign politics according to expediency, not a compulsive constraint on Chinese policy.

Individual leaders may not believe in the importance of a particular border section or the literal necessity of recovering "lost territory," but the manipulative use of such an issue in internal politics may constrain their position, thereby posing foreign policy goals which exacerbate relations abroad. Three instances illustrate the complexity of this problem. Outer Monoglia would seem strategically irretrievable without Soviet acquiescence, and politically undesirable, given fifty years of Mongol escape from Chinese hegemony. Yet authoritative Japanese and Soviet sources attribute statements to Mao which seem to reflect a lingering aspiration to replace Soviet influence there, including an official Soviet claim that Mao raised the issue with Nikita Khrushchev as early as 1954. Are these statements merely an effort to press Soviet influence back, or are they also to advance Chinese influence? Is it Mao's personal *idée fixe*, or is it a shared objective within the elite? While Peking's propaganda publicly lamented Moscow's alleged transformation of the Mongolian People's Republic into a "colony" in 1969–70, Soviet radio broadcasts accused Peking of harboring "chauvinist" ambitions over this vast land of desert and steppe, inhabited by a million or so nomads and herdsmen. Logic may strengthen one or another explanation, but evidence is lacking to provide any definitive answer.

As a second instance, the Sino-Soviet border clashes of 1969 appear to have been initiated by the Chinese. Certainly, Peking's internal propaganda immediately escalated their importance to a matter of highest national prestige and priority, as illustrated by the earlier quotation from *Peking Review*. At the same time, preparations were being completed for the Ninth Congress of the Chinese Communist party, the first in more than ten years and the initial restructuring of the political system since the convulsions and internal upheaval of the so-called Great Proletarian Cultural Revolution of 1966–68. According to Edgar Snow on the basis of his later coversations with Mao Tse-tung, Mao decided to launch the Cultural Revolution because his presumed successor, Liu Shao-ch'i, had advocated patching up the Sino-Soviet quarrel to present a united front in the Indochina war.[5] Was Mao also exploiting sensitivity over borders and "lost territory" to prevail over internal opponents? Or was this a wider design to refashion national unity against an external enemy after the divisive developments of the previous three years? Or was there a genuine coincidence of events, the border clashes being genuinely related to basic Chinese anxieties aroused by the Soviet military buildup in central Asia and the Far East and Moscow's military move into Czechoslo-

vakia in August, 1968? Again, our effort is not to provide a single explanation in the absence of proof, but to illustrate the various ways in which China's borders and territorial problems may interact with domestic and foreign policy.

A final instance concerns Taiwan. Since the founding of the PRC in 1949, its leadership has ritualistically and repeatedly sworn to "recover China's province, Taiwan." Yet after imposition of the U.S. Seventh Fleet in the Taiwan Strait in 1950 and the Mutual Assistance Treaty concluded between Taipei and Washington in 1954, no serious effort from the mainland has sought to recover Taiwan by force or subversion. Is this an issue of genuine irredentism which inevitably must result in reunion with the mainland by one means or another? Is it a political matter linked to the continuing presence on Taiwan of a defeated civil-war enemy, the Chinese Nationalists, who still lay claim to representation of and rule over all China? Is it a whipping-boy for attacking "U.S. imperialism," and if so, are the implications primarily domestic—for mobilizing unity—or foreign—to isolate the United States from Asian affairs? Or is there a changing mixture of motivations, varying according to the changing perceptions and priorities of the leadership in Peking?

Suggesting these various instrumental uses of the question is not to deny objective factors which, from the perspective of those responsible for Chinese security, make China's size a defensive liability and China's borders a vulnerable point of contention. First, vague territorial claims, Chinese or otherwise, based on concepts of suzerainty and tributary relations or on disputed trea-

---

[5]Edgar Snow, "Aftermath of the Cultural Revolution: Mao Tse-tung and the Cost of Living," *The New Republic*, April 10, 1971, p. 19.

ties, are an inadequate basis for determining international boundaries. Chinese Communists and Nationalists alike agree that the use of force against Tibetan leaders, whether in 1950 or 1959, is an internal affair, and does not constitute legal "aggression." Even New Delhi acquiesced, albeit reluctantly, in the earlier instance. But where runs the legal boundary resultant from a line drawn on an inadequate map by a British official before World War I and never surveyed, much less formally ratified by the government in Peking?

Second, even where such boundaries are fixed with rough approximation, precise definition is impeded by the absence of natural lines of demarcation. Except for the coast and the Amur-Yalu river complex in the northeast, none of China's frontiers can be readily identified topographically. Instead, they twist tortuously through jungle, mountain, and desert, according to the temporary dictates of local need and the relative power available to interested parties. The absence of natural demarcation is paralleled by an absence of natural barriers against migration or invasion, complicating the responsibilities facing the central government responsible for its citizens' welfare and defense.

Thus, the ability in 1959 of 80,000 Tibetan refugees to flee through Himalayan passes, in some cases claimed and ostensibly guarded by Indian patrols, raised the possibility of these refugees returning with foreign arms and training to carry on subversion and sabotage, if not actual guerrilla war. Indeed, precisely such clandestine activities followed the exodus, described by foreign participants and correspondents from bases in the sub-Himalayan

area. Again, in 1962, the flight of up to 100,000 Uighur, Kazakh, and Kirghiz refugees across the Sinkiang border to ethnically related areas in adjacent Soviet central Asia raised Chinese fears of their eventual return as instruments of Soviet subversion in a province long known for anti-Chinese revolts among its predominantly Turki-speaking Moslem peoples. Small wonder that under these circumstances the Indian and Soviet borders appear so sensitive to decision makers in Peking.

Few lines of communication traverse the great distances from China's traditional power centers to its remote border provinces, whereas these provinces lie relatively close to rival centers of power. Not until well after establishment of the PRC did a railroad link Outer Mongolia with northern China, although it was circled on the north by the Trans-Siberian Railroad. Only rough roads linked Tibet with China proper until the late 1950s, while Lhasa lay within striking distance of determined troops, traders, and travelers approaching from the Indian subcontinent, as evidenced by British expeditions at the turn of the century. Nor did Peking push a railroad into Sinkiang until the mid-1950s, despite its strategic and economic importance proximate to the highly developed transportation network across the Soviet border. Even today, land communications to most points along China's southern and western boundaries are scarce and subject to the hazards of interruption by recurring natural phenomena as well as to interdiction by potential dissidents. This combination of arduous terrain and traditionally hostile non-Chinese local populaces mocks the image of size and strength projected by simple unidimensional maps of China.

China's traditional attraction for invaders was food and wealth, luring from the interior nomadic groups against whom the Great Wall was originally designed. Modern invaders came after markets (Great Britian), raw materials (Japan), or imperial prestige (Germany). Regardless of the size and distance of the predatory power, during the nineteenth and twentieth centuries China grappled with problems of defense against external pressure to a degree unique among the countries under survey in this volume. Virtually no point along the 12,600 miles of its perimeter has been safe from one or another of these pressures during the last three hundred years. At the turn of the century, many wondered whether China would become the "sick man of Asia," to be carved up by other countries as was the "sick man of Europe," the Ottoman empire.

These physical factors have combined with the behavior of other powers to make defense a major preoccupation of Chinese foreign policy elites, be they Manchu, Nationalist, or communist. We have dwelt at length on the border problem because it looms large in the foreign policy perspective of Peking—not because of communist "expansionism" or "paranoia," but rather as an outgrowth of China's remembered past. Thus, thousands of PLA troops, ostensibly engaged in road-building, occupied two northern provinces of Laos adjacent to China from 1962 into the 1970s. This was not only in response to an agreement with the Royal Laotian government, but to secure a buffer against possible penetration of China by

American CIA-trained Meo hillsmen or by former Chinese Nationalist soldiers living in exile in nearby Thailand. Nor can we understand recurring tensions in the Taiwan Strait around the offshore islands of Quemoy and Matsu in 1954–55, 1958, and 1962 without an appreciation of the recurring raids against the mainland launched from these islands by Chinese Nationalist teams trained and backed by the United States. Indeed, China's only major military actions—in Korea (1950) and on its borders with India (1962) and the USSR (1969)—in the first two decades of the PRC came about in large part because of anxiety over the potential penetration by hostile powers over vulnerable borders, at times when internal tensions, economic and political, heightened fears of invasion and subversion.

### Historical Factors

China's defensive attitudes intermittently explode into xenophobia. Their subjective evaluation of events during the past century convinces Chinese Nationalist and Communist alike that many, if not all, of China's ills stem from contact with the "foreign devil," now castigated as "Western imperialism." Two hundred years ago, Li Shih-yao, viceroy of Kwangtung and Kwangsi, memorialized the throne on regulations for the control of foreigners, warning:

It is my most humble opinion that when uncultured barbarians, who live far beyond the borders of China, come to our country to trade, they should establish no contact with the population, except for business purposes.[6]

[6]Quoted in Hu Sheng, *Imperialism and Chinese Politics* (Peking, 1955), p. 9.

Events since Li Shih-Yao's day show little break in continuity, so far as interpretation of foreign relations is concerned. Chiang Kai-shek blamed the chaotic years of interregnum following the collapse of the Manchu dynasty on "secret activities of the Imperialists, ... the chief cause of civil wars among the warlords."[7] Indeed, he attributed the empire's disintegration to the so-called unequal treaties which "completely destroyed our nationhood, and our sense of honor and shame was lost. ... The traditional structure of the family, the village, and the community was disrupted. The virtue of mutual help was replaced by competition and jealousy. Public planning was neglected and no one took an interest in public affairs."[8]

This simplistic explanation errs in attributing cause and effect where coincidence is the phenomenon. Western pressures hastened the collapse of the empire and its Confucian traditions, but they came after the process of disintegration had begun. The ability of Japanese society to respond to the combined impact of feudal decline and Western influence by adapting the old content to new forms demonstrates the distortion of history in Chiang's analysis.

However, it is not the facts of history that condition political behavior, but the way in which men view those facts. Hence, the similarity of the following communist analysis to those preceding it is highly suggestive of xenophobia as a component of Chinese policy:

[The imperialists] will not only send their running-dogs to bore inside China to carry out disruptive work and to cause trouble. They will not only use the Chiang Kai-shek bandit remnants to blockade our coastal ports, but they will send their totally hopeless adventurist elements and troops to raid and to cause trouble along our borders. They seek by every means and at all times to restore their position in China. They use every means to plot the destruction of China's independence, freedom, and territorial integrity and to restore their private interests in China. We must exercise the highest vigilance. ... They cannot possibly be true friends of the Chinese people. They are the deadly enemies of the Chinese people's liberation movement.[9]

Thus, the Chinese communist devil-theory of imperialism coincides with the popular mythology that evil is inherent in foreign contacts, and produces suspicion and hostility at various levels. The popular mythology derives from experiencing the rape and pillage by Western troops during the nineteenth century. Western insistence on extraterritorial privileges so that their nationals could be tried by foreign law for crimes committed on Chinese territory rubbed salt in the wound. Insult was added to injury. While the Chinese viewed white behavior as barbaric, the whites viewed Chinese punishment as brutal. The inevitable cultural gap, widened by racial prejudice, reinforced the hostility on both sides.

Injustice was also encountered at higher levels of diplomatic relations. Chinese experience in the international arena gave good reason for bitter resentment at being cast in the role of "a melon to be carved up by the powers." Throughout the nine-

---

[7]Chiang Kai-shek, *China's Destiny*, p. 78.
[8]Ibid., pp. 79, 88.

[9]K'o Pai-nien, "Hsin min chu chu yi te wai chiao tse" [The foreign policy of the new people's democracy] *Hsüeh Hsi* [Study] 1, no. 2 (October, 1949):13–15.

teenth century, gunboat diplomacy forced China to abdicate her customary rights of sovereignty without reciprocal privileges. Extraterritorial law, economic concessions, and the stationing of foreign troops in Chinese cities were sanctified by treaty but won by force. Punitive expeditions, in 1860 and 1900, delivered the supreme insult of foreign military occupation of the venerated capital of Peking.

The twentieth century brought little relief. Japan fought Russia on Chinese soil for control of the rich provinces of Manchuria. China's own allies in World War I swept aside her protests at Versailles, and awarded to Japan concessions in China held by defeated Germany. During World War II, the Yalta Conference of 1945 rewarded the Soviet Union with important military, economic, and political privileges in China, all without consultation with Chiang Kai-shek. Although President Roosevelt reminded Premier Stalin that those inducements for Soviet entry into the war against Japan would have to be affirmed by Chiang, Allied pressure left China no alternative but capitulation.

In sum, China was the object of international relations but seldom the agent. Acted on by others, she was unable to act in her own right. Long the primary power in Asia, she has been cut deeply, during the past century, by an induced feeling of inferiority. Her fear of Japan followed a defeat caused by material inferiority. Her resentment against the West followed a capitulation caused by military inferiority and a humiliation caused by sensed political and ideological inferiority. Peking's militant rhetoric which is being heard in regional and world councils strikes a responsive chord among wide sec-

tors of the populace. At long last, a determined elite is working to restore China's place in the sun.

To be sure, irredentist claims to lost territories, denunciation of unequal treaties, and the playing off of power against power—"use barbarians against barbarians"—are all traditional techniques of foreign policy. The difference in their use by the Chinese lies in the psychological convictions behind these techniques. Among Western states, the exploitation of grievances is an accepted stratagem among assumed equals who are struggling for limited gains and for the coveted position "first among equals." Between China and the rest of the world, however, the bitter remembrance of things past heightens the defensive and offensive aspects of foreign policy.

The Communists' emphasis on imperialist aggression fits well into the objective and subjective factors, conditioning Chinese views of world politics. The resulting xenophobia, manifested in exaggerated attitudes of belligerence, has ultimately worked even to the Soviet Union's disadvantage. Whereas originally it was exploited by Soviet leaders against the West, eventually it exploded again over such real and sensed grievances as Soviet looting in Manchuria after World War II, the resentment against dependence on Soviet economic assistance, and the suspected Soviet subversion in Sinkiang. In the decade 1949–1959, official affirmations of the "monolithic unity of Sino-Soviet friendship" sought to repress the hostility with which many Chinese viewed the Sino-Soviet alliance. When Mao challenged Khrushchev for primacy in the communist world, however, such protestations of friendship disappeared in a wave of anti-Soviet invective which probably won enthusiastic support among the majority of the populace always ready to believe the worse of any foreigner in his dealing with China.

## THE PROCESS OF POLICY: THE COMMUNIST COMPONENT

### Ideological Content: Marxism-Leninism

Besides those aspects of continuity in policy which we ascribe to the Chinese component, there are differences in degree or substance which stem from the dedication of the present Chinese leaders to communism. As Mao Tse-tung declared in 1945, "From the very beginning, our Party has based itself on the theories of Marxism, because Marxism is the crystallization of the world proletariat's most impeccable revolutionary scientific thought."[10]

General protestations of fidelity to Christianity, international law, and justice appear throughout statements of Western political figures. Rarely do these protestations enable us to determine the ends and means of these leaders, especially in foreign policy. Marxism-Leninism, however, carries with it a construct of goals and ways of seeking those goals that imparts form to ideology and institutions to a degree unknown in the noncommunist world.

Foremost in this ideology is its determination to advance communism throughout the world. Almost three decades ago, the fugitive Chinese Communist party, beleaguered by Nationalist armies in Kiangsi, proclaimed, "The Provisional Government of the Soviet Republic of China declares that it will, under no condition, remain content with the overthrow of imperialism in China, but, on the contrary, will aim as its ultimate objective in waging a war against world imperialism until the latter is all blown up."[11]

In terms of "progress" and "revolutionary scientific thought," this goal is justified as a desirable one, the "good society" being found in utopian drives common to world philosophies. An additional element, however, distinguishes this compulsion toward ideological expansion from counterparts in Islam, Christianity, Wilsonian democracy, and Nazism. For the Marxist, destruction of the imperialist is not only desirable but necessary. The maximum goal of world conquest is the only guarantee for achieving the minimum goal of communist survival.

Basic to this argument is the assumption of conflict as omnipresent in human relations. The "contradictions of the dialectical process" exist in various forms; conflict need not be military in manifestation. Marx posited all historical development as a process of struggle, whether between classes within a nation or between nations themselves. The highest and final conflict is to come between classes on the international plane, in the world revolution springing from the basic contradiction between international communism and international capitalism. This struggle is not one that is created by the Communists. Accord-

[10] *The Fight for a New China.* A report of April 24, 1945, to the Seventh National Congress of the Chinese Communist party as quoted in O. Edmund Clubb, "Chinese Communist Strategy in Foreign Relations," *The Annals* 277 (September, 1951):156.

[11] *Central China Post* (Hankow), November 25, 1931, as quoted in Clubb, "Chinese Communist Strategy," 157.

ing to their credo, it is the imperialists who are to blame, engaging in a death struggle to stave off the inevitable victory of the communist ideal. As expressed by Peking's official voice, *Jen Min Jih Pao* (People's Daily), "Although we have consistently held and still hold that the socialist and capitalist countries should co-exist in peace and carry out peaceful competition, the imperialists are bent on destroying us. We must therefore never forget the stern struggle with the enemy, i.e., the class struggle on a world scale."[12]

Thus, the minimum goal of survival requires policies employing means which simultaneously serve the maximum goal of world communist domination. One such means is that of applying the classic Chinese dictum of "using barbarian against barbarian" so as to take advantage of the conflict that assumedly exists among capitalists. Mao Tse-tung wrote, in 1940, "Our tactical principle remains one of exploiting the contradictions among . . . [the imperialists] in order to win over the majority, oppose the minority, and crush the enemies separately."[13]

These assumptions of conflict are reinforced by the attitudes and actions of the noncommunist world. In part, this results from Chinese Communist behavior and illustrates the phenomenon of the self-fulfilling prophecy. When Mao Tse-tung pro-

claimed the establishment of the People's Republic of China in October, 1949, Great Britian extended recognition. Twisting the lion's tail, Peking rejected the recognition with protests against the phraseology of the British note, as well as against British consular relations with the Nationalist authorities on Taiwan. The maltreatment of British business concerns in China undermined the economic arguments advanced in England for wooing Peking. The subsequent British refusal to vote for Peking's admission to the United Nations, and British support for the United States' action in Korea, aroused a violent reaction in China against the "Anglo-American imperialist bloc." In one sense, that bloc came about, in spite of the contradictions within it, largely because of the Chinese predisposition to hostility.

To a lesser extent, America's relations with the new regime were also a product of its own actions. As early as 1948, American consular officials were put under house arrest in communist-held Mukden, jailed, tried, and eventually expelled from China. The seizure of Economic Cooperation Administration stocks in 1949, the inflaming of public opinion against American personnel, both official and unofficial, and the confiscation of American consular property held through treaty agreement, in January, 1950, all served to obstruct a rapprochement between Washington and Peking. Chinese intervention in the Korean War, and the attendant defeat of American troops at the Yalu in November, 1950, wiped out whatever possibility remained of normal relations between the two countries, at least for many years to come. Yet, prior to this war, the record shows a number

---

[12]"More on Historical Experience of Proletarian Dictatorship," *Jen Min Jih Pao* (Peking), December 29, 1956. An article prepared by the editorial department of *Jen Min Jih Pao* on the basis of a discussion at an enlarged meeting of the Political Bureau of the Central Committee on the Communist party of China.

[13]"On Policy" (December 25, 1940), as translated in *Selected Works of Mao Tse-tung* (Bombay, 1954), vol. 3, 218.

of instances where normal adherence by Peking to international custom might have strengthened the hand of groups within the United States which were seeking to establish ties with the new regime.

It would be misleading to attribute all Chinese Communist fears and resentments against the United States to this self-fulfilling prophecy. America's support of Chiang Kai-shek in the civil war, its obstruction of Chinese representation in the United Nations, and its promulgation of an economic embargo against Peking exacerbated relations between the two countries during the 1950s. The combination of expectation and realization reinforced the ideological content of Chinese Communist policy, which posits conflict, overt or covert, with the noncommunist world.

The most famous formulation of this principle came in Mao Tse-tung's "lean to one side" declaration on July 1, 1949:

> "You lean to one side." Precisely so. ... Chinese people either lean to the side of imperialism or to the side of socialism. To sit on the fence is impossible; a third road does not exist. ... Internationally we belong to the anti-imperialist front headed by the U.S.S.R. and we can look for genuine friendly aid only from that front, and not from the imperialist front.[14]

The implementation of this principle came quickly, with the signing of the Treaty of Friendship, Alliance, and Mutual Aid of February 14, 1950, between the Chinese People's Republic and the Union of Soviet Socialist Republics. Mao and Stalin agreed that "in the event of one of the Contracting Parties being attacked by Japan or any state allied with her and thus being involved in a state of war, the other Contracting Party shall immediately render military and other assistance by all means at its disposal." A proliferation of subsequent agreements regulated Soviet economic assistance to China (loans and technical assistance), as well as military aid, cultural exchange, and routine international arrangements about telecommunications and postal regulations.

The "lean to one side" policy, precluding assistance from, much less alliance with, noncommunist countries, was antithetical to traditional Chinese politics of playing off one country against another. It can only be explained in terms of the communist component of Chinese foreign policy.

### Ideology: Maoism

So far, we have been discussing aspects of policy that stem from the communist component as developed in Marxism-Leninism. Assumptions of conflict, antagonism against capitalism, and promoting the world revolution are all compatible with the ideological concepts dominant in the Soviet Union, at least until the death of Stalin in 1953. Within this framework, however, divergent strategies emerged with the rise of the Chinese Communist party (CCP). As early as 1946, Liu Shao-ch'i told an American correspondent, "Mao Tse-tung has created a Chinese or Asiatic form of Marxism. His great accomplishment

---

[14]"On People's Democratic Dictatorship," July 1, 1949, as translated in *A Documentary History of Chinese Communism*, ed. C. Brandt, B. Schwartz, and J. K. Fairbank (Cambridge: Harvard University Press, 1952), pp. 449 ff.

has been to change Marxism from its European to its Asiatic form. He is the first who has succeeded in doing so."[15] At that time, the principal Chinese innovation appeared to be Mao's building a Communist party on a peasant guerrilla army based in the countryside, as opposed to the classical Marxist method of a worker's movement which seizes power in the cities. Beneath this question of strategy, of course, lay the deeper question of historical "stages" whereby Marx posited socialism as "naturally" emerging out of advanced capitalism, in contrast with Mao's effort to move directly from China's "semifeudal" state into socialism.

Subsequent to winning power, however, new ideological differences pitted Mao's vision of the "good society" against that manifest in the Soviet Union. We cannot recapitulate the entire Sino–Soviet dispute, nor do we wish to place exclusive emphasis on ideological as contrasted with national interest conflicts. Mao recognized that both factors cause "contradictions between socialist countries and [between] Communist Parties" when he asserted these were "not the result of a fundamental clash of interests between classes but of *conflicts between right and wrong opinions* or of a partial contradiction of interests"[16] (italics added). Mao's reference to "right and wrong opinions" reflects his philosophy of "cure the illness, save the patient," in that "wrong opinions" are to be "struggled against"

instead of either being passively ignored or suppressed by physical force. The "struggle" is necessitated by the importance of "thought" as a guide to "action" and it includes public confrontation between the erring individual and his peers in a "study group." In similar fashion, Mao initiated a theoretical debate with Nikita Khrushchev, conducted in public as well as private channels, beginning with the Soviet leader's sudden denunciation of Stalin at the Twentieth Congress of the Communist Party of the Soviet Union in March, 1956. Again in 1960, Mao moved from indirect, closed debate to direct, open polemics in order to persuade Khrushchev's colleagues at home and abroad of the difference between "right and wrong opinions."

This philosophy and its accompanying tactics were wholly alien to the repressive and secretive style of Stalin, much of which continued to characterize Soviet politics down to the 1970s. But more than style separated Mao from his Soviet counterpart. At issue was nothing less than the fundamental ideological goals of revolution, not merely as manifested in the century-old slogans of Marx and Engels, but in the present practices and future values of the new society. Mao's primary aim in carrying out a revolution in China was to transform the society's ethos from a hierarchical, elitist, authoritarian culture to an egalitarian, mass-oriented, and eventually mass-directed culture. For him, this domestic revolution took priority over such other goals as modernization of the economy, building up national military power, and emulating foreign societies in their definition of national goals and values.

This appreciation of Mao's goals

---

[15]Quoted in Anna Louise Strong, *Dawn Out of China* (Bombay: People's Publishing House, 1948), p. 29.

[16]"More on the Historical Experience of Proletarian Dictatorship," *Jen Min Jih Pao*, December, 1956; later officially attributed to Mao.

did not emerge fully until his Cultural Revolution of 1966–68. In retrospect, however, it provides a clue to the intensity with which Mao waged his attack against "revisionism" as early as 1958, initially masked as "Yugoslav" revisionism and later revealed explicitly as "soviet" when the polemic became public in the 1960s. The important linkage between internal Soviet policy and Chinese foreign policy lay in Mao's recognition that national boundaries and governmental relations provide an inadequate frame of reference for understanding important levels of transnational interaction. Just as the missionaries and businessman of the nineteenth century provided alternative models for emulation in China and transmitted values antithetical to the Confucian ethic, so the Soviet Union threatened to shape the new Chinese society in its own image. Such Soviet "leadership" was a compulsive dictate of Stalin's era whereby emulation of all things Russian seemed mandatory for "membership in the socialist camp," meaning Soviet military and economic support. Even after death removed Stalin's personal tyranny, Soviet methods and motivational values dominated allied regimes through the continuing ascendance of the Soviet model, transmitted by translated texts and articles, technical assistance teams, training in Soviet institutes and research centers, and varying degrees of integration and standardization of technical systems, especially military.

The Sino-Soviet alliance promised to keep China permanently dependent—psychologically if not in fact—on the Soviet Union, since Peking could hardly hope ever to "catch up" with Moscow's technical

and material superiority, especially given China's tremendous imbalance between an enormous, largely untrained population and scarce resources of capital, foodstuffs, and raw materials. Ideologically, the alliance confronted Mao with a model that stressed economic modernization, material incentives, and unequal rewards of power and status for political authority and acquired skill. These values, national interest conflicts apart, threatened his twin goals of developing a China "standing on its own feet" and eliminating the traditional Confucian culture.

Thus, in addition to specific foreign policy conflicts which sharply exacerbated Sino-Soviet tensions in 1958–59, the ideological conflict eroded the alliance because Mao was willing to risk the loss of Soviet military and economic support in order to shield China from Soviet "revisionism." Another ideological dimension, dominant in the polemic at the time, concerned the strategy and tactics best suited for advancing world revolution. Each side tended to caricature the other in this debate, the Chinese accusing the Soviets of "abandoning" the revolution to "peaceful coexistence with imperialism" while sacrificing local Communists through insistence on the "parliamentary path to power," which could only end in frustration or suppression. The Soviets responded by claiming Mao to be a "nuclear madman" who would risk World War III to advance Chinese "chauvinistic, expansionistic" interests while he sacrificed local Communists to bloody "people's wars" which might escalate to global proportions.

Accordingly, China's foreign policy has carried a far more militant, strident tone of support for "people's wars" since 1958 than has that of the Soviet Union. Mao believes that "power grows out of the barrel of a gun" and that "armed struggle in the countryside" is the most reliable path to power. Moreover, his confrontation with Moscow has compelled Peking to champion communist causes throughout the world to "prove" that China is revolutionary while the USSR is revisionist. These two factors illustrate the dialectic of choice and necessity which intertwines Maoist ideology with foreign policy. More important, however, is the root involvement of Mao's domestic ideological concerns which fueled his "struggle" with Khrushchev's "wrong opinions," thereby splitting the "socialist camp" and ultimately the "world revolutionary movement."

A reliable journalist subsequently explained Mao's decisions to launch the Cultural Revolution in the light of two problems. First, his presumed successor and then chief of state, Liu Shao-ch'i, was "taking the capitalist road" and refusing to "repudiate the reactionary bourgeois academic 'authorities' and the ideology of the bourgeoisie and all other exploiting classes." Second, Liu advocated reuniting with the Soviet Union in the face of American military escalation in Vietnam.[17] Liu was villified as "China's Khrushchev," thereby emphasizing Mao's first concern, domestic affairs. Mao refused to mute his dispute with Moscow after Khrushchev's fall in 1964, despite U.S. bombing of North Vietnam and massive U.S. troop involvement in South Vietnam during 1965, deciding instead both to "go it alone" and to purge China's political system of "revisionists." This demonstrates

the extent to which he saw his domestic ideological goals threatened by any affiliation with the Soviet Union.

Mao's suspicions were not without foundation. For instance, the transformation of China's military establishment from a backward army developed in guerrilla warfare against the Japanese into a modern, multiservice force moving toward a nuclear capability resulted wholly from Soviet assistance, both material and human. In Mao's eyes, however, the army is not merely for passive defense, exclusively military in function, but as in the guerrilla years of World War II, it should be intimately associated with civilian political and economic activities, serving both as a model of selfless behavior and as a direct participant in mass campaigns of flood control, reforestation, and agriculture. For him it was no coincidence that opposition to his "Great Leap Forward" experiment of 1958–59 with its mass communes and "backyard furnaces" was spearheaded by top PLA officials whose position paralleled that of Moscow. While Soviet criticism of the communes was accompanied by an apparent scaling down of promised assistance in developing China's atomic weapons, PLA leaders attacked Mao's experiment as endangering the economy. To be sure, their argument was shared by civilian officials. But to the extent it appeared to reflect Soviet priorities of technical efficiency and technological leadership, as well as self-defined (rather than Mao-defined) roles and relationships between the military and civilian systems, the interplay between Khrushchev's "revisionism" and domestic Chinese developments fueled Mao's determination to push the Sino-Soviet dispute.

[17]Snow, "Aftermath of the Cultural Revolution."

Again in 1965, the connection between foreign and domestic politics appeared in the confrontation between top Chinese officials, some of whom seem to have argued for a strategy based on modern professional, military perspectives as against Mao's advocacy of a massive people's militia and a return to defensive strategies of the prenuclear era. Those who argued against Mao, implicitly or explicitly, advocated closer cooperation with the Soviet Union in support of North Vietnam in order to improve China's military capability and to deter further U.S. escalation. The potential fusion of organizational values across national lines threatened Mao's determination to fashion an indigenous, truly revolutionary society in China. In this regard, it is interesting to note that in May, 1965, only a few months after he rejected Soviet Premier Kosygin's proposals in Peking, Mao eliminated all signs of rank in the People's Liberation Army. That fall, he ousted his chief of staff and reactivated his long dormant mass militia program.

What of the external ideological goals of world revolution? How do they weigh in the scales of priority for Peking? Despite their salience in the Sino–Soviet dispute, the goals of revolution appear seriously constrained and of lower priority than other ends of foreign policy, such as national security and international prestige. Of course, "national liberation wars" may strengthen China's security if they weaken "U.S. imperialist bases" in Southeast Asia, and they can promote Peking's prestige, when they succeed, by paralleling Mao's path to power. But Mao seems to have excluded serious support for such foreign ventures, neither affording them success nor saving them from failure by significant contributions of Chinese assistance. In part, this is ideologically determined by the theory that "revolution is not for export," but must be indigenous to a country's problems and won by that country's revolutionary leadership. Quite likely, however, this is not the only constraint which limits Chinese material help to Communist parties abroad. An amalgam of prudence and Sinocentrism reduces Peking's contribution to considerably less than might be inferred from its polemic with Moscow or from its propagandistic pledges of "support" to various insurgencies, whether in adjacent Burma, more distant Malaysia, or far-off Brazil.

In light of the above, the role of ideology in positing goals which require verbal, if not full, commitment should not be overlooked in understanding the constraints which condition choice in Peking. However tempting might seem the gains of disavowing world revolution in general or disowning a Mao-oriented group in a particular country, for purposes of improving diplomatic, economic, or military relations the leadership can move only so far in this direction without betraying its own sense of obligation as ritualistically reiterated virtually every day of its existence. By placing this goal, as well as specific means of achieving it, through "armed struggle" as well as through the "parliamentary road," at issue in the Sino-Soviet debate as far back as 1957, Peking limited its options, at least in public relations, in the competition for international influence with both Moscow and Washington. In some cases, this proved no liability regardless of whether armed struggle with Chinese support was at issue. In Indonesia, for instance, the largest Communist party in Asia (other than the Chinese) steadily expanded its influence by peaceful means from 1955 to 1965, while both it and the government under Sukarno moved ever closer to Peking and further away from Moscow and Washington. In India, however, the local communist movement was splintered over the choice between violence versus peaceful competition, with Moscow clearly winning over Peking at both the governmental and the communist levels of influence. While the Sino-Indian border conflict finally tipped the balance decisively against China at both levels, the prospects for Peking were already dim before the Himalayan clashes of October and November, 1962.

The prospects are uncertain for Mao's ideological influence on future Chinese foreign policy, as contrasted with the more general tenets of Marxism-Leninism, which are certain to complement Chinese components of policy so long as the Chinese Communist party remains in power. It is this very uncertainty which prompted Mao to implement the extreme measures of the Cultural Revolution. If, through bureaucracy, organization, and decision-making processes, routinization and institutionalization invariably dilute revolutionary ideology over time, it is no surprise that twenty years after winning power the policy establishment in Peking was not to Mao's liking. How deep has been the impact of his cultural Revolution and how successful his successors will be in carrying on Mao's heritage remains to be seen. In subsequent conversations with Edgar Snow, Mao insisted that while state differences could be resolved with Moscow, ideological differ-

ences would remain.[18] Presumably these include not only the external differences over how to confront "U.S. imperialism" and support "national liberation struggles," but also the domestic systems of values in the two societies. If so, much will depend on Mao's successors maintaining his revolutionary priorities even if they cut against bureaucratic and "national" interests of "modernization" and economic growth, not to mention individual preferences for promotion and material rewards. Mao's confidence that ideological differences will remain may be somewhat misplaced, but the conflicts of interest on other levels would appear to have cut so deeply into the consciousness of all Chinese involved with Sino-Soviet affairs over the last fifteen years as to preclude any return to the intimacy of the early fifties in the foreseeable future. Insofar as the ideological infusion of the Soviet ethos was a function of that intimacy, then, Mao may have no need for anxiety over his successors' handling of Soviet relations, although China may nonetheless evolve in directions contrary to his own ethos.

### Institutional Structure of Decision-Making

So far, we have focused primarily on such vast aggregate concepts as "China" and "the Chinese," or on individual personalities such as Mao Tse-tung and Liu Shao-ch'i. Moving from these two extreme opposite levels of analysis to the intermediary ground of governmental decision making is essential if we are to project a model of behavior compat-

[18]Snow, "A Conversation With Mao," *Life,* April 30, 1971.

ible with our appreciation of such processes in other large bureaucracies. Rarely, if ever, does foreign policy result from an abstract concept of a monolithic "national interest." Neither is it usually the dictate of a single official acting wholly on his own initiative. Instead, specific interests and responsibilities shape the perceptions, information intake and output, and policy preferences of organized groups whose interaction defines policy in specific situations. That interaction will change over time as different groups' relative power changes within the political system, in addition to changing in response to "feedback" from the international system. These two dynamic processes, internal and external, virtually preclude simplistic assertions of individual roles and rigid projection of future policy.

Even more than in our previous analysis we must now work by inference, since we have virtually no solid data on group interactions in the foreign policy process of China since 1949. Mountains of material reflecting public participation in the form of mass rallies, demonstrations, and petitions are superficial evidence of non-governmental groups organized along economic, educational, and communal lines. This tells us much about the implementation and utilization of foreign policy in domestic politics, but virtually nothing about the masses' prior participation in decision making. In contrast, a few illuminating glimpses into bureaucratic relationships were provided in the turmoil of the Cultural Revolution; otherwise, logical deduction rather than hard evidence must be the primary basis for speculation concerning interactions within the government.

With these reservations in mind, we can sketch the outlines of in-

teracting elements as they probably exist and speculate on how this "mix" might affect future policy. We should be wary of the pure authoritarian models of the individual (Mao) or the institution (party) that are suggested by China's mass media, because it does not seem logical or feasible that so large and complex a problem as Chinese foreign policy can be so simply determined. As we have seen, foreign relations, especially in the Chinese perspective, involve first of all security against attack. This requires estimates of friend and foe and the allocation of scarce resources according to felt needs and sensed future threats. Thus, one large organization necessarily concerned with foreign policy planning, implicit or explicit, is the military. It must play a role in determining the degree of risk to be accepted on behalf of besieged friendly states, such as North Korea or North Vietnam, or in response to threats posed by the Soviet Union, India, or the United States. Its interests were intimately involved in the Sino-Soviet alliance and in the jeopardy to that alliance posed by the dispute. Its modernization and nuclear development are affected by foreign trade and the use to which China's scarce purchasing and export power is put. Intelligence requirements must be met by a clandestine foreign service and Chinese missions abroad, as well as by costly, technologically advanced systems such as satellites and long-range radar. Commitments to foreign recipients of military aid, whether governmental or subversive, involve the PLA at least peripherally. In the cases of Pakistan or the Indochina war, the involvement may become major and prolonged. These matters, while they do not exhaust the interests of the military in foreign policy, demonstrate the unlikelihood of such policy being determined solely within the walls of the Ministry of Foreign Affairs or among party leaders acting exclusively in that capacity.

More obviously, of course, the Ministry of Foreign Affairs acquires its own organizational identity and interests as formal recognition of the PRC increases its size and responsibilities. The advancement of China's prestige through diplomacy —as manifested in the signing of treaties, the establishment of embassies, exchanges of state visits, and Chinese participation in international conferences—is an important substitute for the projection of influence and power through global military and economic aid. Yet, at the same time that the People's Republic aspires to diplomatic preeminence, especially in the "Third World" of Asia, Africa, and Latin America, it professes to be the main base supporting world revolution. These two goals can easily conflict at particular points in time and place, as evidenced by African regimes which have denied recognition to Peking or, after granting recognition, have ousted its diplomats because of Chinese subversive activity. Thus, a presumably sizeable organization within the overall bureaucracy argues for more resources and policy support to promote revolution, even if this conflicts with the dictates of diplomacy advanced by the foreign ministry. Still another point of contention comes with the need to present a public posture in accordance with one or another of these conflicting interests through domestic media and their global counterparts, such as Radio Peking, *Peking Review,* and the tons of pamphlets distributed in a dozen languages, including Esperanto.

So far, we have identified agencies within the government whose responsibilities are primarily, if not exclusively, externally directed. However, no agency concerned with internal development can be wholly disinterested in foreign relations if its activity is in any way dependent on foreign trade, either as a means of acquiring technology to facilitate development or as a demand on domestic production of exports to fund imports. Despite the insistence of both Chiang Kai-shek and Mao Tsetung that China be "self-reliant," foreign trade, while small relative to the country's size, can play an important role in the domestic economy. At the crudest level, maintenance of the delicate food-population balance throughout the 1960s depended on annual imports of wheat from Canada, Australia, Argentina, and France. Improving that balance required major purchases abroad of chemical fertilizers and entire factories for their manufacture. At the minimum, this trade called for avoidance of unnecessary risks which might involve China in hostilities disruptive to seaborne commerce. In addition, the purchasing power for such imports could not be generated in bilateral trade, because China's products had insufficient demand. Consequently, the unique role of Hong Kong, which provided China with $500 million or more in annual trade surplus, made Sino-British relations critical for domestic development. Despite this remnant of imperialism on China's doorstep, occasioning Soviet ridicule of Mao's revolutionary pretensions, the preponderance of nonrevolutionary interests in Peking safeguarded Hong Kong against internal or external takeover.

These linkages virtually preclude the possibility that foreign affairs are the prerogative of a few men, although detailed management undoubtedly falls within narrow sectors of particular competence, with highest-level guidance from the apex of the policy pyramid. Before focusing on that apex, however, we must add one more dimension to our model: time. Over time, developments occur, internally and externally, which affect the weight of each component in the policy process. Capabilities change, threats shift, and projections are borne out or fail to prove correct. Successes and failures affect the credibility of policies and of those who advocate or oppose them. Individuals rise or fall in the process, with changing degrees of influence. While avoiding an exclusive concern with personalities, we cannot ignore the significance of the political game, with its unwritten rules for assuring personal survival and its invisible struggles to win out over one's rival, either within an organization or in opposite areas of interest. The temptation is strong to see all policy decisions as rationally arrived at within a wholly logical and consistent model, thereby explaining why past events occurred and providing hopeful predictability for future events. However, in reality accident and mismanagement are far more frequent than could ever be believed by the outside observer. Tidiness is not the hallmark of large bureaucracies in foreign or domestic affairs. Therefore, not only may the whole be larger than the sum of its parts, but also its shape is subject to change as its parts change in the course of time.

Let us look schematically, then, at the apex of decision-making. The arena of action is the Chinese Communist party's top organ, the political bureau (Politburo)—or, more accurately, the party's Standing Committee. A top-ranking party official, Teng Hsiao-p'ing, analyzed the relationship between party and state in his report to the Eighth National Congress of the CCP, in September, 1956, as follows:

The Party is the highest form of class organization. It is particularly important to point this out today when our Party has assumed the leading role in state affairs. . . . [This] means first, that Party members in state organs and particularly the leading Party members' groups formed by those in responsible positions in such departments should follow the unified leadership of the Party. Secondly, the Party must regularly discuss and decide on questions with regard to the guiding principles, politics, and important organizational matters in state affairs, and the leading Party members' groups in the state organs must see to it that these decisions are put into effect with the harmonious cooperation of non-Party personalities. Thirdly, the Party must . . . exercise constant supervision over the work of state organs.[19]

This frank appraisal lends substance to an analysis of party control of state organs based on interlocking direction by high-ranking party members. The State Council, corresponding to the Council of Ministers in the Soviet Union or to the Western cabinet, allocates controlling positions to party members—the premiership, all twelve vice-premierships, and positions in such key ministries as foreign affairs, defense, public security, finance, state planning agencies, machine industries, electric power, railways, and foreign trade.

Similarly, the Standing Committee of the National People's Con-

[19]"Report on Revision of Party Constitution," delivered to the CCP Eighth National Congress on September 16, 1956, as quoted by NCNA, Peking, September 18, 1956.

gress is dominated by the seven Politburo members and the thirteen Central Committee members. Moreover while this group is vested, by the 1975 constitution with powers akin to those of legislative bodies in the West, it seems politically impotent in view of the extreme range of decree power held by the State Council. The inclusion of such dignitaries as Madame Sun Yat-sen (Soong Ch'ing-ling) and China's outstanding literary polemicist, Kuo Mo-jo, among its vice-chairmen, suggests that this body is an honorific gathering to provide public sanction for decisions arrived at elsewhere. The party's constitution makes clear the absolute duty of all members to carry out policies and practices decreed by the Central Committee:

ARTICLE 5 ... The whole party must observe unified discipline. The individual is subordinate to the organization, the minority is subordinate to the majority, the lower level is subordinate to the higher level, and the entire Party is subordinate to the Central Committee.

That major decisions were seldom those of the Central Committee was evidenced by the infrequency of its sessions, the size of its membership, and the relatively short intervals during which lengthy reports were read and accepted. The Eighth Central Committee, elected in 1956, had more than 190 regular and alternate members. Although it met approximately twice yearly, as stipulated by the party constitution, its plenums seldom lasted more than five days. Moreover, in crisis-ridden 1960, no Central Committee plenum was reported, despite nationwide famines, reorganization of the communes, and the growing differences with

Soviet Russia. The Tenth Central Committee, elected in 1973, has 319 regular and alternate members. It met for only four days in 1973 to adopt a new party constitution and hear reports on the alleged attempt by Mao's successor, Lin Piao, to assassinate the Chairman. In January 1975 it met for an equally brief time to approve a revised state constitution and a new governmental namelist for the first National People's Congress to be chosen in ten years. Key decisions come from a small self-perpetuating CCP elite whose composition remained fairly constant from 1945 to 1966. The active members of the Politburo's Standing Committee—Mao, Liu, Chou, and Teng Hsiao-p'ing—dated their association back to the 1920s. Despite the wealth of reported accusations and other documentation of the Cultural Revolution, we are still unable to pinpoint at what time and over what issues Mao and Liu began to drift apart. In the absence of such information, it may be safe to assume that consensus emerged under the leadership of Mao more readily in foreign than in domestic affairs until the two became inextricably intertwined in the Sino-Soviet dispute. This surmise is supported by the ease with which the PRC resumed established lines of foreign policy in 1969–71, made familiar from its earlier period when Liu was chief of state, and by the continuity of Chou En-lai's service as China's most prominent spokesman in world affairs despite the Cultural Revolution.

While we have cautioned against an exclusive personality focus, it is worth recalling that both Mao and Chou have long shown flexibility and adaptability in foreign relations, in contrast with the more rigid posture adopted by Peking's propaganda at home and abroad concerning world revolution and the struggle against imperialism. This permitted emergent organizational and interest groups to adopt an equally diverse set of approaches to the outside world, as the CCP moved from a beleaguered guerrilla army in the hills and plains of northern China to command of the People's Republic. As early as December, 1944, Mao and Chou requested a secret meeting with President Roosevelt in Washington, and the following spring Mao talked at length with an American official concerning his hope for U.S. investments and industrial assistance after the civil war had been won.[20] Significantly, Mao did not announce his celebrated "lean to one side" formula until 1949, well after CCP experience with U.S. support for Chiang Kai-shek had confirmed expectations of "imperialist" opposition as compared with "socialist" support. In 1946, Chou En-lai had warned Ambassador George C. Marshall, President Truman's special emissary in an abortive attempt to mediate between the Nationalist and Communists, "Of course we will lean to one side, but how far depends upon you."[21] Thus the leadership roles of Mao and Chou permit an overall framework of flexibility for the discussions of for-

eign policy, within which specific interests represented through members of the Politboro contend for different policies. In addition, a ready rationale for different strategies, tactics, and specific policies is provided by the Marxist philosophy of the dialectical progression of history and by Mao's emphasis on understanding "contradictions"— both "antagonistic" and "nonantagonistic"—among foreign powers as well as between a foreign power and China. How these "contradictions" are to be handled, wherein lies "the main threat," and how to "translate theory into practice" become the stuff of policy debate as applied to each situation.

This does not mean that policy disputes never split the leadership or that they never leave an aftermath of bitter acrimony. Clearly, Sino-Soviet relations played an important part in the confrontation between Mao and his Politboro associate Marshal P'eng Teh-huai in 1959. P'eng's role and responsibilities as minister of defense took priority over his collegial role in the party, prompting his challenge to Mao's "Great Leap Forward" and his Soviet policy. P'eng's chief of staff fell with him at this time, as did other military figures and a former ambassador to Moscow.[22] Mao's subsequently named successor, Marshal Lin Piao, became minister of defense, and Lo Jui-ch'ing moved from head of internal security to chief of staff. However, six years afterward, Lo's socialization shifted his identification so close to the viewpoint of professionals in the PLA as to prompt him to challenge Mao's pol-

[20] For details on these and related developments, see the telegram of Ambassador Hurley to Secretary of State Hull, February 7, 1945, paraphrasing message from Mao and Chou sent "eyes only via General Wedemeyer," January 9, 1945, and Mao's conversation with John S. Service of March 13, 1945, *Foreign Relations of the United States: Diplomatic Papers, 1945*, vol. 7, *The Far East: China* (Washington, D.C., 1969), pp. 209 ff.

[21] Personal reminiscence of John F. Melby, foreign service officer on Marshall's staff, as to the author.

[22] David Charles, "The Dismissal of Marshal P'eng Teh-huai," *The China Quarterly*, no. 18 (October-December 1961):63–77.

icy vis-á-vis Moscow in the context of U.S. escalation in Vietnam, and once again, purge settled policy differences. These developments suggest the relative weight of individual predilection as compared with organizational roles and responsibilities.

Of course, no organization is purely monolithic. Differences exist within them on the basis of sectional and subsectional interests and perspectives on issue areas. Dramatic evidence of factionalism in the Ministry of Foreign Affairs came in May, 1967, when Red Guards ransacked the ministry, seized its files, and attacked its leading officials. Led by an official formerly in the Chinese embassy in Jakarta, the militants won control by mid-summer. By August, they had succeeded in pushing China's relations with several countries, most particularly Burma and Great Britain, to the brink of rupture through violent demonstrations against foreign missions and their personnel in Peking as well as through turbulent public demonstrations by Chinese embassy staffs abroad.[23] In Burma, these demonstrations triggered an anti-Chinese reaction in which two Chinese diplomatic personnel and many local Chinese residents were killed. In response, Peking adopted a harsh position, throwing its full propaganda support against the regime of Ne Win and behind the Burmese White Flag (Communist party) insurgents. Meanwhile, in the Chinese capital, massive demonstrations against the missions of the Soviet Union, India, and Britain climaxed

with the sacking of the British chancery on August 22 and the manhandling of its occupants. Beginning in May, coincident with the assault on the foreign ministry, the Cultural Revolution spillover in Hong Kong threw the colony into a summerlong crisis complete with riots, bombings, and border incidents.

These tumultuous events coincided with intense struggles at every level of the political system and throughout the country, threatening civil war as military units and services became divided in their support for contending factions. With this last prospect imminent and with foreign relations in shambles, enough temporary unity emerged at the top to quiet the worst violence. More particularly, control of the Ministry of Foreign Affairs was wrested from the militants, and nominal control was reassumed by the besieged foreign minister, Ch'en Yi, with substantive direction returning to the strong hand of Chou En-lai. In September, Cambodian Prince Norodom Sihanouk's vigorous protest of the undiplomatic behavior of Chinese embassy personnel in Phnom Penh evoked a prompt personal apology from Chou. More quiet and discreet amends were communicated to the British in Peking, while negotiations at the Hong Kong border restored the previous status quo by mutual agreement.

Although the circumstances surrounding the 1967 eruption are unique in the history of the People's Republic, the issues at stake may not have been. The confrontation between radical, revolutionary interests and those of professional diplomacy is inherent in China's dual mission, derived from its national heritage and its Marxist-Maoist ideology. Equally illuminating is the

[23]A detailed examination of this period, based on Chinese sources of the time, is provided by Melvin Gurtov, "The Foreign Ministry and Foreign Affairs in China's 'Cultural Revolution,'" RAND Corporation Report RM-5934-PR (March, 1969).

light this period throws on the linkage between domestic and foreign politics. This linkage is obvious in the case of those noncommunist societies where public opinion or political parties can affect foreign policy issues. It is, nonetheless, even present in the closed authoritarian system when perceptual and interest differences at various levels are permitted to coalesce in concert with struggles within the leadership.

China's 800 million inhabitants also relate marginally to foreign affairs. Special mass organizations, such as the Communist Youth League and the All-China Democratic Women's Federation, link entire sectors of society in a closely coordinated network of communications media directed from the Department of Propaganda of the CCP. Governmental gatherings, such as the National People's Congress, bring together representatives of "democratic parties and mass organizations" to receive reports from leaders and to endorse contemporary policies. Additional ad hoc meetings at provincial, municipal, and county levels provide ritualized support for policy as a prelude to mass rallies and parades, as do small group discussions as places of employment and in neighborhood and commune gatherings.

Thus, both parties and interest-group organizations exist in the PRC, but their function is basically within the context of one-way communication from the top downward, as distinguished from their dual role of influencing and explaining policy in the West. In this sense, public opinion exists to be mobilized by the party but not to direct the party. It may fail to respond to party propaganda, thereby compelling some revision of policy. It may articulate grievances by indirection, thereby stimulating examination of policy at the top. When it comes to placing external pressure on the government, however, public opinion in China is not an articulate force, at least in the realm of foreign policy.

Thus, in the area of "people-to-people diplomacy" a basic asymmetry exists between China and its opposite numbers in the noncommunist world. The public applause for American table-tennis players in Peking and Shanghai provided no constraint on leadership options in handling Sino-American relations, whereas mass media publicity for this event in the United States immediately changed the context of decision making on China policy in Washington. It would be an exaggeration to say that American public opinion in the aggregate forces a particular choice on presidential policy, except when a national election coincides with the existence of an extremely sensitive foreign policy issue such as the Korean War in 1952 and the Vietnam war in 1968. Nonetheless, the degree of support for or opposition to specific foreign policies in the United States, particularly as manifested through congressional responses to perceived public opinion, is wholly without counterpart in the People's Republic, where policy is exclusively the prerogative of elite interactions within the bureaucratic and party hierarchy.

THE SUBSTANCE OF POLICY

Ends

As is clear from our foregoing analysis, the foreign policy of the People's Republic is multifaceted, embracing a wide range of goals derived from Chinese, communist, and standard nation-state components. A giant in territory and population, its international status was nonetheless one of imposed inferiority down to its representatives being seated in the United Nations in 1971. Although its armed forces, now nuclear armed, are the third largest worldwide, Peking is unable to achieve territorial integrity so long as the island of Taiwan remains beyond its control. Paradoxically China's relatively weak power contrasts with its commanding image and assertive stance in world politics. Thus the People's Republic has been singularly preoccupied with the minimal universal goals of equality, territorial integrity, and national security at the same time it has been feared or admired, depending upon the viewer, for its political challenge to the superpowers and its avowed support for "Third World" and revolutionary forces around the globe.

To be sure, true equality is no more possible in international than in domestic politics, despite continued lip-service to the principle. Yet its symbolic manifestations, minimally marked in the granting of diplomatic recognition, are vital to the status and the self-esteem of governments. This is particularly true for the Chinese, whose humiliating treatment by the international community during the century before Mao's coming to power made "unequal treaties" and extraterritoriality the burning issues in the foreign policy councils of Ch'ing advisers, Republican warlords, and Nationalist officials alike. Publicly the PRC rarely voiced its desire for diplomatic recognition. Privately, however, Mao addressed the issue in words that buried his bitterness under exhortations to achieve economic power as a means to this end.

This in 1961, at the depth of a prolonged economic crisis capped by the sudden withdrawal of Soviet technical assistance, Mao articulated Chinese sensitivity to the international consequences of an inferior power position, "Nations which are big or rich despise nations which are small or poor. . . . At present, China still finds itself in a position of being despised. There is a reason people despise us. It is because we have not progressed enough. So big a country and we have so little steel and so many illiterates. But it is good if people despise us because it forces us to strive harder and forces us to advance."[24]

Representation in the United Nations and the presence in Peking of diplomats from more than 100 countries marked the achievement of symbolic equality by the mid-seventies. However territorial integrity, a second goal inherent in the policy of every government, still eluded the regime. Major border disputes with India and the Soviet Union left undefined frontiers subject to incidents and foreign control. Conflicting claims to distant islands in the South China sea and northeast of Taiwan raised the possibility of armed clashes in the absence of international agreement. Overshadowing all these questions was the status of Taiwan, occupied by Chiang Kai-shek's Nationalist regime as a continuing rival claimant to China.

No major speech or official statement addressing national goals since 1949 has failed to include the "liberation of Taiwan" as an explicit

[24]"Notes on the Soviet Union Textbook 'Political Economy' " *Mao tse-tung ssu-hsiang-wan-sui,* 1969, p. 392.

objective. During the first decade massive rallies thundered the theme although Mao privately cautioned against expecting this to be achieved easily, least of all through military attack. In November 1958 after having failed to dislodge Nationalist troops from the islands of Quemoy and Matsu only a few miles from the PRC coasts, Mao warned, "Both inside and outside the Party there are many persons who do not understand the [U.S. imperialism as a] paper tiger problem . . . who say, since it is a paper tiger why do we not attack Taiwan?" He gave a figurative reply, "It is both a real and a paper tiger. Temporarily it appears as real; in the long run it can be seen to be paper," but he spoke more bluntly a few months later in comparing the problems of Tibet and Taiwan, "Tibet has no other country that has signed a treaty with it like Taiwan. Our air force can go there, also our army. Now the Taiwan situation is entirely different. Taiwan signed a treaty with America."[25] During the next decade, while mass campaigns no longer focused on Taiwan the goal nonetheless remained omnipresent in authoritative editorials and regime pronouncements. After the PRC and the United States exhanged "liaison missions" in 1973, pressure increased on Washington to abandon its protection and recognition of Chiang's regime. Even without such protection and recognition, however, the "liberation of Taiwan" at best remains in the distant future and at worst remains uncertain. While it may finally be quietly abandoned as a lost cause paralleling Outer Mongolia, until the issue is formally re-

solved Taiwan retains considerable force as a sensitive question of territorial integrity.

In addition to equality and territorial integrity, national security is a universal goal of governments. Throughout its long history, China has been vulnerable to subversion of its minority peoples and invasion of its remote frontiers. So too in modern times, security considerations have played a prominent role from the inception of the PRC in 1949 down to the perceived threat of Soviet attack in 1969–71. War in Korea (1950–53), tension in the Taiwan Strait (1954–55, 1958, 1962), war with India (1962), the Indochina conflict (1964–72), and Soviet border incidents (Sinkiang, 1962, 1969; Ussuri River, 1969), provide a dramatically visible record of conflict involving China's armed forces and national security. Less visible but nonetheless troublesome were United States and Chinese Nationalist efforts until 1970 to subvert Tibet and South China and recurring Soviet activities aimed at the large non-Chinese population of Sinkiang.

In the absence of countervailing conventional and nuclear power, a PRC posture of belligerent defiance emerged to deter potential and actual aggressors. Sometimes deterrence failed, as in Korea and India. Sometimes it was misinterpreted abroad either as masking expansionist ambition or as manifesting paranoid behavior. On occasion the call to "prepare against war" was internally motivated for mobilization of the population in production campaigns or for strengthening political unity. Basically, however, the main goal of this belligerent posture was the achievement of security against perceived threats.

[25] *Ibid.*, speech of November 30, 1958, p. 255 and of April 14, 1959, p. 289.

This concern lessened in the 1970s. The United States withdrawal from the Indochina war, together with its abandoning the "containment" policy directed against Peking's normal participation in the international community, removed the grounds for apprehension over "imperialist attack." The Shanghai communique marking President Richard Nixon's visit to China in February 1972 pledged the "ultimate" removal of all U.S. forces and bases from Taiwan. Accordingly Washington gradually reduced its military involvement with the Nationalists. Meanwhile acquisition of a credible second-strike nuclear capability against a possible Soviet attack alleviated Chinese fears on this front. As the number of nuclear-tipped missiles aimed at Russian targets increases so too should PRC confidence in achieving the minimal goal of national security.

Nonetheless anxiety over renewed external efforts to exploit China's vulnerabilities at a time of internal crisis may reawaken security concerns and reintroduce a posture of national mobilization against external threats. The assumptions which underlie this anxiety are rooted in classical as well as modern experience. Thus one PRC study noted, "China's history shows that no matter what feudal dynasty ruled, 'danger from without' generally coincided with 'trouble from within'."[26] That such concern could have major impact on perceptions in Peking was shown in 1962 when Foreign Minister Ch'en Yi vividly described the intentions attributed to "Pentagon generals":

... Thinking particularly that the Chinese economic situation is difficult they may attempt to have Chiang Kai-shek land on the mainland and start a civil war.... On the one hand we must overcome the economic difficulties due to the three years of natural calamities and on the other hand, provide against the provocations of a Chiang Kai-shek supported by America. Also we must provide against incidents that may occur on other borders.[27]

Reference to "other borders" included Indian activity in the disputed Himalayan frontier areas and suspected Soviet collusion with unrest in Sinkiang manifested by a mass exodus across the border. Along the Taiwan Strait, PRC concern led to the sudden deployment of more than 100,000 troops to strengthen local defenses and an unprecedented diplomatic warning delivered through the Sino-American ambassadorial channel in Warsaw.

Domestic tensions could accompany a succession struggle after the passing of Mao and Chou or might result from prolonged economic difficulties as in 1961–62. Under these circumstances evidence of external threat is likely to trigger sharper responses in Peking than might otherwise be expected. Alternatively, sensitivity about control over China's sovereign domain, particularly in disputed areas such as the oil-rich continental shelf, may renew postures of belligerent assertiveness that place national security interests ahead of other goals.

These "other" goals can be differentiated as intermediate or

[26]Hu Sheng, *Imperialism and Chinese Politics* (Peking: Foreign Languages Press, 1955), p. 9.

[27]Chen Yi interview of May 29, 1962, *Tokyo Journalist*, June 26, 1962, in *Foreign Broadcast Information Service*, August 13, 1962.

middle-range goals and maximum or long-range goals. Intermediate, middle-range goals common to most states include the use of foreign policy for domestic economic development and the extension of national influence abroad. However the long-range, maximum goal of establishing ideologically like-minded regimes throughout the world is held seriously by only Moscow and Peking, with considerable doubt as to the Russian commitment over time. These objectives coexist in the consciousness of Chinese policy makers, so categorization is admittedly artificial and arbitrary. One intermediate goal, for instance, is to reduce the influence of rival power throughout the arc of Asia traditionally within or proximate to the Middle Kingdom's area of authority. This also serves the minimal goal of national security by reducing the ability of a hostile power to mobilize support among China's neighbors as was done by the United States from 1949 to 1969 and as attempted by the Soviet Union from 1969 to at least 1975. It also serves the maximum goal of establishing communist regimes by increasing Chinese contact with and knowledge about local conditions that can eventually spawn revolution.

The interplay between minimal national security goals and intermediate objectives of extending influence abroad first occurred in the 1950s. The so-called Bandung spirit, named after the 1955 conference of Afro-Asian states, characterized a new "United Front" policy toward noncommunist states that sought to avoid alignment with the rival power blocs of Moscow and Washington. Chou En-lai, then PRC premier and foreign minister, successfully muted the previous years of strident Chinese militancy and manipulated the personalities of rival Afro-Asian leaders so as to fashion a loose community of interests wherein China could play a prominent role while it was excluded from the United Nations. Regionally this offset the Southeast Asian Treaty Organization created by U.S. Secretary of State John Foster Dulles to "contain" the PRC. More widely, it permitted Peking to upstage Moscow by exploiting real and perceived affinities—cultural, developmental, and racial—to the detriment of Russia.

By the 1970s, however, the attempt to extend influence went well beyond the concerns of national security. PRC membership in the U.N. facilitated a more intensive campaign against "hegemony by the two superpowers." No country was too small, such as Malta, and no leader too ideologically remote, such as Archbishop Makarios, to be omitted from inclusion in Peking's defined "Third World" of which the PRC proclaimed itself an active member. No longer was the Sino-Soviet alliance a constraint as in the earlier Bandung period. The Sino-Soviet split now permitted equally virulent attacks against "Soviet social imperialism" and "U.S. imperialism." Whether the issue was war in the Middle East, international maritime law and ocean resources, or the world food and energy crisis, Peking proclaimed its solidarity with the majority of states and world population "in the struggle to stand up against collusion and exploitation by the superpowers." Political influence, not only regional but global, was finally at hand.

Like national security, the effort to increase influence abroad is not unique to Peking. A central assumption of international relations, past and present, is that superior power expands against inferior power. Although Chinese statements ritualistically foreswear hegemony, the game of world politics is too dynamic and potentially too deadly to permit total passivity in the face of constant competition from Russia, the United States, and perhaps Japan or India. This goal also fits in with a long historic pattern of Chinese regional domination that was cultural, political, economic, and at times military, more so than for these other states. The sense of superiority is deeply rooted in Chinese consciousness, once symbolized by tribute missions from abroad and more recently suggested by a steady flow of foreign heads of state to Peking. Rarely have there been reciprocal visits by top Chinese leaders and never by Mao himself.

The range of invitations to bourgeois parliamentary leaders, military dictators, and royal autocrats, all ceremoniously photographed with Mao or Chou, obscured the persistently proclaimed goal of establishing communist regimes throughout the world. Admittedly, this ideological imperative of Marxism-Leninism is an unrealistic objective for the near future. Nonetheless it has played a prominent part in Chinese policy at various times and its continued articulation in authoritative media arouses concern among outside observers, particularly those on China's periphery.

This concern initially stemmed from regime pronouncements in 1949–50 calling on others to follow "the Chinese road of liberation." Although Peking's support was almost wholly verbal at the time, communist insurgencies in India, Burma, Malaya, Indonesia, and the Philippines offered an immediate opportunity to

expand PRC influence, if not control. Only in Indochina, however, did war against the French achieve victory, and that was confined to the northern half of the country. As communist insurgencies elsewhere collapsed or dwindled to insignificant proportions, other policy goals won higher priority. Propagandistic rhetoric recurrently championed the cause of armed struggle throughout the next two decades, but only in 1967, during the most radical phase of the Cultural Revolution, were foreign relations dominated by the maximum goal of world revolution.

Overall, then, revolution abroad has received relatively little support from Peking. However the recurring rhetoric, accompanied by small amounts of weapons, training, and money for insurgent groups in Asia, Africa, and Latin America, serves as a reminder of this goal. Revolution could again receive greater emphasis to the point of jeopardizing influence won through political unity with "Third World" regimes. It is impossible at this juncture to determine how seriously this maximum goal will be pursued over time. In 1967 Mao addressed the question privately in words which reflected the Cultural Revolution ethos, "We —China—are not only the political center of world revolution but moreover in military matters and technology must also become the center of world revolution. If we provide weapons we should stamp them as Chinese (except for some places) and show open support. We must become the arsenal of world revolution."[28] Yet within a few years policy had swung back to the Bandung period of "United Front" at the state-

[28]Remarks of July 7, 1967 in *Mao tse-tung, op. cit.*, pp. 679–80.

to-state level. President Nixon was invited to Peking even while the United States continued to bomb communist armies in Laos, Cambodia, and South Vietnam.

Mao's importance in the definition of Chinese goals, both foreign and domestic, has been greater than that of any other individual. However his own generation of revolutionary colleagues includes critics who have at times ignored and even challenged his views openly. It is unlikely that his revolutionary impulse will be maintained by the next generation of leadership, given the differing priorities of various groups in the policy process. Whatever the individual inclinations, some time will pass before any single figure can truly succeed Mao. This means that groups and factions will determine policy through maneuver and compromise, thus lessening the ability of any individual or interest to impose an extremist goal. As a final consideration, the historical evolution of other self-avowed revolutionary regimes, whether French, American, or Russian, argues against the continued pursuit of revolutionary goals long after the original group that won power has passed from the scene. Nonetheless so long as support for revolution abroad continues to be articulated and actively implemented with material aid, it deserves attention in the analysis of Chinese foreign policy.

Means

Any construct of probable means to be adopted in support of ends must consider both what means are available and how likely they are of being utilized. Our concept of availability rests on two constraints: the objective capability actually at hand in the form of political, economic, and military power; and the subjective perception of what is permitted by ideology and self-definition. Objectively, for example, China's vast population offers an overwhelming superiority of military manpower in comparison with countries in South and Southeast Asia. Subjectively, however, PRC decision makers have not seen territorial expansion as an ideologically acceptable means of extending influence or alleviating internal problems. Therefore external preoccupation with China's population as an aggressive threat is misplaced because it is not seen in Peking as an instrument of military power for foreign conquest.

Our concept of the probability of various means being utilized also assumes two factors as omnipresent in the policy process: continuity and rationality. More than twenty-five years of rule by the same elite in Peking provides ample evidence of continuity for projection at least into the next five to ten years. While individuals will change, institutions such as the ministry of Foreign Affairs and the PLA have developed bureaucratic routines of behavior that have persisted. In addition, this behavior has been almost wholly free of actions that might be termed irrational so far as foreseeable consequences and risk taking are concerned. Of course, miscalculation can occur in Peking as elsewhere. At the height of the 1958 Quemoy crisis, Mao frankly admitted, "When we considered hitting Quemoy and Matsu with a few shells, I simply did not calculate the world would become so disturbed and turbulent."[29] In short, Mao underestimated the American reaction. How-

[29] *Mao tse-tung, op. cit.*, p. 233.

ever, in examining the likely means to be adopted we can draw our parameters of probability with considerable confidence in the continuity and rationality of Chinese policy.

One final general observation must be made. The objective availability of means varies according to internal developments, particularly when a society undergoes rapid change that is simultaneously political, economic, and military. Seen in these terms the China of today has little similarity with that of 1949, much less the China of 1911 or 1894. Even in the relatively short span of fifteen years, from 1961 to 1976, its material power and world image changed from that of a relatively isolated state shaken by three years of economic disaster to one of a prime catalyst in the "Third World" U.N. majority. The China of today is an economically self-sufficient country with oil exports that could provide potential leverage on nearby countries, and a nation capable of launching nuclear strikes against major Soviet cities as well as most Asian capitals.

This dynamic element of change is accounted for in Chinese policy analysis by the concept of dialectics. This concept stresses the elements of contradiction in all existence that result not only in tension and conflict but also in new relationships. Put into crude jargon, while there is "collusion" among "imperialist powers" there is also "contradiction" and "struggle for hegemony" that will lead to war, out of which will emerge new communist states (as after World Wars I and II). Similarly Chinese calculations take the long view for world revolution, accepting losses and setbacks as inevitable but temporary. In January 1975, Premier Chou En-lai summed it up

for the Fourth National People's Congress,

The United States and the Soviet Union are the biggest international oppressors and exploiters today and they are the source of a new world war. Their fierce contention is bound to lead to world war some day. Whether war gives rise to revolution or revolution prevents war, in either case the international situation will develop in a direction favorable to the people and the future of the world will be bright.[30]

This attitude not only avoids a timetable approach to achieving goals but also sanctions a high degree of flexibility to accommodate to new situations. Changing relations among "imperialist" states may call for different tactics. In 1965, for example, the goal was to divide western Europe by focusing on France for favorable attention, while in 1975 tactics were used to stress the need for west European unity to resist alleged Soviet designs. In like manner the waxing and waning of "peoples' war" calls for shifts from revolutionary to diplomatic means to advance goals.

This flexibility invalidates a static analysis attributing permanent priority to one or another means. In the first years of the PRC, revolutionary themes dominated foreign policy pronouncements but these gradually lessened with the "Bandung spirit" of 1955. This in turn gave way to "East Wind prevails over West Wind" in a partial return to confrontation postures in 1957–58. In 1959 virulent attacks on Indian prime minister Nehru mocked the "Five Principles of Peaceful Coexistence" signed with Chou only five years earlier. But Chou's 1965 Afri-

[30] *Peking Review*. No. 4, January 24, 1975.

can tour statement that "revolutionary prospects are good" seemed forgotten when African heads of state ceremoniously shook his hand in Peking a decade later. Perhaps most striking was the shift from the shrill Cultural Revolution attacks against "U.S. imperialism" to the highly publicized meeting between Chairman Mao and President Nixon four years later.

Despite appearances, these policy turns are neither mercurial nor opportunistic. They are seriously and systematically addressed in Chinese internal and external statements on both ideological and pragmatic grounds, reflecting a consistently rational view of foreign policy. Yet despite the explicitness of these statements and their persistence over nearly three decades of rule, such changes can come with stunning surprise to those outside the dialectical frame of reference who place more credence in protestations of "long-lasting friendship" and "immutable alliance." Observers may accuse Peking of perfidy, but Chinese analysts frankly point to the "twists and turns" of international politics and history, which logically dictate corresponding adjustments in policy.

Viewed from Peking's vantage point, it makes sense to change emphases among the various means of policy. In its early years, the regime was politically isolated, economically weak, and militarily vulnerable. Under these circumstances, top priority went to personal contacts, "people to people" diplomacy, and propaganda, thus relegating formal diplomacy to relative insignificance. At the highest level, Chou, uniquely qualified in experience and personality, indefatigably traveled abroad and hosted at home to stress China's desire for peace and its concern with domestic problems. At the same time he offered support, to the limited extent of China's ability, for East Europeans, Africans, and Asians with common interests regardless of ideological differences. This personalized approach proved particularly effective in many countries where individuals, unimpeded by opposition parties or bureaucratic rivals, dominated policy. The greater the personal ego, the more susceptible the individual was to Chou's approach, as exemplified by the cases of Prince Norodom Sihanouk, Pandit Nehru, and Henry Kissinger. It is impossible to exaggerate the role he played in overcoming the political liabilities in Peking's international position between 1949 and 1972.

At a lower level "people to people" diplomacy offered an additional escape from the isolation imposed on the PRC, especially in the 1950s, although it still continues to receive major emphasis. Bilateral "friendship" associations provide local outlets for films and pamphlets. Cultural tours by opera companies, ballet troupes, and acrobatic teams subtly promote the PRC image abroad. International sports competitions mobilize support for punitive moves against targets of "Third World" opprobrium, such as the Union of South Africa. Post-competition commentaries attack "the nefarious superpower tactics" of Soviet teams as against the "comradely unity" of Chinese athletes with those from other countries. Visits of radical and communist groups to China, featuring high-level receptions and corresponding publicity, serve to legitimize Chinese involvement that might otherwise be regarded as subversive interference in the internal affairs of other countries.

In all these activities, propaganda plays an important part, and propaganda as such deserves separate attention as a means of policy. Peking's foreign language output is impressive in volume and scope, as indicated by the following partial subscription list: *Peking Review*, an authoritative weekly magazine of political affairs, commentary, and theory, in English, French, German, Japanese, and Spanish, airmailed worldwide; *China Pictorial*, a large format pictorial monthly in Arabic, Chinese, English, French, German, Hindi, Indonesian, Italian, Japanese, Korean, Russian, Spanish, Swahili, Swedish, Urdu, and Vietnamese; *China Reconstructs*, an illustrated monthly in Arabic, English, French, Russian, and Spanish; *Chinese Literature*, monthly in English, quarterly in French; and *People's China*, a comprehensive monthly in Japanese. Even the "universal" language, Esperanto, wins attention with a monthly, *El Popola Cinio*. Special editions of Mao's writings add Burmese, Mongolian, Persian, and Thai editions. Meanwhile Peking Radio broadcasts in a multiplicity of tongues, transmitting New China News Agency versions of international affairs and domestic developments.

Despite PRC isolation in the world community, Chou and his colleagues in the Ministry of Foreign Affairs negotiated with consummate skill in conferences on Korea and Indochina in 1954, 1962, and 1972. They confronted Indian border experts with voluminous position papers and after the 1962 war issued comprehensively documented compendia to argue Peking's case in foreign chancelleries. Scholars agree

that the People's Republic, like all other states, cites international law and custom selectively when it serves China's interests. An impressive volume of treaties and agreements concluded since 1949 testifies to the seriousness Peking attaches to formal relations, in most cases following standard procedures and precedent established by noncommunist states.

PRC participation in all major international conferences and representation in more than 100 countries assures diplomacy a growing role. This was symbolized by the reappointment of Chou as premier in 1975 and confirmation of his long-time associate, Chiao Kuanhua, as foreign minister. There is no doubt that in addition to its traditional functions PRC diplomacy will act as the self-styled representative of "the rising oppressed peoples throughout the Third World," substituting propagandistic rhetoric for reasoned argument. But political confrontation in public may mask diplomatic compromise in private, and international law and organization will have increasing influence on Peking's policy.

Economic means have similarly grown in importance as capabilities for trade and technical assistance expand. While its overall foreign trade (less than $20 billion) is miniscule compared with the United States, the Soviet Union, and Japan, China nonetheless targets its economic activity abroad so as to pursue foreign political as well as domestic economic goals. Purchases of wheat have not only followed price benefits but also have shifted around among Canadian, American, and Australian sellers according to the desire to influence respective governments. Despite the virulence of the Sino-Soviet dispute and a domestic campaign publicizing the threat of a Russian attack, Peking continued to acquire long-range commercial aircraft from Moscow rather than rely exclusively on newly available Boeing transports. Chinese foreign trade is largely economically determined, but under certain circumstances political considerations can be important, particularly when other factors are in close balance.

Technical assistance programs vary from small-scale road building to extensive ventures such as the Tanzanian railroad, which utilized large amounts of capital, equipment, and manpower. They may operate in relative obscurity as in the Yemen but uniformly appear to avoid any activity that is covertly subversive or overtly political. This does not mean they are wholly devoid of political significance. In Laos roads built at the request of the royal government extended strategic communications lines from China into a potential buffer zone with ready access to Thailand. In Nepal a north-south highway linked Tibet with the main route to India while an extensive east-west project, announced in 1975, made the Chinese presence competitive with that of India.

This competitive role for technical assistance was suggestively alluded to in one authoritative commentary:

... While helping a certain country of the Third World to build a large dock, we came to realize that there existed a fierce struggle concerning dock construction. In point of fact, a certain superpower vainly attempted to control this country through its foreign aid program, but the offer was resolutely turned down by this country. We have come to realize that the assignment of this project is not only an engineering problem but also a struggle for supporting the Third World countries in defending

their sovereignty and combating the hegemonism of the superpowers.[31]

This serves the intermediate goal of extending influence abroad. Although it emulates far larger efforts by Moscow and Washington it may work more to Peking's advantage because Chinese experience better meets the needs of many underdeveloped countries. Moreover, Chinese technicians with their austere lifestyles cost the host government less than the Russian or American counterparts. Indeed, the visible results of social and economic mobilization in China may win selective emulation elsewhere, especially in Africa.

China's potential for the pursuit of policy through economic means is impressive as the world enters an extended period of economic crisis and uncertainty. The internal economy is virtually self-sufficient and thus suffers much less than that of most other states from shortages in raw materials with attendant price inflation. In addition it is only marginally dependent on foreign sales to sustain economic development, remaining relatively immune to the viscissitudes of international monetary and market fluctuations. Finally, China is beginning to emerge as an exporter of oil with limited local leverage in Asia, although nothing comparable to that enjoyed by Middle East nations.

By 1975 Peking could offer high-grade crude oil at competitive prices to Japan and Thailand, with promise of substantial increases in availability by 1980. Completion of a 715-mile pipeline from northeast oil fields to a tanker terminal in the Yellow Sea was announced simultaneous with reports of a 20 percent

[31]*Jen Min Jih Pao,* January 26, 1975.

increase in production for 1974. This approximates a total output of 65 million tons. Because China's economy is largely coal fuelled, the amount available for export should grow commensurate with production increases. In addition to extant fields, heavy investment in off-shore drilling equipment reflects Peking's high expectations for a major source in the continental shelf where its claims extend almost to Okinawa.

China is not alone in this game, of course. On land, the vast reaches of Siberia offer the Soviet Union far greater riches of natural gas and oil with which to tempt Japan, provided that massive amounts of capital, Russian and foreign, become available for exploitation of this forbidding area. In the sea, Seoul, Tokyo, Manila, and Saigon, in addition to Taipei, all have rival sea claims that put them in competition for leases with multinational oil corporations. Whether or not these claims will be resolved by the use of force, as occurred with the Paracel Islands in January 1975 when Chinese naval units eliminated the South Vietnamese presence, remains to be seen. In any event they open a new range of options for PRC policy with respect to both ends and means.

Reference to the use of force raises the question of military means as an adjunct of policy. We have already discounted the likelihood of conquest and annexation being seen by decision makers in Peking as viable options. However, our analysis of territorial integrity and national security goals showed a recurring resort to force between 1949 and 1974. In the overwhelming number of instances the People's Liberation Army fought for defensive reasons, either because deterrence had failed, or because it could best be

pursued by a belligerent posture on or across the frontier. We concluded that as these goals came to be realized over time such actions would become less likely.

Several qualifications to this reassuring prognosis must now be noted. First, China's force posture and hence its capabilities are undergoing qualitative and quantitative change. Attention abroad has understandably focused on nuclear developments, which provide Peking with a growing inventory of short-, medium-, and intermediate-range missiles, in addition to a medium-range bomber force of more than 100 aircraft. An eventual intercontinental capability seems certain although it has apparently held lower priority, probably because fear of a Soviet attack made Russian targets perferred hostages for deterrence rather than more distant American cities.

However China's conventional capability has also improved considerably over the past decade. Its ground forces, numbering some 2,500,000, are significantly stronger in firepower and logistical support. The air force is still preponderantly comprised of obsolete fighters and has limited transport capacity, but it is rapidly introducing new equipment and expanding its strike range. At sea, Chinese capabilities have shown a marked change with a rapid growth of surface and subsurface ships. Although still no match for Russian or American naval power available for use in the West Pacific, Peking's submarine fleet of more than fifty relatively new craft and the increasing number of rocket-equipped destroyers, destroyer escorts, and fast attack vessels is more than sufficient for other potential opponents.

These developments do not yet

signify offensive designs. No effort has gone into acquisition of an amphibious capability sufficient to invade nearby Taiwan, let alone more distant targets such as Japan or the Philippines. No bombers were built before 1969, and those introduced subsequently seem clearly designed for a nuclear deterrent role. China's land armies remain geared to defense against invasion, trading space for time to absorb enemy forces in the vast interior. Nothing in the disposition of transportation networks and base arrangements suggests planning for major fighting on Soviet, Indian, or other foreign soil.

Yet together with these changes in capability it is important to note a change in the policy stakes that may be significant in the future, particularly in East Asia where territorial seas and disputed islands provide a potential for conflict over access to subsurface oil. Whereas Taiwan has thus far been primarily a political issue, secondarily posing a minor threat of attack against the mainland, it may become increasingly important for providing entry to the continental shelf. Uninhabited islands in the South China Sea and northeast of Taiwan, once noted only for coral deposits and fishing, now lie within the range of Peking's air and sea forces. China will vigorously contest foreign claims and foreign concessions, but whether this will be by military or political means, or both, cannot be determined at this juncture.

As we have already noted, PRC interest in revolutions abroad has spawned a large body of literature devoted to "support for armed struggle." Actual assistance, however, has been minimal as compared with what could have been provided had greater priority been given this means of policy. In all cases, except Indochina, it has been marginal to the success of local insurgency. Still, the capability exists for considerable effort in this direction, particularly through training camps in China, multilingual manuals, a virtually unlimited arsenal of light weaponry, and dedicated cadres to advise guerrilla groups in Asia, Africa, and Latin America. China's expanding political and economic relations provide new information and contacts for improving this capability and a growing merchant fleet compensates somewhat for severe logistical limitations that do not similarly constrain Soviet or American subversive activities.

This political-military means of policy is mentioned last because it has been of least importance in recent years and in all likelihood will continue to rank below other means of attaining goals. Marxist-Leninist ideology, expanded upon in the writings of Mao, stresses the need for revolution to be basically indigenous if it is to succeed. "Self-reliance" is a cardinal feature of Chinese advice to foreign insurgents. Both ideologically and pragmatically, it is logical for Peking to keep its role secondary to that of the local leadership and local organization engaged in bringing new communist regimes to power through armed struggle. Support to such groups may provide useful leverage against existing governments, as in Thailand, and demonstrate the regime's continued revolutionary dedication, as in Angola. Basically, however, political-military subversion is not to be relied upon for advancing foreign-policy goals, as has been amply proven by the past record of limited Chinese assistance and the mixed results thereof.

China stands at a potential watershed in its modern history as the leadership of Mao-Tse-tung and Chou En-lai comes to an end. Moreover any attempt to focus on China in isolation from other states runs the risk of ignoring the dynamic interaction that impels international relations and removes it from the control or initiative of any single government. Finally, the genuinely global magnitude of problems that confront humanity in the realm of nuclear weaponry, food, and energy cautions against predicting foreign policy for any nation-state, even one as vast as China. Within these formidable constraints, however, systematic study and analysis should provide an ongoing basis for understanding and anticipating the policy process, ends, and means that will evolve in the People's Republic of China.

## SELECTED BIBLIOGRAPHY

### Books

CHEN, KING C. *Vietnam and China, 1938–1954.* Princeton: Princeton University Press, 1969.

CHIU, HUNGDAH. *China and the Question of Taiwan: Documents and Analysis.* New York: Praeger, 1973.

_____. *The People's Republic of China and the Law of Treaties.* Cambridge, Mass.: Harvard University Press, 1972.

CLUBB, OLIVER EDMUND. *China and Russia: The "Great Game."* New York: Columbia University Press, 1971.

COHEN, JEROME ALAN, ed. *China's Practice of International Law: Some Case Studies.* Cambridge, Mass.: Harvard University Press, 1972.

_____, and CHIU, HUNGDAH. *People's China and International Law: A Documentary Study.* Princeton, 1974.

DOOLIN, DENNIS J. *Territorial Claims in the*

*Sino-Soviet Conflict: Documents and Analysis.* Stanford: Hoover Institute, 1965.

ECKSTEIN, ALEXANDER. *Communist China's Economic Growth and Foreign Trade.* New York: McGraw-Hill, 1966.

ECKVALL, ROBERT B., *The Faithful Echo.* New York: Twayne Publishers, 1960.

FAIRBANK, JOHN K. *China Perceived.* New York: Knopf, 1974.

_____, ed., *The Chinese World Order: Traditional China's Foreign Relations.* Cambridge, Mass.: Harvard University Press, 1968.

_____. *The United States and China.* 3rd. ed. Cambridge, Mass.: Harvard University Press, 1971.

FITZGERALD, STEPHEN. *China and the Overseas Chinese.* New York: Cambridge University Press, 1972.

GITTINGS, JOHN. *Survey of the Sino-Soviet Dispute.* New York: Oxford University Press, 1968.

_____. *The World and China.* New York: Harper & Row, 1974.

GURTOV, MELVIN. *China and Southeast Asia —The Politics of Survival.* Lexington, Mass.: Heath Lexington Books, 1971.

HINTON, HAROLD C. *China's Turbulent Quest.* Bloomington: Indiana University Press, 1973.

_____. *Communist China in World Politics.* New York: Houghton Mifflin, 1966.

HSIUNG, JAMES CHIEH. *Law and Policy in China's Foreign Relations.* New York: Columbia University Press, 1972.

HUCK, ARTHUR. *The Security of China.* New York: Columbia University Press, 1970.

LALL, ARTHUR. *How Communist China Negotiates.* New York: Columbia University Press, 1968.

LARKIN, BRUCE D. *China and Africa, 1949–1970.* Berkeley: University of California Press, 1971.

LEE, LUKE T. *China and International Agreements: A Study of Compliance.* Durham, N.C.: Rule of Law Press, 1969.

LENG, SHAO-CHUAN and CHIU, HUNDAH, eds. *Law in Chinese Foreign Policy: Com-*

*munist China and Selected Problems of International Law.* Dobbs Ferry, N.Y.: Oceana, 1972.

LOVELACE, DANIEL D. *China and "People's War" In Thailand, 1964-1969.* Berkeley: Center for Chinese Studies, 1971.

OGUNSANWO, ALABA. *China's Policy In Africa, 1958-1971.* New York: Cambridge University Press, 1974.

OJHA, ISHWER C. *Chinese Foreign Policy In An Age Of Transition.* 2nd ed. Boston: Beacon Press, 1971.

RANDLE, ROBERT F. *Geneva 1954: The Settlement of the Indochinese War.* Princeton: Princeton University Press, 1969.

REES, DAVID. *Korea: The Limited War.* London: Macmillan, 1964.

SIMON, SHELDON W. *The Broken Triangle: Peking, Djakarta, and the PKI.* Baltimore: Johns Hopkins Press, 1968.

———. *War and Politics In Cambodia.* Durham: Duke University Press, 1974.

SYED, ANWAR H. *China and Pakistan.* Amherst: University of Massachusetts Press, 1974.

TAYLOR, JAY. *China and Southeast Asia: Peking's Relations with Revolutionary Movements.* New York: Praeger, 1974.

VAN NESS, PETER. *Revolution and Chinese Foreign Policy.* Berkeley: University of California Press, 1970.

WATSON, FRANCIS. *The Frontiers of China.* London: Chatto and Windus, 1966.

WENG, BYRON S. *Peking's UN Policy: Continuity and Change.* New York: Praeger, 1972.

WHITING, ALLEN S. *China Crosses The Yalu.* Stanford: Stanford University Press, 1968.

———. *The Chinese Calculus of Deterrence: India and Indochina.* Ann Arbor: University of Michigan Press, 1975.

WILCOX, F. O., ed. *China and the Great Powers: Relations with the United States, the Soviet Union, and Japan.* New York: Praeger, 1974.

WILSON, IAN, ed. *China and the World Community.* London: Augus and Robertson, 1973.

WU, YUAN-LI, ed. *China, A Handbook.* New York: Praeger, 1973.

YOUNG, KENNETH T. *Negotiating With The Chinese Communists.* New York: McGraw-Hill, 1968.

ZAGORIA, DONALD S. *The Sino-Soviet Conflict, 1956-1961.* Princeton: Princeton University Press, 1962.

Periodicals

*Asian Survey* (Berkeley).

*China Quarterly* (London).

*Current Scene* (Hong Kong).

*Far Eastern Economic Review* (Hong Kong).

*Journal of Asian Studies* (Ann Arbor). With annual bibliography.

*Pacific Affairs* (Vancouver).

*Pacific Community* (Tokyo).

*Peking Review* (Peking).

*Problems of Communism* (Washington).

*Survey of the China Mainland Press* (American Consulate General, Hong Kong).

# THE
# FOREIGN POLICY
# OF
# MODERN JAPAN

*7*

*Robert A. Scalapino*

## THE BACKGROUND OF JAPANESE FOREIGN POLICY

In geopolitical terms, there are some obvious reasons for making a rough comparison between Japan and Great Britain. Both are island societies lying within the Temperate Zone and close to a great continental mass. From earliest times, cultural interaction with the continent has been vital in shaping the character of each society; each has definitely been a part of the larger cultural orbit centering upon the continent. The sea, however, has been both a lane and a barrier. It has prevented recent invasions, enabling the development of a relatively homogeneous people who, despite many foreign adaptations, have retained a strong quality of uniqueness. Thus the en-

circling sea has been important to culture as well as to livelihood and defense. It has also been central to the historic dilemma over isolation versus continental involvement. This has been the basic foreign policy issue of both societies throughout their existence. And in recent eras, the interaction between internal and external pressures has been such as to present essentially the same answer to this question in both Japan and Great Britain. The growth of foreign pressures and the needs flowing from modernization—the scarcity of certain domestic resources combined with the rise of unused power—these and other factors led to regional and then global commitment. When the costs of that commitment proved too great, and the power of these societies relative to others declined, a substantial withdrawal took place. Now, in the case of Japan at least, some renewed commitments are being undertaken, reflective of the extraordinary advances made by that nation during the last two decades. To appreciate the new trend, let us turn first to the background against which it emerges.

## The Tokugawa Era

The diplomatic history of modern Japan opened in the mid-nineteenth century on a decidedly reluctant and confused note. Prior to Perry's arrival in 1853, the Japanese government had pursued a rigorous policy of isolation from the outside world for over two hundred years. It abandoned that policy only under strong pressure and with many misgivings. Isolation had first been imposed as a means of maintaining internal stability. When the Tokugawa family came to power in Japan in 1606, the West had already been represented in the country for fifty years. Missionaries and traders had come in a steady stream, first from Portugal and Spain, then from the Netherlands and England. In the first years of the Tokugawa era, however, abuses were regularly reported to the government. Christian converts among the provincial nobility sought Western arms or alliances to fortify their position against the central regime. Western trade also became a means of augmenting local power, especially in the Kyushu area. Between 1616 and 1641, therefore, the Tokugawa government applied a series of anti-Christian and antitrade edicts, leading up to a policy of almost total exclusion of the West. As is well known, only the Dutch were allowed to trade, very restrictedly, at Nagasaki. This, together with some limited relations with China and Korea, constituted Japanese foreign relations until the middle of the nineteenth century.

To draw up a balance sheet for the policy of isolation is not easy. It can be argued that, had Western intercourse been allowed to continue, Japan might well have been plunged into chaos and warfare, subsequently suffering the colonial fate of Southeast Asia. On the other hand, isolation clearly exacted its price. This is true not merely in terms of institutions and material developments, but also in the realm of emotions and attitudes. Isolation always breeds some of the symptoms of the garrison state—exclusivism, ethnocentrism, and mounting fear of the unknown, outside world. Most of these factors have been present in the Japanese scene, helping to shape the foreign policies and attitudes of that nation.

But in its time, isolation seemed to present only one major problem to Japan: How to maintain it? The expansion of the West in Asia was building up an intense pressure on Japan by the beginning of the nineteenth century. From the north, the Russians were moving forward on a broad front; Saghalien, the Kuriles, and even Hokkaido seemed threatened. Overtures for trade and coaling stations were rejected, but, at the same time, English intrusions began to take place in the southwest. These events were climaxed by news of the Opium War and repeated warnings from the Dutch. A debate began to shape up in Japan over fundamental policies.

This debate enabled Japanese nationalism to come forward, borne aloft by intellectuals from the agrarian-military class, and rooted in the primitive mythology of Shintoism. It was a movement with many facets: in part, dedicated to a restitution of imperial prerogatives and their defense against usurpation by Tokugawa; in part, an attack on the longstanding intellectual subservience to China and a simultaneous insistence on the unique character of Japan; and finally, partly a fierce assault on Western encroachment born out of an admixture of condescension and fear. All these factors were implied in the chief slogan of the era, *sonno-joi* ("revere the emperor; oust the barbarians").

In the precise form just described, this movement did not enjoy complete success, but within it was carried the destiny of modern Japan. Its evolution followed, in some measure, the broad stages characteristic of the whole panorama of Asian-Western relations during this period, whether stated in political or intellectual terms: an initial stage, dominated by the total rejection of Westernism as barbarian, inferior, and completely incompatible with the Asian way of life; a second stage, in which Western science and technology—distilled into the unforgettable spectacle of Western power—were accorded a begrudging but nonetheless deeply felt respect, from which followed, after much soul-searching and confusion, a conscious majority decision to attain these sources of power while holding firmly to traditional values; and thence, inevitably, there developed that stage in which such a rigid and unrealistic dichotomy as that between technology and values had to be abandoned in favor of a more broadly based and integral synthesis, the exact ingredients and balance of which have depended on the

background and convictions of each individual or group. It is within this general trend—its various exceptions, time lags, and all-important local distinctions not to be ignored—that the major elements of foreign policy in modern Asia have taken shape. Japan has been no exception.

Even before the arrival of Perry, a small group of Japanese intellectuals had begun to question the policy of rigid isolation. Out of "Dutch learning" had come exciting ideas; and there grew, in some minds, the desirability of leading the commercial revolution rather than fighting it, and of using foreign trade to develop power. How else could the intriguing slogan, "a rich country; a powerful soldiery," be made a reality? How else could Japan defend herself against Western imperialism? But this group was a small minority in the early period. Even the Tokugawa government supported the opening of the country only as a temporary expedient until force could be garnered to throw out the West. In accepting Perry's demands, it decided to accede rather than risk war, but it gave as little ground as possible. With the initial step taken, however, it was impossible to retreat. The first U.S. envoy, Townsend Harris, secured major liberalization of the Perry treaty in 1858, and similar rights were soon granted to other Western powers. From this date, Japan was truly opened up to Western commerce, and shortly the Tokugawa regime was even to seek assistance in developing arsenals and shipyards. "Support the government" and "open the country" seemed to be slogans indissolubly linked.

Yet basically, Tokugawa policy remained more a product of pressure than of purpose, and this fact worked against the effectiveness of the policy. Beset by many problems, the regime grew steadily weaker; its capacity to act vigorously in any direction diminished. It satisfied neither the West, which complained of its inability to control unruly elements, nor the provincial samurai, who regarded the central government as arch-appeasers. As so often happens in history, the regime in power found, by tortuous means, the only feasible policy for national survival—in this case, the policy of opening the country—but in the course of reaching that policy it was itself fatally weakened, so that the actual execution and fulfillment of the policy had to pass to other hands.

## Meiji Foreign Policy

In 1867, the Tokugawa regime was finally overthrown and the young Emperor Meiji was "restored" to the position of ruler, a position which the nationalists claimed the Tokugawa family had stolen. But real power in Meiji Japan gravitated into the hands of a small group of court officials and young leaders of the former military class. Their first major objective in foreign policy became that of removing the blemish of the unequal treaties, thereby attaining "complete independence" and equity with the Western powers. This task proved more difficult than they had expected; to accomplish it took nearly three decades. The Western powers, and particularly Great Britain, saw no reason to revise the treaties until Japanese standards came close to Western norms. The Japanese discovered that treaty revision was closely connected with basic reform

in such fields as law and commerce. Thus the Iwakura mission, which left for the West so hopefully, in 1871, to persuade the powers to abandon the fixed tariffs and extraterritoriality, came home realizing that many internal developments had first to be undertaken.

Through the years, "modernization" progressed by means of German, French, British, and American models. Japanese economic and military power showed remarkable gains. Law and order prevailed despite occasional domestic crises. Finally, in 1894, after repeated failures, the first great objective of Japanese foreign policy was obtained: agreements on basic treaty revisions were concluded with the West, all of which went into effect by 1899. As the nineteenth century ended, Japan had become the first nation of Asia to attain nearly complete parity with the West in legal terms. She had done so, in part, by satisfying the West that she was prepared to abide by the general rules of Western conduct, in part by the obvious facts of her internal progress and stability, and in part by her persistence and by certain clear signs that inequity toward Japan had reached a point of diminishing returns.

In the long struggle for treaty revision, latent elements of antiforeignism occasionally came to the surface in various forms. Officials deemed obsequious to foreign powers, too pro-Western in their personal habits, or disrespectful of Japanese tradition ran grave risks. The history of these years is filled with records of assassination plots, some successful, against more moderate leaders. This was one price to be paid for cultivating a nationalist movement so assiduously, while scarcely daring to admit its excesses. But quite apart from its extremists, Japanese society as a whole tended to react in pendulumlike fashion to the West. In many respects, this was most natural. Periods of intensive borrowing and adaptation at both individual and group levels would be followed by noticeable retreats, with the primary targets being those excesses and absurdities most easily discernible, but with secondary attacks ranging over as broad a front as conditions would permit. On the one hand, Japan wanted to catch up with the West, be accepted as a "progressive" and "civilized" nation, and match the West in the areas of its own talents; in addition, a very genuine fondness for things Western was entertained by many Japanese, great and small. But on the other hand, in this period of intensive nationalist indoctrination, and when the old antiforeign traditions were not yet completely dead, the periodic cry of "excessive Europeanization!" or "un-Japanese practices!" could have telling effect. Moreover, if selected aspects of Westernism appealed to almost everyone, there was no widespread desire to abandon the mainstream of Japanese culture or customs. These factors are not completely absent from contemporary Japan.

During the early Meiji era, there were strong overtones of defensiveness in Japanese policy and psychology. But the climate was also ripe for the rise of expansionism. Northeast Asia was largely a vacuum of power, tended haphazardly by the "sick man of Asia," China, on the one hand, and the somewhat stronger but essentially unstable and overcommitted tsarist forces, on the other. The Japanese mission seemed even clearer when it could

be posed against the prospects of continuous Korean turmoil and the increasing threat of Western imperialism in this entire area. The theme of "Asia for the Asians" was first applied here, and ofttimes by sincere men who had a vision of liberating other Asians from backwardness and Western domination, sharing with them the fruits of the new era in Japan. Private societies like the *Genyosha* (Black Current Society) and the *Kokuryukai* (Amur River Society) emerged, to exercise a great influence on Japanese foreign policy as influential pressure groups on behalf of a forceful continental policy with some such objectives in mind.

The ideology of expansionism was complex, and it knew no single form of expression. Groups like the *Kokuryukai* represented the past: they held firm to Japanese Confucianism, exalted the primitive mythology that surrounded the emperor-centered state, and were composed of ultranationalists of a peculiarly medieval type. Yet, from another point of view, these same men were radicals associated with the new era. Wherever Asian nationalism took root, they were willing to give it nourishment, even when its ideological bases were greatly different from their own. To movements as widely disparate as those of Aguinaldo and Sun Yat-sen their assistance was given freely, and in this they often went beyond what the Japanese government was willing or prepared to do. Moreover, there was an element of radicalism in their approach to internal affairs as well, even though its source might be largely traditional. Decrying the corruption, materialism, and excessive wealth of the new order, they demanded stringent internal reforms, some of which could be considered socialist in character. Thus were connected the themes of internal reform and external expansion as twins that were to have recurrent echoes throughout modern Japanese history.

The expansionists made their first major advance in the extraordinary decade between 1895 and 1905. Prior to that time, Japan had already added the Ryukyu Islands and the Bonins to her domain, and made more secure her northern outpost, Hokkaido, by extensive colonization, but these were not spectacular ventures. By 1894, however, Japanese leadership was ready to challenge China, the weakest of her rivals, for influence on the Korean peninsula. For Japan, the war was unexpectedly short and easy, the first of a series of wars that "paid." The Western-style training and the nationalist indoctrination of her conscript military forces stood the initial test with flying colors. For China, defeat at the hands of a foe long regarded with some contempt, and treated at best as a pupil, was a profound shock. Demands for fundamental reform were now renewed, especially by younger intellectuals, and China was pushed toward accelerated change and revolution despite Manchu resistance.

In Japan, the implications of victory were fourfold. The beginnings of the Japanese empire were laid, and the first tentative steps as a modern continental power were taken; China ceded Formosa, the Pescadores, and, for a time, the Liaotung Peninsula, until the intervention of Russia, France, and Germany forced its return. And China was eliminated as a serious competitor in the Korean contest. Second, the war served as a further stimulus to industrial growth and general economic development. In an atmosphere of patriotic fervor, industrial investment and expansion were undertaken, with an emphasis upon heavy industry. The war boom brought prosperity; and afterward, Japan received both indemnities and new China markets. Third, Japan enjoyed a sharp rise in prestige; most of the West looked on approvingly as their most apt pupil demonstrated her progress and valor, and it was in the aftermath of this victory that Japan began to be received in Western circles with some semblance of equality. Finally, these factors naturally accrued to the credit of the nationalist movement and to the prestige of the military class. The professional soldier, his samurai traditions now supplemented by Western science and by a new sense of mission not present in the Tokugawa era, promised to play a vital role in determining the future of his society.

In the aftermath of the Sino-Japanese War, a crucial decision had to be made. Japan was dedicated to increasing her ties with other Asian societies and providing leadership for them when possible. But to obtain these objectives and to have any basic security for herself, she needed a major alliance with a non-Asian power. This was still the world of the nineteenth century, when Europe collectively exercised a global influence, and when the unfolding of European power politics had a direct and immediate effect upon the non-European world. With the United States, Japan needed only to achieve some general agreement that would serve to neutralize potential conflict; indeed, she could expect no more, since American commitments toward the Pacific were still very limited, even after the annexation of the

Philippines. The major powers in Asia were Great Britain and Russia, and the choice had to be made between these two.

Initially, top political circles in Japan were divided. Men like Ito and Inoue hoped for an agreement with Russia that would establish long-term peace in northeastern Asia on the basis of satisfying mutual interests. Had such an agreement been reached, Japanese expansion might have been directed southward at a much earlier point. An alliance with Great Britain, on the other hand, was recognized as a step toward stabilization in the south and fluidity in the northeast. Not merely in this respect, however, but in every respect, Japanese foreign policy was affected for nearly two decades by the Anglo-Japanese Alliance of 1902. This pact was widely heralded as insuring the peace of Asia. Within certain limits, perhaps it did contribute to that end. England, now finished with isolation, needed global alliances to protect her global interests. In the Western Hemisphere, she cultivated the United States; in Asia, she directed her attentions to Japan. Once established, the alliance not only supported the status quo in southern and Southeast Asia; it also provided, within the limitations of British policy, some protection for China. In exchange, Japanese "special interests" in northeastern Asia were given recognition by the leading power of the world. Under such conditions, Japan could scarcely afford not to advance those interests.

Thus, the first fruit of the Anglo-Japanese Alliance was not peace, but war. The question of Japanese or Russian hegemony over northeastern Asia, having its antecedents back as far as the seventeenth century, was now given over to military decision. As is well known, Japanese victory against a weary and distracted foe was swift. From the Portsmouth Treaty, Japan emerged in control of much of northeastern Asia, and became the first Asian world power. The fruits of defeat and victory were similar to those of the Sino-Japanese War: for the defeated, soul-searching, unrest, and revolution; for the victor, a new gain of territory and fame. Clear title was obtained to the Kuriles, and southern Saghalien was added to the empire; control over Korea could no longer be challenged, although outright annexation did not come until 1910; the Manchurian-Mongolian area also fell under the shadow of expanding Japanese power, a situation placing new pressure upon China. Again, Japanese industry had enjoyed great expansion as a part of the war effort, with some support from British and American loans. And once more Japanese nationalism had risen to the test. Only a handful of intellectual pacifists and radicals denounced the war; the great majority of the people had been deeply loyal to the cause of a greater Japan.

Some of the costs of victory could also be tabulated. One lay on the surface. Nationalist propaganda had been carried so far during the war that many patriots assumed that the peace would be dictated in Moscow, not realizing that a long war of attrition might be dangerous for a smaller country. Consequently, ugly riots broke out over the Portsmouth settlement, and the government had difficulty in restoring order. There were also deeper costs to be tallied. At home, militarism had grown stronger; the nonconformist had little protection, either in law or by the customs of his society. Abroad, Japan was moving into a new orbit of power and influence; but as a result, she was now the object of new suspicions and fears, some of them coming from such traditional supporters as the United States and Great Britain. Already it seemed likely that the critical test might be China.

In partial recompense, immediately ahead lay an era of unprecedented influence for Japan throughout Asia. It was an influence, moreover, derived from much more than mere military prowess. There is no doubt that most of the Asian world experienced a thrill at the Japanese victory over Russia, because it gave hope that the West could be beaten at its own game. But in the broader sense, Japan had become the symbol of the new Asia, a society that had successfully made the transition toward modernization by a process of synthesizing new ideas with its indigenous culture. Western science and progress had come alive within the Japanese context, and from this experience the rest of Asia had much to learn. The success of Japanese nationalism was also a tremendous stimulus, even though its precise ideological forms might not be acceptable elsewhere. Thus, as this era unfolded, Japan embarked upon an extensive career as model, tutor, and leader to eager Asians everywhere. Thousands of students flocked to Tokyo and other Japanese centers of learning and industry. The majority came from China, but every section of Asia was represented in some degree. Likewise, Asian nationalist movements found in Japan a haven and source of support. Their leaders in exile wrote polemics, collected funds, and sometimes obtained official encouragement. Tokyo became a revolutionary center for the Far East. Japan

was riding the crest tide of the developing "Asia for the Asians" movement.

Already, however, the central problem of Japanese foreign policy was becoming that of distinguishing the thin line between acceptable leadership in Asia and unwelcome domination. This problem could be put in various forms. Would Japanese national interests, in the long run, be made compatible with the Asian march toward independence? Would Japanese technological, economic, and political assistance to Asia rest on mutual benefit and truly cooperative bases, or were the methods and intentions such as to be readily labeled the underpinnings of Japanese imperialism? Did the Japanese have, or would they acquire, a fitting psychology for world leadership, or would their actions and attitudes be marked by ethnocentrism, insecurity, and brutality, thereby producing the hatred of those whom they wished to persuade? From these, the universal questions of twentieth-century relations between advanced and lagging societies, Japanese foreign policy was by no means immune. The events of World War I accentuated the issues.

## The Rise of Japan as a World Power

World War I was the third conflict within a generation to pay handsome and immediate dividends to the cause of Japanese prestige. It is not difficult to understand why later glorification of war by Japanese militarists produced such weak rebuttals from the society as a whole. Against the true desires of her ally, Japan entered the war "to fulfill her obligations under the Anglo-Japanese Alliance." She proceeded to capture, without difficulty, the German holdings on the Chinese Shantung peninsula and in certain other parts of the Pacific. With this mission accomplished, she directed her energies to supplying the Asian markets cut off from their normal European contacts, and to providing her Western allies with the materials of war. These tasks required enormous industrial expansion. Indeed, it was at the close of this period that industrial productivity overtook agrarian productivity in yen value, and Japan could thereby claim to have moved into the ranks of industrial societies.

These trends, and complemental factors elsewhere, stimulated the drive for a more intensive policy toward China. The Manchu dynasty had fallen in the revolution of 1911, but that revolution had failed in its major objectives. The Chinese scene was now marked by deep political cleavages, with rival factions striving desperately for both internal and external support. With Europe fully engaged in a bloody "civil war" and the United States prepared to go no further than a policy of moral suasion, Japan was soon heavily involved in Chinese politics. In 1915, the Japanese government demanded an extensive list of concessions from the Yuan Shih-k'ai regime, known as the "Twenty-one Demands." These were bitterly resisted by China, with some success. Japanese influence moved steadily forward by means of loans, advisers, and technical assistance, yet Japan soon acquired a new image in China—that of the chief threat to Chinese nationalism. This era was climaxed by the historic May Fourth Movement, now widely heralded by the Chinese Communists as their point of origin, a fervent demonstration against Versailles and against Japanese imperialism, spearheaded by Peking students and spreading throughout China in May, 1919.

At the close of the World War I, however, there could be no question that Japan had become a world power. She was the one major nation besides the United States to emerge from that war in a stronger position. Her preeminence in eastern Asia could not be doubted, despite the uncertain new force of Bolshevism. What were the ingredients of this power as the third decade of the twentieth century began?

One source of Japan's new power clearly was her evolving economic capacities. Perhaps the full secret of the Japanese industrial revolution still escapes us. However, in its essence, it seems to have involved the capacity of Japanese society to utilize selected elements of Western technique and experience, adapting these to its own culture and timing, without duplicating either the historical context of Western development or the precise set of Western drives, impulses, and incentives. Toward this process were contributed both the conscious purposes of state and the remarkable talents of a people who could display creativeness through integration and discipline. By 1920, Japan was already becoming the workshop of Asia. Her large factories, equipped in many cases with the most modern machinery, contributed such basic products as textiles in great volume; at the same time, an infinite variety of cheap manufactured items flowed out of the thousands of small and medium-sized plants that formed the base of the pyramidal Japanese industrial structure. Sharing with management the credit for such productivity was the new Japanese labor force, abundant in numbers, cheap in cost, malleable (within limits) to its new task, moving out of the paddy fields into the factories, and acquiring sufficient know-how to give Japan an industrial character of which their fathers could not have dreamed.

But if manpower was a strength, it was also a problem—and one that now began to have an overt influence upon policy. Shortly after World War I the Japanese population reached 60 million, more than double the figure at the beginning of the Meiji era. In many respects, the facilities existing within Japan to accommodate this great mass already seemed seriously strained, yet no leveling off was in sight. Increasing talk of *lebesraum* was inevitable. And if the population explosion had produced an abundance of cheap labor, by the same token it had placed certain limits on their consumption of goods, by throwing increased emphasis on foreign trade.

Other factors underlined Japanese dependence on foreign lands. The four main islands of Japan were not richly blessed with those natural resources vital to the industrial development of this period. Coal was present in sufficient quantities (except for high-grade coking coal), but the supply of iron ore was very limited, that of petroleum was negligible, and most essential metals were either absent or available only in modest quantity. Moreover, because of her limited land space and her location, Japan had to import many of the agricultural resources needed for industry; raw cotton and rubber were two prominent examples. The Japanese empire of this period was helpful; from Formosa, Saghalien, and particularly from Korea came important raw materials and foodstuffs. However, the more important supplies lay outside these areas, and the Manchuria-Mongolian region could be depicted in impressive economic terms.

To revert to our discussion of the sources of Japanese power, the military and political ingredients certainly cannot be overlooked. The Japanese navy had become the third largest in the world. Her army, in size, equipment, and training, dwarfed other forces readily available in this part of the world. There was no foreign force that seemed prepared to challenge a Japanese force that was fully committed in its own territories or in any part of eastern Asia. The size and equipment of the Japanese military was a testament to the lavish yearly budgetary contributions of the people; the morale of that force was a tribute to intensive indoctrination, sustained by the realities of great political power and prestige within the society.

Politics, in its broader reaches, was also a wellspring of power. For a society without totalitarian restraints (albeit one strongly paternal and authoritarian in character), Japan presented a picture of remarkable stability up to this point. Besides a handful of intellectual radicals, there were few who would dare (or think) to question *Kokutai*— "the national polity" or, more vaguely, "the Japanese way of life." Thus, decisions of state, especially in the realm of foreign policy, could be taken on the assumption that they would be accepted with a maximum of conformity. The oracles of national interest could speak without fear of discordant responses, at least so long as they spoke within a consistently nationalist framework. What leadership group has not found some advantage in this?

Yet, as the postwar era began, there were indications that Japanese politics might be drastically affected by the democratic tide. The influence of Western liberalism, crowned by the global idealism of Woodrow Wilson, was strongly felt in Japanese intellectual and urban circles. Party government had assumed new importance, the office of premier was held for the first time by a commoner, and the movement for universal suffrage was receiving widespread support. Japan's liberal era was opening, bringing with it some serious efforts to establish parliamentary and civilian supremacy in Japanese politics. Temporarily, at least, the long-entrenched bureaucrats and even the military had to move to the defensive. For the latter, the Siberian expedition was the first clearly unrewarding venture abroad. And however strong the attempt to shift the blame to political timidity and lack of resolution at home, the army could not prevent some questions from arising in the public mind.

Hence, moderation in foreign policy was possible during this period. At the Washington Armament Conference of 1921, Japan accepted the famous 5:5:3 naval ratio with the United States and Great Britain, despite the bitter protests of her naval authorities. She agreed to the return of the Shantung concessions. Withdrawal from Siberia was slowly and cautiously undertaken. One cabinet even had the audacity to cut the military budget sharply, and there were some discussions (although no action) on a permanent reduction in the institutional power of the military in Japanese government. During this era, no figure symbolized moderation in foreign policy more than Kijuro Shidehara, foreign minister under the Minseito cabinets. Shidehara was a conservative, a nationalist, and a loyal servant of the emperor. He believed that Japan had special interests in northeastern Asia and a special responsibility toward China. But he wanted to avoid a "get-tough" policy which would only provoke boycotts, anti-Japanese hostility, and possibly war. Rather, he hoped Japanese influence could be exerted through trade, financial agreements, and political negotiation.

## Militarism and Defeat

The liberal era was short-lived. With its collapse went much of the hope for moderation, either at home or abroad. This is not the place to spell out the story of democratic failure in prewar Japan, but its more immediate causes are familiar: economic crisis and depression; political confusion and corruption; and the consequent rise of opponents from left and right. The repercussions were felt almost immediately in Japanese foreign policy. In 1928, under the Tanaka cabinet, there was a sharp turn toward a more militant nationalism in both the economic and political fields. State support to home industry was combined with a more "positive" program of support for Japanese interests abroad, especially in China. Overtures from Chiang Kai-shek—who had just broken with the Communists—were rejected, partly because of fear that his successful northern expedition would jeopardize the future Japanese position in Manchuria and northern China. Ironically, while the Tanaka China policy was provoking sharp Chinese reaction because of its strengths, it was under simultaneous attack by Japanese military extremists because of its weaknesses. Some of these elements, working through the Kwantung army in Manchuria, engineered the murder of Chang Tso-lin in June, 1928, hoping to force a decisive Japanese move in this area. The Japanese government was posed with the first of a series of direct military challenges to civilian control, challenges which went unmet.

Japanese foreign policy, in the fifteen years between 1930 and 1945, represented the natural culmination of these new trends. To be sure, not all the old themes were reversed, particularly those that could be read with different inflections. Stress continued to be placed upon Sino-Japanese cooperation, and on the need for a stable, friendly China, purged of communist and anti-Japanese elements. But action continually interfered with words. As the Japanese militarists gained control of the strategic heights of policy, especially in the field, any cooperation had to be strained through the tightening net of aggression, fanatical patriotism, and individual, sometimes mass, acts of brutality. Through these field actions, and as a result of a contrived incident, war came to Manchuria in September, 1931. The weaker Chinese forces were quickly defeated, but Manchukuo remained, to the great body of the Chinese, an unacceptable symbol of Japanese aggression.

With the Manchurian region at last under complete Japanese control, the militarists could not avoid spreading outward toward Mongolia and northern China. Thus the Second China Incident erupted, in 1937, and led eventually to total war and defeat. Throughout this entire period, Japan could always find some Chinese allies, whether as a result of the acrid internal rivalries for power in China, sheer opportunism, or some genuine hopes that this route might lead to a new and better Asia, freed from Western control. Indeed, the allies garnered from all of these sources were not inconsiderable either in number or in influence. In Wang Ch'ing-wei, Japan finally found an able if embittered leader. But, as against these facts, Japanese policy achieved what had always been feared most: a union of the dominant wing of the Kuomintang with the Communists and many independents into a nationalist popular front that was bitterly anti-Japanese. Although it had as one of its supreme goals the salvation of Asia from communism, Japanese policy, in the end, contributed more than any other single factor to communist success.

To concentrate solely on China, however, would be to examine only the weakest link of a general Asian policy which, for all its militant, aggressive qualities, had elements of real power and appeal. Building from the old "Asia for the Asians" theme, Japanese policy moved, in the 1930s, toward the concept of a Greater East Asia Co-Prosperity Sphere. The economic background for this policy lay in the rapid strides made by Japanese trade throughout Asia. By means of general deflation, changes in currency valuation, industrial rationalization, and extensive state support, Japanese trade came to enjoy highly favorable competitive conditions in eastern Asia by the mid-thirties. Western Europe complained vigorously about the practice of "social dumping" onto the colonial markets. Japan retorted with charges of economic discrimination and attempted monopoly.

The fact remained, however, that Japanese penetration of the Asian market, during this period, was substantial. The basis was thus provided for later proposals of greater economic integration of an Asian region led by Japan and divorced from Western control.

The center of the Japanese appeal to greater Asia, however, remained in the sphere of political nationalism. As Japan drifted toward the fascist bloc, Western imperialism in Asia could be attacked with less inhibition than in the past. These attacks were particularly effective in areas where nationalism was still treated as subversive by Western governors, and where Japanese policies could not yet be tested. Once again, an attempt was made to develop an expanded program of cultural relations and technical assistance. Students flocked to Japan from all parts of Asia; cultural missions were exchanged on an increasing scale; Japanese technicians went forth; and, as the Pacific war approached, the Japanese government provided underground assistance to various Asian nationalist movements in the form of funds, political advice, and even the training and equipping of military forces.

Most of the presently independent governments of southern and Southeast Asia owe an enormous debt to Japanese propaganda, military successes, and political concessions—even when the latter were self-serving, empty, or last-minute gestures. There can be no doubt that Japan, both in victory and in defeat, contributed mightily to the end of the old era and the emergence of a more independent, dynamic Asia. Yet her record was tarnished, and today she must combat a legacy of suspicion and even hatred in some

of these countries. In part, this can be attributed to such factors as the misconduct of her troops, but, more importantly, it is the product of the great cultural barriers that separated her from the regions she occupied and of her inability—through lack of experience, insecurity, and because of her own traditions—to develop the type of flexibility and broad tolerance necessary in leadership. In considerable degree, Japanese hopes for cooperation and friendship were strangled by the nationalism that pushed them forward.

As a corollary to her new Asian policy, Japan naturally developed a new policy with respect to the West. Nearly a decade earlier, at the time of the Washington conference of 1921, Japan had reluctantly given up the Anglo-Japanese alliance, her shield and support for twenty years. In its place were substituted the more general agreements among the major powers. This concept of collective agreement (not, it should be emphasized, collective security) was especially attuned to the American position. The United States wanted an end to exclusive alliances, but it was prepared to undertake only the most limited of commitments, and it still wished to rely essentially upon moral suasion for policy enforcement. The great symbol of this hope and this era was the famous Kellogg-Briand Pact, outlawing war.

Thus, the decline of Japanese liberalism at home was complemented by the absence of effective external checks or controls. The old system of alliances, and the type of checks they imposed upon unilateral action, had been declared obsolete in the Pacific, but no effective international order had replaced them. Consequently, in the name of her national interests, Japan could successfully defy the Nine-Power Agreement and the League of Nations, with no single nation or group making an effective stand against her. Inevitably, as she challenged the status quo powers, Japan gravitated toward Germany and Italy, the dissidents of Europe. The Anti-Comintern Pact sealed an alliance of mutual interest, though not one of great intimacy.

But the real decision that confronted Japan as the Pacific war approached had a familiar ring: Was she to seek a stabilization of her northern or her southern flanks? Who was to be engaged, the Soviet Union or the Western allies? The decision was not an easy one. In the late 1930s, Japan had participated in large-scale clashes with Soviet forces in the Mongolian region, and her historic rivalry was augmented by her hatred of communism. In the final analysis, however, she decided to count on a German victory on the steppes of Russia, and she turned to the south, whose resources had to be unlocked and whose Western masters had to be overthrown if the Japanese vision of the future were to be attained. Possibilities for agreement with the West to avoid this fateful step were explored, as all the moderates desired, but hopes were broken on the rock of China. Too much had been invested in blood and treasure to concede to Chiang Kai-shek, and so, infinitely more was to be invested—and all in vain.

## THE FORMULATION OF FOREIGN POLICY IN PREWAR JAPAN

In the Tokyo trials of major war criminals that followed the Japanese surrender, the Allied prosecutors repeatedly sought the answer to one central question: Who bears the responsibility for leading Japan toward aggression and war? If they did not obtain a completely satisfactory answer, no blame should be assigned. Few questions involve greater difficulties. The problem has taken on universal dimensions as the modern state has grown in complexity and as foreign policy has developed into the composite, uncertain product of a myriad of technicians, men rigidly compartmentalized, skilled and jealous of these skills, but almost always frustrated by the limits of their power; an indeterminate number of free-roaming generalists, yet not so free, being bound by the limits of the single mind, the niceties of group decision, and the pressures—subtle or direct—of subalterns; and, finally the larger, vaguer public, varying in size but never comprising the whole of its society nor the sum of its parts —alternately indifferent and excited, overwhelmed by the complexities and focusing on some vital issue, ignored and watched with anxiety, molded and breaking out of molds.

Japan was a modern state. In the narrow sense, Japan appeared as a society of great personal absolutism. In both the family and the nation, the head was invested with absolute powers. Inferiors owed complete and unswerving obedience. There seemed no measure of egalitarianism or individualism to alleviate the rigidities of a hierarchical system which, through primogeniture and an emperor-centered mythology, found its apex in a single source. But in fact, the essence of power in Japanese society has not been that of personal absolutism. The vital center of decision making has uniformly lain in its collective or group character, and in its extensive reliance on consensus as the primary technique. It is critical to understand that, despite all superficial signs to the contrary, the basic nature of Japanese society can only be approached by a thorough appreciation of the intricate refinements of small group interaction, the great importance of induced voluntarism, and the generally eclectic quality of final agreements.

In all likelihood, it is only because these things were true that the outward signs of rigid hierarchy and absolutism were so well maintained into the modern era. Elaborate methods had already been developed to integrate theory and appearance with the needs of a dynamic society. Just as the system of adopted sons had long preserved the necessary flexibility in the Japanese family, so the institutions of senior councillor, adviser, and go-between had each, in its own way, facilitated the making of group decisions. That process, giving extraordinary attention to form and status, was often wearisome and prolonged, but every care had to be taken to make concessions and consensus possible, with a minimum of violence to the position and prestige of those involved. Necessarily, equals were wary of confronting each other in person until the formula for consensus seemed assured; and inferiors developed, to a fine art, all forms of subtle pressures and persuasive devices, so that successful superiors paid silent homage to these in the course of final action.

Not all these conditions sound strange to Western ears, although the aggregate process might seem foreign or extreme. In any case, how were such basic factors in Japanese social relations translated into politics and the making of foreign policy? In theory, the Meiji Constitution of 1889 paid its highest tribute to imperial absolutism but, for successful practice, it demanded a unity or consensus of its disparate working parts. The weakest of these, the two-house Diet, its lower house elected, had at least the power to withhold its consent from basic policies. The administrative bureaucracy, culminating in such executives as the prime minister, and the members of the cabinet and the Privy Council, had a vast range of powers and had legal responsibility only to the emperor, but it could not be effective alone. The military also drew their power from the emperor and had direct access to him; in practice, moreover, this branch acquired a potent weapon in that the ministers of war and navy had to come from its ranks, which served to limit sharply the independent power of the Japanese cabinet. The military, however, could operate effectively only in conjunction with the other major branches.

There was never any serious thought of having these forces coordinated by the emperor personally, despite the awesome nature of his stipulated powers. Instead, that task was handled, for some thirty years, by a small oligarchy of Meiji restoration leaders who acted in the name of the emperor as his "chief advisers." Ultimately, this group came to be known as the *genro* or "senior councillors," an institution without a vestige of legal recognition or responsibility, but central to the process of Japanese politics. Every basic policy decision was placed before the *genro,* and their approval was a prerequisite to action. Even the daily affairs of state frequently engaged their attention. With protégés in every branch of government, and with their own vast accumulation of experience, these men were at once the source of integration, the court of final appeal, and the summit of power. To be sure, agreement among them was not always easy; there were deep personal and political cleavages in this, as in other Japanese groups. Timed withdrawals and temporary concessions, however, enabled a consensus to operate with a minimum of crises. Until the close of the World War I, with rare exceptions, the fountainhead of Japanese foreign policy was this group.

With the postwar era, however, basic changes in government began to emerge, paralleling those in society. The members of the *genro* became old, and their ranks were not refilled. No group came forth to undertake the integrative role. Instead, Japanese politics was marked by an increasing struggle for supremacy and control among the parties, the bureaucracy, and the military. It is interesting to note that, at the outset of this era, an attempt was made to establish a liaison council under the aegis for the prime minister for the development of a unified foreign policy. It was intended to include major party, official, and military representation, but it was never accepted by the major opposition party, and it ultimately faded away.

Without a supreme coordinator such as the *genro*, Japanese constitutionalism, in both its written and unwritten aspects, revealed serious flaws. In the hectic party era, foreign policy decisions taken in cabinet or government party circles were subject not only to legitimate attacks in the Diet, but also to extensive sabotage by the ranks of the subordinate bureaucracy, and to angry challenges by the military groups. The parties never attained more than a quasi supremacy and, as they faded, the military moved from verbal challenge to open defiance. Japanese society, in the period after 1928, was a classic example of a government divided against itself. Important segments of the military operated, both in the field and at home, in such a manner as to scorn the government. They received substantial support from within the bureaucracy, and from certain party figures as well. Every branch of government was riddled with dissension. Within the Ministry of Foreign Affairs, various cliques maneuvered for position—the militarist clique, the Anglo-American clique, and numerous others. For a time, consensus was impossible, and conditions close to anarchy prevailed.

Gradually, however, greater stability was achieved. Making full use of traditional procedures, top court officials surrounding the emperor involved themselves in unending conferences with representatives of all major groups; innumerable go-betweens explored the possible bases of compromise; certain voluntary withdrawals, strategic retreats, and silent acquiescences were effected. Slowly, a new basis for interaction developed, one which gave due recognition to military superiority but still was broad enough to include essential elements of the civil bureaucracy, court officials, and important pressure groups. Once again, the basic decisions were reached by consensus, but with somewhat greater cognizance of the realities of power. In this period, a new group of senior councillors, the *jushin*, was organized. Although lacking the influence of the *genro*, it was fashioned after that model, indicating the continuing search for an integrative center. That search was destined never to be completely successful. Another experiment was conducted in a liaison council, the purpose being to pool military and civilian policy with particular reference to the foreign scene. Ultimately, the imperial conference, with the emperor himself presiding over a small group of top military and administrative officials, became the final decision-making body. Indeed, it was this group that determined the Japanese surrender, the emperor personally settling this great issue. Perhaps this was the only basis left for the organic unity envisaged by the Meiji constitution.

The foregoing trends are not completely meaningful without some brief reference to other important social groups. First, however, it should be noted that the type of consensus being developed during the militarist era was abetted by an increasing control over all media of communication. One of the most literate societies in the world, Japan had national newspapers and magazines with massive circulation. After the early thirties, prominent dissent from ultranationalism became increasingly dangerous and, after the Second China Incident, all the public organs were echoing the official line.

Meanwhile, a process of accommodation had been taking place between conservative militarists and the industrial and commercial world of Japan. In the initial stages of the military revolt against liberalism and a weak-kneed foreign policy, the strong notes of a radical, anticapitalist theme were heard; the historic cry of "internal reform, external expansion" once again sounded forth. However, after the February 26th

Incident, in 1936, when army units in Tokyo under radical command rebelled, this type of revolutionary activity was suppressed. Although some liberal business elements were regarded with suspicion, and certain onerous controls were sharply protested by entrepreneurs, still the necessary compromises were made, and all of Japanese industry rose to the war effort.

Japanese labor reacted in the same way. Its radical and liberal elements had long since been silenced, and the great masses worked with patriotic fervor. It was from the rural areas, however, that the bedrock of Japanese conservatism derived. The alliance between peasant and soldier now held more meaning than at any time since the Meiji restoration. As is so frequently the case, rural provincialism bred its own type of ultranationalism. The Japanese common man played a role in the formulation of foreign policy in his own way: he posed no obstacles to expansionism, his complete loyalty was assured, and no sacrifice would be too great if it contributed to the nationalist cause.

## JAPAN SINCE 1945: OCCUPATION AND ITS AFTERMATH

When Japan surrendered in August, 1945, both her leaders and her people were forced to reconcile themselves to being a vanquished nation. By the terms of the Yalta and Potsdam agreements, the Japanese empire was to be dissolved and Japan reduced in size to the approximate boundaries of the restoration era. The homeland was to be occupied for an indefinite period by foreign forces. For the first time in recorded history, Japanese sovereignty was to be superseded by foreign rule. Some of the broad objectives of this rule had already been stipulated: action was to be taken to insure that Japan never again would become a world menace, or a world power. Total disarmament was to be carried out, and those responsible for past aggression were to be punished; even the fate of the emperor was unclear, although Japanese leaders sought desperately to gain assurances on this point during the surrender negotiations. Along with these essentially negative tasks, the occupation was also to encourage Japanese democratic forces and movements, so that Japan could eventually take her place in a peaceful world. Thus was inaugurated, in September, 1945, a radically new era for Japan, one that might well be labeled "the era of the American Revolution."

If the contemporary processes and substance of Japanese foreign policy are to be discussed meaningfully, certain pertinent aspects of this period must be set forth. In the first place, the American occupation and its aftermath can easily be divided into three broad phases: *(a)* the early revolutionary era, when the emphasis was upon punishment and reform; *(b)* the era of reconstruction, when the stress was shifted to stabilization and economic recovery; and *(c)* the era of proffered alliance, which is continuing at present. Each of these eras, in its own way, has contributed to the current nature and problems of Japanese society.

### The Revolutionary Era

The American Revolution in Japan was that of 1932, not that of 1776, although some of the spirit of the latter, as it applied to basic democratic values, was certainly present. The New Deal had new opportunities along the bombed-out Ginza and in the rice fields. But first, the old order had to be eradicated. Japanese military forces were totally disbanded in a remarkably short time; before the end of 1947, some 6 million Japanese troops and civilians had been returned from overseas, demobilized, and poured into the homeland. The military forces within Japan proper had also been completely dissolved. The ministries of war and navy were abolished. And, in an effort to seal these actions with the stamp of permanency, the now-famous Article 9 was written into the new Japanese Constitution:

Aspiring sincerely to an international peace based on justice and order, the Japanese people forever renounce war as a sovereign right of the nation and the threat or use of force as means of settling international disputes.

In order to accomplish the aim of the preceding paragraph, land, sea, and air forces, as well as other war potential, will never be maintained. The right of belligerency of the state will not be recognized.

The American vision for Japan during this period became widely associated with the phrase, "the Switzerland of the Far East," although, in this case, pacifism was added to neutralization. It was a vision that had a powerful appeal to many Japanese who lived amidst rubble, without adequate food or warmth, and with vivid memories of lost ones, fire raids, and the final holocaust of the atom bomb. There could be no question as to whether this war had paid. Moreover, the extraordinary vulnerability of the great Japanese cities had been fully demonstrated during the war's last, terrible months. For most thoughtful Japanese, the early postwar era was a period of deep reflection. Its dominant theme was trenchant criticism of past leaders and institutions. Once more, there was a Japanese surge toward new ideas and ways; MacArthur, no less than Perry, symbolized the end of an old order, and a war-weary people turned hopefully to *demokurashi*, without being precisely sure of its contents. These sentiments, widespread as they were, aided the revolution that was getting under way.

Among the various SCAP[1] actions, none had more long-range implications than those which affected the nature and position of Japanese pressure groups. As we have noted, for more than a decade the most powerful group in Japanese society had been the military. Suddenly it was entirely liquidated, and it has not yet reappeared as a significant political force. Liquidation was not merely demobilization, but also the purge that barred all professional military officers from future political activity, and the war crimes trials, after which the top military men of the nation were executed or sentenced to prison. Although many of these actions were subsequently modified or rescinded, their total effect, combined with other circumstances, has thus far been sufficient to render postwar militarism in Japan weak.

Through the purge and other measures, SCAP ate still further into prewar conservative ranks. For the old guard it seemed like the reign of terror, although without violence or

brutality. Most professional politicians of the old conservative parties had to step aside because they had belonged to some ultranationalist group or had been endorsed by the Tojo government in the elections of 1942. Conservative leadership was hastily thrust into the hands of the one group that could be cleared: the so-called Anglo-American group from within the Foreign Ministry. Kijuro Shidehara, Shigeru Yoshida, and Hisashi Ashida, all from this group, became the top conservative leaders of Japan for nearly a decade. Even the commercial and industrial world felt the shock of reform. Beset by purges, a program to break down the *zaibatsu* ("big combines"), and the general toll of wartime ravage and postwar inflation, most business elements sought merely to survive, as if seeking shelter during a gale.

Meanwhile, with American encouragement, the labor union movement attained a massive size; within a brief period it numbered some 6 million workers, whereas, in the prewar period, bona fide union membership had never exceeded one-half million. These postwar figures masked many divisions and weaknesses, but there could be no doubt that Japanese organized labor was a new force with which to reckon on the economic and political scene. And in the rural areas, the "American Revolution" was operating in the most forceful fashion. Under a far-reaching program of land reform, absentee landlordism was almost completely abolished, tenancy was reduced to less than 10 percent of total agrarian families, and land holdings were equalized beyond the wildest imagination of prewar advocates of land reform. Basically, this program was dedicated to the creation of a huge independent yeo-

---

[1]SCAP is the commonly used abbreviation for "Supreme Commander of the Allied Powers." It is used to designate General MacArthur personally, and the American occupation force collectively.

manry. The political repercussions in the rural areas, especially among younger age groups, have only recently become measurable.

Certain reforms cut across class lines and into the broadest categories of society. Legal attempts were made to abandon primogeniture and to emancipate women. Women were given full equality before the law, including equal rights of inheritance, divorce, and suffrage. Sweeping reforms in education were inaugurated, with the purpose of developing freer, more independent students, unshackled from the old chauvinism and submissiveness. Even that very special category of men, the subordinate government officials, were given lectures on democracy, in the hope that some of the old attitude of *kanson mimpi* ("officials honored, people despised") could be removed.

To recite these various efforts in such bald fashion may lead to the supposition that a total social revolution took place in Japan during the first years after 1945. Any such impression would be false. Conservatism, both in the form of certain dominant classes and in the form of certain traditions that operated in every class, was a sturdy force. Moreover, as might be surmised, not all SCAP experiments were successful and, by the end of 1947, in any case, the era emphasizing reform was drawing to a close. In its ripest forms, it had lasted only about two years. The conservatives definitely survived. Indeed, conservative dominance has been the hallmark of Japanese politics for the past three decades, giving Japan a degree of political stability unequalled by any other advanced industrial society during this era.

It would be equally misleading, however, to underestimate the changes that took place during the Occupation, whether because of SCAP reforms or as a result of the total complex of postwar circumstances. Some of these changes should be regarded as part of the continuum inherited from prewar days. Others were largely the product of foreign intervention or the new conditions prevailing as a result of military defeat. In any case, the changes which developed during this period had a direct influence on the processes and substance of Japanese foreign policy. Most important have been the altered composition of Japanese pressure groups and the accelerated movement toward a mass society.

The nature of Japanese conservatism has been strongly affected by the demise of the military, the declining importance of the agrarian sector, and the tremendous premium upon economic development. The Japanese "left" has also been affected by the greatly expanded freedom as well as the emergence of new generations and issues. In recent years, the drift of Japanese politics has been toward the establishment of leftist enclaves in the polity, especially in the great urban centers, raising questions about the future of conservative dominance. The political path that will be taken in the coming decade remains unclear. One thing, however, seems apparent: the trend has been toward a closer balance of competing pressure groups within that society than there was in the prewar era. As a result of this and other factors, the Japanese common man has become the object of increasing political solicitation and concern.

Stabilization

Before we turn to the current status of foreign policy, some brief consideration should be given to the second and third phases of the occupation and the gradual emergence, once again, of an independent Japan. The shift of emphasis in occupation policy, from punishment and reform to economic stabilization and recovery, began as early as 1947. The change was motivated by many problems. Certain earlier American premises about the postwar world now seemed unjustified. The prospects for a China that would be friendly and democratic by American definition were dim; the honeymoon with the Soviet Union was clearly over and the Cold War was beginning; the threat of communism throughout Europe and Asia, as a result of postwar chaos and economic misery, was a matter of profound concern. In Japan itself, the close relation between economic recovery and the prospects for democratic success could no longer be slighted or ignored. In addition, the expenses of occupation and relief constituted a heavy burden for the American taxpayer; at its peak, the cost ran close to a half-billion dollars a year.

The new emphasis brought many changes. Increasingly, the supreme test to which any policy could be put was: Does it advance productivity and economic stabilization? An assessment was made of the primary obstacles—war damage, inflation, the lack of raw materials, and low industrial morale. SCAP began to interest itself in Japanese productive efficiency, and moved from merely keeping Japan alive to furnishing her with raw materials and acquainting her entrepreneurs with the most advanced machinery and techniques. The complex problem of inflation was finally faced. Under the Dodge Nine-Point Stabilization Program, stringent reforms were put into effect. These were unpopular in many quarters, but the inflationary tide was at last turned.

Meanwhile, other disruptions to production were dealt with. The deconcentration program was relaxed and gradually abandoned, after successful initial attempts to reduce certain large zaibatsu families and cartels. The United States also progressively receded from its early severity on the issue of reparations. By the end of this era, the American government had indicated its acceptance of the thesis that the Japanese ability to repay war damages was strictly limited, that large reparations would indirectly become a responsibility to the United States, and that the heavy industry on which the Japanese future was so dependent could not be used for these purposes. Finally, SCAP took a sterner attitude toward the labor movement, amending its earlier generous legislation on unionism to give the employer, and especially the government, a stronger position.

The net effect of these actions, accompanied by certain broader trends at home and abroad, was to stimulate rapid economic recovery. Japanese society could build on an industrial revolution already well advanced, and on a legacy of technical know-how. Deflation and internal readjustments were followed by new opportunities for industrial expansion. The Korean War and the great prosperity of the free world were of major assistance. Beginning in 1950, therefore, Japan entered a period of amazing economic development. For the next twenty years, the average annual rise in gross national product was approximately 10 percent, one of the most spectacular rates of growth in the world.

This second phase of the occupation, which triggered the economic surge, was not without internal political reverberations. In the revolutionary era, American actions had been an anathema to the conservatives; now, the conservatives became the new allies. The liberal left, which had cheered in the early days, was filled with dismay and resentment at many actions of which it did not approve but from which it had no recourse. Japanese democracy was still under the tutelage of American military rule, and criticism and opposition were strictly limited by that fact. Inevitably, however, the United States and its policies became the central issue in Japanese politics, paving the way for the sharp divergencies that came into the open later. For every political group, moreover, this second era was one of reflection and reconsideration of Western values. There was an unmistakable tendency, at all levels, to emphasize synthesis and adjustment rather than uncritical acceptance of foreign concepts. The pendulum had begun to swing back.

As can be seen, the beginnings of postwar Japanese foreign policy were established in this era, albeit under American direction. These beginnings followed a course that Japanese leadership itself might well have taken and even labeled "in the national interest," had it been an independent agent. Indeed, on issues like reparations and trade, the United States was widely accused of being excessively pro-Japanese. One policy which was emphasized was that of rehabilitating Japanese heavy industry and encouraging its orientation toward the needs and markets of the late-developing societies, particularly those of non-communist Asia. Again, the concept of Japan as the workshop of Asia was advanced, but without certain former connotations. As a concomitant to this policy, the United States also tried to adjust Japanese political and economic relations with erstwhile enemies. Like a benevolent warden convinced of the successful rehabilitation of his charge, the United States pressed for Japanese reentry into the world community.

But with the second phase of the occupation, there also began an intimate and largely new relationship between Japan and the United States, a relationship founded on a rising tempo of economic interaction. Japanese products began to flow into the United States in exchange for American raw materials, foodstuffs, and machinery. Technical assistance from the United States smoothed the way for investments and patent sharing. The economic interaction was thus very broadly based. It was supported, moreover, by an expanding cultural exchange of customs, ideas, and patterns of life.

### The Era of Alliance

Within these trends lay the seeds of the third era, that of alliance proferred by the United States to Japan. By 1949, American authorities realized, on the one hand, that the occupation was reaching a point of diminishing returns, and, on the other, that continuing economic and political ties between the two countries were a mutual necessity. The explorations which led to the San Francisco Peace Treaty of 1951 involved a series of decisions that added to the new Japanese foreign policy and provoked heated political debate.

The critical issue pertained to the question of Japanese defense. Two broad alternatives seemed to exist. One was Japanese pacifism, which involved seeking universal agreements guaranteeing the sanctity of Japanese territory and backing these with pledges of protection by the United Nations, and possibly by the United States, separately. The alternative was to acknowledge the Japanese need for, and right to, military defense, and to underwrite Japanese rearmament with American power. Obviously, the choice between these two broad courses would affect and shape most other aspects of Japanese foreign policy.

The Yoshida government did not hesitate to support the second alternative, that of political, military, and economic alliance with the United States, as the only course compatible with world conditions and Japanese needs. To adopt a policy of neutralism, the conservatives argued, would make Japan dependent on the mercurial policies of the communist world. It would provide neither security nor prosperity. They insisted that both the economic and the political interests of Japan were best served by alignment with the free world, particularly the United States.

These arguments prevailed. While making known its desire for an overall peace treaty, the Japanese government agreed to sign a treaty with the noncommunist allies alone, if necessary. The Cold War had become hot in Korea while preliminary treaty negotiations were getting under way. Because of this, and because of the wide divergence between Soviet and American views on Japan, no serious attempt was made to obtain communist approval for the treaty draft, as the Japanese socialists had wished. In exchange for their willingness to sign a separate treaty, the conservatives were given a treaty considered generous by all, and soft by some. Reparations, and certain territorial issues (the Kurile and Ryukyu Islands), were left open, providing Japan with some bargaining power. The treaty contained no stipulations concerning SCAP reforms. Japan was left free to make any changes desired in her internal institutions. This included the right to rearm.

Official independence for Japan finally came on April 28, 1952, the day on which the San Francisco treaty came into effect. Accompanying the main treaty was a bilateral Mutual Security Treaty with the United States providing for the continuance of American military bases in Japan until adequate defenses were prepared by the Japanese government. At least as early as 1949, the creation of a Japanese defense force was being urged in some American and Japanese circles, and Japanese rearmament was first started in the summer of 1950, shortly after the outbreak of the Korean War. The National Police Reserve was activated in August of that year with an authorized component of 75,000 men. With the coming of Japanese independence, this number was increased to 110,000, and a small Maritime Safety Force was established, in May, 1952. In August, these were brought together under the National Safety Agency. Two years later, on July 1, 1954, the name was changed to the Defense Agency, and the armed forces were brought directly under the office of the prime minister, who was authorized to add a small Air Self-Defense Force. The slow build-up of Japanese defense forces continued. By the end of 1955, there were about 200,000 men in the total defense force. Twenty years later, in 1975, the force numbered some 250,000 men in all branches. While various fears have been voiced that Japan may again become a major military power, the fact remains that this force is entirely defensive in character at present, and in terms of numbers represents the smallest military establishment in Northeast Asia, including the Koreas and Taiwan as well as the People's Republic of China and the USSR.

Meanwhile, economic relations between the United States and Japan have grown to gigantic proportions. By the end of 1974, total Japanese trade was approaching $118 billion, and roughly 21 percent of that trade was still with the United States. Since the trade has grown at the staggering rate of nearly 20 percent per annum during the last decade, two critical facts immediately become clear: first, Japanese-American economic relations provide the foundation for the alliance, being of vital importance to both nations; second, those relations have recently presented serious problems certain of which are likely to remain.

## THE FORMULATION OF FOREIGN POLICY IN POSTWAR JAPAN

Before exploring the basic issues and alternatives currently involved in Japanese foreign policy, let us look briefly at the way in which decision-making and administrative processes in this field operate. The post-1945 state inherited a troubled,

complex record. In the critical Meiji era (between 1867 and 1910), as we have indicated, the apex of the decision-making process lay with a small group of elder statesmen, the *genro*. The political genius of Japan has always lain in oligarchy and a consensus process involving intricate negotiations and compromises. After World War I, however, centripetal forces multiplied, with the *genro* institution fading away. For more than two decades thereafter, the problems of coordination mounted, with various parts of the political-economic-military elite increasingly in conflict.

In this period, the role of the bureaucracy was naturally of critical importance. In theory, this bureaucracy was an instrument of the emperor, not the Diet. Institutional limitations combined with socioeconomic realities to reduce the independent role of the political parties. The parties were significant only as they were linked with one or another faction of the bureaucracy and its senior officialdom. Public opinion was of very limited significance. Divisions within the bureaucracy, however, were serious, and tended to grow deeper with the passage of time. It has been customary to see these divisions largely as reflecting a cleavage between civilian and military. In fact, however, they were much more complex, with many competitive, conflicting civilian-military alliances. As our knowledge of decision making in the foreign policy field for the 1920–1945 era grows, the problems of coordination, the depth of policy conflicts, and the instances of open or subtle insubordination on the part of junior officials in various branches of the government have come into sharp focus. The series of crises preceding Pearl Harbor were built out of deep fissures within the conservative-radical nationalist elites that in some measure shared power during those tumultuous years.

Has the decision-making process been more coordinated in the postwar era? The new Japanese constitution of 1947 did much to clarify the ultimate responsibility for policy, domestic and foreign. Patterned almost wholly after Anglo-American institutions, it drastically altered the old system. Under its provisions, the emperor's functions became ceremonial and symbolic. Sovereignty was assigned to the people, to be exercised by their elected representatives. A parliamentary system modeled after that of Great Britain was established, with certain modifications of a distinctly American flavor.

The Diet, instead of being peripheral to the political process, is now its center, and both houses are elective. The upper house, the House of Councillors, is constructed in a complicated fashion, with both nationwide and prefectural constituencies; the lower house, the House of Representatives, is based on medium-sized election districts (three to five members chosen from each district, depending upon its size). Executive responsibility to the Diet is clearly stipulated. The prime minister must be approved by the Diet or, if the houses disagree, by the lower house. In case of a vote of no confidence, the government must either dissolve the lower house and call for new elections, or resign.

A new law pertaining to the Diet was enacted to accompany the constitution of 1947. Among other things, it provided for a system of standing committees—in contrast to the prewar, British-style, ad hoc committees. Thus, each house of the Diet now has a Foreign Affairs Committee. After agreement among the parties on the allocation of committee seats, members are selected by each party on the basis of training, experience, and political connections. The standing committees exist to hold hearings on government legislation or any policy matters within their general jurisdiction. Special ad hoc committees, however, are still used extensively in the Japanese Diet, sometimes on issues involving foreign policy.

Despite these institutional changes, the Japanese Diet committee system, as it currently operates, does not give either to the Diet as a whole or to individual Diet members the degree of power possessed in the United States Congress. Party or, more accurately, factional discipline interacts with the traditions of Japanese parliamentarism to make this true. Initiative and power in foreign policy continue to lie overwhelmingly with the executive branch of government—in concrete terms, currently with the key leaders of the Liberal Democratic party. In certain respects, of course, party supremacy has been strengthened by the new institutional structure. Under a Western-style parliamentary system, major party leaders constitute the apex of authority. The emperor no longer serves as an independent and legally omnipotent channel of power. The military branch of government is no longer a separate and competitive source of influence. And even the civil bureaucracy is now clearly subordinated in law to a political administration that must be consonant with a majority of the popularly elected members of the House of Representatives.

How do the bureaucracy and the parties cooperate in foreign policy formulation today? The evidence suggests that the dominant leaders of the conservative Liberal Democratic party play the major role in determining the broad framework within which foreign policies shall be developed; then such Ministries as those of Foreign Affairs, Finance, and International Trade and Industry draft specific policies within this framework. The draft is then subject to scrutiny and approval by the party leaders, after which the designated officials proceed to execute policy in its final forms. To understand how this actually works out, however, one must have a general appreciation of the present Japanese party system and bureaucracy.

Perhaps four general trends within the party system are significant for foreign policy. First, the conservatives have continued to hold a commanding position in Japanese politics. They currently hold a wide margin in both houses of the Diet, as has been the case almost continuously during the post-1945 era. Perhaps the major reasons for regular conservative victories have been their prewar ties and strength at local levels, especially in rural areas; their prominent, well-known candidates; the funds at their disposal; the extraordinary prosperity of Japan since 1950; the divided and weak nature of the opposition; and last, but by no means least, the capacity of the conservatives to adjust to changing conditions. Will this LDP dominance continue throughout the 1970s? The signals are mixed.

The conservatives do have some reasons for concern. Their percentage of the total vote in House of Representatives elections has dropped below 50 percent in recent years. It is clear, moreover, that the conservatives are in trouble in the metropolitan areas, where urban issues are becoming of critical importance. In Tokyo, Osaka, and Kyoto, for example, they do badly, especially in local elections. The rural vote upon which the conservatives traditionally counted, meanwhile, continues to decline in percentage terms. These and other factors have led some observers to predict that Japan is enroute to coalition government at some point in the 1970s. It is by no means clear, however, when or even whether such a political shift will take place. The opposition parties continue to be badly split, and with no obvious candidate for central leadership. The *Komeito,* Japan's newest and most novel party, has parlayed religion (Buddhism of the Soka Gakkai sect), Asia-centered nationalism, domestic reform, and antiestablishment imagery into a considerable measure of success. At the moment, however, the *Komeito* appears to have run into problems, both internal and vis-à-vis the Japanese public, making its further advances problematic. The Japan Socialist party has long been deeply divided and politically stagnant, dominated by a preoccupation with ideology and seemingly afraid of actually coming to power. At some point, it is possible that the labor movement will reshape this party— or some successor—in a more moderate, realistic fashion. Until that time, the JSP's impotence will probably continue—unless a major economic crisis were to emerge. The Democratic Socialist party, meanwhile, is a moderate party—closely akin to the British Labour party in some respects. Its base of support, however, has remained small, and there are few signs that this will change. There remains the Communist party of Japan—a party that has finally established an "autonomous" or "independent" position vis-à-vis both Peking and Moscow. The Communists are currently the most dynamic of the opposition parties, and their gains in recent years have been significant. Currently, they poll approximately 10 percent in national elections and substantially more in the great cities. Most observers predict that their share of Diet seats will continue to increase during the next few elections. However, they too appear likely to reach a plateau, assuming an avoidance of prolonged national and international economic crisis—and one considerably below that of the French and Italian Communist parties.

United-front leftist politics thus far has been most easily established and most successful at metropolitan and local-regional levels. In general, however, the conservatives (with almost all of the independents affiliated with them) dominate local and prefectural politics even more thoroughly than at the Diet level. Only in the key cities have they slipped badly. Barring some sustained crisis such as war or depression, therefore, it is difficult to foresee any early demise of the conservatives. In a functional sense, Japan can be said to have a "one and one-half" party system: one dominant party that knows only how to govern, and half-parties that know only how to oppose. If this should change in the near future, the most likely cause would be the deepening fissures within the LDP and the development of new party alignments.

This suggests that there is still another way in which the Japanese party system can be defined and explained: as a system of rival federations within which operate the real

parties—namely, the smaller factions that are based upon intimate personal ties and mutual interests. Each of the major parties is composed of such factions. Thus, the Liberal Democratic party currently has eight to ten principal factions. The shifting alliances among these factions determine leadership of the "federation," or party. Factional loyalty generally takes precedence over loyalty to the federation; hence, in many respects, the real party is the faction.

Considering the circumstances noted above, it is not surprising that bipartisanship on foreign policy issues does not exist in Japan. Indeed, such issues are often used as weapons in the struggle for power among rival factions *within* a major party. Within the Liberal Democratic party, for example, such issues as policies toward the Republic of Korea, adjustments in the Mutual Security Treaty with the United States, and—above all—China policy have been made heated intraparty issues. Sometimes, issue divergence stems from genuine differences of opinion. More frequently, it becomes a means of soliciting public or elitist support.

In sum, Japanese foreign policy is largely determined today by the dominant party, the Liberal Democratic party, and within that party by the so-called "mainstream" factions —namely, those factions closely aligned with the prime minister. Changes of whatever character in Japanese foreign policy are at least as likely to come via the evolution of the Liberal Democratic party itself as via some new party, a coalition government or the emergence of an opposition group into power. It is appropriate, however, to note at this point that the advent of *any* opposition party to power (with the exception of the Democratic Socialists) would result in major foreign policy changes, assuming that current views were retained. The *Komeito* takes a position favoring a gradual phasing out of the Mutual Security Treaty, to be replaced by a policy of "complete neutrality"—that is, of nonparticipation in any military alliance, the maintenance of an "equal distance" from other nations, and the retention of an "absolute minimum force of national guards." The Japanese Socialist party has advocated "unarmed neutrality" (a totally pacifist position in principle, but one linked up with strong anti-American positions) and—on the part of one major faction—a high level of sympathy for the People's Republic of China. The Communists, curiously, have opted for a more nationalistic "armed neutrality" position, and nonalignment with either Peking or Moscow, reflective of the new nationalist currents within many Asian communist movements. Needless to say, however, the JCP is bitterly opposed to the American-Japanese alliance, and to all U.S. policies in Asia.

Thus, when we refer to Japanese foreign policy or government attitudes, the sharp divisions between contending political forces must be constantly kept in mind. One final point, moreover, deserves emphasis. The party system as a whole is still on trial with the Japanese people, although the Japanese political system, in comparison with those in other democratic societies, looks relatively stable at present. Popular commitments to parties and to the party concept may have grown, but they are still weak. There is always the danger that parties and the Diet may be circumvented, with the left protesting via the streets and the ultraright via the knife. That danger, however, does not seem greater at the moment in Japan than in certain other "advanced" nations, including the United States.

Although the LDP leaders play the critical role in setting the basic positions for Japanese foreign policy, the Japanese bureaucracy nevertheless merits special attention. In relative terms, it is probably correct to assert that the prestige of the Japanese official has been declining. The popular homage he receives, his emoluments, and his own attitude toward his status seem to point in this direction. But the changes taking place in these respects are relative to the Japanese past. In comparison with other democratic societies, the Japanese official still enjoys very great prestige and power. And many young Japanese aspire to careers as officials. Indeed, competition for the available civil-service positions is as intense as for top positions in industry or the leading professions.

In some respects, the bureaucracy has changed less than most other facets of postwar Japan. It remains strongly hierarchical, and its modes of operation have been altered only slowly. Yet, in its socioeconomic composition, the Japanese bureaucracy is undergoing significant evolution. Young men from the upper and upper-middle classes still have sizeable advantages—the educational opportunities and the proper social connections—but others have been pushing their way into the civil service in increasing numbers. Tokyo University, moreover, does not have the monopoly on training it possessed before 1945; a larger proportion of successful candidates come from other institutions. Above all, Japanese civil servants are now receiving a much broader college education, on the one hand, and much more advanced technical training, where it is desired, on the other hand. The premium on specialized skills has grown steadily. Some observers believe that the Japanese civil service not only attracts top talent in such fields as economics, but gives it more opportunity than does the academic world.

Another vital fact cannot be ignored. As in the prewar period, an increasing bureaucratic infiltration of the conservative group has been taking place. The percentage of conservative Diet members who have been officials in the national civil service has steadily risen since 1946. Approximately one-fourth of the Liberal Democratic Diet members are in this category, and the percentage of party leaders and cabinet members who are former officials is much higher. This fact explains the close interaction between party leadership and government bureaucracy at the topmost levels in contemporary Japan.

The Ministry of Foreign Affairs (or Foreign Office), it should be noted, is less prestigious than the Ministry of Finance, generally regarded as the most powerful branch of the Japanese bureaucracy. Moreover, the Foreign Office does not handle all matters involving foreign affairs, particularly those dealing with trade, aid, and similar matters. Both the Ministry of Finance and the Ministry of International Trade and Industry (MITI) are of major importance in the foreign policy arena. And like all advanced nations, Japan has major problems of bureaucratic coordination. The Ministry of Foreign Affairs is itself relatively small and simply organized. It has approximately 2,000 men of civil-service

rank. Its major subdivisions are bureaus of two types—those covering geographic areas and those representing specialized functions. The latter include treaties, economic affairs, information and culture, and international cooperation. Within the ministry, there is also a Secretariat which serves as a central coordinating and administrative unit. It includes a policy planning staff charged with overall evaluation and planning of basic policy positions. Official liaison with the Diet is maintained through a parliamentary vice-minister, normally appointed from the Diet membership.

In comparison with the prewar period, the formulation of Japanese foreign policy is clearly more coordinated and efficient. Prior to 1945, as we have noted, the struggle to control foreign policy was a complex one waged by diverse forces. The ultimate cost to Japan was enormous. In the immediate postsurrender period, neither party leaders nor bureaucratic leaders could play a major role. Both foreign and domestic policies were laid down by occupation authorities. The Japanese function was, essentially, to discern what the policy was and then to exercise—with uncertain results—the right of suggestion. Diplomacy had to be directed almost wholly toward the United States. As the occupation drew to a close, Japanese initiative was gradually reasserted. Initially, diplomacy, which was in the hands of Prime Minister Yoshida, himself a former Foreign Office man, was highly personalized. His opponents charged him with "one-man diplomacy." Party participation in foreign policy was very limited, and the Foreign Office still struggled to overcome its earlier weak and ineffectual position.

Down to the present, Japanese prime ministers have continued to keep a firm hand on their nation's foreign policy, and for most, indeed, some major personal accomplishment in this field has tended to mark the climax of each leader's political career. Gradually, however, the base for the conduct of foreign policy has broadened, with elements of the Liberal Democratic party and the various Ministries centrally involved. By the time of the Kishi era (Kishi became prime minister in February, 1957), bureau chiefs in the Ministry of Foreign Affairs had begun to maintain close contacts with party leaders. Many of these contacts were with the pertinent committees of the Liberal Democratic party: the Research Committee on Foreign Relations, the Policy Research Committee, and the General Affairs Board. These committees, particularly the General Affairs Board, officially determine the foreign policy of the party. At least equally important were the contacts maintained with "mainstream faction" leaders.

Relations between career officials and the Liberal Democratic party relating to foreign policy issues have not always been smooth or uncomplicated. As we have noted, the factional character of Japanese parties can be a major problem, especially if a faction is encouraged by external pressure groups. Thus, at the time of negotiations between Japan and the Soviet Union for a treaty of peace, some leaders within the Liberal Democratic party, supported by certain fishery and commercial groups, built up pressure for a rapid settlement. This was resisted by top Foreign Office officials but, for a time, Japan suffered once again from dual diplomacy. The Foreign Office has also faced jurisdictional and policy quarrels with other ministries on occasion. As yet, however, Japan has not had the massive problem of reconciling and integrating a Pentagon-State Department-White House staff triumvirate in the foreign policy field. Nonetheless, recent deepening of issues within the Liberal Democratic party itself during Prime Minister Miki's tenure raises questions about the future.

And, there is another side of the coin. Japanese pressure groups and public opinion, when combined with the opposition parties, have added many new complexities to the scene. As we noted earlier, pressure groups of all types now exist. Their number, diversity, and influence on Japanese foreign policy have increased greatly. On several recent occasions, for example, and notably with respect to textile trade regulations, the evidence suggests that the prime minister himself was not able to prevail over a powerful internal interest group. It is not appropriate here to attempt any detailed discussion of this development; only a few salient points can be presented. As in the prewar era, the commercial and industrial groups have the greatest single influence on the Liberal Democratic party, especially in the field of foreign policy. These speak through the Japan Employers Association and many similar organizations. It would be a mistake, however, to assume that the Japanese business and industrial world speaks with a single voice. On such an issue as China policy, for example, it is far from unanimous. Still, the broad outlines of Japanese foreign policy at present are deeply influenced by the interests and views of leading industrial and commercial pressure groups. They remain the chief financial support for the Liberal Democratic party, they include the most intimate confidants of conservative politicians, and, hence, they are the most powerful unofficial influence on public policy, domestic and foreign.

The pressures emanating from rural Japan have decreased substantially in recent years, particularly in the area of foreign policy. While the farmer continues to vote conservative in substantial measure, he has progressively become a smaller fraction of the Japanese electorate, and very frequently, in occupational terms, he now represents a mixed element, with some of his income derived from labor or small to medium-sized business.

The more serious of the factors that complicate the formulations of Japanese foreign policy are not the traditional Japanese pressure groups, but certain new ones, in addition to the force of public opinion as it is revealed in countless polls. Among the opposition pressure groups, the most important is organized labor. *Sohyo,* the General Council of Trade Unions of Japan, has been especially vocal on foreign policy. It has hewed closely to, and helped to shape, the socialist positions on neutralism, on relations with the communist world, on "American imperialism," and on many other issues. In addition, it has supported these positions with demonstrations, work stoppages, and quantities of political literature.

*Sohyo,* with 4.2 million members, is probably the most formidable of the opposition pressure groups (although it should not thereby be implied that it can commit all its members on any issue). There are, however, a number of others. Most of them represent intellectual, student, and labor elements in Japanese society. As in the case of "conservative" interest groups, these diverse forces by no means speak with a single voice. At the same time, such groups cannot totally be ignored by the governing elite, particularly since they maintain a substantial forum by means of newspapers, magazines, TV, and radio. Their various messages now reach the Japanese public—especially the urban public—regularly. Hence, in the last twenty years, foreign policy has become a central part of the political battlefield in Japan, sometimes the most vital part. The conservatives have been forced to recognize a far more significant opposition than any experienced in the prewar era, despite the weaknesses in that opposition noted earlier. Suppression or indifference is no longer feasible. Consequently, the conservatives are also resorting to the media and other forms of public appeal.

It is very difficult to assess the present influence of Japanese public opinion on foreign policy. In recent years, polling has become popular in Japan. It is carried out by a number of organizations, the most widely regarded polls being those which resemble the leading American polls. The major Japanese newspapers, in particular, poll the public at regular intervals on a wide variety of subjects, including many issues of foreign policy. Opinions on rearmament, the Mutual Security Treaty, the Middle East, constitutional revision, and relations with China have been frequently requested. And, in a number of cases, the polls have indicated that either a large minority or an actual majority of those polled differed with government policy. They also revealed a considerable amount of public apathy and ignorance.

There is little doubt that public

opinion, now being presented in these concrete, measured forms, has had a rising impact on decision making in Japan. Increasingly, it is a factor which Japanese leaders take seriously. Sometimes, to be sure, public opinion is used to justify a decision based mainly on other grounds. But more frequently, when the polls indicate substantial public opposition to a given policy, conservative leaders respond with modifications, a shift in timing, or a more intensive public relations campaign. However, the reluctance of recent conservative administrations to rearm rapidly or to seek the repeal of Article 9 of the Constitution, the long and fairly firm Japanese bargaining in connection with the revised Mutual Security Treaty, and the cautious ambivalent position toward China are all indications of the new political power of the Japanese common man.

At the same time, the Japanese conservatives are well aware of the fact that elections in Japan are not won primarily on the basis of issues of foreign policy. To the extent that elections hinge on issues in Japan, domestic concerns have been of overwhelming importance. Throughout their long tenure in office, the conservatives have consequently played upon such themes as prosperity and progress; and they count heavily upon their superior organization, their greater funds, and their local leadership. And where they have lost elections, as noted earlier, domestic issues have been paramount.

Thus, the Liberal Democratic leaders can afford to take some chances in the area of foreign policy, even when they know or suspect that there is strong public opposition to specific policies. When confronted with evidence of hostile public opin-

ion, the government tactic is to camouflage or alter a policy slightly, so as to disarm some of the opposition, but rarely if ever to make basic changes. With respect to the socialists (and other elements of the "left") also, a caveat must be entered regarding the influence of public opinion: the record would indicate that such parties have often ignored public opinion when it conflicted with their ideological stance.

In sum, the process of formulating, executing, and defending Japanese foreign policy today is in the hands of a conservative elite. The formal and informal institutional processes have been greatly refined in the postwar era, and now operate at a fairly high level of efficiency. Collaboration between the Liberal Democratic party and the Ministry of Foreign Affairs (or other appropriate branches of government) is close and continuous. The prime minister continues to play the dominant role, together with the factions supporting him, and, in the final analysis, the political rather than the bureaucratic element now tends to predominate on most basic issues of foreign policy (although many top conservative leaders have been ex-officials). The military has been very subordinate thus far, but it is likely that its influence will increase somewhat in the decade ahead—how much depending upon both internal and external developments. Meanwhile, the newer generations of Ministry officials are more broadly recruited and trained than they were before World War II, and they possess a higher level of technical proficiency.

The conservative elite that directs Japanese foreign policy is sustained and influenced mainly by the industrial, commerical, and agrarian segments of Japanese society. Contradictory pressures, however, sometimes flow from these elements. In any case, no simple economic analysis does justice to the realities of the situation. Japan is becoming, among other things, a mass society in which the conservative elite is forced to pay increasing attention to public opinion. While not of commanding importance, public opinion now serves to effect modifications both of substance and of timing in certain policies, and causes the Japanese leaders to give more attention to the public image of their policies.

## CONTEMPORARY ISSUES IN JAPANESE FOREIGN POLICY

At present, three dominant considerations underlie the debates and decisions pertaining to foreign policy in Japan. First, there is the high priority that must be accorded economic considerations in foreign policy—the importance still attached to maintaining Japanese economic growth, but the increasing need to face the problems which that phenomenal growth has already bequeathed. Second, there is the major issue of security, an issue involving Japanese relations with the United States, the communist nations, and the world—particularly the Pacific-Asian world. Finally, there is the broader, vaguer question of what role Japan should play in the world, and what mix of economic, political, and military commitments is desirable, both from the standpoint of her national interest and from the standpoint of the changing psychological needs of the Japanese people.

## The Economic Basis of Japanese Foreign Policy

Today, Japan is an economic giant, with an annual productivity exceeded only by the United States and the Soviet Union. In 1974, her GNP (gross national product) was $456 billion, her foreign trade was approaching $118 billion, her overseas investments totaled over $10 billion, and the average annual income of an employed individual was $6257 making her people the most prosperous in eastern Asia by a wide margin. As is well known, this series of achievements did not occur suddenly. In the decade after 1960, the Japanese GNP averaged a gain of approximately 12 percent per annum, with exports growing at an average annual rate of 16.5 percent, imports at 15 percent.

This accomplishment is all the more remarkable when one considers certain basic socioeconomic facts with which Japan must live. In 1974, the population of the relatively small four islands comprising this nation had reached 110 million. Present trends indicate that that population will increase at the rate of approximately 1 million per year for the next decade, with Japan being the first society in Asia to practice population planning on a massive (and effective) scale. This means, of course, that the Japanese labor force will gradually become older, and the problem of labor scarcity will become more serious. Meanwhile, only 14 percent of the land is currently under agricultural cultivation, with about 20 percent of the population engaged in agricultural pursuits. Under these circumstances, it is remarkable that Japan is able to achieve over 70 percent total food self-sufficiency, with rice production completely meeting current needs.

The events of recent years, however, have indicated those areas of vulnerability to which this extraordinarily successful economy is prone. For many years, Japan—pleading its poverty—maintained a number of protectionist policies. This, combined with the unique working relation established between government and industry, enabled Japan to detect promising markets and then exploit them with great intensity. Meanwhile, labor productivity was rising at a rapid rate, and the costs of energy sources and raw materials were relatively modest.

Beginning in the mid-1960s, these circumstances produced a growing crisis in Japanese-American relations. At this point, nearly one-third of all Japanese foreign trade was with the United States. Specific industries, including such politically sensitive ones as textiles, felt themselves coming under great pressures, as Japanese goods flooded the market. The voluntary quota system, a system whereby the two governments agreed upon specific percentage increases for select products, agreements then enforced within Japan, provided some amelioration. In overall terms, however, the situation grew worse from an American perspective. Adverse trade balances grew to astronomical proportions.

Clearly, the fault did not lie wholly with Japan. By the late 1960s, the American economy was in trouble, partly as a result of the guns *and* butter policies of successive administrations. The weakening American dollar combined with declining rates of growth in labor productivity and a series of other problems to reduce American competitiveness and stimulate a growing crisis in the advanced industrial world. Those twin pillars of economic stability since World War II—the International Monetary Fund and the General Agreement on Tariffs and Trade—were undermined by inflation and the rising instability of the international currency system.

Under the circumstances, Japanese resistance to such basic measures as devaluation and a sweeping reform of existing protectionist policies was certain to induce American retaliation. That retaliation came in the form of the so-called Nixon shocks in mid-1971, when measures were taken to float the dollar and impose a ten percent surcharge on all foreign imports. The Japanese response was one of panic, then action. Within a few years, Japan had not only repeatedly revalued the yen, but had also moved to reduce tariff and nontariff barriers in a serious, sustained fashion. Liberalization extended to the thorny field of foreign capital investment as well. It could be argued, indeed, that Japan was enroute to becoming the most economically open society within the advanced world. Certainly, the comparison with the Common Market countries of West Europe was striking. There, various forms of discrimination were still pursued, many of them directed against Japan.

American business leaders continued to complain that despite legal changes, the Japanese economic system itself made truly fair and equal competition difficult, if not impossible. For example, in Japan, governmental agencies like the Ministry of International Trade and Industry worked to promote rather than patrol business. Such aspects of industry as the distribution system, moreover, defied American practices. Japanese spokesmen retorted that none of these difficulties were insurmountable, and that the real problem lay in the fact that American ingenuity and productivity were flagging, with a softness having developed that put American enterprises at a handicap when competing with the more energetic Japanese.

Despite complaints, the new Japanese policies—together with other developments—had alleviated the immediate problems by 1973. The massive trade imbalances had disappeared, at least temporarily, and a new trend had commenced, namely, the flow of Japanese investments into the United States. Meanwhile, the percentage of economic intercourse with the United States compared to total trade declined, moving from close to 30 percent to slightly over 20 percent by the end of 1974. That trade, however, in absolute figures steadily rose, and the United States still represented Japan's single most important source of economic interaction by a huge margin.

Events during this period, however, continued to demonstrate Japan's high degree of dependence upon external developments. The widespread recession in the West had immediate reverberations in Tokyo. More seriously, the oil embargo and subsequent rise in oil prices confronted Japan with its most critical challenge since World War II. A nation that enjoyed trade surpluses now found itself confronted with a multibillion dollar deficit ($6–7 billion). In 1974, inflation reached 24 percent, one of the higher rates for the advanced world. Even the optimists of yesteryear began to question the viability of the Japanese economy as they looked

ahead to a period of increasing competition for raw materials and energy sources, and a time when certain historic advantages were slipping: cheap labor and steady gains in labor productivity, low social overhead, high political stability, and excellent planning.

Temporarily, at least, Japan once again appears to be defying those proclaiming doom. By the beginning of 1975, as a result of rigorous policies and finely tuned government-industry coordination, the trade imbalance had been closed, despite high oil prices, as Japan registered a phenomenal 46 percent increase in exports. Inflation had been cut in half. From its first negative growth rate (–1.7 percent) in the postwar era, moreover, Japan expected 1975 to produce a real GNP increase of 2.2 percent, modest in comparison with past figures but not bad when compared to the probabilities in the United States and West Europe.

However, many of the basic problems confronting the nation's economy remain, and some of them are not susceptible to solution by Japan alone. No modern nation has such a stake in a peaceful, open world. The Japanese economic miracle was a product of access to advanced technology and cheap resources, with these transformed into salable products via an economy that operated on the basis of great spurts in labor productivity, a very high savings ratio (over 20 percent of disposable income), and enlightened planning at the national level. Now, labor costs are steadily rising in relation to productivity; raw material and energy costs also seem destined to advance; and the spector of economic nationalism in various parts of the world looms ahead. Moreover, the domestic climate is changing, with greater emphasis upon quality of life and social services.

Against this background, what are Japan's economic goals and how do these affect its alternatives in foreign policy? Those goals have been spelled out in recent long-range projections prepared by governmental agencies, and now incorporated in partial form into the 1975 budget. Naturally, like all projections, they may be based upon erroneous information or negated by unforeseen events. Nonetheless, they are the best possible indication of where Japan intends to go, and how it intends to get there.

As might be expected, the future emphasis will be upon high technology industries, and the tertiary sector of the economy will grow rapidly. Japan will seek to export many of its heavy industries abroad in an effort to take advantage of cheaper labor and reduce pollution problems on her four small, crowded islands. There will thus be a major premium upon direct investment overseas. At the same time, expenditures at home for social services will rapidly increase, reflective of popular demands. Housing, antipollution measures, welfare programs and many other "quality of life" activities will be undertaken.

Under these conditions, Japanese officials project an average GNP increase of 6 percent in real growth over the next decade. Private capital investments overseas are expected to increase tenfold by 1985. Inflation will be reduced, not eliminated —with a tolerable rate of 5–8 percent anticipated, slightly higher in the initial years. Wage increases will continue, but on a diminishing scale.

To achieve these goals, what is necessary? First, the economic health of the world, and particularly the so-called advanced industrial world, must be good, and a return to economic nationalism must be avoided. Japan anticipates that her trade and investment with the United States will continue to be vitally important, albeit gradually declining in percentage terms. With West Europe also, Japan counts upon an expanding market. However, the great advances are anticipated in the so-called "developing" world—notably Asia, Africa and Latin America. Naturally, the Middle East now looms up with special significance. Already, the recycling of petrodollars in Japan has exceeded $7 billion, and it is expected to reach $10–14 billion in 1975. With the Communist states also, Japan looks toward major trade expansion. Intercourse with these states, including both the Chinese People's Republic and the USSR, now accounts for a mere 7 percent of total Japanese trade.

In sum, Japan can afford to ignore no sector of the world in its quest for market and investment expansion. Together with the United States, it represents today one of the world's truly universal powers, using that term here in an economic sense. For Japan, the effort to separate economics and politics is likely to continue. Tokyo will enter into economic relations with all available parties. At the same time, economic considerations will dictate or at least influence political positions on some issues. On the Middle East problem, for example, Japan can be expected to tilt toward the Arabs. By the same token, the special ties with the United States are powerfully underwritten by economic realities. There is no current evidence, however, to support the thesis that Japan is destined to move toward a high political-military posture in its foreign relations, a subject to which we shall shortly turn. The Japanese do hope to expand their cultural and political as well as economic ties with the so-called Third World, a vast heterogeneous group of states now accounting for some 45 percent of Japanese trade. In the future as in the past, however, economics will dominate Japanese foreign policy.

### The Security Issues in Japanese Foreign Policy

Let us now move to issues within the realm of the political—more specifically, issues relating to the security of this unique nation. If Japan is an economic giant, she is currently a political pygmy. Nor is her military strength impressive at present, all of the charges of an incipient Japanese militarism notwithstanding. It is true, as noted earlier, that the Japanese military establishment is a highly modern one, geared to the use of the latest defensive techniques on land, in the air, and at sea. The total personnel involved, however, number less than one-quarter of a million individuals. If the Fourth Defense Plan is completed in 1976, the target year, the ground self-defense forces will consist of 180,-000 men, 820 tanks, 650 armored personnel carriers, and 350 tactical aircraft in addition to various other weapons. The maritime self-defense force will total 214,000 tons, being comprised mainly of destroyers and submarines. The airforce will number 770 aircraft, and there will be 6 groups of NIKE nonnuclear missiles.

Given the severe inflation, it now seems likely that some aspects of the plan will be postponed or aban-doned. Even if these figures are reached, however, this is a very modest military structure, the smallest in Northeast Asia. Certainly it is not one capable of playing the earlier American role in Asia, as some observers suggested might come to pass. But is there a possibility of a major shift in Japanese thought and planning in the military field?

At the outset, let us note the two basic factors that have governed Japanese security policies in the post-1945 era. The single most critical determinant of those policies has been the military alliance with the United States via the Mutual Security Treaty. In essence, Japan has had her security underwritten by the American nuclear umbrella, and by the sizeable American conventional force present in eastern Asia, some of it utilizing bases in Japan and Okinawa. With such a formidable shield available, it was considered neither necessary nor desirable to develop a large independent military capacity. Consequently, to date, Japan has spent less than 1 percent of its annual GNP on defense. In 1968, for example, when Japan was allocating 0.8 percent of its GNP to such expenditures, the German Federal Republic was spending 3.9 percent, Great Britain 5.3 percent, the Chinese People's Republic 9 percent, the United States 9.2 percent, and the Soviet Union 9.3 percent.

It is true, of course, that because her GNP was rising very rapidly, Japan in actuality was spending substantially increased amounts on defense. Indeed, those expenditures have doubled approximately every six years since 1952, and in the Fourth Defense Plan, the budgetary expenditure over five years was set at $15 billion. Nevertheless, in the crucial years between 1950 and

1970, capital investment could be concentrated in industries vitally important to the total Japanese economy in unprecedented degree because defense spending was very low in comparison with those nations against whom Japan found herself in primary competition.

A second factor of equal significance relates to the political-psychological environment in which Japanese defense policy has evolved. The postwar era began with the shattering impact of the war breeding in most Japanese varying commitments to pacifism, withdrawal, and minimal risk. These sentiments were particularly strong among the immediate postwar generations. As we shall shortly suggest, there are now signs that the psychological trends of yesteryear are changing. To date, however, the Japanese public has not had a deep sense of external threat to its security. Public opinion polls are revealing in this respect.

On the one hand, the Japanese public dislikes the Soviet Union more than it dislikes any other major nation, although antipathy to Korea also runs very high. On occasion, moreover, such as after the initial nuclear tests and during the Cultural Revolution, antagonism to the People's Republic of China increased markedly. In recent years, positive sentiments toward China have shot up, with a sizeable number of Japanese expressing the desire for closer ties with the PRC, perhaps a natural development in the light of international trends. Meanwhile, attitudes regarding the United States, overwhelmingly favorable in the decades immediately after 1945, have inclined toward increasing negativism or doubt, reflective of the events of the mid- and late 1960s. The most general trend, however, has been toward increasing independence, with a refusal, when polled, to identify any country as "most liked."

What have been the attitudes concerning the American military ties? When questioned about the purpose of American military bases in Japan, most Japanese see these as primarily intended for the defense of the United States and other Asian nations, *not* for the defense of Japan. Moreover, many Japanese perceive the threat of becoming involved in war via the American alliance as equally great as, or greater than, the threats emanating from the Soviet Union or the People's Republic of China. There is a disposition to rate the dangers of an attack by these or other states upon Japan as very low.

Naturally, these views—shared by a certain portion of the Japanese political elite—have influenced policy in various ways. Even the most security-conscious leaders are not disposed to seek a repeal of the so-called antiwar clause (Article 9 of the Japanese Constitution), because under present conditions there would be no public support for such a move. The public apparently supports limited rearmament—for defense purposes only—at approximately the levels currently established. But all recent public opinion polls register strong opposition to extensive rearmament, the use of Japanese military forces abroad, or the acquisition of nuclear weapons. It is not surprising, therefore, that Japanese leaders speak cautiously when discussing security policy alternatives—and even among the conservative elite, there are presently substantial differences of opinion on security issues and the basic direction to be pursued in the future.

Before exploring these differences, and the policy alternatives which they imply, it might be wise to note that, under certain conditions, public opinion is subject to radical changes. Within a few years, the Chinese People's Republic will have operational ICBMs quite capable of being directed at Japan. The military power of the Soviet Union in the Pacific-Asian area has sharply increased in recent years. Meanwhile, the Japanese economic-political stake in eastern Asia steadily grows. If one or both of the major communist powers were to undertake political-military blackmail against Japan, or view Japanese economic expansion as contrary to their national interests, present Japanese public opinion could presumably change as dramatically as Japanese policies. There is also the complex phenomenon of a new Japanese nationalism, to which we shall refer shortly—a phenomenon having uncertain bearings upon attitudes toward power and security.

Thus, Japanese security policies will evolve in the context of a swiftly changing international scene, and one marked' by many uncertainties. Not the least of these, of course, are trends in the East Asian policies of the United States. Today, the "Nixon doctrine" sets the basic outlines of American policy. In security terms, the central theme of the Nixon doctrine is that, while the United States will maintain its treaty commitments, each of its allies will be expected to provide for its own ground defense, and that the American contribution will be primarily that of a deterrent to major-power involvement—by virtue of its nuclear weapons, and by supplying aerial-naval aid if necessary. For many Japanese, however—and for many other Asians as well—the issue is not the merits of the Nixon doctrine, but whether that doctrine can withstand the heavy tides of isolationism that are now sweeping over the American scene.

Any precipitous American withdrawal from Asia would almost certainly produce an increased polarization within Japan over the basic direction to be taken in foreign policy. Three quite different possibilities suggest themselves. One would be an accelerated nationalism of a Gaullist character, manifesting itself initially in some combination of an independent political-military program (including the development of nuclear weapons) and a new/old type of pan-Asianism. It is some variant of this policy that has been most widely discussed and predicted, from communist and noncommunist sources alike.

An entirely opposite set of policies might flow from the same set of circumstances: the fears and antagonisms caused by an abrupt American withdrawal might further strengthen the political position of the Japanese left, with a coalition government emerging which would in turn opt for "nonalignment," with the premium upon friendly relations with the communist bloc and a very low military profile. This would require a dramatic reorientation, and one probably involving economic as well as political and psychological dimensions.

There is yet a third response that might develop as a response to American isolationism—one which seems more probable than the second course outlined above, and at least as possible as the first course suggested: American withdrawal and the psychological pangs accompanying it might well result in locking Japan into a position of uncertainty—and hence, inaction—for the next few crucial years. During this time, such signs of greater political initiative and of concern over the security of northeastern Asia as have appeared would fade away. A moderate leadership, remaining in power, would revert to an exceedingly cautious economics-only policy, one involving the minimum possible risks and commitments. The effect would be to freeze Japanese foreign policy in the mold of the recent past, with Japan unable or unwilling to accept any new role in the absence of confidence in American policy or in the American will.

In all probability, such a "freeze" could not be sustained beyond a few years. Pressures would surely rise, both at home and abroad, pushing Japan in the direction of one or the other of the first two policies set forth above. Indeed, the pressures would probably accelerate on behalf of both policies simultaneously, with differences over Japanese foreign policy becoming a growing source of political instability. In any case, however, the element of timing under the circumstances just outlined could be crucial. If uncertain Japanese leaders felt themselves forced to follow a minimal, weak foreign policy, while at the same time widespread American withdrawal became an accomplished fact, the Asian-Pacific area would be cast into a state of political-military disequilibrium. If the international peacekeeping mechanisms remained as inadequate as they are at present, and the military capacities of some states as formidable, the temptations to engage in "wars of liberation" might increase, casting a long shadow over the peace of the region.

Let us assume, however, that the Nixon doctrine in its basic outline prevails. Even under those conditions, a considerable reduction of the American presence in eastern Asia will take place, particularly in military terms. Questions concerning American credibility will mount, and debate will revolve around the basic alternatives set forth above.

In the near future, Japan will continue to allocate about 1 percent of her GNP to defense expenditures. If projected growth rates are realized, this means that by 1980 Japan will be spending about $5 billion annually in the military field. Such expenditures, moreover, will be oriented most heavily toward modern military aircraft, missiles, and naval expansion. Japan has now assumed defense responsibilities for Okinawa, as well as for the air and sea approaches to Japan proper. The presence of American military personnel in the Japan-Okinawa military base complex is continuing to be phased out, with naval facilities being the primary bases in Japan proper.

Under these circumstances, at most, Japan will be a "middle power" militarily by 1980, spending approximately one-half the amount being spent in the military field by each of the major European states or by the People's Republic of China. The Mutual Security Treaty will continue to be the linchpin in Japan's defense program, providing as it does America's nuclear guarantee, and the Japanese government will continue to be deeply concerned about the credibility of the American defense pledge. There will be no move to develop nuclear weapons; but, in the broadest sense, the nuclear option will be kept open, with the ultimate decision dependent upon developments throughout the world, and particularly in northeastern Asia.

Under such circumstances, Japan will not be capable of engaging in any military confrontation with China or the Soviet Union, nor will she be prepared—militarily or psychologically—to play any power role in southern Asia. Her first security concern after that involving her own territory will be with the Republic of Korea. Given the complex political relations that have existed historically between these two societies, however, as well as the reluctance of the Japanese people to accept any overseas military obligations, the Japanese commitment is not likely to go beyond certain forms of economic and military aid, together with permission for the United States to use Japanese bases in the event of strife on the Korean peninsula.

Developments in foreign policy during the late 1970s and early 1980s are more difficult to project. Certainly, there are no financial inhibitions upon a more extensive military buildup, should that course become necessary or desirable in the eyes of Japanese leaders. Given the present and probable future rate of growth, Japan could raise her military expenditures to 2 percent of her GNP or more without major financial strain. Nor are there serious technical restraints. Japan manufactures modern fighter planes, and such missiles as the Nike-Hercules and Hawk missiles are already being constructed there. Japan could also construct nuclear weapons in a very brief period of time, if she chose to do so.

The arguments for developing nuclear weapons generally put forth in private discussions include the following: The American defense commitment cannot be trusted, especially in the light of recent trends in U.S. foreign policies and the growing nuclear threat likely to be presented by the PRC; only nuclear powers have major political status; and without nuclear weapons, Japan will be subject to blackmail by either China or the Soviet Union. Additional reasons are presented for substantially augmenting Japan's conventional defenses: the protection of her vital sea lanes to the Middle East and throughout eastern and southern Asia; the critical importance of South Korea and Taiwan to Japan's own defenses; and the likelihood that the conventional forces of both China and the Soviet Union will grow, enabling them to bargain—or threaten—from a position of power.

The arguments against nuclear weapons are at least equally potent: nuclear power has conferred upon neither France nor Great Britain a significantly enhanced political position, while representing a massive drain on their economies; as a state containing a huge population concentrated in a very small area, Japan is at a unique disadvantage in contemplating any nuclear conflict, even one involving only tactical nuclear weapons; and a large-scale military arsenal has not proven particularly useful in protecting overseas markets and investments.

Whatever the logic of these various arguments, many outside observers believe that as her economic strength steadily grows and her global position becomes both massive and critical to her future, Japan will not be able to tolerate military-political dependence upon others and the status of a mere medium-sized power. Thus, it is argued that by carefully measured but steadily accelerating stages, Japan will once again be a major military power by the 1980s probably with nuclear weapons—unless vastly more effective steps toward worldwide nuclear disarmament have been taken in the interim. Under any circumstances, it is assumed that the Japanese military establishment would place primary emphasis upon air and sea power, as befits an island nation heavily dependent upon her overseas markets. Will this prediction prove correct? At this point, no one can be certain. The new Japanese nationalism may abet such a tendency. But the truly decisive influence is likely to be the nature of the perceived threat (specifically, the policies and attitudes of China and the Soviet Union); the perception of the American commitment and the American will; and the degree of progress attained in such fields as those of disarmament and "peaceful coexistence," especially as these relate to eastern Asia. On balance, the immediate trends are running decidedly against the remilitarization of Japan.

Meanwhile, certain special problems will exist with respect to the Japanese bases. Officially, Japan holds to the three "nonnuclear" positions: no production, no possession, no presence of nuclear weapons on Japanese soil. Hence, a political storm was raised when information was received to the effect that American warships entering Japanese harbors possessed nuclear weapons on occasion. Noise, pollution, and other inconveniences connected with the bases also give leftist forces handy issues. At present, however, the base issue is not as controversial as it was during the 1960s. Interestingly, both the People's Republic of China and the Soviet Union have indicated that they have no objection to the U.S.-Japan Mu-

tual Security Treaty at this time—since both would prefer the risks of an American presence to those of a Gaullist Japan or a Japan aligned elsewhere.

### The Quest for the Japanese Role in World Affairs

Thus far, we have been discussing the two vital sets of problems with which contemporary Japan must concern itself in constructing its foreign policy—those in the economic field and those in the military-security arena. Beyond such specific issues, however, there lies a broader question: What is the Japanese role to be in the late-twentieth-century world? Here, we are involved in probing the political culture of this remarkable society, and the deeper psychological as well as economic-political trends now governing the Japanese people. As was suggested earlier, Japanese political culture has been traditionally based upon strictly hierarchical relations; consequently, the concept of equality in foreign as well as domestic relations has been extremely difficult to accept or to practice. Thus, the American occupation of Japan in 1945 began with a little appreciated advantage—a people conditioned to accept tutelage if they could not exercise dominance. On the other hand, the United States was fully prepared to assume leadership—not necessarily in terms of her specialized knowledge of the area, but in terms of her moral and political self-confidence. Total victory in a global war, unprecedented prosperity at home, and the accelerating, upward thrust of the "American Revolution" in Japan combined to abet those psychological qualities that had always underwritten American internationalism in its most expansive forms: great self-confidence in one's abilities; a pervasive optimism concerning the future; a strong belief in the efficiency that stems from total commitment (and thus produces policies wedded to an impressive use of resources and a brief time-span of operations); and finally, a genuine humanistic attitude, sometimes resting uneasily with deeply rooted feelings of political and racial superiority.

The post-1945 American-Japanese relationship was successful in part because it was consonant with both the underlying psychological traits of the two societies *and* their prevailing political moods. Americans undertook the costly, dangerous tasks of rehabilitation and security, not merely for Japan but for various other parts of Asia as well. The Japanese, for their part, accepted a dependent status, one with minimal external responsibilities, as they set about the reconstruction of a devastated society. What division of labor could have accorded better with the psychological proclivities of these two diverse societies at that time?

The times have changed. Once again, after an enormous expenditure of resources, material and human, the United States is tired, querulous, and in a "withdrawal" mood. Meanwhile, complex and somewhat contradictory psychological trends are manifesting themselves in Japan. Any individual living outside the Japanese cultural orbit seeks to define these trends with trepidation. Japanese observers are themselves by no means agreed upon their import. However, we appear to be witnessing a shift away from the mood that dominated the generation of Japanese deeply scarred by World War II. Many in that generation harbored intense feelings of inferiority and guilt, and showed a proclivity for dependency and withdrawal. This proclivity was naturally abetted by the harsh economic conditions that prevailed.

How substantial has the change in Japanese psychology been? To equate the newest generation of adult Japanese and their counterparts of the 1920s and 1930s, or to draw close parallels between Japanese nationalism in that era and today, is to commit a major error. Political institutions and values on the one hand, and socioeconomic developments on the other, have undergone radical changes. Moreover, the regional environment is entirely different. A new mood, however, is emerging in Japan. Recent Japanese generations seem more self-confident, more optimistic concerning their personal future and that of their nation, less inhibited in personal and group relations, and more willing to stand comparison with others—Asian and Western. Naturally, such qualities vary with the individual and also with the socioeconomic group, but it is impossible to overlook their increasing importance. In the aggregate, these and related trends can be said to constitute the new Japanese nationalism.

It would be surprising, indeed, if this new nationalism did not contain some xenophobic—and, more specifically, anti-American—elements. Dependency upon the United States, after all, has been the most enduring symbol of the post-1945 era. As yet, however, this is not the predominant characteristic of the new atmosphere. The current thrust appears more in the direction of a willingness and a desire to assert Japanese "self-interest"—especially in the economic sphere, and more strongly in bargaining relations at the official level and in other forms of interchange at the private level. Will this mood ultimately project a demand in Japan for recognition in all fields, the political and military as well as the economic? Will the new nationalism combine with unprecedented economic power to make Japan a major actor on the political stage by the 1980s?

Thus far, the Japanese government has contented itself with the pledge to attain an "independent diplomacy," and with pursuing a foreign policy in keeping with the nation's "national interests, economic and security"—words that are suitably flexible and vague. Full cognizance, moreover, should be given the fact that the enormous success of Japan's minimal-risk—maximal-gain foreign policy operates against any rapid or massive changes. Why should one abandon a policy that has been extraordinarily successful, unless altered circumstances force such an abandonment? Nor can the Japanese ignore the fact that dramatic changes in military technology in recent decades have tended to enhance the relative power of continental-mass societies. It is difficult to conceive of a restoration of the nineteenth-century principles of military and political power that favored Japan's geography.

These facts are not lost upon the leaders of Japan. When they talk of playing a greater role in the international community, they are currently thinking of an enhanced role in the United Nations and in other international bodies, particularly those involved in social and economic activities; an enlarged political role for Japan in Asia, via ASPAC and similar regional groups; a middleman position between Asia and the West, and possibly, if circumstances permit it, a peacekeeping role as well. The most immediate problem, therefore, should American withdrawal from Asia be substantial, is more likely to be Japan's minimal performance, not her maximal performance; in the longer run, however, the picture still remains cloudy.

In the meantime, despite the strains to which it is currently subject, the American-Japanese alliance is likely to remain the cornerstone of Japanese foreign policy in the coming years. For both countries, this alliance is of vital importance. Indeed, modern Japan has never had a relationship so significant, not merely in economic and military terms, but in political and cultural terms as well. It can also be assumed that Japan will seek a further expansion of her relations with both the People's Republic of China and the Soviet Union, as noted earlier. Such a development, however, even if it occurs, is more likely to be a supplement to, rather than a substitute for, close Japanese-American ties. The prospects for truly close relations between Japan and the communist giants are dim. The great differences in stages of development, ideological-political systems, current cultural trends, and economic structures preclude a Japanese-Chinese or Japanese-Soviet alliance in the foreseeable future. At best, Japan can achieve a form of peaceful coexistence with these countries that permits improved economic and political interaction.

Thus, the prospects are for modifications of past foreign policies, but no sharp break with the traditions of the last twenty-five years. Japan will add to her economic role certain political and military increments in the years that lie immediately ahead, but she will not seek to play the role of a superpower—in Asia or elsewhere. Her dilemma, however, lies in the fact that whether she wills it or not, she is becoming an economic superpower, with enormous influence upon the policies of many nations and the lives of their peoples. How to mesh this fact, and its implications, with her relatively limited military capacity and her still low political profile constitutes the central problem for Japanese policy makers in the 1970s, and the approach taken to this problem will powerfully affect every nation in the Pacific Asian region.

## SELECTED BIBLIOGRAPHY

There is a wealth of primary and secondary source materials on Japanese foreign policy for the reader who can use the Japanese language. Memoirs of prominent statesmen are abundant; a number of documentary collections and good secondary works exist; and many of the Japanese Foreign Office Archives, having been microfilmed during the American occupation, are obtainable through the Library of Congress. To list even the most essential Japanese materials would be a lengthy task, and one not appropriate here. Fortunately, the reader of Japanese can refer to a number of sources for bibliographic assistance. We shall merely suggest some English-language materials, with emphasis upon more recent books.

Although English-language materials are still far too limited, the last fifteen years have seen an increasing number of worthy articles, monographs, and general studies, many of which deal in some fashion with Japanese foreign policy. To start with the historical background of Japanese international relations, one might mention the older work

of R. H. Akagi, *Japan's Foreign Relations, 1542–1936* (Argus, 1936); but the historical writings of Sir George Sansom provide an excellent introduction to this subject as well as to other facets of traditional Japan: *Japan—A Short Cultural History*, Rev. ed. (Englewood Cliffs, N.J.: Prentice-Hall, 1962). *A History of Japan to 1334* (Stanford, Calif.: Stanford University Press 1958), *A History of Japan, 1334–1615* (Stanford, Calif.: Stanford University Press, 1960), and *The Western World and Japan* (New York: Alfred A. Knopf, 1950). See also Herschel Webb, *The Japanese Imperial Institution in the Tokugawa Period* (New York: Columbia University Press, 1968).

To these should be added C. R. Boxer's *Christian Century in Japan* (Berkeley: University of California Press, 1951) for a careful exposition of initial Western contacts.

For the modern period, a few general works include materials on foreign policy. One might select Hugh Borton's *Japan's Modern Century* (New York: Ronald Press Co., 1955) and Chitoshi Yanaga's *Japanese People and Politics* (New York: Wiley, 1956) as recent works of this type.

For those particularly interested in early Meiji period, we are fortunate in having the work of W. C. Beasley. His *Great Britain and the Opening of Japan, 1834–1858* (Luzac, 1951) was followed by *Select Documents on Japanese Foreign Policy, 1853–1868* (London: Oxford University Press, 1955). These serve as an admirable introduction to the problems of the early Meiji era, which began in 1867. The memoirs and accounts of Western diplomats and other residents are also of interest: E. M. Satow, *A Diplomat in Japan* (Philadelphia: J. B. Lippincott Co., 1921); Sir Rutherford Alcock, *The Capital of the Tycoon*, 2 vols. (London, 1963); J. H. Gubbins, *The Progress of Japan, 1853–1871* (London: Oxford University Press, 1911).

There are also a few monographs of special interest, mainly pertaining to the later Meiji period. Two of these are Marius B. Jansen, *The Japanese and the Chinese Revolutionary Movements, 1895–1915,* and Shumpei Okamoto, *The Japanese Oligarchy and the Russo-Japanese War* (New York: Columbia University Press, 1970). The Taisho period (1912–1926) is rather sparsely covered as yet. Masamichi Royama has written one work in English, *The Foreign Policy of Japan, 1914–1939* (Tokyo, 1941); the older work by T. Takeuchi, *War and Diplomacy in the Japanese Empire* (Garden City, N.Y.: Doubleday & Co., 1935), may still have some utility.

The books by A. M. Young, especially his *Japan in Recent Times, 1912–1926* (New York: William Morrow & Co., 1928), are of interest as contemporary accounts and the Young newspaper, the *Kobe* (later *Japan*) *Chronicle*, is a most important source for many events of the entire period between the mid-Meiji and prewar Showa eras.

For most readers, the Showa period is likely to be of greatest interest. For the militarist era of the 1930s, the most important materials are contained in two memoirs: the so-called *Harada-Saionji Memoirs* and the *Kido Diary;* neither of these has been published in English, but both are available at certain leading libraries in the United States in mimeographed form, in whole or in part.

Perhaps no single English source is as valuable as the voluminous *War Crimes Trial Documents*, running into thousands of pages, which were translated for the famous Tokyo trials. These also can be obtained; a complete set exists, for instance, at the University of California, Berkeley library.

Among existing Western memoirs, special mention should be made of J. C. Grew, *Ten Years in Japan* (New York: Simon & Schuster, 1944), and Sir R. Craigie, *Behind the Japanese Mask* (London: Hutchinson & Co., 1946). From the Japanese side, see Mamoru Shigemitsu, *Japan and Her Destiny* (New York: E. P. Dutton & Co., 1958).

We have a general account of this wartime period in F. C. Jones, *Japan's New Order in East Asia: Its Rise and Fall, 1937–1945* (London: Oxford University Press, 1954).

A growing number of monographs dealing with this general period are available. Yale Maxon explores the problems involved in formulating Japanese foreign policy in his *Control of Japanese Foreign Policy: A Study of Civil-Military Rivalry, 1930–1945* (Berkeley: University of California Press, 1957).

For other worthy studies, see Harry J. Benda, *The Crescent and the Rising Sun* (Institute of Pacific Relations, 1958); Robert Butow, *Japan's Decision to Surrender* (Stanford, Calif.: Stanford University Press, 1955), and *Tojo and the Coming of the War* (Stanford, Calif.: Stanford University Press, 1961); Willard H. Elsbree, *Japan's Role in Southeast Asian Nationalist Movements, 1940–1945* (Cambridge: Harvard University Press, 1953); James B. Crowley, *Japan's Quest for Autonomy* (Princeton: Princeton University Press, 1966); Ernst Preusseisen, *Germany and Japan: A Study in Totalitarian Diplomacy, 1933–1941* (The Hague, 1958); Sadako N. Ogata, *Defiance in Manchuria—The Making of Japanese Foreign Policy, 1931–1932* (Berkeley: University of California Press, 1954); and Paul Schroeder, *The Axis Alliance and Japanese-American Relations, 1941* (Ithaca, N.Y.: Cornell University Press, 1958).

Japanese accounts of the war are available in Saburo Hayashi, in collaboration with Alvin D. Cox, *Kogun: The Japanese Army in the Pacific War* (Marine Corps Association, 1959) and Nobutaka Ike (trans. and ed.), *Japan's Decision for War* (Stanford, Calif.: Stanford University Press, 1967); T. Kase, *Journey to the Missouri* (New Haven: Yale University Press, 1950); M. Kato, *The Lost War* (New York: Alfred A. Knopf, 1946); and Mamoru Shigemitsu, *Japan and Her Destiny* (New York: E. P. Dutton, 1958).

Various aspects of the postwar period are covered in certain general books: Ardath Burks, *Government in Japan* (New York: Praeger, 1961); Allan B. Cole, *Japanese Society and Politics* (Boston, 1956); Esler Dening, *Japan* (New York: Praeger, 1961); Nobutaka Ike, "Japan," in *Major Governments of Asia*, ed. George Kahin (Ithaca, N.Y.: Cornell University

Press, 1958); Kazuo Kawai, *Japan's American Interlude* (Chicago: University of Chicago Press, 1960); Ivan Morris, *Nationalism and the Right Wing in Japan* (London: Oxford University Press, 1960); and Harold Quigley and John Turner, *The New Japan: Government and Politics* (Minneapolis: University of Minnesota Press, 1956). See also *Parties and Politics in Contemporary Japan* by Robert A. Scalapino and Junnosuke Masumi (Berkeley: University of California Press, 1962).

In his book *The Japanese People and Foreign Policy* (Berkeley: University of California Press, 1962), Douglas Mendel, Jr., presents an important collection of public opinion polls pertaining to foreign policy issues.

Naturally, the American reader will tend to have a special interest in American-Japanese relations. A substantial number of books have been written on this subject. Among the older works, those of Payson J. Treat are well known: *Japan and the United States*, rev. ed. (Stanford, Calif.: Stanford University Press, 1928), and *Diplomatic Relations between the United States and Japan*, 3 vols. (Stanford, Calif.: Stanford University Press, 1932, 1938). See also Foster Rhea Dulles, *Forty Years of American-Japanese Relations* (New York: Appleton-Century-Crofts, 1937).

A broad cultural account is to be found in T. Dennett, *Americans in Eastern Asia* (New York: Macmillan Co., 1922). More recently, such an approach has been effectively used by Robert Schwantes in his *Japanese and Americans: A Century of Cultural Relations* (New York: Harper & Row, 1955).

For current political relations, the reader can refer to E. O. Reischauer, *The United States and Japan*, rev. ed. (Cambridge, Mass.: Harvard University Press, 1957); Herbert Passin, ed., *The United States and Japan* (Englewood Cliffs, N.J.: Prentice-Hall, Spectrum Books, American Assembly Series, 1966); Donald C. Hellman, *Japanese Domestic Politics and Foreign Policy* (Berkeley: University of California Press, 1969); Gerald L. Curtis, ed., *Japanese-American Relations in the*

*1970's* (Washington, D.C.: American Assembly, 1970); Herman Kahn, *The Emerging Japanese Superstate: Challenge and Response* (Englewood Cliffs, N.J.: Prentice-Hall, 1970); Martin E. Weinstein, *Japan's Postwar Defense Policy, 1947–1968* (New York: Columbia University Press, 1970); John K. Emmerson, *Arms, Yen and Power: The Japanese Dilemma* (New York: Dunellen, 1971); Zbigniew Brzezinski, *The Fragile Blossom* (New York: Harper and Row, 1972); Gerald L. Curtis, *Japan and East Asia—The New International Order* (New York: Praeger, 1972); James M. Morley, *Forecast for Japan: Security in the 1970's* (Princeton: Princeton University Press, 1972); Robert A. Scalapino, *American-Japanese Relations in a Changing Era*, The Center for Strategic and International Studies, Georgetown University, Washington, D.C. (New York: Library Press, 1972); Frank Langdon, *Japan's Foreign Policy* (Berkeley: University of California Press, 1973); and Ralph N. Clough, *East Asia and U.S. Security* (Washington, D.C.: The Brookings Institution, 1975).

Official publications from the U.S. State Department, such as the series *Foreign Relations of the United States and Japan*, contain useful major documents. See also various congressional hearings, especially those of the Senate Committee on Foreign Relations, *United States Security Agreements and Commitments Abroad—Japan and Okinawa*, 91st Congress, 2d sess., on January 26–29, 1970, pt. 5.

In addition, there are a number of more specialized accounts, limited in scope or time. Only four will be mentioned here: H. L. Stimson, *The Far Eastern Crisis* (New York: Harper & Row, 1936); Herbert Feis, *The Road to Pearl Harbor* (Princeton: Princeton University Press, 1950); Ray W. Curry, *Woodrow Wilson and Far Eastern Policy* (Twayne, 1957); and Dorothy Borg and Shumpei Okamoto, ed., *Pearl Harbor as History: Japanese-American Relations, 1931–41*, (New York: Columbia University Press, 1973).

No serious study of Japanese foreign policy should be undertaken, of course, without reference to the periodical literature. Among the English-language journals, those carrying articles of significance at rather regular intervals include *Contemporary Japan, Japan Quarterly* (formerly *Far Eastern Quarterly*), *Foreign Affairs, Pacific Affairs,* and *Asian Survey* (formerly *Far Eastern Survey*).

Some reference should also be made to the increasing number of English-language materials being published by the Japanese government, including valuable items, pertaining to foreign policy problems and policies, from the Ministry of Finance, the Ministry of Trade and Commerce, and the Foreign Office. In reference to contemporary issues, it will be helpful to consult the translations of the vernacular press and of selected articles from Japanese vernacular magazines which are put out by the American embassy, if one can obtain access to these.

Such newspapers as the *Japan Times* (formerly *Nippon Times*), the *Osaka Mainichi* (English-language edition), and the *Asahi Evening News* should also be examined. Naturally, many of the above materials will contain further leads and much fuller biographies.

# INDIA'S FOREIGN POLICY

8

*Richard L. Park*

Twenty years ago one could outline India's foreign policy with a sense of precision. Independence had come following the end of World War II—not easily but decisively—and there was an atmosphere of optimism on domestic as well as external fronts. The goal of the nationalists had been to achieve freedom from British control first. The next steps were to move rapidly to improve the lot of the average Indian citizen, and at the same time to influence the rest of the world in the direction of peace. Compromise and rational discourse over conflicting issues, and not violence, were to be the rules at home and abroad, as Gandhi taught. Jawaharlal Nehru expressed his people's views eloquently and persuasively, gaining the attention of the outside world, as well as adulation at home.

The years since independence have been hard and sometimes bitter, despite advances on many fronts. The winter war with Pakistan over Kashmir in 1947–48 was only the first of three conflicts between these neighbors on the subcontinent. The war of 1965 was harmful enough, but the armed struggle of 1971 resulted in the formation of Bangladesh, thus reducing Pakistan to its western sector, further refueling Indo-Pakistani antagonisms. Perhaps even more devastating was the border war with the People's Republic of China in 1962 that was a debacle for the Indian Army. This disaster was only partially ameliorated by the smooth and successful military campaigns in East Bengal that liberated Bangladesh from Pakistan.

Wars were not the only forces that hardened and reshaped India's worldview. "Police actions" in Portuguese India (Goa and others) and Hyderabad, as well as lengthy negotiations with France for possession of French India (Pondicherry et al.), were deemed necessary to establish the national unity of the country. Criticism came from many sides because of these actions. During the same Cold War period the United States, the USSR, and China concentrated on wooing India, effectively complicating the internal development process. In the United Nations, where India expected to be influential, the Kashmir case, raised by India as a charge of aggression against Pakistan in late 1947, induced a debate that turned out to be more favorable to Pakistan than to India. Nevertheless, reliance on the United Nations, over the long run, remains an important segment of India's policy. At home, inadequate or erratic monsoons, inexperienced and inept planning, overly ambitious industrialization, substantial population growth, dependence on the outside world for food, and administrative failures led, year after year, to a realization that economic development was going to be a long, costly, and demanding process. There was no golden path to a quick prosperity, despite independence.

It is not surprising that India's foreign policy, while not abandoning its fundamentals established in the early Nehru years, has toughened. The national interest, always present in Nehru's mind, turned out to be more central and unbending as the years of experience and occasional disillusionment became more evident. India, as an important world power in Asia in the late 1970s, carries the language of its earlier foreign policy, but without any misunderstanding about the requirements of being prepared to argue hard and fight if necessary for national aims.

The emergency declared by the Government of India on June 26, 1975, resulted in dramatic changes in the domestic political affairs of India, but Prime Minister Gandhi made clear that India's foreign policy would not be affected. Time and circumstances will determine the longer range consequences of the emergency on the political system at home and the ramifications of these domestic consequences on foreign affairs.

History, geography, personalities, and political circumstances have helped to shape the foreign policies of India today. A review of this legacy is in order.

## INTRODUCTION

The emergence of India as an independent state in 1947, and the coming to power of the Chinese Communists two years later, represent the consequences of two major forces in the social and political revolutions that have been waged in Asia throughout the present century. More than half the people on earth are encompassed in the great arc of nations from Japan and Korea in eastern Asia westward to Pakistan and the Middle East. What happens in India and in China, and between them, will affect the whole of Asia. For the noncommunist as well as the communist worlds, what comes of the Indian experiment with democratic government will not be of immediate significance only; it may well have repercussions in every other part of the globe. From this point of view, the stability of India's domestic politics, her effectiveness in developing her economy, and her ability to solve her social problems would seem to outweigh, by far, India's external influence on contemporary world affairs.

The leaders of India view their role in international politics from a different perspective. They place special emphasis on the fact that the whole of Asia, and increasingly the Middle East and Africa as well, at last are escaping from the dominance and imposed economic tutelage of Western power. With freedom attained, the next objective is to raise living standards appreciably and to revitalize old civilizations with the best of modern technology and the most far-reaching of social reforms. The communist issue, according to leaders in the highest political circles in India, cannot be allowed to obscure the fact that internal national development must take priority over external involvement, and for reasons of domestic rather than ideological or international concern. Communism and Asian nationalism have grown up together and have come to critical junctures calling for commitment and decision at about the same time, but for India, at least, foreign policy must be exercised in the immediate interests of India, and not in accordance with the wishes and interests of other world powers. India believes that her own national interests are best served by creating conditions of peace, encouraging cultural and economic cooperation on an unrestricted international scale, and fostering conditions favorable to political coexistence between competing forms of government. Under these circumstances, it is felt India might enjoy an international atmosphere conducive to the

development of her own material and human resources. In this view, domestic and foreign policies necessarily interlink; foreign policy is a safeguard for the national interest.

The failure of India's effort to reach an understanding with China, and the continuation of heated and sometimes violent relations with Pakistan over Kashmir and related boundary issues, have compelled India to modify her foreign policy and her defense arrangements. The commitment to nonalignment nevertheless remains the backbone of India's posture in international politics.

To understand the dynamics of India's foreign policy, it is advisable to look with some care at the factors that have influenced her outlook on the world community, and to examine India's pattern of domestic problems and her plans for their solution, out of which stem policies for external affairs.

## THE NATIONAL BACKGROUND

### Political History

Any full-scale inquiry into Indian foreign policy would lead one to range widely through history to identify the infinite variety of influences which flowed between India and her neighbors and which characterized the early relations among the peoples of Asia. The relative isolation of segments of the region during the past few centuries was, in large part, the result of the parceling out of spheres of influence between the several Western imperial powers. But cultural memories are lasting. Although India is a young nation, its civilization is ancient. Contemporary leaders are mindful of past greatness at home and abroad, and are unwilling to build toward anything less than a new image of greatness that will efface the memories of subordination during centuries of Western dominance.

The cultural vehicles of the Hindu and Buddhist ways of life carried Indian philosophy, art, and literature throughout Asia. No major part of that continent was untouched by Buddhism, which arose in India but flourished on its borders and beyond. Pilgrims from the Buddhist world were drawn back to India, the birthplace of Gautama Buddha, bringing with them new ideas and taking back to their own countries diaries of their observations in the holy land. Through this interchange of culture and faith, ties were made that centuries of neglect could not entirely break.

From the north and west came the Islamic invasions which culminated in the Mogul empire from the sixteenth century, splendidly exemplified by the rule of the Emperor Akbar. Akbar, like the Hindu-Buddhist Asoka long before him, is an Indian hero, remembered for combining compassion with strength, and honor with efficiency—terms now reserved for modern leaders such as Mahatma Gandhi and Jawaharlal Nehru. Akbar represents Islam and the tie of India to the cultural traditions of the Middle East.

Much later, particularly after the seventeenth century, when European powers battled for trading rights in the Indian subcontinent, Western and Indian ideas and institutions met, clashed, and in part coalesced in the creation of a pattern of political and social doctrine and forms of social organization that have persisted to a remarkable extent, and are clearly represented in

the constitution of the Republic of India.

Our concern must be directed toward more recent history, to the direct line of development of independent India's foreign policy. In concentrating on these latter years, however, it would be well to remember that India's leaders keep at least one eye reserved for 5,000 years of history, and not a few of their contemporary decisions are made with due regard for this background of experience.

By the middle of the nineteenth century, India had become an administrative and political unity. Between 1600, when Elizabeth I chartered the British East India Company for trading rights in the East, and about 1858, most of the lands of the Indian subcontinent were brought under British administration and control. The rapid decline of the Mogul empire in the eighteenth century, plus the skill of the British in administration and in warfare, had led to the gradual absorption and political control of local Indian rulers' lands. This process involved, first, revenue collecting and imposition of law and order to assure trading rights, and, then, possession itself, for the ultimate assurance of commercial security that such political control allows.

India had never before had an opportunity to draw together the many cultural strands that formed the basis of its unique community. In the Sanskritic tradition and in Indian philosophy, there were ties that for millennia had given a sense of unity to the many Hindu peoples who inhabited the larger part of the subcontinent. But diversity of expression—in language, art, literature, religious belief, and intensity of loyalty—was the rule rather than the exception before the nineteenth century and the age of British dominance. The institutions of caste and the joint family, cemented by local symbols of loyalty and social custom, contributed to the patchwork quilt of subcultures on the subcontinent—a condition, incidentally, which continues to divide the Indian people into competing regional groups, but also creates much of the color and grandeur that are the special qualities of the country.

British administration, to be effective and efficient, had to be tightly organized and centralized. Thus the country was divided and subdivided, not always rationally or in accordance with an integrated plan, but in any event in line with considerations that would bolster imperial British control. The objective was to organize an administrative state: one where revenues could be collected regularly and sufficiently; where a few top British political officers, and a small corps of Indian civil-service members, could funnel orders from the top of the hierarchy to the grass roots, and conversely, where local sentiments could be channeled upward; where law and order—and proximate justice—could be enforced; and where British ideas about the ultimate destiny of the Indian people could be carried forward by the Indians by means of education, imitation of colonial behavior, and experience in the use of Western social and political institutions.

The year 1858 was a turning point in Indian history. The year before, a mutiny, now often called the First War of Indian Independence, had broken out in several parts of northern India. The ostensible objective of the mutiny was to restore the Mogul emperor to his throne in Delhi. Underneath, however, were a number of grievances against the East India Company's rule, grievances based on its failure to give adequate attention to the social and economic needs of the people. Agreements with local rulers had been set aside, often without consultation, and, in general, the social well-being of the population was subordinated to the personal and economic interest of the rulers themselves. Often ignorant of local customs, and sometimes oblivious to the social consequences of enforced rules and regulations, the East India Company was suddenly confronted with crises on many fronts that led to outright revolt against the company's power. London's response to the situation was to give control of India to the British crown, and for Parliament to assume the supervisory responsibilities for the conduct of state affairs.

## Nationalism

From 1858 to 1947, authoritarian British rule in India conceded gradually to the liberal British view that a people should be trained to govern themselves, at least in local affairs. Indian nationalist opinion developed with the view that a people *must* be allowed to govern themselves. It was perhaps inevitable that the growth of Indian nationalism would be encouraged by the liberal British tradition that dominated the Indian educational system from the middle of the nineteenth century.

Indian nationalism commenced more as a movement for social and religious reform than as a political and economic movement. Faced with the facts of an earlier Muslim domination of a basically Hindu society, and then with the rapid take-over of Mogul reins by the British, nineteenth-century Indian leaders were led to question the inherent strength of Hindu social institutions. Men such as Raja Rammohan Roy, often called the "father of Indian nationalism," vigorously fought, in the early nineteenth century, for a liberalization of Hindu social institutions, and for English education so that the new ideas of Europe might be brought to bear on the reform of Indian life. Rammohan Roy founded the *Brahmo Samaj*, in 1828, as an institutionalized means for giving opportunities to liberal Indians to make over Hindu society along more enlightened lines. Other reformers, such as Dayananda Saraswati, founder of the *Arya Samaj*, urged a return to the purer—less historically and socially overladen—philosophy of the ancient Vedic age, unhindered by caste divisions, as his more indigenous response to the impact of the West. Late-nineteenth-century developments along the same general lines, but in more modern terms, included the work of Annie Besant of the Theosophical Society and Swami Vivekananda of the Ramakrishna Mission.

But poverty, illiteracy, and disease, deep-rooted and widespread, were the facts of Indian life that served as the mainsprings for a vigorous nationalism and, later, for the insistent demand for freedom from British rule. Centralized imperial administration provided the means for improving transportation and communication, broadening markets for industry and agriculture, and encouraging modern finance and commerce. In the process, British capital, more than Indian, reaped the profits. It was British industry and commerce that benefited more by the construction of a colonial economy in which India provided the raw materials for a profitable European industry. And in the Indian backwaters, the relatively self-sufficient village economy broke down as middle-scale industrialization came to India. No longer could village craftsmen hope to compete with the factories of the towns and cities. The tightly woven fabric of Indian village society, with its ancient system of interrelated economic functions and social services, was struck a heavy blow. The economy and the related aspects of the society grew in a lopsided manner. The tiny fraction that was urban India grew further apart from the four-fifths that was village India. Education, better health, and the benefits of modern technology hardly touched the countryside; indeed, even in the towns and cities the cleavages between the well-off and the down-and-out were all too evident.

## Indian National Congress

It was under these conditions of dominance by British power, of internal division between the several layers of Indian society, of separatist tendencies between Hindu and Muslim and between linguistic regions, plus a pervasive stagnation in the culture and in the general economy, that the Indian National Congress was founded in 1885. The Congress, destined to be the vehicle of the Indian nationalist movement and the organization in which the main lines of independent India's foreign policy would be tested and formed, was a moderate body with modest objectives in the years preceding World War I. Congress leaders of those days, such as Pherozeshah Mehta,

Surendranath Banerjea, and G. K. Gokhale, were mainly concerned with increasing Indian membership in the Indian Civil Service, extending the benefits of higher education, and arguing a persuasive case to the Parliament and people of Great Britain for a greater measure of Indian participation in running the affairs of India. In this effort, the Congress was encouraged by liberal British leaders in both Great Britain and India. It was the belief of those concerned with this early phase of nationalist expression that, with experience and time, the good sense of the British would recognize the obvious need for a loosening of British control over Indian affairs. Such optimism proved unwarranted, and a vigorous but uniquely nonviolent nationalist movement, led by Mohandas K. Gandhi from 1919 onward, was the result. The National Congress-backed nationalist movement expanded its program of action to the masses of the Indian people, pressing harder and harder for the concessions from their rulers that ultimately led to an independent India in 1947.

As freedom came near, however, the bitter feeling between the Hindu and Muslim communities grew more intense. The common nationalist cause against an alien ruler broke down and, after 1940, a large proportion of the Muslims demanded a separate state, Pakistan, in which to develop a nation based on Islamic brotherhood. Pakistan was founded in 1947, after widespread rioting, terrible blood-shed, and the fearful migration of millions of people had forced the issue. Needless to say, the circumstances of partition contributed much to the mutual fear and enmity that have colored relations between Pakistan and India ever since.

This brief survey of the Indian nationalist movement and of the general conditions of nineteenth- and twentieth-century India is intended to convey one important lesson in the better understanding of India's view of world affairs: Indians have been concerned—one might almost say obsessed—during the past half-century with the imperial or colonial question. Almost everything else in world history has been read in terms of the colonial theme, including the communal rivalry between Muslims and Hindus, which is felt to be the product of a British imperial policy of "divide and rule." It is understandable that leaders like Nehru, who fought for independence for over a quarter-century, would not easily forget their experiences in earlier years. As a colony, India considered herself isolated from active participation in world affairs, and yet subject to the forces of world politics because she was bound to the decisions of Great Britain. In particular, India resented its involuntary, if legal, involvement in two world wars. This involuntary alignment with Great Britain and its allies in times of war and peace undoubtedly contributed to India's decision to develop its foreign policy along lines of nonalignment with blocs of power, especially with the Western alignment with which she had been all too familiar.

### Economic Geography

However internationally isolated, in a formal sense, the Indian National Congress may have been in the years before independence, Indian leaders certainly were alert to the geographical, economic, and political facts of Indian life which formed the conditions of any Indian foreign policy, even as interpreted by Great Britain.

First, India was recognized as being strategically located in the west of Asia: her peninsula stretches across the main lines of sea and air communications from west to east, and her northern, mountainous boundaries touch important centers of the Middle East, central Asia, and the Far East. India's near neighbors include several of the most powerful nations in the world—particularly the Soviet Union and China—but also Burma, Malaysia, Sri Lanka, Indonesia, and the other countries of South and Southeast Asia with which India feels she has much in common. India has been relatively isolated, historically, by mountains to the north and seas on her peninsular sides; nevertheless, it has been recognized that India's geographic location, in the age of air travel, involves a natural intercourse with the many economic, political, and cultural forces that cross or abut on its territory. Not only is protection from invasion the crucial question; also of importance is the skill with which India may take advantage of interrelations with the many who come her way.

Economically, India has been and remains a country poor in the level of its exploited natural resources, in the rate of its industrial and agricultural development, and in the prospect for rapid rises in its standards of living. These facts were early recognized by the Indian National Congress. One of the great urges of the nationalist movement was the hope that, with greater freedom to plan and legislate, adequate steps might be taken to improve the economic lot of the Indian people. Nationalist thinking on foreign affairs was never far removed from the economic implications of whatever steps might be taken abroad. And the first major step toward sound economic development was the attainment of the political freedom which would permit national economic planning.

## Competing Ideologies

The geographic and economic facts affecting India's international position discussed above, however, are of relatively minor significance to National Congress leaders when these facts are compared with the influence of political ideas. The first major ideological influence was that of liberalism; the second, closely following on the first in historical sequence, was socialism.

The farthest-reaching legacy of the period of British rule in India was the infusion of a liberal philosophy of government in the mental frame of India's educated hierarchy of leadership. The process by which this intermixture of ideas and institutions took place over the past 150 years is, in large part, the total social history of India of the period. Education in English from the mid-nineteenth century on, both at the secondary and higher educational levels, brought to Indian students the story of western European political achievement which assumed that law, politics, and civil and military administration would be subject to the responsible control of the people. The connection between a vital liberal democracy and rapid economic and social development was not lost on those Indians who examined European experience. Moreover, significant numbers of Indian students took their higher degrees in London, or at Oxford or Cambridge, and a few on the continent, thus pouring back into Indian society leaders fully on a par, intellectually and informationally, with their European classmates.

As the British administrators of India faced novel problems for which no ready indigenous solution seemed present, it was only natural that they looked to British experience for ideas and institutions applicable in India. Indian judges and lawyers, accountants and teachers, agricultural economists and engineers, editors and reporters, and, of course, politicians as well, grew up in an institutionalized milieu that was reflective of the British liberal view of society's proper organization. Although this process of macrocosmic acculturation was largely an urban phenomenon and affected only a small segment of India's society, the influence was nevertheless great, for it touched the lives of the greater part of India's educated ruling classes. By the 1920s, when the Indian National Congress under Gandhi opened its mass campaign for political freedom, liberalism was well established as the common core of political agreement concerning the kind of government and the kind of society that India's leaders wished to develop under their own guidance. In fact, one of the most powerful weapons that leaders of the National Congress used against the British was the assertion that Great Britain was denying to the Indian people the goals of liberal democracy extolled so vociferously in London.

The second major ideological influence in twentieth-century India has been socialism. For many, socialism was seen as a combination of utopian propositions and Fabian interpretations of social democracy. These ideas equated rather easily with the main tenets of liberalism as they had been developed in India. For others, Marxism and Marxian socialism were more influential, although organized political parties favoring Marxian socialism did not gain prominence until the 1930s. Most Indian intellectuals, and many politicians, were convinced that India's economic and social conditions required active, regularized legislative and administrative direction if needed social and economic changes were to come about. The Russian Revolution was closely followed by Indian leaders, since it was felt that here was an experiment in a social and economic situation not fundamentally unlike that of India. The fact that the Soviet Union and spokesmen for the Comintern endorsed India's aspirations for independence and condemned British imperial power, at a time when others were silent, has not been forgotten. At least a portion of the sympathetic hearing now given to Soviet views on world affairs may be traced to the communists' early support of Indian nationalism.

Ideologically, then, India's leaders had grown accustomed, by the mid-1920s, to the liberal democracy of western Europe, combined with an infusion of socialist solutions to economic problems, and they were fully committed to the perpetuation of such a mixed form of government in an independent India. This was true even though it was well understood by these leaders that some of the principles of liberal democracy, when applied in India, would conflict with the localized groups of village India, which relied more on caste, class, or community, and less on the individual, for the exercise of political responsibilities.

### Foreign Policy in the Making

The Indian National Congress did not, of course, have a foreign policy, in any formal sense, until it became the body conducting the government of the Republic of India. But as a strategy in the nationalist movement, the Congress adopted a policy of expressing itself by resolutions on foreign affairs at its annual sessions, or through statements by its officers at other times. The same policy was adopted for matters of domestic concern. This process was called "parallel government": the Congress, in this case, speaking for the Indian people who were unable to speak effectively through British-Indian organs of government.

By the mid-1920s, the National Congress turned its attention more regularly to international politics. The new emphasis arose partially as a consequence of India's failure to secure a greater measure of freedom following the end of World War I, but perhaps more so because of the insistence of a young Congressman from the United Provinces, son of a then-prominent Congress leader, Motilal Nehru.

Jawaharlal Nehru, a London-trained lawyer educated first at Harrow and Cambridge, began to make his influence felt in circles of the National Congress by the mid-1920s. Although he was primarily interested in domestic politics, his special contribution to the nationalist movement was the education of several generations of Indians in the facts of international life. Nehru believed that India was inevitably to play an important role in international affairs, and that the Indian National Congress had the responsibility of preparing the people for the years ahead. An examination of the resolutions of the Congress from 1926 to 1947 reveals an acute awareness of the dangers in the growth of fascism, a sympathetic approach to the aspirations of the Soviet Union, a consistent criticism of the continuation or expansion of Western imperial power anywhere in the world, and a sensitive exposure of all forms of racial, social, and economic discrimination. Such an examination of the record reveals the development of the view that international disputes require peaceful means of solution, and that peaceful means for resolving disputes would be encouraged by a world organized to enforce the exclusive use of such means. The influence of Gandhi in the growth of this policy of nonviolent methods in international affairs is obvious. Jawaharlal Nehru, as general secretary of the Indian National Congress, reestablished, in 1936, a Foreign Department (originally formed in 1925) to study world affairs and to disseminate literature on the subject throughout India. Although it is not accurate to credit Prime Minister Nehru for the whole construction of India's foreign policy, it can be said that he was the architect and the guide who prepared the way, from 1926, for policies that, by 1947, were acceptable to and taken for granted by the vast majority of the citizens of India.

### THE POLICY-MAKING PROCESS

For the personal and historical reasons outlined above, Jawaharlal Nehru was able to impress his personal stamp on the foreign policy of India. One measure of Mr. Nehru's lasting influence on foreign policy has been the pledge made by his successors, the late Lal Bahadur Shastri and Nehru's daughter, Mrs. Indira Gandhi, to continue the policies he shaped. As a politically powerful, highly intelligent nationalist leader with a deep concern for world affairs, Mr. Nehru articulated a policy based on his view of the present and future, bearing in mind the strengths and weaknesses of his country and people, and that policy was affirmed by all but rather small sectors of Indian political opinion. After the Sino-Indian dispute over the Himalayan border in 1962, there was a sharp increase in public criticism of foreign policy, criticism which brought into focus the bureaucratic and legislative apparatus that supports the voice of the prime minister on matters of foreign policy.

### Governmental Agencies

*The Executive Authority.* India's constitution places formal executive responsibility with the president of the republic. But, like Great Britain's queen, the president acts on the advice of his Council of Ministers. The cabinet, which does not necessarily include all ministers, is composed of senior ministers nominated by the prime minister and appointed by the president, who then act with collective responsibility to Parliament.

From 1947 to 1964, India had one prime minister, Jawaharlal Nehru, who continuously held the portfolio for external affairs as well. Since Nehru's Congress party enjoyed a substantial majority in every session of Parliament over that period, continuity in foreign policy was sustained to the degree that Nehru wished to sustain it. Although, as

minister of external affairs, Mr. Nehru could and did take counsel with his colleagues in the cabinet, as prime minister he held such broad responsibility for the domestic and external well-being of his country that explanations, rather than questions, appear to have been his normal presentations to the cabinet on foreign matters. The holding of the two portfolios by a man of such experience—one, moreover, who was held in near-reverence by the bulk of his people—combined with the Congress party's control of a substantial majority in Parliament, gave Mr. Nehru what amounted to a free hand in constructing and executing India's foreign policy. Following Mr. Nehru's death in 1964, the new prime minister, Lal Bahadur Shastri, selected Sardar Swaran Singh to head the Ministry of External Affairs. M. C. Chagla and then Dinesh Singh led the ministry during Mrs. Indira Gandhi's first term starting in 1966, but Sardar Swaran Singh was returned to the post after Mrs. Gandhi's sweeping victory in 1971. Other politicians have held the post since, but Mrs. Gandhi has not elected to run the ministry herself. She is, of course, a powerful force in the conduct of foreign policy nonetheless.

The Ministry of External Affairs is a large and professionally staffed organization. The Minister is assisted at political levels by Congress Party associates from Parliament. At operational and administrative levels, the Foreign Secretary is the key figure, assisted by Secretaries I and II who hold broad responsibilities for various world areas, and an Additional Secretary for administration. A Foreign Service Board, chaired by the Foreign Secretary, has as members the other senior secretaries, plus the Secretary for Foreign Trade and

Supply. Many important advisory opinions on India's foreign policy implementation come from this Board.

It is from the "county desks," from the research and intelligence branches, and from the technical staffs that analytical materials flow upwards to the Minister, providing the raw materials and statements of alternative policies on which foreign policy tends to be based.

*The Foreign Service.* Over 7,000 staff members man the Ministry of External Affairs and its offices abroad. Personnel recruited into the foreign service—now scattered throughout the world in the high commissions and commissions within the Commonwealth of Nations, in the embassies, legations, consulates-general, and consulates, and in the United Nations and international missions elsewhere—are carefully selected by competitive examination and thoroughly trained for their positions. At the highest levels—ambassadors and high commissioners—what might be called "political appointments" sometimes occur. But the tradition is to use the professional service to the maximum.

The foreign service, somewhat similar to its counterpart in Great Britain, is an elite service, admission to which is much sought after by some of India's most able university graduates. The pressure to expand India's external representation rapidly was very great after 1947, but trained personnel were in short supply. Now the service is stabilized, and its standards of performance have increased year by year. Protected from personal criticism by the restraints of responsible ministers, the foreign service has been able to give an even greater maturity to India's assessment of the facts of international affairs. More adequate linguistic skills, an improvement in the analysis of intelligence, and much greater information on world situations provide the Ministry of External Affairs with substantial resources to use in pursuing the global implications of India's foreign policy.

*Parliament.* Parliament is not concerned constitutionally with the day-to-day making or execution of foreign policy. But debates in the *Lok Sabha* (House of the People) or the *Rajya Sabha* (Council of State)—initiated by the prime minister or the minister of external affairs, or by questions raised during the question period, or following the president's addresses opening Parliament or concerning the budget—give several opportunities for members to influence policy. Since the prime minister necessarily is concerned daily with foreign affairs, reports tend to be made to Parliament regularly, often, and in detail. Seldom is Parliament in doubt about the government's views. But Parliament does not have a standing committee on foreign affairs. This prerogative remains with another organ of Parliament, the cabinet, and, of course, with the minister of external affairs and the prime minister. The president, also, keeps informed on foreign affairs, and occasionally undertakes trips abroad to "show the flag" in support of India's policies. When the president speaks out personally on domestic or foreign policy, as most presidents have from time to time, the prime minister usually finds an appropriate moment, privately or publicly, to take the president to task for such invasions of the principles of cabinet responsibility.

It should not be assumed, however, that members of Parliament are not an integral part of the process of making foreign policy. To the contrary, articulate members of the Opposition, including several members of the Communist party of India, as well as Congress party members who disagree with accepted policy, often are heard, their words recorded, and the debate disseminated widely throughout the country in official records and in the press. Spokesmen in Parliament help to identify the controversial issues for the public. Public opinion, in turn, acts as a restraint upon the Congress party's parliamentary majority. Members of Parliament have become far more vocal in their criticism of government policy since India's confrontation with China in 1962. The emergency of 1975 resulted in the closing off of the opposition's role in the shaping of foreign policy; the most articulate and experienced members of the opposition were jailed. Whether this situation will be temporary or more lasting is not yet possible to determine.

## Nongovernmental Agencies

*Political Parties.* The Congress party, through its annual sessions (usually held in December), through its policy-suggesting organ—the Working Committee—and through the party's administrative secretariat—the All-India Congress Committee—regularly discusses foreign policy and proposes policy changes to the parliamentary Congress party. The prime minister, as a prominent leader of the party, remains in close communication with party headquarters and party leaders, on foreign as well as on domestic matters. The considered opinion of the Congress party today is likely to be official policy tomorrow.

As we have already mentioned, certain respected leaders from other parties, or from among the independents, can be influential, in Parliament or from the public platform, on matters relating to foreign affairs —but only to the extent that their personal standing is high in the country. For example, the various socialist parties have not been effective critics of foreign policy. But a socialist leader of proven ability can personally have significant impact, as can a former socialist like Jayaprakash Narayan, who holds no political office at all. (His recent "popular" movement against the Government of Bihar is an indication, in domestic terms, of the influence he could generate, if he wished, on foreign affairs as well.) The communists, too, are not backward in voicing opposition to given policies. The pro-Peking and pro-Moscow Communist parties both express opinions on foreign affairs, in and out of Parliament.

But since the Congress party rules India more or less as if India were, in fact, a one-party state, debate *within* the Congress party is the most critical locus of political controversy on domestic and world affairs. The Congress party is not inclined, substantively and for good political reasons, to deny the prime minister's conclusions if a positive stand is taken and support is requested. The exceptional cases tend to be issues involving China or Pakistan, where debate is less disciplined.

*Interest Groups.* For the most part, interest groups do not have much influence in shaping India's foreign policy. Tradition excludes them from indirect involvement as informal advisers, and the law bars them from direct pressures. Such groups do, of course, have spokesmen in Parliament; they publish their views; they influence individuals. But groups such as the trade unions, student movements, professional societies, commercial, financial, and industrial organizations, and caste lobbies have a most limited scope of direct influence. To the extent that these groups find a congenial home in a political party, their interests can be more effectively passed on through recognized political channels.

The Indian Council of World Affairs, at its Sapru House headquarters in New Delhi and in its many branches throughout the country, as well as in its publications, can be influential. However, the Council has tended to be tender in its criticism of established policy in foreign affairs.

*Media of Mass Communications and Public Opinion.* World news is given extended and generally fair treatment in the English-language newspapers, and in the best of the Indian-language newspapers, and in the thousands of weeklies, fortnightlies, and monthlies published in all parts of the country. The reasons for this attention to world affairs are not entirely noble. Most Indian publications are run on thin budgets that do not permit much investigative reporting, field offices, or reporters trained for highly specialized studies. Since world news flows in regularly and copiously from international news agencies, editors tend to print it. Many in India are better informed on world affairs than they are on the conditions prevailing in India.

Indian newspapers are inclined to carry very long articles and informative editorials, which may run two full columns, about crucial foreign affairs questions. These publications also attempt to influence foreign policy in their editorials. Newspapers of the quality of the *Hindu* (Madras), the *Times of India* (Bombay and New Delhi), the *Hindustan Times* (New Delhi), and the *Statesman* (Calcutta and New Delhi) are read meticulously by officers in the Ministry of External Affairs. Party organs such as *Vigil* and the *Organiser,* or papers of opinion like the *Economic and Political Weekly* (Bombay), *Seminar* (Delhi), and *Quest* (Bombay), to name a few of the special publications, help to shape opinion indirectly. Television is not yet an important means of communication in India, and the All-India Radio is nationalized and without significant editorial influence on foreign policy. Increasingly, serious academic studies are making a difference on policy. Twenty years ago academic influence was close to nil.

These stimuli of public opinion, plus books, pamphlets, and lectures, appear to have made an impact on the urban intelligentsia. But India is 70 percent illiterate, and much of the country is out of the range of radios that function. Thus, public opinion, even at best, is expressed only by relatively few people, and these largely in urban centers.

On the whole, the Indian press supports the government's conclusions on foreign affairs, and such criticism as does appear is usually minor. The exceptions have involved the Sino-Indian disputes and the old Kashmir question. In these two cases, India's territorial integrity is at stake, and critics, including many journalists and editors, have been outspoken—and perhaps, thereby, somewhat influential. Strategic and military considerations, especially following the underground nuclear explosion in 1974, have led some editors to speculate on the policy implications more trenchantly than used to be the case.

India is not a country of opinion pollsters. However, the Indian Institute of Public Opinion (New Delhi) has produced two serial publications, one on public issues and one on economic matters (using George Gallup's methods), which supply useful material on public attitudes.

## The Substance of Foreign Policy

The remarkable consistency in public expressions of India's foreign policy can, as we have already noted, be traced to the continuity of leadership held by Jawaharlal Nehru and the Congress party from 1947 to 1964.

The trying circumstances of India's political and economic life have induced wide public support for the government of India's stand on world affairs, particularly since this stand has resulted in the growth of India's prestige. Although the cases of Kashmir, Korea, Suez, Hungary, Israel, China, and East Pakistan (1971) have produced bends and kinks in the main lines of foreign policy, India's principal international objectives and her diplomatic strategy have not been changed fundamentally since independence.

On September 26, 1946, Mr. Nehru, as the leader of the Interim Government, issued the following statement on foreign policy—a statement that would be applicable, in large measure, today:

In the sphere of foreign affairs India will follow an independent policy, keeping away from the power politics of groups aligned one against another. She will uphold the principles of freedom for dependent peoples and will oppose racial discrimination wherever it may occur. She will work with other peace-loving nations for international cooperation and goodwill without exploitation of one nation by another.

It is necessary that, with the attainment of her full international status,

India should establish contact with all the great nations of the world and that her relations with neighboring countries in Asia should become still closer. . . .

Towards the United Nations Organization India's attitude is that of wholehearted cooperation and unreserved adherence, in both spirit and letter, to the Charter governing it. To that end, India will participate fully in its varied activities and endeavor to play that role in its Councils to which her geographical position, population and contribution toward peaceful progress entitle her. In particular, the Indian delegate will make it clear that India stands for the independence of all colonial and dependent people and their full right to self-determination.[1]

One finds in this statement a number of principles that highlight the main strands of India's foreign policy:

1. the independence in outlook of a people who had been dominated for too long;
2. the fear that involvement in the affairs of others would restrict India's ability to construct a new and better social and economic order for itself;
3. the determination to assist others in attaining the political freedom for which India fought for so many years;
4. the hatred of second- and third-class citizenship, and particularly of an inferior status awarded because of race;
5. the confidence in cooperation and mutual goodwill, exemplified by the United Nations; and
6. the urge for international contacts throughout the world, but with special attention given to neighboring countries in Asia.

The signing of the "Treaty of Peace, Friendship, and Cooperation Between the Republic of India and

[1] Statement issued at a press conference in New Delhi on September 26, 1946, and published in *Indian Information* (New Delhi: Government of India Information Bureau), October 15, 1946.

the Union of Soviet Socialist Republics" on August 9, 1971,[2] may mark the beginning of a policy of close association with the Soviet Union that, over time, may change the character of India's independence in foreign policy. It is too early to say.

## Theory in Practice

In practice, the principles enumerated above have made it relatively easy to anticipate the government of India's response to issues as they have arisen in world politics. *Nonalignment.* The policy of nonalignment (or of "neutralism," as some prefer to call it) assured that India would not participate in the Southeast Asia Treaty Organization (SEATO) or the Baghdad Pact (later CENTO). What was (and is) less well known is that India, in order to help create "conditions of peace," would exercise its influence to lessen the effectiveness and the range of membership in such mutual defense arrangements, particularly those which, like SEATO and CENTO, impinge on the region of southern Asia. To the extent possible, it appears that India has advised its diplomats to endorse nonmilitary, peaceful solutions, and to bring into question military solutions. The exceptions, perhaps, are those military agreements (e.g., the North Atlantic Treaty or the Warsaw Pact) that do not relate directly to Asian concerns and are geographically distant from India. Also, when India's own national interests are involved, such as in the "Bangladesh War" of 1971, India can be remarkably military in its strategy.

During the period of negotiations leading to the signing of the Mutual Defense Assistance Agreement between the United States and Pakistan on May 19, 1954, India pushed its nonalignment policy one step further, in this case arguing that a military agreement entered into by Pakistan—a country whose eastern and western sectors enclose India like bookends—inevitably involved India in dangerous military consequences not of India's choosing and without mutual consent. In Parliament, Mr. Nehru explained why he felt it necessary to object to Pakistan's decision to sign such an agreement, even though Pakistan, a sovereign state, claimed that the matter was none of India's business:

Of course, they are a free country; I cannot prevent them. But if something affects Asia, India especially, and if something, in our opinion, is a reversal of history after hundreds of years, are we to remain silent? We have thought in terms of freeing our countries, and one of the symbols of freedom has been the withdrawal of foreign armed forces. I say the return of armed forces from any European or American country is a reversal of the history of the countries of Asia, whatever the motive. . . .

I am not prepared to express my opinion except in the most philosophic manner about the distant problems of Europe. India has not the slightest desire to impose its views or wishes on any other country. But because in Asia we have passed through similar processes of history in the last two hundred years or so, and thus can understand each other a little better, it is likely that I am in tune with some of my neighbor countries when I speak. If the great powers think that the problems of Asia can be solved minus Asia or minus the views of Asian countries, then it does seem to be rather odd.[3]

[2]For the full text, see *Aspects of Renewal, 1971–1973* (New Delhi: All India Congress Committee), 1973, p. 15 ff.

[3]Speech of February 22, 1954, given in full in *Jawaharlal Nehru's Speeches*, vol. 3, March, 1953–August, 1957 (New Delhi: Ministry of Information and Broadcasting, 1958), pp. 344–46.

Pakistan did sign the agreement, of course, and India's earlier differences with Pakistan, especially those over Kashmir, were hardened. Whether the defense agreement was wise, or not, depends on one's point of view. But from the perspective of India's foreign policy and India's sense of the situation in Asia, an American offer of a similar defense arrangement with India to parallel the Pakistan arrangement, intended to offset the charge of upsetting the balance of power in southern Asia, was both ill-advised and impertinent. Leaders in India could read the United States' offer only as a total misunderstanding or, worse, an indifference to India's policy of nonalignment and to the diplomatic strategy which India felt helped to create conditions of peace. India's foreign policy gave a clear indication of its probable response to a proposal for a defense agreement with the United States, but the United States ignored the signs. This case provides a useful lesson in the dilemmas of international politics. Assuming a mutual understanding of the issues involved in a dispute, a resolution need not necessarily follow. Indeed, a sharp identification of the issues may well make an agreement less likely, particularly if the probable ramifications of alternative solutions are rendered explicit.

Another case in point was the lifting in 1975 by the United States of the arms embargo imposed on India and Pakistan at the time of the subcontinental war of 1965. The United States offered arms both to India and to Pakistan. Since India had been well supplied by the Soviet Union and from internal manufactures, the United States clearly was opening a way for Pakistan to recharge its military batteries. The offer to India was ceremonial and, to India, insulting.

Needless to say, conditions changed radically after 1962. Pakistan, originally closely tied to American strategy in Asia, later sought an accommodation with China—and at the very time that Pakistan's enemy, India, became embroiled in border conflicts with China. As India had anticipated, American arms in Pakistan, intended to contain China, were used by Pakistan against India in 1965.

The independence movement of 1971 in East Pakistan again involved India and Pakistan in a controversy over styles of nonalignment. The government of Pakistan in Islamabad accused India of interference in Pakistan's internal affairs because of India's sympathy for the "freedom fighters" and criticism of the Pakistan army's effort to quell revolt in East Pakistan. Prime Minister Gandhi replied that India could not remain still when military force was used against an unarmed public. In the end, after providing training stations and arms to Bangladeshi freedom fighters, the Indian Army moved into East Bengal in December of 1971, defeated the Pakistani military contingent, and made possible the independence of Bangladesh. The East Bengal case again shows the tendency for India's foreign policy to be more narrowly self-interested the closer the case in dispute is to home.

Indeed, the coup in August of 1975 in Bangladesh that resulted in the killing of the "father" of Bangladesh, Sheikh Mujibur Rahman, posed a serious problem for India's foreign policy. Mujibur Rahman had maintained reasonably close ties with India and with the Soviet Union, whereas the new government seemed to favor the United States, Pakistan, and perhaps China. India has no intention of losing a special role in Bangladesh, if it can be managed.

*Nationalist Movements.* India's foreign policy has led, in the past, to consistent support of groups aspiring to national independence from Western imperial control. On the subcontinent itself, French Indian territory was claimed by India and eventually was handed over without a struggle. The dispute with Portugal over Goa and the rest of Portuguese India was ended when India occupied these territories by force of arms in 1961. In the neighboring country of Nepal, whenever influence could be exercised, it has been intended to maintain Nepal's independence and to encourage internal changes that would transfer political power from authoritarian leaders to responsible political hands. In recent years, Nepal (with Bhutan) has been subjected to firmer influence from India because of the critical importance of these regions to India's policy of defense of the territory which borders China. Recently the Indian Parliament has taken action to incorporate Sikkim into the Indian republic, thus ending the semiautonomous domestic administrative status of this border state. But Nepal, in particular, has resisted Indian influence, and Bhutan has successfully sought membership in the United Nations to assert its independence. Thus far, India has not been very successful in courting friendships with its immediate neighbors. On the other hand, India's immediate neighbors know very well that they are no match against Indian power, if and when India chooses to exercise it.

Nationalists further afield—in Algeria, Kenya, Malaysia, the Congo, Angola, Egypt, and many other areas—have enjoyed India's open support. In the more recent cases, especially after the tempering years of experience in the United Nations, India has been somewhat more cautious about supporting nationalist movements in Africa. But her support of the principles of self-determination and the national right to independence remains firm. This firmness has been challenged seriously in the Israeli case, but India has not altered its support to the Arab cause, despite the rapid rise in the price of oil that has been a severe handicap to India's economic development.

India has been unwilling, however, to apply this principle to the communist world, except in the case of Yugoslavia—where a solution other than national revolt was found. The uprisings in Poland and the notorious cases of Hungary and Czechoslovakia tested India's intentions. India was not, in these cases, willing to stretch her policy to help to sustain national strivings behind the communist shield. The contrast between India's reluctant and basically neutral reaction to the Soviet Union's behavior in Hungary and Czechoslovakia and her immediately hostile reaction to British, French, and Israeli behavior in Suez in 1956 underscores an inconsistency that would appear to be difficult to explain except in ideological or opportunistic terms. India's official reaction to revolts in Tibet and to the escape of the Dalai Lama from the Chinese also was cautious and noncommittal, at first. After 1959, when the Sino-Indian border dispute, involving Tibet, touched directly on the national interests of India, she altered her previous strategy of fostering peace by recognizing the complex character of the communist world system. Under the pressure of the struggle with China over the Sino-Indian boundaries in the Himilayas and Ladakh, India recognized more clearly the nature and substance of Tibetan resistance to Chinese cultural and political absorption. The Indian government's implication that a communist form of imperialism exists—especially in Asia, from China—has been made more explicit in public and private forums over the past years, although little solid evidence has been produced to prove the case against China. The legend that imperialism is uniquely the final stage of capitalism, grounded on Lenin's analysis and known to every schoolboy in India, dies hard.

*Racial Discrimination.* For many years preceding independence, Indian leaders objected to discrimination based upon race or creed. Mahatma Gandhi established his world reputation, before World War I, by organizing effective nonviolent resistance to such discrimination in South Africa. The continuation in South Africa of racial policies, and the enactment of permanent and legal discrimination in the form of apartheid, have led India to boycott South Africa and sever diplomatic relations. The withdrawal of South Africa from the British Commonwealth of Nations is in no small part due to the adamant stand against apartheid taken by India, Pakistan, Ghana, and other African and Asian Commonwealth members, powerfully supported by Canada. India has followed a similarly strong stand against the racist policies of the all-white government of Southern Rhodesia.

The South Africa case is only the most dramatic instance of India's involvement in international anti-discriminatory policies. Australia's "white" policy, the plight of the Negro in the United States, and the Sinhalese-Buddhist attacks on the rights of the minority of Tamil-speaking Hindus in Sri Lanka are three among the many other instances in which India speaks, but more cautiously, in behalf of equality.

*The United Nations and the Afro-Asian Bloc.* India's record in the United Nations is far too extensive to review here. The record reveals the great importance she places on the United Nations as an international forum for the resolution of conflicts, the prevention of possible conflicts, and the spreading of mutual understanding and cooperation, especially through the work of the specialized agencies and the General Assembly. The Kashmir case, first brought to the attention of the United Nations by India in late December of 1947, resulted in some disillusionment for India, since the Security Council's actions did not coincide with India's wishes. The handling of the Kashmir dispute by the United Nations was a lesson in the political operations of the Security Council. It is not likely that India will again bring a case of that sort to the United Nations, except after the most careful consideration.

The Afro-Asian consulative conference within the United Nations has become, since its formation in 1950, a significant force in the General Assembly, especially as the number of Afro-Asian member nations increases yearly. India and Egypt have played leading roles in this group. Although several shades of political outlook are encompassed in the bloc, it is dominantly neutralist. Partially by means of this informal organization of states, India has been able to advance its formula for the conditions of peace, by limiting military defense arrangements in Africa and Asia and by gaining United Nations membership for potential members of the bloc. The growing power of this group was shown in the steady rise in the proportion of states willing to vote for the admission of the People's Republic of China to the United Nations. This now is an accomplished fact, and the Republic of China on Taiwan no longer holds a seat in the United Nations. India supported these actions, but without much enthusiasm.

### Circles of Interest

*Pakistan.* India's most important foreign policy problem is neighboring Pakistan. Partition was the consequence of bloodshed, arson, rape, abduction, tremendous losses of property, the transfer of 12 million people, plus a general ill will of a virulent and lasting variety. India's conciliatory and generous approach to more distant problems has not been applied to Pakistan.

Almost three decades have passed since partition, and functional ties between the two countries—in transportation, communications, exchange of persons, commerce, and culture—have not been restored to any significant extent. Piecemeal, a few of the thorny differences over trade, boundaries, and the like have been settled. And with the help of the International Bank, a spectacular technological solution to the Indus valley (canal waters) dispute, one which benefited both countries, was achieved. On the other hand, Indians and Pakistanis seldom meet each other on the subcontinent. Customs rules make it difficult for Indians to read about Pakistan, and vice versa. What could be a natural avenue for the exchange of goods on the subcontinent now is almost devoid of Indo-Pakistani traffic.

The fight for Bangladesh (Bengali nation) in the area of East Pakistan was the most recent—and most serious—confrontation between India and Pakistan since 1965. The Pakistani elections of December of 1970 resulted in the spectacular political rise of East Pakistan's Awami League and of the party's leader, Sheikh Mujibur Rahman, who won so handsomely that he was declared prime minister-designate. The Sheikh's demand for radical autonomy for East Bengal, however, led from March 25, 1971, to a deadly purge of intellectuals and followers of Rahman by the Pakistani Army, the arrest of the Sheikh, and a sweeping military suppression of the independence movement for Bangladesh—a movement spearheaded by the guerrillas, the Mukti Bahini (freedom fighters). In the turmoil and fear thus created, ultimately more than nine million East Bengalis, mostly Hindus, fled to India, presenting to India an intolerable refugee problem in border regions. India assisted the guerrilla movement with military training and armaments, and provided artillery cover for guerrillas seeking safety in Indian territory after completing operations in East Bengal. When no political solution was offered by Pakistan by the winter of 1971, the Indian Army moved early in December in direct support of the Mukti Bahini and forced the surrender of the Pakistani Army in the East after two weeks of fighting. A western front had opened in the meantime, but it too closed with a ceasefire at the time of surrender. India had occupied 1400 square miles of Pakistani territory in the western sector, and Pakistan had occupied about 60 square miles of India. By 1975 the aftermath of the war had been healed to a large extent. Pakistani troops were released from Indian custody, and the leaders of India and Pakistan were speaking together once more. Unfortunately, severe economic distress, corruption in government, and a lack of firm political leadership in Bangladesh resulted in the coup of August 1975 and the imposition of martial law. Freedom has proved to be a bitter pill.

The 1971 war was local, but Peking and Washington supported the Pakistan case, whereas Moscow encouraged the Indian case. As a result of the war, Indo-American relations hit a new low, and the Soviet Union's reputation in India could not be higher. The Treaty of Peace, Friendship, and Cooperation . . ., signed by India and the Soviet Union in 1971, links India and the USSR in ways that may prove to be an obstacle to India's restoration of full accord with the United States.

Kashmir currently remains the most vivid symbol of past differences and deep antagonisms between India and Pakistan. The issue is too complex to detail here. In sum, each country proceeds from different premises. Pakistan argues that possession of the territory should be settled by a plebiscite, as recommended by the United Nations; India argues that the state of Jammu and Kashmir is an integral part of India by reason of the accession agreement of 1947, and that referral to the people already has taken place during elections conducted legally in the state.

The case has not advanced a step toward solution over the years, except that time has tended to stabilize India's possession of the larger part of the area. This, in turn, has resulted in an authoritarian rule in Jammu and Kashmir, in order to squash opinion favoring secession to Pakistan or Kashmiri independence from both India and Pakistan. Azad ("Free") Kashmir, on Pakistan's side, is equally disturbed, and also ruled with a hard hand.

In 1965, a major armed conflict broke out between India and Pakistan over Kashmir, threatening to engulf the subcontinent in a war going far beyond the Kashmir controversy. Pressure from the United Nations, the United States, and the Soviet Union led to a ceasefire. The Soviet Union, in 1966, invited the president of Pakistan and the prime minister of India to meet in Tashkent to work out an amicable solution. The Tashkent declaration, drawn up at the conclusion of the meetings, resulted in a gradual reduction of militant feelings in both countries, and the two armies have moved back to the boundaries existing before the conflict opened in the late summer of 1965, except for the military movements opened by the Bangladesh war of 1971.

There are several feasible solutions to the Kashmir problems: (a) the territory could be ceded, in whole, to one party or the other; (b) they could agree on the status quo; (c) they could agree on a repartitioning; (d) they could agree on a partition, plus a plebiscite in the Vale of Kashmir; (e) Kashmir could be granted condominium status, supported by India and Pakistan; or (f) Kashmir could be granted independence. And there are variations on these themes, of course. But solutions have been barred, thus far, because India sees in Kashmir not only an important link in its geographic line of security and in its economy, but also a largely Muslim area, possession of which tends to justify India's secular political philosophy. Pakistan, in turn, sees Kashmir as advantageous to her military security; as a largely Muslim area of some economic value; and as a land contiguous to Pakistan, one that should, under the principles of partition, have come to Islamic Pakistan. Military, political, and economic issues are here intertwined with questions of religion and prestige, a deadly combination. Only India can resolve the deadlock, since India controls the richest, largest, and most populous part of the territory. Such initiative has not been forthcoming, and her reluctance to move has undoubtedly reduced her effectiveness in world affairs. In fairness, it should be said that India's reluctance to take initiative stems, in part, from the inability or unwillingness of many world powers to try to comprehend the position of India and to understand the enormous complexities of the case. The basically communal argument of Pakistan has convinced the majority of impatient ears, since that side of the matter is much easier to present. Only one willing to dig deeply will ever understand the Indian case and, even when one understands, it is possible to disagree with India's solutions.

In March of 1975 the Parliament of India approved an accord reached between Prime Minister Indira Gandhi and Sheikh Abdullah, the famous leader of Kashmir, that sent Sheikh Abdullah back to Kashmir to head the government. India, it seems clear, has accepted a political solution based on the status quo.

*China.* India was one of the first to recognize the People's Republic of China in 1949, has worked for its recognition elsewhere, and has argued for China's membership in the United Nations from the start. Under the ambassadorship of K. M. Panikkar, India developed a policy of friendship toward China based on a large nation's shrewd respect for a more powerful neighbor. India's was a strategy of functional and cultural involvement. Rather than allow China to become isolated, and thus ever more closely tied to the Soviet Union, India hoped for a China that would be at least as Asian as it was communist—and the more Asian, the better.

In the process of building these relationships, India withstood many a Chinese affront: first over Tibet, then over trading rights, and finally over territory. In retrospect, it must be conceded that India's policy toward China was misconceived. India failed adequately to weigh China's traditional territorial claims along India's northern borders, and she underestimated the militancy of the Chinese Communists in confrontations with Asian bourgeois nationalist regimes, which challenged what Peking felt were legitimate demands.

Since at least 1957, China has laid positive claim to over 50,000 square miles of land in Ladakh, in the North East Frontier Agency, and elsewhere along the Himalayan frontier, and has actually entered and occupied some of this territory, including large segments in the Ladakhi sector of Kashmir. In 1959, when these Chinese military maneuvers were announced in Parliament, an uproar rose in India. The fact that Parliament was kept in the dark for so long on a matter of national concern also led to an unusually heated and extended debate. The armed conflict with China, in October of 1962, resulted in a military defeat for India that approached a catastrophe. China quietly occupied most of the key areas it claimed and then drew back its armies unilaterally.

*Others.* India is interested in safeguarding Nepal and Bhutan as integral parts of the subcontinental security line. Afghanistan, to the northwest, is given special attention because of its proximity to the Soviet Union. Relations with Sri Lanka, to the south, and with Burma, Malaysia, Singapore, and Indonesia, to the southeast, are mutually supportive of nonalignment and neutralism. Members of SEATO are less cordially viewed, and Taiwan is officially ignored. Japan is increasingly of special interest to India, as more detailed knowledge of Japan is accumulated, but their foreign policies clash. The Philippines remains a curiosity, largely a mystery, even to well-informed Indians.

India's relations with the Soviet Union and with the United States have been alternately cordial and testy, in both cases in response to Cold War pressures that have tended to make India suspicious of proposals coming from either side. When, more recently, economic aid and technical assistance began to predominate over ideological wooing, and continued aid from the United States showed its goodwill to be genuine, some shift toward the United States occurred. However, India has nevertheless given higher priority to her relations with the Soviet Union, especially to offset pressure from China. Soviet military assistance to India since 1971 has been substantial, and the enhancement of political accord has accompanied military cooperation.

The British Commonwealth of Nations is another of India's links around the world. Membership in the Commonwealth provides an easy means for maintaining close relations with Great Britain, and is also a comfortable and noncommital way for India to keep informed on the affairs of old Commonwealth friends and new members from Asia and Africa. At first, the most valuable assets of Commonwealth membership were the sterling balances held in London to India's credit and the consulative facilities in London. Now, India, rapidly taking on the status of an old constituent, is in a position to lead in discussions and to use the Commonwealth as a forum to promote the Indian outlook on world affairs. But one should not overemphasize the Commonwealth tie. For India, the Commonwealth is *a* connection, not *the* connection above all others. The Commonwealth, nevertheless, does provide exclusive and clublike contacts with Canada, New Zealand, Australia, and with the many members in Africa and Asia.

Relations with Western Europe—especially France, West Germany, Italy, and the Scandinavian countries —tend to be commercial and cultural, except as colonial issues arise. Latin America, to all but a few in India, is a distant mystery of no great significance, except when votes are counted in the United Nations.

### Panch Shila

*Panch Shila* ("the five principles") of India's diplomacy were first incorporated in the communiqué on the Trade and Intercourse Agreement between India and China issued in Peking on April 29, 1954.[4] This communique put forward the principles as follows:

Both parties agreed to negotiate on the basis of the principles of [1] mutual respect for each other's territorial integrity and sovereignty, [2] mutual nonaggression, [3] mutual non-interference in

[4]The full text can be found in *Foreign Policy of India: Texts of Documents, 1947–1958* (New Delhi: Lok Sabha Secretariat, 1958), pp. 87–93.

each other's internal affairs, [4] equality and mutual benefit, and [5] peaceful coexistence.

Since the signing of the 1954 agreement, India has signed similar agreements with a good many countries in Asia. The hope was that promises to respect one another's territory and national aspirations would, in time, strengthen the likelihood of peace. The outbreak of conflicts between *Panch Shila* nations, especially after the seven-point adaptation was affirmed at the 1955 Bandung Conference, was disappointing to India. China's demand, in 1957, for substantial segments of territory occupied and claimed by India, and the conflict with China in 1962, seemed to have dealt a devastating blow to the *Panch Shila* ideal. One hears little of it today.

### International Trade and Economic Aid

India's chief economic problem is to raise living standards as quickly as possible, with limited material and excessive human resources. Customs, tariff, taxation, and import-export rules are closely calculated to promote industrialization, to discourage or prohibit imports, to extend the exploitation of India's natural resources and to decrease their import, and to increase exports of all kinds. A favorable balance of trade is the object. But the fact is that India can go only so far in developing her economy. Savings are relatively modest and, in any event, inadequate to the necessary investment; goods and services must be imported from hard-currency countries, especially the United States; and food still must be bought outside the country.

India's international economic policy is, therefore, directed at the regulation of trade and also at the gaining of economic aid from abroad in massive amounts. The United States has been the largest subscriber of help since 1947. Loans and grants from the United States have been more than four times as extensive as those from the Soviet Union. The United States is expected to guarantee some in the future, but at much lower levels than in earlier years, as is the Soviet Union. In addition, Great Britain, Canada, West Germany, and Japan, to name a few, have contributed a good deal as well, and probably will continue to do so, but also at reduced levels.[5]

### Nuclear Testing

India has not been a supporter or signer of the Non-Proliferation Treaty. Indeed, India has taken the position that the Treaty is intended to safeguard the rights of the five nuclear powers (the U.S., U.S.S.R., Great Britain, France, and China) at the expense of experiments for peaceful uses of nuclear energy by the developing countries. India sees nothing altruistic in the Treaty, especially when underground nuclear testing, to say nothing of stockpiling multiple-overkill numbers of nuclear weapons by the Great Powers, are not prohibited by the Treaty. India made clear as early as 1967 that she intended to develop nuclear technology and to engage in underground testing for peaceful purposes as soon as possible.

[5]For an analytical treatment of economic aid to India and to the rest of southern Asia, see Charles Wolf, Jr., *Foreign Aid: Theory and Practice in Southern Asia* (Princeton: Princeton University Press, 1960). See also John P. Lewis, *Quiet Crisis in India* (Garden City, N.Y.: Doubleday & Company, Inc., 1963).

On May 18, 1974, at Pokharan on the Rajasthan desert, India conducted its first successful underground nuclear test, thus admitting India to the nuclear club as number six. There was an immediate critical outcry in much of the world's press, but the criticism has died down, except in Pakistan; India's spokesmen have been making increasingly cogent arguments in support of India's position. Whether India's decisive action will lead other weaker powers to "go nuclear" has yet to be seen. If so, the Non-Proliferation Treaty will become a nullity, and the drafting of a new cooperative approach to controls will be necessary.

### The Emergency of 1975

This analysis was written in the summer and fall of 1975—a critical period in Indian politics. In early June 1975 Prime Minister Indira Gandhi was judged guilty by the Allahabad High Court of breaking two electoral laws in the 1971 General Election. Her right to serve as Prime Minister was granted by a judge of the Supreme Court, but without the right to vote in Parliament. In the interim, Prime Minister Gandhi recommended and the President of India declared an emergency on June 26, 1975, that resulted in the jailing, without legal remedies, of many of the most important members of the opposition in Parliament, some members of Mrs. Gandhi's Congress Party, some Maoists, and leaders of several radical dissident groups, both right and left, in India. The Parliament changed the electoral law, with retrospective effect, to protect Mrs. Gandhi from the Supreme Court's review. Relatively rigorous efforts have since been made to lower prices on staple goods, arrest smugglers, encourage land re-

form, and generally alter the malaise into which the country's economy and politics had fallen. The Supreme Court on November 7, 1975, upheld Mrs. Gandhi's appeal, and she regained her right to participate fully in Parliamentary affairs.

The justification for moves to authoritarian modes of governance was the spectre of a collapse of the Indian political and economic order, encouraged by persons the Government alleged were irresponsible. Evidence of such a potential collapse is yet to be forthcoming. Investigations are underway by Mrs. Gandhi's party to seek new constitutional styles to further strengthen executive authority.

The rapid sweep of internal events precludes firm conclusions about the foreign affairs of India. The following summary represents the optimistic view that the emergency will be limited in tenure, that constitutional revisions will be significant but not incompatible with democratic processes, and that a substantial opposition will again arise to lend balance to the political system. In such a situation, it is likely that continuity will be the characteristic pattern of India's future foreign policy. Fundamental changes in the Indian political system, especially increased and long continued authoritarian practices, will affect not only the internal political system, but foreign policy as well.

### SUMMARY

The foreign policy of India has three, interrelated, main themes:

1. the policy of nonalignment, to obviate direct involvement in military or political commitments, thus permitting each issue to be decided on its intrinsic merits as it arises;

2. the policy of positive neutralism, as a technique for unrestricted cultural and personal interrelationships on a global basis, thus opening opportunities for extending the area of peace by all legitimate means; and

3. the policy of national self-interest, to assure the military security of the country and the social and economic well-being of its citizens.

The last point has gained in importance since 1962. Defense policies are now more adequately geared to meet immediate threats to India's territorial interests than they were before the conflict with China.

Nonalignment provides the independent status that, in turn, makes neutralism possible; these two policies seem best calculated, in an interdependent world, to satisfy the national goals of the third and crucial policy, security and progress.

The long range political aspirations of India rest on the democratic base of parliamentary and party government, on adult suffrage, on the rule of law, on responsible administrative and military services, and on the positive search for individual liberty and national freedom. India's foreign policy, as its leaders see it, is devised to serve these ideals of national life.

## SELECTED BIBLIOGRAPHY

AIYAR, S. P. *The Commonwealth in South Asia.* Bombay: Lalvani Publishing House, 1969.

*Asian Survey: A Monthly Review of Contemporary Asian Affairs.* Berkeley: University of California Press. [See January and February numbers each year for a review of Indian and other Asian domestic and foreign developments of the previous year.]

AYOOB, MOHAMMED. *India, Pakistan and Bangladesh: Search for a New Relationship.* New Delhi: Indian Council of World Affairs, 1974.

———, and SUBRAHMANYAM, K. *The Liberation War.* New Delhi: S. Chand, 1972.

BARNDS, WILLIAM J. *India, Pakistan and the Great Powers.* New York: Praeger, for the Council on Foreign Relations, 1972.

BHATIA, KRISHAN. *The Ordeal of Nationhood: A Social Study of India since Independence, 1947–1970.* New York: Atheneum, 1971.

BOWLES, CHESTER. *Ambassador's Report.* New York: Harper & Row, 1954.

BRECHER, MICHAEL. *India and World Politics: Krishna Menon's View of the World.* New York: Praeger, 1968.

———. *Nehru: A Political Biography.* New York: Oxford University Press, 1959.

———. *The Struggle for Kashmir.* New York: Oxford University Press, 1953.

BRINES, RUSSELL. *The Indo-Pakistani Conflict.* London: Pall Mall, 1968.

BROWN, W. NORMAN. *The United States and India, Pakistan, Bangladesh.* 3rd ed. Cambridge, Mass.: Harvard University Press, 1972. (See Chaps. 16 and 17.)

BURKE, S. M. *Mainsprings of Indian and Pakistani Foreign Policies.* Minneapolis: University of Minnesota Press, 1974.

CHOUDHURY, G. W. *Pakistan's Relations with India, 1947–1966.* New York: Praeger, 1968.

CRABB, CECIL V., Jr. *The Elephants and the Grass: A Study of Nonalignment.* New York: Praeger, 1965.

DATAR, ASHA. *India's Economic Relations with the USSR and Eastern Europe, 1953–1969.* Cambridge: Cambridge University Press, 1972.

DONALDSON, ROBERT H. *Soviet Policy Toward India: Ideology and Strategy.* Cambridge, Mass.: Harvard University Press, 1974

FISHER, MARGARET W., ROSE, LEO E., and HUTTENBACK, ROBERT A. *Himalayan Battleground: Sino-Indian Rivalry in Ladakh.* New York: Praeger, 1963.

GALBRAITH, JOHN KENNETH. *Ambassador's Journal: A Personal Account of the Kennedy*

*Years.* Boston: Houghton Mifflin, 1969.

GANDHI, INDIRA. *Aspects of Our Foreign Policy: From Speeches and Writings of Indira Gandhi.* New Delhi: All India Congress Committee, 1973.

GUPTA, SISIR. *Kashmir: A Study of India-Pakistan Relations.* New York: Taplinger Publishing Co., 1966.

HARRISON, SELIG S., ed. *India and the United States.* New York: Macmillan, 1961.

HEIMSATH, CHARLES H., and MANSINGH, SURJIT. *A Diplomatic History of Modern India.* Bombay: Allied Publishers, 1971.

HIGGINS, ROSALYN. *United Nations Peacekeeping, 1946–1967: Documents and Commentary.* Vol. 2, *Asia.* London: Oxford University Press, 1970.

*India Quarterly* (journal). New Delhi: India Council of World Affairs.

KAPUR, HARISH. *The Soviet Union and the Emerging Nations: A Case Study of Soviet Policy towards India.* London: Joseph, for the Graduate Institute of International Studies, Geneva, 1972.

KORBEL, JOSEPH. *Danger in Kashmir.* Rev. ed. Princeton: Princeton University Press, 1966.

LAMB, ALASTAIR. *The China-India Border: The Origins of the Disputed Boundaries.* New York: Oxford University Press, 1964. Issued under the auspices of the Royal Institute of International Affairs.

MAXWELL, NEVILLE. *India's China War.* London: Jonathan Cape, 1970.

MEHTA, BALRAJ. *India and the World Oil Crisis.* New Delhi: Verry Publishers, 1974.

MISRA, K. P., ed. *Studies in Indian Foreign Policy.* Delhi: Vikas Publications, 1969.

MORAES, DOM. *The Tempest Within.* New Delhi: Vikas, 1971.

NEHRU, JAWAHARLAL. *Independence and After: A Collection of Speeches, 1946–1949.* New York: John Day, 1950.

————. *India's Foreign Policy: Selected Speeches, September 1946–April 1961.* New Delhi: Government of India, 1961.

————. *Speeches, 1949–1953.* New Delhi: Government of India, 1954.

————. *Speeches, 1954.* New Delhi: Government of India, 1955 (and annually thereafter to 1964).

NOORANI, A. G. *The Kashmir Question.* Bombay: Manaktalas, 1964.

NORMAN, DOROTHY, ed. *Jawaharlal Nehru: The First Sixty Years.* 2 vols. New York: John Day, 1965.

PALMER, NORMAN D. *South Asia and United States Policy.* Boston: Houghton Mifflin, 1966.

RUSHBROOK-WILLIAMS, L. *The East Pakistan Tragedy.* London: Stacey, 1972.

SEN GUPTA, BHABANI. *Communism in Indian Politics.* New York: Columbia University Press, 1972.

————. *The Fulcrum of Asia: Relations among China, India, Pakistan and the USSR.* New York: Pegasus, 1970.

STEIN, ARTHUR. *India and the Soviet Union: The Nehru Era.* Chicago: University of Chicago Press, 1969.

SUBRAHMANYAM, K. *The Indian Nuclear Test in a Global Perspective.* New Delhi: India International Centre, 1974.

VARMA, S. P., and MISRA, K. P., eds. *Foreign Policies in South Asia.* Bombay: Longmans, Green, 1969.

WHITING, ALLEN S. *The Chinese Calculus of Deterrence: India and Indochina.* Ann Arbor: University of Michigan Press, 1975.

WILCOX, WAYNE. "China's Strategic Alternatives in South Asia," in Tang Tsou, ed., *China in Crisis*, vol. 2. Chicago: University of Chicago Press, 1968, pp. 395–431.

————. *The Emergence of Bangladesh: Problems and Opportunities for a Redefined American Policy in South Asia.* Washington, D.C.: American Enterprise Institute for Public Policy Research, 1973.

WOLF, CHARLES, JR. *Foreign Aid: Theory and Practice in Southern Asia.* Princeton: Princeton University Press, 1960.

# AMERICA'S FOREIGN POLICY: A HISTORICAL PERSPECTIVE

9

*Robert J. Art*

## INTRODUCTION

### The Rise and Decline of Pax Americana

The age of Pax Americana is over. From 1945 until the early 1970s, the United States experienced a world preeminence that only a few nations throughout history have enjoyed. During these years America reigned as the world's foremost military and economic power. She forged a network of alliances that committed her to come to the defense of over fifty nations if they were subject to attack. When she chose to intervene somewhere with military force, she did so at will. For over twenty-five years, she maintained a military force of over a half million men stationed overseas. Through her nuclear might she faced down her foremost adversary in their singular test of wills over Cuba in 1962. Through the sheer size and dynamism of her economy, she generated an economic presence throughout the world that left few areas untouched. She was and still remains the world's best single national market for the sale of manufactured goods and raw materials. Her multinational corporations dominated the economies of some nations and significantly affected those of many others. For hundreds of millions of non-Americans, the American standard of living was the yardstick by which to measure progress. With the exception of the Vietnam War, America's foreign policy for over thirty years, as measured by the objectives she set for herself, was mostly a string of successes, not a series of failures.

The age of Pax Americana was brief but brilliant.

By the early 1970s, America had passed the zenith of her power. It was not that she was becoming weaker absolutely, bur rather that others were becoming stronger in relation to her and were thereby narrowing the gap between their power and hers. By 1972 the Soviet Union had effectively closed the gap between her strategic nuclear forces and those of the United States. In signing the Strategic Arms Limitation Accords of 1972, America publicly accepted this fact and gave to the Russians something that had become central to their foreign policy objectives—official recognition by America of their coequality in nuclear armaments. Although not yet possessing conventional forces as transportable and flexible as those of the United States, the Soviet Union was rapidly developing the sea and air transport capabilities that would enable her to act, not merely as a regional, but also as a global conventional power.

While the SALT Accord of 1972 officially marked the end of America's nuclear preeminence, the devaluation of the dollar in 1971 symbolically marked the passing of America's overweening economic dominance. No longer the fixed bedrock of international economic dealings, the dollar became subject to the same types of pressures that had caused other currencies before it to be devalued. Underlying the dollar's devaluation was a host of structural changes in the noncommunist international economy, but prime among them was the revived prosperity of Western Europe and Japan. Her two erstwhile dependents, after extremely rapid growth throughout the 1960s, had become America's toughest economic competitors by the early 1970s. Reflective of America's recognition of this fact was the dual nature of the 1974 Trade Reform Act: it provided both for the lowering or virtual elimination of tariff and quota barriers *and* their reimposition should foreign competition prove too severe to American industry.

If the United States had passed the zenith of its power by the early 1970s, it nevertheless remained quite powerful. Among the four power centers of the world, the United States still retained the preeminent position. The Soviet Union could not match America's economic strength; Western Europe could not match her military strength; Japan could match neither. But because the gap between her power and that of the other three was narrowing, America could no longer command the same degree of obedience from her allies nor the same degree of restraint from her prime adversary that she once could. While still preeminent, the United States could no longer convert that preeminence into the virtual dominance she once held.

Future historians will record that ironically it was America's very dominance that caused her influence to decline. Largely by design, not by inadvertence, did American statesmen use their nation's power in ways that ultimately caused its singular preeminence to wane. It was the *successes* of post-1945 American foreign policy that brought about the demise of Pax Americana. First was the generosity that America exhibited towards Western Europe and Japan. Prostrate after World War II, these two were rebuilt through American aid, both direct and indirect. With respect to Western Europe, the United States not only poured in over 12 billion dollars in grant aid from 1948 through 1952, but also encouraged and aided the development of the European Economic Community that eventually became the world's largest free trade zone by population size. The EEC now rivals the United States for the world's trade. Through American benevolence Japan was given an access to sell in the American market such that by the early 1970s the United States took over one-third of Japan's total annual exports, exports being the basis for Japan's postwar economic resurgence. For some twenty-odd years, American businessmen never had the same degree of access to sell and invest in the Japanese market that Japanese businessmen had in the American market. Moreover, both Western Europe and Japan were rebuilt and aided in their economic flowering by America's bearing the major military burdens of protecting them. The fact that the United States derived significant economic and other benefits from these actions towards Europe and Japan is important to remember, but it does not alter the central point: the net effect of America's actions was to help fashion her wards into her foremost competitors in the world's markets.

Second, through the exercise of her overweening nuclear superiority in the early 1960s and through her subsequent commitment in the later 1960s to arms control, the United States taught the Soviet Union the disadvantages of strategic inferiority, thereby demonstrated the necessity of acquiring nuclear parity with the United States, and, finally, tolerated the eventual rough parity in nuclear armaments that Russia acquired by the early 1970s. In the history of modern international relations of the last 100 years, no other great power has willingly and con-sciously permitted its foremost military rival to acquire a coequal military preeminence unless constrained by the limits imposed by its own resources. For whatever the reasons that Russia poured offensive missiles into Cuba in 1962, the fact that the United States forced her to take them out caused a worldwide humiliation for Soviet foreign policy that the Politburo determined never to suffer again. The Russians subsequently engaged in a massive ballistics missile building program that brought them up to the levels of America's strength by the early 1970s. Whether American decision makers thought this would be the eventual outcome of the Cuban missile crisis is interesting to speculate upon. But such speculation does not alter the central point: the net effect of America's actions, both in using her nuclear superiority to humiliate Russia and then in deciding not to maintain her own overwhelming superiority, was to allow the Russians to acquire a military preeminence that now rivals America's.

The third reason for the decline of American predominance—her entanglement in Vietnam—is, paradoxically enough, just like the other two factors, a direct result of the successes of post-1945 American foreign policy. But while the first two factors reduced America's power relative to that of her rivals, the third affected her will to use the considerable power that she still retained. From the War of 1812 until Vietnam, the United States had never lost a major war when it had chosen to commit the necessary resources. As much as anything else, Vietnam signified a failure in America's willpower, not in her military power. No nation allied with the type of governments in South Vietnam to which America had tied herself may ever have won that war; but due to their estimates of what the American public would tolerate, successive Administrations did not persevere with the levels of assistance long enough to find out whether such a war was in fact winnable. The net effect of America's failure in Vietnam was to make the nation's foreign policy elite quite reluctant to commit America's military power to situations that do not promise quick, decisive results. Vietnam must be seen as the post-World War II watershed for that most intangible factor—the deference, based on consensus, that a people gives to its government to conduct the foreign affairs of the state. The Vietnam intervention undermined the faith of the American people in the wisdom and integrity of their governmental officials. Just as World War II discredited the virtues that an entire generation of Americans thought neutrality held, so too did Vietnam destroy the consensus that the post-1945 generation had developed in America's internationalist world role. Vietnam was an imperial war fought to preserve the credibility of America's global commitments. Ironically enough, it resulted in their lessened credence because of the disillusionment it produced both at home and abroad.

Within this context of the rise, exercise, and waning of America's singular global dominance, two central questions about post-1945 American foreign policy arise. First, what were the underlying factors responsible for producing America's overweening world power? Second, to what ends did the United States choose to utilize that power? These two broad questions in turn give rise to a host of others. Why did the American public accept such an activist foreign policy when previously it had overwhelmingly favored an isolationist posture? Why was isolationism such a powerful force in pre-1945 American foreign policy? To what lengths did the American government have to go in order to persuade the American people to accept an internationalist role? What political, military, and economic instruments did America fashion in order to implement her global role? How have the Executive and Congressional branches interacted in the setting and implementing of American foreign policy? The remainder of the chapter will deal with these questions.

## ISOLATIONISM BEFORE 1945

No contemporary student of American foreign policy can fully appreciate the revolution that World War II wrought in American thinking unless he understands the profound grip that isolationism held over most Americans before 1941. The central feature of America's foreign policy before then was its political-military nonentanglement with the other great powers. Only once from 1778 until 1949 did America conclude an alliance with another nation that bound her to come to the ally's aid with military force if the ally were attacked.[1] From 1800 until 1949, the United States did enter into treaties

[1]The sole exception was the alliance signed with France in 1778 in order to secure her aid for the colonies' revolt against England. The French alliance enabled the colonies to obtain their independence, but it was not honored by the United States when France found herself at war with England in 1793 and was finally abrogated by America in 1800 as part of an effort to extricate herself from the revolutionary and Napoleonic wars consuming the European great powers.

and understandings with other nations, but none of them involved binding commitments for military assistance of any kind. Isolationism did not mean America's indifference to the actions of other nations, nor did it imply that America pursued a passive foreign policy. But isolationism did mean that for over 150 years Americans refused to commit themselves to a defensive pact with another power.

Two factors were responsible for producing such a remarkable consistency in policy. First were the lessons that the founding statesmen drew from their colonial experience, lessons that were reinforced by the events of the first twenty-five years of independence. Second was the apparent success of the isolationist policy throughout most of the nineteenth century, a success that elevated the founding principles to a virtually unquestioned religion. The grip of isolationism over Americans was thus due to America's earliest experiences and her subsequent successes.

The lessons that the founding fathers drew from their colonial experience were simple. That experience taught them that every time the European great powers fought among themselves, the war spread to the new world. In the heyday of eighteenth-century mercantilism, when colonies were seen as sources of national wealth and prizes to be fought for, Europe's wars quickly became the colonies' wars. Although control over the colonies of the new world was considered of signal importance to the European balance of power, the colonies were nevertheless treated as mere pawns by England and France in the struggle that they waged throughout the eighteenth

century for dominance in Europe.[2] The purpose of the republic's early statesmen in avoiding entangling alliances was thus to isolate the new nations from the one area of the world, namely Europe, that could threaten it with attack. During the first twenty-five years of her existence, moreover, America's colonial experience was repeated once again, for the European great powers were at almost continual war with one another from 1793 until 1815. From 1796 to 1800, America found herself in a quasi-naval war with France. From 1805 until 1812, her trade was subject to severe harassment by England. From 1812 to 1815, she found herself at war with the British and invaded by them.

It is within the context of both her colonial experience and her first twenty-five years of independence that Washington's Farewell Address of 1796 and Monroe's Doctrine of 1823 must be viewed. When Washington urged his countrymen to avoid entangling alliances, he was not stating a general principle against all alliances, but rather one directed against those of a permanent nature. Temporary alliances based on expediential needs of the moment were not ruled out. What was ruled out was the type of alliance that America had signed with France in 1778, a truly "entangling" alliance since it was stated in the text that the alliance would endure "forever." Washington was not con-

[2]See Max Savelle, "The American Balance of Power and European Diplomacy, 1713–1778," in *The Era of the American Revolution: Studies Inscribed to E. B. Greene,* edited by Richard B. Morris (New York, 1939), pp. 140–69; and Max Savelle, "Colonial Origins of American Diplomatic Principles," *Pacific Historical Review,* 3 (1934): 334–50.

cerned solely with the foreign policy implications of such alliances, although the effects of the Franco-American alliance on Anglo-American relations disturbed him. Of equal concern were his perceptions of the disturbances to America's domestic politics that such alliances had and could be expected to have. He saw the debate in the mid-1790s over whom to side with, France or England, as leading to ideological polarization in the United States and to the concomitant development of partisanship and parties, a phenomenon that neither he nor the other founding fathers had either anticipated or desired. Washington's call for the avoidance of entangling alliances was a call for the cessation of ideological polarization. He wanted his fellow citizens to remain neutral to Europe's wars, to desist from allowing their personal preferences for England or France to affect their attitudes and sense of trust toward one another.[3] He did not want America's domestic politics, in short, to become entangled with Europe's power struggles.

Not until the Monroe Doctrine do we see the intellectual codification of the lessons of the early phase of American diplomacy. Monroe's famous message to Congress in December of 1823, actually written by his Secretary of State, John Quincy Adams, was consciously intended by these two men to serve as the beacon to guide America's subsequent foreign policy. It was the first time that all alliances, be they permanent or temporary, were ruled out. Monroe's

[3]See Felix Gilbert, *To the Farewell Address* (Princeton: Princeton University Press, 1961); Alexander de Conde, *Entangling Alliance* (Durham: Duke University Press, 1958) and Joseph Charles, *The Origins of the American Party System* (New York: Harper and Row, 1961).

call for the Old World (Europe) to cease meddling in the New (the United States and Latin America) and for the New to stay out of the Old was directed to both Europeans and Americans. To Europeans, the Administration declared the New World to be off limits for further colonization; to Americans, it declared that Europe's squabbles were beyond the power of the United States to affect and were therefore not objects worthy of American energy. These two statements comprised the "Two Spheres' Principle" of Monroe's Doctrine—that Europe and the New World were two distinct regions, physically isolated from one another, politically disjunct, each with a separate set of concerns. In its earliest official formulation, isolationism as set forth in the Monroe Doctrine was thus a European-oriented policy designed to keep America out of Europe's squabbles by keeping her insulated from them. Not until 1823, therefore, was isolationism proclaimed as the natural and permanent state for America.

That America's early statesmen pointed the nation toward isolationism is not sufficient to explain why isolationism had such a powerful hold over Americans until 1941. It is also necessary to realize that subsequent Americans believed that their interests were best served by adopting such a posture. Developments throughout the nineteenth and early twentieth centuries appeared to confirm the wisdom of the course set by the early statesmen. By 1900 America had expanded to the Pacific and had fulfilled her "natural and manifest destiny" to do so. By 1910 her economy had developed to the point that, by most indicators of economic strength, she had surpassed Europe and had become the world's foremost economic power. By 1905, after forcing England to back down in her border dispute with Venezuela, after evicting Spain from Cuba and Puerto Rico, and after securing from England the right to be the sole builder and owner of a canal across the isthmus, the United States had established unchallenged supremacy over the Caribbean and Latin America. While the European great powers had continued to squabble among themselves, the United States had remained aloof from their quarrels and had built a continental empire that rivaled any that the European powers, save Great Britain, had carved out overseas. Even America's incursion into the western Pacific and East Asia at the turn of the century was effected in a typically American manner. For in attempting to secure access to the China market, the United States took the Philippines from Spain and issued the "Open Door Notes" in 1899 and 1900 that called for respect for China's territorial and administrative integrity and for the right of all interested powers to trade freely within China. The United States shunned a joint Anglo-American or Japanese-American protectorate over the Philippines, rebuffed England's attempts to enlist American aid in preventing China from being carved up the way Africa had been, and instead pursued a strictly unilateral approach in injecting itself into East Asian affairs.

On the eve of World War I, America was the world's greatest power, if measured by potential, not actual, military strength. She clearly was the world's strongest economic power. She had established dominance over Latin American affairs and had laid claim to being a Pacific and East Asian power. All this had been done without having contracted any entangling alliances. In short, isolationism had worked.

The isolationism of the interwar period (1921–1941) and particularly that of the 1930s, however, possessed an urgency and self-consciousness it had never had before 1914. Pre-1914 isolationism was a habitual state of mind for most Americans, bordering on an almost unconscious reflex towards foreign affairs. In the 1920s and 1930s, it was almost as if Americans had constantly to remind themselves that World War I was an aberration and that they had decided to return to normalcy, to political nonentanglement with the rest of the world. During the 1930s, as events in both Europe and the Far East took ominous turns, America's quest for insulation from external developments became more frenzied. She switched from a passive isolationism to an active neutrality. Before the 1930s isolationism simply meant not concluding military pacts. Now, concerned about how and why the United States had become embroiled in World War I, Congress passed a series of laws designed to prevent American citizens and American Presidents from taking actions that could eventually lead to such alliances or even embroil the United States in a war without having contracted any. On the eve of World War II, the United States experienced the era of the neutrality acts, the heyday of Congressional hobbling of Presidential flexibility in foreign affairs. From an Executive declaration in 1823 about the merits of an isolationist posture, the United States by 1937 had passed to a Congressional action designed to force the Executive branch to adhere permanently to such a posture.

Isolationism was thus the most potent force in American foreign policy before 1945. It did not mean strict nonintercourse with the rest of the world. It did not mean cessation of trade with other nations. It did not mean abstinence from meddling in the internal affairs of countries in Latin America or in the Far East. It did not even mean refraining from imperial conquests overseas. What it meant, first and foremost, was a deliberate attempt to keep aloof from Europe's power struggles through a pure unilateralism in making and implementing foreign policy.

## THE NATURE OF CONTAINMENT SINCE 1945

Viewed in historical perspective, America's foreign policy after 1945 has been truly revolutionary. For almost 150 years, from 1800 until 1945, the United States shied away from entangling commitments. In the space of the next 20 years, she became entangled with literally most of the world. Instead of isolationism, she pursued an internationalist policy under the guise of containment, the intent of which was to prevent the spread of communism.

Although containing communism has been the consistent underpinning for post-1945 American foreign policy, containment has nonetheless gone through three distinct phases. During the first phase, from 1945 until 1950, the United States evolved a coherent policy with respect to Europe, but not towards the Far East. The major instruments of policy were political and economic, not military. Containment was

mostly a European policy, certainly not a global one. The policy developed gradually, not all at once, due to the Executive branch's concern over how much activism in foreign affairs the Congress and the public would tolerate. During the second phase, 1950 through 1968, the United States globalized and corrupted its containment policy. The major instruments of policy were alliances, foreign aid, and reliance on military force. The Executive generally had little difficulty in obtaining from the Congress what it considered essential in order to achieve its goals. During the third phase, not yet over, from 1969 onwards, containment was muted but not ended by détente with Russia and China. The instruments of policy began to shift back to prime reliance on political-economic means. The Congress began increasingly to challenge the President's predominance in foreign affairs and slowly but steadily to circumscribe the flexibility he had enjoyed for over twenty years.

During the first phase, the primary threat perceived by American decision makers was, not a direct attack by Russian troops on Western Europe or in the Far East, but rather the internal decay of those nations into communism as a result of the economic disintegration and chaos that they were experiencing in the mid and late 1940s. During the second phase, there were two prime threats. As a consequence of the Korean War, the fear of the fifties was of a direct attack by Russia on Western Europe; as a consequence of Castro's rise to power in Cuba by successful guerrilla warfare and because of Khrushchev's declaration in 1961 that such wars of national liberation were communism's strategy for the future, the fear of the sixties became one of internal subversion in the Third World. During the third phase, the prime threat was no longer external to the United States but came from within: fear that the American public would withdraw its commitment to contain communism and lapse back into isolationism.

Throughout most of this period, then, America's pursuit of containment remained steadfast, but the means she chose in each period to implement it were tailored to the particular form the threat was perceived to have taken. Containment was simply a reactive policy designed to counter Russian initiatives. From 1945 onward, the United States became committed, first, to shoring up the 1945 status quo and then to preserving it essentially unchanged. As with all status-quo powers, America's foreign policy became defensive in tone and precedent-conscious. The foreign policy elite became obsessed with the fear that if America failed to fulfill the terms of any one of her commitments, then the rest would lose their credibility, her foreign policy edifice would crumble, and her world influence would rapidly unravel. This obsession with setting and enforcing precedents created a "domino-mania": if one commitment (domino) that America made was not honored, then all the rest would lose their credibility (would fall). This obsession with precedents created a peace-is-indivisible mentality, in which any action that America took was seen as inextricably linked to every other that she had taken and would take. Foreign policy became a seamless web.

Ultimately, this policy turned reactionary. In defense of democracy, America began to resort too readily to military force in order to solve political problems. In defense of the freedom of peoples to determine their own fate, she gradually tolerated more and more of her client states' right-wing military dictatorships that repressed the very freedom of choice America was supposedly defending. Throughout the containment era, American decision makers were motivated more by the negative than the positive: their actions were designed primarily to forestall communist takeovers than to create or preserve democracy. When there was a risk that democracy could lead to socialism or communism, that risk was not taken. President Kennedy epitomized this mentality when he was deciding what policy to pursue toward the Dominican Republic after the long-lived dictator, Trujillo, was assassinated at the end of May 1961: "There are three possibilities in descending order of preference: a decent democratic regime, a continuation of the Trujillo regime, or a Castro regime. We ought to aim at the first, but we really can't renounce the second until we are sure that we can avoid the third."[4] The long-term goal of democracy was often sacrificed for the short-term expediency of stopping communism. The reason was simple: communism was permanent, irreversible; right-wing military dictatorships, it was thought, could be changed.[5] America could eventually lean on its military clients, but once a state went

[4]Quoted in Arthur Schlesinger, Jr., *A Thousand Days* (Boston: Houghton Mifflin, 1965), p. 769.
[5]I am in debt to Kenneth Waltz for impressing upon me the importance of this point.

communist, all hope for exerting influence over its internal political evolution was lost. Discrimination is the essence of wise statecraft. America's commitment to democracy, framed by an aversion to risks that could significantly alter the status quo, ironically pushed her into the indiscriminate defense of military dictatorship.

### The Forging of Containment, 1945–1949

In 1945 the United States faced a world that had changed radically from that which had prevailed before 1941. All the traditional landmarks were gone. Europe ceased to exist as an independent actor able to exert influence beyond its borders. It became instead the object of the actions of more powerful actors. In the Far East, Japanese power was shattered; China was rent by civil war; Indochina was poised on the verge of one. The wartime policy of cooperation with Russia was dissolving. Russia was in the process of installing communist-dominated governments in Eastern Europe. Alone among the great powers, only the United States emerged unscathed from World War II; America had in fact become the stronger for having fought it. Unlike the situation in 1919 after the end of World War I, after World War II there was not even the façade of a world order, much less a structure for it, behind which the United States could retreat.

*America's European Policy.* Confronted with these circumstances, the Truman Administration's prime concern lay with preserving anticommunist governments in Western Europe, not with imposing democratic governments on Eastern Europe. Some commentators have argued that the Truman Administra-

tion overestimated Russia's power immediately after World War II, that it did not realize how seriously the war had weakened her, and that it was therefore too cautious in dealing with her. Others have argued the reverse: the Truman Administration was well aware of Russia's weakness and tried to exploit it in order to create an American sphere of influence in Eastern Europe, thus denying Russia what was rightfully hers by virtue of the tremendous sacrifices she had made during the war. Both views are wide of the mark. With regard to the latter, the Truman Administration talked long, loudly, and forcefully about the violations to the Yalta Declaration of February 1945 that Russia was committing. (The Declaration promised that free elections would be held in the liberated countries of Eastern Europe.) But the Truman Administration did virtually nothing other than talk, nothing that could have significantly influenced what was occurring there, such as the threat to use military force unless Stalin desisted. If the intensity of a commitment to a goal is measured by the resources devoted to attain it, then America's commitment to preserving democracy in Eastern Europe, or to keeping the door open to American capitalism there, or whatever one calls it, had to rank near the bottom of her list of priorities. All nations have desires that surpass their resources to fulfill them. How scarce resources are allocated among competing goals determines their true relative worth. Preserving the right to hold free elections in Eastern Europe was not worth much to the Truman Administration, if measured by what it was willing to pay in order to get them.

With regard to the first view, the Truman Administration's overestimation of Russia's power or, for that matter, her underestimation of it is relevant only if the Administration was bent on wresting Eastern Europe from the Soviet Union. True, the Administration could have been as vapid as it was in its response to Stalin's actions there because it overestimated Russian strength. But consider the facts. Russian troops were in Eastern Europe; America had none there. Tough talk had been used and proved futile. Stalin had not desisted. The next effective step after tough talk is threats to use force. And such threats always carry with them the risk that they might have to be made good. Only the issuance of such threats could have determined how strong Stalin felt he was, how firm was his resolve, and thus whether the Truman Administration had over-, under-, or correctly estimated Russian power.

Harry Truman chose not to issue such threats for two reasons. First, he calculated, almost certainly correctly so, that the American public would not support another war following immediately on the heels of one they had just finished fighting and one against their recent ally to boot. Immediately after the war's end, the tug of demobilization was too strong to resist, unless one wished to commit political suicide. (Roosevelt had even felt it during the war: at the Teheran Conference in November of 1943, he had told Stalin that American troops would remain in Europe for at most only up to two years after the war's end and that upon victory America would quickly begin to demobilize her armed forces.) If such threats to use force were made with full knowledge that they were not likely to receive the public backing necessary to carry them out, and if they were then called, Truman would have thereby

subjected his diplomacy to a severe loss of credibility at a time when he was desperately trying to muster all the credibility he could. Given the other more important interests to be protected, as will be discussed, such a gamble over Eastern Europe proved too risky to take.

Second, if the United States were to have any hope of reversing the evolution of political events within Eastern Europe by mere threats to resort to force, it had to act sometime before the end of 1945 at the latest. After that, Russia's position there would be so entrenched that mere threats to use force would have even less of a chance of working than they had in 1945; and, consequently, the surety of the need to resort to force would increase. In 1945, however, the Administration was reluctant to issue such threats, strangely enough, out of a fear of endangering the American public's support for an activist, internationalist-oriented postwar foreign policy. The key to the apparent puzzle of how in 1945 an activist, threatening policy towards Russia over Eastern Europe could have undermined the American public's support for an activist foreign policy elsewhere lies with the Truman Administration's view of the political function that the United Nations was to play *within* the United States. Well aware of the mistakes that Wilson had made in not carrying along the American public and the Senate in support of the League of Nations, Roosevelt was quite careful during the war to do everything possible to ensure the public's support for the United Nations, going to such lengths as enlisting Republican Senatorial involvement in the planning for it that went on during the war. Truman continued this policy. To both Presidents the United Nations was to be the guise through which a postwar internationalist foreign policy would be sold to what had historically been a profoundly isolationist public. Given the nature of the Security Council, however, with the veto power that each of the permanent members possessed, it was thought at the time that the United Nations could not function effectively without Russian-American cooperation. To have taken actions in 1945 that threatened war against Russia would have meant risking such cooperation. That, in turn, would have risked discrediting the United Nations as a viable body. And, finally, that would in turn have risked the American public's support for it and by extension their backing for a nonisolationist postwar foreign policy. Thus, both the peculiar linking of events in Eastern Europe to the status of the United Nations and the special role that the United Nations was intended to play within the United States hamstrung the Truman Administration in Eastern Europe.

Clearly, immediately after the war's end, it was the perceived domestic constraints on the use of force, not any estimation regarding the relative strengths of the United States and the Soviet Union, that explains why the Truman Administration reasoned that it could do little more than talk tough in Eastern Europe.[6] But would not the same do-

mestic limits on action also apply to Western Europe? And if that was the case, would it not be cause for the gravest concern because by culture, by tradition, by economic and security interests, Western Europe was the area valued most in America's postwar calculations? The answer to the first question is not definite, but clearly if it were even a tentative "yes," then the answer to the second would be a resounding "yes." But, from 1945 until 1950, these questions, and their answers, were largely academic; therefore, a "yes" answer to each loses most of its force. "Yes" answers to these questions would have been significant only if the Truman Administration had feared that Russian armies were poised in Eastern Europe, ready to march at a moment's notice straight across Western Europe to the Atlantic. The Administration feared no such thing during the first phase, which suggests that it did have a good sense of Russia's capabilities even if it could not with certainty plumb her intentions. From the end of World War II until the beginning of the Korean War in June of 1950, the prime fear concerned the political leverage that the large communist parties of France and Italy could gain from the economic chaos prevailing there. And if these two nations were "subverted" from within, then the political fate of the rest of Europe would be in doubt. During the first phase of containment, the overriding concern of policy makers was to keep Western Europe from going communist; but military means were not used because the

---

[6]In fact, it was not really predisposed to do more than that. The reasons Roosevelt and Truman even talked tough were again mainly to domestic political considerations. Powerful Republican Senators, like Arthur Vandenberg, were making their support for the United Nations dependent upon the Administration's taking a tough stance against Truman's actions in Eastern Europe, even though they, too, were not prepared to risk war in order to reverse events there. These Senators felt pressure from their Eastern Eu-

ropean constituents. For more on the electoral factors, see John Lewis Gaddis, *The United States and the Origins of the Cold War, 1941–1947* (New York: Columbia University Press, 1972); and Lynn Etheridge Davis, *The Cold War Begins* (Princeton: Princeton University Press, 1974).

threat was considered to be primarily political and economic.

It is only in this light that the three major actions of America towards Europe from 1945 to 1949 make sense. Each in their own way, the Truman Doctrine, the Marshall Plan, and the NATO Alliance, were designed to deal with the political-economic aspects of the situation. The Truman Doctrine was the first postwar manifestation of the domino theory. The Truman Administration sent economic aid and some military arms to Greece and Turkey in order to enable the Greek monarchy to win the civil war against the communists and to bolster Turkish resistance against the political pressure that the Soviet Union was placing on her. If Greece and Turkey were allowed to fall under Russian influence, the gateway to the Middle East would be opened, with the attendant threat to the vast oil reserves there. And, so it was reasoned, if the Middle East became fertile field for Russian penetration, then Western Europe, with its dependence on Middle East oil, would ultimately find it necessary to accommodate itself to Russia. Greece and Turkey were the first dominoes that could ultimately lead via the Middle East to the "fall" of Western Europe, to its detachment, that is, from America's influence. If the United States failed to show its mettle in Greece and Turkey, then it would be less able to persuade the noncommunist political forces in France and Italy that their fortunes lay with the United States, or that their efforts to preserve noncommunist governments had a good chance of success. The short-term strategic consequences of the "fall" of Greece and Turkey might not be severe, but the long-term political consequences for Western Europe would

be. Inaction now, it was feared, could very well breed irreversible defeat later on.

The aid to Greece and Turkey embodied in the Truman Doctrine was thus aimed at influencing political developments within Western Europe. The same was true for the Marshall Plan and the NATO Alliance. The Marshall Plan was designed to bring about the economic recovery of Western Europe in order to forestall a communist electoral victory arising from the economic chaos prevailing there. In a little over four years the United States sent to Western Europe over $12 billion in grant aid in order to provide the capital required to reconstruct their war-shattered economies. Economic recovery was deemed so crucial that the United States pressured England and France to amalgamate their two occupation zones in Germany with that of the United States in order to create a West German state. The Americans argued that the economic recovery of France, Italy, and England could not occur unless Germany were also revived. Not American altruism toward her former enemy, but the need to revive Western Europe in order to prevent the emergence of parliamentary communism, was responsible for the beneficial treatment that West Germany received from the United States.

Similarly, the NATO Alliance (The North Atlantic Treaty Organization) was designed to foster the development of strong noncommunist governments in Western Europe. In 1948 the Berlin Blockade, but more particularly the communist coup in Czechoslovakia, clearly demonstrated the political leverage that Russia could gain from mere proximity to a nation, though not actual use within it of her large conventional forces. Russian troops massed on the border of Czechoslovakia intimidated the noncommunist forces within, and prevented them from resisting the bloodless coup staged by the communists. Fearful that Russia might try to repeat this in Western Europe, worried that this coup would demoralize the noncommunist forces there unless something were done, and anxious to offset the profound psychological shock that the fall of Czechoslovakia had produced, the United States formed the NATO Alliance in early 1949. With this pact the United States tied its fate to that of Europe by declaring "that an armed attack against one or more of them [the signatories] in Europe or North America shall be considered an attack against them all." The intent of NATO, however, was not to provide an effective defense against a Russian attack but to deter such an attack. Yet, American policy makers rated the likelihood of such an attack as quite low. Why, then, was the need felt to deter something not thought likely to occur? The answer lies with the larger perspective within which Western Europeans viewed what had happened in Czechoslovakia, and it illustrates the political motive the Truman Administration had in entering into this alliance. Europe's historical memory was much longer than America's; it was replete with duplicity in dealing with allies. Czechoslovakia, moreover, had a special symbolism. It had been sacrificed by France and England to Hitler in order to protect themselves from war in 1938. Europeans had also not forgotten that America's commitment to them after World War I was short-lived. What the Europeans had once done to Czechoslovakia, what the Americans had once done to Europe, could happen again. In order to erase Europe's fears that America would lapse back into isolationism and sell them out once the going got tough, the Truman Administration formed NATO. The essence of the alliance was political: to convince Europeans that America had "staying power."[7] Only if they were confident of this could they be expected to throw their lot in with the United States. NATO was thus to be Europe's security blanket behind which the aid provided by the Marshall Plan would resurrect her.

*America's Far Eastern Policy.* The policy toward Europe was clear and coherent. A definite distinction was made between America's interest in Western as opposed to Eastern Europe. A series of steps, mainly political and economic, was taken in order to do that which was necessary to keep Western Europe in America's camp. Unlike its European policy, however, America's Far Eastern policy had no such coherency. Instead it was marked by temporizing and expediency, with no overarching strategy of containment applied there. That did not come until after the outbreak of the Korean War, when America's policy toward the Far East as a whole finally crystallized.

There was in fact not one Far Eastern policy, but really four—one for Indochina, one for China, one for Korea, and one for Japan—with no clear-cut linkages among them. The policy toward Indochina was reluctant deference to the French, who were in the process of reimposing their colonial control there. The United States was officially opposed to imperialism, but it tacitly sup-

[7]See Robert E. Osgood, *NATO: The Entangling Alliance* (Chicago: University of Chicago Press, 1962), Chap. 2.

ported the French effort because that was the price they demanded for their participation in NATO and for the creation of a West German state. America's strategy in Europe thus dictated her policy toward Indochina. Before 1950 the most the United States did there was to urge the French to give autonomy or independence to Indochina so as to be able to co-opt the cause of antiimperialism and to weaken the political appeal of the Vietminh. It is important to stress the tacit and reluctant nature of America's political support for the French effort at this time. For while the French were in fact fighting Ho Chi Minh and the communists, the United States saw no Russian design to take over Asia; or if it did, it certainly did not get exercised about it and did not proclaim a holy war against Vietnamese communism or even communism in Asia. Thus the Truman Administration made no linkage before June of 1950 between the communists in Vietnam and those in China, but instead kept them quite distinct. By 1948, in fact, it had written off the Chinese Nationalists, had concluded that the Chinese communists would ultimately triumph, and was searching for ways to accommodate itself to a communist China. This search yielded an initial estimate that a China gone communist would not be harmful to American interests because of the calculation that the traditional hostility between Russia and China and the antagonistic force of their nationalisms would easily override any of the ties that might arise from the sharing of a common Marxist ideology. There was even no fear that a communist China would be out to take over all of Asia.[8] Here is

clear evidence that not until somewhere between July 1949 and June 1950, the year during which the Truman Administration began to clarify a containment policy in the Far East and worldwide, did the United States see a monolithic communist threat, a central direction by the Soviet Union over world communism, or a Russian design to take over the world.

The policy with regard to Japan was clear concerning how to deal with her domestic affairs, but not beyond that. The United States had prevented Russia from involving herself in Japan's postwar occupation and kept her as a sole American preserve. Japan was being democratized under America's tutelage, but with the collapse of Chinese power in the region, no definite plans had yet been made with regard to the role Japan might play in Far Eastern politics, because the United States had no coherent policy toward the region. It did not sign a peace treaty with Japan until 1951 and did not permit her to rearm until 1955. Again, not until after the outbreak of the Korean War did America's thinking about Japan's foreign role begin to crystallize. Finally, planning towards Korea was probably the most muddled. The United States had rushed troops into Korea to accept a Japanese surrender there so that the Soviet Union could not occupy the entire peninsula. But with Russian armies in the north and American troops in the south, Korea quickly became divided. The United States pledged itself to the peaceful reunification of Korea, but by late 1947 had decided that its troops stationed

[8]See Tang Tsou, *America's Failure in China,*

*1941–1950* (Chicago: University of Chicago Press, 1963), Chap. 12.

there were a liability and withdrew them in 1948. Economic aid and defensive arms were sent, but there were no plans for using American troops if South Korea were attacked.

What is most remarkable about American thinking towards Korea before June of 1950, in view of the dramatic reversal in policy that occurred at the outbreak of the Korean War, is this: until South Korea was attacked, the Truman Administration saw no significant linkage between a communist military conquest of the Korean peninsula and the political situation within Japan. The only potential linkage made was a military, not a political one; and because it was thought easy to deal with, the linkage was of no real concern. From 1945 until the Korean War, America's defense planning centered on a general war with Russia, not on a limited one with either her or one of her client states. If in such a war the Soviet Union occupied the entire Korean peninsula, the disadvantage which that might pose for America's defense of Japan would be tactical, not strategic, and could be handily dealt with by America's sea and air power based in Japan. Through interdiction the United States could thus quickly neutralize any Russian military threat to Japan from the mainland. Unlike Europe, where the Truman Administration saw a clear linkage between the proximity of Russian military power and the evolution of political events within America's sphere of influence, it saw no such thing, or chose to discount it, in the relation of Korea to Japan. Before June of 1950, the Administration did not conclude that a Korea gone communist might influence the political debate then raging in Japan over the future course that

her foreign policy should take, a debate which pitted the neutralists who favored nonalignment for Japan against the conservatives who wished to throw Japan's fortunes in with the United States. There was no calculation that a Korea having recently fallen to the communist camp might help tilt Japan towards neutralism.

The reason this calculation was not made may have been due to the gap developing between America's foreign policy commitments and the military power available to back them up. Until she began a major rearmament effort in 1950, America's military power was stretched thin. In the order of priorities, the defense of Korea loomed small. Japan was the prime concern, and because any military threat to her from Korea would occur only in the context of a general war with Russia, such a threat could be handled from Japan. Necessity may thus have fathered policy: the lack of sufficient forces to defend Korea may have led to deeming her unimportant to America's Far Eastern interests. Another reason the above calculation was not made may also have been due to the estimate that a general war with Russia in the near future was not likely. A limited war was not even envisioned. If these calculations were correct, there was no urgency to anticipate how highly unlikely events in Korea might influence political developments within Japan. Until June of 1950, in fact, the primary worry of the Truman Administration about Korea was, not that the North Koreans and Russians would march south, but that the South Koreans would march north. For whatever reasons, by its actions the United States put Korea in a never-never land. America had pledged herself to reunify Korea, but had no plans for how to do so other than to call for elections supervised by the United Nations. The United States had deliberately refrained from giving the South Koreans the offensive weapons that might have enabled them to achieve reunification by force of arms. America was pledged to the existence of an independent South Korea, but had made no commitments to defend her if she was attacked. Her importance to the United States was not intrinsic but derivative by virtue of her proximity to Japan. By deliberate omission she was publicly excluded from the defensive perimeter that American officials drew in the Far East in late 1949 and early 1950 and that clearly delineated the nations which the United States would protect by force of arms. Before the Korean War, in effect, the United States had liquidated its commitment to preserve an independent South Korea.

## The Globalization of Containment, 1950–1968

By 1949, then, the United States had developed a clear containment policy for Europe but not for the Far East. In both areas the likelihood of war with Russia was deemed low, and that estimate governed the policy pursued in each. As had historically been the case, mainland Asia ran a poor second to concern for Europe. In fact, as we have seen, the only reason that the United States had backed France in Indochina was to gain her support for NATO. The same was true for the Truman Administration's backing of the Chinese Nationalists after 1947. Even though it thought their defeat inevi-

table, the Truman Administration continued to send economic and military aid to the Nationalists only because that was the price demanded by the Republicans in Congress for their support of the Democrats' European policy. In a curious way, then, events in the Far East were linked to those in Europe, but only in the sense that the exigencies of her European policy—the need to buy French and Congressional support—shaped much of America's Far Eastern policy. In no way, however, were they linked in the sense that the Administration was operating on the basis of a belief in the indivisibility of peace or upon a conviction about the monolithic nature of communism. Commitments were being made and honored in the Far East, but not because they were believed to reflect on American credibility in the minds of Europeans. (The Administration in fact viewed the China policy it had to pursue in just the reverse manner: because resources were so scarce, aid to China detracted from its commitments to Europe.) In this regard, therefore, the Truman Administration acted as if events in Europe and the Far East were discrete and disjunct.

*Planning for Global Containment: July 1949 to June 1950.* The Korean War soon changed that. But before its outbreak, the United States began to take tentative steps in two directions —one toward adopting a containment policy in the Far East and another toward planning for a systematic containment policy for the entire world that would relate America's global interests to her military power.

With regard to the Far East, there were two events—Mao Tse-tung's foreign policy pronouncement of July 1, 1949 and the Sino-Soviet

Treaty of Friendship and Alliance—
that pushed the Truman Administration towards planning for a coherent containment policy there.
Mao's speech shattered the Administration's initial calculation that
Sino-Soviet relations would be antagonistic rather than harmonious.
In his speech Mao proclaimed essentially what Secretary of State Dulles
was to say later on in the 1950s, that
is, "if you're not with us, then you're
against us," that neutrality in the
communist-capitalist struggle was
not possible, that one was forced to
choose sides. Mao aligned China
with the Soviet Union in the worldwide struggle against the forces of
imperialism led by the United States.

> The Chinese people must lean either
> to the side of imperialism or to that of
> socialism. There can be no exception.
> There can be no sitting on the fence;
> there is no third road. . . . Not only in
> China but throughout the world, one
> must lean either to imperialism or to so-
> cialism. There is no exception. Neutral-
> ity is merely a camouflage; a third road
> does not exist.[9]

This speech could have been dismissed as mere rhetoric for internal
domestic consumption, but it was
followed by the Sino-Soviet Treaty
in which Stalin returned to China
most of the territorial concessions
that he had wrested earlier from the
Nationalists as his price for Russia's
entry into the Pacific War. Here was
concrete proof that the binds of
ideology between them were
stronger than the repellent forces of
their nationalisms. As a consequence of Mao's speech, the Truman Administration began to take
tentative steps towards formulating
a containment policy in Asia. Secre-

[9]*Ibid.*, p. 505.

tary of State Acheson instructed Ambassador at Large Philip Jessup that
"it is a fundamental decision of
American policy that the United
States does not intend to permit further extension of communist domination on the continent of Asia or in
the southeast Asia area," that the
United States must "make absolutely certain that we are neglecting
no opportunity that would be within
our capabilities to achieve the purpose of halting the spread of totalitarian communism in Asia," and that
he should "draw up . . . possible programs of action relating to various
specific areas not now under communist control in Asia under which
the United States would have the
best chance of achieving this purpose."[10]

This policy must be termed highly
tentative, however, because of the
other actions that the United States
was pursuing in the area. At the
same time that Acheson was calling
for a commitment to containment in
Asia he was also removing South
Korea from America's defense perimeter; he was failing to support the
French war in Indochina in any way
except verbally; he was not lifting a
finger to reverse the tide of events
within China; he was not proposing
to interject the United States again
in a military way into the Chinese
civil war by defending the Nationalists from a communist attack in their
redoubt on Taiwan; he was not,
finally, pushing for a rapid rearmament of Japan that a containment
policy could logically require. Acheson was doing, in short, what Amer-

[10]Memorandum for Ambassador Jessup,
July 18, 1949, in United States Senate, Committee on Foreign Relations, *Hearings on the
Nomination of Philip Jessup to be the U.S. Representative to the Sixth General Assembly*, 82nd Congress, 1st Session, p. 603.

ica had traditionally done in her policy towards the Far East: making commitments far in excess of what she was willing to commit in resources to back them up. Until all the documents are available for this period, therefore, we must conclude that at this time the containment policy towards the Asian mainland and beyond was highly tentative, that it was not likely to be implemented if it proved too costly, and that before June of 1950 there was in fact no real containment policy towards the Far East but only the *desire* to have one.

With regard to the second tentative step, the Truman Administration began systematically to assess the relation between its security and that of the entire free world and to analyze the type of military force that such a global containment policy would require. This effort resulted in what became known as NSC-68 (National Security Council Study #68), the first high-level review since 1945 of America's evolving foreign and military policies. NSC-68 took stock of what the nation had done over the last five years and of where it should be going over the next several. The immediate catalysts for the study were the Russian explosion of an atomic bomb in August of 1949, three years before the American intelligence community predicted it would occur, the triumph of the communists on mainland China in late 1949, and Truman's uncertainty over whether the United States should begin development of a hydrogen bomb now that the Russians had the atomic one. The combined effect of these developments was to produce a belief among some, but not all, top level decision makers that America

may have been too piecemeal in its approach to containment, that a worldwide perspective which would integrate all the various parts into a coherent whole was necessary, and that recent Russian military developments required the United States to build up her military forces significantly if she were to be able to deter Russian aggression.

The four central recommendations of NSC-68 flowed directly from the impetuses for the study. First, because Russia had obtained the atomic bomb, the United States needed to improve its massive destructive capabilities. Second, because the mutual possession of nuclear weapons would weaken America's ability to deter war and especially local wars through her nuclear weapons alone, she needed to develop a conventional capability sufficient to deter or fight them. Third, as a consequence of the first two, a major rearmament effort was necessary; and it was one the United States could well afford to undertake. Fourth, the reason these three steps were necessary was because the United States could no longer afford to "distinguish between national and global security." In the words of Paul Hammond, NSC-68 analyzed

... the relationship between the strength of the United States as the center of the free world, with the strength of the countries on its periphery, the relationship of economic and military programs to each other, and of both to psychological factors of strategy. It stressed the importance of allies to American security, the inadequate military preparedness of the free world, hence the need for improving it. ... [NSC-68] concluded that the best way to build free-world military strength would be to begin at the "center" with the building up of American military capabilities. . . .[11]

NSC-68 was thus a call for major American rearmament because of a communist threat more potent and pervasive than had theretofore been realized. NSC-68 asked for major rearmament, in short, because it predicated the need for a global containment policy.

What must be stressed, however, is that NSC-68 *asked* and *predicted*. It was not a program the President had made his own, but rather a joint State-Defense recommendation to the President about what type of national security program he should make his own. It was a staff study, not a policy ready for implementation. NSC-68 was completed in the late spring of 1950. For that reason its exact effect on American foreign policy is difficult to assess, since the Korean War came only a few months later. Its significance, however, is clear: it demonstrates that just before the Korean War, which was the catalytic event that globalized containment, the United States government was moving toward an indivisibility-of-peace view of its security and toward a containment policy heavily laden with military overtones. NSC-68 marked the beginning of the shift from a restricted political-economic containment policy to an open-ended military one. Once Korea occurred, NSC-68 provided the intellectual justification for the major rearmament that subsequently followed. Whether containment would have been globalized and militarized without the Korean

[11]The definitive study of NSC-68 is that by Paul Y. Hammond, "NSC-68: Prologue to Rearmament," in Warner R. Schilling, Paul Y. Hammond, and Glenn H. Snyder, *Strategy, Politics, and Defense Budgets* (New York: Columbia University Press, 1962), pp. 267–379.

War is anybody's guess. What is not is that America's foreign policy was showing distinct, even if preliminary, signs of evolving that way right before June of 1950.

*The Effects of Korea on American Foreign Policy.* The Korean War, together with the Vietnam War, are the two most important single events for shaping the general contours of post-1945 American foreign policy. The Korean War served as the catalyst that helped forge a global containment policy; the Vietnam War was the one that helped shatter it. The Korean War had two general effects on American foreign policy. First, it undermined all the key assumptions that had governed the conduct of foreign policy in the previous five years. Second, it reinforced the predisposition, which was shared by most top level decision makers, not to repeat in the post-1945 world the mistakes that America had made in the interwar period (1919–1939). With the outbreak of the Korean War, therefore, a "mind-set" was crystallized that significantly influenced the next twenty years of American foreign policy.

There were three key assumptions of the 1945–49 period that Korea helped to undermine. First, instead of viewing separate national communisms as discrete phenomena, the United States took the view that communism was monolithic, that is, that it was centrally directed and controlled by the Soviet Union. The Truman Administration had already begun to think this way starting with its reassessment towards the implications of a communist China in mid-1949. In early 1950, after China and Russia recognized Ho Chi Minh, the United States applied the same attitude toward Indochina and began to view the French effort not as anticolonial but as anticommunist. Korea clinched the process, but in a dramatic way that had wide public recognition and effect. The Truman Administration assumed that North Korea would not have attacked South Korea had it not had Russia's orders, support, or merely encouragement to do so. Whether Russia gave such support, whether she even knew of the attack before it was launched, is still not known. But such knowledge is irrelevant to the central point: the Truman Administration did not know either. However, in a situation where a state was created, politically supported, and militarily armed by the Soviet Union, it was *reasonable* to assume that such a state was indeed under Russian control. Events since 1947 in Eastern Europe must have contributed to this assessment. For with the beginning of the Marshall Plan, Stalin imposed the rigid Stalinist system on Eastern European communism—total subjection to Stalin's personal authority and whims, not merely to Russian control—in order to prevent the states there from being weaned away from Russia to an economically revived Western Europe.[12] Given the ignorance prevailing in the American government about the North Korean regime, there was no reason *not* to believe that Stalin exerted the same control over North Korea that he had over Eastern Europe, especially since both these areas, unlike China or Indochina, had been occupied by Russian armies. Decision makers must always act before they have complete information about the events with which they must deal. The Tru-

man Administration jumped to a conclusion that was justifiable to make at the time, *even if it may have been wrong*, something which the West to this day still does not know.

Second, because the Korean attack seemed to give dramatic proof that the Soviet Union was the world control center of communism, the Truman Administration concluded that the United States could no longer treat events in the Far East and Europe as if they were disconnected. The Korean War was what tied the Far East to Europe. It drove home the indivisibility-of-peace proposition in a way that no staff paper could. Such a blatant act, so reasoned the Truman Administration, could not go unanswered by the United States; for if it did, America's word would have no credibility elsewhere, to friend and foe alike. Korea per se was again not intrinsically important; it was the psychological effects that would be produced by not fighting there which were. Unless it responded, the Truman Administration worried that the Europeans, who had just concluded a defensive pact with the United States, and the Japanese, who were in the process of deciding whether to conclude one, would have no faith in alliances with America. Korea was thus a war fought by the United States initially in order to demonstrate the credibility of its commitments to its European and prospective Japanese allies.

Finally, the Korean attack demonstrated that internal subversion through economic and political chaos was not the sole or even primary threat. Direct military attack had now to be accounted for. After Russia had exploded the atomic bomb in 1949, the American intelligence community calculated that no

---

[12] Adam B. Ulam, *Expansion and Coexistence* (New York: Frederick A. Praeger, 1968), Chap. 8.

military action would occur before Russia had built up a nuclear arsenal, which would not be before the middle 1950s. NSC-68 had reasoned that local wars were more likely now that the Soviet Union had the security with which to wage them and now that the mutual possession of nuclear weapons decreased the chances of a direct, general war between Russia and America. But neither foresaw an attack upon Korea; neither predicted military action was inevitable. The Truman Administration had unconsciously extended its view of what was the primary threat in Europe—internal subversion—to Korea when it had discounted the likelihood of a military attack there. Once Korea was attacked, the Administration consciously transferred this materialized threat in the Far East back to Europe. If Russia could order a military action by a nation in which she no longer had combat troops, then she certainly could do so in those where she had large armies. Once again Korea provided what seemed to be incontrovertible proof that the threat had changed in form and, therefore, that the means to counter it had better change too. Rearmament became the order of the day. America's defense budgets throughout the 1950s achieved a level three times greater than they had been in the late 1940s, reaching $45 to $50 billion as opposed to $15 billion. And as further illustration that Europe still counted more in America's calculations than the Far East, most of the rearmament effort during the Korean War went to build up the military forces in the United States and Europe, not in Korea.

Korea thus gave immediate proof that communism had to be viewed in a worldwide perspective, but the full force of the Korean War on American policy makers cannot be understood unless it is seen in the broader historical context that they themselves at the time placed it. For the generation of policy makers that have run America's foreign affairs from 1945 to the present, Korea threatened a repetition of what they had lived through in the 1930s, to wit, piecemeal aggression that was abetted by dealing with it on a piecemeal basis. For these men the lessons of the 1930s were clear. Appeasement stimulates an aggressor; it does not satiate him. Aggression is monolithic; if one aggressor gets away with it, others will be emboldened to try. Had England, France, and America only stood up to Japan in China or Mussolini in Ethiopia, so these men at the time and later argued, Hitler might well have been deterred in Europe. The appeasement of Hitler at Munich, at Czechoslovakia's expense, moreover, only emboldened him to go for Poland next and subsequently brought on World War II.

Truman was a product of the 1930s in this regard. As President, he was determined not to allow this sequence to be repeated. Aggression could only be dealt with effectively if it were met forcefully and decisively at its first showing. Truman clearly describes the parallel that he drew between Korea and the 1930s after he had just been notified of the North Korean attack. On the plane from Missouri to Washington, he ruminated:

The plane left the Kansas City Municipal Airport at two o'clock, and it took just a little over three hours to make the trip to Washington. I had time to think aboard the plane. In my generation, this was not the first occasion when the strong had attacked the weak. I recalled how each time that the democracies failed to act it had encouraged the aggressors to keep going ahead. Communism was acting in Korea just as Hitler, Mussolini, and the Japanese had acted ten, fifteen, and twenty years earlier. I felt certain that if South Korea was allowed to fall, Communist leaders would be emboldened to override nations closer to our own shores. If the Communists were permitted to force their way into the Republic of Korea without opposition from the free world, no small nation would have the courage to resist threats and aggression by stronger Communist neighbors. If this was allowed to go unchallenged, it would mean a third world war, just as similar incidents had brought on the second world war. It was also clear to me that the foundations and the principles of the United Nations were at stake unless this unprovoked attack on Korea could be stopped.[13]

Truman acted in Korea because he viewed it as the test of America's willingness to assume the leadership of the free world that NSC-68 had called for. This is how the United States portrayed its actions to its allies:

> Our allies and friends abroad were informed through our diplomatic representatives that it was our feeling that it was essential to the maintenance of peace that this armed aggression against a free nation be met firmly. We let it be known that we considered the Korean situation vital as a symbol of the strength and determination of the West. Firmness now would be the only way to deter new actions in other portions of the world. Not only in Asia but in Europe, the Middle East, and elsewhere the confidence of peoples in countries adjacent to the Soviet Union would be very adversely affected, in our judgment, if we failed to take action to protect a coun-

try established under our auspices and confirmed in its freedom by action of the United Nations. If, however, the threat to South Korea was met firmly and successfully, it would add to our successes in Iran, Berlin, and Greece a fourth success in opposition to the aggressive moves of the Communists. And each success, we suggested to our allies, was likely to add to the caution of the Soviets in undertaking new efforts of this kind. Thus the safety and prospects for peace of the free world would be increased.[14]

The Korean War was thus the pivotal event in America's foreign policy from 1945 to 1965. It was not that Korea radically altered the general contours of policy as they had been evolving since 1945, but rather that Korea solidified, crystallized, and broadened them. The Truman Doctrine is often taken as the proof that the United States had quite early on decided to adopt a global containment policy. Certainly the words that Truman used in order to defend his aid request support this view: "I believe that it must be the policy of the United States to support free peoples who are resisting attempted subjugation by armed minorities or by outside pressures." But these words were rhetoric designed to obtain support from a public that had traditionally thought more in ideological than in balance-of-power terms when thinking about foreign affairs. The rhetoric used belied the policy intended. For immediately after Truman's speech to the Congress, then Under Secretary of State Acheson in his testimony to the Senate Foreign Relations Committee qualified the unlimited nature of the Doctrine:

> Any requests of foreign countries for aid will have to be considered according

---

[13]Harry S. Truman, *Memoirs,* Vol. 2 (Garden City: Doubleday, 1956), 332–33.

[14]*Ibid.,* pp. 339–40.

to the circumstances in each individual case. In another case we would have to study whether the country in question really needs assistance, whether its request is consistent with American foreign policy, whether the request for assistance is sincere, and whether assistance by the United States would be effective in meeting the problems of that country. It cannot be assumed, therefore, that this government would necessarily undertake measures in any other country identical or even closely similar to those proposed for Greece and Turkey.[15]

Acheson's qualifiers could, of course, have been a ploy by the Administration to lead Congress on, to ask piecemeal with full knowledge that the ultimate intent was to obtain a global reach. Certainly the request for the Marshall Plan a few months later could support this view. But none of the other actions until 1950 do. The Truman Administration limited itself primarily to Europe. It was, in fact, trying to keep down governmental spending, which a huge foreign-aid program would not have helped. It is fair to conclude, therefore, that the Truman Doctrine's rhetoric did not reflect its intent. It was the Korean War, not anything before, that marked and forged a globalized containment policy.

*Deterrence and Subversion in the 1950s and 1960s.* With Korea, the main contours of American foreign policy were set until the Vietnam War challenged them and until the Nixon Administration began subtly to alter them. The mind-set towards communism that Korea crystallized by no means wholly predetermined America's subsequent actions, but because it was the framework with

[15]Quoted in George F. Kennan, *Memoirs,* Vol. 1 (Boston: Little, Brown, 1967), pp. 321–22.

which decision makers approached and interpreted succeeding events, it did shape the general tenor of America's response to them. Korea was one of those pivotal decisions that influences much of what follows them. What the United States did from 1950 through 1968 was not inevitable, but neither was it wholly accidental. During these years there were, of course, differences in tone, style, and substance between Democratic and Republican Administrations. By comparison with Democrats, Republicans were more restrained in their activism, even if their rhetoric sounded more fearsome. Under Kennedy and Johnson the Democrats gave more attention to fashioning effective means for military interventions than did the Republicans under Eisenhower. Europe loomed large and primary for both, but by comparison with Republicans, Democrats tended to give more nearly equal attention to the Far East. The Republicans worried mostly about direct military attack by the communists on the nations bordering on, or in close proximity to, their spheres of influence and, consequently, directed American resources to fashioning these states into strong, defensible, military bastions. The Democrats continued that policy in the 1960s, but decolonization brought an obsession with communist wars of national liberation and their concomitant counterinsurgency techniques. The differences in Democratic and Republican policies, however, are clearly overshadowed by the basic similarities. None of these Administrations intervened in every area they could have, but all viewed every situation from the standpoint of how America's specific actions there would affect her general relation with the Russians. Not every adverse situation was contained, but each was scrutinized with a view as to whether not acting would cause America's general world position to deteriorate. Containment in the *conceptual approach to events*, not in omnipresent interventionism, was the essence of a global policy. The basic continuity of this approach over four different Administrations suggests that global containment was a bipartisan foreign policy.

There were three central hallmarks to this twenty-year global policy: a proliferation of new commitments and a strengthening of old ones; a reliance on military power and a quest for general military superiority in order to deter attack and to maintain a political offensive against communism; and a willingness to resort to military intervention where the threat of force did not suffice. The need to make new commitments and to strengthen old ones stemmed directly from Korea. America's policy toward South Korea before the attack seemed to give incontrovertible evidence that a prior commitment to defend a nation against attack was necessary in order to prevent it. By immediate hindsight, the omission of South Korea from America's defensive perimeter was viewed as directly responsible for bringing on the North Korean invasion. As a consequence, the United States proceeded to conclude a whole series of such commitments: with Japan in 1951 through the Japanese-American Security Treaty; with New Zealand and Australia in 1951 through the ANZUS Pact; with nations in the Middle East and South Asia in 1955 through CENTO; with nations in Southeast Asia in 1954 through SEATO; and over the years with a host of nations,

like Spain, Thailand, and the Philippines, through numerous base rights' agreements. Most of these commitments were made in the 1950s, but all were honored during the 1960s. The Korean War thus pushed American policy makers one step beyond Munich: it was no longer sufficient to stand fast against aggression once in order to deter it again; now it was necessary to commit in advance to prevent aggression. Ambiguity of intent, flexibility in purpose, unpredictability in response—these were not viewed as diplomatic virtues during this period. As a consequence of the Korean War, the United States globalized its NATO policy; that is, it proliferated deterrent pacts around the world. In the space of little over eight years from 1949 through 1956, the United States went from having no such commitments to endorsing well over twenty-five of them.

Strengthening old commitments meant bolstering the NATO Alliance, which was only one year "old." Beginning with Korea, three successive Administrations thought it necessary to take significant steps designed to enhance in European eyes the credibility of America's commitment to them. The Truman Administration sent four combat divisions to Europe as tangible symbols, hostages in effect to a Russian attack, of the depth of the American commitment to defend Europe. It also worked to turn NATO into a semiintegrated multilateral military force, rather than permit it to remain merely a loose coalition of separate national military forces. In order to redress NATO's presumed inferiority in conventional forces vis-à-vis the Warsaw Pact, the Eisenhower Administration sent thousands of tactical nuclear warheads to Europe (though they were to remain under American control). The troops were guarantees that America would fight if Europe were attacked; the tactical nuclear weapons were guarantees that America would use her nuclear arsenal in such an attack. But Europe wished neither to be used. It did not want another war of liberation fought on its soil, nor did it wish to have nuclear weapons devastating the very soil they were intended to defend. The NATO allies were persuaded, largely by the United States, that the troops and nuclear weapons were the means best suited to deter war.

The Kennedy Administration went two steps further. In order to offset any lingering doubts that Russia had a nuclear superiority over the United States, the Administration engaged in a massive missile-building program at home. The main intent was to persuade the Europeans that America had the strategic nuclear wherewithal to take care of them and thereby that they need not acquire or keep their own national nuclear forces. America's own nuclear buildup was meant to restore Europe's confidence in American power in order to discourage further proliferation of nuclear forces there. The Kennedy Administration also launched a large conventional buildup at home and pushed the Europeans to do so too. The logic was that these forces would give greater credence to deterrence because they would demonstrate that NATO had a true conventional war-fighting capability. Enhancement of its conventional capability would add to its deterrent power, reasoned the Administration, because if the Russians knew NATO could fight a conventional war, they would not launch one. To

the Europeans, however, such a buildup only weakened nuclear deterrence, because it signaled the Russians that the Americans did not put much credence in the deterrent value of their nuclear forces; otherwise, why would they build up their conventional ones?

It is not possible to know which view is correct. Strangely enough, both might be. Nor is it possible to state with certainty whether the Europeans over the years have been as worried about a Russian attack on them as have the Americans, though they probably have not. What is clear is that successive Administrations were worried enough about the credibility of the American commitment to NATO that they took vigorous steps to counter Russia especially when she was presumed to have an advantage. In the age of the nation state, however, no one country can be absolutely assured that another will come to its aid if it is attacked. The age of nuclear weapons has compounded this problem. By its commitment to use its nuclear forces against Russia if she attacks Europe, the United States has opened up the American homeland to possible nuclear devastation by Russia. There will always be a degree of doubt in European minds about America's reliability, as long as Europe is dependent upon the United States for its security. But during this period of globalized containment, the United States went to extraordinary lengths to reduce Europe's doubts to that irreducible minimum by concentrating on her capability to defend Europe in the event of a Russian attack. In short, the United States thought and acted largely as if its ability to *deter* a Russian attack was measured by Europeans in terms of its ability to *de-*

*fend* them if they were attacked. In American eyes, the deterrent value of its commitment to NATO became a function of its defensive capability. But to the Europeans, who wanted to prevent war, not wage it, such defensive measures were approved only when they did not appear to weaken the deterrent value of the American commitment. The clash of interests was inevitable because of the clash in national perspectives. Europe wanted to heighten deterrence so as to avoid war, and the United States wanted to do that but also to minimize damage to itself should deterrence fail. Understandably, the United States wanted to localize any war to Europe; and equally understandably, the Europeans did not want one there.[16]

The second and third hallmarks of these years were integrally related to the first. In an era when prior commitment per se was not thought sufficient to hold the line against further communist expansion, the United States built a military force that would enhance the credibility of its commitments. It did not begin a major rearmament in 1950 nor significantly increase its defense budgets in the early 1960s because it feared a Russian attack was imminent. The United States created and tried to maintain through the late 1960s a marked military superiority over Russia, not for its own security, but for that of its allies. The point of having the military edge was psychological—to convince both the Soviet Union and America's allies that the United States had more than enough power to back up its commitments.

Whether the United States ever had an overall force superior to that of Russia cannot be definitively known. Only the test of their arms could have determined which was the stronger. There was a clear desire by the United States to have the appearance of superiority; and it was reflected in America's commitment to have a nuclear force "second to none." During these twenty years every Administration operated under the belief that a superiority in numbers and quality of nuclear forces could be turned to America's political advantage. Belief in "the more the better" caused the Truman Administration to rush development of the hydrogen bomb to stay ahead of the Russians, once they developed the atomic bomb. Three years before Russia's Sputnik launching of 1957, the Eisenhower Administration committed the country to a massive intercontinental ballistic missile development program. Soon after the Kennedy Administration came into office, and even after aerial intelligence indicated that the United States had a marked superiority in ICBMs, the Administration nevertheless programmed a further increase in America's strategic nuclear forces. During the mid-1960s, the Johnson Administration used the "greater-than-expected-threat" estimate as the basis for determining America's nuclear forces. This process estimated the outer limits of Russia's capabilities, then multiplied *that* figure by some number, which then became the basis for America's needs. Even the second Eisenhower Administration, which was at the time lambasted as laggard for not countering the Russian nuclear threat dramatized by Sputnik, nevertheless proceeded with a rapid

[16]For a further discussion of these points, see Robert J. Art and Kenneth N. Waltz, "Technology, Strategy, and the Use of Force," in Art and Waltz, eds., *The Use of Force* (Boston: Little, Brown, 1971), pp. 1–25.

ICBM development program, shipped still more tactical nuclear weapons to Europe, and sent hundreds of intermediate range ballistic missiles there. In the era of global containment, the quest for nuclear superiority was a permanent feature of America's foreign policy.

Viewed in this light, the differences over military doctrine that occurred between the Republicans in the 1950s and the Democrats in the 1960s signify differences over means not ends. The Eisenhower Administration had accused the Truman Democrats of failing to take an active enough posture against the Russians. "Massive retaliation" was its answer. Exploit America's nuclear prowess, said Secretary of State Dulles, by threatening to blow up the Soviet Union should it engage in acts of aggression. Such a posture would throw the communists on the defensive. The Kennedy Administration retorted that such a posture paralyzed America's military power. If faced with the need to make that threat good, the United States had only two choices—blow them up and risk nuclear retaliation, or do nothing and suffer humiliation. Rather than choose between devastation or surrender, the Kennedy and Johnson Administrations pursued the strategy of "flexible response." If the United States built up both its nuclear and conventional forces, then it would have the capability to respond to the entire spectrum of threats Russia could make. Flexible response, argued the Democrats, gave the United States the flexibility to select the response most appropriate to the threat made or the action taken. How much of a difference there actually was between these two

postures is interesting. Whether there actually was "a bigger bang for the buck" under the Republicans, or "a greater range of bangs for more bucks" under the Democrats, the overall goal never varied: maintain America's military preeminence in order to wage a successful political offensive against communism.

The third hallmark of these years was a logical extension of the first two. If the commitment to use force, backed up by enough military power to make it credible, did not work, then force was used where the interests involved dictated it. From 1950 through 1968, the United States engaged in the whole spectrum of military interventionism. There were the overt uses of significant numbers of combat troops, as in Korea in 1950, Lebanon in 1958, the Dominican Republic in 1965, and Vietnam in 1965. There were the covert paramilitary uses of force or the severely circumscribed overt uses of force, as in Iran in 1953, Guatemala in 1954, and Cuba in 1961. There were, finally, the clearly communicated threats to intervene with force, as in Laos in 1961 and Cuba in 1962. Despite the differences in circumstances, all of these interventions shared either or both of two overriding aims: preventing communists from coming to power and/or preventing the appearance of Russia's gaining at America's expense. Military interventionism was the last resort of cold-war liberalism's attempt to preserve the status quo.

In the global containment era, Korea and Vietnam were the two most significant military interventions. Both were fought for the same reason, namely to protect America's global commitments. Korea was fought to consolidate them; Vietnam, to keep them from eroding. In this regard, however, Korea was a plausible war. Vietnam was not. Korea came at a time when America's fidelity to Europe had yet to be demonstrated and in the midst of Japan's debate over whether to opt for neutralism or alignment with the United States. Monolithic communism was a new and reasonable proposition. Vietnam came at a time when the unity of the communist world had been proved a sham, when America had demonstrated her loyalty to her Japanese and European allies for fifteen years, and after America had repeatedly demonstrated her will to intervene militarily against communism. Yet, successive Administrations saw Vietnam as the test of America's continuing determination. It was the United States alone, not Russia, China, the Vietnamese communists or noncommunists, nor any of America's allies, that made Vietnam into such a symbol.

Apart from the generous and laudable motive of preserving the chance for democracy in South Vietnam, Vietnam per se was never important to the United States. None of the rationales for standing there, save one, ever made sense. Saving the other dominoes in Southeast Asia made little sense when considered in view of the tangible interests that the United States had in Cambodia, Laos, or Thailand. Such interests she may have acquired came after, and as a result of, the Vietnam intervention. If Vietnam was important because of the domino-type effect it could have on larger nations in the area, then the United States should have left Vietnam at the end of 1965. For by then the noncommunist forces in Indonesia, the fifth largest nation in the world by population, had succeeded in overthrowing Sukarno, physically liquidating many of the communists, and thereby preventing their coming to power. All this had been done (as far as we know) without American assistance. If the goal was to contain Chinese communist expansion into Southeast Asia, then a better way would have been to have brought about a united, not a divided, Vietnam. Whether ruled by communists or noncommunists, the Vietnamese are no lovers of the Chinese. To the extent that Southeast Asia could ever be free from Chinese domination, a united Vietnam, and one even incorporating Laos and Cambodia, had the best chance. Only if viewed in America's global perspective, therefore, does the Vietnam war make even the slightest sense. Vietnam was America's imperial war. Just as the British during the Boer War once feared the effects that the loss of the South African Cape Colony might have on her other colonial holdings, so too did the Americans fear the effects of the loss of Vietnam on her other commitments. Edward Gibbon, the historian of Rome, said that one of the tell-tale signs of an imperial power in decline was its waging of wars far from the imperial center and with little or no tangible benefits to the empire as a whole. The imperial government, in short, did not know when it was prudent to stop fighting and when to avoid taking on new commitments. Although the parallel between Rome and America is not exact, still the Vietnam War must be viewed in the Gibbonian sense. It was the tell-tale sign of America's loss of prudence and the overreaching of her power.

## THE RETRENCHMENT OF CONTAINMENT

Since 1969 America has retrenched. The three hallmarks of the global containment era have begun to erode, but have by no means been totally discarded. Rather than proliferate commitments, the United States has gradually begun to cut back—the withdrawal from Indochina being the first step. Rather than rely on military superiority in order to achieve political ends, the United States, because it has accepted a rough parity with Russia, has been forced to return to the diplomatic maneuvering reminiscent of the classical balance-of-power days, even though the world remains militarily bipolar. Rather than an easy and quick resort to military intervention, the President, because of the passage of the 1973 War Powers Act (to be discussed below), has found his flexibility circumscribed. For example, he was unable to launch B-52 strikes in Vietnam in 1975 in order to prevent a South Vietnamese collapse. Retrenchment has meant consolidation and a withdrawal from positions of weakness. From the standpoint of the Presidency to date, however, it has not meant a retreat from the goal of containing communism, but rather the search for new means in order to persevere with the old goal. Retrenchment has had two key aspects —détente with America's adversaries and difficulties with her allies, with the first a significant cause of the second.

*Détente with Adversaries.* President Nixon's desire to insure his reelection in 1972 probably affected the timing of his trip to China and his signing of the SALT I Accord with Russia, but it had little to do with the basic decision to pursue détente with America's two foremost adversaries. The détente with Russia and China was a personal triumph for Nixon's acumen and toughness and Kissinger's negotiating talents, but neither or both of these is sufficient to explain the shift in America's strategy towards these two countries. Rather, in order to explain the desire to mute hostilities, we must look to the basic change that occurred in the 1960s in the international balance of forces. Genius in statecraft, said the gifted French statesman, Talleyrand, is to recognize the inevitable and then to exploit it. What was inevitable was something that Secretary of Defense Robert McNamara realized as far back as the early 1960s, that Russia would eventually acquire nuclear parity with the United States. It was the tremendous military power that Russia had acquired during the 1960s, when America was dissipating part of hers in Indochina, that made détente with Russia and China highly advantageous, if not inexorably inevitable. Nixon understood the consequences for the United States of this structural shift and tried to turn it to America's advantage.

Détente with China is not difficult to explain. Viewed in historical perspective, the American-Chinese hostility that prevailed from 1953 to 1972 was neither necessary nor advantageous for the larger purposes of American foreign policy. Neither was this hostility "natural." Aside from their differences over Taiwan, there were no life and death matters of conflict between them, nor any disputes that involved significant clashes of material interests. America's hostility to Communist China was an indirect by-product of America's global containment policy, not a direct result of a fundamental clash in their national interests. As a consequence of the outbreak of the Korean War, the United States had reinjected itself into the Chinese civil war by deciding to interpose the seventh fleet between the Communists on the mainland and the Nationalists on Taiwan. After all, it would have looked politically incongruous to fight the communists in Korea and meanwhile allow them to take Taiwan without lifting a finger to prevent it. As a consequence of its miscalculation about Chinese interests, warnings, and perceptions of American actions in Korea, the United States became embroiled in a needless war with China. Even if ill-considered and unintentional, these American actions gave good grounds for the hostility between the two nations to linger for awhile after the 1953 truce. But this hostility persisted long after it made reasoned sense from the standpoint of America's self-interest, largely because of the exigencies of American electoral politics. Particularly after the Sino-Soviet rift became apparent in the early 1960s, the United States was foolhardy not to attempt to consort with the Chinese Communists. Fears of the Democrats over another Republican campaign about China deterred them from making any overtures of significance. The lack of any compelling foreign policy need to open up contacts with China gave the Democrats no political incentive to take the risk and make the case to the American electorate. America's rigid nonintercourse with and nonrecognition of Communist China after the mid-1950s were thus ideological, reflecting Dulles' desire not to give an ounce of legitimacy to the communists where he did not have to, and electoral, reflecting the

Democrats' sensitivity to the China issue. The internal deterrents to détente with China were powerful; the external "compellents" were weak. Still, the United States could have gained a degree of flexibility in her Far Eastern policy had she tried to come to terms with China sooner than she did. It would have been advantageous, though it was not essential.

By the early 1970s, however, such a rapprochement was necessary. Just as the twenty-two years of American-Chinese hostility was a product of America's globalizing her containment policy, so too was the American-Chinese détente, from the American side, a product of America's retrenching on that global policy. And the same factor that caused the United States to become hostile to the Chinese Communists, namely the Soviet Union, also caused her to warm up to them. Certainly there was a strictly Far Eastern interest in détente with China—obtaining any assistance the Chinese could give in extricating the United States from the Vietnamese War. But this was only a contributing factor. Fundamentally, it was the need to offset the expansion of Russian military power and concomitant influence that dictated the move. Despite Nixon-Kissinger denials to the contrary, the détente with China was clearly anti-Russian in motivation and purpose. No longer able to count on the political leverage that her vast military superiority over Russia had afforded her, America had to resort to other means to maintain a global posture against the Soviet Union. Operating under the old dictum that "the enemy of my enemy is my friend," Nixon moved toward China in order to be in a position once more to extract concessions from

Russia. Détente with China can therefore be understood only in the context of the change in American-Russian relations.[17] It was the means to preserve a flexibility for the United States vis-à-vis Russia that America's military superiority had once yielded. The achievement of military parity between the world's two foremost military powers dictated the once dominant power's switch to diplomatic tactics. The détente with China heralded in the age of "balance of maneuver" diplomacy.

There were two basic motives for seeking a détente with the Soviet Union, and both derived from the same increase in Russian power that made détente with China a logical step. Although we cannot dismiss Nixon's desire to obtain Russia's help in extricating the United States from Vietnam, nevertheless this must, as with the case of China, remain a secondary motive. Rather it was the search for a new basis for American-Russian *security* relations and for American-Russian *global* relations, both of which were altered by the emergence of Russian-American nuclear parity, that impelled the Nixon Administration toward détente.

Russia's pulling roughly even with the United States did not mean that the American-Russian nuclear arms race had come to an end, but rather that if the United States wished to continue it, then it would prove exceedingly expensive and perhaps even more dangerous than before. Russia's actions since her humilia-

tion in the Cuban missile crisis had demonstrated how tenacious was her determination to have strategic nuclear forces "second to none." Within the Nixon Administration, moreover, there developed a gradual acceptance of the view that "more was not necessarily better" and that when both sides had such huge numbers of nuclear forces, superiority in numbers had no clear military or political meaning.[18] As long as each could retaliate upon the other if attacked first and cause the other to suffer extreme devastation, the military value of ever larger forces became questionable. Such increases would not add to either nation's security, but only cause each to spend billions more in order to end up where they both were before. By drawing even with the United States, Russia ended any appearance there might have been of the United States having possessed a first strike capability vis-à-vis her, and the political value of superior forces became increasingly tenuous. If the United States could no longer use a nuclear threat to intimidate the Russians and exact political concessions from them, as was the case in Cuba, what would be the political use of a military superiority that yielded only a larger number of missiles? If there was no longer a meaningful military potential in superiority, then there could be little practical political value in it. In short, if Russia was determined to maintain parity with America, and if both nations had strategic forces that were invulnerable to a surprise attack for the foreseeable future, then America's quest for military superiority would be

[17]See Michel Tatu, "The Great Power Triangle—Washington—Moscow—Peking," reprinted in Robert J. Art and Robert Jervis, eds., *International Politics: Anarchy, Force, Imperialism* (Little, Brown, 1973), pp. 452–74.

[18]See the account, which remains the only detailed one available to the public, by John Newhouse, *Cold Dawn* (New York: Holt, Rinehart, & Winston, 1973).

costly, illusory, and of no real advantage.

Nixon accepted the logic of this position. Nixon the candidate spoke of the need for continued American superiority, but Nixon the President spoke instead of sufficiency, an oblique reference to his acceptance of parity. The SALT I Accord, if followed up by a SALT II Accord, will signal the official end of America's quest for superiority. The SALT I Accord had two principal features: 1) a quantitative and qualitative freeze on antiballistic missile systems (ABMs) and 2) a quantitative freeze only on offensive ballistic missiles. By severely limiting ABMs, the SALT I Accord signified an American and Russian acceptance of MAD, or mutual assured destruction. The ABM agreement meant that each nation accepted the ability of the other to retaliate as the foundation for their present and subsequent relations. Each nation had in effect officially guaranteed the existence of the other. The 1974 Ford-Brezhnev statement of intent for a SALT II agreement signified a mutual desire to make permanent and equal the offensive freeze of SALT I, which was only to be a five-year agreement and which gave the Russians more missiles than the Americans. If achieved, these two accords taken together will mean that the United States and the Soviet Union will have reduced the danger of surprise attack significantly. Neither nation will be able to gain a decisive advantage in offense or defense without violating the accords. Ironically enough, America's acceptance of the SALT accords may very well bring her to a sense of security about her relations with the Russians that she has not experienced since 1945.

The muting of the nuclear arms race, together with the concomitant reduction in the danger of general nuclear war, was the first impulse for and the only tangible achievement thus far of détente with the Russians. Paradoxically, it is precisely because the two superpowers have put their security relations with one another on a firmer footing than ever before that their global relations have become more unpredictable than ever and may very well be characterized by more intense competition than in the heyday of the cold war. There is a linkage between their security relations and their global relations because of the spill-over effects of the former on the latter. When America had an overweening nuclear superiority, and when Russia lacked a global conventional capability, the Russians, despite all their bluster, were quite restrained in their actions. Their putting offensive missiles into Cuba in 1962 is the exception that proves the rule. Once the Americans publicly announced in October of 1961 what the Russians had known since 1957, to wit, that America was far superior in nuclear strength, Khrushchev reasoned that he had to resort to his own "quick fix" in order to reduce the clear gross disparity in forces between the two nations. Khrushchev took a gamble and poured intermediate-range offensive missiles into Cuba in order to reacquire (this time on the basis of actual capability, not bluff) the nuclear strength he believed necessary for a vigorous foreign policy. Khrushchev's actions in Cuba in 1962 and Brezhnev's since then clearly demonstrate that the Russians have always understood the basis of America's global influence: a sophisticated, large, and visible nuclear force. This has been the precondition since World War II for waxing strong on the world's stage.

Russia now has such a force. With each nation feeling more secure about its physical survival, both may be emboldened by that very sense of security to enhance their political-economic competition for world-wide influence. Parity has brought an assurance of mutual survival, no mean feat, but little else to date. Thus, the cold war is not over; it has only changed its coloration. Limiting nuclear competition has required each nation to reduce its ideological mudslinging, but there is no evidence that the elites of either nation have any lessened sense that they are fierce rivals or that they can trust the good intentions of the other and therefore not have to compete. From their actions to date, we can only surmise that this is the case with the Russians; but for the Americans we have Henry Kissinger's words on it:

The factors which perpetuated that rivalry [between the United States and the Soviet Union] remain real and deep. We are ideological adversaries, and we will in all likelihood remain so for the foreseeable future. We are political and military competitors, and neither can be indifferent to advances by the other in either of these fields.[19]

Therefore, now that both nations have their security vis-à-vis each other assured, and now that both have the conventional capability to be global players, the cold war may be of a worldwide scope and intensity that it never was before. And, then again, it may not. For the desire to limit the chances of nuclear war

may impel both to collude with each other against the interests of others so that each does not become drawn into regional conflicts in such a way that both feel they cannot back down. Parity may thus bring a more intense but safer competition; or, it may produce a much more muted rivalry.

Whichever is the case, the point remains that parity has brought with it a change in the status quo and a greater degree of unpredictability in American-Russian global relations. This was the starting point for the Nixon Administration's second motive for seeking détente with the Soviet Union. It was precisely to tilt those relations away from unpredictability that Nixon tried to link advances in the nuclear arms talks to Russian cooperation on other matters or areas where the interests of both nations were engaged. The second intent of détente was to work out with Russia a set of agreed upon "rules of the game" that would permit rivalry but allow for no surprise moves and the risk of direct confrontation. Again, as Kissinger puts it:

Although we compete, the conflict will not admit of resolution by victory in the classical sense. We are compelled to coexist. We have an inescapable obligation to build jointly a structure for peace. Recognition of this reality is the beginning of wisdom for a sane and effective foreign policy today.[20]

The Nixon goal was thus to build a superpower consensus on how the two should conduct their worldwide relations, a consensus that resembled in spirit if not in detail the vision that Franklin Roosevelt had for American-Russian relations after the defeat of Germany and Japan. Not a

[19]Congressional Briefing by Henry A. Kissinger, Assistant to the President for National Security Affairs, on the SALT I Accord, *The Washington Post*, June 16, 1972, p. A18.

[20]*Ibid.*

cessation of competition between them, but an agreement to respect their respective spheres of influence and to abide by rules where they compete—this was the Nixon-Roosevelt vision. Since 1969, however, the evidence on this score is mixed. We cannot state whether such a superpower consensus will be, or is in the process of being, realized.

*Difficulties with Allies.* If America's relations with her adversaries have improved since 1969, those with her allies have worsened. The improvement in relations with the former has been a significant, though by no means the only, cause of the worsening in relations with the latter. America's alliances with Japan and Western Europe are intended to deter and defend them against a Russian attack. It should not be surprising that when the United States improved relations with Russia, America's foremost allies would begin to worry about American-Russian collusion at their expense. With Europe, particularly, past periods of relaxation in East-West tensions had usually been accompanied by a lessening in the political cohesion of NATO and in the need, as seen by Europeans, to maintain a high level of conventional military preparedness. Détente in the era of mutual assured destruction has brought this phenomenon to the fore again, but with a clarity and force that was missing in the earlier periods of relaxation in tensions. This superpower détente has an appearance of durability, seriousness, and perhaps even permanency that none of the earlier ones had. If the essence of détente—American-Russian cooperation to avoid those confrontations that bring with them the risks of nuclear war—persists, then

the Europeans must worry about the likelihood of one of two logical occurrences. In order to avoid a nuclear war, either the United States would not risk defending Europe from a Russian attack or Russia would never risk attacking Europe. If the first is the case, the Europeans would have to draw the obvious conclusions: NATO would be worthless, Europe would have to unite politically if it ever could hope to match Russian strength, and the odds on its doing so are no better than even. If the second is the case, then the NATO alliance per se may be necessary but not all the military paraphernalia that has come with it since 1950, at America's insistence, such as elaborate planning and joint exercises, integrated command and staff structures, and the quest for a conventional capability that could match that of the Warsaw Pact forces. In the first case, NATO itself is irrelevant; in the second, NATO's associated military structure is worthless. These two cases are the clearcut extremes, but any path between them will partake of the difficulties associated with one of them. In all cases, America's perseverance with détente will cause it to experience conflicts in its security arrangements with its European allies.

Roughly the same two choices will confront the Japanese. Either the United States will not risk its own destruction for the defense of Japan, or the Soviet Union would never risk its devastation for the conquest of Japan. But the choices for Japan look even starker than for Europe. Since they do not yet have nuclear weapons, the Japanese have no claim even to the pretensions of independence that the French and British have. Their dependence on the United States appears all the more complete, if not abject. The Japanese themselves have publicly said as much. In early 1973, the Japanese military calculated that, in a conventional attack by Russia, if Japan received no immediate American military assistance, her air force would be knocked out in a matter of hours; her navy would cease to function after four days; and her army could hold out for no more than ten.[21] The military assumed, moreover, that the United States could not give military assistance immediately after Japan invoked her security treaty because of the nature of the treaty. That is, the American-Japanese defense treaty pledges American aid, but only after the United States has gone through its due constitutional processes. In short, while the Congress and the Executive were consulting on what to do, Japan could not defend herself and would not receive aid in sufficient time to survive destruction. Doubt over the degree of immediacy of America's aid is thus an oblique reference to doubts over whether such aid would in fact ever be forthcoming. The conclusion the military drew was obvious: unless she rearmed, Japan's defeat was inevitable and surrender the only possible course. What makes the conclusion significant is not that it has been widely accepted within Japan, but merely that it has been presented for public debate. This was

[21] See *The New York Times*, March 4, 1973, p. 16. These figures could have been exaggerated, for obvious political effect, to aid the Self-Defense Forces in making a case for larger defense budgets. But even if they are exaggerated, they are still reflective of her dependence on the United States. Even if these figures are to be viewed as the beginning of the debate in Japan over whether to rearm, the point is that Japan is practically defenseless without America. Quibbling over the exact figures does not affect the central point.

the military's first comprehensive reassessment of Japan's security position in twenty-two years. And by no accident did it come after Nixon proclaimed in the Nixon Doctrine that America's allies must henceforth provide the bulk of the combat troops for their own defense.

American-Russian détente has thus brought a degree of uncertainty in America's security relations with her most important allies. From 1950 through 1968, in the heyday of the cold war, there were gross shifts in the perceived strategic nuclear balance between America and Russia; but there was also clarity and firmness in America's relations with her major allies. Strategic uncertainty was combined with diplomatic certainty. In the age of détente, these factors have reversed themselves: strategic certainty has produced diplomatic uncertainty. The chances of nuclear war between the two superpowers may be less now than ever before, but America and perhaps Russia are experiencing a lessening in the clarity and purpose of their relations with their allies. As each superpower moves closer to the other, both open up the distance between themselves and their respective allies.

For the United States, at least, adversaries have been transmuted into competitors. But so too have allies. Instead of friends and foes, America now faces competitors of two types, "friendly" and "unfriendly." The cause of the competition with Japan and Europe is economic, but it derives from the interests both share with the United States, as well as from the disparity in economic strength between them and America. Europe and Japan need the United States for both trade and investment; and, similarly, the United

States needs them. The economic stake that each has in the other's market makes each a competitor in that market. Mutual dependence, however, does not create automatic harmony. Competition can and does occur within a broad framework of shared interest. America, moreover, retains an economic position that makes her dominant in her bilateral relations with Japan and Europe, and this economic dominance causes suspicion and resistance from her allies whenever America asserts a leadership role. What America views as necessary to protect the overall shared interest, Europe and Japan see as a further entrenchment of America in her dominant position. The oil crisis is a case in point. In an attempt to lessen the dependence of Europe, Japan, and itself on OPEC oil, the United States pushed its allies to set a floor price under oil. The intent was to encourage the development of alternate energy supplies by guaranteeing their competitiveness with oil. A floor price for oil would insure that the OPEC nations could not manipulate the price of oil in order to drive alternate energy sources out of the market. Because Europe as a whole is poor in natural energy sources compared to America, Europe viewed America's proposal with suspicion, no matter how sound was its economic logic. The Europeans viewed the United States as trying to get them to underwrite the costs of America's acquisition of energy self-sufficiency, something Europe could probably never achieve. Whether the United States intended this is irrelevant; the point is that it could be a logical outcome.

When allies are economic competitors, differences in relative strength will enhance the competition and produce greater chances for discord.

When one ally is dependent on another for its security, the temptation for the stronger to use that dependence for its own advantage is powerful. Until quite recently, America resisted the temptation. It tolerated economic measures by Europe and Japan that enhanced their economic strength—measures that often did not benefit the United States and sometimes actually hurt it. The reason was America's calculation that anything that made these allies stronger in relation to the Soviet Union was in America's overall interests. But the costs of this tolerance are becoming high, if not prohibitive, for the United States. If the trend continues, the United States will resort to using the security it provides Europe and Japan as a bargaining lever to wrest the economic concessions it wants from them. The results will be, of course, that economic and security issues will become inextricably intertwined and that conflicts in the one area will exacerbate those in the other. In the era of global containment, economic factors tended to cement America's relations with Europe and Japan. In the era of superpower détente, these factors will corrode them.

America's alliances with Europe and Japan are the centerpieces of her global commitments. When the United States experiences conflicts of interests with these two, its relations with secondary allies are likely to become even more strained. For a period after the collapse of South Vietnam, this will not be readily apparent because the United States will make strenuous efforts to assure these allies of the credibility of its commitments to them. As Vietnam recedes from memory and if détente continues, the pressures on America and her allies to rethink their relations with one another will mount.

During this transition period, the Nixon Doctrine will serve as a half-way house, a holding operation, between America's past indivisibility-of-peace view and her as yet undefined constricted role. The Nixon Doctrine is an attempt to preserve the indivisibility-of-peace role for the United States, but to present it in a more tolerable guise to the American public. It has three components. First, the United States will extend its nuclear shield over non-nuclear states in order to prevent any of them from being subject to nuclear blackmail. Second, the United States will honor all the commitments it had made. And, third, in actual combat situations, the United States will furnish financial aid and arms, but would look to the ally concerned to provide the bulk of combat troops. The import of the Nixon Doctrine applies least forcefully to Europe because the United States has 300,000 combat troops stationed there. It is also only marginally applicable to Japan because of her perceived intrinsic importance to the United States. The logic of the Doctrine applies most forcefully to those nations in which America may even have combat troops stationed or military bases operating, but whose intrinsic importance to the United States is clearly secondary. If mutual assured destruction has weakened the credibility of America's security pledges to Europe and Japan, it will obviously do so for these secondary allies. If the third tenet of the Nixon Doctrine is taken seriously, then doubt over America's credibility will be all the more exacerbated. The Nixon Doctrine was an attempt to assuage the American public by telling them that there would be no more Vietnams, that

their world role would not be so burdensome in the future as it was in the past. The Nixon Doctrine was largely for domestic consumption. In the age of détente, however, the net effect of the attempt to buy the American public's support for a continued global role will probably be to accelerate the global decay of its secondary alliance commitments.

## POLICY AND THE POLICY-MAKING PROCESS

American foreign policy is clearly at the second major crossroads since the end of World War II. What shall be her future course? The grand alternatives are clear: a continued, if somewhat retrenched world role, with all its attendant burdens; or, a retreat into an isolationist posture, with all its short-run gains and long-term dangers. The choices are easy to portray, but not so the path that will be taken. For the foreign policy a nation pursues is a result of both the external forces it confronts and the manner in which it formulates and implements its policy. Therefore, no discussion of the past contours and future prospects of American foreign policy is complete without an analysis of the internal factors affecting foreign policy.

Within the United States, there are three factors to consider: the relation between Congress and the executive branch of government; bureaucratic policies within the executive branch; and the nature of public opinion with its attendant effects on foreign policy. All are significant, but each exerts influence only within the context of America as a representative democracy. American democracy is by no means perfect. There is no one-to-one correspondence between what the people want and what its government does. There are special interests and important elites exercising a powerful role over certain aspects of foreign policy. With all these caveats, nevertheless, the representative nature of the American political system does make a difference. For the elites must appeal to, get elected by, and carry along, the publics to whom they are in some way accountable. The elites may very well cater to special interests, but they cannot do so for a long time without the public's support or apathy. How, then, does the manner in which the United States makes its foreign policy decisions affect the substance of those decisions?

## Congressional-Executive Relations

Next in importance to the representative nature of the American political system is the dispersal of power in its governmental structure. In foreign as well as in domestic policy, neither the Congress nor the president monopolizes any single function or issue. The fact that power is dispersed means that it is shared. The most significant substantive effect of this sharing of power is the anticipatory influence that Congress can have on foreign policy. The president may often appear to be supreme and unchallenged in his conduct of foreign policy, but the appearance of reality can belie its substance. When the president needs to obtain congressional approval or merely tolerance for his policies, as he ultimately must, he needs, before he goes to the congressional leaders, to anticipate their probable reactions and to tailor his proposals accordingly. Or, in anticipating what he needs from them, he will meet with the leaders,

solicit their advice, determine what will be acceptable to them, and then formally present his proposals to the Congress as a whole. Thus, although congressional influence may be hard to locate and, once found, difficult to measure, it is, nevertheless, always present and usually significant. Lyndon Johnson, for example, is reputed to have intervened in Vietnam in 1965 partly because of his anticipation of the reaction from powerfully placed congressional conservatives if he did not. He feared that they would use his "softness on communism" to attack his Great Society programs. John Kennedy deferred overtures to Communist China, after the Sino-Soviet rift made it advantageous for the United States to do so, largely for fear of the political costs to his Presidency from an attack by the conservatives.[22] Whether these calculations were correct is irrelevant; the point is that presidents made them on the basis of the anticipated congressional reaction to a contemplated policy. That in itself illustrates the potency of the role that Congress can play.

The Congress and the president share power in foreign policy, but usually not equally. Congress will always exert influence on foreign policy because of the American structure of government, but the exact amount of its influence and its type will vary largely as a consequence of the general attitudes prevailing within the body politic as a whole. The extremes of congressional influence have been either total deference to the president or severe con-

[22]See David Halberstam, *The Best and the Brightest* (New York: Random House, 1972), pp. 425–26, and James C. Thompson, Jr., "On the Making of China Policy, 1961–1969," *The China Quarterly* 50 (April/June, 1972), 220–44.

striction of his flexibility. The former characterized congressional-executive relations from 1950 through 1968; the latter, from 1919 to 1941. In the interwar period Congress restricted the president's ability to carry on an active foreign policy because of the isolationist sentiment that prevailed in the nation. Fearful that the president could embroil the country in war if his power to do so were not limited, Congress assumed a negative role. It told the president what he could not do. In the age of global containment, Congress went to the other extreme and gave the president a free hand, though not a blank check, to do what he thought best. The Congress deferred to the president, or perhaps better put, mandated presidential predominance because of the containment sentiment that prevailed in the nation. Congressional support was the prerequisite for presidential predominance.

Congressional constrictions on presidential freedom and the neutrality legislation of the 1930s was a direct product of the lessons drawn from how America became embroiled in World War I and were intended to keep her out of World War II. Similarly, congressional deference to executive activisim during the 1950s and 1960s resulted from the lessons drawn from how America became embroiled in World War II and were intended to prevent the occurrence of another world war. If isolationism produced a hamstrung president who could not wage an effective diplomacy against aggressors, then containment needed unfettered presidents who would have the diplomatic tools to deter or defeat aggression. Whether Congress was deferential or restrictive depended on the larger generational mind-sets of the day, which, in turn, were products of lessons drawn from earlier days.

It is in this sense that one must interpret the moves that Congress has made since 1967 to restrict the president. Just as World War I produced its congressional reaction to presidential predominance, and just as World War II produced its congressional reaction to presidential constrictions, so, too, has the Vietnam War produced its congressional reaction to the unfettered presidency. As seen by Congress in retrospect, Vietnam was not a war of presidential inadvertence, but of presidential duplicity. When Congress passed the Tonkin Gulf Resolution in August of 1964, it thought it was helping Johnson make a threat to the North Vietnamese more credible so that the United States would *not* have to go to war. Senator Fulbright, floor manager of the resolution, made this clear, though obliquely, in a colloquy with Senator Brewster:

Mr. Brewster: I would look with great dismay on a situation involving the landing of large land armies on the continent of Asia. So my question is whether there is anything in the resolution which would authorize or recommend or approve the landing of large American armies in Vietnam or in China.

Mr. Fulbright: There is nothing in the resolution, as I read it, that contemplates it. I agree with the Senator that that is the last thing we would want to do. However, the language of the resolution would not prevent it. It would authorize whatever the Commander in Chief feels is necessary. It does not restrain the Executive from doing it. ... Speaking for my own committee, everyone I have heard has said that the last thing we want to do is to become involved in a land war in Asia. . . .[23]

At the time, it was reasoned that passage of the resolution would strengthen the president's bargaining position by making the country appear united behind him. It was not publicly known, however, as the Pentagon Papers subsequently revealed, that the United States had been waging a low-level, covert war against North Vietnam for four years and, therefore, that North Vietnam's action in the Tonkin Gulf was either retaliatory or precautionary. Johnson's motive may very well have been to enhance his deterrent threat to North Vietnam, but the fact that he never told the Congress about the context within which North Vietnam's actions could be viewed led to congressional charges of presidential deception when the facts became known. Congress subsequently came to view the Tonkin Gulf Resolution, not as a presidential bluff, but as a presidential blank check. It had the effect of putting the president in a stronger position vis-à-vis Congress in order to wage war, not vis-à-vis North Vietnam in order to deter it.

In retrospect, Congress came to feel that it had abdicated its role in foreign policy. The War Powers Bill of 1973 was its attempt to redress the situation. This act requires that a president, when he uses military forces before obtaining congressional authorization, must then report to Congress within sixty days of such an action and defend it. If Congress chooses not to approve it, the president has no authority to continue. The War Powers Bill, in effect, gives Congress a veto power over presidential use of the nation's military forces. It can be viewed as a mechanism that provides for a delayed recognition of war, or for a refusal to declare war. Liberal attackers of the bill argued that it gave the president too much power because it gave him something the Constitution never intended—the power to wage war *before* Congress had authorized it. And once in a war, they argued, the political pressures to back the president would make refusal to go along nearly impossible. Conservative attackers of the bill argued that it limited the president's power too much and would thereby reduce the credibility of America's diplomacy. For if the president could not make credible military threats, the nation would not have a credible diplomacy. In the abstract, both arguments make sense. But both neglect what the supporters of the bill claimed for it. In contemplating a military intervention, future presidents would know that soon after they intervened somewhere they would have to come to Congress for approval. The very need to gain approval or to avert refusal would affect the president *when* he was contemplating any such intervention. It would be the anticipated response of the Congress to his action that the president would have to take into account in deciding whether to take action and, if so, of what type. The War Powers Bill may given presidents more power than they have had before; or, it may weaken the nation's diplomacy because it reduces its credibility. What it definitely does do, however, is to force presidents to take Congress seriously when formulating military interventions, to consider quite carefully the merits of

---

[23]Quoted in Theodore Draper, *The Abuse of Power* (New York: Viking Press, 1967), pp. 65–66.

any contemplated intervention, and, therefore, restrains presidents from intervening unless they think they have a persuasive case. The War Powers Bill marks the end of nearly automatic congressional deference to the presidential use of force, a deference that has characterized most of post-1945 American foreign policy.

The reassertion of congressional prerogatives in the realm of military intervention has already spilled over into other foreign policy areas. In approving the 1972 SALT Accord, for example, the Senate mandated that in the next accord there must be an equality in strategic missiles between the United States and the Soviet Union. In approving the 1974 Trade Reform Act, Congress blocked most favored nation treatment for the Soviet Union unless it reformed its emigration laws and also refused to give preferential treatment to the manufactured goods of developing nations that belonged to cartels. In 1975, Congress suspended aid to Turkey until substantial progress was made on the Cyprus problem. All these congressional interventions are significant, because the president had vehemently opposed them, and because they seriously constrained presidential flexibility. Such interventions by Congress are likely to continue, not only because of the momentum that Congress has developed, but also because economic issues are increasingly intruding into the core concerns of American foreign policy. In the era of global containment, when foreign policy problems were framed in terms of the survival of freedom and the need to use force, Congress and the public deferred to what they thought to be presidential expertise and the necessity for swift

action. In the era of détente, however, when foreign policy problems seem to be less problems of the survival of liberty and more problems of the prosperity of the United States in a highly competitive world, Congress will take an active role. Economic issues impinge more directly and more quickly on a greater part of the American electorate than do most of the military issues it has confronted. Congress is acutely responsive to these "pocketbook" issues and has no choice but to intrude. Thus, a more assertive Congress is a product both of the aftereffects of the Vietnam War and the shift in the priorities, if not the concerns, of American foreign policy.

## Executive Bureaucratic Politics

If Congress is the place where foreign policy must be approved and where, since 1945, it has often been rubber-stamped, the executive branch is where it has been formulated and implemented. The executive consists of the president, his White House advisors and Cabinet agency appointees, and the career bureaucrats who staff the executive agencies. There are therefore two distinct layers within the executive branch—the top level, politically elected and politically appointed layer, which extends from the president down to the deputy assistant secretary tier; and the nonelected, nonappointive permanent layer, which extends from the deputy assistant tier all the way down to the bottom of the hierarchy. In addition, there are many agencies involved in the making and implementing of foreign policy, such as the State Department, the Defense Department, the Treasury Department, the Agriculture Department, to name only a few. If we look closely at these two layers and many agencies, two distinct sorts of conflicts emerge. First, there is the struggle between the political layer and the careerist layer, between the short-term superiors and the long-term subordinates, between those who have a specific mandate to carry out and only a short time in which to do it and those who seek to protect their established, entrenched prerogatives and all the time in which to do it. Second, there is the struggle that cuts across the political-permanent dichotomy and that pits the political and permanent members of one agency against those of another to win the president's favor, to gain bigger budgets for themselves, to seize and maintain control over important issues, or merely to protect their "turf" from encroachment by other agencies.

Both types of conflict have an effect on the conduct of American foreign policy. Both really resolve themselves into one fundamental problem: how can the president get what he wants from the executive branch? In the first case, he and his advisors sit astride a huge bureaucracy from which they try to wrest control over foreign policy; in the second, he must wage battles with his own men in order to get them to do his own bidding. These struggles can produce results that alter policy from what the President initially wanted.[24] In short, bureaucratic politics within the executive branch can significantly reduce the president's

predominance in foreign policy. It can be a mistake to view the president solely in terms of his relations with the Congress. For while he may prevail in executive-legislative battles, he is not always master in his own house.

When is this the case? When does the president not get what he wants from his executive subordinates, be they his political appointees or the bureaucratic careerists? The answer is simple: it depends on the president's specific political calculations and general political power. What gives executive officals clout vis-à-vis the president is their ability to muster allies outside of the executive branch, the most important of which are the congressional committee or subcommittee chairmen, or other highly visible senators and representatives. When presidents are able to predominate within the executive branch, these executive subordinate-congressional alliances are not strong. When, in turn, is that the case? The answer is: it depends on the issue in contention, and because that is so, it is difficult to generalize. There is, however, an important qualification to the last point. Because the power of executive officials vis-à-vis the president derives from the support that they gain from outside of the executive branch, in general their ability to muster such support will be low in periods when the Congress and the public defer to the president on foreign policy and high in periods when they do not. When the Congress and the public defer to the president, the effects of bureaucratic politics are minimal and are influential at the edges of policy rather than in its core. When these two do not defer to the president, the effects on the core of policy can

[24]See Graham T. Allison, *Essence of Decision* (Boston: Little, Brown, 1971), especially Chapter 5; and Morton H. Halperin, *Bureaucracy and Foreign Policy* (Washington, D.C.: The Brookings Institution, 1974).

be significant.[25] Succinctly put, bureaucrats are strong when presidents are weak; and bureaucrats are weak when presidents are strong.

It should be obvious, therefore, that the same factors that enable presidents to "get their way" in foreign policy vis-à-vis the Congress enable them to do so vis-à-vis their executive subordinates. These factors include the president's personal prestige, the margin of his electoral victory, whether his party controls the Congress, the nature of the foreign policy issues he must deal with, what problems he has inherited from past administrations, what the other important nations are doing, the extent to which foreign policy is a partisan issue, and so forth. Presidential predominance or presidential constriction in the realm of foreign policy is thus in part an amalgam of many highly variable factors, none of which any president can exclusively control. Fundamentally, however, there is an underlying factor that largely determines the degree of presidential predominance or constriction, no matter how variable the other factors are. Throughout America's history, there have been extended periods of presidential predominance or constriction in foreign affairs, irrespective of the party affiliation, personal prestige, or all the other variable factors associated with presidents enumerated above. During these periods there has been a continuity in the public's distrust of, or deference to, the presidential conduct of foreign affairs that derives from the mind-sets, fears, and hopes of the

public as a whole. Since 1919, at least, these periods have coincided roughly with generational turnover. In the interwar years, presidents were weak in foreign affairs because of the public's preference to be isolated from them. In the post-1945 years, presidents have been strong because of the public's belief that the times required a vigorous foreign policy and strong presidents. In the post-Vietnam periods, we are witnessing a reduction in presidential power, but probably not to the level that prevailed in the interwar years. In the last analysis, therefore, who predominates over whom within the national government is basically a product of what the public believes the times require. What, then, determines this belief?

## Public Opinion and the Future of American Diplomacy

Unfortunately, there is no simple, wholly satisfactory answer to this question. What a democratic nation does with its foreign policy is a product of what its policy-making elites think the configuration of external forces requires them to do, what they wish to do with their nation's power, what they can do with it, and what of this blend of necessity, desirability, and capability they can convince the public to support or at least tolerate. No matter how much it may be maligned by analysts for its ignorance or emotionalism, the public's active support or passive tolerance is the fundamental basis of America's foreign policy.

The study of the nature of public opinion on foreign policy can become a thing in and of itself. Analysts have correlated public attitudes with party affiliation or lack of it,

---

[25]For a more extended analysis, see Robert J. Art, "Bureaucratic Politics and American Foreign Policy: A Critique," *Policy Sciences,* 4 (December, 1973): 467–90.

with age, sex, education, geographic region, and so forth. All of these correlations are interesting, but none really gets to the heart of the matter: what is the relation between what elites do and what the public wants or will tolerate? There are three generalizations that are useful in trying to clarify this relation. First, the public, historically at least, generally approves of presidential initiatives in foreign policy, with little attention paid to the substance of the initiative taken. Within broad constraints, initial approval is given to presidents who appear to be doing *something*. Style, or the appearance of exercising forceful leadership, counts more than the substance of the policy, at least for a time. Second, the public prefers success to failure. It is willing to give the president latitude to try something, but when the policy begins to appear to cost more than seems reasonable in light of its potential benefits, the public gradually withdraws its support. Presidents have been able to gain the public's backing or tolerance for initiatives at the beginning, but they can keep either only if their policies work. Third, the public is willing to support very costly policies at the outset only when it is convinced that there are vital interests at stake. This means that it must perceive that there is much to lose if action is not taken.

The first proposition is most valid in periods of public deference to the president's role in foreign policy. The second and the third hold irrespective of presidential predominance, although the greater the deference the longer the public will support a policy that appears not to be working and the more readily it will extend initial support to a costly one. Do these three propositions,

however, really tell us much? On the face of it, all they say is that when the public defers to the president, he has tremendous latitude for taking initiatives and much time to try to make the policy work. But to state the matter that way only forces us back to the original question—why is it that the public at some times more than others believes that strong presidential leadership in foreign affairs, and the deference that accompanies it, is necessary?

Ultimately, the answer must be a historical one. We are all creatures of history in the sense that we try, even if we fail, not to repeat the mistakes of the past. Decision-makers and their publics are obsessed with the past. Whether anything can in fact be learned from the past, or whether American decision makers and their publics have learned anything from it, is irrelevant. They believe they can do so, and they try to do so. In learning from the past, people are motivated by the negatives, not the positives. They are concerned first and foremost with what to avoid, not with what to achieve. They are out to minimize losses, not to maximize gains. If this be the manner in which decision makers and their publics calculate, then both are guided by the failures of the past, by their sense of what did not work and by their judgments of why not. Perhaps the best explanation for a nation's foreign policy is to understand, not its people's hopes, but rather its fears. The fear of another great war led to the isolationism of the thirties. The fear of more Munichs and another world war led to containment. Where the fear of another Vietnam will lead us is still moot. It is this uncertainty that provides foreign policy analysis with its ultimate mystery and excitement.

## SELECTED BIBLIOGRAPHY

ADLER, SELIG. *The Isolationist Impulse.* New York: Collier Books, 1961.

ARON, RAYMOND. *The Imperial Republic.* Cambridge, Mass.: Winthrop Publishers, 1974.

BEARD, CHARLES. *The Idea of the National Interest.* Chicago: Quadrangle Books, 1966.

BEMIS, SAMUEL FLAGG. *A Diplomatic History of the United States.* 5th Ed. New York: Holt, Rinehart, & Winston, 1965.

BROWN, SEYOM. *The Faces of Power.* New York: Columbia University Press, 1968.

CALLEO, DAVID P., and ROWLAND, BENJAMIN M. *America and the World Political Economy.* Bloomington: Indiana University Press, 1973.

GADDIS, JOHN LEWIS. *The United States and the Origins of the Cold War, 1941–1947.* New York: Columbia University Press, 1972.

KENNAN, GEORGE F. *American Diplomacy, 1900–1950.* Chicago: University of Chicago Press, 1951.

KOLKO, GABRIEL. *The Politics of War.* New York: Random House, 1968.

KOLKO, JOYCE, and KOLKO, GABRIEL. *The Limits of Power.* New York: Harper & Row, 1972.

MAY, ERNEST R. *"Lessons" of the Past.* New York: Oxford University Press, 1973.

OSGOOD, ROBERT E. *NATO: The Entangling Alliance.* Chicago: University of Chicago Press, 1962.

PERKINS, DEXTER. *The American Approach to Foreign Policy.* Cambridge, Mass.: Harvard University Press, 1952.

SCHLESINGER, ARTHUR M., JR. *The Imperial Presidency.* Boston: Houghton Mifflin, 1973.

TUCKER, ROBERT W. *Nation or Empire?* Baltimore: Johns Hopkins Press, 1968.

ULAM, ADAM B. *The Rivals.* New York: Viking Press, 1971.

WALTZ, KENNETH N. *Foreign Policy and Democratic Politics.* Boston: Little, Brown, 1967.

WILLIAMS, WILLIAM APPLEMAN. *The Tragedy of American Diplomacy.* New York: Dell Publishing, 1962.

# INDEX